Masters of Sociological Thought

Ideas in Historical and Social Context

SECOND EDITION

Masters of Sociological Thought

Ideas in Historical and Social Context

SECOND EDITION

LEWIS A. COSER

STATE UNIVERSITY OF NEW YORK AT STONY BROOK

Under the General Editorship of Robert K. Merton

COLUMBIA UNIVERSITY

Harcourt Brace Jovanovich, Inc.

NEW YORK CHICAGO SAN FRANCISCO ATLANTA

PORTRAIT DRAWINGS BY JACK FARAGASSO

ISBN: 0-15-555130-2

Library of Congress Catalog Card Number: 77-72745

Printed in the United States of America

COPYRIGHTS AND CREDITS

MARY E. COOLEY AND ROBERT C. ANGELL for excerpts from *Sociological Theory and Social Research* by Charles Horton Cooley, published in 1930 by Holt, Rinehart and Winston, Inc. Reprinted with permission of Mary E. Cooley and Robert C. Angell.

HARCOURT BRACE JOVANOVICH, INC. for excerpts from *Ideology and Utopia* by Karl Mannheim. Reprinted with permission of Harcourt Brace Jovanovich, Inc., and Routledge & Kegan Paul Ltd.

THE MACMILLAN COMPANY for excerpts from *Race and Culture* by Robert E. Park. Reprinted with permission of The Macmillan Company, copyright 1950 by The Free Press.

THE PARETO FUND for excerpts from *The Mind and Society* by Vilfredo Pareto, published in 1935 by Harcourt Brace Jovanovich, Inc. Reprinted with permission of The Pareto Fund.

PRENTICE-HALL, INC. for the table entitled "The Contrast Between Militant and Industrial Societies," constructed from Herbert Spencer, *The Principles of Sociology,* Volume I, Chapter 10, and Volume II, Chapters 17 and 18 by Neil J. Smelser in his *Essays in Sociological Explanation*. Copyright 1968 by Prentice-Hall, Inc. Reprinted by permission of Prentice-Hall, Inc., and Professor Smelser.

THE UNIVERSITY OF CHICAGO PRESS for excerpts from *The Evolution of Society: Selections from Herbert Spencer's Principles of Sociology,* edited by Robert L. Carneiro. Copyright 1967 by The University of Chicago Press. Reprinted with permission. For excerpts from *Mind, Self and Society* by George H. Mead. Copyright 1934 by The University of Chicago Press. Reprinted with permission. For excerpts from *Introduction to the Science of Sociology* by Robert E. Park and Ernest R. Burgess. Copyright 1921 by The University of Chicago Press. Reprinted with permission. For excerpts from *The Polish Peasant in Europe and America* by William I. Thomas and Florian Znaniecki. Copyright 1918 by The University of Chicago Press. Reprinted with permission.

THE VIKING PRESS, INC. for excerpts from *The Theory of the Leisure Class* by Thorstein Veblen. Reprinted by permission of The Viking Press, Inc. For excerpts from *The Portable Veblen,* edited by Max Lerner. Copyright 1948 by The Viking Press, Inc. Reprinted by permission of The Viking Press, Inc., Ann B. Sims, and Esther Meyer Johnson.

C. A. WATTS & CO. LTD. for excerpts from *Karl Marx: Selected Writings* by T. B. Bottomore, as reprinted in *Karl Marx: Selected Writings in Sociology and Social Philosophy,* published in paperback edition in 1964 by McGraw-Hill Publishing Company Limited. Reprinted by permission of C. A. Watts & Co. Ltd.

Was Du ererbt von deinen Vaetern hast, erwirb es, um es zu besitzen.

GOETHE

What you have inherited from your fathers, you must earn in order to possess.

Foreword

Once in a great while a textbook comes along that leaves an enduring impress on generations of students. The field of medicine has such notable examples as Gray's *Anatomy,* Starling's *Physiology,* and Osler's *Principles and Practice;* the social sciences in turn have Samuelson's *Economics,* Kroeber's *Anthropology,* and Sutherland's *Criminology.* Lewis Coser's *Masters of Sociological Thought,* a long-needed and altogether exemplary book, has, I am happy to say, joined this rare company.

Now the book appears in an expanded second edition. To his roster of twelve outstanding social theorists—Comte, Marx, Spencer, Durkheim, Simmel, Weber, Veblen, Cooley, Mead, Park, Pareto, and Mannheim—Professor Coser has added Pitirim A. Sorokin (Chapter 13) and W. I. Thomas and Florian Znaniecki (Chapter 14). Professor Coser rounds out the gallery of past masters in his new concluding chapter—a survey of major American theorists whose theories have come to the fore in recent decades.

Professor Coser's evident skill for epitomizing complex ideas without trivializing them enables him to cut deep below the surface to their assumptions. As a result, this exposition of classical sociological thought is critical in tone, comprehensive in scope, and conscientious in its attention to detail. I know of no other book that so thoroughly and so compactly sets out the essentials of this wide range of classical theory.

Masters of Sociological Thought is more than just another history of sociological ideas written as though the ideas issued from disembodied minds, free from the constraints and stimulations of time, place, history, society, and culture. To be sure, Professor Coser traces the intellectual antecedents of each major mode of sociological thought and, to a degree, follows up its later fate as well. But beyond this concern with the filiation of ideas, he adopts perspectives drawn from the discipline of sociology itself to analyze and interpret the development of those ideas. He instructively connects the work of each theorist to his life-history (in both its social and psychological aspects), to the ebb and flow of his career, to his location within the social structure, and, in a particularly effective fashion, to his distinctive audiences and reference groups. By relating the ideas of a Weber or a Durkheim, a Cooley or a Pareto, to the distinctive contexts of their respective biography, history, and social structure, Professor Coser broadens and deepens our understanding of their thought while alerting us to their tacit assumptions and value commitments.

Professor Coser does all this in lean and lucid prose, a happy contrast to the wordy and obscure language that has for so long afflicted the sociology of knowledge. What is more, his critical analyses remain scholarly throughout, far removed from the popular cloak-and-dagger variety of "ideological analysis," which consists largely in denigrating and "unmasking" minds of the first class by the simple tactic of substituting self-righteous *ad hominem* attacks for intellectual analyses.

In treating the acknowledged masters of sociology, this book brings to mind two maxims that have long seemed to me excellent guidelines for the sociologist as well as for other scholars and scientists. One is the apparently brusque aphorism by Alfred North Whitehead: "A science which hesitates to forget its founders is lost." The other is by the young mathematical genius Niels Abel: "It appears to me that if one wants to make progress in mathematics, one should study the masters and not the pupils."

At first glance, these two statements may seem somewhat at odds, if not downright contradictory. Whitehead appears to be saying that the early masters should be put aside, their works ignored, and their memory no longer kept green, while Abel is apparently advocating a closer study of their work. But such surface interpretations are gross misinterpretations arising from neglect of the contexts of the statements—precisely the kind of error Professor Coser tries to teach us to avoid. Can one seriously believe that Whitehead, with his addiction to the history of ideas, would repudiate as worthless a knowledge of that history? Rather, as the immediate context of his maxim makes plain, he was issuing a warning to us all: when we confine ourselves to pious commentary on the founding fathers instead of trying to develop their ideas through further cumulative efforts, we decline into scholasticism rather than advance into scholarship. And Abel is suggesting that the direct study of masterworks helps us to acquire intellectual taste and style, a sense for the significant problem and for the form of its solution.

It is only fitting that Professor Coser should adopt as the epigraph for his book the aphorism by Goethe, which in effect consolidates the Whitehead and Abel maxims: "What you have inherited from your fathers, you must earn in order to possess." In this book Professor Coser invites us to read the masters of sociology in a new light. He helps us to earn and possess our legacy of sociological thought by doing for the masters what they could not readily do for themselves, namely, fathoming the effects that their own life-styles and the milieus in which they lived and worked had on the character and substance of their thought.

In the present developing state of sociology, there is prime need for a "disciplined eclecticism"—close familiarity with the distinctive strengths and limitations of a plurality of theoretical orientations, rather than pursuit of the chimera of a single unified theory that would be competent to deal with the entire range of sociological problems. From this standpoint, it is important to introduce the student to as diverse an array of theoretical perspectives as feasible. The larger the arc of choice provided, the better for both students and instructors. The great value of the first edition of this work is thus substantially increased by the addition of the three new chapters.

With the publication of *Masters of Sociological Thought,* Second Edition, Lewis Coser takes an even more commanding place than before as sociologist and historian of sociological theory.

ROBERT K. MERTON

Acknowledgments

Robert K. Merton, my former teacher and long-term friend, not only suggested the idea of this book and assisted at its inception, but he gave crucial support in bringing to completion both the first and second editions. Without his sustained attention, searching discussion, and painstaking comment on each chapter, *Masters of Sociological Thought* would never have become what it is.

My wife, Rose Laub Coser, is closely associated with this book, as she has been with all my previous work. She has been my critical superego, sternly insisting on logical and semantic clarity in the formulation of my thought and mode of expression.

A number of colleagues have been good enough to read specific chapters and to give me the benefit of their advice. I am grateful to all of them. Robert C. Angell read the chapter on Cooley, Herbert Blumer on Mead, Everett C. Hughes on Park, Frank E. Manuel on Comte, and Arthur Mitzman on Weber. Helena Znaniecki Lopata (Znaniecki's daughter), Theodore Abel, and Everett C. Hughes read the chapter on Thomas and Znaniecki. I have greatly benefited from their comments and from the supplemental information they provided. Concerning Chapter 15, "Recent Trends in American Sociological Theory," I wish to record my indebtedness to Nicholas C. Mullins's *Theories and Theory Groups in Contemporary American Sociology* (1973) and to Jonathan H. Turner's *The Structure of Sociological Theory* (1974). I have profited a great deal and borrowed quite liberally from both these volumes. A number of my colleagues at the Center for Advanced Study in the Behavioral Sciences and at the State University of New York at Stony Brook read portions of the book and offered many helpful comments.

The major part of the first edition was completed during the year (1968–69) when I was a Fellow at the Center for Advanced Study in the Behavioral Sciences. I am in deep debt to its officers and staff for providing an ideal environment to pursue this work. The new chapters in this enlarged edition were written in 1976 during my stay at Clare Hall, Cambridge, England, as a Fellow of that college and as a recipient of a Guggenheim Fellowship. I wish to thank that institution as well as the Graduate School of the State University of New York at Stony Brook for providing funds for the final typing of the manuscript.

LEWIS A. COSER

Introduction

Some years ago a student came to my office to discuss the idea of "value neutrality" in the work of Max Weber. I talked with him for a while, but finally, with a somewhat contemptuous gesture, he summed up his feelings about the man and the issue: "Well, after all, he was just looking for a way to cop out."

Though I had been vaguely toying for some time with the idea of writing a book on the history of sociological theory, this interview was decisive in crystallizing that intention, and the character of the book I wished to write began to take shape in my mind.

It now occurred to me that for an American student really to understand the history of sociological theory more is required than a knowledge of formal propositions and theoretical structures. In order to grasp their import a student needs to acquire some familiarity with the social and intellectual milieu in which these theories emerged. This is not to suggest, of course, that a knowledge of the social and historical source of ideas would ensure assessment of their truth or validity, but a correct appraisal of a particular thought is often difficult, if not impossible, if the social context in which it took root cannot be understood. This book is intended to furnish just that kind of knowledge—to contribute to what might be called the social ecology of sociological ideas.

There are a number of first-rate histories of sociological thought, among which Raymond Aron's earlier work on German sociology[1] and his more recent *Main Currents in Sociological Thought*[2] are perhaps the most outstanding. These works provide a critical exposition of the thoughts of some important scholars, an account of ideas as refracted through the mind of the expositor or interpreter. In some cases there is an effort at relatively neutral exposition; in others, as in the two histories of sociological thought by Pitirim A. Sorokin,[3] there is a running combat with the writers discussed. Sometimes, as with Parsons's *The Structure of Social Action,* the purpose is to integrate a series of different approaches to arrive at a new synthesis.[4] But rarely has there been any

[1] Raymond Aron, *German Sociology* (New York, The Free Press, 1957).

[2] Raymond Aron, *Main Currents in Sociological Thought,* 2 vols. (New York, Basic Books, 1965 and 1967).

[3] Pitirim A. Sorokin, *Contemporary Sociological Theories* (New York, Harper & Row, 1928), and Pitirim A. Sorokin, *Sociological Theories of Today* (New York, Harper & Row, 1966).

[4] Talcott Parsons, *The Structure of Social Action* (New York, The Free Press, 1949), and in a very different vein, Robert Nisbet, *The Sociological Tradition* (New York, Basic Books, 1966).

effort to place the work in its socio-historical context. We have a great number of books that attempt to elucidate what Marx or Weber or Pareto *really* meant but only few and scattered efforts to use the tools of the sociologist to investigate the role of sociological theorists within the social structure in which they are variously placed. There has been no sustained attempt to show how social origin, social position, social network, or audience found a reflection in the problems that a theorist addressed himself to or in the overall orientation of his life's work.

It is indeed curious, as Robert K. Merton has remarked,[5] that while historians of science have increasingly come to use in their work sociological conceptualizations and methodological tools, historians of sociology have largely been remiss in this respect, if one can judge from the dearth of any serious sociological study of sociologists.[6] This suggests an extension of the well-known impression that sociologists feel most at ease studying status inferiors, be they workers or students, army privates or thieves, while they find it much more difficult to study status superiors, whether top managers or university presidents, generals or senators. But apparently sociologists find it still easier to study status superiors than to study themselves. Auguste Comte claimed that before humankind could study itself, it first had to go through a number of stages and steps in which the focus of cognitive intention was on the nonhuman surrounding. While I hesitate to defend this Comtean "law" in general, I nevertheless venture the hunch that something of the same order might have been at play in regard to the late emergence of a sociology of sociologists. We discover ourselves as the focus of possible study only after we have directed our attention to a variety of outsiders who are not of the tribe.

Yet the time now seems ripe to move beyond critical summaries of past theories[7] or elaborate classificatory schemes[8] to a true sociological history of sociological theory. Such a history will require the collaborative effort of a number of scholars, and it would be foolhardy to think that any single volume can do more than pilot work.[9] This book is an attempt to acquaint the student with those social circumstances and winds of doctrine that help account for the shape and character of the sociological thought of fifteen masters. It examines

5 Robert K. Merton, *Social Theory and Social Structure,* enlarged ed. (New York, The Free Press, 1968), Ch. 1.

6 For a few exceptions, see H. Stuart Hughes, *Consciousness and Society* (New York, Vintage Books, 1961); John Staude, *Max Scheler* (New York, The Free Press, 1966); Arthur B. Mitzman, *The Iron Cage, An Historical Interpretation of Max Weber* (New York, Alfred A. Knopf, 1970); and Arthur B. Mitzman, *Sociology and Estrangement: Three Sociologists of Imperial Germany* (New York, Alfred A. Knopf, 1973). See also several of the studies in the selected reading list of this book.

7 Harry Elmer Barnes, ed., *An Introduction to the History of Sociology* (Chicago, The University of Chicago Press, 1948), and Nicholas S. Timasheff, *Sociological Theory,* 3rd ed. (New York, Random House, 1957).

8 Don Martindale, *Nature and Types of Sociological Theories* (Boston, Houghton Mifflin, 1960).

9 For promising beginnings in this direction see the *Transactions of the Fourth World Congress of Sociology,* esp. the papers by Raymond Aron and Robert K. Merton.

the overall contribution of each man as well as the more specific conceptualizations that went to make up the many strands of his life work.

Let me illustrate what I have in mind by returning to the student who thought that Max Weber had been "copping out." Had he had the patience to listen and had I had the patience to break through his armor of ideological conviction and prejudice, I would have said something like this: "You cannot understand Weber's thought if you fail to place yourself, through an imaginative leap, in the intellectual and social climate in which he wrote. Weber was appalled by the fact that the social sciences were dominated by men who felt obliged, out of a sense of patriotism, to defend the cause of the Reich and the Kaiser in their teachings and writings. They oriented their research toward enhancing the greater glory of the Fatherland. It is against this prostitution of the scientific calling that Max Weber directed his main effort. His appeal for value neutrality was intended as a thoroughly liberating endeavor to free the social sciences from the stultifying embrace of the powers-that-be and to assert the right, indeed the duty, of the investigator to pursue the solution to his problem regardless of whether his results serve or hinder the affairs of the national state. In Weber's view, value neutrality in the pursuit of disciplined and methodological inquiry would emancipate the social sciences from the heavy hand of the political decision-makers. It would end the heteronomy of the social sciences and clear the way for their autonomous growth. . . ."

These are some of the things I wanted to say to that student, but there is so much more that has to be explained. Hence this book, which will attempt to explain—regarding Weber and fourteen other theorists who have rightly come to be considered major figures in our discipline—the focus of their attention, the choice of their problems, and the general drift of their orientation through an elucidation of the social and intellectual contexts in which they worked.

No claim is made that the sociological factors and intellectual influences discussed are the only ones that account for the specific cast of the work of a thinker; individual psychological dispositions, for example, certainly play a part that historians have only begun to consider seriously.[10] The tools I have used are not the only ones that can be employed in the history of sociological ideas, but they have allowed me to proceed in searching out that most elusive of preys, the working of the minds of fifteen distinguished scholars who have made the sociological enterprise what it is today.

Each of the first fourteen chapters follows a parallel organization. The first section is a capsule summary of the master's work—his main orientations, ideas, and contributions. Here I have included many direct quotations to immerse the reader at the outset in the thought and style of the man. No summary, of course, can do justice to all the intricacies of a man's thought; it is only meant to serve as a kind of paradigm to which the rest of the chapter can be anchored.

10 See, for example, Erik Erikson, *Young Man Luther* (New York, Norton, 1958), and Frank Manuel, *A Portrait of Isaac Newton* (Cambridge, Harvard University Press, 1968).

There follows a short sketch of the life of the theorist that takes into account the man's struggles and successes; the influences of his family, peers, and superiors; and his involvement, or lack of involvement, in community affairs. The third section proceeds to locate him and his work in the texture of a particular moment in intellectual history. What were the major doctrinal trends when the author appeared on the scene? What were the sources on which he drew? What were major opposing currents against which he pitted himself? These are some of the questions asked.

The concluding section of each chapter is concerned specifically with sociological questions. What were the social origins of the theorist? Did the distinctive location of his parents in the class structure color his early formative experiences and later outlook? Did specific generational ties link him to others in the same age cohort, whose outlook was colored like his own by the impact of historical events? Did crucial events such as war, depression, or revolution help fashion his orientations in ways similar to or deviant from those of others in his generation? Also considered is the influence of social position on the theorist's life-style and scholarly orientation. Did he manage to carve a niche for himself among the intellectual elite of his time or did he pursue his work in a marginal position located in the interstices of society? Did he attain a position in the academy or was he an academic outsider?

Closely linked to, in fact inseparable from, the discussion of status and position is an elucidation of the audience or public to which a particular thinker addressed himself, whether by choice or necessity. The social role of the man of knowledge[11] is shaped by the circle of appreciative listeners or dissenting ones, as the case may be. Hence, the study of the audience that bestows or withholds recognition and appreciation is an essential ingredient of the sociological investigation of a thinker's contributions. So, too, we must consider the theorist's social network, that is, his significant friends and enemies as well as the reactions of those who might be mildly interested in, though basically indifferent to, his work.

The notion of audience must be further specified by reference to specific organizational settings. Is that audience mainly academic or extra-academic? What specific demand structures for intellectual offerings are present in what specific organizational environment? Here attention is paid to the media of communication open to each theorist. Did he find access to academic and professional publications or was he dependent on more general publications? Did he propagate his message by addressing a formal academic audience or did he lecture in extra-academic settings? Finally, and perhaps most importantly, did he have access to colleagues or was he forced to function in a setting where he was deprived of colleagues?

Yet it is not enough to limit attention to the actual audience of a particular

[11] Cf. Florian Znaniecki, *The Social Role of the Man of Knowledge,* new ed., with an introduction by Lewis A. Coser (New York, Harper & Row, 1968).

sociologist. We need consider not only those who listened to his message but those prospective or anticipated audiences a thinker wished to reach even though he might have failed in this endeavor. It may turn out that an author's work was shaped by his prepotent desire to acquire a specific circle of readers and listeners, despite the fact that they never bothered to hear or decode his message.

These are some of the sociological notions that have guided my study of each theorist. My main concern has not been an antiquarian preoccupation with historical "background," but rather an attempt to increase the understanding of a man's work. If, for example, certain eccentric aspects of a man's work can be explained by his ex-centric location in the social structure, then I would consider this a vindication of the fruitfulness and power of a sociological interpretation of sociology.[12]

At the request of many friends and colleagues, this new edition deals with the more recent developments in sociological theory as well as with the master theorists. The final chapter, "Recent Trends in American Sociological Theory," provides a discussion of the major theoretical orientations that have emerged between the 1940's and the 1960's. Since most of the authors presented are, happily, still among the living, the chapter is purely expository. I felt it inappropriate to consider these authors in the same biographical detail and with the same sociology of knowledge approach that were used in the case of their predecessors.

[12] For a much fuller and elaborate scheme in the sociology of knowledge than I shall utilize here, see Robert K. Merton, "The Sociology of Knowledge" in his *Social Theory and Social Structure,* enlarged ed. (New York, The Free Press, 1968), esp. pp. 514 ff. Cf. also Lewis Coser, *Men of Ideas* (New York, The Free Press, 1965).

Contents

GEORGE HERBERT MEAD 1863–1931

ROBERT EZRA PARK 1864–1944

VILFREDO PARETO 1848–1923

Masters of Sociological Thought

Ideas in Historical and Social Context

SECOND EDITION

Auguste Comte

1798-1857

THE WORK

Comte's aim was to create a naturalistic science of society, which would both explain the past development of mankind and predict its future course. In addition to building a science capable of explaining the laws of motion that govern humanity over time, Comte attempted to formulate the conditions that account for social stability at any given historical moment. The study of *social dynamics* and *social statics*—of progress and order, of change and stability—are the twin pillars of his system.

The society of man, Comte taught, must be studied in the same scientific manner as the world of nature. It is subject to basic laws just as is the rest of the cosmos, even though it presents added complexities. Natural science, Comte argued, had succeeded in establishing the lawfulness of natural phenomena. It discovered that these phenomena, from the falling of stones to the movement of planets, followed ordered sequences of development. In the world of nature, science had succeeded in progressively contracting the realm of the apparently nonordered, the fortuitous and the accidental. The stage was now set for a similar endeavor in the study of society.

Natural scientists, since the days of Newton and his immediate predecessors, had developed explanatory schemes in which the previous vain quest for first and final causes had been abandoned and had been replaced by the study of laws, that is, of "invariable relations of succession and resemblance."[1] Instead of relying on the authority of tradition, the new science relied on "reasoning and observation, duly combined"[2] as the only legitimate means of attaining knowledge. Every scientific theory must be based on observed facts, but it is equally true that "facts cannot be observed without the guidance of some theory."[3]

The new social science that Comte sought to establish he first called "social physics"; later, when he thought that the term had been "stolen" from him by the Belgian social statistician, Adolphe Quetelet, he coined the word "sociology," a hybrid term compounded of Latin and Greek parts. It was to

[1] *The Positive Philosophy of Auguste Comte,* in three volumes, translated and condensed by Harriet Martineau (London, Bell, 1896), Vol. I, p. 2. I have used this Martineau version throughout since it is easily available in most college libraries and since it was personally approved by Auguste Comte.

[2] *Ibid.* [3] *Positive Philosophy,* I, p. 4.

be patterned after the natural sciences, not only in its empirical methods and epistemological underpinnings, but also in the functions it would serve for mankind. Far from being of theoretical interest alone, the social sciences, like the natural sciences, must ultimately be of concrete benefit to man and play a major part in the amelioration of the human condition.

In order for man to transform his nonhuman environment to his advantage, he must know the laws that govern the natural world, "For it is only by knowing the laws of phenomena, and thus being able to foresee them, that we can . . . set them to modify one another for our advantage. . . . Whenever we effect anything great it is through a knowledge of natural laws. . . . From Science comes Prevision; from Prevision comes Action." (*Savoir pour prévoir et prévoir pour pouvoir.*)[4] In a like manner, social action beneficial to mankind will become possible once the laws of motion of human evolution are established, and the basis for social order and civic concord is identified.

As long as men believe that social events "were always exposed to disturbance by the accidental intervention of the legislator, human or divine, no scientific previsions of them would be possible."[5] As long as they believe that social actions followed no law and were, in fact, arbitrary and fortuitous, they could take no concerted action to ameliorate their lot. Under these circumstances men naturally clashed with one another in the pursuit of their differing individual interests. When this was the case, a Hobbesian model of society, in which only power and the willing acceptance of power permit a semblance of order, seemed appropriate and plausible. But things are different once sociology can teach men to recognize the invariable laws of development and order in human affairs. At that time men will learn to utilize these laws for their own collective purposes. "We shall find that there is no chance of order and agreement but in subjecting social phenomena, like all others, to invariable natural laws, which shall, as a whole, prescribe for each period, with entire certainty, the limits and character of social action."[6]

The discovery of the basic laws of society will cure men of overweening ambition; they will learn that at any historical moment the margin of societal action is limited by the exigencies of the proper functioning of the social organism. But at the same time, men will also be enabled to act deliberately within given limits by curbing the operation of societal laws to their own purposes. In the realm of the social, as elsewhere, "the office of science is not to govern, but to modify phenomena; and to do this it is necessary to understand their laws."[7] Above all, once the new scientific dispensation comes into its own, men will no longer think in absolute terms, but in terms relative to a particular state of affairs in society. It is impossible, for example, to talk about political aims without considering the social and historical context of political action. By recognizing and acknowledging the constraint that any social order

[4] *Ibid.*, pp. 20–21. [5] *Positive Philosophy*, II, p. 215. [6] *Positive Philosophy*, I, p. 216.
[7] *Positive Philosophy*, II, p. 240.

imposes on action, men will at the same time be enabled freely to order their society within the bounds imposed by necessity.

The new positive science dethroned the authority of perennial tradition. Comte's oft-repeated insistence that nothing is absolute but the relative lies at the very core of his teaching. Instead of accepting canonical truths as everlastingly valid, he insisted on the continued progress of human understanding and the self-corrective character of the scientific enterprise. "All investigation into the nature of beings, and their first and final causes, must always be absolute; whereas the study of the laws of phenomena must be relative, since it supposes a continuous progress of speculation subject to the gradual improvement of observation, without the precise reality ever being fully disclosed. . . . The relative character of scientific conceptions is inseparable from the true idea of natural laws."[8]

But by no means did Comte reject all authority. Once men recognize the overriding authority of science in the guidance of human affairs, they will also abandon the illusory quest for an unfettered "right of free inquiry, or the dogma of unbounded liberty of conscience."[9] Only those willing to submit themselves to the rigorous constraints of scientific methodology and to the canons of scientific evidence can presume to have a say in the guidance of human affairs. Freedom of personal opinion makes no sense in astronomy or physics, and in the future such freedom will be similarly inappropriate in the social sciences. It is an insufferable conceit on the part of ordinary men to presume that they should hold opinions about matters of scientific fact. The intellectual reorganization now dawning in the social sciences "requires the renunciation by the greater number of their right of individual inquiry on subjects above their qualifications."[10] Just as is the case in the natural sciences today, so in the sociology of the future, "the right of free inquiry will abide within its natural and permanent limits: that is, men will discuss, under appropriate intellectual conditions, the real connections of various consequences with fundamental rules universally respected."[11] The exigent requirements of scientific discourse will set firm limits on vain speculation and unbridled utopianism.

METHODS OF INQUIRY

What then are the resources upon which sociology can draw when it sets itself the task of explaining the laws of progress and of social order? They are, first of all, the same that have been used so successfully in the natural sciences: *observation, experimentation,* and *comparison.*

Observation does not mean the unguided quest for miscellaneous facts. "But for the guidance of a preparatory theory," the observer would not know what facts to look at.[12] "No social fact can have any scientific meaning till it is

[8] *Ibid.,* p. 213. [9] *Ibid.,* p. 151. [10] *Ibid.,* p. 153. [11] *Ibid.,* p. 152. [12] *Ibid.,* p. 243.

connected with some other social fact"[13] by a preliminary theory. Hence, observation can come into its own only when it is subordinated to the statical and dynamic laws of phenomena.[14] But within these limits it remains indispensable.

The second scientific method of investigation, *experimentation,* is only partly applicable in the social sciences. Direct experimentation is not feasible in the human world. But "experimentation takes place whenever the regular course of the phenomenon is interfered with in any determinate manner. . . . Pathological cases are the true scientific equivalent of pure experimentation."[15] Disturbances in the social body are "analogous to diseases in the individual organism,"[16] and so the study of the pathological gives, as it were, privileged access to an understanding of the normal.

The scientific method of inquiry of central importance to the sociologist is *comparison,* above all, because it "performs the great service of casting out the . . . spirit [of absolutism]." Comparisons of human with animal societies will give us precious clues to "the first germs of the social relations"[17] and to the borderlines between the human and the animal. Yet comparisons within the human species are even more central to sociology. The chief method here "consists in a comparison of the different co-existing states of human society on the various parts of the earth's surface—these states being completely independent of each other. By this method, the different stages of evolution may all be observed at once."[18] Though the human race as a whole has progressed in a single and uniform manner, various populations "have attained extremely unequal degrees of development"[19] from causes still little understood. Hence, certain phases of development "of which the history of [Western] civilization leaves no perceptible traces, can be known only by this comparative method,"[20] that is, by the comparative study of primitive societies. Moreover, the comparative method is of the essence when we wish to study the influence of race or climate on human affairs. It is indispensable, for example, to combat fallacious doctrines, "as when social differences have been ascribed to the political influence of climate, instead of that inequality of evolution which is the real cause."[21]

Although all three conventional methods of science must be used in sociology, it relies above all on a fourth one, the *historical method.* "The historical comparison of the consecutive states of humanity is not only the chief scientific device of the new political philosophy . . . it constitutes the substratum of the science, in whatever is essential to it."[22] Historical comparisons throughout the time in which humanity has evolved are at the very core of sociological inquiry. Sociology is nothing if it is not informed by a sense of historical evolution.

[13] *Ibid.,* p. 245. [14] *Ibid.* [15] *Ibid.,* p. 246. [16] *Ibid.* [17] *Ibid.,* p. 248. [18] *Ibid.,* p. 249. [19] *Ibid.,* p. 250. [20] *Ibid.* [21] *Ibid.,* p. 251. [22] *Ibid.*

THE LAW OF HUMAN PROGRESS

As early as 1822, when he was still an apprentice to Saint-Simon, Comte set himself the task "to discover through what fixed series of successive transformations the human race, starting from a state not superior to that of the great apes, gradually led to the point at which civilized Europe finds itself today."[23] Applying what he conceived to be a method of scientific comparison through time, Comte emerged with his central conception, *The Law of Human Progress* or *The Law of Three Stages.*

The evolution of the human mind has paralleled the evolution of the individual mind. Phylogeny, the development of human groups or the entire human race, is retraced in ontogeny, the development of the individual human organism. Just as each one of us tends to be a devout believer in childhood, a critical metaphysician in adolescence, and a natural philosopher in manhood, so mankind in its growth has traversed these three major stages.

> Each of our leading conceptions—each branch of our knowledge, passes successively through three different theoretical conditions: the Theological or ficticious; the Metaphysical or abstract; and the Scientific or positive. . . . In the theological state, the human mind, seeking the essential nature of beings, the first and final causes (the origin and purpose) of all effects . . . supposes all phenomena to be produced by the immediate action of supernatural beings. In the metaphysical state . . . the mind supposes . . . abstract forces, veritable entities (that is, personified abstractions) . . . capable of producing all phenomena. . . . In the final, the positive state, the mind has given over the vain search after Absolute notions, the origin and destination of the universe, and the causes of phenomena, and applies itself to the study of their laws—that is, their invariable relations of succession and resemblance.[24]

For Comte, each successive stage or sub-stage in the evolution of the human mind necessarily grew out of the preceding one. "The constitution of the new system cannot take place before the destruction of the old,"[25] and before the potentialities of the old mental order have been exhausted. "The highest order of minds cannot discern the characteristics of the coming period till they are close upon it."[26]

Although Comte focused mainly on stages in the development and progressive emancipation of the human mind, he stressed that these stages correlated with parallel stages in the development of social organization, of types of social order, of types of social units, and of the material conditions of human life. All these, he thought, evolved in similar manner as the changes in progressive mental developments.

[23] Auguste Comte, *Système de politique positive,* 4 vols., 4th ed. (Paris, Crès, 1912), Vol. IV, Appendix. [24] *Ibid.,* pp. 1–2. [25] *Ibid.,* p. 149. [26] *Ibid.*

would be a mistake, Comte averred, to expect a new social order, any han a new intellectual order, to emerge smoothly from the death throes old: "The passage from one social system to another can never be continuous and direct."[27] In fact, human history is marked by alternative "organic" and "critical" periods. In organic periods, social stability and intellectual harmony prevail, and the various parts of the body social are in equilibrium. In critical periods, in contrast, old certainties are upset, traditions are undermined, and the body social is in fundamental disequilibrium. Such critical periods—and the age in which Comte lived, seemed to him preeminently critical—are profoundly unsettling and perturbing to men thirsting for order. Yet they are the necessary prelude to the inauguration of a new organic state of affairs. "There is always a transitional state of anarchy which lasts for some generations at least; and lasts the longer the more complete is the renovation to be wrought."[28]

It can hardly be questioned that Comte's Law of Three Stages has a strongly mentalistic or idealistic bias. Yet, as has been noted, he correlated each mental age of mankind with its characteristic accompanying social organization and type of political dominance.[29] The theological stage is dominated by

priests and ruled by military men (Comte subdivides this stage, as he does others, into a variety of substages, but discussions of these are not pertinent

for an understanding of the Law.) The metaphysical stage—which corresponds very roughly to the Middle Ages and the Renaissance—was under the sway of churchmen and lawyers. The positive stage, just dawning, will be governed by industrial administrators and scientific moral guides. Similarly, in the first stage the family is the prototypical social unit, in the second the state rises into societal prominence, and in the third the whole human race becomes the operative social unit.

Furthermore, though Comte insists repeatedly that "intellectual evolution is the preponderant principle"[30] of his explanation of human progress, he nevertheless admits other causal factors. Increases in population, for example, are seen as a major determinant of the rate of social progress. The "progressive condensation of our species, especially in its early stages" brings about

> such a division of employment . . . as could not take place among smaller numbers: and . . . the faculties of individuals are stimulated to find subsistence by more refined methods. . . . By creating new wants and new difficulties, this gradual concentration develops new means, not only of progress but of order, by neutralizing physical inequalities, and affording a growing ascendancy to those intellectual and moral forces which are suppressed among a scanty population."[31]

Comte sees the division of labor as a powerful impellent of social evolution.

[27] *Ibid.*, p. 148. [28] *Ibid.* [29] *Ibid.*, p. 143. [30] *Positive Philosophy*, II, p. 307.
[31] *Ibid.*, p. 305.

HIERARCHY OF THE SCIENCES

Comte's second best known theory, that of the hierarchy of the sciences, is intimately connected with the Law of Three Stages. Just as mankind progresses only through determinant stages, each successive stage building on the accomplishments of its predecessors, so scientific knowledge passes through similar stages of development. But different sciences progress at different rates. "Any kind of knowledge reaches the positive stage early in proportion to its generality, simplicity, and independence of other departments."[32] Hence astronomy, the most general and simple of all natural sciences, develops first. In time, it is followed by physics, chemistry, biology, and finally, sociology. Each science in this series depends for its emergence on the prior developments of its predecessors in a hierarchy marked by the law of increasing complexity and decreasing generality.

The social sciences, the most complex and the most dependent for their emergence on the development of all the others, are the "highest" in the hierarchy. "Social science offers the attributes of a completion of the positive method. All the others . . . are preparatory to it. Here alone can the general sense of natural law be decisively developed, by eliminating forever arbitrary wills and chimerical entities, in the most difficult case of all."[33] Social science "enjoys all the resources of the anterior sciences"[34] but, in addition, it uses the historical method which "investigates, not by comparison, but by gradual filiation."[35] "The chief phenomenon in sociology . . . that is, the gradual and continuous influence of generations upon each other—would be disguised or unnoticed, for want of the necessary key—historical analysis."[36]

Although sociology has special methodological characteristics that distinguish it from its predecessors in the hierarchy, it is also dependent upon them. It is especially dependent on biology, the science that stands nearest to it in the hierarchy. What distinguishes biology from all the other natural sciences is its holistic character. Unlike physics and chemistry, which proceed by isolating elements, biology proceeds from the study of organic wholes. And it is this emphasis on organic or organismic unity that sociology has in common with biology. "There can be no scientific study of society either in its conditions or its movements, if it is separated into portions, and its divisions are studied apart."[37] The only proper approach in sociology consists in "viewing each element in the light of the whole system. . . . In the inorganic sciences, the elements are much better known to us than the whole which they constitute: so that in that case we must proceed from the simple to the compound. But the reverse method is necessary in the study of Man and Society; Man and Society as a whole being better known to us, and more accessible subjects of study, than the parts which constitute them."[38]

[32] *Positive Philosophy,* I, p. 6. [33] *Positive Philosophy,* III, pp. 383–84. [34] *Ibid.* [35] *Ibid.*
[36] *Positive Philosophy,* II, p. 261. [37] *Ibid.,* p. 225. [38] *Ibid.,* pp. 225–26.

CIAL STATICS AND DYNAMICS

Just as in biology it is useful to separate anatomy from physiology, so it is desirable to make a distinction in sociology between statics and dynamics. "The distinction is not between two classes of facts, but between two aspects of theory. It corresponds with the double conception of order and progress: for order consists . . . in a permanent harmony among the conditions of social existence, and progress consists in social development."[39] Order and Progress, statics and dynamics, are hence always correlative to each other.

In order to supplement his theory of stages, Comte set out to investigate the foundations of social stability. "The statical study of sociology consists in the investigation of the laws of action and reaction of the different parts of the social system—apart, for the occasion, from the fundamental movement which is always gradually modifying them."[40] It studies the balance of mutual relations of elements within a social whole. There must always be a "spontaneous harmony between the whole and the parts of the social system."[41] When such harmony is lacking, we are confronted by a pathological case.

When Comte deals with the components of a social system, he emphatically refuses to see individuals as elementary parts. "The scientific spirit forbids us to regard society as composed of individuals. The true social unit is the family—reduced, if necessary, to the elementary couple which forms its basis. . . . Families become tribes and tribes become nations."[42] A social science that takes as its point of departure the needs and propensities of individuals is bound to fail. In particular, it is erroneous to derive man's social tendencies, "which are now proved to be inherent in his nature,"[43] from utilitarian considerations. In the early ages of humanity the individual advantages of association were doubtful. "It is thus evident that the social state would never have existed if its rise had depended on a conviction of its individual utility."[44]

It is within the family that the elementary egotistical propensities are curbed and harnessed to social purposes. "It is by the avenue [of the family] that man comes forth from his mere personality, and learns to live in another, while obeying his most powerful instincts."[45] The family is the most elementary social unit and the prototype of all other human associations, for these evolve from family and kinship groups. "The collective organism is essentially composed of families which are its true elements, of classes and castes which form its true tissue, and finally of cities and townships which are its true organs."[46]

Although Comte conceived of society by analogy with a biological organism, he was aware of the difficulties that such analogical thinking brings in its wake. A biological organism is, so to speak, encased in a skin and hence

[39] *Ibid.*, p. 218. [40] *Ibid.*, p. 219. [41] *Ibid.*, p. 222.
[42] *Positive Philosophy*, II, p. 281, and *Système*, II, p. 181. [43] *Positive Philosophy*, II, p. 275.
[44] *Ibid.*, p. 276. [45] *Ibid.*, p. 281. [46] *Système*, II, p. 293.

has material boundaries. The body social, however, cannot be held together by physical means, but only by spiritual ties. Hence, Comte assigned central importance to language, and above all, religion.

Language is the vessel in which the thought of preceding generations, the culture of our ancestors, is stored. By participating in a linguistic universe, we are part of a linguistic community. Language binds us to our fellows and at the same time connects us to the long chain that links a living community to its remote ancestors. Human society has more dead than living members. Without a common language men could never have attained solidarity and consensus; without this collective tool no social order is possible.

A common language is indispensable to a human community, but it is only a medium, not a positive guide, to behavior. What is needed in addition is a common religious belief. Religion furnishes the unifying principle, the common ground without which individual differences would tear society apart. Religion permits men to overcome their egoistic propensities and to transcend themselves in the love of their fellow men. It is the powerful cement that binds a society together in a common cult and a common system of beliefs. Religion is at the root of social order. It is indispensable for making legitimate the commands of government. No temporal power can endure without the support of spiritual power. "Every government supposes a religion to consecrate and regulate commandment and obedience."[47]

Beyond language and religion, there is a third factor that links man to his fellows: the division of labor. Men are

> bound together by the very distribution of their occupations; and it is this distribution which causes the extent and growing complexity of the social organism.
>
> The social organization tends more and more to rest on an exact estimate of individual diversities, by so distributing employments as to appoint each one to the destination he is most fit for, from his own nature . . . , from his education and his position, and, in short, from all his qualifications; so that all individual organizations, even the most vicious and imperfect . . . , may finally be made use of for the general good.[48]

Comte believed in principle that the division of labor, while it fostered the development of individual gifts and capacities, also contributed to human solidarity by creating in each individual a sense of his dependence on others. Yet at the same time, he was perturbed by what he considered certain negative aspects of the modern industrial division of labor.

> If the separation of social functions develops a useful spirit of detail, on the one hand, it tends on the other, to extinguish or to restrict what we may call the aggregate or general spirit. In the same way, in moral relations, while

[47] *Ibid.*, p. 194. [48] *Positive Philosophy*, II, p. 292.

> each individual is in close dependence on the mass, he is drawn away from it by the expansion of his special activity, constantly recalling him to his private interest, which he but very dimly perceives to be related to the public. . . . The inconveniences of the division of functions increase with its characteristic advantages.[49]

As a result, Comte expressed the fervent hope that in the future both temporal and spiritual power would unite "to keep up the idea of the whole, and the feeling of the common interconnection."[50]

Comte always considered social institutions, whether language or religion or the division of labor, not so much in their own right as in terms of the contribution they make to the wider social order. To this extent, he must surely be regarded as one of the earliest functional analysts of society, for he not only considered the consequences social phenomena have on social systems, but he stressed the interconnectedness of all these phenomena. "There must always be a spontaneous harmony between the parts and the whole of the social system. . . . It is evident that not only must political institutions and social manners, on the one hand, and manners and ideas on the other, be always mutually connected; but further that this consolidated whole must always be connected, by its nature, with the corresponding state of the integral development of humanity."[51]

To Comte, the study of social statics, that is, of the conditions and preconditions of social order, was inevitably linked to the study of social dynamics, which he equated with human progress and evolution. Though he failed to specify this link and to show how it operated concretely, he reiterated this position in programatic form. Despite the fact that it seemed desirable for methodological and heuristic purposes to separate the study of statics and dynamics, in empirical reality they were correlative. Functional and evolutionary analyses, far from contradicting each other, were in effect complementary.

THE NORMATIVE DOCTRINE

To the preceding outline of Comte's scientific writings must be added a summary of his normative theory, which he sketched out in his earliest papers and developed in his later work, from the *Positive Philosophy* on. He elaborated a complex blueprint of the good positive society of the future, a society directed by the spiritual power of priests of the new positive religion and leaders of banking and industry. These scientific sociologist-priests would be, as were their Catholic predecessors in the theological age, the moral guides and censors of the community, using the force of their superior knowledge to recall men to their duties and obligations; they would be the directors of education

[49] *Ibid.*, p. 293. [50] *Ibid.*, p. 294. [51] *Ibid.*, p. 222.

and the supreme judges of the abilities of each member of society. In the positive sociocracy of the future, the scientist-priests of the religion of humanity, having acquired positive knowledge of what is good and evil, would sternly hold men to their collective duty and would help suppress any subversive ideas of inherent rights. Saint-Simon had suggested that in the future the domination of men over men would be replaced by the administration of things. Comte now argued that the "things" to be administered were in fact human individuals. Human relations would become "thingified." Just as in the eleventh century Pope Hildebrand had for a brief moment extended his spiritual power over all temporal power, so the High Priest of Humanity, armed with a scientific knowledge the Pope could not yet command, would institute a reign of harmony, justice, rectitude, and equity. The new positivist order, to quote some of Comte's favorite formulae, would have Love as its Principle, Order as its Basis, and Progress as its Aim. The egoistic propensities to which mankind was prone throughout previous history would be replaced by altruism, by the command, *Live for Others*. Individual men would be suffused by love for their fellows, and they would lovingly venerate the positivist engineers of the soul who in their wisdom would incarnate the scientific knowledge of man's past and present and the lawfully determined path into a predictable future.

Comte, especially in his later years, considered himself not only a social scientist but also, and primarily, a prophet and founder of a new religion that promised salvation for all the ailments of mankind. These normative aspects of Comte's thought, although important for the historian of ideas, are only of peripheral concern here, where the focus is on sociology as a scientific enterprise. Yet this aspect of Comte's work must be kept in mind in relation to his life and to the social and intellectual context in which his work emerged.

THE MAN

Auguste Comte[52] was born on January 19, 1798, on the first of Pluviôse in the Sixth Year of the Republic, in the southern French city of Montpellier. His father, a fervent Catholic and discreet Royalist, was a petty government official, an earnest, methodical, and straightlaced man, devoted to his work, his religion, and his family, whose only pastime was to cultivate his garden. The older Comte despised the Revolution and decried the persecution of Catholicism it had brought in its wake but never forgot that he was in the

[52] My main sources for this section have been Henri Gouhier's monumental *La Jeunesse d'Auguste Comte*, 3 vols. (Paris, Vrin, 1933–1941), as well as his *La Vie d'Auguste Comte* (Paris, Gallimard, 1931). I have also profited a great deal from Frank E. Manuel's *The New World of Henri Saint-Simon* (Cambridge, Harvard University Press, 1956) and the chapter on Comte in his *The Prophets of Paris* (Cambridge, Harvard University Press, 1962). Emile Littré's *Auguste Comte et la philosophie positive*, 3rd ed. (Paris, Aux Bureaux de la Philosophie Positive, 1877) has also been helpful.

service of the government, no matter how quickly its form and composition changed in these turbulent times. He was, above all, a man attached to order.

Small, delicate, and subject to many illnesses, the young Auguste Comte nevertheless proved to be an outstanding student at the imperial *lycée* of his native town, which he had entered at the age of nine. He was studiously devoted to his work, but he was also among the most recalcitrant and rebellious of the students. Very early in his school career he lost the faith of his parents and substituted for it a fervent republican faith in liberty. He hated the reigning Emperor and dreamed of a revival of the glorious days of the Revolution.

The only teacher who made a very strong impression on the young Comte was his professor of mathematics, a former Protestant pastor named Daniel Encontre, a man of broad learning and catholic concerns. It was probably he who awoke in the young Comte his interest in mathematics and also served as a role model for the wide-ranging intellectual that Comte was to become.

In August 1814, Comte entered the competition for the entrance examinations of the prestigious *Ecole Polytechnique,* a kind of governmental M.I.T., but even more difficult to enter, and was admitted as the fourth man on the entrance list. He registered in October and moved to Paris—a city he was never to leave again, except for relatively short periods.

The Emperor had never been very popular in the *Ecole Polytechnique,* which had been created by the *Convention* as a scientific school. He had reorganized it on a military model and had it directed by a military governor and his general staff. From the point of view of Napoleon, the school ought to have trained mainly officers, even though it was also set up to furnish engineers for the major public services. The students, still having the original scientific character of the school clearly in their minds, saw themselves as budding scientists and disagreed with Napoleon's practical emphasis.

Early in 1814, when the Allies attacked Paris, young *polytechnicians* fought in the suburbs against the enemy, but in November the school operated again as usual, and the young Comte, though a bit bored, could enjoy the privilege of sitting at the feet of many of the eminent scientists of France. He soon felt that this was *his* school, a school from which he not only wished to graduate with honors, but where he hoped to teach after the end of his studies. Yet the young Comte, whom most of his comrades already considered the leader of his class, continued the disorderly and unruly behavior of his Montpellier *lycée* days. Then the ardent hater of Napoleonic tyranny, he now found the restoration of the Bourbon kings even less to his taste. He shared the Republican faith of the majority of his schoolmates; with the reestablished monarchy and its mediocre servants, even the Napoleonic Empire appeared beautiful.

When Napoleon returned, the school as a whole enthusiastically joined his camp, and Comte was one of the leaders of his revolutionary fellows. But the hundred days passed quickly. After Waterloo and the capitulation of

Paris, order was reestablished and the school routine began all over again. Comte returned to his course of studies—and to his usual insubordinate and insolent behavior toward the school authorities.

In April 1816, six students protested to the administration against its antiquated mode of examination. When these six were to be punished, the whole student body expressed its solidarity. The administration appealed to the minister in charge. Soon the governor announced that the school was to be closed. It was to be reorganized, and those students who had behaved themselves could apply for readmission at a later date. Boiling with rage, Comte went home. But Montpellier did not hold him for long. The action was in Paris.

Returning to the capital in July, Comte supported himself by tutoring and lived in hopes of the imminent overthrow of the Bourbon oppressors. He met a general who had a number of connections in the United States and who promised to find him a position in an American version of the *Ecole Polytechnique,* which was about to be organized. Comte, full of Republican ardor, dreamed of emigrating forever to the land of the free. But the project fell through. Congress approved in principle the idea of creating an American *Polytechnique* but postponed the opening indefinitely.

Comte continued to give private lessons in mathematics and helped translate a book on geometry from the English, but the future looked bleak. He did not even try to gain readmission to the *Ecole Polytechnique,* which was being reopened. And then came the *coup de foudre,* which was to change the direction of his life.

THE ALLIANCE WITH SAINT-SIMON

In the summer of 1817 Comte was introduced to Henri Saint-Simon, then director of the periodical *Industrie,* a creative, fertile, disorderly, and tumultuous man who was to have a major and lasting influence on Comte's life and works. Saint-Simon, at this point nearly sixty years old, was attracted by the brilliant young man who possessed a trained and methodical capacity for work, which Saint-Simon so conspicuously lacked. Comte became his secretary and close collaborator.

The two men worked for a while in intimate conjunction. In the beginning Comte was paid three hundred francs a month, but when Saint-Simon again experienced those financial straits with which he was frequently afflicted, Comte stayed on without pay both for intellectual reasons and in hopes of future reward.

A number of scholars have argued the question of who benefited the most from the close collaboration, Comte or Saint-Simon. There is no need to take sides in this somewhat byzantine quarrel. It suffices to say that Comte was influenced in a major way by his patron, even though his close contact with

Saint-Simon may have brought to fruition ideas that had already germinated in Comte's mind. It is certain, in any case, that the young Republican advocate of equality was converted to an elitist point of view soon after meeting Saint-Simon; one of Comte's first essays, written in July 1819, testifies to this fact. The elitist conception stayed with him throughout his career.

The sketches and essays that Comte wrote during the years of close association with Saint-Simon, especially between 1819 and 1824, contain the nucleus of all his later major ideas. One finds here not only the major scientific ideas he was to develop in his *Cours de philosophie positive,* but also, and this is often overlooked, the beginnings of his later conceptions concerning the need for a unifying communal order based on a newly instituted spiritual power.

In 1824 Comte finally broke with his master. The immediate cause concerned a somewhat involved and rather squalid fight over the form in which one of Comte's essays was to be published. Should it be under Saint-Simon's name as in the past? Or as Auguste Comte's *Système de politique positive,* first volume, first part? Comte was given one hundred copies of his work under his own name. At the same time, Saint-Simon put out one thousand copies entitled *Catechisme des industriels* by Henri de Saint-Simon, Third Installment, a work that included Comte's essay, with an unsigned preface written by Saint-Simon in which he found fault with his disciple. Comte now repudiated the master whose name became anathema to him during the rest of his life. The master once denied was rejected over and over again.

The quarrel had intellectual as well as material causes. To be sure, Comte had begun to chafe under the pretension of the old man who continued to treat him as the obedient pupil he had once been rather than as a member of a kind of competitive alliance. Comte had already begun to make a name for himself in the world of liberal journalism and among an elite of scientists. But the two collaborators now also diverged in regard to the strategy to be used for winning consent and influence among the public. Saint-Simon, ever the activist, wished to emphasize the need for immediate reform. What he wanted above all was to inspire the liberal industrialists and bankers who were his backers to take prompt steps for the reorganization of French society. Comte, in contrast, emphasized that theoretical work had to take precedence over reform activities, and that establishing the foundations of the scientific doctrine was more important for the time being than effecting any practical influence. Furthermore, and such are the ironies of intellectual history, Comte, the future High Priest of Humanity, objected strenuously to the religious cast that Saint-Simon now began to give to his doctrine.

And so, although he now basked in the glory of having received letters of admiration and encouragement for his last work from such eminent scientists as Cuvier and von Humboldt, as well as from a variety of liberal deputies and publicists, Comte again stood alone—a marginal intellectual, only tenuously connected with the Parisian world of letters and science. There was now a Comtean system, but its author was without position or office, without chair or salary.

In the meantime, Comte thought that he had at least found some security in his personal life. In February 1825, he decided to marry Caroline Massin, a young woman whom he had known for several years, more recently as the owner of a small bookstore and earlier as a streetwalker in the neighborhood of the Palais Royal. The marriage was a tempestuous one—they separated several times and finally parted ways forever—but for a time Comte felt that he had found domestic anchorage, although he was still adrift in his search for professional recognition and social position.

Comte refused to accept a proffered position as a chemical engineer, continuing instead to eke out a meager living by giving private lessons. In this way he could devote himself to theoretical rather than practical problems and was sometimes able to establish close ties with the high-born families whose sons he taught. For a while he also gained some additional income from writing, more particularly for the *Producteur,* a journal founded by the spiritual sons of Saint-Simon after the death of their master.

During these years Comte's major preoccupation was centered in the elaboration of his positive philosophy. When the work seemed advanced enough to be presented to a wider audience, Comte, having no official chair from which to expound his theories, decided to offer a private course to which auditors would subscribe in advance and where he would disclose his *summa* of positive knowledge. The course opened in April, 1826. Some illustrious men graced the audience. Alexander von Humboldt, several members of the Academy of Sciences, the economist Charles Dunoyer, the duc Napoléon de Montebello, Hippolyte Carnot, the son of the organizer of the revolutionary armies and brother of the great scientist Sadi Carnot, and a number of former students of the *Ecole Polytechnique* were in attendance.

Comte gave three of his lectures, but when the audience came for the fourth, they found the doors closed. Comte had fallen ill, having suffered a serious mental collapse. For a while he was treated for "mania" in the hospital of the famous Dr. Esquirol, where this author of a *Treatise on Mania* attempted to cure him by cold-water treatment and bloodletting. When Madame Comte finally decided to bring him back to their home, Esquirol objected. The register of discharge of the patient had a note in Esquirol's hand, "N.G." (*Non Guéri*—not recovered.)

After returning home, Comte fell into a deep melancholic state, and he even attempted suicide by throwing himself into the Seine. But in the course of the year 1827, and after an extended trip to his native Montpellier, the patient slowly recovered. In August 1828, he symbolized his victory over the illness by writing a review of a book entitled *Irritation and Folly.*

The course of lectures was resumed in 1829, and Comte was pleased again to find in the audience several great names of science and letters. Yet, the small reputation he enjoyed proved a fragile support. A number of eminent men continued to stand by him, but as time went on he gradually became an object of ridicule in the scientific community. Specialists of every field united in condemnation of a man who seemed to have the promethean ambition to encompass the development of all the sciences in his encyclopedic enterprise.

Comte now resumed his wretched life in neglect and isolation. During the years 1830–1842, when he wrote his masterwork, the *Cours de philosophie positive,* he continued to live miserably on the margin of the academic world. All attempts to be appointed to a chair at the *Ecole Polytechnique* or to a position with the Academy of Sciences or the *Collège de France* were of no avail. He only managed in 1832 to be appointed "répétiteur d'analyse et de mécanique" at the *Ecole;* five years later he was also given the position of external examiner for the same school. The first position brought a meager two thousand francs, the second little more. He also taught mathematics at a private school, and these three positions, together with unused *per diem* fees paid him as a traveling examiner for the *Ecole,* allowed him to live just above the margin of poverty.

During the years of intense concentration when he wrote the *Cours,* he not only was troubled by financial difficulties and continued academic rebuffs, but by increasing marital difficulties. Slowly Comte withdrew further and further into his shell. The system he elaborated began to dominate the man. For reasons of "cerebral hygiene," he no longer followed the current literature in all the many fields he wrote about. In fact, he decided in 1838 that he would no longer read any scientific work, limiting himself to the reading of fiction and poetry. In his last years the only book he read over and over again was the *Imitation of Christ.*

Yet despite all these adversities, Comte slowly began to acquire disciples. Perhaps more gratifying than the conversion of a few remarkable French disciples, such as the eminent scholar Emile Littré who became his close follower, was the fact that his positive doctrine now had penetrated across the Channel and received considerable attention there. Sir David Brewster, an eminent physicist, welcomed it in the pages of the *Edinburgh Review* in 1838 and, most gratifying of all, John Stuart Mill became a close admirer and spoke of Comte in his *System of Logic* (1843) as "among the first of European thinkers." Comte and Mill corresponded regularly, and Comte told his British correspondent not only of his scientific work but of the trial and tribulations of his marital life and the difficulties of his material existence. Mill even arranged for a number of British admirers of Comte to send him a considerable sum of money to tide him over his financial difficulties.

Soon after the *Cours* was finally finished, Comte's wife left him forever. Lonely and isolated, he continued to assail those scientists who refused to recognize him. He complained to ministers, wrote quixotic letters to the press, needled his enemies, and taxed the patience of his few remaining friends. In

1844, having created too many enemies at the *Ecole Polytechnique,* his appointment as examiner was not renewed. Hence, he lost about half of his income. (He was to lose his other position with the *Ecole* in 1851.)

The year 1844, when he had been publicly humiliated by not being reappointed at the *Ecole,* was also, it turned out, the year of his greatest elation. He fell in love with Clothilde de Vaux, an upper-class woman not yet thirty years old, who had been abandoned by her husband, a petty official. He had absconded with government funds and had gone to Brussels, leaving her, as well as his gambling debts, in Paris. Comte met her at a young disciple's house and fell passionately in love with her. Suddenly the cool and methodical mask that Comte had presented to the outside world seemed to dissolve. Comte in love was a Comte transformed. All the previously repressed passionate elements of his nature now came to the fore. The encounter with Clothilde, short as it was to be, proved as important to the middle-aged Comte as the encounter with Saint-Simon had been to the young man.

The *grande passion* never led to physical fulfillment. Clothilde resisted all his entreaties and kept the affair on a lofty platonic and romantic plane. And, only a few months after they had exchanged their first love letters, Clothilde took to her bed, stricken by that most romantic of illnesses, tuberculosis. Almost a year after the beginning of the affair she died.

Comte now vowed to devote the rest of his life to the memory of "his angel." The *Système de politique positive,* which he had begun to sketch in 1844, was to become a memorial to his beloved. In its pages, Comte now hailed the primacy of emotion over intellect, of feeling over mind; he proclaimed over and over again the healing powers of warm femininity for a humanity too long dominated by the harshness of masculine intellect.

When the *Système* finally appeared between 1851 and 1854, Comte lost many, if not most, of those rationalist followers he had acquired with so much difficulty over the last fifteen years. John Stuart Mill and Emile Littré were not willing to concede that universal love was the solvent for all the difficulties of the age. Nor could they accept the Religion of Humanity of which Comte now proclaimed himself the High Priest. The multiple ritual observances, the special calendar, the whole elaborate rigmarole of the cult now unveiled appeared to them a repudiation of Comte's previous message. The prophet of the positive stage seemed to fall back into the darkness of the theological stage. The intimation of things to come, which can already be found in his earliest writings, had not commanded their attention.

Comte was undismayed by the loss of disciples. Let them go; he would attract others to the bosom of the new Church. Comte decided that he would henceforth sign all his circulars "The Founder of Universal Religion, Great Priest of Humanity." From the seat of the new pontiff now poured letters to the powerful of the world—the Czar Nicholas, the Grand Vizier of the Ottoman Empire, the head of the Jesuits—trying to convert them to the new order. And at home, Comte now lectured to diverse audiences, more particularly the working class, to convert them to the new creed. He wrote appeals to the workers, a *Positive Catechism, Appeals to Conservatives*—in fact, appeals to anybody and everybody who seemed at all disposed to listen.

In 1848, a few days after the February Revolution, he had founded the *Société Positiviste,* which became in the early fifties the main center of his teaching. The members tithed themselves to assure the livelihood of the master and vowed to spread his message. Comte now sent weekly messages to his disciples in the provinces and abroad, which he compared to Saint Paul's epistles. Missions functioned in Spain, England, the United States, and Holland. Every evening, from seven to nine, except on Wednesday when the *Société Positiviste* had its regular meetings, Comte received his Parisian disciples at home. Former polytechnicians and future politicians, intellectuals and manual workers, here intermingled in their great love for the master. He who had been denied so often finally found rest in the knowledge that he had at last found disciples who, unlike the former false friends, did not come together admiring his intellect alone, but basked in the emanation of his love and loved him in return.

Comte had travelled far from the republican and libertarian enthusiasms of his youth. The rebellious student from Montpellier now preached the virtues of submission and the necessity of order. The twin motto of the Positive Church was still Order and Progress, but in these last years the need for order assumed ever greater weight in the eyes of its founder. Revulsion from the bloody events of the June days of 1848 had finally brought Comte into the camp of Napoleon III, and it was this rage for order that now made him see Czars and Grand Viziers, even the head of the Jesuits, as brothers under the skin.

On the seventeenth of June, 1857, Comte, for the first time in eleven years, failed to visit the grave of Clothilde at the Père Lachaise cemetery. The early symptoms of an internal cancer kept him at home. The illness progressed swiftly, and he died on the fifth of September. The following Tuesday, a small group of disciples, friends, and neighbors followed his bier to the Père Lachaise. Here his tomb became the center of a small positivist cemetery where, buried close to the master, are his most faithful disciples.

THE INTELLECTUAL CONTEXT

Auguste Comte was a son of the Enlightenment carrying on the tradition of the philosophers of progress of the late eighteenth century, especially the tradition established by Turgot and Condorcet. This much is beyond dispute; yet, standing by itself, this statement is a serious distortion of his intellectual portrait.

Auguste Comte was a thinker in the tradition of de Bonald and de Maistre, a resolute antagonist of the individualistic approach to human society that had predominated throughout the eighteenth century. Appalled by the breakdown of social order in his days, he called, just as did the traditionalist thinkers, for the reconstruction of a moral community. Since he was scandalized by "the anarchy which day by day envelops society," a rage and quest for order hovers over his work. This, too, is beyond dispute, though later commentators have not always seen this aspect of Comte's work quite as clearly as his link to the tradition of enlightenment.

Auguste Comte was a liberal. This statement is much less defensible than are the first two, yet it too contains more than a grain of truth. During a period of his life, especially in his formative years, he was deeply influenced by liberal thinkers and especially by the liberal political economists from Adam Smith to Jean Baptiste Say.

One could list still other intellectual traditions to which Comte can be linked in one way or another. He knew, for example, some of the writings of Immanuel Kant, more particularly his seminal *Idee zu einer allgemeinen Geschichte in weltbuergerlicher Absicht.* Comte considered Kant "the metaphysician most close to the positive philosophy," and wrote in 1824 that, had he read him earlier, this would have "spared him much effort."[53]

Comte saw himself as the continuator of the dissimilar scientific traditions of Bacon and Descartes, but he was also much impressed with Bossuet's Catholic vision. Montesquieu and Hume, de Condillac and the *idéologues,* as well as the major natural scientists from Newton's day until his own, all exercised considerable influence on his thought. In debt to many traditions but not fully belonging to any, he assimilated various doctrines in order to present a synthesis which, even when it is juxtaposed to the work of Saint-Simon that so deeply influenced him, is uniquely his own. From his young manhood till his middle thirties when he ceased reading other men's works, Comte drew on many sources and selected from them the multiple strands that he wove into the rich texture of his own *summa.* This chapter does not attempt a complete intellectual history, and so only a few of these strands can be considered in some detail.

THE TRADITION OF PROGRESS

In 1750, the Baron Anne Robert Jacques Turgot, the future minister of Louis XVI, then only twenty-three years of age, delivered two lectures at the Sorbonne that were, in Frank Manuel's words, "the first important version in modern times of the ideology of progress."[54] Contrasting the order of nature with its eternal sameness to the world of man, Turgot wrote: "The succession

[53] Letter to d'Eichthal, quoted in Littré, *op. cit.,* pp. 150–51.
[54] *The Prophets,* p. 13.

of men . . . presents a changing spectacle from century to century. . . . All ages are linked to each other by a series of causes and effects which binds the present state of the world with all those which have preceded it." Language and writing were the vehicles by which men transmitted their culture so that "all detailed forms of knowledge constitute a common treasury, which one generation transmits to another like a legacy that is ever being augmented with the discoveries of each century, so that the human race appears . . . to be one immense whole which, like every individual, has its infancy and its progress."[55] Turgot was convinced of the inevitability of progress. There could be no stop to the continuous enlargement of man's intellectual inheritance, and although science, morality, technology, and the arts might each develop at a different pace, thus creating some unequal developments and temporary dislocations, science, and more particularly the mathematical sciences, would always be in the vanguard of progress. The march of science, and hence the forward thrust of mankind, could never be stopped.

The stress on necessary linkages between the ages of mankind, the emphasis on the inevitable increase in the cultural inheritance of humanity, the belief in the powers of science—these and many other elements clearly are major ingredients in Comte's synthesis and make him a continuator of the tradition that was started by Turgot.

Comte was even more deeply indebted to the Marquis Jean-Antoine-Nicolas Caritat de Condorcet, whose *Esquisse d'un tableau historique des progrès de l'esprit humain,* written while he was hiding from Robespierre's police, continued Turgot's emphasis on the long historical chain of progress now culminating in modern rational man. "We pass by imperceptible gradations from the brute to the savage and from the savage to Euler and Newton."[56] Like his predecessor, Condorcet believed that he could document the operation of progress in the past. Its projection into a future of infinite perfectibility was to him a foregone conclusion. Like Turgot, he saw in science and technology the means by which mankind had been propelled forward as well as the main engine of future advances. But while Turgot had still relied on the regular appearance of men of genius to spur the movement of progress, Condorcet thought that with enlightenment and state-supported mass instruction, the number of productive scientists could be deliberately increased, and hence the rate of progress could be enormously accelerated. Taking his clue from Bacon's *New Atlantis,* he elaborated a plan for a new scientific society of the future in which an elite of scientists would collaboratively share their labors and enhance scientific productivity. These men of science would be in the vanguard of humanity. The progress of the ordinary run of mankind would be more sluggish than that of men of scientific training, but common men would eventually accept scientific guidance to reach for further perfectibility. Certain inequalities would continue to exist, but, given the high

[55] Quoted in *ibid.,* p. 21. [56] *Ibid.,* p. 62.

level of achievement of the race as a whole, they would no longer lead to suffering and deprivation. In the tenth epoch of human history (Condorcet had described the previous march of humanity in terms of nine key epochs), mankind would come into its kingdom. Rejecting the last remnants of superstition and clerical domination, men, trusting in the authority and high mission of science, would all move forward and become free and rational citizens. Intellectual and moral progress would go hand in hand, and the heightened pace of scientific discovery and invention would accelerate the rate of general advance.[57]

Comte's close kinship to the major ideas of the author of the *Esquisse* is clearly evident, and he recognized repeatedly the great debt he owed to Condorcet. However, he never followed Condorcet in two of the Marquis' major tenets: the belief in individualism and in relative equality. Comte's doctrine had a strongly hierarchic, anti-individualist and inegalitarian cast. Although in this respect the influence of Saint-Simon was a decisive element, the impact of the traditionalist thinkers was equally marked.

THE TRADITION OF ORDER

Comte heaped high praise on the traditionalists. He referred to them as "that immortal school which emerged . . . under the noble leadership of de Maistre and was dignifiedly brought to completion by de Bonald with the poetic assistance of Chateaubriand."[58] The encomium was justified; Comte owed a great deal to these enemies of the promises and the premises of the Enlightenment—at least as much as he owed to the Enlightenment itself.

The major traditionalists had all been among the *émigrés.* Some of them had not initially been hostile to the Revolution; de Maistre, for example, had even been considered close to the Jacobins in the early years of the Revolution. But they all turned their backs on it during its later radical stages. Writing from foreign shores, they castigated their fellow Frenchmen for the errors of their ways. Devout Catholics and royalists, they saw in the later stages of the Revolution the work of the devil. And the names of the devil's work were individualism, secularism, and the notion of natural rights.

A society not bound together by the ties of moral community, they taught, must collapse into a sandheap of unrelated individuals. A society without the firm support of legitimate authority and without hierarchy was a nonviable monstrosity. Society was an organic whole or it was nothing. The attempt to base social living on contracts between individuals, or to reconstruct society on the basis of natural individual rights, was inspired by hubris or madness, or both. Men had duties rather than rights.

Rousseau and Condorcet were the particular targets of the traditionalists'

[57] My account of Turgot and Condorcet is deeply indebted to Manuel's *The Prophets.*

[58] *Système,* III, p. 605.

contempt. Rousseau had asserted that man, unspoiled by society, had been naturally good. "Coming from the hand of the author of all things," began his *Emile,* "everything is good; in the hand of men everything degenerates." In reply, de Bonald asserted the primacy of society. Society had humanized, it had created, man. "We are bad by nature," he stated, "good through society. The savage is not a man, he is not even a childish man, he is only a degenerate man."[59]

Condorcet had dreamed of perfecting the society of man—an absurd undertaking in the eyes of the traditionalists. "Condorcet wants men to perfect society," wrote de Bonald, "and I maintain on the contrary that it is only society which perfects man in his intellectual and physical aspects."[60] The cardinal error of the Enlightenment, the traditionalists believed, had been to consider that society served the purposes of men. "Man does not exist for society," snorted de Bonald, "society forms him only for its own purposes."[61] The social dimension had primacy over the individual dimension both logically and morally.

To the rationalist and utilitarian image of society as an aggregate of individuals engaged in the pursuit of their private ends, the traditionalists counterposed the notion of the social group. The Revolution, they argued, had destroyed those security-giving groupings that shielded individuals and structured their pursuits. Without such intermediary groupings there could be no community. The family, taught de Bonald, is the nucleus of primitive society. He quoted Cicero, "Prima societas in ipso conjugio est." Domestic societies in their turn form larger groups. All these stand in hierarchical relations to one another, the whole culminating in the spiritual power of the Pope and the secular power of the king. Without religious institutions to keep individual propensities and drives in check, no society can endure. Without religion there is no moral community, and without moral community social living is a lonely ordeal. Devoid of morally sanctioned ties to superiors and inferiors, the society of men decays into a collection of isolated, insulated, and acquisitive persons. The liberated individual of the Enlightenment, the traditionalists contended, is in reality the socially alienated individual.

Society is healthy only when the different orders of which it is composed stay in harmony. The good society of the traditionalists is a pluralistic society, like the medieval world. (Though, it should be remarked in passing that the traditionalists have no monopoly on the notion of pluralism—it is held by many liberals as well.) The family, the estates, the guild, the local community all have their proper sphere of authority, and so, on a higher plane, have the Church and the State. Only through a proper adjustment of these

[59] de Bonald, *Oeuvres* (Paris, J. P. Migne, 1864), Vol. III, pp. 360–61.

[60] de Bonald, *Théorie du pouvoir,* quoted in *La Jeunesse,* II, p. 339.

[61] de Bonald, *Essai analytique sur les lois naturelles* (Paris, 1882), p. 15.

institutions and groups to one another can social stability and harmony be assured. The social order exists in a delicate and finely adjusted balance that men tamper with only at their peril. "Oh, when degree is shaked," the traditionalists might have quoted Shakespeare, "the enterprise is sick."[62]

Order, hierarchy, moral community, spiritual power, the primacy of groups over individuals—these and many other themes of the traditionalists find an echo in Comte. In fact, there is but little in his social statics that cannot be traced to their influence. Yet he could not accept their retrograde vision; to him the good society was not to be found in the medieval past but in a future yet to come. Even though he shared with them an admiration for the medieval papacy and the glory that was the Church, he was not willing to relinquish the optimistic and futuristic vision that he had imbibed from the Enlightenment. He clung to the idea of progress, even though beholden to the vision of social order. He appreciated and admired the traditionalists' view of past organic society; nevertheless, he also believed that this view did not equip them to do justice to the new critical forces that had come to the fore in his day.

To understand the Industrial Revolution, Comte had to turn toward its most determined analysts and apologists, the liberal economists from Adam Smith to Jean Baptiste Say and their allies among the political thinkers of French liberalism.

THE TRADITION OF LIBERALISM

Comte had high praise for Adam Smith, though not for most of his successors. He called Smith "the illustrious philosopher" and referred to his "luminous analyses relating to the division of employments."[63] But he was also critical of Smith, and particularly his successors, for their belief in the self-regulating character of the market. *Laissez faire,* Comte believed, "systematizes anarchy." In as far as the political economists set up "as a dogma, the absence of all regulating intervention whatever,"[64] Comte naturally regarded them as the sworn enemies of his world view.

Comte's belief in the beneficial effects of the division of labor derives directly from Smith. He agreed with Smith that the industrial form of the division of labor had brought in its wake a specially potent form of social cooperation, which allowed men to increase their production immeasurably. In Smith's view, with which Comte concurred, a nation was a vast workshop

[62] On the traditionalists see Robert Nisbet, *The Sociological Tradition* (New York, Basic Books, 1966) as well as his earlier papers quoted therein and several essays in his *Tradition and Revolt* (New York, Random House, 1968). Cf. also Dominique Baggs, *Les Idées politiques en France sous la restauration* (Paris, Presses Universitaires, 1952); Jacques Godechot, *La Contre-révolution* (Paris, Presses Universitaires, 1961); and, for a sharply critical account, Roger Soltau, *French Political Thought in the 19th Century* (New York, Russell and Russell, 1959).

[63] *Positive Philosophy,* II, p. 204. [64] *Ibid.,* p. 206.

where the labor of each, however diverse in character, added to the wealth of all.[65]

It would not be correct to say that Comte's realization of the detrimental consequences of the division of labor, which appeared concomitantly with its beneficial results, derived solely from his reading of economists, such as Sismondi, who were critical of prevailing liberal doctrine. There, too, he was beholden to Adam Smith. Most readers of the *Wealth of Nations* confine their reading to the first two or three books of that work. Were they to read the fifth book, they would find formulations as critical of the division of labor as those of Sismondi:

> In the progress of the division of labor, the employment of the far greater part of those who live by labor, that is, of the great body of the people comes to be confined to a few very simple operations; frequently to one or two. . . . But, the man whose whole life is spent in performing a few simple operations, of which the effects too are, perhaps, always the same, or very nearly the same, has no occasion to exert his understanding, or to exercise his invention. . . . He naturally loses, therefore, the habit of such exertion, and generally becomes as stupid and ignorant as it is possible for a human creature to become.

Such pessimistic views about the effects of the division of labor were, of course, extended and enlarged upon by later socialist and left-Catholic reformers but were neglected in the main writings of liberal political economists. It remains, however, that Comte stood in the line of the Smith tradition both when he praised the new industrial division of labor and when he was sharply critical of its human effects.

There is still one other point for which Comte is directly indebted to the liberal economists: his recognition of the major creative functions of "industrialists" or, in modern parlance, *entrepreneurs*. In this Comte followed Smith's French disciple, Jean Baptiste Say, whose *Le Traité d'économie politique,* which first appeared in 1803, was essentially a work of popularization of ideas from across the Channel. But in at least one aspect it went beyond Smith, who spoke of capitalists, alongside workers and landowners, as the major agents of production. Say distinguished the capitalist from the entrepreneur. He stressed the special and distinct function of entrepreneurship and delineated the role of the entrepreneur. It is he, rather than the capitalist, who directs and superintends production and distribution. The entrepreneur, through his guiding and directing activities, becomes for Say the true pivot of the new industrial system.

Adam Smith had talked about the creative contributions of labor. Say corrected him by pointing out that what was needed was not simply labor but

65 Charles Gide and Charles Rist, *A History of Economic Doctrines* (Boston and New York, Heath, n.d.), p. 57.

"industry," that is, the creative conjunction of labor and capital. Say maintained that the entrepreneur is a man who uses initiative to create value through the judicious employment of factors of production. An industrial product emerges only when raw material is transformed through labor under the directing guidance of an entrepreneur.[66]

Say had not only written a cool description of the new creative role of the "industrieux" as he called them; he had in fact exalted their functions and attempted to make them into the heroes of the dawning industrial world. His influence on his contemporaries and more particularly on the liberal political thinkers of the Restoration was profound. Thus Benjamin Constant, for example, could write, "Industrial property amounts to the amelioration of the whole of society, and one might call it the legislator and the benefactor of the human kind."[67]

Saint-Simon and the Saint-Simonians were to expand on the creative functions of enterprising industrialists, and it may well be that Comte first fully appreciated Say's work under the guidance of his one-time master. Be this as it may, it is readily apparent that the exaltation of the role of the industrial entrepreneur in the work of Comte, as in that of Saint-Simon, had its roots in the liberal teaching of Jean Baptist Say. Comte, though he was assuredly not a liberal, still stands in major aspects of his work under the shadow of Adam Smith and his French disciple.

THE INFLUENCE OF SAINT-SIMON

The notion of a positive Science of Man and that of the hierarchy of the sciences can be found, though in an unsystematic and often only embryonic form, in the work of Saint-Simon. Saint-Simon's knowledge of the natural sciences was rudimentary; yet some of his writings during the Empire already sound surprisingly Comtean. "All sciences," he wrote then, "began by being conjectural, the greater order of things has ordained that they all become positive." The sciences were developed in a series, Saint-Simon contended, which went from the relatively simple to the highly complex. The time had now come for the emergence of a fully positive Science of Man that would revolutionize the institutions of Europe. At this point, "Morals will become a positive science. Politics will become a positive science. Philosophy will become a positive science. The religious system will be perfected. The clergy will be reorganized and reconstituted. The reorganization of the clergy can only mean the reorganization of the scientific corps because the clergy must be the scientific corps."[68] Such notions abound, and one could go on quoting.

Not only the embryo of the general philosophy of positivism but also

[66] *Ibid.*, p. 113, and M. Girard, *Le Libéralisme en France de 1814 à 1848* (Paris, Les Cours de la Sorbonne, n.d.), pp. 86 ff. [67] Girard, *op. cit.*, p. 157. [68] *The New World*, esp. pp. 133–36.

many specific Comtean notions are adumbrated in Saint-Simon's writings: the emphasis on the key role of industrialists in ordering the temporal affairs of society; the stress on the need to reconstitute spiritual power in the hands of an elite of scientists; the distinctions between organic and critical epochs in history, and the realization that after the critical work of the Enlightenment and the Revolution had been accomplished, there was an urgent need to build the foundations for a new organic unity; the stress on social engineering and planning and the concomitant revulsion from the anarchy of the age; the emphasis on the need for hierarchy and on the creative powers of elites—these, and many other Comtean notions, can be found in the work of Saint-Simon.

There are, nevertheless, major differences in Saint-Simon's and Comte's approach. To cite only one, the aristocratic Saint-Simon never failed to put great stress on the ideal of individual self-realization in all his Utopian dreams. His followers would develop this notion and stress sexual liberation, the "rehabilitation of the flesh." In contrast, Comte, the son of a petty functionary, pictured the man of the future as an ascetic—a self-abnegating, self-denying creature totally devoted to the Whole.[69]

THE EFFECTS OF INTELLECTUAL COMPETITION: A NOTE ON COMTE AND QUETELET

Comte came upon the term "social physics," which he used quite explicitly in his 1822 paper, through an extension of the notions of the natural sciences. "We now possess," he wrote, "a celestial physics, a terrestrial physics, either mechanical or chemical, a vegetable physics and an animal physics; we still want one more and last one, social physics, to complete the system of our knowledge of nature. I understand by social physics the science which has for its subject the study of social phenomena."[70] This was a terminological (and partly conceptual) analogue. A few years later, Comte abandoned the term "social physics" in favor of the neologism "sociology." This was not because he now judged organismic analogies to be more appropriate in the study of society than physical ones; rather, he dropped the term because it had been used by a Belgian statistician, Adolphe Quetelet (1796–1874). Not knowing of Comte's usage, Quetelet had published in 1835 a book called *On Man and the Development of Human Faculties,* which bore the subtitle, *An Essay on Social Physics.* Comte was outraged, especially since Quetelet's system was based on the notion that the normal curve of distribution of social phenomena points to the crucial importance of "the average man," and hence contradicted Comte's hierarchical notions.

To distinguish his system from that of Quetelet, Comte coined the hybrid term sociology. This episode is worth recounting if only because it evidences, once again, how decisions of thinkers are affected by their interactions with other scholars in their significant environment, and by their concern to be

[69] *The Prophets,* pp. 280–81. [70] *Système,* IV, Appendix.

distinctively identifiable in their own thinking. There is, beyond that, however, more than a terminological aspect. Quetelet introduced the notion of "social physics" as an off-shoot of his empirical mode of investigation in which he demonstrated, for the time being, statistical uniformities in man's behavior. Comte went at it in quite another way, through the philosophical style of analogy. This highlights marked differences in the intellectual currents of the time. Quetelet and Comte represent opposite poles in sociological thinking, and it is hence fortunate that they came to employ different terminologies.

THE SOCIAL CONTEXT

Auguste Comte lived through seven political regimes and an untold number of insurrections, uprisings, and popular revolts. For more than fifty years France had experienced an almost continuous series of upheavals punctuated by only fairly short periods of relative calm. The major revolutions resulted not only from political causes but also from acute and widespread economic and social unrest in an age of rapidly quickening social change. They marked the belated coming of the Industrial Revolution.

While France was in this period a seedbed of disorder and upheaval, she was also the undisputed and unrivaled center of scientific advance in Europe. In all the natural sciences and in mathematics, French scholars took the lead and made key contributions that were to determine the future course of European scientific development. These same scholars, moreover, were also instrumental in efforts to unify and synthesize the hitherto dispersed scientific findings of a variety of disciplines.

George Sabine, commenting on Bodin's development of the doctrine of the "divine right of kings" in sixteenth century France, remarked upon the fact that Bodin's *Republic* was written only four years after the Massacre of Saint Bartholomew and in the midst of the instability and violence of religious wars that tore apart the fabric of French society. Sabine suggests that Bodin exalted the role and authority of the king so as to bring order and stability to a society that floundered in endless civil war.[71] Comte's concern with order can be understood in similar terms. But he lived in an age in which science had made major strides so that he was enabled to wed the traditionalist appeal for order to the Enlightenment tradition of scientific progress.

THE GENERAL SCENE

When Comte was born, France was ruled by the Directory, which had been established by the moderate Thermidoreans after the overthrow of Robespierre's regime of terror. Within two years Napoleon staged his *coup*

71 George H. Sabine, *A History of Political Thought* (New York, Holt, Rinehart and Winston, 1961), p. 399.

d'état and became first consul; five years later he was crowned Emperor of the French. After Napoleon's defeat in 1814, the brother of the king who had died on the guillotine returned to France as King Louis XVIII. A year later Napoleon escaped from Elba and began the short rule generally called the Hundred Days. In June 1815 he abdicated for the second time, and Louis XVIII was reinstalled. The Restoration, as his regime and that of his brother Charles X who succeeded him was called, lasted till 1830, when it was overthrown by the July revolution which led to the reign of Louis Philippe, Duke of Orléans. The February revolution of 1848 inaugurated the short-lived Second Republic. In December 1851 Louis Napoleon, who had been President of the French Republic since 1848, staged a *coup d'état* and assumed dictatorial powers. In 1852 the Empire was reestablished and Napoleon III was proclaimed Emperor.

This period of political revolutions and popular revolts was also the period of the Industrial Revolution which, in France, came into its own only during the post-Napoleonic years. From 1816 to 1829, the French cotton industry tripled its production. There were 7,000 silk looms in Lyons in 1817; there would be 42,000 in 1832. The production of pig iron doubled from 1818 to 1828.[72] By 1832 there were only 525 steam engines in all of France (in 1818, there had been no more than 200), but in 1841 there were 2,807, and six years later there were 4,853. (In England there were already 15,000 such engines in 1826.)[73]

During the first part of the nineteenth century, a modern French working class slowly and painfully emerged out of what had been largely a mass of small artisans, craftsmen, and handicraft workers. Most workers still continued to be employed in very small enterprises, but by the middle forties, industrial establishments employing more than ten workers had already more than a million employees.[74] Salaries varied considerably from region to region and among craftsmen, factory workers, and farmer-artisans in the countryside. In general, salaries were very low, and rural workers suffered most. The urban craft workers formed an aristocracy of labor, while industrial workers lived in acute misery. Working and hygienic conditions in the new factories were horrible. The long work day, which had been endurable in the family workshop, became an ordeal in larger manufacturing enterprises.

Wages declined steadily from 1820 onward. In 1830 the Lyons silk weavers earned only a third of their 1810 wages. Economists have estimated that during the Restoration, the average annual wage of a worker varied between 400 and 500 francs, and that the minimum living wage for a family of three was around 900 francs. Hence, a family could escape abject poverty only if women

[72] Guillaume de Bertier de Sauvigny, *The Bourbon Restoration* (Philadelphia, The University of Pennsylvania Press, 1966), pp. 223 ff.

[73] Sébastien Charléty, *La Monarchie de Juillet,* Vol. V of Ernest Lavisse, ed., *Histoire de France contemporaine* (Paris, Hachette, 1921), p. 187. [74] *Ibid.,* p. 213.

and children became additional breadwinners. The number of utterly destitute men and women who had to be assisted by welfare payments increased enormously, especially in those areas in which industrial production had begun to hit its stride. In 1828, out of 224,000 workers in the Département du Nord, 163,000 had to be helped by welfare agencies.[75] Conditions among displaced artisans were equally frightening. In all, welfare agencies assisted 700,000 persons in 1833 and double that number fourteen years later.[76]

The revolutionary movements between 1830 and 1848 were not yet dominated by the new industrial working class but still consisted mainly of urban craftsmen and journeymen in the skilled trades. These men often expressed their discontent through unorganized rioting, smashing of machines, and the like. But when the times were propitious, they would also appear in the vanguard of more organized political movements in the capital or in major industrial centers such as Lyons.[77]

The Bourbons were overthrown by a combination of a political crisis and popular unrest caused by economic depression. "The people" or the "laboring poor" who manned the barricades were composed not only of craftsmen or journeymen as in the past, but also of industrial workers.[78] Those workers assumed even more of the burden of fighting in 1848.

Post-revolutionary France, in part during the Restoration but to a full extent after 1830, was a bourgeois society dominated by *nouveaux riches*. Their elemental greed was hardly tamed by the *noblesse oblige* that characterized older ruling classes. They were usually self-made men of lowly origin who owed little to family background or education. What they lacked in refinement and status, they more than made up for by their ferocious energy and self-confidence. They were generally considered a crude and unappetizing lot, and Balzac has drawn their collective portrait in the *Comédie humaine* with deep loathing and revulsion.

These new men also possessed an iron will to succeed, unlike the older ruling strata, which had by now settled into a routinized style of life. They became the daring entrepreneurs of the new age. They managed the venturesome banking houses, organized railroads, and built new factories. Many of these new men, especially among the bankers, had yet another incentive for their extraordinary exertion: they were of Protestant or Jewish origin and attempted to compensate for their minority status by special assiduity in the amassing of wealth and fortune.

These, sketched with very broad strokes, were some of the salient characteristics of the scene which Comte entered when, as a young man from the provinces, he registered at the *Ecole Polytechnique* and became a Parisian intellectual.

[75] Sauvigny, *op. cit.*, pp. 250–57. [76] Charléty, *op. cit.*, p. 216.
[77] E. J. Hobsbawm, *The Age of Revolution* (New York, Mentor Books, 1967), p. 152.
[78] *Ibid.*, pp. 145–46.

COMTE'S GENERATION—LE MAL DU SIÈCLE

Coming into manhood during the Restoration was fraught with both material and spiritual frustrations. The opportunities for careers that had existed in the revolutionary and Napoleonic period were blocked. Since so many political and administrative places had been filled in the earlier period by very young men, there were now but few openings. Promotions of young men who had been appointed under the Empire naturally delayed appointments and promotions for those who came later. Moreover, the *émigrés* who had returned from exile preempted many places that would normally have gone to younger men. As a consequence, the age structure of employment changed by favoring the middle-aged over the young in public office. For example, the proportion of prefects over the age of fifty was 15 percent in 1818, but changed to 55 percent by 1830. In 1828, a Genevan author, James Fazy, expressed the discontents of the young in a pamphlet called *On Gerontocracy, or the Abuse of the Wisdom of Old Men in the Government of France.* "They have reduced France," he said, "to seven thousand or eight thousand asthmatic, gouty, paralytic, eligible candidates with enfeebled faculties."[79]

Some openings could be found in the new industrial enterprises, but these developed slowly and really came to matter only during the latter part of the July monarchy.

Just because France had created an excellent educational system, the educated youth of 1820, whose supply exceeded the demand, faced what they considered a bleak future. The France of the Restoration abounded in doctors without patients, lawyers without clients, and young men spending their time in the waiting rooms of the high and mighty.[80] Not really being in demand, these young men suffered not only from material discontent but also from a deep-seated spiritual malaise that came to be called *le mal du siècle*. They had no ideological explanations for their fate, nor did they have firm beliefs and commitments as guidelines for their existence. Although the Church was now again in an honored position and the altar was a prized ally of the throne, religion failed to regain its old moral authority. It had not recovered from the shock administered by the Revolution. The romantic Catholic revival led by men like Chateaubriand did not succeed in capturing the imagination of most young men. Nor was there any other system of values available to fill the vacuum. "Alas, alas," wrote Alfred de Musset of his generation in *La Confession d'un enfant du siècle,* "religion is vanishing. . . . We no longer have either hope or expectations, not even two little pieces of black wood before which to wring our hands. . . . Everything that was is no more. All that will be is not yet." A young generation, dissatisfied with the official smugness and self-confidence of the Restoration and the July monarchy, was thirsting for a

[79] Quoted in Sauvigny, *op. cit.*, pp. 238–39. [80] *Ibid.*, pp. 239–40.

new faith to give sense to what seemed devoid of meaning, to fill the aching void of loneliness and despair.

THE PROMISE OF SCIENCE

The *Ecole Polytechnique,* founded in 1794, was, in Comte's days, the foremost scientific school in France, and France was in the first part of the nineteenth century the unrivaled center of European scientific advance. The list of illustrious scientists who taught at the *Ecole* is impressive. Lagrange, Monge, Fourier, and Poinsot were among the early teachers of mathematical and physical science; Berthollet taught chemistry. The second generation, which began to take over during the latter part of Napoleon's reign, included Poisson, Ampère, Gay-Lussac, Arago, Fresnel, and Cauchy.

Although eminent theoretical scientists taught at the *Ecole,* the school was mainly devoted to the applied sciences. The teaching centered around descriptive geometry, the art of blueprint making, since, in contrast to the *Ecole Normale* that had been organized at the same time, its students were prepared to become civil or military engineers rather than theoretical scientists.[81]

Although the majority of students became expert engineers and applied mathematicians, a significant minority refused to accept the prospect of such quotidian careers. They fused longing for a new faith and a new order with the positivistic and scientific spirit they were imbued with at the *Ecole,* and they decided to become scientific reformers. Not only Auguste Comte, but Prosper Enfantin, the future Pope of the Saint-Simonian Church, Victor Considérant, the future spokesman of Fourierist doctrine, and Frédéric Le Play, the Catholic sociologist and reformer, had been students of the *Ecole,* as were several hundreds of later Saint-Simonians and many of Comte's disciples.[82]

When Comte entered the *Ecole,* he soon found a group of young *polytechniciens* with whom he could share his ideas and ideals. Gouhier, who has followed the careers of a good number of Comte's schoolmates, documents the fact that his class contained an especially large number of social reformers, Saint-Simonian or otherwise. Comte, the provincial novice, found here a sustaining group of young men from all over France, activated like himself by scientific ardor and the reformer's zeal. An unkind commentator, Albert Thibaudet, once remarked that these young men thought that "one could create a religion in the same way as one learned at the *Ecole* to build a bridge."[83] Although the remark is on the caustic side, it touches upon an important point. These men tended to think that social engineering—even the engineering of a new faith—was not essentially different from the trade of the

[81] Frederick A. Hayek, *The Counter-Revolution of Science* (New York, The Free Press, 1952), pp. 110 ff.

[82] *Ibid.; La Jeunesse,* I, pp. 146 ff; and *La Vie,* p. 56.

[83] Quoted in Gouhier, *La Jeunesse,* I, p. 146.

civil engineer. One had but to apply the laws of science to the creation of new structures, be they physical or social.

Of the eminent men who taught at the *Ecole* many made major contributions to their particular discipline, but there were also men given to generalization and to attempts to bridge the gap between the natural and the social sciences. They saw themselves as the nineteenth-century continuators of a synthesizing trend, which was already pronounced in Diderot's and d'Alembert's *Encyclopédie*. Among them, and in French science in general, it was felt that the time had come to put together many heretofore disjointed pieces of theorizing and research and to build a unified scientific system that would encompass both the natural and the social sciences. "The scientists of this generation," writes Sébastien Charléty, "accomplished or prepared a work which has the mark of a general conception of the world similar to that of the social and political theoreticians."[84] The scientists of the day attempted to prove the connectedness of phenomena hitherto thought to be distinct. They began to assert the essential unity of all forces of nature, and certain scientists, especially those pondering the laws of probability, began to conjecture about the basic similarity of the laws of nature and those governing the life of man.

It is no wonder, then, that the young *polytechniciens* looked upon their teachers as men who, through their own work or through their teaching, provided models of a generalizing and synthesizing approach. No wonder also that they studied modern writers in the social sciences, such as Jean Baptiste Say, in the hope of learning from them the operation of social laws.[85]

Those polytechnicians who suffered from *mal du siècle* attempted in one way or another to substitute a faith based on the authority of science for their lost religious beliefs at the same time as they espoused a variety of reforming doctrines, all of which included the notion of social engineering. Frederick Hayek summed this up when he wrote:

> The very type of the engineer with his characteristic outlook, ambition, and limitations was created [at the *Ecole Polytechnique*]. That synthetic spirit which would not recognize sense in anything that had not been deliberately constructed, that love of organization that springs from the twin sources of military and engineering practices, the aesthetic predilection for everything that had been consciously constructed over anything that had "just grown," was a strong new element which was added to—and in the course of time began to replace—the revolutionary ardor of the young polytechniciens.[86]

Comte, while he made his unique contribution, is quite typical of his generation at the *Ecole Polytechnique*. The *Ecole* provided him with an intellectual milieu in which he could evolve his peculiar views through daily

[84] Sébastien Charléty, *La Restoration,* Vol. IV of Ernest Lavisse, ed., *Histoire de France contemporaine,* p. 223. [85] Cf. Gouhier, *La Jeunesse,* I, p. 152. [86] Hayek, *op. cit.,* p. 113.

contacts with like-minded equals and with superiors who, even though they may not have shared all the enthusiasms of the young, stimulated them through their teachings. Among the few human ties that Comte maintained throughout most of his life were those he had established with co-students and with some of his teachers. When he first attempted to find a sympathetic audience for his innovating ideas, he sent his early (1824) version of the *Système de politique positive* to former students of the *Ecole* and to his teachers Gay-Lussac, Hachette, Ampère and Poisson.[87] Throughout most of his life, although he had dropped out of the school before graduating, Comte signed his letters, "Auguste Comte, former student of the *Ecole Polytechnique.*"

COMTE WITHOUT COLLEAGUES

Although it had been Comte's fortune in his brief years as a student to find role models, like-minded peers, and a willing audience for his ideas, it was his abiding tragedy that he could not find similar intellectual companionship and support during his subsequent career.

Many of his letters testify that during the first part of his association with Saint-Simon, he experienced an intense elation through his close intellectual exchange with the older man. But the period in which Comte looked upon Saint-Simon as his master was short-lived. Latent disputes over intellectual priorities cooled their relationship even before the final break. It proved impossible to establish a genuine peer relationship between men who belonged to different generations and had sharply dissimilar social and intellectual backgrounds.

Through Saint-Simon Comte made the acquaintance of a number of progressive and liberal journalists and writers, and he no doubt profited from intellectual exchanges with them. But most of these contacts were lost again when Comte broke with the master. From then on, Comte had hardly any friends with whom he could deal on the basis of intellectual equality. A few men, like the physiologist de Blainville, remained close to him for over a quarter of a century, but even that friendship broke in the end. Relatively early in his career Comte acquired a few disciples. But like the young Gustave d'Eichthal, who admired him greatly for a while in the twenties only to leave him for the Saint-Simonians soon after, most of these disciples remained close for a short while only; and most of them, moreover, were hardly his intellectual peers.

Neither did Comte have academic colleagues. It will be remembered that he never attained a regular academic position and hence never profited from the sustained benefits of structured colleagueship that fall to most academic men. The give-and-take of critical stimulation and appraisal, which forms

[87] *La Jeunesse*, I, p. 219.

the sustaining medium in which most scholars operate, was forever denied him.

Yet Comte was not a total academic outsider as Darwin had been throughout his life and Nietzsche through most of his. He was relegated to the margin of the academy, performing lowly academic tasks. In constant contact with academic scientists, he was yet clearly their status inferior. He examined students to find out what they had retained of the lectures of other men or, as a *répétiteur,* he repeated to them the lessons of the masters. Rebuffed again and again in all his efforts to become a regular academic man, he was condemned through most of his career to gain his livelihood as a lowly assistant to men he soon came to look upon as his scientific inferiors.

For years on end Comte went through a process of anticipatory socialization. He prepared to develop the attitudes and values necessary for full academic position, without ever having the chance to enact the role he had learned with so much assiduity. When it finally became clear that he would never attain the hoped-for institutionalized role, he resolved to create a new role for himself, that of a prophet. But prophets are lonely men who may have disciples but lack co-equals. In his later years, Comte, though now surrounded by adoring followers, still remained without colleagues. He managed from time to time to establish a semblance of colleague-type relationships—the most notable being with John Stuart Mill with whom he entertained an intensive correspondence for many years. But one ventures to think that this relationship would have been shorter than it was had Mill lived in Comte's proximity rather than in England.

Progressively removed from sustaining relations with peers, and rebuffed, or feeling rebuffed, by the eminent men of science whose critical comments he had once craved, Comte increasingly withdrew from the current intellectual scene. And as he became deprived of critical commentary by equals, he relied increasingly on fawning approval by disciples. The bizarre character of many of his later ideas is in some measure the result of a partly involuntary and partly willed insulation from colleagues.

THE SEARCH FOR AN AUDIENCE

During the days in which he worked for and with Saint-Simon, Comte had begun to create for himself an audience among liberal writers and journalists and among powerful leaders in the world of business and politics. He wrote for influential publications, first under Saint-Simon's name and then under his own. Readers of the leading liberal periodicals began to pay attention to him. Moreover, scientists he had known at the *Ecole,* and others he met later, eagerly listened to his message. When he published the first version of his *Système* in 1824, Cuvier wrote a flattering letter in the name of the Academy of Sciences; French scientists of the stature of Poinsot, de Blainville, de Broglie, and Flourens applauded the work. The German scientist-explorer Alexander von Humboldt responded with enthusiasm.

But after the break with Saint-Simon, this audience slowly dwindled, whether because of Comte's self-destructive capacity to irritate friends and foes alike or because the competition of the Saint-Simonians undercut his appeal. Apart from his brief collaboration with the new Saint-Simonian publication, *Le Producteur,* Comte found no regular journalistic outlets. Academic audiences were not available either. Whatever teaching Comte now did, be it in private schools, in private lessons, or in his humdrum menial work for the *Ecole Polytechnique,* did not allow him to test his own ideas. Whatever audience was provided through teaching was an audience for the ideas of other men, whom, moreover, Comte came increasingly to loathe.

Being deprived of an institutional setting, Comte resolved single-handedly to create one by offering a course of public lectures to an invited audience of eminent men. There were a good number of status equals and superiors among his listeners, and for once he had an appreciative audience. But, perhaps because he had been deprived of it for so long, he felt unequal to the task—and fell ill. The strain of the situation appears to have contributed, or so one may surmise, to his breakdown after he had given only a few lectures.

He resumed lecturing after his illness and again enjoyed a number of eminent men in the audience, among them four members of the Academy of Sciences. His "Opening Discourse" was soon published by the *Revue Encyclopédique,* and subsequent chapters of the *Cours* now appeared in installments. But these successes were not to last. The first full volume of the *Cours* came off press in July 1830—when, in the midst of revolution, it attracted but little attention. Soon afterward, the publisher went bankrupt. These were temporary mischances, of course, but it soon became apparent that Comte had permanently lost the intellectual audience he first seemed to attract. And, as subsequent parts of the *Cours* appeared in print, most of the scientists who had once stood high in Comte's estimation turned against him. When the six volumes of the *Cours* were finally published, it did not receive a single review in all the French press!

In the middle forties, Emile Littré, a newly found disciple, published six major articles on Comte's work in *Le National* and attracted some attention to positive philosophy. Slowly, some other disciples were recruited in France; in England men like Mill and George Lewes were receptive to Comte's message. But these admirers again left the fold when Comte turned to the Religion of Humanity. Intellectuals, so Comte reasoned, were a fickle audience.

Comte now turned to other publics. As early as December 1830 he proposed to the *Association Polytechnique* to give a free public course in elementary astronomy—a course he was to continue to give for eighteen years and which became more important to him when he had lost his academic audience. Here his public consisted of men who were but partly educated.

They were not his peers or his status superiors within the academy. Comte now exalted the virtues of the Parisian workers who formed a significant part of the audience. ("The rest [of the audience]," he said, "is composed of a variegated mixture in which old men are strongly represented.")[88] His further description of this audience is most revealing and worth quoting at some length.

> The fortunate absence among them of our stupid scholastic culture enables them . . . to seize directly, though necessarily in a very confused manner, the true spirit of a philosophical renovation which is reached only with great difficulty, and very imperfectly at that, by the badly trained intellectuals who abound in the world of letters. Among minds who are not professionally philosophical, it is amidst true workers (watchmakers, mechanics, printers, etc.) that I have found up till now the sanest appreciation . . . of the new philosophy.[89]

Shunned by his intellectual peers, the philosopher scorned chose for himself a less critical audience of intellectual inferiors.

To complement his oral teaching, Comte wrote a *Philosophical Treatise of Popular Astronomy,* the preamble of which is the well known *Discourse on the Positive Spirit* of 1844. Already in this work, and increasingly in all that was to follow, Comte's style changed significantly. In contrast to the *Cours* and his early works, which were written in a dry, ponderous, and methodical style that would appeal to fellow intellectuals and scientists, Comte's new style was florid, emotional, and imprecise. Whether deliberately or unwittingly, he now tried to capture the feelings of his audience at least as much as he tried to capture their minds. His style and thought became increasingly flaccid and flabby as he abandoned his hopes for an audience of peers and attempted instead to broaden his intended public to include the educated as well as the uneducated, workers as well as intellectuals, in fact the whole of mankind. As the circle to which he addressed himself became wider and wider in his mind, his thought and style became less and less controlled. Deprived of social control exercised by peers, he seemed to lose his own control over his ideas. His earlier writings had resembled the Cartesian order of a well tended French garden; now his work came to look like an untamed tropical forest.

Finally, after 1849, Comte retired completely into the security of the sect he had founded. The warm esoteric and encapsulated universe of his Religion of Humanity now eclipsed for Comte the surrounding hostile world of unbelievers. Preaching every Sunday at the Palais-Royal, lecturing to his beloved disciples at his home, sending epistles and missives to recruits in other lands and to foreign potentates, Comte became increasingly bizarre in his pronouncements. No wonder that the unconverted came to regard him as a madman.

[88] *La Vie,* p. 219. [89] *Ibid.,* pp. 218–19.

Perhaps he was mad in these last years. In any case, his almost total insulation from the intellectual currents of his day (remember that he had long since ceased to read other men for reasons of "cerebral hygiene"), as well as his being reduced to an audience of mostly half-educated but admiring followers, can account for at least a part of that madness. The Pope of positivism now lashed out against intellectuals whom he failed to reach: "Those so-called positivists who think of themselves as intellectuals are the least intellectual of all."[90] Comte now asserted that the workers "have a natural aptitude to become the auxiliaries of spiritual power."[91] He relied on the untutored feelings of the simple in spirit—or on those who pretended for a while that they were "simple." Among the disciples who sat at the feet of the Pope in those last years were mechanics, carpenters, and unsuccessful poets, as well as librarians, future politicians, and past students of the *Ecole Polytechnique*. The appeal for funds to insure Comte's livelihood in the last years of his life is signed by the following: Ch. Jundzill, professor of mathematics; Belpaume, shoemaker; Fili, mechanic; Pascal, student of philosophy; Ch. Robin, medical doctor; F. Magnin, carpenter; Littré, member of the *Institut;* Second, medical doctor; Contreras, medical student; Francelle, watchmaker; Leblais, professor of mathematics; A. Ribet, law student.[92] When preaching to this motley crew, Comte used a hortatory and florid language that had little in common with the precise and purposeful style that he had once employed to convince his peers by rational argument. Having moved very far indeed from the intellectual center and occupying as he did an ex-centric position in the society of his time, Comte had become eccentric in the extreme in his writings and preachments.

In the days of his youth Comte must have perceived, and correctly so, that there was a demand for a new intellectual and moral synthesis such as he proposed to fashion. Not only Saint-Simon but, as Gouhier has shown, a number of lesser minds attempted in their diverse way to supply this demand.

Yet it appears that Comte was nevertheless out of step with the demands of the time. When the *mal du siècle* was at its height, Comte limited himself in the main to severely scientific writings, leaving the field of moral regeneration to Saint-Simonian and other peddlers of nostrums of salvation. When he finally turned to the new role of religious prophet, after the upheavals of 1848, France had already begun to adjust to what were to become the routines of Louis Napoleon's Empire, and many of the earlier devotees of new religions had already settled in comfortable positions in banking, politics, and industry. While the Saint-Simonians had attracted in their day the intellectual flower of young France, Comte was reduced to preaching to the untutored and the

90 *Ibid.*, p. 277.

91 Quoted in Maxime Leroy, *Histoire des doctrines sociales en France* (Paris, Gallimard, 1954), Vol. III, p. 234.

92 Littré, *op. cit.*, pp. 600–01.

unadjusted. His doctrine was much more successful in Latin America, where liberal intellectuals and aspiring bourgeois politicians could use it for their purposes. But in his native France, demand and supply were never properly balanced. Though Comte had a deep influence on later generations of French social scientists and historians—Renan, Taine, Lucien Lévy-Bruhl, and Durkheim among them—and though part of his message was to be picked up by men like Charles Maurras on the right and by many of the luminaries of the Third Republic on the left, there never developed a Comtean school of intellectual consequence. What survived of his doctrine was his method rather than the specific content. His influence, though great, remained diffuse.[93]

IN SUMMARY

Comte's was an enormously creative mind. Sociology cannot attempt to penetrate to the sources of such creativity, but it can help to explain the particular shape and form of the work of creative intelligence.

The product of a constricting provincial environment, Comte was lucky enough to escape to Paris, the center of all things political and intellectual. Having been trained in the foremost scientific school of his age and exposed to brilliant teachers and schoolmates, Comte absorbed the diverse intellectual currents of his day with rapidity and thoroughness. Courses and lectures, as well as informal bull sessions, were formative experiences. The later association with Saint-Simon completed the intellectual formation of the young man.

Growing up in a critical age of breakdown and anarchy, of loss of faith and certitude, he resolved early to fashion a philosophical system that would bring mankind back to that organic wholeness that seemed so conspicuously lacking. The appeal and the rage for order pervade all his work. But at the same time, this progressive scientist was firmly convinced that a new order was to be sought in the future, rather than in some return to the *ancien régime*. Like Saint-Simon, he was the spiritual son of both de Maistre and Condorcet.

Comte lived through most of his life on the margin of the academic establishment. The lack of control by disciplined and methodical colleagues may explain, at least in part, the boldness and daring of his intellectual efforts, while at the same time it helps account for the decline of his work in later years. The distance from colleagues and the lack of a secure audience may initially have enabled Comte to plow his lonely furrow, unimpeded by the ordinary requirements of academic discipline, but later he paid a heavy price for it.

And so we are left with twin images of the man: The creator of the first

[93] Cf. Donald G. Charlton, *Positivist Thought in France During the Second Empire* (Oxford, Clarendon, 1959), and Walter M. Simon, *European Positivism in the Nineteenth Century* (Ithaca, New York, Cornell University Press, 1963).

major sociological synthesis, and the pathetic Pope of Humanity; the originator of sociological insights, which later generations can ignore only at the risk of a serious impoverishment in their heritage, and the little old man piously preaching to his audience of carpenters and intellectual failures; the flaming spirit who wished to provide a unified vision of the past and future of mankind, and the fearful old man who counseled the Czar to tighten his censorship to prevent the emergence of subversive ideas.[94]

Perhaps it is only just that sociology, which has done so much to analyze the profound ambiguities of modern society, should have had its beginning in the work of a man who was himself so ambiguous and Janus-faced a figure. If he was torn between the twin demands of order and progress, so are we.

[94] *Système,* III, p. xxix.

Karl Marx

1818-1883

THE WORK

Karl Marx was a socialist theoretician and organizer, a major figure in the history of economic and philosophical thought, and a great social prophet. But it is as a sociological theorist that he commands our interest here.

THE OVERALL DOCTRINE

Society, according to Marx, comprised a moving balance of antithetical forces that generate social change by their tension and struggle. Marx's vision was based on an evolutionary point of departure. For him, struggle rather than peaceful growth was the engine of progress; strife was the father of all things, and social conflict the core of historical process. This thinking was in contrast with most of the doctrines of his eighteenth century predecessors, but in tune with much nineteenth century thought.

To Marx the motivating force in history was the manner in which men relate to one another in their continuous struggle to wrest their livelihood from nature. "The first historical act is . . . the production of material life itself. This is indeed a historical act, a fundamental condition of all history."[1] The quest for a sufficiency in eating and drinking, for habitation and for clothing were man's primary goals at the dawn of the race, and these needs are still central when attempts are made to analyze the complex anatomy of modern society. But man's struggle against nature does not cease when these needs are gratified. Man is a perpetually dissatisfied animal. When primary needs have been met, this "leads to new needs—and this production of new needs is the first historical act."[2] New needs evolve when means are found to allow the satisfaction of older ones.

In the effort to satisfy primary and secondary needs, men engage in antagonistic cooperation as soon as they leave the primitive, communal stage of

[1] Karl Marx, *Selected Writings in Sociology and Social Philosophy,* newly translated by T. B. Bottomore (London, McGraw-Hill, 1964), p. 60. I have used this useful volume throughout, since it is easily available. Other easily available editions, such as the Moscow edition of Karl Marx and Friedrich Engels, *Selected Works,* 2 vols. (Moscow, Foreign Language Publishing House, 1962), have also been used extensively so as to facilitate students' search for relevant materials. In some cases, where the translation was outmoded, I have slightly modified it.

[2] *Selected Writings.*

development. As soon as a division of labor emerges in human society, that division leads to the formation of antagonistic classes, the prime actors in the historical drama.

Marx was a relativizing historicist according to whom all social relations between men, as well as all systems of ideas, are specifically rooted in historical periods. "Ideas and categories are no more eternal than the relations which they express. They are historical and transitory products."[3] For example, whereas the classical economists had seen the tripartite division among landowners, capitalists, and wage earners as eternally given in the natural order of things, Marx considered such categories as typical only for specific historical periods, as products of an historically transient state of affairs.

Historical specificity is the hallmark of Marx's approach. When he asserted, for example, that all previous historical periods were marked by class struggles, he immediately added that these struggles differed according to historical stages. In marked distinction to his radical predecessors who had tended to see history as a monotonous succession of struggles between rich and poor, or between the powerless and the powerful, Marx maintained that, although class struggles had marked all history, the contenders in the battle had changed over time. Although there might have been some similarity between the journeymen of the late Middle Ages who waged their battle against guildmasters and the modern industrial workers who confronted capitalists, the contenders were, nevertheless, in a functionally different situation. The character of the overall social matrix determined the forms of struggle which were contained within it. The fact that modern factory workers, as distinct from medieval journeymen, are forever expropriated from command over the means of production and hence forced to sell their labor power to those who control these means makes them a class qualitatively different from artisans or journeymen. The fact that modern workers are formally "free" to sell their labor while being existentially constrained to do so makes their condition historically specific and functionally distinct from that of earlier exploited classes.

Marx's thinking contrasted sharply with that of Comte, as well as of Hegel, for whom the evolution of mankind resulted primarily from the evolution of ideas or of the human spirit. Marx took as his point of departure the evolution in man's material conditions, the varying ways in which men combined together in order to gain a livelihood. "Legal relations as well as form of state are to be grasped neither from themselves nor from the so-called general development of the human mind, but rather have their roots in the material conditions of life, the sum total of which Hegel . . . combines under the name of 'civil society.' . . . The anatomy of civil society is to be sought in political economy."[4]

The change of social systems could not be explained, according to Marx, by extra-social factors such as geography or climate, since these remain relatively

[3] Karl Marx, *The Poverty of Philosophy,* Chapter II, p. 1. [4] *Selected Works,* I, p. 362.

constant in the face of major historical transformations. Nor can such change be explained by reference to the emergence of novel ideas. The genesis and acceptance of ideas depend on something that is not an idea. Ideas are not prime movers but are the reflection, direct or sublimated, of the material interests that impel men in their dealings with others.[5]

It was from Hegel, though perhaps also from Montesquieu, that Marx learned the holistic approach that regarded society as a structurally interrelated whole. Consequently, for Marx, any aspect of that whole—be it legal codes, systems of education, religion, or art—could not be understood by itself. Societies, moreover, are not only structured wholes but developing totalities. His own contribution lay in identifying an independent variable that played only a minor part in Hegel's system: the mode of economic production.

Although historical phenomena were the result of an interplay of many components, all but one of them, the economic factor, were in the last analysis dependent variables. "The political, legal, philosophical, literary, and artistic development rests on the economic. But they all react upon one another and upon the economic base. It is not the case that the economic situation is the *sole active cause* and that everything else is merely a passive effect. There is, rather, a reciprocity within a field of economic necessity which *in the last instance* always asserts itself."[6]

The sum total of the relations of production, that is, the relations men establish with each other when they utilize existing raw materials and technologies in the pursuit of their productive goals, constitute the real foundations upon which the whole cultural *superstructure* of society comes to be erected. By relations of production Marx does not only mean technology, though this is an important part, but the social relations people enter into by participating in economic life. "Machinery is no more an economic category than is the ox which draws the plough. The modern workshop, which is based on the use of machinery, is a social relation of production, an economic category."[7]

The mode of economic production is expressed in relationships between men, which are independent of any particular individual and not subject to individual wills and purposes.

> In the social production which men carry on they enter into definite relations that are indispensable and independent of their will; these relations of production correspond to a definite stage of development of their material powers of production. The totality of these relations of production constitutes the economic structure of society—the real foundation, on which legal and political superstructures arise and to which definite forms of social conscious-

[5] I have relied heavily in this paragraph, and in those that follow, on Sidney Hook's brilliant article, "Materialism," in the *Encyclopedia of the Social Sciences* (New York, Macmillan, 1933).

[6] *Selected Works,* II, p. 304. This is a late formulation, earlier statements are considerably more dogmatic in their insistence on the priority of economic factors.

[7] *Selected Writings,* p. 93.

> ness correspond. The mode of production of material life determines the general character of the social, political and spiritual processes of life. It is not the consciousness of men that determines their being, but, on the contrary, their social being determines their consciousness.[8]

Basic to these observations is that men are born into societies in which property relations have already been determined. These property relations in turn give rise to different social classes. Just as a man cannot choose who is to be his father, so he has no choice as to his class. (Social mobility, though recognized by Marx, plays practically no role in his analysis.) Once a man is ascribed to a specific class by virtue of his birth, once he has become a feudal lord or a serf, an industrial worker or a capitalist, his mode of behavior is prescribed for him. "Determinate individuals, who are productively active in a definite way, enter into . . . determinate social and political relations."[9] This class role largely defines the man. In his preface to *Das Kapital* Marx wrote, "Here individuals are dealt with only in so far as they are personifications of economic categories, embodiments of particular class-relations and class-interests." In saying this, Marx does not deny the operation of other variables but concentrates on class roles as primary determinants.

Different locations in the class spectrum lead to different class interests. Such differing interests flow not from class consciousness or the lack of it among individuals, but from objective positions in relation to the process of production. Men may well be unaware of their class interests and yet be moved by them, as it were, behind their backs.

Despite his emphasis on the objective determinants of man's class-bound behavior, Marx was not reifying society and class at the expense of individual actors. "It is above all necessary to avoid postulating 'society' once more as an abstraction confronting the individual. The individual is a *social being.* The manifestation of his life—even when it does not appear directly in the form of *social* manifestation, accomplished in association with other men—is therefore a manifestation and affirmation of social life."[10] Man is inevitably enmeshed in a network of social relations which constrain his actions; therefore, attempts to abolish such constraints altogether are bound to fail. Man is human only in society, yet it is possible for him at specific historical junctures to change the nature of these constraints.

The division of society into classes gives rise to political, ethical, philosophical, and religious views of the world, views which express existing class relations and tend either to consolidate or to undermine the power and authority of the dominant class. "The ideas of the ruling class are, in every age, the ruling ideas: i.e., the class which is the dominant *material* force in society is at the same time its dominant *intellectual* force. The class which has

[8] *Ibid.,* p. 51. [9] *Ibid.,* p. 74. [10] *Ibid.,* p. 77.

the means of material production at its disposal, has control at the same time over the means of mental production."[11] However, oppressed classes, although hampered by the ideological dominance of oppressors, generate counter-ideologies to combat them. In revolutionary or prerevolutionary periods it even happens that certain representatives of the dominant class shift allegiance. Thus, "some of the bourgeois ideologists, who have raised themselves to the level of comprehending theoretically the historical movement as a whole"[12] go over to the proletariat.

Every social order is marked by continuous change in the material forces of production, that is, the forces of nature that can be harnessed by the appropriate technologies and skills. As a consequence, "the social relations of production are altered, transformed, with the change and development of the material means of production, of the forces of production."[13] At a certain point the changed social relations of production come into conflict with existing property relations, that is, with existing divisions between owners and nonowners. When this is the case, representatives of ascending classes come to perceive existing property relations as a fetter upon further development. Those classes that expect to gain the ascendancy by a change in property relations become revolutionary.

New social relationships begin to develop within older social structures and result from contradictions and tensions within that structure at the same time as they exacerbate them. For example, new modes of industrial production slowly emerged within late feudal society and allowed the bourgeoisie, which controlled these new modes of production, effectively to challenge the hold of the classes that had dominated the feudal order. As the bourgeois mode of production gained sufficient specific weight, it burst asunder the feudal relations in which it first made its appearance. "The economic structure of capitalist society has grown out of the economic structure of feudal society. The dissolution of the latter sets free the elements of the former."[14] Similarly, the capitalist mode of production brings into being a proletarian class of factory workers. As these men acquire class consciousness, they discover their fundamental antagonism to the bourgeois class and band together to overthrow a regime to which they owe their existence. "The proletariat carries out the sentence which private property, by creating the proletariat, passes upon itself."[15] New social and economic forms are fashioned in the matrix of their predecessors.

[11] *Ibid.*, p. 78. [12] *Selected Works*, I, p. 43. [13] *Selected Writings*, p. 147. [14] *Ibid.*, p. 133.
[15] *Ibid.*, p. 232.

CLASS THEORY

Marx's class theory rests on the premise that "the history of all hitherto existing society is the history of class struggles."[16] According to this view, ever since human society emerged from its primitive and relatively undifferentiated state it has remained fundamentally divided between classes who clash in the pursuit of class interests. In the world of capitalism, for example, the nuclear cell of the capitalist system, the factory, is the prime locus of *antagonism* between classes—between exploiters and exploited, between buyers and sellers of labor power—rather than of functional collaboration. Class interests and the confrontations of power that they bring in their wake are to Marx the central determinant of social and historical process.

Marx's analysis continually centers on how the relationships between men are shaped by their relative positions in regard to the means of production, that is, by their differential access to scarce resources and scarce power. He notes that unequal access need not at all times and under all conditions lead to active class struggle. But he considered it axiomatic that the potential for class conflict is inherent in every differentiated society, since such a society systematically generates conflicts of interest between persons and groups differentially located within the social structure, and, more particularly, in relation to the means of production. Marx was concerned with the ways in which specific positions in the social structure tended to shape the social experiences of their incumbents and to predispose them to actions oriented to improve their collective fate.

Yet class interests in Marxian sociology are not given ab initio. They develop through the exposure of people occupying particular social positions to particular social circumstances. Thus, in early industrial enterprises, competition divides the personal interests of "a crowd of people who are unknown to each other. . . . But the maintenance of their wages, this common interest which they have against their employer, brings them together."[17] "The separate individuals form a class only in so far as they have to carry on a common battle against another class; otherwise they are on hostile terms with each other as competitors."[18]

Class interests are fundamentally different from, and cannot be derived from, the individual interests imputed by the utilitarian school and classical British political economy. Potential common interests of members of a particular stratum derive from the location of that stratum within particular social structures and productive relations. But potentiality is transformed into actuality, *Klasse an sich* (class in itself) into *Klasse fuer sich* (class for itself),

[16] *Selected Works,* I, p. 34. [17] *Selected Writings,* p. 186.

[18] Karl Marx and Friedrich Engels, *The German Ideology* (New York, International Publishers, 1930), pp. 48–49.

only when individuals occupying similar positions become involved in common struggles; a network of communication develops, and they thereby become conscious of their common fate. It is then that individuals become part of a cohesive class that consciously articulates their common interests. As Carlyle once put it, "Great is the combined voice of men." Although an aggregate of people may occupy similar positions in the process of production and their lives may have objectively similar determinants, they become a class as a self-conscious and history-making body only if they become aware of the similarity of their interests through their conflicts with opposing classes.

To Marx, the basis upon which stratification systems rest is the relation of aggregates of men to the means of production. The major modern classes are "the owners merely of labor-power, owners of capital, and landowners, whose respective sources of income are wages, profit and ground-rent."[19] Classes are aggregates of persons who perform the same function in the organization of production. Yet self-conscious classes, as distinct from aggregates of people sharing a common fate, need for their emergence a number of conditions among which are a network of communication, the concentration of masses of people, a common enemy, and some form of organization. Self-conscious classes arise only if and when there exists a convergence of what Max Weber later called "ideal" and "material" interests, that is, the combination of economic and political demands with moral and ideological quests.

The same mode of reasoning that led Marx to assert that the working class was bound to develop class consciousness once the appropriate conditions were present also led him to contend that the bourgeoisie, because of the inherent competitive relations between capitalist producers, was incapable of developing an overall consciousness of its collective interests.

The classical economists picture the economic system of a market economy as one in which each man, working in his own interest and solely concerned with the maximization of his own gains, nevertheless contributes to the interests and the harmony of the whole. Differing sharply, Marx contended, as Raymond Aron has put it, that "each man, working in his own interest, contributes both to the necessary functioning and to the final destruction of the regime."[20]

In contrast to the utilitarians who conceive of self-interest as a regulator of a harmonious society, Marx sees individual self-interest among capitalists as destructive of their class interest in general, and as leading to the ultimate self-destruction of capitalism. The very fact that each capitalist acts rationally in his own self-interest leads to ever deepening economic crises and hence to the destruction of the interests common to all.

The conditions of work and the roles of workers dispose them to solidarity

[19] *Selected Writings,* p. 178.

[20] Raymond Aron, *Main Currents in Sociological Thought* (New York, Basic Books, 1965), Vol. I, p. 135.

and to overcoming their initial competitiveness in favor of combined action for their collective class interests. Capitalists, however, being constrained by competition on the market, are in a structural position that does not allow them to arrive at a consistent assertion of common interests. The market and the competitive mode of production that is characteristic of capitalism tend to separate individual producers. Marx granted that capitalists also found it possible to transcend their immediate self-interests, but he thought this possible primarily in the political and ideological spheres rather than in the economic. Capitalists, divided by the economic competition among themselves, evolved a justifying ideology and a political system of domination that served their collective interests. "The State is the form in which the individuals of a ruling class assert their common interests."[21] "The ideas of the ruling class are . . . the ruling ideas."[22] Political power and ideology thus seem to serve the same functions for capitalists that class consciousness serves for the working class. But the symmetry is only apparent. To Marx, the economic sphere was always the finally decisive realm within which the bourgeoisie was always the victim of the competitiveness inherent in its mode of economic existence. It can evolve a consciousness, but it is always a "false consciousness," that is, a consciousness that does not transcend its being rooted in an economically competitive mode of production. Hence neither the bourgeoisie as a class, nor the bourgeois state, nor the bourgeois ideology can serve truly to transcend the self-interest enjoined by the bourgeoisie. The bourgeois reign is doomed when economic conditions are ripe and when a working class united by solidarity, aware of its common interests and energized by an appropriate system of ideas, confronts its disunited antagonists. Once workers became aware that they are alienated from the process of production, the dusk of the capitalist era has set in.[23]

ALIENATION

For Marx, the history of mankind had a double aspect: It was a history of increasing control of man over nature at the same time as it was a history of the increasing alienation of man. Alienation may be described as a condition in which men are dominated by forces of their own creation, which confront them as alien powers. The notion is central to all of Marx's earlier philosophical writings and still informs his later work, although no longer as a philosophical issue but as a social phenomenon. The young Marx asks: In what circumstances do men project their own powers, their own values, upon objects that escape their control? What are the social causes of this phenomenon?

To Marx, all major institutional spheres in capitalist society, such as re-

[21] *Selected Writings*, p. 223. [22] *Ibid.*, p. 78.

[23] In the preceding pages I have used a number of ideas first developed in "Karl Marx and Contemporary Sociology," by Lewis A. Coser, *Continuities in the Study of Social Conflict* (New York, The Free Press, 1967).

ligion, the state, and political economy, were marked by a condition of alienation. Moreover, these various aspects of alienation were interdependent. "Objectification is the practice of alienation. Just as man, so long as he is engrossed in religion, can only objectify his essence by an *alien* and fantastic being; so under the sway of egoistic need, he can only affirm himself and produce objects in practice by subordinating his products and his own activity to the domination of an alien entity, and by attributing to them the significance of an alien entity, namely money."[24] "Money is the alienated essence of man's work and existence; the essence dominates him and he worships it."[25] "The state is the intermediary between men and human liberty. Just as Christ is the intermediary to whom man attributes all his own divinity and all his religious *bonds,* so the state is the intermediary to which man confides all his non-divinity and all his human freedom."[26] Alienation hence confronts man in the whole world of institutions in which he is enmeshed. But alienation in the workplace assumes for Marx an overriding importance, because to him man was above all *Homo Faber,* Man the Maker. "The outstanding achievement of Hegel's *Phenomenology* . . . is that Hegel grasps the self-creation of man as a process . . . and that he, therefore, grasps the nature of *labor* and conceives objective man . . . as the result of his own labor."[27]

Economic alienation under capitalism is involved in men's daily activities and not only in their minds, as other forms of alienation might be. "Religious alienation as such occurs only in the sphere of *consciousness,* in the inner life of man, but economic alienation is that of *real life.* . . . It therefore affects both aspects."[28]

Alienation in the domain of work has a fourfold aspect: Man is alienated from the object he produces, from the process of production, from himself, and from the community of his fellows.

"The object produced by labor, its product, now stands opposed to it as an alien being, as a power independent of the producer. . . . The more the worker expends himself in work the more powerful becomes the world of objects which he creates in face of himself, the poorer he becomes in his inner life, and the less he belongs to himself."[29]

"However, alienation appears not merely in the result but also in the *process of production,* within *productive activity* itself. . . . If the product of labor is alienation, production itself must be active alienation. . . . The alienation of the object of labor merely summarizes the alienation in the work activity itself."[30]

Being alienated from the objects of his labor and from the process of production, man is also alienated from himself—he cannot fully develop the many sides of his personality. "Work is *external* to the worker. . . . It is not

[24] *Karl Marx: Early Writings,* trans. and ed. by T. B. Bottomore (New York, McGraw-Hill, 1964), p. 39. [25] *Ibid.,* p. 37. [26] *Ibid.,* p. 11. [27] *Ibid.,* p. 202. [28] *Ibid.,* p. 156. [29] *Ibid.,* p. 122. [30] *Ibid.,* p. 124.

part of his nature; consequently he does not fulfill himself in his work but denies himself. . . . The worker therefore feels himself at home only during his leisure time, whereas at work he feels homeless."[31] "In work [the worker] does not belong to himself but to another person."[32] "This is the relationship of the worker to his own activitiy as something alien, not belonging to him, activity as suffering (passivity), strength as powerlessness, creation as emasculation, the *personal* physical and mental energy of the worker, his personal life . . . as an activity which is directed against himself, independent of him and not belonging to him."[33]

Finally, alienated man is also alienated from the human community, from his "species-being." "Man is *alienated* from other *men*. When man confronts himself he also confronts *other* men. What is true of man's relationship to his work, to the product of his work and to himself, is also true of his relationship to other men. . . . Each man is alienated from others . . . each of the others is likewise alienated from human life."[34] Marx would have liked the lines of the poet, A. E. Housman, "I, a stranger and afraid/In a world I never made." Only Marx would have replaced the poet's *I* with *We*.

The term alienation cannot be found in the later writings of Marx, but modern commentators are in error when they contend that Marx abandoned the idea. It informs his later writings, more particularly *Das Kapital*. In the notion of the "fetishism of commodities," which is central to his economic analysis, Marx repeatedly applies the concept of alienation. Commodities are alienated products of the labor of man, crystallized manifestations, which in Frankenstein fashion now dominate their creators. "The commodity form," writes Marx in *Das Kapital,*

> and the value relation between the products of labor which stamps them as commodities, have absolutely no connection with their physical properties and with the material relations arising therefrom. It is simply a definite relation between men, that assumes in their eyes the fantastic form of a relation between things. To find an analogy, we must have recourse to the nebulous regions of the religious world. In that world the productions of the human brain appear as independent beings endowed with life, and entering into relation both with one another and with the human race. So it is in the world of commodities, with the products of men's hands. This I call the fetishism which attaches itself to the products of labor, as soon as they are produced as commodities.[35]

Explicitly stated or tactily assumed, the notion of alienation remained central to Marx's social and economic analysis. In an alienated society, the whole mind-set of men, their consciousness, is to a large extent only the re-

[31] *Ibid.*, pp. 124–25. [32] *Ibid.*, p. 125. [33] *Ibid.*, p. 126. [34] *Ibid.*, p. 129.
[35] *Selected Writings*, pp. 175–76.

flection of the conditions in which they find themselves and of the position in the process of production in which they are variously placed. This is the subject matter of Marx's sociology of knowledge, to which we now turn.

THE SOCIOLOGY OF KNOWLEDGE

In an attempt to dissociate himself from the panlogical system of his former master, Hegel, as well as from the "critical philosophy" of his erstwhile Young Hegelian friends, Karl Marx undertook in some of his early writings to establish a connection between philosophies, ideas in general, and the concrete social structures in which they emerged. "It has not occurred to any of these philosophers," he wrote, "to inquire into the connection of German philosophy with German reality, the relation of their criticism to their own material surroundings."[36] This programmatic orientation once established, Marx proceeded to analyze the ways in which systems of ideas appeared to depend on the social positions—particularly the class positions—of their proponents.

In opposing the dominant ideas of his time, Marx was led to a resolute relativization of those ideas. The eternal verities of dominant thought appeared upon inspection to be only the direct or indirect expression of the class interests of their exponents. Marx attempted to explain ideas systematically in terms of their functions and to relate the thought of individuals to their social roles and class positions. We must go astray, he believed, "if . . . we detach the ideas of the ruling class from the ruling class itself and attribute to them an independent existence, if we confine ourselves to saying that in a particular age these or those ideas were dominant, without paying attention to the conditions of production and the producers of these ideas, and if we thus ignore the individuals and the world conditions which are the source of these ideas."[37]

Ideas, Marx maintained, must be traced to the life-conditions and the historical situations of those who uphold them. For example, it is not sufficient to state that the ideas of bourgeois writers are the ideas of the bourgeoisie. Distinctions must be made between those ideas that emerge at the beginning of the bourgeois era and those that come at its height. Utilitarian notions in the writings of Helvétius and d'Holbach differed from those that made their appearance with James Mill and Bentham. "The former correspond with the struggling, still undeveloped bourgeoisie, the latter with the dominant, developed bourgeoisie."[38]

It is with revolutionary ideas as it is with conservative ideas. "The existence of revolutionary ideas in a particular age presupposes the existence of a revolutionary class."[39] "The ruling ideas of each age have ever been the ideas

[36] *The German Ideology*, p. 6. [37] *Selected Writings*, pp. 79–80. [38] *Ibid.*, p. 164.
[39] *Ibid.*, p. 79.

of the ruling class. When people speak of ideas that revolutionize society, they do but express the fact that within the old society the elements of a new one have been created, and that the dissolution of the old ideas keeps even pace with the dissolution of the old conditions of existence."[40]

The ideologists and the political representatives of a class need not share in all the material characteristics of that class, but they share and express the overall cast of mind.

> One [must not] imagine that the democratic representatives are indeed all shopkeepers or enthusiastic champions of shopkeepers. According to their education and their individual position they may be as far apart as heaven from earth. What makes them representatives of the petty bourgeoisie is the fact that in their minds they do not go beyond the limits which the latter do not get beyond in life, that they are consequently driven, theoretically, to the same problems and solutions to which material interest and social position drive the latter practically.[41]

Moreover, Marx granted that particular individuals might not always think in terms of class interests, that they "are not 'always' influenced in their attitude by the class to which they belong."[42] But categories of people, as distinct from individuals, are so influenced.

In his more polemical writings Marx used his functional analysis of the relations between ideas and the social position of their proponents as a means of unmasking and debunking specific opponents and specific ideas. His aims were wider, however. Karl Mannheim perceived this when he wrote:

> [Marx's] undertaking . . . could reach its final goal only when the interest-bound nature of ideas, the dependence of 'thought' on 'existence,' was brought to light, not merely as regards certain selected ideas of the ruling class, but in such a way that the entire 'ideological superstructure' . . . appeared as dependent upon sociological reality. What was to be done was to demonstrate the existentially determined nature of an entire system of *Weltanschauung,* rather than of this or that individual idea.[43]

In Marx's later writings, and in particular in a remarkable series of Engels' letters that date from the 1890's, some of the sharp edges of earlier polemical writings were smoothed out. Marx and Engels were now led to repudiate the idea that the economic "infrastructure" alone determined the character of the "superstructure" of ideas and only held onto the assertion that it "ultimately" or "in the last analysis" was the determining factor.

> According to the materialist conception of history, the *ultimately* determinant element in history is the production and reproduction of real life. . . .

[40] *Selected Works,* I, p. 52. [41] *Selected Writings,* p. 82. [42] *Ibid.,* p. 202.

[43] Karl Mannheim, *Essays on the Sociology of Knowledge* (New York, Oxford University Press, 1952), p. 143.

> Hence if somebody twists this into saying that the economic element is the *only* determining one, he transforms that proposition into a meaningless, abstract and senseless phrase. The economic situation is the basis, but the various elements of the superstructure . . . also exercise their influence upon the course of the historical struggle and in many cases preponderate in determining their *form*.[44]

In their later writings, both Marx and Engels were led to grant a certain degree of intrinsic autonomy to the development of legal, political, religious, literary, and artistic ideas. They now stressed that mathematics and the natural sciences were exempt from the direct influence of the social and economic infrastructure, and they now granted that superstructures were not only mere reflections of infrastructures, but could in turn react upon them. The Marxian thesis interpreted in this way gained considerable flexibility, although it also lost some of its distinctive qualities.[45]

DYNAMICS OF SOCIAL CHANGE

Marx's focus on the process of social change is so central to this thinking that it informs all his writings. The motor force of history for Marx is not to be found in any extra-human agency, be it "providence" or the "objective spirit." Marx insisted that men make their own history. Human history is the process through which men change themselves even as they pit themselves against nature to dominate it. In the course of their history men increasingly transform nature to make it better serve their own purposes. And, in the process of transforming nature, they transform themselves.

In contrast to all animals who can only passively adjust to nature's requirements by finding a niche in the ecological order that allows them to subsist and develop, man is active in relation to his surroundings. He fashions tools with which to transform his natural habitat. Men "begin to distinguish themselves from animals as soon as they begin to *produce* their means of subsistence. . . . In producing their means of subsistence men indirectly produce their actual material life."[46]

Men "who every day remake their own life"[47] in the process of production can do so only in association with others. This is what makes man a *zoon politicon*. The relations men establish with nature through their labor are reflected in their social relationships.

[44] *Selected Works*, II, p. 488.

[45] In this section I have used a few sentences from my article "Sociology of Knowledge," in the *International Encyclopedia of the Social Sciences* (New York, Macmillan, 1968). For a comparison of Marx's sociology of knowledge with that of others, see Robert K. Merton, *Social Theory and Social Structure* (New York, The Free Press, 1968), Chapters 14 and 15.

[46] *Selected Writings*, p. 53. [47] *Ibid.*, p. 61.

> The production of life, both of one's own by labor and of fresh life by procreation, appears at once as a double relationship, on the one hand as a natural, on the other as a social relationship. By social is meant the cooperation of several individuals, no matter under what conditions, in what manner or to what end. It follows from this that a determinate mode of production, or industrial stage, is always bound up with a determinate mode of cooperation, or social stage, and this mode of cooperation is itself a 'productive force.'[48]

In their struggle against nature, and to gain their livelihood through associated labor, men create specific forms of social organization in tune with specific modes of production. All these modes of social organization, with the exception of those prevailing in the original stage of primitive communism, are characterized by social inequality. As societies emerge from originally undifferentiated hordes, the division of labor leads to the emergence of stratification, of classes of men distinguished by their differential access to the means of production and their differential power. Given relative scarcity, whatever economic surplus has been accumulated will be preempted by those who have attained dominance through their expropriation of the means of production. Yet this dominance never remains unchallenged. This is why "the history of all hitherto existing society is the history of class struggles."

Free men and slaves, patricians and plebeians, barons and serfs, guildmasters and journeymen, exploiters and exploited have confronted one another from the beginning of recorded time. Yet Marx insisted on the principle of historical specificity, that is, he thought it essential to note that each particular class antagonism, rooted in particular productive conditions, must be analyzed in its own right. Each stage in history is conceived as a functional whole, with its own peculiar modes of production, which give rise to distinctive types of antagonisms between exploiting and exploited classes. Not all exploited classes have a chance to assert themselves in successful combat against their exploiters. The revolts of the slaves of antiquity or of the German peasantry at the time of the Reformation were doomed to failure because these classes did not represent a mode of production that would dominate in the future. On the other hand, the bourgeoisie in the last stages of feudalism and the proletariat in modern times were destined to be victorious since they represented a future mode of production and social organization.

While Marx can be considered a historical evolutionist, it would be a mistake to think of him as a believer in unilinear evolution. He was acutely aware of periods of relative stagnation in human history—for example, in Oriental societies—and he knew of historical situations characterized by a stalemate, a temporary equilibrium, between social classes. His writings on

[48] *Ibid.*, p. 62.

the regime of Napoleon III illustrate in masterful fashion a historical situation in which the forces of the old class order and of the new are so nearly balanced that neither is able to prevail, thus giving rise to a "Bonapartist" stalemate. Moreover, though throughout his life Marx held fast to the belief that the future belongs to the working class, which will lead the way to the emergence of a classless society, he was nevertheless willing to consider the possibility that the working class may not be equal to its "historical task" so that mankind would degenerate into a new kind of barbarism.

Marx conceived of four major successive modes of production in the history of mankind after the initial stage of primitive communism: the Asiatic, the ancient, the feudal, and the modern bourgeois form. Each of these came into existence through contradictions and antagonisms that had developed in the previous order. "No social order ever disappears before all the productive forces for which there is room in it have been developed; and new higher relations of production never appear before the material conditions of their existence have matured in the womb of the old society."[49]

Class antagonisms specific to each particular mode of production led to the emergence of classes whose interests could no longer be asserted within the framework of the old order; at the same time, the growth of the productive forces reached the limits imposed by previous productive relations. When this happened, the new classes, which represented a novel productive principle, broke down the old order, and the new productive forces, which were developed in the matrix of the old order, created the material conditions for further advance. However, "the bourgeois relations of production are the last antagonistic form of the social process of production."[50] When they have been overthrown by a victorious proletariat, "the prehistory of human society will have come to an end,"[51] and the dialectical principle that ruled the previous development of mankind ceases to operate, as harmony replaces social conflict in the affairs of men.

Marx's emphasis on the existential roots of ideas, his stress on the need to view thinking as one among other social activities, has remained—no matter what qualifications have to be made—one of the enduring parts of his work. Together with his economic interpretation of the course of human history, his theory of class relations, and his focus on the alienating aspects of social life in modern society, it has become a permanent part of the sociological enterprise.

[49] *Ibid.*, p. 52. [50] *Ibid.* [51] *Ibid.*, p. 53.

THE MAN

Karl Marx, the eldest son of Heinrich and Henrietta Marx, was born on May 5, 1818 in the Rhenish city of Trier, where his father practiced law and later rose to become head of the bar. Both his mother and father came from long lines of rabbis, Heinrich's in the Rhineland and Henrietta's in Holland.[52]

Marx's father, the first in his line to receive a secular education, had broken with the world of the ghetto and had become a disciple of the Enlightenment —of Leibniz and Voltaire, of Kant and Lessing. His native Trier had once been the seat of a Prince-Archbishop, but early in the century it had been occupied by the French and incorporated by Napoleon in the Confederation of the Rhine. Under the French regime, the Jews, who had suffered from grievous civil disabilities earlier, achieved equal rights as citizens. The doors of trades and professions hitherto closed to them were now open. Since the Jews of the Rhineland owed their emancipation to the Napoleonic regime, they supported it with ardor. They faced a major crisis, however, when, after Napoleon's defeat, the Rhineland was assigned by the Congress of Vienna to Prussia, where Jews were still deprived of their civil rights. Threatened with the loss of his legal practice, Marx's father decided in 1817 to convert to the mildly liberal Lutheran Church of Prussia. Being a vague deist and having had no contacts with the synagogue, he regarded conversion as an act of expediency without great moral significance.

The young Marx grew up in a bourgeois household where tensions stemming from its minority status were at best subjacent. His mother, a fairly uneducated woman who never learned to write correct German or to speak it without an accent, does not seem to have had a major influence on him. In contrast, relations with his father, despite some strain, remained close almost throughout the latter's life. He introduced the young Marx to the world of human learning and letters—to the great figures of the Enlightenment and to the Greek and German classics. Although Marx was early repelled by his father's subservience to governmental authority and the high and mighty, the intellectual bonds that had been created between father and son began to be severed only in the last year of the father's life, when the son became a Young Hegelian rebel at Berlin University.

52 This section is based in the main on standard biographies among which Franz Mehring's classic, *Karl Marx: The Story of His Life,* trans. by Edward Fitzgerald, new ed. (Ann Arbor, University of Michigan Press, 1967), is still most helpful, though it is superseded in much detail by later work. E. H. Carr's *Karl Marx, A Study in Fanaticism* (London, Dent, 1934) has much new detail not available to Mehring, and counterposes a very sceptical view to Mehring's worshipful attitude. Isaiah Berlin's *Karl Marx, His Life and Environment,* 2nd ed. (New York, Oxford University Press, 1948) is by far the best short study in English or in any other language. I have relied on it heavily here. Nothing that has appeared since (and there have been whole shelves of books written on Marx since the forties) overshadows it.

The young Marx was fortunate to have another role model besides his father, the Freiherr Ludwig von Westphalen, a next-door neighbor. Westphalen, though socially his superior, enjoyed cordial relations with Marx's father: they were both at least nominal Protestants in a largely Catholic city, and they shared an admiration for the Enlightenment and for liberal ideas. An uncommonly cultivated man, Westphalen spoke several languages, knew Homer by heart, and was exceedingly well read in ancient and modern philosophy and literature. He soon found himself attracted to his neighbor's son; he encouraged him, lent him books, and took him on long walks during which he talked to him about Shakespeare and Cervantes and also about the new social doctrines, especially that of the Saint-Simonians, which had lately created such a stir in Paris. The bond between the two was close, and the distinguished upper-class Prussian government official became the spiritual mentor of the future leader of proletarian socialism.

MARX BECOMES A YOUNG HEGELIAN

After uneventful years at the Trier *Gymnasium,* the young Marx, following his father's advice, registered at the age of seventeen at the faculty of law in the University of Bonn. In 1836 he left Bonn to transfer to the University of Berlin. Although this transfer seems to have been motivated by nothing more than the desire of a provincial to move to the more exciting and lively atmosphere of the capital, it was to prove the decisive turning point in the young man's career.

Hegel was already dead when Marx entered the University of Berlin, but his spirit still dominated it fully. And Marx, after but a short period of resistance, surrendered to that spirit.

His teachers at the faculty of law, Savigny in jurisprudence and Gans in criminal law, exerted some influence over the young Marx. Savigny, the founder of the Historical School of Jurisprudence, impressed him with his historical erudition and his power of argumentation. Gans taught him methods of theoretical criticism in the light of philosophy of history. But it was not these older Hegelians or near-Hegelians who converted the young man to his new vision; it was a group of near-contemporaries, the Young Hegelians. These young philosophers had formed a little band of heretics who, though in many respects beholden to the master, had moved away from his teachings. Through them Marx was initiated into the Hegelian world system at the same time as he became a member of a group of iconoclasts who irreverently began to raise awkward and critical questions about major parts of the great man's synthesis.

The informal *Doktorklub,* of which Marx now became a member, was comprised of young marginal academics—a radical, somewhat antireligious, and more than slightly bohemian lot. Outstanding among them were the brothers Bruno and Edgar Bauer, both radical and freethinking Hegelians of the Left, and Max Stirner, the later proponent of ultra-individualistic anarchism. Under the influence of these men Marx abandoned law and resolved to devote himself to philosophy. He also became a "man-about-town," frequenting the advanced salons of the capital, as well as the beer cellars, where the Young Hegelians debated for hours on end the fine points of Hegelian doctrine.

In these student years Marx saw himself as a future professor of philosophy. In fact, Bruno Bauer, who had recently been appointed to the University of Bonn, promised that he would find him a position there. But soon after this, Bauer himself was dismissed for his antireligious, liberal views, and Marx abandoned forever his hope for an academic position. His student days came to an end with the submission to the University of Jena in 1841 of his thesis, *On the Differences between the Natural Philosophy of Democritus and Epicurus*. The dissertation was a fairly traditional exercise, except for a flaming antireligious preface which, upon the advice of his friends, was not submitted to the academic authorities. Marx faced an uncertain future: he was now twenty-three years of age, an amateur philosopher who had made a marked impression in advanced salons and bohemian gatherings, but had otherwise no prospects for a career.

It is no wonder that when an early admirer, the socialist firebrand Moses Hess, asked him to become a regular writer for the new liberal-radical and bourgeois paper *Rheinische Zeitung* in Cologne, he grasped the opportunity. He became its editor-in-chief ten months later after writing a number of outstanding contributions. Back in his native Rhineland as an editor of a leading radical publication, Marx for the first time became involved in the immediate practical battles of the day. He wrote a series of articles on social conditions, among them, the misery of the Moselle vine-growing peasantry and the harsh treatment the poor received for the theft of timber in forests to which they thought they had a communal right. These articles attracted considerable attention, and Marx began to be regarded as a leading radical publicist. But his editorship was short-lived. He had to battle with the censor continuously and to use all his ingenuity to get his thinly veiled democratic and republican propaganda past their scrutiny. When he acidly portrayed the Russian government as the chief bulwark of reaction in Europe, his own government's tolerance gave out. The Russian Emperor Nicholas I, who happened to have read one of Marx's attacks, complained to the Prussian ambassador, and consequently the *Rheinische Zeitung* was suppressed. The whole adventure had lasted only half a year and Marx was again without a position.

Soon afterward, in April 1843, he married his childhood sweetheart, Jenny von Westphalen, to the dismay of most of her family who grumbled about the misalliance with a social inferior, indeed, one who had no standing whatever.

Following their marriage, the young couple stayed in Bad Kreuznach for several months. During those idyllic months of honeymoon and young love, Marx filled five large exercise books with extracts from nearly a hundred volumes of political and social history and theory, including Montesquieu's *Spirit of the Laws* and Rousseau's *Social Contract.* In November 1843, despairing of any hope to attain a position in the increasingly reactionary atmosphere of Germany, Marx and his wife left for Paris.

PARISIAN DAYS: MARX BECOMES A SOCIALIST

The Paris years, from 1843 to 1845, were as decisive for Marx's intellectual development as the years of association with the Young Hegelians in Berlin. Under the relatively tolerant July monarchy, Paris had become the center of social, political, and artistic activity and the gathering place of radicals and revolutionaries from all over Europe.

During the Paris years, Marx plunged into the study of various reformist and socialist theories that had been inaccessible in Germany. He read Proudhon and Louis Blanc, Cabet and Fourier, Saint-Simon and the Saint-Simonians, as well as the revolutionary disciples of Babeuf such as Blanqui. In addition, he became familiar with the British political economists from Adam Smith to Ricardo and with their liberal and radical critics such as Sismondi.

In Paris Marx not only had an opportunity to study novel doctrines, but he also was able to meet a number of radicals in person. Among the émigrés, he was especially attracted to the Russian revolutionary Michael Bakunin, and among the Germans, he frequented the radical poets Heinrich Heine and Ferdinand Freiligrath, the revolutionary itinerant tailor Wilhelm Weitling, and the radical left-Hegelian writer Arnold Ruge. Among the Frenchmen Marx met in person, Proudhon may have made the strongest impression. Marx had already read his *What Is Property?* in Cologne and had praised it very highly. At first the two seemed to be made for each other, but after a fairly short period the friendship dissolved. A few years later Marx savagely attacked Proudhon's *Philosophy of Misery* in his *The Misery of Philosophy,* charging him with a misuse of Ricardo's economic concepts and with doing away with the movement of history by neglecting and neutralizing the thrust of dialectical contradictions.

Above all, it was in Paris that the remarkable lifelong friendship with Friedrich Engels began. Here Marx became intimate with the textile manufacturer's son who had turned socialist from revulsion about the conditions of the working class, which he had observed both in his native Rhineland and in England, where he was now a manager of one of his father's enterprises. It was through Engels and his work that Marx was introduced to an understanding of the concrete conditions and the misery of working-class life.

Besides the leading intellectuals of the radical and liberal movement whom

Marx had an occasion to meet in Paris, he also encountered for the first time those artisan and craftsman radicals, German and French, who, in alliance with intellectuals, were the mainstay of the socialist and revolutionary movement. In almost daily commerce with them, Marx, although often contemptuous of their simple-mindedness and lack of intellectual distinction, was impressed by this new type of man, so very different from the academically trained intellectual with whom he had associated before.

Marx, the radical liberal, completed his conversion to socialism in the heady atmosphere of Paris. It was here that, sometimes alone and sometimes in collaboration with Engels, he wrote those early works that served to define his new philosophical and political position and helped to sever the ties that had bound him to his erstwhile Young Hegelian companions. Some of these writings appeared as articles in a short-lived review, *Deutsch-Franzoesische Jahrbuecher,* which he edited with Arnold Ruge. Most, however, like the now famous *Economic and Philosophical Manuscripts* and *The German Ideology* (which was completed in Brussels), were never published during his lifetime, having been written primarily as a means for intellectual self-clarification. *The Holy Family,* his final settling of accounts with the key figures of the Young Hegelian "family," appeared in Frankfort in 1845. It received little attention since it appeared to most readers, not without reason, as a tedious family quarrel within the ranks of the Hegelian Left. *The Misery of Philosophy* was published in French in 1847.

In the beginning of 1845 Marx was expelled from Paris by the Guizot government. Just as the Prussian government had once terminated Marx's editorial career as a result of protests from Russia, so the French government now acted to expel him upon representations of Prussia, which had been offended by the antiroyalist comments of the socialist paper *Vorwaerts* on which he collaborated. Marx moved to Brussels and established contacts with the German refugees who had taken shelter there. In particular, he sought out the remaining members of the dissolved radical League of the Just, an international revolutionary organization influenced by the aforementioned Weitling. Marx now saw himself as a member of the international revolutionary movement and eagerly cultivated relations not only with German but also with Belgian and other socialist individuals and organizations. He had become a professional revolutionary, writing, lecturing, and conspiring in the service of a revolution which he, like his newly found comrades, believed imminent. From then on, as Isaiah Berlin has said, "His personal history which up to this point can be regarded as a series of episodes in the life of an individual [became] inseparable from the general history of socialism in Europe."[53]

[53] Berlin, *op. cit.,* p. 146.

THE END OF APPRENTICESHIP

Among the socialist organizations Marx made contact with in Brussels was the German Workers' Educational Association, headed by a type-setter (Schapper), a cobbler (Bauer), and a watchmaker (Moll); its headquarters were in London, and it was affiliated with a federation called the Communist League. In 1847 this group commissioned Marx to write a document expounding its aims and beliefs. Reworking a first draft provided by Engels, Marx wrote *The Communist Manifesto* in a burst of creative energy and dispatched it to London early in 1848. It was published, without having any major impact, a few weeks before the outbreak of the Paris revolution. The by now familiar first sentence, "The history of all hitherto existing society is the history of class struggle," adumbrates what is perhaps the most distinctive aspect of all of Marx's later work. His period of apprenticeship was over. He would elaborate and refine his message later on, and his specific political views and orientations would undergo many changes, but the main line of his intellectual development was determined.

When the 1848 revolution broke out in Germany, Marx returned to the Rhineland, after having spent some time in revolutionary Paris, and once again assumed the editorship of a radical newspaper, the *Neue Rheinische Zeitung*. He and Engels now worked for an alliance of the liberal bourgeoisie with the incipient working-class movement against the reactionary government. When the revolution failed, Marx, back again in exile, entertained for a while the will-o'-the-wisp of an impending new revolutionary outbreak. Castigating the liberals for their failure and their cowardice, Marx still expected that the revolutionary flame would be rekindled in the very near future.

In August 1849, Marx was presented by the French government with the alternatives of retiring into a distant provincial retreat or leaving the country. He made his decision and embarked for London. He was never to leave this city again for any length of time.

During the first phase of his stay in London, Marx considered the city a temporary port he would soon leave when the Continental revolution came again. In these early years he wrote his most brilliant historical pamphlets, *The Class Struggles in France* (1850) and *The Eighteenth Brumaire of Louis Bonaparte* (1852). These works are informed by a burning revolutionary ardor, but perhaps more importantly, they show Marx at his best in his new role as a social historian of distinction.

As the London years went on, Marx, although never despairing of the coming of a new revolutionary upsurge, realized that the fires of 1848 had burned out. Refusing to participate in a variety of insurrectionary conspiracies advocated by Continental revolutionaries, Marx and Engels withdrew from most of their fellow refugees. Since he had not managed to make many contacts in the British labor and socialist movement, Marx now retired almost completely into the narrow circle composed of his family, Engels and a few other devoted friends and disciples. He remained in this isolated condition throughout most of his life. When he wrote to Engels about "our party" he was referring to Engels and himself.

In June 1852 Marx obtained an admission card to the reading room of the British Museum. There he would sit from 10:00 A.M. to 7:00 P.M. every day, pouring over Blue Books of factory inspectors and perusing the immense documentation about the inequities of the operation of the capitalist system that was to become an important part of *Das Kapital.* Here also, filling notebook after notebook, he deepened his knowledge of the British political economists whom he had begun to study during the Paris days.

Throughout most of the London period Marx lived in dire and abject poverty. Only once had he attempted to find regular gainful employment (as a clerk in a railway office) but was turned down because of his illegible handwriting. Being entirely devoted to his work and absolutely convinced that the anatomy of the political economy of capitalism, which he now was describing, would provide an indispensable instrument for the "necessary" emancipation of the working class, Marx continued his scholarly tasks even when he and his family were pursued by angry creditors and found it hard to obtain lodging. Three of his children died from malnutrition or lack of proper care. When one of them died, he had no money to pay for a coffin until a fellow refugee came to his rescue. He and his family were exhausted by a variety of illnesses, some of which clearly stemmed from their miserable living conditions. But Marx persevered. Had it not been for the financial support that the devoted Engels gave to the full measure of his ability, the family might have gone down completely.

Meanwhile, work on what was to become *Das Kapital* proved even more time-consuming than had been anticipated. A first sketch entitled *A Contribution to the Critique of Political Economy* had been published in 1859 but attracted little attention. The first volume appeared in 1867. Marx never completed the subsequent volumes; they were finally published by Engels and Kautsky after his death.

Marx's grinding poverty was slightly relieved for a time when the foreign editor of the *New York Daily Tribune,* then probably the world's largest newspaper and one with a radical orientation to boot, asked him to become its regular correspondent for European affairs at one pound sterling for each article. He was to send them regular weekly dispatches for almost ten years. When ill health, lack of detailed knowledge, or the pressure of work on *Das Kapital* prevented him from writing, Engels, much more the facile journalist, took over. Recently, efforts to establish which of the unsigned articles were written by Marx and which by Engels have proved a profitable occupation for Marxicologists. In any case, these occasional writings provide privileged access to the operation of Marx's mind. The articles range over a variety of subjects—diplomatic events, social histories of England and the Continent, analyses of the secret sources of war and crisis, analytical accounts of the consequences of British domination in India—and reveal his reactions to the passing scene that are otherwise available only in his *Correspondence,* particularly with Engels.

Throughout the fifties, Marx and Engels watched expectantly for signs of the major economic crisis that would inaugurate a new period of revolutions. None came for many years. When a serious slump finally occurred in 1857, it had no revolutionary consequences. Marx then concentrated less on the expected economic breakdown and more on organizing the working class, but here too he was disappointed for a long time. To be sure, Ferdinand Lassalle, the romantic firebrand of German socialism, had created a German labor movement. But Marx disapproved of its political orientation even more than of Lassalle's histrionic manners. Jealousy of Lassalle, who had borrowed most of his theoretical weapons from Marx, may have been one of the motives for Marx's hostility, but there were more objective reasons. He was suspicious of Lassalle's tendency to build a socialist movement upon some sort of unspoken alliance with Bismarck and the Prussian government.

On the rest of the Continent, more particularly in France, the working-class movement was quiescent, not having fully recovered from the disasters of 1848. As for England, Marx never managed to have much sympathy for the stolid, unideological and pragmatic labor leaders who dominated the union movement there. He regarded most of them with withering contempt and they, in turn, to the extent that they knew him at all, returned the compliment.

THE FOUNDING OF THE FIRST INTERNATIONAL

The great change came in the year 1863. In that year, a delegation of French workers was given permission to visit England for the opening of the London Exhibition of Modern Industry in order to study industrial developments and to establish contact with their English counterparts. English and French labor leaders soon resolved to create a continuing economic and political cooperation, to invite representatives of other Continental nations to join them, and to constitute an international federation of working men pledged to end the prevaling economic system and to replace it with some form of collective ownership. The *International,* as it was to be called, was composed of various elements. Among the French, the Proudhonists and Blanquists were in the majority; among the Italians, there were nonsocialist radical democrats of Mazzini's persuasion; among the British, nonpolitical unionists and radical reformers, some of whom were followers of Comte, worked side by side.

Marx, contrary to his previous aloofness from organizations that were not fully committed to his own view, sensed the importance of this gathering and resolved not only to join it but to become its directing genius. German artisans residing in London made him their representative, and soon after the first meeting, Marx took full command. The *Inaugural Address of the International,* which Marx composed and which was adopted by the organization, is a historic document hardly less important in the Marxist canon than *The Communist Manifesto* penned fifteen years earlier.

During the next ten years of his life, Marx devoted a major part of his energies to the affairs of the *International.* He fought for his theoretical orientation against middle-class reformers and Bakuninist anarchists alike; he waged a continuous battle with the disciples of Blanqui and Proudhon in France and with the Lassalleans in Germany. Throughout these years he strove to make what had started as a loose alliance with divergent ideologies into a united movement informed by that one revolutionary ideology which he had forged in the many years of loneliness and isolation during his British exile.

The *International* soon became a powerful movement, inspiring fear in the defenders of the status quo. Branches of the *International* were formed in all the principal countries of Europe. From then on, Marx, as head of the General Council of the *International,* was in effective control of the movement and insisted on rigid adherence to the line he had set down. The specter of Communism that Marx had seen haunting Europe in 1847 seemed much more real to the men of power of the late sixties than it had been twenty years earlier. The obscure scholar from the British Museum suddenly became an object of choice attention for the various intelligence services that combed the world of London revolutionaries for information about subversive activities.

When the first volume of *Das Kapital* was published in 1867, Marx was already in the limelight as the leader of the *International.* Although the book did not attract as much immediate attention as he had no doubt expected, it soon gained an audience, particularly among Continental socialists. In England there was only one critical review, which amusingly remarked that "the presentation of the subject invests the driest economic questions with certain peculiar charm"; but on the Continent there was a more understanding reaction. A number of Marx's friends propagandized it strongly, and some of his old German associates sent him praise. In Russia, in particular, reviews were very favorable and more searching than anywhere else. Generally, quite apart from its scientific merits, the book was widely read by members of the *International.* Marx's previous books had been neglected even in German speaking countries. The first volume of *Das Kapital* was translated into Russian, French, English, and Italian within ten years of its publication.

In the late sixties, Marx, as head of the *International* and author of a book that sought to lay bare "the economic law of motion of modern society," must have felt that he had finally achieved the union of socialist theory and revolutionary practice that he had aimed for ever since 1847. He had provided the intellectual foundation for a socialist movement over which he exercised full organizational control. Yet that dream was soon shattered.

Ironically, the Paris *Commune* of 1871, the first instance of the working class achieving power for itself and thus seemingly vindicating Marx's vision, also proved the undoing of the *International.* Although the Paris *Commune* was dominated by Proudhonians and latter-day Jacobins rather than by Marxists, Marx had risen to its defense in an eloquent address published under the title, *The Civil War in France.* But soon after the *Commune* was drowned in blood, the latent dissensions in the ranks of the *International* came to a head. The English trade unionists grew frightened; they feared to be associated in the mind of peaceful British workers with the "red terrorists of Paris." The French movement was shattered, and its exiled leaders, as is the wont of émigré politicians, fell to quarreling among themselves. Followers of Bakunin now attempted to grasp the opportunity to wrest control from Marx. In order to insure his continued domination of the *International,* Marx managed to have its seat transferred to the United States where his followers were in full control. This proved to be the fatal blow. The *International* finally expired in Philadelphia in 1876.

In the few years that remained, Marx, wrecked by illness, produced no major work. When his followers and those of Lassalle united in 1875 to form a united socialist party at a congress in Gotha, he wrote a series of marginal and highly critical notes on its program in which he formulated for the last time his conception of the theory and practice that should guide the socialist movement. This *Critique of the Gotha Program,* published after his death, was his last major writing.

Toward the end of his life Marx finally achieved a measure of comfortable living. Engels, by now quite prosperous, settled an annuity on him, enabling him to spend his last few years in relative ease. He had become a famous man, and socialists from all over Europe consulted him by letter or in person. Russian radicals in particular—to the astonishment of Marx who for thirty years had attacked Russia as the charnel house of Europe—now flocked to him and asked for his advice. In addition, the young leaders of the now united German Social Democratic movement—Bebel, Bernstein and Kautsky—visited him and consulted him on all important issues. The German movement flourished, and one of the leaders of the revived French movement, Jules Guesde, consulted Marx on the program to be adopted. Slowly, the Bakuninist influence was pushed back by Marxist leaders in Italy and Switzerland, with whom Marx also carried on a long correspondence.

A revered figure in the growing socialist movement, Marx had finally found an audience and a satisfying role. But his creative powers were diminished. He still read voraciously; he even taught himself new languages such as Russian and Turkish, but, to Engels' despair, he wrote less and less, and more obscurely than ever.

In 1881, his wife died of cancer. A year later his eldest daughter, the wife of the French socialist leader Jean Longuet, also died. Marx never recovered from these blows. He died in an armchair in his study on March 14, 1883. Only a few friends and socialist representatives from abroad accompanied the casket to Highgate cemetery. His death was hardly noticed by the general public.

THE INTELLECTUAL CONTEXT

It has often been said the Marx fashioned his doctrine out of three major elements: German idealism, especially in its Hegelian version, French socialist tradition, and British political economy. Though not incorrect, this is hardly the whole truth. Other streams of thought, primarily the German and French Enlightenment, were equally important to him. Even before he came into contact with most other doctrines, Marx had already acquired from his father and from Ludwig von Westphalen a deep love for the Enlightenment and for the philosophy of Spinoza.

An omnivorous reader throughout his life, Marx managed to fuse in his thought a variety of previous intellectual traditions. He had above all a synthesizing mind. In the words of Isaiah Berlin, "What is original in the result is not any one component element, but the central hypothesis by which each is connected with the others, so that the parts are made to appear to follow from each other and to support each other in a single systematic whole."[54] Marx was not the bull in the china shop of Western culture as he is sometimes pictured by the uninformed. On the contrary, his work stands in a direct line of descent from the mainstream of European thought. He was in debt to many past doctrines and to his contemporary thinkers as well.

Among the significant themes in the works of his predecessors that are important for the understanding of Marx, four major ones stand out: the idea of progress, whether peaceful or conflictive; the idea of alienation; the idea of perfectibility; and the holistic view of society and of historical epochs.

THE IDEA OF PROGRESS

The notions of growth, development, becoming, and the like were central to the German philosophical tradition ever since Leibniz. At the beginning of the eighteenth century, Leibniz had stressed that each growing entity went through stages of development, that "nature never makes leaps" and that at each moment it was "charged with the past and pregnant with the future." He wrote but little about historical matters, but his religious writing on the theodicy and his secular considerations on the advancement of science docu-

[54] *Ibid.*, p. 13.

ment his view that mankind would progressively reach greater happiness and perfection, above all through the further spread of science.[55]

As the eighteenth century advanced, the notion of progress became secularized. Lessing, in *The Education of the Human Race,* couched his picture of the progressive moral development of mankind in a three stage theory—a theory that was still rooted in Christian tradition although fundamentally secular. To Lessing, human history appears divided into the pre-Christian moral world of harsh punishment and tangible reward, the Christian stage of more refined and spiritual morality, and a third imminent stage in which moral man would no longer be in fear of external punishment or internal guilt but would freely and autonomously make reasoned moral judgments. In the future, the whole human race would enjoy the fruits of rational mastery and moral autonomy.

The doctrines of the Enlightenment, which stressed the gradual and more or less harmonious progress of mankind, were countered, toward the end of the century, by a harsher philosophy. Kant in particular, although holding onto the belief in human progress, injected a more pessimistic note. For him, antagonism between men was the ultimate driving force in history. Far from associating harmoniously with one another, men were given to an "unsociable sociability." Men, he argued, had an inclination to associate because only in this way could they develop their natural endowment. Yet they were also inclined to hold themselves apart because of their unsociable desire to have everything their own way. Progress came about through antagonistic cooperation. Men may wish concord, but nature has created discord to stir people from their sheeplike passivity. The progress of the race was but the result of innumerable antagonisms among individuals.[56] Natural potentialities for growth and perfection manifest themselves not in individuals but only in the race as a whole.

The Kantian view of the centrality of conflict became one of the points of departure of Hegelian doctrine. The Leibnizian conception of progress as smooth development from potentiality into actuality was abandoned there. The history of mankind is indeed the history of the gradual unfolding of the Spirit, but it is also a history of bloody battles, of wars and revolution, of rival claims and tragic entanglements. Man's history is marked by necessary stages in which the Absolute Spirit gradually comes into its own. Mankind slowly arrives at true self-consciousness, but this history is tragic if viewed from the perspective of the historical actors. Advance can be perceived only from the vantage point of the Whole. "This may be called the cunning of reason—that

[55] Cf. Frank E. Manuel, *Shapes of Philosophical History* (Stanford, California, Stanford University Press, 1965), pp. 78 ff.

[56] Cf. *Kant on History,* trans. by Beck, Anchor and Fackenheim (Indianapolis, Bobbs-Merrill, 1963).

it sets the passions to work for itself, while that which develops its existence through such impulsion pays the penalty, and suffers loss. . . . The particular is for the most part of too trifling value as compared with the general: individuals are sacrificed and abandoned."[57]

For Hegel, the question of freedom, to give just one example, can never be answered in terms of individual desires and propensities; it is an historical question. For Hegel as for Spinoza, freedom is only the recognition of necessity. In previous stages of the progress of the world spirit, only a few could attain freedom, and they could gain it only at the expense of the many who were not free. Solely in the new era that had dawned with the French Revolution could man begin to envisage the possibility of general freedom.

The German doctrine of progress, at least since the later eighteenth century, was considerably less optimistic and less simple than the French view at that time, which is discussed in the previous chapter. Marx was influenced by both. He was a son of the French Enlightenment as well as of the German Enlightenment. But the influence of the German tradition was perhaps more profound, as is apparent in his notion of alienation.

THE IDEA OF ALIENATION

Rousseau's *Second Discourse* is among the chief early sources of the notion of alienation. His vivid depiction of the natural goodness of men and of their corruption by society, his stress on "the equality which nature established among men" and "the inequality which men have instituted," the horror with which he contemplated the havoc that society had created in its impact upon human nature—all these later stimulated critical views of the fallen condition of man.

Rousseau's influence, however, was not limited to "the defiant individualism of the *Discours sur l'inégalité,*" in which he depicted how men had been cut from their natural moorings by oppressive and unjust social laws. He also showed in his *Social Contract* how, by associating together in a new community they could voluntarily forge new bonds that would overcome their suffering through common subjection to the General Will. The individualism of the *Second Discourse* was followed by "the equally defiant collectivism of the *Social Contract.*"[58] The work of Rousseau can be read, and no doubt was often read, as a secular version of the old story of man's sin and subsequent redemption.

Many of Rousseau's German readers were unimpressed by his idyllic description of the nobility of savages. Schiller, for example, called it "the tranquil nausea of his paradise." But Rousseau's indictment of society and its

[57] F. W. Hegel, "Introduction," *The Philosophy of History* (New York, Bohn Library, n.d.), p. 34.
[58] C. E. Vaughn as quoted in George H. Sabine, *A History of Political Thought* (New York, Holt, Rinehart and Winston, 1961), p. 580.

deleterious effects became a common theme among many German thinkers of the late eighteenth and early nineteenth centuries. In particular, these men, although sceptical about the alleged wholeness of the life of savages, still deplored with him the torn condition of man in contemporary society. Communal integration and individual wholeness in antiquity were contrasted with the disintegration of community and the separateness of man's existence in the modern age. Schiller, for example, claimed that man was torn asunder by the modern division of labor; a specialized cog in the clockwork of modern society, he could no longer develop his full potentialities. "Eternally bound to but a small fraction of the whole, man himself becomes but a fraction . . . and never develops the harmony of his being. Instead of representing the totality of mankind in his own nature, he becomes but a replica of his business or his science." "We see not only single individuals but whole classes of men develop but a part of their gifts, while the rest, as in the case of crippled plants, only faintly suggest the given potentialities." Not only is the individual harmony of men aborted in the present fallen condition; society is likewise crippled. "State and Church have been torn apart and so have law and morality; fulfillment has been severed from labor, the means from the end, exertion from remuneration."[59]

Similar indictments of the alienation of modern man are common among other representatives of German idealism. Fichte, for example, characterized the modern age as marked by "breakdown," "absolute sinfulness," "destruction of everything positive," "anarchy." But these thinkers were united not only by their criticism of present conditions but by a common straining toward a future of reintegration and positive synthesis. Man and society having been sundered, they must be made whole again. Mankind must rationally construct a future in which what has been separated can be reunited, so that individuals can again become whole and find their place in a harmoniously organized society.

THE IDEA OF PERFECTIBILITY

If there is one idea that united the otherwise divergent doctrines of the French and English Enlightenments, it was the idea of human perfectibility. Whether rationalists in the manner of most French *philosophes,* or sensationalists like most of the British, including Locke, or materialists like La Mettrie, the philosophers of the Enlightenment were at one in their common belief in the possibility of altering the human environment in such a way as to allow a fuller and more wholesome development of human capacities. They were in

[59] Friedrich Schiller, *On the Aesthetic Education of Man in a Series of Letters,* ed. by Wilkinson and Willoughby (New York, Oxford University Press, 1967). See also Heinrich Popitz, *Der Entfremdete Mensch* (Basel, Verlag fuer Recht und Gesellschaft, 1953). I have relied heavily on this superb introduction to the ideas of the young Marx.

accord that man has no divine soul, that he is an object in nature, but that he has the capacity for self-improvement through education and environmental changes. When men's minds are released from the fetters of superstition and irrational belief, when they are enabled through education to make full use of their intelligence, the human race will come into its own. Men are the creatures of circumstances and upbringing. Hence changed circumstances and changed upbringing will result in better men.

THE IDEA OF TOTALITY

In contrast to most of the *philosophes,* who tended to be individualistic and atomistic in their views and to have a fairly weak historical imagination, Hegel stressed cultural totalities and historical determinism.

In Hegel's doctrine, two dimensions, the vertical or historical and the horizontal or structural, have to be examined simultaneously.[60] In the first, history is viewed as a temporal succession, as a series of necessary stages. Each point in time must be considered in its double aspect of being determined by what went on before and as containing within it the seeds of the future. In the horizontal perspective, on the other hand, the focus is on the structural unity of a society or an epoch as an interconnected whole with a unitary pattern or form.

Hegel taught that the error of all previous thinkers had been to assume the relative independence of the various spheres of culture. They had severed the study of warfare from the study of art; they had separated philosophy from daily life. The historians had isolated phenomena which could only be understood as parts of a totality. In contrast, the modern historian, according to Hegel, must be holistic in his orientation. "He must," to quote Isaiah Berlin, "endeavor to paint a portrait of an age of movement, to collect that which is characteristic, to distinguish between its component elements, between the old and the new, the fruitful and the sterile, the dying survivals of a previous age and the heralds of the future, born before their time."[61] Historians must describe cultural phenomena in their fullest historical context. Henceforth, the history of art or the history of philosophy were to be treated as complementary elements in a general history of culture, and even activities that had been regarded as trivial by the old history, such as trade, commerce, the mechanical arts, now had to be considered essential elements in the "organic" institutional history of mankind.

The intertwined notions of progress and perfectibility, of alienation and integration, were all part of the intellectual heritage Marx assimilated even before he set upon writing his own synthesis with the ideas gathered from his contemporaries and near-contemporaries.

[60] The following is deeply indebted to Berlin, *op. cit.,* especially pp. 35–60.
[61] *Ibid.,* p. 52.

MARX'S DEBT TO HIS CONTEMPORARIES

The criticism of Hegel, which Marx encountered among the Young Hegelians, deeply influenced his thought. During the later stages of his Berlin career, Hegel had become increasingly conservative in his orientation. The young Hegel had welcomed the French Revolution with fervent enthusiasm, but he had now stiffened into an old man who feared any further revolution and most reform, and considered the Prussian state under Frederick William III the very embodiment of freedom and rationality and as close to perfection as any human institution was ever likely to be. He now proclaimed that, "Whatever is real is reasonable, and whatever is reasonable is real," which was generally thought to mean that all that existed was reasonable and hence worthy of support, although he himself denied this interpretation.

It was this political and philosophical quietism of the old master that his young erstwhile disciples turned against in the 1830's. Seizing upon some remarks that Hegel had made toward the end of his life, they asserted that the truly real was the perfectly ideal, and that the struggle to attain it was still on the agenda of history.[62] Hegel had taught them to see how throughout mankind's past, philosophical thought had always been critical of a given state of affairs, how the negative critique of philosophy had been a key instrument for destroying the complacency of the given and for preparing the way for the birth of new cultural possibilities. The need for corrosive criticism of the status quo, they argued, had by no means ceased in the present age. Philosophy still had as its central mission the need to be critical. Suffering from the spiritual oppression that marked the reign of the King whom Hegel extolled, they turned their critical weapons to an examination of the culture of their time.

The state of Germany, the Young Hegelians asserted, was marked by blind unreason and spiritual chaos, and therefore it could hardly be considered "real" in the metaphysical sense. In particular, German culture was still dominated by an unenlightened and oppressive religiosity. Hence, the critique of religion became to them the major philosophical task of the day.

In 1835, David Strauss, one of the Young Hegelians, published a critical *Life of Jesus* in which he used the Hegelian historical method to show that certain portions of the Gospels were pure invention whereas others were only reflections of semimythological beliefs common in primitive Christian communities. Bruno Bauer, a more radical Young Hegelian, followed suit by denying the historical existence of Jesus altogether and treating the Gospels as works of pure imagination, as simple reflections of the ideology of the time.

[62] Cf. Sidney Hook, *From Hegel to Marx* (New York, Reynal and Hitchcock, 1936), p. 20. The whole of this work remains indispensable for an understanding of Marx's relationships to the Young Hegelians.

Finally, Ludwig Feuerbach, in his *Essence of Christianity* (1841) and in other philosophical works, defined religious beliefs as only the projection of elements of human experience into objects of worship.[63]

Utilizing Hegelian notions for his purposes, Feuerbach depicted religious phenomena as alienated reifications that can be analyzed in terms of the social relations to which they owe their origins. To Feuerbach, anthropology is the secret of theology. The existence of religion testifies that man is alienated from himself. Through religion, men are ruled and oppressed by their own unconscious creation. Feuerbach urged that the time had come for a truly Copernican turn in the history of ideas. Men, acting in relation with their fellows, rather than Gods or the Hegelian Absolute Spirit, must now be the focus for the understanding of man's past and his future. The God-centered world of the imprisoned past must give way to the man-centered universe of the liberated future. This liberation once accomplished, man will truly become the measure of all things.

Marx's own philosophical development was considerably furthered by the critical philosophy of the Young Hegelians who saw in religious beliefs only the reflection of "real" social phenomena. Marx was impressed in particular with Ludwig Feuerbach's turn from a spirit-centered or God-centered world to the analysis of those unhappy social conditions which had led men to find consolation in a world of religious entities of their own creation. Other elements of Young Hegelian philosophy, such as the activist radicalism of Arnold Ruge and the iconoclastic individualism of Max Stirner, also influenced him in various ways. But there is still one other figure, the socialist rebel Moses Hess, who contributed in considerable measure to Marx's conversion from critical liberalism to a radical socialist analysis of social relations.

Feuerbach had mainly used the notion of alienation in his attack on religion, but Moses Hess employed it in a corrosive critique of current social and economic arrangements. To Hess, the reign of money and of private property symbolized the alienated condition of mankind just as much as, if not more than, the existence of revealed religion. In his earlier writings, Hess had tended to indulge in the rather cloudy abstractions of an ethereal socialism, but by 1847 he turned to a realistic analysis of economic phenomena. In the words of Sidney Hook, "In [his essay "The Consequences of the Revolution of the Proletariat"] will be found . . . the theory of the concentration and centralization of capital, the theory of increasing misery, the theory of overproduction to account for the periodicity of crisis, the doctrine that the collapse of capitalism is inevitable . . . theories which were to receive classic formulation . . . a few months later, in the *Communist Manifesto*."[64] Though largely unacknowledged by Marx, his debt to Hess is considerable.

The Young Hegelians in general, and Ludwig Feuerbach in particular,

[63] Cf. *ibid.*, p. 221. [64] *Ibid.*, p. 204.

provided Marx with elements of that theoretical equipment which enabled him "to stand Hegel on his head." That is, they led him to anchor his views in an examination of the social system—of the social relationships in which men were enmeshed—rather than the world of disembodied ideas and the Spirit.

But it was only in his Paris years that he was converted to socialism through contact with some of its major protagonists and through a thorough reading of their works—some of which he had already begun to peruse in Germany, having been guided in this respect by Hess and by Lorenz von Stein's *Socialism and Communism in Contemporary France* (1842).

Marx's specific socialist doctrine is not relevant in this context. What is relevant, however, is the extent to which he utilized certain aspects of contemporary and near-contemporary French social thought in rounding out his own view of history and of the social order. From Saint-Simon and the Saint-Simonians, as well as from "bourgeois historians" such as Guizot and Thierry, he took elements of his theory of class struggle. To Saint-Simon, in particular, he owes the notion that human history is largely the history of wars between classes. In the words of Frank Manuel, "Classes were the key to Saint-Simon's philosophy of history. In its very fabric history was the conflict of classes, and the historical process could be explained solely in these terms."[65]

In Saint-Simon can be found not only the notion of the struggle between classes, but also that property relations rather than governmental forms are central to an understanding of history. "The form of government," he wrote, "is but a form, and property relations are the basis; hence property relations are the real basis of the social edifice."[66] In contrast to the Hegelian tradition, which had focused on the State, the tradition of Saint-Simon focused on social relations. Moreover, it will be remembered, Saint-Simon was one of the first who saw society as a gigantic workshop of industrial relationships.

Class struggle, the crucial importance of the working class in the modern industrial world, the emphasis on the centrality of industry and labor, and, above all, the emphasis on an activistic social philosophy that called not only for interpreting the world but for changing it—all these elements of Marx's synthesis were stimulated through his reading of French socialist or near-socialist doctrine, more particularly of the Saint-Simonian variety. Marx and Engels later denied this inheritance as much as possible and came to regard the French socialists as "utopians" whom they contrasted unfavorably with their own "scientific" version of socialism. But the historian of ideas need not accept their judgment; they owed to these utopians much more than they were later prepared to acknowledge.

While in Paris, Marx turned from his preoccupations with philosophy to

[65] Frank E. Manuel, *The New World of Henri Saint-Simon* (Cambridge, Massachusetts, Harvard University Press, 1956), p. 244.

[66] Quoted in Rubel's "Introduction" to Karl Marx, *Selected Writings, op. cit.*, p. 10.

the analysis of the contradictions and struggles within civil society—that is within social structures. It was also during the Paris days that he turned to the idea that "the anatomy of civil society is to be sought in political economy." The classical economists from Smith to Ricardo and Malthus, as well as their heterodox critics such as Sismondi, loomed large in Marx's final synthesis. This tradition will not be detailed here since it mainly concerns his economic doctrine and has often been analyzed, most perceptively by Joseph Schumpeter.[67]

Enough has been said to document the claim that Marx's thought stood at the confluence of a wide variety of European streams of thought: the French and German Enlightenments; German idealism, especially as represented by Hegel; the critical tradition of the Young Hegelians and the anthropological vision of Feuerbach; French social thought, especially in its Saint-Simonian version; and British political economy.

THE SOCIAL CONTEXT

THE GENERAL SCENE

The eighteen thirties and early forties, the years of Marx's young manhood, were years of profound despair for the German educated classes. A blanket of repression covered all those who attempted to think independently. The Holy Alliance, established by the powers that had defeated Napoleon in order to repress the forces of libertarian revolution, of radicalism and the Rights of Man, seemed forever able to stifle even faintly liberal stirrings.

The repressive regime was especially galling to those who, like the inhabitants of the Rhineland, had breathed the air of comparative freedom under Napoleonic administration. But even in other parts of Germany great hopes had been aroused by the war of National Liberation and the reforms that had been made in order to enlist the population at large, especially the educated classes, in the anti-Napoleonic crusade. These hopes were now dashed. Patriotic liberals, who had dreamed of thorough reform after Napoleon's defeat, instead found themselves in a police regime considerably more efficient than its predecessors. Especially in Prussia under the reign of Frederick William III, all expectations for political and social reform were disappointed. And when the Crown Prince, a romantic who had prattled a good deal about allying patriotism, democratic principles, and constitutional monarchy, and who had been the great hope of the liberals, ascended the throne in 1840, it soon became apparent that the liberals' aspirations would again remain unfulfilled. What he

[67] Joseph Schumpeter, *Capitalism, Socialism and Democracy,* 3rd ed. (New York, Harper & Row, 1950); *History of Economic Analysis* (New York, Oxford University Press, 1954); *Ten Great Economists: From Marx to Keynes* (New York, Oxford University Press, 1951).

sought to attain was not liberal unity through constitutionalism, but a revival of the mystic glories of a divinely consecrated and patriarchal monarchy.

German intellectuals, especially students, had organized liberal societies (*Burschenschaften*). They had gotten together in large gatherings such as the Wartburg Festival of 1817, at which the emblems of reaction were burned, and the Hambach Festival of 1832, where 25,000 men drank to Lafayette and demanded a unified German Republic. All this had been to no avail.

Since 1819, the sovereigns of the German Confederation had pledged themselves to control the universities in their territories through special commissions and had provided for strict censorship of all publications. In the thirties, in response to the threat of an extension to Germany of the French July revolution, additional repressive measures were instituted, including the prohibition of all political meetings, the surveillance of suspicious political "agitators," and even tighter control of universities. Germany had no parliament, no trial by jury, no rights of free speech or assembly. It is no wonder that Germany in general, and especially its pivotal state, Prussia, appeared to the liberals among the educated classes as a formidable bulwark of reaction.

Germany was lagging behind France and England not only in its political development, but socially and economically as well. The middle classes had failed to attain power, and various traditional, sectional, and religious interests divided the country, thus preventing the emergence of a unified middle-class movement. Germany was still predominantly agricultural; it lacked a self-conscious bourgeoisie and was largely dominated, especially in its Prussian part, by a semifeudal nobility. To be sure, manufacturing, mining, and shipping grew fairly rapidly in the post-Napoleonic period and increased national wealth, but the middle classes, fragmented as they were within the boundaries of thirty-nine German states, were preoccupied with parochial concerns and were unwilling, by and large, to think in terms of national interests.

The Krupps of the Ruhr installed their first steam engine in 1835, and the first shafts of the Ruhr coal-fields were sunk in 1837. New industrial areas developed, such as the textile towns of Barmen and Krefeld in Prussia. Transportation networks were being built, and the new rapid mail, which linked Berlin to Magdeburg after 1824, shortened travel time from two and a half days to fifteen hours. But all these were only islands of modernity still largely submerged in an ocean of tradition. The bulk of production was still centered in the shop of the artisan rather than in factories. The traditional guild system of master, journeyman, and apprentice continued to prevail and prevented mobility of labor and business enterprise.

Moreover, government supervision hampered the growth of a free capitalism. Until the thirties each mercantilist and paternalistic state government regulated export and import. Later a custom union between the states did away with barriers to interior commerce, but each state continued to control productive activities within its boundaries. The Prussian government, for example, controlled the quality and fair price of handicraft production, the activities of the Silesian domestic line-weaving industry, and the operations of mine owners in the Rhineland. Government permission was required before a mine could be opened; it could also be withdrawn after the owner was already in business.[68]

Under such social and economic conditions, the lower and middle strata of the professionals, the administrators, and the intellectuals, in other words the educated, became the major proponents of nationalism and liberalism. Young men not yet encumbered by responsibility and position were in the lead of this movement. Yet, these educated men, while being permitted to spin intricate abstract theories about freedom in general, were firmly prevented from engaging in any practical activities that might bring about concrete freedom. These general conditions form the background against which Marx's peculiar circumstances can be assessed.

MARX'S PARENTAL BACKGROUND AND EARLY COMPANIONS

If ever there was a man who fitted the notion of marginality to the full, it was Karl Marx. Marx's family, it will be remembered, had converted to Christianity for prudent reasons. They had become Lutherans. But Protestants, although imbued with prestige, were only a small minority in predominantly Catholic Trier where the Marx family resided. Moreover, although the specifically racial notion of Jewish inferiority was not yet prevalent, even converted Jews suffered from discrimination and prejudice. As a consequence, Marx's contemporaries or near-contemporaries among Jewish intellectuals, whether they were converted or not, usually felt uneasy about their Jewishness. For example, Ludwig Boerne, Heinrich Heine, Ferdinand Lassalle, and Rahel Varnhagen, as well as many others, were still considered socially inferior in spite of having attained intellectual eminence.[69] Many of them suffered deeply from status contradictions, which resulted, to a greater or lesser degree, in an expression of Jewish self-hatred.

Marx was no exception. As a matter of fact, his lifelong attempts to dissociate himself from a Jewishness that was imposed on him from the outside, led him to equate it with all the detestable and vile characteristics and activities he despised. In Marx's writings the Jew appears typically as the usurer and moneychanger; the Children of Israel are portrayed as forever dancing before the Golden Calf. (Marx's lifelong aversion to the making of money is probably connected with this struggle against his Jewishness.) Among the most unattractive features of Marx is the profusion of deprecating references to Jews and Jewishness that are to be found in his letters. Such expressions as, "There

68 Cf. Hobsbawm, *The Age of Revolution* (New York, Mentor, 1967), pp. 210–11 and *passim.*

69 Cf. Hannah Arendt, *The Origins of Totalitarianism,* new ed. (New York, Harcourt Brace Jovanovich, 1960), Chapter 3.

are many Jews and fleas here," or references to Lassalle as "the Jewish nigger" are painfully abundant. In his later career, Marx was subject to a good deal of anti-Semitic abuse, but it is evident that even before that time he suffered intensely from his marginal status as a Jew and never came to terms with it.

The status disequilibrium that characterized Marx's position was compounded by what might be termed a disequilibrium in his role models. His father, whom he admired on other counts, exhibited attributes that he associated in his mind with a specifically Jewish defect: weakness and submissiveness. Ludwig von Westphalen, on the other hand, seemed to exhibit admired *Zivilcourage,* but he was of much higher status than Marx and his family could dream of attaining.

Only once in his life had Heinrich Marx taken a courageous public stand. He had spoken at a public dinner on the desirability of reform. However, when the police inquired, Marx's father retracted at once. This submissive attitude made a definitive impression on the son, who was then sixteen years old. Forty years later, when one of his daughters submitted to him one of those characteristically Victorian questionnaires that required him to state "the vice you most detest," he entered: "Servility."

It is probable that Marx's admiration for Ludwig von Westphalen, to whose memory, rather than to his father's, he dedicated his dissertation, may have been connected with his feeling that Westphalen possessed those admired virtues, especially courage, which he felt his father so conspicuously lacked. The high-status Westphalen, imbued with *noblesse oblige,* became a role model to the lower-status Marx, thus increasing his sense of marginality.

Marx's sense of being on the margin of things was reinforced by the associates he sought out in his student days in Berlin. Here he dealt almost exclusively with men who refused to come to terms with academic proprieties in the university, and who saw themselves as principled opponents of the political regime. Some of them, to be sure, toyed with the idea of attaining academic positions, and a very few managed temporarily to gain a foothold in the academy. By and large, however, their point of reference was no longer the university but a diffuse public of dissatisfied liberals and revolutionaries among the professional and educated strata, loosely attached, if at all, to specific institutional settings.

Like their French contemporaries discussed earlier, they were young men who had been highly educated and yet felt that in the stultifying atmosphere of Germany they had been trained for what we would today call "growing up absurd." Hence, they would sit for hours on end in coffee houses and beer halls, or flit from salon to salon, where they were lionized by the more staid of the liberals as daring young men *who really meant it.* They did gain some gratification from all of this, and they surely sharpened their wits in the scintillating intellectual exchanges that marked their gatherings. But all this nervous intellectual activity was like a powerful motor running idle.

Marx had found among peers in Berlin friends and allies with whom he now shared the marginality previously suffered in loneliness.

Marx's writing style in his early work shows the environment in which his ideas matured. It is a style that was intended to appeal not to the *vulgus,* but to the small and esoteric group of fellow outcasts. It is full of obscure references to family quarrels among the young Hegelians, which the ordinary reader could hardly be expected to understand. But it also displays brilliant dialectical skills, a joyous manipulation of words remindful of the informal debates in which it indeed originated. No doubt, some of this language represents an attempt to match that of Hegel, but more of it is in the style of sectarian discussions among rhetorically proficient friends and peers. No wonder that Marx decided not to publish much of it. By the time he left for Paris, he had already broken with most of his erstwhile associates. Although he had begun to discount these men as an audience, he in fact still conducted a kind of internal dialogue with them, attacking them with the ferocious dialectic skills he had acquired in their company.

Yet, even in these early writings one also finds analytical and descriptive passages that seem far indeed from the dialectical fireworks Marx used in his infightings with his former associates. One may surmise that his all too brief experience as a writer and editor for the daily press, when he addressed himself to a larger educated public, stood him in good stead. The expository style of his writings for the *Rheinische Zeitung,* though still distinguished by dialectical skills of a high order, is markedly different from that of his other early writings. Here he does not try to overwhelm the antagonist by the brilliant manipulation of his intellectual rapier but rather attempts to reason and to convince by methodical argument and factual evidence.

Both the style of thought and argumentation that Marx developed as a young rebel in the heady atmosphere of Berlin's bohemia and the dissimilar way of thinking and writing that marked his journalistic contribution were later to be fused in the writings of the mature man.

THE WORKING-CLASS AUDIENCE

The educated middle-class strata in France provided French authors with the type of audience that was not available to their German counterparts. Except for some literary men such as Heine, German authors in exile had to depend mainly on their own circles and on whatever public back home the censor allowed them to reach. This may explain, in part, the crabbed, confined, and ingrown quality of much of émigré writing. But, in addition to the company of status-equal exiles, the left-wing writers among them discovered in Paris one group they could address themselves to both in person and in writing: skilled artisans and handicraft workers who had, like themselves, left the homeland where they had been persecuted for their activities and beliefs.

In his almost daily commerce with such men, as well as through his gradual acquaintance with socialist writers who had in one way or another endeavored to express their desires and to put into words their inchoate aspirations, Marx was converted to socialism. From this time on, his almost demonic intellectual energies were no longer operating in a void; they were purposefully put to the service of his revolutionary goals. The philosopher's task of interpreting the world took a back seat to the revolutionary's willed resolve to change it.

During his years in Paris and Brussels, Marx associated as an equal with various powerful intellects, including Heine and Ruge, Proudhon and Bakunin, who were more diverse in their origins and casts of mind than the relatively homogeneous group of young bohemians who had been his companions in Berlin. And as his circle of friends and acquaintances widened, so did his readings. Moreover, he was now in contact with German and foreign workmen who, although they could not pretend to the education and erudition of his intellectual peers, exhibited that moral fortitude and strength of character Marx so much admired. To be sure, he was to quarrel with most of them sooner or later, just as he was to break away from almost all the intellectual companions of his Paris years. Nevertheless, workers were to remain the privileged audience he would address, if only in imagination, when, as in the years of almost total isolation in London, he had no direct contact with any of them.

Although both Marx and Comte (in the later stages of his career) addressed themselves to workers, it needs to be stressed that the nature of their relation to their audience differed fundamentally. Comte talked down to his working-class admirers. They were the simple in spirit who had to be brought to the gospel by means of an emotional appeal to their limited intellectual equipment. Marx, on the contrary, never talked down to the workers. He attempted instead to educate them in such a way that they could share with him the fruits of the new science that he was developing on their behalf. By trying to instill in them an awareness of their own misery and deprivation, by making them conscious, he wished to elevate them above the level to which their deprived social condition had condemned them. What the German idealistic tradition and its Greek forebears had attempted to teach individual men—that the unexamined life was not worth living and that man attained his dignity only through consciousness—Marx now endeavored to teach a whole class of men.

There are propagandistic elements in Marx's message, and it was on these that Sorel later attempted to build his notion of useful myths. But the main thrust of Marx's writings is otherwise. Through rational enlightenment and scientific education, he would show the working class how things *really* were. They would be energized into action not by vain moralistic exhortations or by appeals to their emotions, but by the portrayal of reality as it could be perceived once ideological blinders had been discarded. Underlying all of Marx's mature writings is *the search for social reality*. It is for this reason that Marx, in his attempt to fashion a "scientific" doctrine in the service of the working class, also left a legacy to those who, sharing his social passions only partly if at all, were still at one with him in their concern for understanding the social dimensions of man's vicissitudes on earth.

Men search for other men to whom they think their message will appeal. In this strict sense, they seek congenial, kindred minds. Marx, after having found a small public among sympathetic left-wing intellectuals and workmen, went out to create an audience. By educating workers through word of mouth and the written word, he helped them appreciate the intricacies of his own constructions, thereby providing an outlet for his doctrines. This was in contrast to Comte who suffered so slight a demand for his work that he was at last reduced to cheapening it in a desperate effort to be heard.

At the same time, Marx always wished to appeal to the highest standards of the scientific community of his time. Although he wrote about his "bourgeois" antagonists with withering contempt, he was far from the stance of his later mediocre disciples who thought that Marxism gave them a warranty to ignore the "bourgeois science" of their contemporaries. For these men, Marxism became the last refuge of the untalented and inept who could not make their way in the official groves of academe. Marx himself was far removed from such conceits. It is probably true that in his last years his mind grew rigid, so that what Vernon Parrington once said about Increase Mather—"he closed the window of his mind against the winds of new doctrine"—could also apply to Marx. Through most of his life, however, he did the major minds of the "bourgeois" world the honor of taking them seriously. Darwin's work impressed him deeply. And, as his voluminous notebooks as well as his published work amply testify, he continuously conducted a close combat with his antagonists in the "bourgeois world," thus making them worthy objects of his polemical wrath.

Since the Paris and Brussels days, Marx had fashioned a new image for himself as the purveyor of a new truth about social reality for the working class. He would bring to the workers a message he had forged through independent investigation and through close critical engagement with the major social thinkers of his and preceding generations. Engels summed it up when he wrote: "We had no wish to propound these new scientific conclusions in ponderous tomes for professional wiseacres. On the contrary. We had both of us entered bag and baggage into the political movement; we had certain connections with the educated world . . . and close ties with the organized proletariat. We were in duty bound to base our point of view upon a firm scientific foundation; but it was no less incumbent upon us to convince the European proletariat."[70]

ISOLATION AND DOUBLE MARGINALITY

In the Paris and Brussels days, Marx had been able to work for a relatively short period in a setting in which congenial peers and an appreciative working-class audience were present at the same time. It was in this setting that *The Communist Manifesto* was born. But when Marx settled in London after the short and disillusioning revolutionary interlude of 1848, he was deprived of that fortunate conjunction of stimulating companions and receptive audiences he had enjoyed on the Continent.

Partly because of his quarrelsome and overbearing temperament, but mainly for objective reasons, Marx was almost totally isolated in the first period of his London exile. He soon realized that the revolutionary dreams of his fellow exiles were just that: dreams divorced from a serious base in reality. Hence he withdrew as much as possible from their company. Yet he shared with them the sociological location as a stranger, a man who, to use Georg Simmel's terminology, is not a sojourner, here today and gone tomorrow, but who is bound to stay, without, however, developing those organic ties with the surrounding world that characterize the native. Edmund Wilson's superb literary imagination grasped the peculiarities of the exile's condition:

> The life of political exiles becomes infected with special states of mind which are unimaginable for men who have a country. Those precisely whose principles and interests have raised them above the ordinary citizen, now lacking the citizen's base and his organic relation to society, find themselves contracted to something less. And, even aside from the difficulties that the exile encounters in finding work and making friends in a foreign country, it is hard for him to take hold in a new place, to build himself a new career there, because he lives always in hope of going home when the regime by which he has been banished shall have failed.[71]

In the early London years Marx lived in double exile; he had little contact with Germany or with British thinkers and he was also isolated from the émigrés. In February 1851 Engels wrote to Marx: "One comes to understand more and more that emigration is an institution in which everybody who does not withdraw from it necessarily becomes a fool, an ass and a common scoundrel." And Marx replied that he welcomed "the open and authentic isolation in which we two, you and I, now find ourselves. It corresponds to

[70] Cited in Edmund Wilson, *To the Finland Station* (New York, Harcourt Brace Jovanovich, 1940), p. 163. [71] *Ibid.*, p. 221.

our position and our principles."[72] In the same letter Engels also told Marx that they must now write "substantial books" in which they need not even "mention these spiders of the émigré world." Isolation and marginality, the severing of almost all bonds to former comrades and associates, enabled Marx to gain the necessary distance from everyday affairs and to devote himself fully to his major work on *Das Kapital* in the protective shadow of the British Museum.

In those years, Marx had only a few devoted disciples, but he had Engels as a stable alter ego. The importance of Engels in Marx's life can hardly be overestimated. Engels agreed with all of Marx's theoretical ideas, yet he was by no means an automatic yea-sayer; he was himself a very gifted man capable of critical judgment of a high order. Because of his profound admiration for Marx, he tended to fall into the role of a superbly gifted and respectful son, although he was only two years younger. This meant that Marx was not wholly alone in his isolation and that he could accept the burden of marginality with greater ease, being backed by at least one man who was willing to share it with him to the hilt.[73]

Engels was a more earthy, more concrete, and less troubled man than Marx; he represented for Marx the stable pole of reality from which, without his guidance, Marx would be tempted to depart too far into the realm of abstractions. "Engels," Edmund Wilson has written, "was to fill in the blank face and figure of Marx's abstract proletarian and to place him in a real house and a real factory."[74] It is likely that without Engels Marx would never have managed to extract himself from the abstruse ratiocinations to which the lonely researcher in the British Museum was temperamentally prone.

Apart from his paid journalism for *The New York Tribune,* Marx never wrote for non-socialist publications. He made no attempt to find a public among the educated readers who patronized the distinguished weekly or monthly reviews of Victorian England. Only occasionally did he contribute to radical émigré publications in England and on the Continent. His two historical works on the Revolution of 1848 and its aftermath were still written for an audience of European radicals. In these works Marx had anticipated the renewal of the Revolution, and when, during the fifties and sixties it failed to occur, he had no public whatsoever, having cut himself off from the survivors of 1848. Those were years of physical and psychological misery for Marx. But he was sustained by Engels, Marx's privileged audience of one, as well as by the imaginary audience of socialist workmen on whose behalf he was writing *Das Kapital.*

The expository prose of *Das Kapital* and related writings varies a great deal from chapter to chapter. Sometimes, as in the famous chapter on "The

[72] Marx-Engels, *Correspondence, 1846–1895* (New York, International Publishers, 1934).
[73] Arnold Kuenzli, *Karl Marx: Eine Psychographie* (Wein, Europa Verlag, 1966), p. 377.
[74] Wilson, *op. cit.,* p. 147.

Working Day," the style is lucid, informed by moral passion and the will to persuade. At other times, as in certain chapters of the first volume and even more pronouncedly in the later volumes, the style is abstruse and cryptic. It is as tight and dense at the atmosphere of the unventilated, smoke-filled rooms in which Marx was forced to write. Then again, one finds a profusion of violent images: rape, repression, mutilation and massacre, premature burial, the stalking of corpses, the vampire living on the victims' blood, all of which suggest the enormous psychic costs and the buried furies that underlay the calm, though overbearing, face that Marx usually presented to the world.

Marx's location on the extreme margin of his society, together with his rejection of the actually extant public for an imaginary one yet to come, accounts for some of the deficiencies as well as for the lucidity of his vision. As an outsider, he was able to discern fissures in the imposing edifice of capitalist society that would remain hidden from more settled denizens. Marx's crucial insights into the conflicts and built-in contradictions of capitalist society were achieved at the price of loneliness and exile. Edmund Wilson is probably correct when he writes that Marx found in his own experience the key to the larger experience of society under capitalism. "His trauma reflects itself in *Das Kapital* as the trauma of mankind under industrialism; and only so sore and angry a spirit, so ill at ease in the world, could have recognized and seen into the causes of the wholesale mutilation of humanity, the grim collisions, the uncomprehended convulsions, to which the age of great profits was doomed."[75]

Social indignation and the vision of a better world to come were the spur that drove Marx into ever closer, ever more detailed, investigations of the operation of the capitalist system. Without them, there would have been no *Das Kapital.* His personal situation, the acute misery of isolation and marginality, in its turn fueled and refueled the sense of outrage and indignation that informs his works. His tension-ridden and conflictive private life predisposed him to see in conflict and contention the ultimate hidden motive force of all history.

Marx's vision and perceptiveness derived in large part from his social position. But the very isolation that enabled him to disregard the conventional wisdom of the day and to penetrate into layers of social reality hitherto untouched by the research of specialist scholars also contributed to the defects of the work. His lack of peers and colleagues shows up in the dogmatism and the rigidity of many of his assertions. Admittedly, he always attempted to write in tune with the canons of scholarly evidence, which he shared with his "bourgeois" antagonists. Nevertheless, the lack of informed critics most probably accounts for a number of the logical and substantive mistakes in *Das Kapital*—mistakes that later critics delighted in pointing out.

[75] *Ibid.,* p. 316.

Before the founding of *The International* in 1863, Marx could never be sure for whom he wrote. Afterward, he again achieved that happy conjunction of political and scholarly roles he had briefly enjoyed in the late forties. The labor movement he had called into being became the consumer of his works. *The International* created the demand structure for his writings that had been absent for so long. He no longer needed to write for Engels and for an imaginary audience of the future, but could now write for the concrete living men who were beginning to look at him as the fountainhead of scientific socialism. It is hard to imagine what would have been the fate of *Das Kapital* had it been brought out before *The International* was founded. To judge from the initial reception, or rather non-reception, in the world of scholarship and in the public at large, it is quite conceivable that it might have shared the fate of earlier radical and often penetrating treatises in economics, such as those of the Ricardian socialists Thomas Hodgkins, William Thompson and John Gray, or of Sismondi. Who reads them now?

As it was, *Das Kapital,* and other writings of Marx, soon gained almost canonical stature in the labor movement, especially in the German speaking countries. However, when this occurred, Marx was already nearing the end of his creative energies. The addresses he wrote in the sixties and early seventies in the name of *The International* show him at the height of his rhetorical and analytical powers, but after the final duel with his great adversary, Bakunin, and the dissolution of *The International,* little of consequence came from his pen. He had by now found the public for which he had craved all these years. He bathed in the glory of devoted followership. But the volcano had burnt out.

IN SUMMARY

Raised in a country and a region whose educated classes suffered deeply from a spiritual malaise induced by repressive governmental measures and general backwardness, having come to perceive himself as a marginal man deeply discontented with the existing state of affairs, Marx was prepared to become a principled critic of the existing order. His critical weapons were sharpened in the heady atmosphere of radical sects and esoteric philosophical cliques; his dialectical skills were developed in the give-and-take of debate between fellow sectarians.

Marx devoted himself to uncovering for the working class the ideological veil that hid from them the actual operation of the existing state of affairs. His depiction and analysis of the anatomy of civil society is his enduring life work. Like many of his forebears, he stood on the shoulders of giants. But the penetration of his vision was not due to this alone, but equally to his status as a perennial outsider and to his firm anchorage in a vision of the future—a vision that his working-class audience was "destined" to bring into being. The sociologist does well to distinguish prophecy from analysis, but he needs always to keep in mind that in Marx's case the second would not have been realized without the first. And, the supreme irony, the labors of the suffering outsider benefit not only the wretched of the earth, as he had wished, but also those dispassionate scholars of the academy, whom he scorned during his lifetime.

Herbert Spencer

1820-1903

THE WORK

Herbert Spencer was a theorist whose valuable insights have often been drowned in a sea of irrelevance and specious reasoning. What is relevant in his work will therefore have to be selected in a manner recommended by Richard Hofstadter when he wrote about Frederick Jackson Turner, "The most valid procedure with a historical thinker of his kind is not to try to have sport with his marginal failings but to rescue whatever is viable by cutting out what has proved wrong, tempering what is overstated, tightening what is loosely put, and setting the whole in its proper place among usable perspectives."[1] This account of Spencer's work will be severely selective. Here, as elsewhere in this book, only the writer's sociological contributions, and among these only the central ones, will be considered. Spencer's general metaphysics, or antimetaphysics, will be touched upon only tangentially. This is all the easier since critics now seem to be of the opinion that deep down Spencer was a rather shallow philosopher.

Some historians of sociology tend to see Spencer as a continuator of Comte's organicist and evolutionary approach. Although Spencer seems to have protested too much in disclaiming any profound influence of Comte's thought on his own, it is true that his general orientation differs significantly from Comte's. Spencer described their different approaches in this way:

> What is Comte's professed aim? To give a coherent account of the progress of *human conceptions*. What is my aim? To give a coherent account of the progress of the *external world*. Comte proposes to describe the necessary, and the actual, filiation of *ideas*. I propose to describe the necessary, and the actual, filiation of *things*. Comte professes to interpret the genesis of our *knowledge of nature*. My aim is to interpret . . . the genesis of the *phenomena which constitute nature*. The one is subjective. The other is objective.[2]

Comte was, of course, not only interested in the development of ideas but also in the correlative changes in social organization, and he dealt with social order as well as with progress. Nevertheless, Spencer correctly perceived the essential differences between them. Spencer's first and foremost concern was

[1] Richard Hofstadter, *The Progressive Historians* (New York, Alfred A. Knopf, 1968), p. 119.

[2] Herbert Spencer, *An Autobiography*, 2 vols. (New York, Appleton, 1904), Vol. II, p. 570.

with evolutionary changes in social structures and social institutions rather than with the attendant mental states. To Spencer, like to Marx, ideas were epiphenomenal. "The average opinion in every age and country," he writes, "is a function of the social structure in that age and country."[3]

Evolution, that is, "a change from a state of relatively indefinite, incoherent, homogeneity to a state of relatively definite, coherent, heterogeneity, "[4] was to Spencer that universal process, which explains alike both the "earliest changes which the universe at large is supposed to have undergone . . . and those latest changes which we trace in society and the products of social life."[5] Once this master key to the riddles of the universe is used, it becomes apparent, Spencer argued, that the evolution of human societies, far from being different from other evolutionary phenomena, is but a special case of a universally applicable natural law. Sociology can become a science only when it is based on the idea of natural, evolutionary law. "There can be no complete acceptance of sociology as a science, so long as the belief in a social order not conforming to natural law, survives."[6]

It is axiomatic to Spencer that ultimately all aspects of the universe, whether organic or inorganic, social or nonsocial, are subject to the laws of evolution. His sociological reflections concentrate, however, on the parallels between organic and social evolution, between similarities in the structure and evolution of organic and social units. Biological analogies occupy a privileged position in all of Spencer's sociological reasoning, although he was moved to draw attention to the limitations of such analogies. Because Spencer was a radical individualist, organic analogies caused him some sociological and philosophical difficulties, which Comte, with his collectivist philosophy, was spared.

Spencer's most fruitful use of organic analogies was his notion that with evolutionary growth come changes in any unit's structure and functions, that increases in size bring in their wake increases in differentiation. What he has in mind here, to use a homely example, is the idea that if men were suddenly to grow to the size of elephants, only major modifications in their bodily structures would allow them to continue being viable organisms.

[3] Herbert Spencer, *The Study of Sociology* (New York, Appleton, 1891), p. 390.

[4] *The Evolution of Society: Selections from Herbert Spencer's Principles of Sociology*. Edited and with an introduction by Robert L. Carneiro (Chicago, The University of Chicago Press, 1967), p. xvii. This is a later and simplified definition. The more elaborate definition can be found in Herbert Spencer, *First Principles* (New York, Appleton, 1898), pp. 370–73, and *passim*.

[5] *First Principles*, p. 337. [6] *The Study of Sociology*, p. 394.

GROWTH, STRUCTURE, AND DIFFERENTIATION

Both organic and social aggregates are characterized by Spencer according to progressive increases in size. "Societies, like living bodies, begin as germs—originate from masses which are extremely minute in comparison with the masses some of them eventually reach."[7] Societal growth may come about through two processes, "which go on sometimes separately, and sometimes together."[8] It results either from an increase in population, "by simple multiplication of units," or from the joining of previously unrelated units by "union of groups, and again by union of groups of groups."[9]

Increases in the size of units is invariably accompanied by an increase in the complexity of their structure.[10] The process of growth, by definition, is to Spencer a process of integration. And integration in its turn must be accompanied by a progressive differentiation of structures and functions if the organism or the societal unit is to remain viable—that is, if it is to survive in the struggle for existence. Animals that are low on the evolutionary scale, just like embryos of those higher on that scale, have but few distinguishable parts; they are relatively homogeneous. So it is with society. "At first the unlikeness among its groups of units is inconspicuous in number and degree, but as population augments, divisions and subdivisions become more numerous and more decided."[11]

Social aggregates, like organic ones, grow from relatively undifferentiated states in which the parts resemble one another into differentiated states in which these parts have become dissimilar. Moreover, once parts have become unlike, they are mutually dependent on each other; thus, with growing differentiation comes growing interdependence and hence integration. "While rudimentary, a society is all warrior, all hunter, all hut-builder, all tool-maker: every part fulfills for itself all needs."[12]

> As [society] grows, its parts become unlike: it exhibits increase of structure. The unlike parts simultaneously assume activities of unlike kinds. These activities are not simply different, but the differences are so related as to make one another possible. The reciprocal aid thus given causes mutual dependence of the parts. And the mutually dependent parts, living by and for another, form an aggregate constituted on the same general principle as is an individual organism.[13]

"This division of labor, first dwelt on by political economists as a social phenomenon, and thereupon recognized by biologists as a phenomenon of living

[7] *The Evolution of Society,* p. 9. Wherever possible I have quoted from this easily available volume. [8] *Ibid.*, p. 10. [9] *Ibid.* [10] *Ibid.*, p. 3. [11] *Ibid.* [12] *Ibid.*, pp. 4–5.
[13] *Ibid.*, p. 8.

bodies, which they called the 'physiological division of labor,' is that which in the society, as in the animal, makes it a living whole."[14]

In simple hunting tribes, specialization of functions is still only crudely developed. The same men are typically both hunters and warriors. But as settled agricultural societies arise, the roles of cultivator and warrior become more distinct. Similarly, small tribal groupings have but rudimentary political institutions, but as larger political units arise, increasing political complexity and differentiation appear with the emergence of chiefs, rulers, and kings. With further increases in size, "a differentiation analogous to that which originally produced a chief now produces a chief of chiefs."[15]

As the parts of a social whole become more unlike and the roles individuals play become in consequence more differentiated, their mutual dependence increases. "The consensus of functions becomes closer as evolution advances. In low aggregates, both individual and social, the actions of the parts are but little dependent on one another, whereas in developed aggregates of both kinds that combination of actions which constitutes the life of the whole makes possible the component actions which constitute the lives of the parts."[16] It follows as a corollary that, "where parts are little differentiated they can readily perform one another's functions, but where much differentiated they can perform one another's functions very imperfectly, or not at all."[17] In simple societies, where the parts are basically alike, they can be easily substituted for one another. But in complex societies, "the actions of one part which fails in its function cannot be assumed by other parts."[18] Complex societies are therefore more vulnerable and more fragile in structure than their earlier and ruder predecessors. Contemporary examples come to mind when one thinks, for example, of the contrast between American society and a simple agrarian society such as that of Vietnam.

The increasing mutual dependence of unlike parts in complex societies, and the vulnerability it brings in its wake necessitate the emergence of a "regulating system" that controls the actions of the parts and insures their coordination. "It inevitably happens that in the body politic, as in the living body, there arises a regulating system. . . . As compound aggregates are formed . . . there arise supreme regulating centers and subordinate ones and the supreme centers begin to enlarge and complicate."[19] Early in the process of social evolution, regulating centers are mainly required for dealing with the outside environment, with the "enemies and prey"; but later such regulating systems assume the burden of internal regulation and social control when complexity of functions no longer allows the entirely spontaneous adjustment of parts to one another.

The stringency and scope of internal regulation was to Spencer a major distinguishing mark between types of societies, and he attempted to classify

[14] *Ibid.*, p. 5. [15] *Ibid.*, p. 15. [16] *Ibid.*, p. 25. [17] *Ibid.* [18] *Ibid.*, p. 26. [19] *Ibid.*, p. 46.

them in terms of the scope of internal controls. At the same time he also used another criterion of classification—degrees of evolutionary complexity. These two ways of establishing social types were related, yet largely independent of each other and led to certain difficulties for Spencer's overall scheme.

SOCIAL TYPES: MILITANT AND INDUSTRIAL SOCIETIES

When attempting to classify types of societies in terms of their evolutionary stage, Spencer arranged them in a series as simple, compound, doubly compound, and trebly compound. The terminology is rather obscure, but what he seems to have had in mind is a classification according to degrees of structural complexity. More specifically, he distinguished between simple societies, which were headless, those with occasional headship, those with unstable headship, and those with stable headship. Compound and doubly compound societies were likewise classified in terms of the complexity of their political organization. Similarly, various types of societies were ranked according to the evolution of their modes of settlement, whether nomadic, semisettled, or settled. Societies generally were said to evolve from simple to compound and double compound structures through necessary stages. "The stages of compounding and re-compounding have to be passed through in succession."[20]

In addition to this classification of societies by their degree of complexity, Spencer proposed another basis for distinguishing between types of societies. In this other scheme the focus is on the type of internal regulation within societies. To distinguish between what he called militant and industrial societies, Spencer used as the basis a difference in social organization brought about through forms of social regulation.[21] This classification, it needs to be emphasized, is at variance with that based on stages of evolution. It is rooted in a theory of society that states that types of social structure depend on the relation of a society to other societies in its significant environment. Whether this relation is peaceful or militant affects the internal structures of a society and its system of regulations. With peaceful relations come relatively weak and diffuse systems of internal regulations; with militant relations come coercive and centralized controls. Internal structure is no longer dependent, as in the first scheme, on the level of evolution, but rather on the presence or absence of conflict with neighboring societies.

The characteristic trait of militant societies is compulsion.

> The trait characterizing the militant structure throughout is that its units are coerced into their various combined actions. As the soldier's will is so suspended that he becomes in everything the agent of his officer's will, so is the will of the citizen in all transactions, private and public, overruled by that

[20] *Ibid.*, p. 52. [21] *Ibid.*, p. 53.

> of the government. The cooperation by which the life of the militant society is maintained is *compulsory* cooperation . . . just as in the individual organism the outer organs are completely subject to the chief nervous center.[22]

The industrial type of society, in contrast, is based on voluntary cooperation and individual self-restraint. It is

> characterized throughout by the same individual freedom which every commercial transaction implies. The cooperation by which the multiform activities of the society are carried on becomes a *voluntary* cooperation. And while the developed sustaining system which gives to a social organism the industrial type acquires for itself, like the developed sustaining system of an animal, a regulating apparatus of a diffused and uncentralized kind, it tends also to decentralize the primary regulating apparatus by making it derive from numerous classes its disputed powers.[23]

Spencer stressed that the degree of societal complexity is independent of the militant-industrial dichotomy. Relatively undifferentiated societies may be "industrial" in Spencer's sense (not in today's usage of "industrial society"), and modern complex societies may be militant. What determines whether a society is militant or industrial is not the level of complexity but rather the presence or absence of conflict with the outside.

While the classification of societies in terms of increasing evolutionary complexity gave Spencer's system an optimistic cast—where he later used the term evolution, he earlier spoke of progress—the militant-industrial classification led him to less sanguine views of the future of mankind. Writing toward the turn of the century, he stated:

> If we contrast the period from 1815 to 1850 with the period from 1850 to the present time, we cannot fail to see that all along with increased armaments, more frequent conflicts, and revived military sentiment, there has been a spread of compulsory regulations. . . . The freedom of individuals has been in many ways actually diminished. . . . And undeniably this is a return towards the coercive discipline which pervades the whole social life where the militant type is pre-eminent.[24]

Spencer was by no means, as he is often depicted, the unalloyed believer in continued unilinear progress. This becomes even more evident in his general scheme of evolution.

22 *Ibid.*, pp. 58–59.
23 Herbert Spencer, *The Principles of Sociology* (New York, Appleton, 1896), Vol. I, p. 569.
24 *Ibid.*, p. 587.

THE CONTRAST BETWEEN MILITANT AND INDUSTRIAL SOCIETIES*

Characteristic	*Militant Society*	*Industrial Society*
Dominant function or activity	Corporate defensive and offensive activity for preservation and aggrandizement	Peaceful, mutual rendering of individual services
Principle of social coordination	Compulsory cooperation; regimentation by enforcement of orders; both positive and negative regulation of activity	Voluntary cooperation; regulation by contract and principles of justice; only negative regulation of activity
Relations between state and individual	Individuals exist for benefit of state; restraints on liberty, property, and mobility	State exists for benefit of individuals; freedom; few restraints on property and mobility
Relations between state and other organizations	All organizations public; private organizations excluded	Private organizations encouraged
Structure of state	Centralized	Decentralized
Structure of social stratification	Fixity of rank, occupation, and locality; inheritance of positions	Plasticity and openness of rank, occupation, and locality; movement between positions
Type of economic activity	Economic autonomy and self-sufficiency; little external trade; protectionism	Loss of economic autonomy; interdependence via peaceful trade; free trade
Valued social and personal characteristics	Patriotism; courage; reverence; loyalty; obedience; faith in authority; discipline	Independence; respect for others; resistance to coercion; individual initiative; truthfulness; kindness

* This table has been constructed from Herbert Spencer, *The Principles of Sociology*, Vol. I, Chapter 10, and Vol. II, Chapters 17 and 18, by Neil J. Smelser in his *Essays in Sociological Explanation* (Englewood Cliffs, New Jersey, Prentice-Hall, 1968), p. 246.

EVOLUTION—UNILINEAR OR MULTILINEAR

In many passages Spencer expresses what seems to be a belief in the unilinear evolution of mankind, in which it appears that mankind's progress through stages of development is as rigidly determined as the evolution of individuals from childhood to maturity. "As between infancy and maturity there is no shortcut by which there may be avoided the tedious process of growth and development through insensible increments; so there is no way from the lower forms of social life to the higher, but one passing through small successive modifications. . . . The process cannot be abridged and must be gone through with due patience."[25] At times, especially in his earlier writings, Spencer pictures the process of evolution as unremitting, unrelenting, and ever present. "The change from the homogeneous to the heterogeneous is displayed in the progress of civilization as a whole, as well as in the progress of every nation; and it is still going on with increasing rapidity."[26]

Yet the mature Spencer, perhaps under the impact of his disappointment over the "collectivist" course English society was taking toward the end of the nineteenth century, recognized that, though the evolution of mankind as a whole was certain, particular societies may retrogress as well as progress. "Though taking the entire assemblage of societies, evolution may be held inevitable . . . yet it cannot be held inevitable in each particular society, or even probable."[27] "While the current degradation theory is untenable, the theory of progression, in its ordinary form, seems to me untenable also. . . . It is possible and, I believe, probable, that retrogression has been as frequent as progression."[28] "A social organism," Spencer argued, "like an individual organism, undergoes modifications until it comes into equilibrium with environing conditions; and thereupon continues without further change of structure."[29] Once such equilibrium has been reached, evolution continues "to show itself only in the progressing integration that ends in rigidity [and] practically ceases."[30]

Although passages to the contrary could be quoted, Spencer by and large believed that societies do not develop irreversibly through predetermined stages. Rather, it was his general view that they developed in response to their social and natural environment.

> Like other kinds of progress, social progress is not linear but divergent and re-divergent. . . . While spreading over the earth mankind have found environments of various characters, and in each case the social life fallen into,

[25] *The Study of Sociology*, pp. 402–03.
[26] Herbert Spencer, *Essays, Scientific, Political and Speculative* (New York, Appleton, 1892), Vol. I, p. 19. [27] *The Principles of Sociology*, I, p. 96. [28] *Ibid.*, p. 95. [29] *Ibid.*, p. 96.
[30] *Ibid.*, p. 95.

> partly determined by the social life previously led, has been partly determined by the influences of the new environment; so that the multiplying groups have tended ever to acquire differences, now major and now minor: there have arisen genera and species of societies.[31]

Spencer specifically distinguished his own thought from that of rigid upholders of theories of unilinear stages, such as Comte, when he wrote, "Hence arose, among other erroneous preconceptions, this serious one, that the different forms of society presented by savage and civilized races all over the globe are but different stages in the evolution of one form: the truth being rather that social types, like types of individual organisms, do not form a series, but are classifiable only in divergent and re-divergent groups."[32]

By introducing the factors of stagnation and retrogression, Spencer no doubt made his theory more flexible, but it thereby lost some of its appeal as a universal key to the riddles of the universe. Beatrice Webb reports in her autobiography, *My Apprenticeship,* that her father, a successful businessman, once told her in dispraise of Spencer, "Some businesses grow diverse and complicated, others get simpler and more uniform, others go into the Bankruptcy Court. In the long run and over the whole field there is no more reason for expecting one process rather than the other."

FUNCTIONALISM

We have considered Spencer's emphasis that changes in structure cannot occur without changes in functions and that increases in size of social units necessarily bring in their wake progressive differentiations in social activities. Indeed, much of Spencer's discussion of social institutions and their changes is expressed in functional terms. In these analyses Spencer's point of departure is always the search for the functions subserved by a particular item under analysis. "To understand how an organization originated and developed, it is requisite to understand the need subserved at the outset and afterwards."[33] Spencer analyzed social institutions in relation to the general matrix in which they were variously embedded. He expressed the conviction "that what, relative to our thoughts and sentiments, were arrangements of extreme badness had fitness to conditions which made better arrangements impracticable."[34] He warned against the common error of regarding customs that appeared strange and repugnant by contemporary standards as being of no value to particular societies. "Instead of passing over as of no account or else regarding as purely mischievous, the superstitions of primitive man, we must inquire what part they play in social evolution."[35]

In his discussions of social institutions, Spencer makes great efforts to

[31] *The Principles of Sociology,* III, p. 331. [32] *The Study of Sociology,* p. 329.
[33] *The Principles of Sociology,* III, p. 3. [34] *The Study of Sociology,* p. 399. [35] *Ibid.*

show that they are not the result of deliberate intentions and motivations of actors—he had a very acute sense for the unanticipated consequences of human actions—but that they arise from functional and structural exigencies. "Conditions and not intentions determine. . . . Types of political organization are not matters of deliberate choice."[36] Spencer enjoins us to study institutions under the double aspect of their evolutionary stage and of the functions they subserve at that stage.

INDIVIDUALISM VERSUS ORGANICISM

Spencer had to find a way of reconciling his thoroughgoing individualism with his organicist approach. In this he differed sharply from Comte, who, it will be remembered, was basically anti-individualistic in his general philosophy and developed an organicist theory in which the individual was conceived as firmly subordinated to society. Spencer, in contrast, not only conceived of the origins of society in individualistic and utilitarian terms, but saw society as a vehicle for the enhancement of the purposes of individuals.

According to Spencer, men had originally banded together because it was advantageous for them to do so. "Living together arose because, on the average, it proved more advantageous to each than living apart." And once society had come into being, it was perpetuated because, "maintenance of combination [of individuals] is maintenance of conditions . . . more satisfactory [to] living than the combined persons would otherwise have."[37] In line with his individualistic perspective, he saw the quality of a society as depending to a large extent on the quality of the individuals who formed it. "There is no way of coming at a true theory of society, but by inquiry into the nature of its component individuals. . . . Every phenomenon exhibited by an aggregation of men originates in some quality of man himself."[38] Spencer held as a general principle that "the properties of the units determine the properties of the aggregate."[39]

In spite of these individualistic underpinnings of his philosophy, Spencer developed an overall system in which the organicist analogy is pursued with even more rigor than in Comte's work. The ingenious way Spencer attempted to overcome the basic incompatibility between individualism and organicism is best described in his own words. After having shown the similarity between social and biological organisms, he turned to show how they were unlike each other. A biological organism is encased in a skin, but a society is bound together by the medium of language.

36 *The Evolution of Society*, p. 141.
37 Herbert Spencer, *The Principles of Ethics* (New York, Appleton, 1904), Vol. I, p. 134.
38 Herbert Spencer, *Social Statics* (London, Chapman, 1851), p. 16.
39 *The Study of Sociology*, p. 52.

> The parts of an animal form a concrete whole, but the parts of society form a whole which is discrete. While the living units composing the one are bound together in close contact, the living units composing the other are free, are not in contact, and are more or less widely dispersed. . . . Though coherence among its parts is a prerequisite to that cooperation by which the life of an individual organism is carried on, and though the members of a social organism, not forming a concrete whole, cannot maintain cooperation by means of physical influences directly propagated from part to part, yet they can and do maintain cooperation by another agency. Not in contact, they nevertheless affect one another through intervening spaces, both by emotional language and by the language, oral and written of the intellect. . . . That is to say, the internuncial function, not achievable by stimuli physically transferred, is nevertheless achieved by language.[40]

The medium of language enables societies, though formed of discrete units, to exhibit a permanence of relations between component parts. But there is a more important difference still.

> In the [biological organism] consciousness is concentrated in a small part of the aggregate. In the [social organism] it is diffused throughout the aggregate: all the units possess the capacity for happiness and misery, if not in equal degree, still in degrees that approximate. As, then, there is no social sensorium, the welfare of the aggregate, considered apart from that of the units, is not an end to be sought. The society exists for the benefit of its members; not its members for the benefit of society.[41]

This is not the place to judge whether Spencer really managed to reconcile his individualism and his organicism—I rather think that he did not—but only to note that Spencer thought he had done so by stressing that no social body possessed a collective sensorium. Thus, despite functional differentiations between men, they all still aspired to a measure of "happiness" and satisfaction.

NONINTERVENTION AND THE SURVIVAL OF THE FITTEST

Spencer was at one with Comte in firmly believing in the operation of social laws, which are as deterministic as those governing nature. "There is no alternative. Either society has laws, or it has not. If it has not, there can be no order, no certainty, no system in its phenomena. If it has, then they are like the other laws of the universe—sure, inflexible, ever active, and having no exception."[42] But while Comte stressed that men should aim at discovering the laws of society in order to act collectively in the social world, Spencer argued with equal conviction that we should study them in order *not* to act

[40] *The Evolution of Society*, pp. 7–8. [41] *The Principles of Sociology*, I, p. 479.
[42] *Social Statics*, p. 42.

collectively. In contrast to Comte, who wanted to direct society through the spiritual power of his sociologist-priests, Spencer argued passionately that sociologists should convince the public that society must be free from the meddling of governments and reformers. "As I heard remarked by a distinguished professor," Spencer wrote, " 'When once you begin to interfere with the order of Nature there is no knowing where the result will end.' And if this is true of that sub-human order of Nature to which he referred, still more is it true of that order of Nature existing in the social arrangements of human beings."[43] Given the complexity of causes operating in society and the fact that human actions are likely to result in consequences that can not be anticipated, Spencer urges us to let things well enough alone.

The only power Spencer was willing to grant the state was protection of the rights of the individual and collective protection against outside enemies. The state had "the duty not only of shielding each citizen from the trespasses of his neighbors, but of defending him, in common with the community at large, against foreign aggression."[44] Everything else was to be left to the free initiative of individuals making contracts and agreements with one another.

> For the healthful activity and due proportioning of those industries, occupations, and professions, which maintain and aid the life of a society, there must, in the first place, be few restrictions on men's liberties to make agreements with one another, and there must, in the second place, be an enforcement of the agreements which they do make. . . . The checks naturally arising to each man's actions when men become associated are those only which result from mutual limitations; and there consequently can be no resulting check to the contracts they voluntarily make.[45]

A good society, in Spencer's view, is based on contracts between individuals pursuing their respective interests. Whenever the state intervenes in these contractual arrangements, whether for reasons of social welfare or any other, it either distorts the social order or leads to a retrogression from the benefits of industrial society to early forms of tyrannical and militant social order.

Although Spencer's extremely anticollectivist views can be traced to a number of extrascientific influences, it is also grounded in the doctrine of the survival of the fittest, which he, like Darwin, derived from Malthus. His own theory of population was somewhat more optimistic than that of the dismal parson. He argued that an excess of fertility stimulates greater activity because the more people there are, the more ingenuity is required to stay alive. The least intelligent groups and individuals die off; hence, the general level of intelligence is bound to rise gradually. "Those whom this increasing difficulty of getting a living, which excess of fertility entails, does not stimulate to

[43] *Social Statics,* abridged and revised, together with *The Man Versus the State* (New York, Appleton, 1892), p. 359. [44] *Ibid.,* p. 117. [45] *Ibid.,* p. 404.

improvements in production—that is, to greater mental activity—are on the high road to extinction; and must ultimately be supplanted by those whom the pressure does so stimulate."[46]

Spencer argued that the general level of intelligence will rise to the extent that only those with superior intelligence survive in the battle for existence. But this beneficial evolutionary mechanism will be fatally upset, he contended, once governmental intervention in the form of poor laws or other measures of social welfare is allowed to distort the beneficial processes of natural selection.

> That rigorous necessity which, when allowed to operate, becomes so sharp a spur to the lazy and so strong a bridle to the random, these paupers' friends would repeal. . . . Blind to the fact that under the natural order of things society is constantly excreting its unhealthy, imbecile, slow, vacillating, faithless members, these unthinking, though well-meaning, men advocate an interference which not only stops the purifying process, but even increases the vitiation—absolutely encourages the multiplication of the reckless and incompetent by offering them an unfailing provision, and discourages the multiplication of the competent and provident by heightening the difficulty of maintaining a family.[47]

The intervention of government in social affairs, Spencer argued, must distort the necessary adaptation of society to its environment. Once government intervenes, the beneficent processes that would naturally lead to man's more efficient and more intelligent control over nature will be distorted and give rise to a reverse maleficent process that can only lead to the progressive deterioration of the human race.

OBSTACLES TO OBJECTIVITY

In sharp contrast to Comte and Marx, Spencer gave much thought to the question of objectivity in the social sciences. Although Comte preached a good deal about the need for scientific standards in the study of society, he was never unduly perturbed by the thought that he himself might be found wanting in scientific objectivity, nor did he reflect on sources of possible bias in his own work. Marx, of course, denied altogether that there could be a detached and objective social science. Theory to him was intimately linked to socialist practice.

Spencer, on the other hand, was aware of the special problems of objectivity that arise in the investigation of a social world in which the investigators themselves take part, and he saw in this a complication that does not arise in the study of natural phenomena. The social scientist, he claimed, must make

[46] Quoted in Marvin Harris, *The Rise of Anthropological Theory* (New York, Crowell Collier, 1968), p. 127. [47] *Social Statics*, p. 151.

a deliberate effort to free himself from biases and sentiments that are entirely appropriate and necessary for the citizen but that would vitiate the enterprise of the scientist were he tempted to carry them over into his scientific role. "In no other case," he writes,

> has the inquirer to investigate the properties of an aggregate in which he is himself included. . . . Here, then, is a difficulty to which no other science presents anything analogous. To cut himself short from all his relationships of race, and country, and citizenship—to get rid of all those interests, prejudices, likings, superstitions generated in him by the life of his own society and his own time—to look at all the changes societies have undergone and are undergoing, without reference to nationality, or creed, or personal welfare, is what the average man cannot do at all, and what the exceptional man can do very imperfectly.[48]

No less than half of Spencer's *The Study of Sociology* is devoted to a close analysis of sources of bias and of the "intellectual and emotional difficulties" that face the sociologist in his task. Chapter headings include, "The Bias of Patriotism," "The Class-Bias," "The Political Bias," "The Theological Bias." Spencer here develops a rudimentary sociology of knowledge in which he attempts to show how the defense of ideal or material interests tends to shape and distort perceptions of social reality. Spencer clearly deserves a place, if only a minor one, among those who, beginning with his great compatriot Francis Bacon, have developed the sociology of knowledge.

This account of the major doctrines of Herbert Spencer has emphasized some of their difficulties and contradictions. It would have been intellectually irresponsible to try to explain them away. An examination of Spencer's life and of the social and intellectual contexts in which he worked will help explain them.

THE MAN

George Eliot once remarked of Herbert Spencer, whom she knew well, that "the life of this philosopher, like that of the great Kant, offers little material for the narrator."[49] She was right. There is nothing in his life that compares to the rich texture of experience, of tragedy, of trials and tribulations that one encounters in Comte's career or in Marx's.

Spencer was born on April 27, 1820, in Derby, in the bleak and dismal

[48] *The Study of Sociology*, p. 74.

[49] Quoted in J. W. Burrow, *Evolution and Society* (Cambridge, England, Cambridge University Press, 1966), p. 179.

English Midlands, the heart of British industry. He was the oldest of nine children and the only one to survive. His father, George Spencer, and his whole family were staunch nonconformist Dissenters, highly individualistic in their outlook. George Spencer, a rather eccentric man who combined Quaker sympathies with Benthamite radicalism and rabid anti-clericalism, taught school in Derby. Aggressively independent, he would not take his hat off to anyone and would never address his correspondents as "Esquire" or "Reverend" but always as "Mr." Keenly interested in science and politics, he was for a time honorary secretary of the local Philosophical Society and one of the mainstays of local Dissent. Spencer's mother Harriet is described as a patient and gentle woman whose marriage to his irascible and irritable father seems not to have been happy.

Being sickly and weak as a child, Herbert Spencer did not attend a regular school. His father educated him at home. At the age of thirteen, he moved to the home of a clerical uncle near Bath, from whom he received his further education. This clergyman, who was also an advanced social reformer, a Chartist sympathizer, and an advocate of temperance, taught young Herbert the principles of Philosophical Radicalism as well as the rigid code of dissenting Protestantism. When the Reverend Spencer was asked one day at a gathering why the young Spencer wasn't dancing, he replied, "No Spencer ever dances."

The education Spencer received from his father and uncle leaned heavily on the scientific side. His grounding in Latin and Greek was weak, and he never became even a tolerable linguist. He received no formal instruction in English, and his knowledge of history was superficial. At the age of sixteen he had a good background in mathematics and the natural sciences, but he was not, nor was he ever to become, a generally cultivated man.

Feeling himself unfit for a university career and unwilling to attend Cambridge as his father had done, Herbert Spencer decided to follow his scientific interests, and in 1837 joined the staff of the London and Birmingham Railway as an engineer. A year later he took up a better position as a draftsman with the Birmingham and Gloucester Railway. In addition to his regular duties, Spencer here busied himself with a variety of minor inventions, which he thought much of but which came to little. When the construction of the railroad was finished in 1841, he was discharged and returned home to Derby.

In the next few years Spencer published several articles in the radical press, first on engineering but soon after on social and political questions as well. A series of letters to a dissenting paper, *The Nonconformist,* already indicate the direction of his later course; these letters, entitled "The Proper Sphere of Government," argued for an extreme restriction of the scope of government. He contended that the whole field of human activity, except for policing, should be left to private enterprise. There were to be no poor laws, no national education, no established church, no restrictions on commerce, and no factory legislation.

For a number of years, Spencer struggled on the fringes of radical journalism and of radical politics. Finally, having despaired of making a livelihood as a writer, he returned for a while to the employment of the Birmingham and Gloucester Railway. For two years thereafter he was without settled employment, dabbling in mechanical inventions and radical journalism and even dreaming for a time of emigrating to New Zealand. At last, in 1848, he found a stable position and assured income as a subeditor with the London *Economist.*

THE LONDON YEARS

During the five years with the *Economist,* Spencer built up his relations in the world of advanced journalism in London. He met John Chapman, the publisher, G. H. Lewes, the radical writer, and Lewes' future consort George Eliot (Mary Ann Evans). Soon afterwards he also met the distinguished scientists Thomas Huxley and John Tyndall, who were to remain his close friends through most of his life.

While working on the *Economist,* Spencer finished his first book, *Social Statics,* which was published in 1851. Expounding ideas first adumbrated in "The Proper Sphere of Government," the book was well received by the radical public, which welcomed him as a new recruit to the creed of laissez faire. Spencer now started to write with some regularity for a variety of journals, from the Benthamite *Westminster Review* to the Whig *Edinburgh Review.* A paper on "The Developmental Hypothesis" dating from 1852, seven years before Darwin's *Origin of Species,* expounded and advocated a theory of evolution based on Lamarckian principles—that is, a pre-Darwinian theory of evolution stressing the notion of the inheritance of acquired characteristics—and initiated a concern with evolution that was to last through Spencer's long life.

When his uncle died in 1853, he left Spencer a sizable sum of money. In view of this, as well as the connections he now had at a number of reviews, Spencer felt encouraged to give up his job with the *Economist.* From then on he lived the life of a private scholar without regular employment or institutional attachment. A lifelong bachelor, having been brought up in the strict abstemious discipline of Derby Dissent, he lived frugally and parsimoniously in successive lodgings and rooming houses about London. For a while it had seemed that his friendship with George Eliot would lead to marriage. Spencer had even gone so far out of his habitual ways as to take her to the opera and to restaurants. But although she seems to have been willing, he finally recoiled. One knows of no later amatory experience; there is every likelihood that Spencer died not only a bachelor but a virgin.

In 1854, Spencer began writing his second book, *The Principles of Psychology.* It was published the next year but, unlike *Social Statics,* was not well received. Soon after he suffered from a nervous illness, the nature of which is unclear. (Modern psychiatrists would probably diagnose the illness as a severe neurotic disorder.) All day long he wandered aimlessly about town, unable to concentrate, unable to write, unable even to read. The doctors could find no clear organic cause and talked of overstrain or some obscure lesion of the brain. After a year and a half of enforced idleness Spencer slowly returned to work. But he was to remain a semi-invalid and psychic cripple throughout the rest of his life. Suffering from acute insomnia, which he at times attempted to overcome with a fairly heavy dose of opium, Spencer was henceforth never able to work more than a few hours a day. To work longer would lead to undue nervous excitement and hence insomnia.

The retreat into illness was also for Spencer a retreat from social intercourse. Treating himself with a variety of nostrums, watching his every symptom with the assiduity of the hypochondriac, he increasingly led the life of a semihermit. Among his many eccentricities was the wearing of a special set of ear stoppers, which allowed him, when necessary, to escape from listening. At his clubs he could be seen browsing through the papers or playing a game of billiards, but otherwise he shunned the company of all but a few trusted friends, admirers, and disciples. In his worst periods he found company almost unbearable, and in his later years even the idea of a public lecture became intolerable.

THE SUCCESSFUL AUTHOR

All the while, books poured from his pen in a steady stream; his intellectual processes seem not to have suffered from his nervous ailments. *First Principles* (of his overall *Synthetic Philosophy*) was published in 1862. The several volumes of *Principles of Biology* were issued between 1864 and 1867. *The Study of Sociology* appeared in 1873, and the many volumes of *Principles of Ethics* and *Principles of Sociology* were published between the seventies and the nineties. *The Man Versus the State* appeared in 1884 and the *Autobiography* in 1904. He published, in addition, several volumes of essays and *Fragments* as well as the many volumes of *Descriptive Sociology,* mainly written by several secretaries and collaborators. Many of these books were issued to a select group of subscribers before being released for general publication.

The first few volumes of Spencer's *Synthetic Philosophy* attracted scant interest in the British press. Most comments dealt with peripheral issues such as his agnosticism. But Spencer enjoyed the esteem of a number of radical thinkers and advanced scientists such as John Stuart Mill, Huxley, and Tyndall, men who helped spread his message. Many of them belonged to the famous dining club that Spencer had joined contrary to his usual custom of withdrawal. This company exercised considerable scientific and public influence, for it included among its members three who became presidents of the Royal Society, five who became presidents of the British Association for the Advancement of Science, as well as a president of the College of Surgeons and a president of the Chemical Society.

When *Principles of Biology* was completed, Spencer calculated that he had spent altogether nearly £ 1,100 in writing and publishing books that had met with indifferent success. Obliged every year to dip into his inherited capital, he issued a notice of cancellation to the few hundred persons who had subscribed to the *Synthetic Philosophy*. A circular was then drawn up by Mill, Huxley, Tyndall, and others, inviting a wider public to subscribe to the series. At the same time, the death of his father brought Spencer another legacy, and his devoted American follower Edward L. Youmans collected a considerable sum of money from Spencer's American admirers. Soon afterwards his books began to sell well, and he suffered no further material difficulties.

From the seventies on, Spencer became a very successful author. *The Study of Sociology,* for example, was published serially both in England and America, as well as in book form, netting Spencer more than £ 1,500 profit. Many later works also appeared serially in the *Fortnightly Review* in England and the *Popular Science Monthly* in America, and in book form as well. Apart from his major works, Spencer also continued to contribute to the leading reviews, such as the *Contemporary Review* and the *Nineteenth Century*. From the seventies onward, he was a renowned scientist, one of the most eminent Victorians.

Toward the end of his life, Spencer commented bitterly that his *Social Statics,* which he considered a weak work, had received more critical acclaim than any of his mature writings. But in fact he enjoyed considerable recognition. *Principles of Biology* was used as a textbook at Oxford. William James assigned both *First Principles* and *Principles of Psychology* as textbooks to his Harvard students. William Graham Sumner taught Spencerism in American dress at Yale, and the large printings of Spencer's more popular works indicate his wide appeal among the educated lay public in England and especially in America. By the turn of the century, most of his work had appeared in French, German, Spanish, Italian, and Russian translations.

Throughout his life Spencer refused nearly all honors offered him by universities, the government, or scientific bodies. He had no official position and no university degree. Yet during the last quarter of the century he enjoyed an international reputation and influence almost comparable to that of Charles Darwin.

In the last years of his long life, what little time he had for writing he devoted to a wider variety of controversial issues of the day, from opposition to the Boer War to a proposal for the adoption of the metric system in England. An unhappy old man, almost wholly at variance with the political trends of the time, he lived these last few years in almost complete withdrawal from human intercourse. He died on December 8, 1903, at the age of eighty-three. His body, following the provisions of his will, was cremated.[50]

THE INTELLECTUAL CONTEXT

ANTECEDENTS

Spencer never read widely in philosophy, history, or literature. He seems to have practiced almost from the beginning of his career that "cerebral hygiene" that Comte adopted in his middle years.

Until the early fifties, when he began his friendship with George Lewes, the author of a *Biographical History of Philosophy,* Spencer had hardly any acquaintance with philosophy. He admits this with disarming candor in his *Autobiography*: "Up to that time questions in philosophy had not attracted my attention. . . . It is true that . . . I had in 1844 got hold of a copy of Kant's *Critique* . . . and had read its first pages: rejecting the doctrine in which, I went no further. It is also true that though . . . I had read no books on either philosophy or psychology, I had gathered in conversations or by references, some conceptions of the general questions at issue."[51]

Reading Lewes's work of popularization made Spencer "acquainted with the general course of philosophical thought."[52] But one gains the distinct impression that he never attempted to push that acquaintanceship very far. His secretary, John Collier, reports that "He wrote his final treatise on ethics without reading Mill, Kant, Whewell, or any of the recognized authorities on morals, excepting portions of Sidgwick."[53] In Spencer's library, Collier writes,

> There was not a single work on philosophy other than those sent to him; . . . no book of Hobbes, Locke, Reid, Hume, Kant, or Hamilton. There were even few books in science; there were no histories or biographies, and in the way of pure . . . literature there was only a much prized copy of *Tristram Shandy*. . . . In fact, he was not a reader at all, in the ordinary sense of the word, but only a gleaner. He did not "tear the entrails out of books" like Sir William Hamilton; he left them, for the most part, severely alone.[54]

All this may seem surprising to anyone who has read the heavily footnoted major works of Spencer. But here again Collier explains:

[50] This account is based on Spencer's *An Autobiography;* David Duncan, *Life and Letters of Herbert Spencer,* 2 vols. (London, Methuen, 1908); Hugh Elliot, *Herbert Spencer* (New York, Holt, Rinehart and Winston, 1917); and the "Personal Reminiscences of James Collier," included in Josiah Royce's *Herbert Spencer* (New York, Fox, Duffield, 1904).

[51] *An Autobiography,* I, p. 438. [52] *Ibid.,* p. 439. [53] John Collier in Royce, *op. cit.,* p. 208.

[54] *Ibid.,* pp. 212–13.

> He *picked up* most of his facts. Spending a good part of every afternoon at the Athenaeum Club, he ran through most of the periodicals, reading little in the way of disquisitions, but lynx-eyed for every fact that was grist to his mill. . . . At the same institution he habitually met with all the leading savants, many of whom were his intimates. From these, by a happy mixture of suggestion and questioning, he extracted all that they knew. At home he pillaged the two or three critical and scientific periodicals he took in. His assistants . . . supplied him with a mass of sociological materials.[55]

There is no doubt that Spencer pursued his work in the manner of an engineer (which he was) who searches for relevant facts to be fitted into a preconceived scheme. This scheme was never questioned or revised in the light of other conceptions; yet it was not woven out of whole cloth. Spencer did, after all, owe a debt of gratitude to a few predecessors.

Among these, Malthus' *Essay on Population* ranks very high. This book, which by Darwin's own report helped give birth to the *Origin of Species,* also exerted the most potent influence on Spencer's *Synthetic Philosophy*. When, a decade before the publication of the *Origin,* Spencer worked out the social implications of the doctrine of "survival of the fittest," it was under Malthus' influence, though he disagreed with many of Malthus' pessimistic conclusions. In "A Theory of Population," an article published in 1852, Spencer based his thesis on Malthusian doctrine, even when making it "yield an optimistic conclusion by making progress the result of population pressure by means of what was, in fact, though not yet in name, natural selection among human beings."[56]

The fact that Spencer's admiration for Malthus was matched by his high esteem for Adam Smith brings to mind Mr. Gradgrind, that desiccated utilitarian man of affairs who in Dickens' withering portrait named his two sons Malthus and Adam Smith. Spencer too ranked Adam Smith next to Malthus and probably derived much of his laissez faire philosophy from the author of the *Wealth of Nations*. Another Scotch scholar, Sir William Hamilton, was praised by Spencer for clarifying his ideas on "ultimate questions" of philosophical method.[57] Spencer read the *Logic* of his friend John Stuart Mill and presumably some other writings of the radical utilitarians, but the few names mentioned seem to exhaust the list of writers that had some influence on his general thought.

The notion of evolution, or development, first came to Spencer when, as a young man of twenty, he read Lyell's *Principles of Geology* and, "rejecting his adverse arguments . . . adopted the hypothesis of development."[58] He then went on to proclaim the doctrine of evolution in its Lamarckian form. He alludes to both Lamarck and Erasmus Darwin, and it must be supposed that he was influenced by their writings.

[55] *Ibid.*, pp. 208–09. [56] Burrow, *op. cit.*, p. 188. [57] *Essays,* II, p. 125.
[58] *An Autobiography,* II, p. 309.

Some of his specific ideas on evolution can be traced to the influence of others. In particular, the notion of the change from homogeneity to heterogeneity developed, Spencer notes, from Harvey's embryological inquiries, which were "put into definite shape by Von Baer,"[59] from whom Spencer borrowed it. He also remarks in this connection that "the acquaintance which I accidentally made with Coleridge's essay on *The Idea of Life,* in which he set forth, as though it were his own, the notion of Schelling, that Life is the tendency to individuation, had a considerable effect."[60] When speaking of his idea of the mutual dependence of parts of organic and social wholes, he expresses his debt to the physiologist Milne-Edwards who coined the phrase, "the physiological division of labor."[61]

There remain only a few observations on Spencer's relationship with Comte. He met Comte once, toward the end of the latter's life, but was not particularly impressed by him. He noted though that Comte, hearing of his nervous disorder, "advised me to marry; saying that the sympathetic companionship of a wife would have a curative influence."[62] As to Comte's general influence on his thought, Spencer denied it with vehemence, in a number of impassioned statements. Goaded into action by allegations from across the Channel that he was a disciple of Comte's Positive Philosophy, he even went so far as to solicit from John Stuart Mill and others public statements to the effect that this was not the case. It is true that in 1852, George Eliot had made him read the Introduction to the *Cours de philosophie positive,* and two years later he also read, sketchily as it turned out, Harriet Martineau's translation. But by this time, he had already developed the lineaments of his evolutionary approach, which lends support to his claim to originality in this respect.

When it comes to his specific sociological doctrine, however, the matter is by no means so clear. Spencer admitted that, "To [Comte] I believe, I am indebted for the conception of social consensus."[63] He adopted the words "sociology" and "altruism" from Comte,[64] and he gave Comte credit for teaching that "the principles of organization are common to societies and animals . . . and . . . that the evolution of structures advances from the general to the special."[65] Beyond this, it would seem that Spencer's general interest in matters sociological was to some extent kindled by his reading of Comte and by the many conversations he had with George Lewes and George Eliot, who were at the time close admirers of the French theorist.

This about closes the list of past writers to whom Spencer may have been indebted. In the indexes to his books, names of authors are sparse, and those who are listed are mentioned only once or twice in connection with a particular fact or assertion with which Spencer happened to agree or disagree.

[59] *Essays,* II, p. 137. [60] Duncan, *op. cit.,* II, p. 315. [61] *Ibid.,* p. 322.
[62] *An Autobiography,* I, p. 578.
[63] *Essays,* II, p. 135. [64] *An Autobiography,* I, p. 517.
[65] *The Principles of Sociology,* I, p. 591.

One has the strong suspicion that these quotations were mostly supplied to Spencer by his researchers and that he himself did not fully read the authors in question.

INFLUENCE OF CONTEMPORARIES

Among contemporary figures who influenced Spencer, his lifelong friend Thomas Huxley stands out. The two met in the early fifties at a time when Huxley, who was later to become Darwin's "bulldog," his most vocal supporter and defender, was not yet convinced of the truth of the evolutionary hypothesis. In their many long discussions, Huxley forced Spencer to refine his arguments and sharpen his logic; Huxley's objections were grounded in a knowledge of facts, which, Spencer admitted, was "immensely greater than mine." Huxley probably did not have a fundamental influence on Spencer, but he introduced him to many scientific findings, and to many exponents of these findings of whom Spencer was ignorant.

When Darwin's *Origin of Species* appeared in 1859, Spencer welcomed it warmly. He accepted the idea that natural selection was indeed the key mechanism of evolution, although he continued to cling to a Lamarckian explanation that "the inheritance of organic modifications produced by use and disuse has been a cause of evolution."[66] Darwin, in his turn, expressed his esteem of Spencer's "development theory" even before the *Origin* was published. He was even moved to call Spencer "about a dozen times 'my superior.'"[67] The two men were correspondents ever after and influenced each other to some degree. But it is surely incorrect to call Spencer a "social Darwinist," for his main doctrine was developed before Darwin had published anything on evolution.

Through Huxley Spencer met various eminent British scientists, above all John Tyndall, an associate and successor of Faraday. Huxley introduced Spencer to Tyndall with a line from *Faust,* as, "Ein Kerl der spekuliert"[68] (a fellow who speculates). It would seem indeed that the many scientists whom Spencer later met in the *X Club* or elsewhere considered him a speculative fellow who had interesting ideas ranging more widely than they, as strict specialists, would dare to venture. In turn, it is probable that they helped Spencer a good deal through critical arguments on specific points, and by supplying him with the scientific facts that he used so greedily as building blocks for his theories. Spencer absorbed his science to a large extent as if through osmosis, through critical discussions and interchanges with his scientific friends and associates.

Spencer was aided similarly by his relationships with philosophers and

[66] Duncan, *op. cit.,* I, p. 360.
[67] Quoted in Carneiro's "Introduction" to *Herbert Spencer: The Evolution of Society,* p. ix.
[68] Duncan, *op. cit.,* I, p. 85.

literary men. Spencer, it will be recalled, was very close to George Lewes, the writer and popularizer of philosophy, and to George Eliot, who became Lewes's devoted consort. He was almost equally close to John Stuart Mill. These writers introduced him to some of the heritage of philosophy and to some contemporary thinking such as that of Comte. George Eliot had finished a translation of Strauss's *Life of Jesus* and Feuerbach's *Essence of Christianity* (see chapter on Marx), but there is no indication that these works entered into their conversation. These literary friends helped him through critical argument, but, as in the case of his scientific associates, they did not seem to have had a profound influence on Spencer's thought.

Spencer had some familiarity with most of the works of the other classical social evolutionists—Tylor, Morgan, Maine, McLennan, and Lubbock. But he rarely alluded to them, and when he did, it was generally to disagree with their views. What he derived from them, as from others, were facts rather than novel ideas.[69] The conclusion seems inescapable: Spencer's mind was made up at a fairly young age and did not basically change later.

Sir Isaiah Berlin has classified writers and thinkers in terms of a distinction made by a Greek poet: "The fox knows many things, but the hedgehog knows one big thing." Berlin called foxes those thinkers "who pursue many ends, often unrelated." The hedgehogs, in contrast, "relate everything to a central single vision, one system less or more coherent or articulate . . . a single universal organizing principle."[70] Clearly, Spencer was a hedgehog. Although there are contradictory aspects to his thought, he generally adhered to one single central vision. Friends and associates would help him sharpen details, tighten his arguments, and, above all, furnish new facts to fit into the scheme, but they never succeeded in diverting him in any major way from the theoretical path he had chosen. All this was expressed in Huxley's laughing remark that, for Spencer, the definition of a tragedy was the spectacle of a deduction killed by a stubborn fact.

THE SOCIAL CONTEXT

THE GENERAL SCENE

The Victorian world of Herbert Spencer is far removed from the strife-torn and convulsed social universe of Comte and of Marx. Although Marx and Spencer were near-contemporaries and even lived in the same city a long time, they responded in their writings not to their immediate environment but to the widely different social conditions on the Continent and on the British Isles.

[69] Cf. Carneiro, *op. cit.*, p. xxx.

[70] Isaiah Berlin, *The Hedgehog and the Fox* (New York, Mentor Books, n.d.).

While revolution or its threat marked the societies in which Marx and Comte grew to intellectual maturity, mid-Victorian England was as far removed from the dangers of revolution and violent upheaval as a modern society can be.

The mid-Victorian age may conveniently be dated from the opening of the Crystal Palace by Queen Victoria in 1851, the same year in which Spencer's first book was published. It was a confident and complacent period: the trials and tribulations that had marked the Industrial Revolution were over; the Chartist agitation had died down; the worst consequences of the New Poor Law had been overcome; the hardships of the hungry forties lingered only faintly in memory; popular radicalism was set at a discount; it seemed to most contemporaries that England was now safely settled on a course that would bring it ever-increasing affluence and prosperity.

England's growing material prosperity, its industrial production and foreign trade, had put it far ahead of all other countries. Britain had become the workshop of the world. In 1848 she produced half the pig iron of the world, and she tripled her output in the next thirty years. In 1830 the coal production of the country was thirty million tons; forty years later it reached a hundred and thirty million. By 1870 the foreign trade of the United Kingdom was larger than the combined foreign trade of France, Germany, and Italy, and nearly four times that of the United States. Britannia ruled the waves, her naval supremacy was uncontested. And while the nations of the Continent were embroiled in wars and revolution, England enjoyed peace at home and abroad.

The general standard of living of the British population was rapidly rising. To be sure, at the bottom there was still a "submerged tenth" of the population living in utter misery and destitution. And the mass of unskilled and unorganized laborers were underfed and underpaid, living out the miserable routines of their lives under conditions that were little better than those to which the wholly destitute were condemned. But artisans, farmers, and skilled workers did well on the whole. And the rapidly growing middle classes enjoyed such significant increases in prosperity that the Panglossian optimism of the age, the mood of comfortable self-satisfaction that characterized its spokesmen, is understandable.

This mood of complacency permeated much of British literature, history, and philosophy in the twenty years after the opening of the Crystal Palace. Tennyson put it into mediocre verse:

> For I dipt into the future, far as human eye could see,
> Saw the Vision of the world, and all the wonder that would be;
> Saw the heavens fill with commerce, argosies of magic sails,
> Pilots of the purple twilight, dropping down with costly bales.

The idea of progress was securely anchored in the consciousness of most mid-Victorian intellectuals. It seemed confirmed by convincing examples as years of prosperity were followed by years of even greater prosperity.

To the middle class and most of its intellectual spokesmen, it seemed that all these advances were due to the thrift and methodical application of private individuals, whose disciplined efforts had built the industrial apparatus on which Britain's prosperity was moored. The best government, they felt, was a government that governed least. They favored a nightwatchman state that protected its citizens within and without but otherwise left the field open to private initiative. Few of them noticed that, in the same years in which free enterprise was at its height, the modern state was beginning to accumulate powers mid-Victorian gentlemen would have found horrifying. The English historian G. Kitson Clark puts it well:

> In fact, in the second and third quarter of the nineteenth century, at the very time when private industry was putting on the strength of a giant, when men were prating of the benefits of freedom and the dangers of Government interference, unnoticed, unplanned and certainly as far as most men were concerned absolutely undesired, the modern State with its delegated powers imposing on the community the rule of experts and officials was beginning to take shape.[71]

This new role of the state would not come to the awareness of the ordinary middle-class man as long as prosperity lasted. But things changed drastically in the last quarter of the century when Britain began to lose her prominence on the world scene, and severe crises racked the economy and society.

By the close of the mid-Victorian age, England had already ceased to be the *primus inter pares* among world powers. The golden age of British agriculture came to an end around 1875. Under the impact of the huge imports from the new farmlands of North America and Argentina, the price of wheat was halved, and since other farm products suffered similarly, British agriculture was ruined. Conditions were by no means as bad in industry and commerce, but there, too, danger signs multiplied. From 1870 to the turn of the century, the total value of foreign trade continued to increase considerably, but the rate of German and American increases was still greater. By 1900, German steel output had caught up with that of Britain, and American output nearly equalled the combined German and English totals. Britain's industry now paid what Thorstein Veblen has called the penalty for taking the lead—that is, it was being outclassed by modern technologies recently installed in Germany and the United States while it still was forced to make do with some-

[71] G. Kitson Clark, *The Making of Victorian England* (Cambridge, Mass., Harvard University Press, 1962), p. 109.

what antiquated equipment. Britain's difficulties were increased by the very completeness of her earlier successes. Up to about 1880, all major technological inventions and discoveries were of British origin; after that there were hardly any, and Britain was reduced to adopt the ideas of foreigners.[72]

By the last quarter of the century, the bulk of the working class, with the exception of the "submerged tenth," had experienced a notable improvement in material welfare. But far from decreasing its discontents, as the Tories had hoped, this development had exacerbated them. Trade union activity, which had been largely confined to the skilled trades, began to make headway among the semi- and un-skilled. In the depression of the 1890's Britain experienced an unprecedented wave of strikes, which included, for the first time, all types of workers. Although Marxism did not make progress, the Independent Labour Party, founded in 1893, began to attract previously apolitical trade unionists. And the Fabian Society, founded in 1884, caught the attention of middle-class intellectuals and professional men with its propaganda for efficient social planning.

By the last quarter of the century, Englishmen, although not yet English women, had the vote. As a consequence, both of the old parties now competed energetically for the votes of the working class, which had not been admitted to the political arena until the sixties. (The Second Reform Bill of 1867 granted urban workers the vote and thereby doubled the number of voters.) The working class wanted above all greater social and economic security through legislation. The Liberals were to respond to this demand under Lloyd George early in the next century, but the Tories (now called the Conservatives) first responded to it in the seventies and after. Disraeli's ministry of 1874–80 concentrated on social reform and passed legislation on public health, factory legislation, and trade unions. The Education Act of 1870 introduced general education, and subsequent legislation soon made it free as well as compulsory.

The machinery of local government was completely overhauled. Elected County and Borough Councils replaced the appointed Justices of the Peace. In the larger boroughs and counties, of London and Birmingham for example, local authorities, elected by popular majority, began to provide a variety of social services to citizens. Although the national welfare state was still only a dim vision for the future, municipal socialism began to be a realistic alternative, at least in the main urban areas.

The gradual extension of social services and governmental control led to a huge expansion of the civil service and of local authorities. The whole civil service employed a little more than 20,000 men in 1832; by 1880 it had a staff of over 50,000 and by 1914, some 280,000. The number of civil servants multi-

[72] Cf. R. J. Evans, *The Victorian Age: 1815–1914,* 2nd ed. (New York, St. Martin's, 1968), p. 268.

plied by five within the generation before 1914 when the modern state had finally come into its own.

At the same time modern government extended its controls over domestic areas of jurisdiction (which had previously been left to private enterprise and voluntary activities of gentlemen), it also began to assume a more active role in foreign affairs. The age that saw the emergence of the notion of social security also saw the inception of a new type of British imperialism. Spurred by the growing competition of France and Germany, England embarked upon an unprecedented expansion of her colonial domain. Colonies came to be valued as sources of raw material and markets for manufactured goods, as well as visible embodiments of national grandeur.

The race for colonies began between France and Britain in the eighties, with Germany joining in somewhat later. In the last quarter of the century most of Africa was partitioned between the major powers. In 1898 Britain added control of the Sudan to her previous control over Egypt. In the nineties, Kenya and Uganda became British protectorates, and Cecil Rhodes' grandiose plan to establish a united British dominion stretching from South Africa to Egypt finally led to the outbreak of the disastrous Boer War in 1899. Britain expanded in Asia as well, and Victoria, who had accepted the title of Empress of India in 1876, added British New Guinea, North Borneo, and Upper Burma to the British empire in the eighties.

By the turn of the century the comparatively little England of the mid-Victorian age had become an enormous colonial power. While England had lost her preeminence as the workshop of the world, she still dominated the seas. The British empire extended over major parts of all five continents.

Domestically Britain had travelled far from the laissez faire of mid-Victorianism. The regulating, controlling, active state protecting the welfare of its citizens, even though still very insufficiently, had little in common with the passive nightwatchman state of the first half of the century.

Herbert Spencer, in his long life span, witnessed the whole of this change, and his work bears witness to it. He came to maturity in the mid-Victorian age, never altered the political opinions he formed then, and hence reacted with horror and dismay to the changes that later took place. The buoyant optimistic prophet of progress gradually grew into the dyspeptic old man for whom the whole drift of modern English history represented a descent into a new barbarism of imperialist expansion without and militant state control within.[73]

[73] This account is based on Clark, *op. cit.,* Evans, *op. cit.,* and David Thomson, *England in the Nineteenth Century* (Baltimore, Penguin Books, 1950).

BACKGROUND

All through his early youth and adolescence, Spencer grew up in an atmosphere permeated by Nonconformity and religious Dissent. Nonconformity was not just another religious denomination. In early nineteenth-century England, Dissenters were not only discriminated against and made to suffer for religious reasons, but they were also treated as social inferiors. "The disabilities imposed on Dissenters," writes the historian G. Kitson Clark, "were probably at least in part maintained because of the low esteem in which classes lower than their own were held by those who governed the country."[74] By the Test and Corporation Acts, Dissenters were prevented from holding office in the Corporate towns. Those who associated with the Church of England governed the town, and those associated with the Chapels were in opposition to them. If the Churchwardens so decreed, Dissenters might have to pay a rate for the upkeep of the parish church of which they were not members. In most cases, they were forced to be married in the parish church, although they were often prevented from being buried in the parish churchyard. The universities were closed to them so that even their brightest sons could not avail themselves of the channels of mobility that matriculation at Oxford or Cambridge provided for middle-class members of the Church.

Given these indignities, it is hardly surprising that new radical ideas found an ideal breeding ground among Nonconformists. Many, among them Spencer's father, no longer held coherent religious beliefs, yet acquired a burning and passionate commitment to secular radicalism and liberalism. Whether it be the propaganda for the repeal of the Corporation and Test Acts, the anti-Corn Law agitation, or the drive to mitigate the primitive brutality of the Criminal Law, Nonconformists were found everywhere in the vanguard. The first bill for the reform of Parliament, which gave the vote to the middle classes, owed a great deal to Dissenting agitation.

Nonconformity stood in the forefront of the battle for social emancipation and justice, but only the historically unsophisticated would surmise, therefore, that its representatives were "free" and "spontaneous" personalities. The very opposite was the case. The men who fought the good battle for freedom were dour, repressed, and "puritanic" personalities. Even though many had already shed their specific religious beliefs, they still exhibited in their lifestyles all the characteristics of their puritan ancestors. These were not "self-actualizing" personalities, but rather severely ascetic, self-denying, and pleasure-loathing men, who were single-minded in the regular and methodical application of their energies to the business at hand.

Spencer, a typical product of this Nonconformist milieu, was once moved

[74] Clark, *op. cit.*, p. 39.

to reflect on some of the consequences of such an ascetic upbringing. "In families brought up from generation to generation ascetically, and acting up to the belief that the pursuit of pleasure is wrong, it happens that while there is a frequent witnessing of suffering . . . there is a relatively infrequent witnessing of pleasure . . . and consequently a relative inability to sympathize with pleasure. [In these circumstances] the temptation to give pleasure must be less than usual." He went on to quote from a paper of the Reverend Martineau about his sister Harriet, in which he talks about the starving of emotions and the lack of tenderness in Nonconformist families, and remarks that "the Puritan tradition and reticence of a persecuted race had left their austere impress upon speech and demeanor unused to be free."[75]

Inner-directed, conscience-driven, and ascetic, the Nonconformists were also intensely lonely men whose mode of upbringing made it difficult to form bonds of understanding and sympathy that would tie them to their fellow men. They found it hard to emerge from the shell of self-denial and self-absorption that had been fashioned by all those adults—parents, teachers, preachers—who had surrounded them in their formative years.

The self-denying atmosphere of his youth left its permanent mark on Spencer. He never went to school (except for three months) and hence had no chance to form ties of friendship with peers. Nothing drew him out of his shell. Having had no companions to help him escape, at least in part, from the moral dominance of his stern elders, he remained psychically crippled for the rest of his life. At the risk of engaging in casual psychoanalysis, one may surmise that Spencer's life-long inability to establish meaningful erotic relationships was related to his general inability to form bonds with others.

Spencer's early background probably also accounts for his later psychic breakdown and invalidism. For him there was not even the alternative of rebelling against the social order. He could permit himself only those minor gestures of disdain for official society, such as the refusal of all its honors, which were in tune with his Nonconformist upbringing. As a result, the repressed furies turned inward: he became sick. The only defiance of society that he would permit himself was symbolic, through withdrawal into sickness and eccentricity.

FRIENDS AND ASSOCIATES

In all the years he lived in London, until his father's death, Spencer faithfully reported to him, as he must have done when still a child, all that was happening. Spencer was still the man from Derby. Although he widened his intellectual horizon, he did not significantly depart from the general orientation he had embarked on while still in the Midlands. He was ever open to new

[75] *An Autobiography,* II, pp. 502–03.

facts but not to ideas that might unsettle his fixed scheme. His is not the usual story of the young man from the provinces who grows into a man of the world when he comes to the capital. Nor is it a story of that "becoming," which the German *Bildungsroman* ever since Wilhelm Meister liked to portray. Spencer became what he had always been. He only grew older.

What is striking about his relationships in London is that he used almost all his associates for particular purposes. He used people as he used books. He did not read books that did not profit his purpose at hand nor did he seek out people who had no utility. In this sense he was the very embodiment of the utilitarian morality that he preached. This is not to make him into a moral monster—there must have been occasions when he was graced by the milk of human kindness, but such occasions, as he admits himself, were rare. His correspondence conveys the impression that most of his associations were occasioned by his need to get something from his correspondents, whether information or recognition, advice or support.

One other aspect of his individualism and self-absorption was his intense concern about priorities in his work. He was morbidly sensitive about any claims that others might make to a finding that he held to be his own. He interpreted any such claim as an assault not only upon his work, but upon his very being. Those who wished to deny him his property in matters intellectual were seen as intent upon destroying the man who had created these intellectual products. His was the kind of acquisitive individualism in which intellectual products assume the symbolic significance that money has for misers.

In his fight for the priority of his work, Spencer did not adhere to a pattern followed by many scientists, as analyzed by Robert K. Merton.[76] As Merton showed, scientists themselves do not always enter the arena when it comes to fights about their own priorities. Some may leave it to their followers and disciples to fight the battle. They tend in this manner to resolve the dual pull which comes from the norms of science prescribing that discoveries belong to the scientific collectivity rather than to individual scientists, and the opposing scientific norm that those who contribute to science must be given due acknowledgment. It seems as if this dilemma is frequently resolved by letting disciples fight for their master's deserts so that the master can abstain from making "selfish" claims to what is rightfully a property of the entire scientific community. In such structural circumstances, neither master nor disciples fight for their own property and hence do not violate the taboo on property rights of the scientific community. But Spencer did not claim belong-

[76] Robert K. Merton, "Priorities in Scientific Discoveries: A Chapter in the Sociology of Science," *American Sociological Review*, XXII, pp. 635–59; and "Resistances to the Systematic Study of Multiple Discoveries in Science," *European Journal of Sociology*, IV, 2, pp. 237–82. Cf. also Merton's "Singletons and Multiples in Scientific Discovery: A Chapter in the Sociology of Science," *Proceedings of the American Philosophical Society*, CV (October, 1961), p. 5.

ingness to a delimited scientific community. He saw himself as a kind of free lance, and hence treated the products of his brains as an engineer would treat his inventions. He behaved as if he had a desire to obtain a patent for what was his due.

The question of recognition raised similar difficulties. Although in the last part of his long life he had become a world figure of immense renown, Spencer continued to claim that he was not being sufficiently recognized for his later work. He writes in the *Autobiography* that his first book, *Social Statics,* "was more extensively, as well as more favorably, noticed than any one of my later books: a fact well illustrating the worth of current criticism."[77] A man the sales of whose books in America alone, from the sixties to his death, came to 368,755 volumes, an unparalleled figure in such difficult spheres as philosophy and sociology, could still maintain that he was not being recognized. Being so empty within, he was even more insatiable for praise to recharge his flaccid sense of worth of self than many other men of science.[78]

There were, it is true, a number of objective factors, which in the last twenty-five years of his life led him to become even more bitter, self-centered, and irritable than he had been earlier. In biology, he witnessed the gradual decline of his favorite theory of the inheritance of acquired characteristics. On the social scene, the growing trend toward collectivism and militaristic imperialism ran counter to his whole philosophical orientation in favor of laissez faire. But even so, the heightened egotism and accentuated concern with self that accompanied his bitterness about the public world must be explained in terms of roots that were only partly related to the current scene. One of his biographers says that in those years he "became emotionally barren," and "his emotions withered from lack of sustenance."[79] Yet all these were conditions that had plagued him throughout his adult life. A man who condescended toward the end of his career to write for posterity a detailed account of the state of his teeth was only pushing to the point of absurdity a preoccupation with the self that had been there all along.

THE SOCIAL SETTING

Spencer, it would seem, was as eccentric in his behavior as Comte; yet, unlike Comte, he was not a marginal man in the intellectual world. Similar psychological predispositions and similar obnoxious behavior in regard to one's fellows do not necessarily have similar social consequences. Whether an eccentric becomes marginal depends a great deal on the social setting in which he finds himself. Comte was ostracized because his doctrine seemed repellent

[77] *An Autobiography,* I, p. 422.

[78] Richard Hofstadter, *Social Darwinism in American Thought,* rev. ed. (Boston, Beacon Press, 1955), p. 34.

[79] Hugh Elliot, *op. cit.,* p. 46.

to most of the key thinkers of his day, and not only because he was an unappealing and eccentric man. Spencer, in contrast, was accepted despite his personal eccentricities because what he taught hit a responsive chord among at least a significant stratum of both lay readers and fellow intellectuals; also, there is a long tradition in Britain with regard to the tolerance of eccentricity.

But there is more: Comte, it will be recalled, aspired to an academic position all his life and had, by training, a claim to it. He was rebuffed and spent most of his life being only tangentially connected with the academic world. Spencer was not of the academy either, nor did he have any claim to an academic appointment. But since he had no desire for one, he did not feel deprived when none was forthcoming.

As a consequence, Spencer, unlike Comte, never competed with academic specialists. Also, unlike Comte's contemporaries, these men, in turn, did not see him as a rival, since he was engaged in a line of research that did not compete with their more specialized work. Spencer was free to avail himself of their advice and criticism, to meet with them in private homes and in clubs, though not in faculty dining halls. He had no colleagues, in the strict sense of the word; colleagues are always competitors. To a highly generalizing theorist like Spencer, specialists could provide needed information and criticism while remaining noncompetitive. It is significant that Spencer had no sustained contact with his fellow social evolutionists such as Maine or Tylor. They *were* competitors.

Huxley not only provided general expert criticism but read the proofs of both *First Principles* and *The Principles of Biology*. Spencer reported that he habitually submitted his "biological writing to [Huxley's] castigation."[80] Though nobody seems to have taken Huxley's place in so far as the nonbiological writings are concerned, it is still true that Spencer benefited from advice and criticism by a number of specialist friends.

Nor is Spencer's situation comparable to that of Comte in regard to publications. It will be remembered that after his association with Saint-Simon had ended, Comte found practically all channels of periodical publication were closed to him. Spencer, in contrast, had throughout his life the chance to publish in the leading liberal periodicals and scientific journals of the day, among them, the *Westminster Review*, the *Leader*, the *Edinburgh Review*, the *North British Review*, the *National Review*, the *British Quarterly Review*, the *Fortnightly Review*, and the *Contemporary Review*. He also wrote for the scholarly *Nature* and *Mind*, as well as for the American *Popular Science Monthly*, the *Transaction of the Linnaen Society*, and the London *Times*.

[80] *An Autobiography*, II, pp. 553–54.

AUDIENCE AND DEMAND

In style of writing and exposition Spencer was influenced by his audience. Though his writings are distinctly awkward (partly because he hardly ever revised first drafts), they all exhibit the desire to convey to the large public as well as to his fellow intellectuals the fruits of his thought. He addressed himself not only to Mill and Huxley, to Macauley and Grote; he also wanted to communicate with the audience represented by Mr. Gradgrind—the educated middle class who read the liberal reviews in which he published. In this sense his writings remind one of the Comte of the *Cours,* when Comte was still intent upon communicating his ideas to his peers and to the educated public. But his works differ entirely from the style of the later Comte who no longer wished to persuade rationally but to overwhelm his audience by a flow of emotions.

The widespread success of Spencer's early contributions and of his first programmatic work, *Social Statics,* indicated that there was a demand for what he had to say. His evolutionary theory provided the solution for a dilemma that faced men of ideas at the time. His theory made it possible to reconcile the newly discovered variety of human behavior in different cultures with the principle of the psychic unity of mankind.

In the late forties and early fifties, many among the educated middle class had sensed a loss of moral direction. Harriet Martineau put the matter well in 1853 in the preface to her translation of Comte's *Positive Philosophy:* "The supreme dread of everyone who cares for the good of the nation or the race is that men should be adrift for want of anchorage for their convictions. I believe that no one questions that a very large part of our people are now so adrift. . . . The moral dangers of such a state of fluctuation . . . are fearful in the extreme.[81]

Harriet Martineau here alludes to the crisis of belief that came to be widespread in the forties. Educated men were increasingly deprived of the kind of certainties that used to be provided by traditional religion. Whereas earlier in the century those who had lost faith were sustained by the utilitarian morality of Bentham and the elder Mill, this alternative was no longer viable for the later generation. These men could not accept the ahistorical logic of the utilitarians according to which the principles of legislation and the common morality appropriate for any nation were said to flow from a few basic utilitarian principles, such as the principle of the greatest happiness of the greatest number. They came under the sway of historical relativism, which had originated on the Continent and which stressed the unique character of different historical epochs. Continental historicism rejected alleged universal

[81] *Positive Philosophy of Auguste Comte,* trans. and cond. by Harriet Martineau (London, Bell, 1896), Vol. I, p. viii.

laws of human nature deduced from some fundamental principles of associationist psychology. More generally, to quote Graham Walles, "Bentham's utilitarianism was killed by the unanswerable refusal of the plain man to believe that ideas of pleasure and pain were the only source of human motive."[82] Benthamite utilitarianism appeared too simplistic in its basic assumptions. It was unable to provide credible answers to the attacks of historical relativists who stressed the changes in "human nature" that were disclosed by historical scholarship.

However, history and historiography were not the only sources from which questions arose about the certainties of the utilitarians. Evidence had accumulated about the basic differences between the conduct of Englishmen and that of the many primitive peoples with whom they became increasingly familiar in this age of colonial expansion. Observers were hard put to explain behavior in primitive societies in terms of the rational pursuit of pleasure and the avoidance of pain. The conduct of primitives seemed neither useful, nor practical, nor calculating, and hence could hardly be captured by the categories provided by the rationalist Benthamite dispensation.

If one had to admit that primitive people acted from principles fundamentally at variance with those that governed modern men, must one not relinquish the idea that there was a basic unity to all mankind, that men, under all climes and in all conditions, were basically the same? Would this not be tantamount to rejecting the whole inheritance of the Enlightenment? Liberal opinion was by no means prepared to envisage such a rejection of the fundamental premises of advanced thought.

Evolutionary doctrine, whether in Spencer's dress or in some others', found a ready audience precisely because it seemed to offer a way out of some of these dilemmas. It made it possible to maintain the belief in the psychic unity of mankind in the face of human variability. In the light of evolutionary doctrine, differences in behavior, whether in the past or in far-away places, did not refute the assumption of the universality of human reason but were explained by reference to the process of evolution. Mankind, like any organism, was subject to the laws of evolutionary growth. Just as the child is not basically different from the adult, though distinguished from him by as yet undeveloped capacities, so the savage, the evolutionists asserted, is not less of a man but simply a less evolved man.

Evolutionary doctrine did not require relinquishing belief in the unity of mankind or abandoning the utilitarian principle of the greatest happiness of the greatest number. It only asserted that such thinking did not come naturally at earlier stages in man's evolution, being characteristic only of a stage in which man had reached maturity. Evolutionism hence provided a

[82] Quoted in J. W. Burrow, *op. cit.*, p. 70. I have leaned heavily on Burrow's very fine book in the pages that follow.

scheme of explanation that allowed the liberal Victorian public to retain its belief in the superiority of its way of life, at the same time as it provided an explanation for facts which previously had seemed to challenge accustomed modes of explanation. As J. W. Burrow puts it, "The specific attraction of evolutionary social theories was that they offered a way of reformulating the essential unity of mankind, while avoiding the current objections to the older theories of a human nature everywhere essentially the same. Mankind was not one because it was everywhere the same, but because the differences represented different stages in the same process."[83]

Beyond this general appeal that evolutionary thought had in the Victorian age, Spencer's specific scheme appealed to the public because of the comprehensiveness of his system. While other social evolutionists, men like Maine or Tylor, were relatively modest in the scope of their claims, limiting themselves to a theory of the evolution of human culture and social structure, Spencer purported to supply a universal key for understanding not only the growth of the human race but the evolution of the cosmos. His theory seemed to explain the laws governing the universe, the organic and inorganic realm, as well as the history and destiny of mankind. Spencer formulated a universal explanatory scheme for those in quest of certainty, which in a previous age only religious doctrines could provide. Moreover, his attempt to explain diverse phenomena in terms of a single explanatory principle gave to many the same esthetic satisfaction that the Newtonian synthesis had provided earlier. Spencer's doctrine seemed to be in tune with the findings of the geological, physical, and biological sciences that had made such amazing strides in the recent past.

At the same time Spencer's theory satisfied the quest for an explanation in terms of universal principles, it satisfied the self-righteous quest for moral superiority. As Burrow shrewdly observes, "By agreeing to call the [evolutionary] process progress one could convert the social theory into a moral and political one."[84] It now seemed to turn out that the more evolved a society, the more it could be said to be morally superior. "Progress," wrote Spencer, "is not an accident but a necessity. Surely must evil and immorality disappear; surely must man become perfect."[85] It could be asserted with the authority of "science" that more developed modes of behavior, such as those of contemporary Englishmen, represented a distillation of the moral excellence toward which mankind had unconsciously been striving for many generations. When Spencer "proved" to his audience that the more evolved forms of behavior were superior to earlier forms not only in affording a better adjustment of man to his environment, but also in being more pleasurable for the individual and less detrimental for the community at large, he reinforced the sense of smug self-satisfaction that had permeated so much of the Victorian age; at the

[83] Burrow, *op. cit.*, pp. 98–99. [84] *Ibid.* [85] *Social Statics* (1892 ed.), p. 32.

same time, he stilled some of the anxieties aroused by loss of religious faith and by doubts about the Benthamite doctrine.

There was yet another factor contributing to the appeal of Spencer's doctrine. The fundamental transformation that the Industrial Revolution had brought to British styles of life was still vivid in the collective memory of the mid-Victorians. One of the main aspects of this transformation had been the disappearance of many relatively simple crafts and the emergence of a much more complex division of labor, with the accompanying "alienation" that industrial forms of production had brought in their wake. Spencer's explanation of change in terms of progressive differentiation of functions may have proved attractive to those who were not satisfied with the usual utilitarian schemes. Evolutionary necessity made intellectually palatable what might have appeared morally unsettling. It helped reduce cognitive dissonance among men who might earlier have been torn between the appeals of the modern industrial world and the evidence of the destructive impact it had on previously cherished styles of living.

Spencer's teaching, especially his doctrine of the survival of the fittest, served some other legitimating functions as well. The doctrine that those who had managed to survive thereby proved that they were fitter than those who had not managed to do so legitimized the possessive individualism of the age and provided a rationale for energetic striving for success at a time when the Protestant Ethic had lost some of its appeal in the minds of the educated public. Spencerianism seemed even more serviceable as a justification of acquisitive individualism than Benthamite doctrine had been. Benthamite thought was also committed to individualism, but it nevertheless stressed the positive aspect of legislation in social reform. Spencer, however, rejected any legislative intervention as ultimately detrimental to the overall welfare of mankind and its optimal adjustment to its environment. He provided a good conscience for those who singlemindedly pursued their private interests, by showing that those who resolutely strove to maximize "pleasure" thereby contributed, albeit unwittingly, to the greater benefit of mankind as a whole, and to its evolutionary progress.

The generally optimistic climate of opinion that prevailed in the mid-Victorian age proved receptive to Spencer's teaching. His theory of evolution, which revealed the operation of generally beneficent social laws, gratified the hunger for an explanation of recent or more remote social change; at the same time the theory gave assurance that the future course of mankind was bound to be forever upward and onward.

However, with the onset of economic crisis and labor unrest in the 70's, the optimism of the mid-Victorian period came to an end and Spencer's doctrine went into an eclipse. He was successful with *Social Statics* because he had been so perfectly in tune with his time; but when the times changed, he refused to follow and he lost touch with his public. In the seventies and after, British public opinion slowly moved away from laissez faire to various collectivist orientations in the field of social welfare and elsewhere. Now Spencer's extreme individualism seemed quaintly unfashionable; it was a voice of the past. Moreover, the idea that technological achievement and moral improvement would necessarily go hand in hand seemed out of touch with social surveys, such as those of Charles Booth, which revealed the extent of human wretchedness in the midst of the affluence—the fruit of the machine age. Even Spencer's old friend and ally in the good fight for evolution, Thomas Huxley, felt obliged to admit that moral progress, far from following naturally in the wake of evolutionary development, could be attained only by controlling the effects of nature. "Social progress," he wrote, "means a checking of the cosmic process at every step and the substitution for it of another, which may be called an ethical process."[86]

Spencer, it will be remembered, attempted to account for the new, and to him distasteful, developments on the English scene in the last quarter of the century by various modifications in his evolutionary doctrine designed to make it more flexible. But as he introduced qualifications, he destroyed the unitary basis of the theory, which had been one of its main appeals. Moreover, the new classification of societies in terms of the militant-industrial dichotomy, which he now placed alongside his older evolutionary classification, seemed so fraught with anti-collectivist ideology that it encountered much opposition from the collectivist liberals of the eighties and nineties. Only in America, still in its most determined laissez faire and free-enterprise phase of development, did Spencer's appeal still hold unalloyed sway and prove irresistible to men otherwise as dissimilar as Andrew Carnegie and John Fiske. The story has been told in magisterial fashion by Richard Hofstadter in his *Social Darwinism in American Thought.*

IN SUMMARY

At the time when Spencer entered the intellectual scene, he found a setting that was favorable and a public that was willing to lend an attentive ear to his answers to a number of puzzling questions. Social evolutionism in Spencerian dress seemed to account for the trials and tribulations of man's life on earth in terms of the slow evolution of mankind from its savage beginning to its glorious culmination in mid-Victorian civilization. It seemed to prove that, on the whole, the story of mankind was a success story. It provided intellectual comfort to a generation that was determined to be as comfortably settled in its

[86] Quoted in Burrow, *op. cit.*, p. 270.

moral and spiritual life as it had increasingly become comfortable in its material life.

Because there was a demand for his theories, Spencer, despite his personal idiosyncrasies, was not pushed to the margin of British intellectual life as Comte had been in France. But when the intellectual tide turned, Spencer's fortunes in England turned with them. Although still a highly respected man of science, he lost much of his audience. But as Englishmen turned away from him, a new American public eagerly embraced his message and provided a new receptive public. Furthermore, admirers of his doctrine were to be found in all of Western Europe and his fame had by then spread to a world audience. Although he died a bitter and disappointed man, at variance with the intellectual climate of his homeland, Spencer made an impact so widespread and profound that, even when the ideological aspects of his system have long been forgotten, he is remembered as one of the masterminds of sociology.

Though Spencer suffered an eclipse in his reputation after his death, his work nevertheless continued to inspire British social thought in a major way. L. T. Hobhouse, G. C. Wheeler, and, in a later generation, Morris Ginsberg continued work in his general evolutionary tradition while rejecting his anti-reformist individualism. In America, while only William Graham Sumner, among the founding fathers of sociology, may be said to have been a disciple of Spencer, almost all of them were deeply influenced by his thought. Ward, Cooley, Veblen, Giddings, Ross, and Park, whether agreeing with his ideas or using them as a springboard for dissent, were all in Spencer's debt.

Despite some evidence of continued interest in his work, Spencer was, by and large, a rather forgotten man in the social sciences during the inter-war years. However, many contemporary sociologists in quest of a serviceable theory of social change have recently been moved to read Spencer again. For example, Talcott Parsons introduced his first major treatise, *The Structure of Social Action,* with the rhetorical question: "Who reads Spencer now?"—implying that nobody did, and justifiably so. Thirty years later, not quite the same Parsons wrote an admiring introduction to a re-issue of Spencer's *The Study of Sociology*.[87] Whereas Franz Boas's strictures against evolutionary theories led to a long neglect of Spencer among anthropologists, more recently, partly under the impact of that inveterate evolutionist Leslie White, anthropology seems to have rediscovered Spencer.

After more than three-quarters of a century, the present generation of social scientists seems about to reestablish as intimate a relation with the thought of Spencer as Emile Durkheim established in his time. Like many Continental sociologists, Durkheim created his own theoretical structure through sustained critical confrontation with the work of Spencer. He did not wish to praise him but to bury certain of his main assumptions. And yet, as a

[87] Herbert Spencer, *The Study of Sociology,* new ed. (Ann Arbor, The University of Michigan Press, 1961).

result, he helped preserve through a period of neglect some of Spencer's central insights.

Shorn of its ideological trappings and overweening pretensions, Spencer's thought remains a vital part of the perennial inheritance of the social sciences. He will be read not only now, but much later.

Emile Durkheim

1858-1917

THE WORK

GENERAL APPROACH

The main thrust of Durkheim's overall doctrine is his insistence that the study of society must eschew reductionism and consider social phenomena *sui generis*. Rejecting biologistic or psychologistic interpretations, Durkheim focused attention on the social-structural determinants of mankind's social problems.

Durkheim presented a definitive critique of reductionist explanations of social behavior. Social phenomena are "social facts" and these are the subject matter of sociology. They have, according to Durkheim, distinctive social characteristics and determinants, which are not amenable to explanations on the biological or psychological level. They are external to any particular individual considered as a biological entity. They endure over time while particular individuals die and are replaced by others. Moreover, they are not only external to the individual, but they are "endowed with coercive power, by . . . which they impose themselves upon him, independent of his individual will."[1] Constraints, whether in the form of laws or customs, come into play whenever social demands are being violated. These sanctions are imposed on individuals and channel and direct their desires and propensities. A social fact can hence be defined as "every way of acting, fixed or not, capable of exercising on the individual an external constraint."[2]

Although in his early work Durkheim defined social facts by their exteriority and constraint, focusing his main concern on the operation of the legal system, he was later moved to change his views significantly. The mature Durkheim stressed that social facts, and more particularly moral rules, become effective guides and controls of conduct only to the extent that they become internalized in the consciousness of individuals, while continuing to exist independently of individuals. According to this formulation, constraint is no longer a simple imposition of outside controls on individual will, but rather a moral obligation to obey a rule. In this sense society is "something beyond us and something in ourselves."[3] Durkheim now endeavored to study social

[1] Emile Durkheim, *The Rules of Sociological Method* (New York, The Free Press, 1950), p. 2.
[2] *Ibid.*, p. 13.
[3] Emile Durkheim, *Sociology and Philosophy* (New York, The Free Press, 1953), p. 55.

facts not only as phenomena "out there" in the world of objects, but as facts that the actor and the social scientist come to know.[4]

Social phenomena arise, Durkheim argued, when interacting individuals constitute a reality that can no longer be accounted for in terms of the properties of individual actors. "The determining cause of a social fact should be sought among the social facts preceding it and not among the states of the individual consciousness."[5] A political party, for example, though composed of individual members, cannot be explained in terms of its constitutive elements; rather, a party is a structural whole that must be accounted for by the social and historical forces that bring it into being and allow it to operate. Any social formation, though not necessarily superior to its individual parts, is different from them and demands an explanation on the level peculiar to it.

Durkheim was concerned with the characteristics of groups and structures rather than with individual attributes. He focused on such problems as the cohesion or lack of cohesion of specific religious groups, not on the individual traits of religious believers. He showed that such group properties are independent of individual traits and must therefore be studied in their own right. He examined different rates of behavior in specified populations and characteristics of particular groups or changes of such characteristics. For example, a significant increase of suicide rates in a particular group indicates that the social cohesion in that group has been weakened and its members are no longer sufficiently protected against existential crises.

In order to explain regular differential rates of suicide in various religious or occupational groupings, Durkheim studied the character of these groups, their characteristic ways of bringing about cohesion and solidarity among their members. He did not concern himself with the psychological traits or motives of the component individuals, for these vary. In contrast, the structures that have high suicide rates all have in common a relative lack of cohesion, or a condition of relative normlessness.

Concern with the *rates* of occurrence of specific phenomena rather than with *incidence* had an additional advantage in that it allowed Durkheim to engage in comparative analysis of various structures. By comparing the rates of suicides in various groups, he was able to avoid ad hoc explanations in the context of a particular group and instead arrive at an overall generalization. By this procedure he came to the conclusion that the general notion of cohesion or integration could account for a number of differing specific rates of suicide in a variety of group contexts. Groups differ in the degree of their integration. That is, certain groups may have a firm hold on their individual members and integrate them fully within their boundaries; others may leave component in-

[4] Cf. Talcott Parsons, "Emile Durkheim," *International Encyclopedia of the Social Sciences* (New York, Macmillan, 1968). Cf. also Georges Sorel's acute observations on this point in his "Les Théories de M. Durkheim," *Le Devenir Social,* I (1895), esp. p. 17.

[5] *Rules*, p. 110.

dividuals a great deal of leeway of action. Durkheim demonstrated that suicide varies inversely with the degree of integration. "When society is strongly integrated, it holds individuals under its control."[6] People who are well integrated into a group are cushioned to a significant extent from the impact of frustrations and tragedies that afflict the human lot; hence, they are less likely to resort to extreme behavior such as suicide.

For Durkheim, one of the major elements of integration is the extent to which various members interact with one another. Participation in rituals, for example, is likely to draw members of religious groups into common activities that bind them together. Or, on another level, work activities that depend on differentiated yet complementary tasks bind workers to the work group. Related to the frequency of patterned interaction is a measure of value integration, that is the sharing by the members of values and beliefs. In collectivities where a high degree of consensus exists, there is less behavioral deviance than in groups in which consensus is attenuated. The stronger the credo of a religious group, the more unified it is likely to be, and therefore better able to provide an environment that will effectively insulate its members from perturbing and frustrating experiences. Yet Durkheim was also careful to point out that there are special cases, of which Protestantism is the most salient, in which the credo of the group stresses a shared belief in individualism and free inquiry. Protestantism "concedes a greater freedom to individual thought than Catholicism . . . it has fewer common beliefs and practices."[7] In this case, higher rates of such deviant behavior as suicide cannot be explained as a lack of consensus, but as a response to the group-enjoined autonomy of its members.

The difference between value consensus and structural integration can now be more formally approximated in terms of Durkheim's own terminology. He distinguished between *mechanical* and *organic solidarity*. The first prevails to the extent that "ideas and tendencies common to all members of the society are greater in number and intensity than those which pertain personally to each member. This solidarity can grow only in inverse ratio to personality."[8] In other words, *mechanical solidarity* prevails where individual differences are minimized and the members of society are much alike in their devotion to the common weal. "Solidarity which comes from likeness is at its maximum when the collective conscience completely envelops our whole conscience and coincides in all points with it."[9] *Organic solidarity,* in contrast, develops out of differences, rather than likenesses, between individuals. It is a product of the division of labor. With increasing differentiation of functions in a society come increasing differences between its members.

[6] Emile Durkheim, *Suicide* (New York, The Free Press, 1951), p. 209. [7] *Ibid.,* p. 159.
[8] Emile Durkheim, *The Division of Labor in Society* (New York, The Free Press, 1956), p. 129.
[9] *Ibid.,* p. 130.

Each element in a differentiated society is less strongly tied to common collective routines, even though it may be bound with equal rigor to the differentiated and specialized tasks and roles that characterize systems of organic solidarity. While the individual elements of such a system have less in common, they are nevertheless much more interdependent than under mechanical solidarity. Precisely because they now engage in differentiated ways of life and in specialized activities, the members are largely dependent upon one another and networks of solidarity can develop between them. In such systems, there can be some release from external controls, but such release is in tune with, not in conflict with, the high degree of dependence of individuals on their fellows.

In his earlier work, Durkheim stated that strong systems of common belief characterize mechanical solidarity in primitive types of society, and that organic solidarity, resulting from the progressive increase in the division of labor and hence increased mutual dependence, needed fewer common beliefs to tie members to this society. He later revised this view and stressed that even those systems with a highly developed organic solidarity still needed a common faith, a common *conscience collective,* if they were not to disintegrate into a heap of mutually antagonistic and self-seeking individuals.

The mature Durkheim realized that only if all members of a society were anchored to common sets of symbolic representations, to common assumptions about the world around them, could moral unity be assured. Without them, Durkheim argued, any society, whether primitive or modern, was bound to degenerate and decay.

INDIVIDUAL AND SOCIETY

To Durkheim, men were creatures whose desires were unlimited. Unlike other animals, they are not satiated when their biological needs are fulfilled. "The more one has, the more one wants, since satisfactions received only stimulate instead of filling needs."[10] It follows from this natural insatiability of the human animal that his desires can only be held in check by external controls, that is, by societal control. Society imposes limits on human desires and constitutes "a regulative force [which] must play the same role for moral needs which the organism plays for physical needs."[11] In well-regulated societies, social controls set limits on individual propensities so that "each in his sphere vaguely realizes the extreme limits set to his ambitions and aspires to nothing beyond. . . . Thus, an end or a goal [is] set to the passions."[12]

When social regulations break down, the controlling influence of society on individual propensities is no longer effective and individuals are left to their own devices. Such a state of affairs Durkheim calls *anomie,* a term that

[10] *Suicide,* p. 248. [11] *Ibid.* [12] *Ibid.,* p. 250.

refers to a condition of relative normlessness in a whole society or in some of its component groups. Anomie does not refer to a state of mind, but to a property of the social structure. It characterizes a condition in which individual desires are no longer regulated by common norms and where, as a consequence, individuals are left without moral guidance in the pursuit of their goals.

Although complete anomie, or total normlessness, is empirically impossible, societies may be characterized by greater or lesser degrees of normative regulations. Moreover, within any particular society, groups may differ in the degree of anomie that besets them. Social change may create anomie either in the whole society or in some parts of it. Business crises, for example, may have a far greater impact on those on the higher reaches of the social pyramid than on the underlying population. When depression leads to a sudden downward mobility, the men affected experience a de-regulation in their lives—a loss of moral certainty and customary expectations that are no longer sustained by the group to which these men once belonged. Similarly, the rapid onset of prosperity may lead some people to a quick upward mobility and hence deprive them of the social support needed in their new styles of life. Any rapid movement in the social structure that upsets previous networks in which life styles are embedded carries with it a chance of anomie.

Durkheim argued that economic affluence, by stimulating human desires, carries with it dangers of anomic conditions because it "deceives us into believing that we depend on ourselves only," while "poverty protects against suicide because it is a restraint in itself."[13] Since the realization of human desires depends upon the resources at hand, the poor are restrained, and hence less prone to suffer from anomie by virtue of the fact that they possess but limited resources. "The less one has the less he is tempted to extend the range of his needs indefinitely."[14]

By accounting for the different susceptibility to anomie in terms of the social process—that is, the relations between individuals rather than the biological propensities of individuals—Durkheim in effect proposed a specifically sociological theory of deviant behavior even though he failed to point to the general implications of this crucial insight. In the words of Robert K. Merton, who was the first to ferret out in this respect the overall implications of Durkheim's thought and to develop them methodically, "Social structures exert a definite pressure upon certain persons in the society to engage in nonconforming rather than conforming conduct."[15]

Durkheim's program of study, the overriding problem in all his work, concerns the sources of social order and disorder, the forces that make for regulation or de-regulation in the body social. His work on suicide, of which the discussion and analysis of anomie forms a part, must be read in this

[13] *Ibid.*, p. 254. [14] *Ibid.*

[15] Robert K. Merton, *Social Theory and Social Structure* (New York, The Free Press, 1968), p. 186.

light. Once he discovered that certain types of suicide could be accounted for by anomie, he could then use anomic suicide as an index for the otherwise unmeasurable degree of social integration. This was not circular reasoning, as could be argued, but a further application of his method of analysis. He reasoned as follows: There are no societies in which suicide does not occur, and many societies show roughly the same rates of suicide over long periods of time. This indicates that suicides may be considered a "normal," that is, a regular, occurrence. However, sudden spurts in the suicide rates of certain groups or total societies are "abnormal" and point to some perturbations not previously present. Hence, "abnormally" high rates in specific groups or social categories, or in total societies, can be taken as an index of disintegrating forces at work in a social structure.

Durkheim distinguished between types of suicide according to the relation of the actor to his society. When men become "detached from society,"[16] when they are thrown upon their own devices and loosen the bonds that previously had tied them to their fellows, they are prone to *egoistic,* or individualistic, suicide. When the normative regulations surrounding individual conduct are relaxed and hence fail to curb and guide human propensities, men are susceptible to succumbing to *anomic* suicide. To put the matter differently, when the restraints of structural integration, as exemplified in the operation of organic solidarity, fail to operate, men become prone to egoistic suicide; when the collective conscience weakens, men fall victim to anomic suicide.

In addition to egoistic and anomic types of suicide, Durkheim refers to *altruistic* and *fatalistic* suicide. The latter is touched upon only briefly in his work, but the former is of great importance for an understanding of Durkheim's general approach. Altruistic suicide refers to cases in which suicide can be accounted for by overly strong regulation of individuals, as opposed to lack of regulation. Durkheim argues in effect that the relation of suicide rates to social regulation is curvilinear—high rates being associated with both excessive individuation and excessive regulation. In the case of excessive regulation, the demands of society are so great that suicide varies directly rather than inversely with the degree of integration. For example, in the instance of the Hindu normative requirement that widows commit ritual suicide upon the funeral pyre of their husbands, or in the case of harikiri, the individual is so strongly attuned to the demands of his society that he is willing to take his own life when the norms so demand. Arguing from statistical data, Durkheim shows that in modern societies the high rates of suicide among the military cannot be explained by the deprivations of military life suffered by the lower ranks, since the suicide rate happens to be higher for officers than for enlisted men. Rather, the high rate for officers can be accounted for by a military code of honor that enjoins a passive habit of obedience leading

[16] *Suicide,* p. 212.

officers to undervalue their own lives. In such cases, Durkheim is led to refer to too feeble degrees of individuation and to counterpose these to the excesses of individuation or de-regulation, which account, in his view, for the other major forms of suicide.

Durkheim's discussion of altrustic suicide allows privileged access to some of the intricacies of his approach. He has often been accused of having an overly anti-individualistic philosophy, one that is mainly concerned with the taming of individual impulse and the harnessing of the energies of individuals for the purposes of society. Although it cannot be denied that there are such tendencies in his work, Durkheim's treatment of altruistic suicide indicates that he was trying to establish a balance between the claims of individuals and those of society, rather than to suppress individual strivings. Acutely aware of the dangers of the breakdown of social order, he also realized that total control of component social actors by society would be as detrimental as anomie and de-regulation. Throughout his life he attempted to establish a balance between societal and individual claims.

Durkheim was indeed a thinker in the conservative tradition to the extent that he reacted against the atomistic drift of most Enlightenment philosophy and grounded his sociology in a concern for the maintenance of social order. As Robert Nisbet[17] has shown convincingly, such key terms as *cohesion, solidarity, integration, authority, ritual,* and *regulation* indicate that his sociology is anchored upon an anti-atomistic set of premises. In this respect he was like his traditionalist forebears, yet it would be a mistake to classify Durkheim as a traditionalist social thinker. Politically he was a liberal—indeed, a defender of the rights of individuals against the state. He also was moved to warn against excesses of regulation over persons even though the major thrusts of his argument were against those who, by failing to recognize the requirements of the social order, were likely to foster anomic states of affairs. Anomie, he argued, was as detrimental to individuals as it was to the social order at large.

Durkheim meant to show that a Spencerian approach to the social realm, an approach in which the social dimension is ultimately derived from the desire of individuals to increase the sum of their happiness, did not stand up before the court of evidence or the court of reason. Arguing against Spencer and the utilitarians, he maintained that society cannot be derived from the propensity of individuals to trade and barter in order to maximize their own happiness. This view fails to account for the fact that people do not trade and barter at random but follow a pattern that is normative. For men to make a contract and live up to it, they must have a prior commitment to the meaning of a contract in its own right. Such prior collective commitment, that is, such a non-contractual element of contracts, constitutes the framework of

[17] Robert A. Nisbet, *Emile Durkheim* (Englewood Cliffs, New Jersey, Prentice-Hall, 1965).

normative control. No trade or barter can take place without social regulation and some system of positive and negative sanctions.

Durkheim's main shafts against individualistic social theories notwithstanding, he was by no means oblivious of the dangers of overregulation to which Spencer's social philosophy had been especially sensitive. Durkheim saw man as *Homo duplex*—as body, desire, and appetite and also as socialized personality. But man was specifically human only in the latter capacity, and he became fully human only in and through society. Hence, true moral action lies in the sacrifice of certain individual desires for the service of groups and society. But such sacrifices redound in the last analysis to the benefit of individuals, as well as society, since unbridled desires lead to frustration and unhappiness rather than to bliss and fulfillment. Modern society seems to contain, for Durkheim, the potentialities for individualism within social regulation. In contrast to earlier types of social organization based on mechanical solidarity that demanded a high degree of regimentation, modern types of organization rest on organic solidarity obtained through the functional interdependence of autonomous individuals. In modern societies, social solidarity is dependent upon, rather than repressive of, individual autonomy of conduct.

Though Durkheim stressed that in modern societies a measure of integration was achieved through the intermeshing and mutual dependence of differentiated roles, he came to see that these societies nevertheless could not do without some common integration by a system of common beliefs. In earlier social formations built on mechanical solidarity, such common beliefs are not clearly distinct from the norms through which they are implemented in communal action; in the case of organic solidarity, the detailed norms have become relatively independent from overall beliefs, responding as they do to the exigencies of differentiated role requirements, but a general system of overall beliefs must still exist.[18] Hence Durkheim turned, in the last period of his scholarly life, to the study of religious phenomena as core elements of systems of common beliefs.

THE SOCIOLOGY OF RELIGION

Durkheim's earlier concern with social regulation was in the main focused on the more external forces of control, more particularly legal regulations that can be studied, so he argued, in the law books and without regard to individuals. Later he was led to consider forces of control that were internalized in individual consciousness. Being convinced that "society has to be present within the individual," Durkheim, following the logic of his own theory, was led to the study of religion, one of the forces that created within individuals a sense of moral obligation to adhere to society's demands.

[18] Talcott Parsons, *op. cit.*

Durkheim had yet another motive for studying the functions of religion—namely, concern with mechanisms that might serve to shore up a threatened social order. In this respect he was in quest of what would today be described as functional equivalents for religion in a fundamentally a-religious age.

Durkheim stands in the line of succession of a number of French thinkers who pondered the problem of the loss of faith. From the days when the Jacobins had destroyed Catholicism in France and then attempted to fill the ensuing moral void by inventing a synthetic Religion of Reason, to Saint-Simon's New Christianity and Comte's Religion of Humanity, French secular thinkers had grappled with the modern problem of how public and private morality could be maintained without religious sanctions. They had asked, just like Ivan Karamasov: "Once God is dead, does not everything become permissible?" Durkheim would not have phrased the question in such language, but he was concerned with a similar problem. In the past, he argued, religion had been the cement of society—the means by which men had been led to turn from the everyday concerns in which they were variously enmeshed to a common devotion to sacred things. By thus wrenching men from the utilitarian preoccupations of daily life, religion had been the anti-individualistic force *par excellence,* inspiring communal devotion to ethical ends that transcended individual purposes. But if the reign of traditional religious orientations had now ended, what would take their place? Would the end of traditional religion be a prelude to the dissolution of all moral community into a state of universal breakdown and anomie?

Such questions intensified Durkheim's concern with the sociology of religion, adding to the intrinsic interest he had in terms of the internal logic of his system. Basic to his theory is the stress on religious phenomena as communal rather than individual. "A religion is a unified system of beliefs and practices relative to sacred things, that is to say, things set apart and forbidden—beliefs and practices which unite in one single moral community called a Church, all those who adhere to them."[19] In contrast to William James, for example, Durkheim was not concerned with the variety of religious experience of individuals but rather with the communal activity and the communal bonds to which participation in religious activities gives rise.

Durkheim argued that religious phenomena emerge in any society when a separation is made between the sphere of the profane—the realm of everyday utilitarian activities—and the sphere of the sacred—the area that pertains to the numenous, the transcendental, the extraordinary. An object is intrinsically neither sacred nor profane. It becomes the one or the other depending on whether men choose to consider the utilitarian value of the object or certain intrinsic attributes that have nothing to do with its instrumental value. The

[19] Emile Durkheim, *The Elementary Forms of Religious Life* (New York, The Free Press, 1954), p. 47.

wine at mass has sacred ritual significance to the extent that it is considered by the believer to symbolize the blood of Christ; in this context it is plainly not a beverage. Sacred activities are valued by the community of believers not as means to ends, but because the religious community has bestowed their meaning on them as part of its worship. Distinctions between the spheres of the sacred and the profane are always made by groups who band together in a cult and who are united by their common symbols and objects of worship. Religion is "an eminently collective thing."[20] It binds men together, as the etymology of the word religion testifies.

But if religion, the great binding force, is on its deathbed, how then can the malady of modern society, its tendency to disintegrate, be healed? Here Durkheim accomplished one of his most daring analytical leaps. Religion, he argued, is not only a social creation, but it is in fact society divinized. In a manner reminiscent of Feuerbach, Durkheim stated that the deities which men worship together are only projections of the power of society. Religion is eminently social: it occurs in a social context, and, more importantly, when men celebrate sacred things, they unwittingly celebrate the power of their society. This power so transcends their own existence that they have to give it sacred significance in order to visualize it.

If religion in its essence is a transcendental representation of the powers of society, then, Durkheim argued, the disappearance of traditional religion need not herald the dissolution of society. All that is required is for modern men now to realize directly that dependence on society which before they had recognized only through the medium of religious representations. "We must discover the rational substitutes for these religious notions that for a long time have served as the vehicle for the most essential moral ideas."[21] Society is the father of us all; therefore, it is to society we owe that profound debt of gratitude heretofore paid to the gods. The following passage, which in its rhetoric is rather uncharacteristic of Durkheim's usual analytical style, reveals some of his innermost feelings:

> Society is not at all the illogical or a-logical, incoherent and fantastic being which has too often been considered. Quite on the contrary, the collective consciousness is the highest form of psychic life, since it is the consciousness of consciousnesses. Being placed outside of and above individual and local contingencies, it sees things only in their permanent and essential aspects, which it crystallizes into communicable ideas. At the same time that it sees from above, it sees farther; at every moment of time it embraces all known reality; that is why it alone can furnish the minds with the moulds which are applicable to the totality of things and which make it possible to think of them.[22]

[20] *Ibid.* [21] Emile Durkheim, *Moral Education* (New York, The Free Press, 1961), p. 9.
[22] *The Elementary Forms*, p. 444.

Durkheim did not follow Saint-Simon and Comte in attempting to institute a new humanitarian cult. Yet, being eager as they were to give moral unity to a disintegrating society, he urged men to unite in a civic morality based on the recognition that we are what we are because of society. Society acts within us to elevate us—not unlike the divine spark of old was said to transform ordinary men into creatures capable of transcending the limitations of their puny egos.

Durkheim's sociology of religion is not limited to these general considerations, which, in fact, are contained in only a few pages of his monumental work on *The Elementary Forms of Religious Life*. The bulk of the book is devoted to a close and careful analysis of primitive religion, more particularly of the data on primitive Australian forms of cults and beliefs. Here, as elsewhere, Durkheim is concerned with elucidating the particular functions of religion rather than with simply describing variant forms. In a well-known critique, the Durkheimian scholar Harry Alpert[23] conveniently classified Durkheim's four major functions of religion as disciplinary, cohesive, vitalizing, and euphoric social forces. Religious rituals prepare men for social life by imposing self-discipline and a certain measure of asceticism. Religious ceremonies bring people together and thus serve to reaffirm their common bonds and to reinforce social solidarity. Religious observance maintains and revitalizes the social heritage of the group and helps transmit its enduring values to future generations. Finally, religion has a euphoric function in that it serves to counteract feelings of frustration and loss of faith and certitude by reestablishing the believers' sense of well-being, their sense of the essential rightness of the moral world of which they are a part. By countering the sense of loss, which, as in the case of death, may be experienced on both the individual and the collective level, religion helps to reestablish the balance of private and public confidence. On the most general plane, religion as a social institution serves to give meaning to man's existential predicaments by tying the individual to that supra-individual sphere of transcendent values which is ultimately rooted in his society.

THE SOCIOLOGY OF KNOWLEDGE

Durkheim's sociology of knowledge is intimately tied to his sociology of religion. In the latter, he attempts to show that man's religious commitments ultimately can be traced to his social commitments (the City of God is but a projection of the City of Man). His sociology of knowledge postulates that the categories of man's thought—his ways of conceiving space and time, for example—can be traced to his mode of social life.

[23] Harry Alpert, *Emile Durkheim and His Sociology* (New York, Columbia University Press, 1939), pp. 198–203.

Durkheim maintained that spatial, temporal, and other thought classifications are social in origin, closely approximating the social organization of primitive people. The first "classes" were classes of men, and the classification of objects in the world of nature was an extension of the social classification already established. All animals and natural objects belonged to this or that clan or phratry, residential or kinship group. He further argued that, although scientific classifications have now become largely divorced from their social origins, the manner in which we still classify things as "belonging to the same family" reveals the social origins of classificatory thought.

Durkheim attempted a sociological explanation of all fundamental categories of human thought, especially the central concepts of time and space. These, he claimed, are not only transmitted by society, but they *are* social creations. Society is decisive in the genesis of logical thought by forming the concepts of which that thought is made. The social organization of the primitive community is the model for the primitive's spatial organization of his surrounding world. Similarly, temporal divisions into days, weeks, months, and years correspond to periodical recurrences of rites, feasts, and ceremonies. "A calendar expresses the rhythm of the collective activities, while at the same time its function is to assure their regularities."[24]

Although in the light of later critical discussions of this thesis it can be said that Durkheim failed to establish the social origins of the categories of thought, it is important to recognize his pioneering contribution to the study of the correlations between specific systems of thought and systems of social organization. It is this part of Durkheim's contribution, rather than some of the more debatable epistemological propositions found in his work, that has influenced later development in the sociology of knowledge. Even when one refuses assent to the proposition that the notions of time and space are social in origin, it appears that the particular conceptions of time and space within a particular society and at a particular time in history are derived from specific social and cultural contexts. Here, as in his study of religion, Durkheim was concerned with functional interrelations between systems of beliefs and thought and the underlying social structure.

FUNCTIONAL EXPLANATION

It is Durkheim who clearly established the logic of the functional approach to the study of social phenomena, although functional explanations, it will be recalled, played a major part in Spencer's approach, and the lineaments of functional reasoning were already discernible in the work of Comte. In particular, Durkheim set down a clear distinction between historical and

[24] *Elementary Forms*, pp. 10–11.

functional types of inquiry and between functional consequences and individual motivations.

> When . . . the explanation of a social phenomenon is undertaken, we must seek separately the efficient cause which produces it and the function it fulfills. We use the word "function," in preference to "end" or "purpose," precisely because social phenomena do not generally exist for the useful results they produce. We must determine whether there is a correspondence between the fact under consideration and the general needs of the social organism, and in what this correspondence consists, without occupying ourselves with whether it has been intentional or not.[25]

"The determination of function is . . . necessary for the complete explanation of the phenomena. . . . To explain a social fact it is not enough to show the cause on which it depends; we must also, at least in most cases, show its function in the establishment of social order."[26]

Durkheim separated functional analysis from two other analytical procedures, the quest for historical origins and causes and the probing of individual purposes and motives. The second seemed to him of only peripheral importance for sociological inquiry since men often engage in actions when they are unable to anticipate the consequences. The quest for origins and historical causes, however, was to Durkheim as essential and legitimate a part of the sociological enterprise as was the analysis of functions. In fact, he was convinced that the full explanation of sociological phenomena would necessarily utilize both historical and functional analysis. The latter would reveal how a particular item under consideration had certain consequences for the operation of the overall system or its component parts. The former would enable the analyst to show why this particular item, rather than some others, was historically available to subserve a particular function. Social investigators must combine the search for efficient causes and the determination of the functions of a phenomenon.

The concept of function played a key part in all of Durkheim's work from *The Division of Labor,* in which he sees his prime objective in the determination of "the functions of division of labor, that is to say, what social needs it satisfies," to *The Elementary Forms of Religious Life,* which is devoted to a demonstration of the various functions performed in society through religious cults, rites, and beliefs. An additional illustration of Durkheim's functional approach is his discussion of criminality.

In his discussion of deviance and criminality, Durkheim departed fundamentally from the conventional path. While most criminologists treated crime as a pathological phenomenon and sought psychological causes in the mind of the criminal, Durkheim saw crime as normal in terms of its oc-

25 *Rules,* p. 95. 26 *Ibid.,* p. 97.

currence, and even as having positive social functions in terms of its consequences. Crime was normal in that no society could enforce total conformity to its injunctions, and if society could, it would be so repressive as to leave no leeway for the social contributions of individuals. Deviance from the norms of society is necessary if society is to remain flexible and open to change and new adaptations. "Where crime exists, collective sentiments are sufficiently flexible to take on a new form, and crime sometimes helps to determine the form they will take. How many times, indeed, it is only an anticipation of future morality—a step toward what will be."[27] But in addition to such direct consequences of crime, Durkheim identified indirect functions that are no less important. A criminal act, Durkheim reasoned, elicits negative sanctions in the community by arousing collective sentiments against the infringement of the norm. Hence it has the unanticipated consequence of strengthening normative consensus in the common weal. "Crime brings together upright consciences and concentrates them."[28]

Whether he investigated religious phenomena or criminal acts, whether he desired to clarify the social impact of the division of labor or of changes in the authority structure of the family, Durkheim always shows himself a masterful functional analyst. He is not content merely to trace the historical origins of phenomena under investigation, although he tries to do this also, but he moves from the search for efficient causes to inquiries into the consequences of phenomena for the structures in which they are variously imbedded. Durkheim always thinks contextually rather than atomistically. As such he must be recognized as the direct ancestor of that type of functional analysis which came to dominate British anthropology under the impact of Radcliffe-Brown and Malinowski and which led, somewhat later, to American functionalism in sociology under Talcott Parsons and Robert K. Merton.

The sections that follow will provide more information on Durkheim the man, and on his activities as an applied scientist and engaged reformer. This section was limited to his theoretical work, but it could not possibly do justice to all the facets of the work of so complicated a social theorist as Emile Durkheim. Space did not permit a discussion of Durkheim's contributions to the sociology of education, although they are considerable; nor could justice be done to Durkheim's fascinating if highly speculative work on the importance of professional associations as intermediary links between individuals and the all-encompassing, and possibly suffocating, powers of the state. Even his important contributions to the sociology of law could be alluded to only in passing.

As a social theorist, Durkheim, to quote him directly, had as his "principal objective . . . to extend scientific rationalism to human behavior."[29] And al-

[27] *Ibid.*, p. 71. [28] *Division of Labor,* p. 103. [29] *Suicide,* p. xxxix.

though he may have failed in many particulars, the fact that his work has become part of the foundation for all modern sociology testifies to his overall success.

THE MAN

Emile Durkheim was the first French academic sociologist. His life was dominated throughout by his academic career, even though he was intensely and passionately involved in the affairs of French society at large. In his well-established status he differed from the men dealt with so far, and his life may seem uneventful when compared with theirs. Undoubtedly their personal idiosyncrasies had a share in determining their erratic course. But in addition, they were all devoted to a calling that had not yet found recognition in the university. In their attempts to defend the claim to legitimacy of the new science of sociology, they faced enormous obstacles, which contributed in large measure to their personal difficulties.

Emile Durkheim, as well as the theorists who will be dealt with in subsequent chapters, faced a different set of circumstances. They were all academic men but were still considered by their colleagues as intruders representing a discipline that had little claim to legitimate status. As a result, theirs was by no means an easy course. Nevertheless, they fought from within the halls of academe rather than from outside, and so their lives tended to be less embattled than those of their predecessors.

Emile Durkheim was born at Epinal in the eastern French province of Lorraine on April 15, 1858. Son of a rabbi and descending from a long line of rabbis, he decided quite early that he would follow the family tradition and become a rabbi himself. He studied Hebrew, the Old Testament, and the Talmud, while at the same time following the regular course of instruction in secular schools.

Shortly after his traditional Jewish confirmation at the age of thirteen, Durkheim, under the influence of a Catholic woman teacher, had a shortlived mystical experience that led to an interest in Catholicism. But soon afterwards he turned away from all religious involvement, though emphatically not from interest in religious phenomena, and became an agnostic.

Durkheim was a brilliant student at the *Collège d'Epinal* and was awarded a variety of honors and prizes. His ambitions thus aroused, he transferred to one of the great French high schools, the *Lycée Louis-le-Grand* in Paris. Here he prepared himself for the arduous admission examinations that would open the doors to the prestigious *Ecole Normale Supérieure,* the traditional training ground for the intellectual elite of France.

After two unsuccessful attempts to pass the rigorous entrance examinations, Durkheim was finally admitted in 1879. At the *Ecole Normale* he met with a number of young men who would soon make a major mark on the intellectual life of France. Henri Bergson, who was to become the philosopher of vitalism, and Jean Jaurès, the future socialist leader, had entered the year before. The philosophers Rauh and Blondel were admitted two years after Durkheim. Pierre Janet, the psychologist, and Goblot, the philosopher, were in the same class as Durkheim. The *Ecole Normale,* which had been created by the First Republic, was now having a renaissance and was training some of the leading intellectual and political figures of the Third Republic.

Although admission to the *Ecole Normale* was an achievement in a young man's life, Durkheim, once admitted, seems not to have been happy at the *Ecole*. He was an intensely earnest, studious, and dedicated young man, soon nicknamed "the metaphysician" by his peers. Athirst for guiding moral doctrines and earnest scientific instruction, Durkheim was dissatisfied with the literary and esthetic emphasis that still predominated at the school. He rebelled against a course of studies in which the reading of Greek verse and Latin prose seemed more important than acquaintance with the newer philosophical doctrines or the recent findings of the sciences. He felt that the school made far too many concessions to the spirit of dilettantism and tended to reward elegant dabbling and the quest for "novelty" and "originality" of expression rather than solid and systematic learning.

Although he acquired some close friends at the school, among whom Jean Jaurès was the most outstanding, his earnestness and dedication made him in the eyes of the other students an aloof and remote figure, perhaps even somewhat of a prig. His professors, in their turn, repaid him for his apparent dissatisfaction with much of their teaching by placing him almost at the bottom of the list of successful *agrégation* candidates when he graduated in 1882.

All this does not mean that Durkheim was uninfluenced by his three years at the *Ecole Normale*. Later on, he spoke almost sentimentally about these years and, if many of his professors irked and annoyed him, there were a few others to whom he was deeply in debt. Among these were the great historian Fustel de Coulanges, author of the *Ancient City* who became director of the school while Durkheim attended it, and the philosopher Emile Boutroux. He later dedicated his Latin thesis to the memory of Fustel de Coulanges, and his French thesis, *The Division of Labor,* to Boutroux. What he admired in Fustel de Coulanges and learned from him was the use of critical and rigorous method in historical research. To Boutroux he owed an approach to the philosophy of science that stressed the basic discontinuities between different levels of phenomena and emphasized the novel aspects that emerged as one moved from one level of analysis to another. This approach was later to become a major mark of Durkheim's sociology.

DURKHEIM'S ACADEMIC CAREER

At about the time of his graduation, Durkheim had settled upon his life's course. His was not to be the traditional philosopher's calling. Philosophy, at least as it was then taught, seemed to him too far removed from the issues of the day, too much devoted to arcane and frivolous hairsplitting. He wanted to devote himself to a discipline that would contribute to the clarification of the great moral questions that agitated the age, as well as to practical guidance of the affairs of contemporary society. More concretely, Durkheim wished to make a contribution to the moral and political consolidation of the Third Republic which, in those days, was still a fragile and embattled political structure. But such moral guidance, Durkheim was convinced, could be provided only by men with a solid scientific training. Hence he decided that he would dedicate himself to the scientific study of society. What he considered imperative was to construct a scientific sociological system, not as an end in itself, but as a means for the moral direction of society. From this purpose Durkheim never departed.

However, since sociology was not a subject of instruction either at the secondary schools or at the university, Durkheim embarked upon a career as a teacher in philosophy. From 1882 to 1887 he taught in a number of provincial *Lycées* in the neighborhood of Paris—except for one year when he received a leave of absence for further study at Paris and in Germany. Durkheim's stay in Germany was mainly devoted to the study of methods of instruction and research in moral philosophy and the social sciences. He spent most of his time in Berlin and Leipzig. In the latter city the famous Psychological Laboratory of Wilhelm Wundt impressed him deeply. In his subsequent reports on his German experiences, Durkheim was enthusiastic about the precision and scientific objectivity in research that he had witnessed in Wundt's laboratory and elsewhere. At the same time he stressed that France should emulate Germany in making philosophical instruction serve social as well as national goals. He heartily approved of the efforts of various German social scientists and philosophers who stressed the social roots of the notion of moral duty and sought to make ethics an independent and positive discipline.

With the publication of his reports on German academic life, Durkheim became recognized at the age of twenty-nine as a promising figure in the social sciences and in social philosophy. In addition to his German studies, he had already published a number of critical articles, including reviews of the work of the German-language sociologists Gumplowicz and Schaeffle, and the French social philosopher Fouillé. It was not surprising, therefore, that he was appointed to the staff of the University of Bordeaux in 1887. What was surprising, however, was that at the instigation of Louis Liard, the Director of Higher Education at the Ministry of Public Education, a social science course was created for him at the Faculty of Letters at that university. This was the first time a French university opened its doors to this previously tabooed subject. Only a decade earlier, the furious examiners at the Faculty of Letters of Paris had forced the sociologist Alfred Espinas, a future colleague of Durkheim at Bordeaux, to suppress the introduction to his thesis because he refused to delete the name of Auguste Comte from its pages!

At Bordeaux, Durkheim was attached to the department of philosophy where he was charged with courses in both sociology and pedagogy. Some commentators seem to feel that the teaching of pedagogy was a kind of academic drudgery that Durkheim was forced to accept. This was not the case. He continued to teach in the field of education throughout his career, even when he was clearly free to determine for himself the courses he would offer. Education, as will be seen later in more detail, remained for Durkheim a privileged applied field where sociology could make its most important contribution to that regeneration of society for which he aimed so passionately.

At about the time of his academic appointment to Bordeaux, Durkheim married the former Louise Dreyfus. They had two children, Marie and André, but very little is known of his family life. His wife seems to have devoted herself fully to his work. She followed the traditional Jewish family pattern of taking care of family affairs as well as assisting him in proofreading, secretarial duties, and the like. Thus, the scholar-husband could devote all his energies to his scholarly pursuits.

The Bordeaux years were a period of intense productive activity for Durkheim. He continued to publish a number of major critical reviews, among others of Toennies' *Gemeinschaft und Gesellschaft,* and the opening lectures of some of his courses were published in the form of articles. In 1893, he defended his French doctoral thesis, *The Division of Labor,* and his Latin thesis on Montesquieu. Only two years later *The Rules of Sociological Method* appeared, and within another two years *Le Suicide* was published. With these three major works, Durkheim moved into the forefront of the academic world. He noted in the preface of *Suicide* that sociology was now "in fashion." Not that his work was universally praised; on the contrary, it created a number of famous controversies and polemical exchanges. But the fact that so many theorists were moved to regard Durkheim as their privileged adversary testifies to his impact on the intellectual world. Then, as later, Durkheim was the center of continued controversy and disputation.

Once having established sociology as a field of interest to a wider public, Durkheim soon felt the need to consolidate these gains by setting up a scholarly journal entirely devoted to the new discipline. *L'Année Sociologique,* which he founded in 1898, soon became the center for an extraordinarily gifted group of young scholars, all united, despite a variety of specific disciplinary interests, in a common devotion to the Durkheimian approach to sociology. Each year the *Année* analyzed the current literature of sociology in France and elsewhere.

These critical accounts allowed the French public for the first time to gain an overall view of the depth and breadth of the sociological enterprise. The *Année* also contained independent major contributions from the pen of Durkheim and from his close collaborators. The reviews and papers were all meant to emphasize the need for building conceptual bridges between the specialized fields of the social sciences and the correlative need for factual, specific, and methodical research. The *Année* was successful from the beginning, and the continued collaboration of its key contributors helped to weld them together into a cohesive "school," aggressively eager to defend the Durkheimian approach to sociology against all who opposed it.

In the same year the *Année* was born, Durkheim published his famous paper on *Individual and Collective Representations,* which served as a kind of manifesto of sociological independence for the Durkheimian school. A series of other seminal papers, some published in the *Année* and some elsewhere, followed in the next decade and a half. These included "The Determination of Moral Facts," "Value Judgments and Judgments of Reality," "Primitive Classification" (with Marcel Mauss), and "The Definition of Religious Phenomena."[30]

Nine years after having joined the faculty of the University of Bordeaux, Durkheim was promoted to a full professorship in social science, the first such position in France. He occupied this chair for six years. In 1902, now a man of fully recognized stature, he was called to the Sorbonne, first as a *chargé de cours* and then, in 1906, as a Professor of the Science of Education. In 1913, the name of Durkheim's chair was changed by a special ministerial decree to "Science of Education and Sociology." After more than three quarters of a century, Comte's brainchild had finally gained entry at the University of Paris.

During his Paris years, Durkheim continued to edit the *Année* and offered a wide range of courses in ethics, education, religion, the philosophy of pragmatism, and the teachings of Saint-Simon and Comte. He appears to have been a masterful lecturer who held his audience so much in thrall that one of his students could write, "Those who wished to escape his influence had to flee from his courses; on those who attended he imposed, willy-nilly, his mastery."[31]

[30] The first two papers, as well as the essay on "Individual and Collective Representations" are available in English translations in *Sociology and Philosophy. Primitive Classification* has recently been translated by Rodney Needham (Chicago, The University of Chicago Press, 1963). The last essay appeared in *L'Année Sociologique,* II (1897–98).

[31] Quoted in Harry Alpert, *Emile Durkheim and His Sociology* (New York, Columbia University Press, 1939), p. 62. This section is mainly based on his fine work which, though published thirty years ago, is still the best general account of Durkheim's life. I have also consulted George Davy's "Emile Durkheim," *Revue de métaphysique et de morale,* XXVI (1919), pp. 181–98. His *Emile Durkheim* (Paris, Louis-Michaud, 1911) contains some fine photographs of Durkheim, his co-students at the *Ecole Normale,* and his lecture audience at the Sorbonne. Various contributions to Kurt H. Wolff, ed., *Emile Durkheim 1859–1917* (Columbus, The Ohio State University Press, 1960) were also helpful.

During the last few years of his stay in Bordeaux, Durkheim had already become interested in the study of religious phenomena. At least in part under the influence of Robertson Smith and the British school of anthropology, he now turned to the detailed study of primitive religion. He had published a number of preliminary papers in the area, and this course of studies finally led to the publication in 1912 of Durkheim's last major work, *The Elementary Forms of Religious Life.*

PUBLIC INVOLVEMENT

His scholarly work in the Paris period, though extensive, by no means exhausted Durkheim's energies. He played a major role in the general intellectual life of France, as well as in the university. He was an active defender of Dreyfus during the heyday of the affair and attained eminence as a left-of-center publicist and spokesman. Durkheim also became a key figure in the reorganization of the university system. He served on innumerable university committees, advised the Ministry of Education, helped to introduce sociology into school curricula, and in general did yeoman's work to make sociology the cornerstone of civic education. In these years he came nearest to realizing his youthful ambition of bulding a scientific sociology that would be applied to moral re-education in the Third Republic and at the same time to the development of a secular civic morality.

When the war came, Durkheim felt obliged to aid his beleaguered fatherland. He became secretary of the Committee for the Publication of Studies and Documents on the War, and published several pamphlets in which he attacked pan-Germanism and more particularly the nationalistic writings of Treitschke.

Just before Christmas, 1915, Durkheim was notified that his son André had died in a Bulgarian hospital from his war wounds. André had followed his father to the *Ecole Normale* and had begun a most promising career as a sociological linguist. He had been the pride and hope of a father who had seen him as his destined successor in the front rank of the social sciences. His death was a blow from which Durkheim did not recover. He still managed to write down the first paragraphs of a treatise on ethics on which he had done preparatory work for a long time, but his energy was spent. He died on November 15, 1917, at the age of fifty-nine.

Emile Durkheim, the agnostic son of devoted Jews, had managed during his career to combine scientific detachment with intense moral involvement. He was passionately devoted to the disinterested quest for truth and knowledge, and yet he was also a figure not unlike the Old Testament prophets, who castigated their fellows for the errors of their ways and exhorted them to come together in a common service to moral unity and communal justice. Although a Frenchman first and foremost, he did not waver from his allegiance to a cosmopolitan liberal civilization in which the pursuit of science was meant to serve the enlightenment and guidance of the whole of humanity. A man made of whole cloth, he still managed to play a variety of roles in a distinctive intellectual and historical context.

THE INTELLECTUAL CONTEXT

In contrast to Spencer, who read very little, Durkheim was an omnivorous reader, a highly cultivated man open to a variety of intellectual currents. It is therefore difficult to establish all the major influences on his thought. The task is further complicated by the fact that an intellectual biography of Durkheim has not been written, and his private papers have been destroyed. Accordingly, what follows must be regarded as highly tentative.

DURKHEIM'S ROOTS IN FRENCH INTELLECTUAL HISTORY

Although Durkheim was considerably affected by both German and British social thought, his ideas were rooted "overwhelmingly in French intellectual history," as Talcott Parsons correctly observes.[32] Within that history Durkheim's major roots are in the tradition of the Enlightenment, especially in the work of Rousseau and Montesquieu. Rousseau's conception of the *volonté générale* can be considered one of the foremost influences on Durkheim's thought. This notion of the general will conceived of society as an expression of *social* solidarity,[33] being based neither on economic self-interest as seen by the utilitarians nor on a Hobbesian subjection of the citizen to the political sovereign. Moreover, Durkheim recognized his debt to Rousseau in regard to the distinction between social and psychological phenomena when he wrote that "Rousseau was keenly aware of the specificity of the social order. He conceived it clearly as an order of facts generically different from purely individual facts. It is a new world superimposed on the purely psychological world."[34]

Similarly, Durkheim owed an indebtedness to Montesquieu, which he clearly expressed when he wrote in his Latin doctoral thesis: "In pointing to the interrelatedness of social phenomena, Montesquieu foreshadowed the unity of our science."[35] The idea of the connectedness of all social and cultural phenomena, which Marx derived mainly from Hegel, Durkheim learned from Montesquieu. "Montesquieu," he wrote, "saw quite clearly that all these ele-

[32] Talcott Parsons, "Emile Durkheim," in *International Encyclopedia of the Social Sciences*.
[33] *Ibid.*
[34] Emile Durkheim, *Montesquieu and Rousseau* (Ann Arbor, The University of Michigan Press, 1960), p. 83. [35] *Ibid.*, p. 57.

ments form a whole and that if taken separately, without reference to the others, they cannot be understood. He does not separate law from morality, trade, religion, etc. and above all he does not consider it apart from the form of society, which affects all other social phenomena."[36]

Although Durkheim's holistic view of society owes much to Montesquieu, and his notion of solidarity grew, at least in part, out of his reading of *The Social Contract,* his debt to Comte and Saint-Simon was even greater. He never tired of reiterating that he saw himself as the continuator of the train of thought they had initiated. He said of Saint-Simon that, "although he was the first to have a clear conception of what sociology had to be, strictly speaking, Saint-Simon did not create sociology." That honor Durkheim accorded Comte.

The Division of Labor contains no fewer than seventeen references, most of them highly favorable, to the author of the *Cours de philosophie positive.* And Durkheim took pains to point out that "Comte recognized that the division of labor is a source of solidarity." Durkheim's emphases on the binding force of moral beliefs as the basis of solidarity and on the integration that the division of labor creates between interdependent individuals are, in some measure, derived from Comte and Saint-Simon.

Biographers have stressed that Durkheim began to read Comte only after he had already begun to clarify his own approach to the social sciences through thorough study of such philosophers as Emile Boutroux and Charles Renouvier. This is correct, of course, but no reader of the work of Comte and Durkheim can remain unimpressed by the close affinity of their thoughts. To be sure, Durkheim was not at all taken by Comte's later "theological" writing or by his metaphysics, and in many other particulars Durkheim found himself in disagreement with the Comtean approach. Nevertheless, he was at one with Comte in his general methodological approach, that is, in the quest for positive laws of social behavior not fundamentally at variance with, although certainly more complicated than natural laws. It should also be apparent that Durkheim's *conscience collective* is a variant of Comte's *consensus,* and that Durkheim's concern with the interrelatedness of social phenomena owes much to Comte, as it does to Montesquieu.

Although highly critical of some traditions of the Enlightenment, especially the atomistic aspects of much eighteenth century thought, Comtean positivism can be considered the lineal descendant of the Enlightenment, sharing its rationalism and its secularism. That Durkheim related himself both to the Enlightenment and to positivism is therefore not at all surprising. The matter is more complicated, however, when the claim is made that Durkheim was also deeply influenced by the anti-Enlightenment of such great French traditionalist thinkers as de Bonald and de Maistre and their con-

[36] *Ibid.,* p. 56.

temporaries and successors. Robert Nisbet has made a persuasive case for this in several of his writings.[37] He says, for example, "It was Durkheim's feat to translate into the hard methodology of science ideas and values that had made their first appearance in the polemics of Bonald, Maistre, Haller, and others opposed to reason and rationalism, as well as to revolution and reform."[38] By emphasizing that individuals depend on society and its code and are not the self-sustaining and self-realizing persons they appear to be in the writings of most of the *philosophes;* by stressing the necessity for authority and binding obligations; by seeing in religion, the family, the local community, and the guild those necessary institutions that tie the individual to society, the traditionalist thinkers indeed put forward ideas that found a central place in the Durkheimian canon.

Yet there exists no evidence, as Nisbet readily admits,[39] that Durkheim ever read any of these thinkers. To be sure, he must have been familiar with Comte's admiring references to their thought, and it is quite possible that he absorbed some traditionalist ideas through the writers of the Social Catholic movement. This movement was quite influential in his days and attempted to combine the teaching of the liberal Catholic thinkers, such as Lamenais and Lacordaire, with the traditionalists' interpretation of the organic nature of social bonds. But all this is in the realm of conjecture. One can point to startling similarities and significant differences in the thinking of Durkheim and that of the traditionalists but cannot prove any direct influence.

CONTEMPORARY INFLUENCES

It is much easier to trace the direct impact of thinkers who were still alive and active in Durkheim's days. As mentioned earlier, the influence of two of his teachers at the *Ecole Normale* is beyond dispute. From the great historian Fustel de Coulanges he learned much of the careful historical method of research that is especially evident in the historical sections of the *Division of Labor*. Fustel de Coulanges' stress on the central role of domestic religion and religious associations in his classical book *The Ancient City* influenced Durkheim, if not in his student days, then at a later period when he came to be fascinated by religious phenomena.

From his other major teacher, the philosopher Emile Boutroux, Durkheim learned the distinction between different levels of reality and the notion of emergence as a crucial aspect of the philosophy of science. Boutroux, in the words of one of his recent commentators, Peter A. Bertocci,

[37] Nisbet, *op. cit.;* Robert A. Nisbet, *Tradition and Revolt* (New York, Random House, 1968), esp. Chapters 2 and 4; and Robert A. Nisbet, *The Sociological Tradition* (New York, Basic Books, 1966).

[38] Nisbet, *Emile Durkheim,* p. 25.

[39] Personal communication, dated January 5, 1969.

> stressed that there is a basic discontinuity separating different levels of being —material, instinctive, thinking—each of which displays an element not present in its predecessor and not deducible from it, and that consequently it is impossible to reduce the science of any one level to that of the others. Higher forms of life, despite their physical and chemical characteristics, are not wholly explicable in terms of the mechanical laws that govern matter.[40]

Boutroux's antireductionist doctrine, which took sharp issue with the physico-chemical materialism of the school of Taine, surely served Durkheim well when he set about the task of showing that society was a reality *sui generis* that could not be explained by reductionist arguments from psychology or biology.

Another French figure who had a demonstrably important effect on Durkheim's thought is the neo-Kantian philosopher Charles Renouvier. Renouvier's long life (1815–1903) bridges the gap between the world of Comte and of Durkheim. Educated at the *Ecole Polytechnique,* Renouvier had been influenced by Saint-Simon in the early thirties and had sat at the feet of Auguste Comte when the latter was a *répétiteur* at the school. He had been an active socialist propagandist during the revolution of 1848 but retired from active political participation to become a private scholar during the Empire. In the last years of Napoleon III's reign and during the first thirty years of the Third Republic, Renouvier exerted a major influence on French thought through the journal, *La Critique philosophique,* which he edited, and through the many books he wrote, particularly the *Essais de critique générale.* Renouvier's general position is called neo-criticism because it derived from Kant's method though often diverging from Kant's conclusions. Renouvier's indeterminism and rejection of historical laws probably did not have much of an influence on Durkheim's thought, but there were other Renouvier themes that found an echo in his work. Among these were, to quote Harry Alpert, "the beliefs that ethical and moral considerations occupy a central position in philosophical thought, that there is need for a science of ethics, that philosophy should serve as a guide to social action, that it should specifically contribute to the reconstruction of the moral unity of the Third Republic, that a fundamental, if not *the* fundamental moral concept of modern society is the dignity of the human person."[41] Renouvier identified conflict, both between persons and groups of persons, with evil, and this thought is also likely to have had reverberations in Durkheim's work.[42]

The French sociologist and social philosopher Gabriel Tarde must also be considered important in Durkheim's intellectual development, for Tarde

[40] Peter A. Bertocci, "Emile Boutroux," in *Encyclopedia of Philosophy* (New York, Macmillan, 1967). [41] Alpert, *op. cit.,* pp. 26–27.

[42] George Boas, "Charles Renouvier," in *Encyclopedia of Philosophy,* and Chapter I in John A. Scott, *Republican Ideas and the Liberal Tradition in France* (New York, Columbia University Press, 1951).

was his major antagonist. The many polemical exchanges between them undoubtedly helped Durkheim sharpen and refine his own views; as a result, Tarde, his major adversary, may be said to have been as effective a force in his intellectual development as many of those men from whom he learned directly. Tarde was a provincial magistrate, not an academician, but his legal career provided adequate financial support and free time to let him devote much of his energy to developing a system of social theory.[43] In the eighties and nineties Tarde published a number of works in criminology and social theory of which *The Laws of Imitation* (1890) is the most noteworthy. During the last few years of his life Tarde occupied a chair of modern philosophy at the prestigious *Collège de France* in Paris. His overall theory focused on the premise that new ideas and inventions, although often initiated through impersonal communication, are diffused throughout society by a process of imitation. Influence, he asserted, typically flows from social superiors to social inferiors; thus, economic, religious, or military innovations are spread by elite groups who gather around themselves numerous and vocal supporters who imitate their actions and help propagate their ideas among the population at large. Tarde's was a social psychology predicated on the idea that social processes are always anchored in the imitation of the leaders' actions by the led. Society to him is an aggregate of individuals in interaction. By emphasizing in his writings a methodology and a philosophy that stood at the opposite pole to Durkheim's, Tarde was an ideal target for critical rebuttals. Durkheim had an opportunity to define and refine his contrary notion that society was a reality *sui generis,* so that explanations of human behavior must be couched in structural rather than in social psychological terms.

A more detailed listing of French intellectual influences on Durkheim would have to mention still a host of other figures, including his Bordeaux colleague, the sociologist Alfred Espinas, whose doctoral dissertation (*Des Sociétés animales*) is frequently quoted in the *Division of Labor* in support of Durkheim's holistic and structural approach.[44]

EXTRA-FRENCH INFLUENCES

The extra-French influences on Durkheim, although not as profound as those coming from the French tradition, often affected the direction of his ideas. Among these, Herbert Spencer's work is the most important. There are forty references to Spencer in the *Division of Labor,* many more than to any other theorist. Although Durkheim disagreed with most of Spencer's funda-

43 Terry Clark, "Gabriel Tarde," in *International Encyclopedia of the Social Sciences.*

44 The best introduction to overall trends in French philosophy in the nineteenth and early twentieth century is J. Benrubi, *Les Sources de la philosophie contemporaine en France,* 2 vols. (Paris, Alcan, 1933). This work not only contains detailed critical discussions of the work of all the Frenchmen mentioned in this section, but also has a full chapter on Durkheim and subchapters on most of his major disciples.

mental premises, he remained under his spell, especially during the period he was writing the *Division of Labor.*

Durkheim dissented completely from Spencer's individualistic premises; instead he stressed that individual self-interest and the striving for happiness could not account for social order. Moreover, Durkheim argued, the striving for happiness, far from being at the root of human sociability, was itself a social creation in that it appeared only in certain types of societies and in certain specific historical periods. Durkheim would probably have agreed with the French revolutionist Saint-Just who exclaimed in one of his great speeches: "Le bonheur est une idée neuve en Europe." Durkheim rejected Spencer's basically individualistic idea that contracts between individuals are the building stones of social order, and stressed instead that contractual agreements between parties are always subject to the existence of antecedent general norms.

But in many other respects Durkheim was deeply obliged to Spencer. Most of Durkheim's evolutionary views derive from him. It is evident, for example, that Durkheim's conception of evolution as moving from systems of mechanical to systems of organic solidarity is similar to, though by no means as vague as, Spencer's observation about the evolution from incoherent homogeneity to coherent heterogeneity. Durkheim's emphasis on progressive differentiation in human societies and on the historical movement from societies in which all men are alike to societies in which the division of labor makes men very unalike yet mutually dependent, is derived in large part from the writings of Spencer, though it also owes something to Adam Smith. As will be remembered, major elements of Durkheim's functionalist approach are at least foreshadowed in the work of his British predecessor. Although separated from Spencer by a wholly different set of philosophical and methodological premises, Durkheim may nevertheless be said to have continued in new directions many lines of inquiry in which Spencer had made pioneering contributions.

One other British scholar, the anthropologist William Robertson Smith, author of *Lectures on the Religion of the Semites* (1889), exerted considerable influence on Durkheim in his later years. A point of departure for Durkheim's later work was Smith's conception that because early religions were anchored in ritual practice, analytical attention ought to be directed to the social relations of believers and the working of religious institutions, rather than to belief systems as such. Particularly in his writings on sacrifice, which he regarded as "the central problem of ancient religion," Smith focused his attention on the community of worshippers as they partook of the commensal meal, asserting that the intentions of the actors were relatively unimportant. He maintained that ceremonial eating together created a bond similar to that of kinship; therefore, the social activity itself and not the motivations of religious believers should be the subject matter of the study of religious phenomena.

Smith saw in the unity of the religious group the core of religion, and Durkheim made this notion the core of his own theory of religion.[45]

In regard to German thinkers, the philosopher closest to Durkheim was Immanuel Kant. Durkheim was not so much attracted by Kant's epistemology and general philosophy as by his stern philosophy of moral duty. When Durkheim developed his theory of the social origins of the notions of time and space, he specifically rejected the Kantian doctrine of the inherent categories of the human mind. But he was careful to point out that his sociology of morality, which emphasized the *desirability* of moral acts, was only supplementing Kant's notion of duty and moral obligation. "We cannot perform an act which is . . . in some way meaningful to us simply because we have been commanded to do so. It is psychologically impossible to pursue an end to which we are indifferent. . . . Morality must, then, be not only obligatory but also desirable and desired."[46] Even when he was moved to modify what he saw as Kant's overemphasis on duty in the analysis of moral acts, Durkheim remained deeply attached to this notion. Kantian sternness was clearly congenial to a man who seems to have modeled himself after the Old Testament prophets he had so assiduously studied in his youth.

Durkheim, it will be recalled, wrote lengthy critical reviews of the work of Simmel, Schäffle, Gumplowicz, and Toennies, among others. Undoubtedly, German organicist thought was for a while as attractive to him as the Spencerian version. The influence of Ferdinand Toennies, author of *Gemeinschaft und Gesellschaft,* can easily be traced in Durkheim's similar distinction between mechanical and organic solidarity, although the underlying tone of Toennies' work is very different from that of Durkheim. For Toennies, who was in tune with a German tradition going back at least to Herder, the older form of social organization, *Gemeinschaft,* is the more "organic," the more attractive, the more "natural." In contrast, Durkheim, the heir of French Enlightenment, found the modern form of solidarity the more organic, the more "progressive," the more desirable. While much of German thought continued to hanker after the Golden Age of the past, French thought tended mainly to look to the Golden Age in the future.

One last German figure, Wilhelm Wundt, whom Durkheim knew personally, will be examined in some detail. Wundt has been called the father of experimental psychology, but he worked in other areas of the social sciences as well. He lectured and wrote on logic and ethics and contributed a ten-volume natural history of man called *Voelkerpsychologie,* in which he tried to analyze the laws of evolution of language, myth, and morals. Wundt's notion of the *Volksseele* (the group soul), which he substituted for the more

[45] E. L. Peters, "William Robertson Smith," in *International Encyclopedia of the Social Sciences.*
[46] *Sociology and Philosophy,* pp. 44–45.

common Hegelian *Volksgeist,* may have played a part in Durkheim's formulation of the *conscience collective.* Wundt's output was enormous. As Boring once noted, in the almost seventy years of his productive life, Wundt wrote or revised 53,735 pages—nearly one word every two minutes day and night.[47] How much of this influenced Durkheim we do not know. What is certain, however, is that Durkheim was impressed by the rigor and scientific thoroughness that he witnessed in Wundt's famous psychological laboratory at Leipzig. The method and style of scientific work done there seemed exemplary to him and provided him with a model of how scientific research ought to be conducted in other fields of the social sciences. Here, he felt, was a perfect antidote to the spirit of dilettantism that had so appalled him in his years at the *Ecole Normale.*

A fuller account would have to discuss Durkheim's reading in the works of the German *Kathedersozialisten* (socialists of the chair), those social reformers who tried to persuade the government that it must recognize the central importance of the "social question" in modern industrial society. He was certainly familiar with the writings of their major figure, Gustav Schmoller, and with other writers in that tradition as well, but whether these men specifically influenced Durkheim in his role as an applied social scientist and reformer has not been established.

THE SOCIAL CONTEXT

THE GENERAL SCENE

The Third Republic was in its infancy and suffering from severe disorders at the time Durkheim grew into young manhood. France was slow in recovering from the wounds of the lost war with Germany and the trauma of the Paris Commune. Its constitution of 1875 was framed by monarchists who expected the Republic soon to give way to a return of the Bourbons. After the constitution was adopted, the Republic was plunged into a new crisis. The President of the Republic, Marshal Marie de MacMahon, tried to establish a strong presidential system of government largely independent of parliament and with a weak cabinet that could be recalled at will. In the course of the ensuing struggles, the President dissolved the Chamber of Deputies for the only time in the history of the Third Republic. His actions pitted the Church, the landowners, the upper bourgeoisie, and the forces of law and order against the Republican Left, which was mainly composed of the lower middle classes, the anticlericals among the educated, and a working class weakened by the bloodletting of the Commune. In 1879, the Republicans

47 Edwin G. Boring, "Wilhelm Wundt," in *International Encyclopedia of the Social Sciences.*

decisively defeated MacMahon after he had dissolved the Chamber, and thus put an end to his dictatorial ambitions.

Even after these turbulent years, when Durkheim was at the *Collège d'Epinal* and at the Parisian *Collège Louis-le-Grand,* the Republic was far from secure. The moderate Republican Left under Jules Grévy and his successors remained in control for the next two decades, but it was never able to summon enough energies for a truly innovating response to France's major social and economic problems. Called the Opportunist Republic because of its vacillations and lack of principles, the governments missed the chance of establishing the regime on secure foundations. But moved by the Church's opposition to the Republic, it proceeded energetically in one area at least, that of secular education. The more rabid anticlericals demanded the total suppression of all Church-controlled schools and the establishment of a state monopoly on education. The legislation that was adopted did not go quite that far, but it outlawed religious training in the public schools and substituted civic education. Catholic institutions of higher learning were no longer allowed to call themselves universities, and after a transitional period members of Catholic orders were denied the right to teach in public schools. The Chamber provided funds to build many new schools, especially for girls, and it made provisions for setting up vastly expanded facilities for the training of teachers urgently required by the new secular system.

The sharp confrontation between the clerical Right and the secular Left over the issue of education had hardly settled down when France was again shaken by the tragicomic Boulanger affair. In the elections of 1885, both the monarchist and Bonapartist Right and the radical Left made startling gains, and the Opportunist middle lost its previous majority. During the period of instability that followed, a previously unknown general, Georges Boulanger, suddenly rose in popularity. He had been made Minister of War as the candidate of the Left, which saw him as a protector of the Republic. Having gained widespread support as the public became increasingly dissatisfied with corruption in high places, he started to emulate both Napoleon the First and Napoleon the Third and made moves toward becoming a dictator. The moment was ideal for a coup d'état. But the General was tricked by the Minister of the Interior into believing that the government had evidence of his treasonable activities and that he would shortly be put up for trial. Boulanger panicked, fled to Belgium, and soon afterwards committed suicide at the grave of his mistress in Brussels. In retrospect, the whole episode had the flavor of a comic opera. Nevertheless, the Republic once again had a close call.

In the early nineties the political scene was somewhat more peaceful. Young men of Durkheim's generation, who had lived through a period of almost continual turmoil, may have felt that they could at long last settle down and devote themselves to their professional interests. Durkheim himself was now teaching at Bordeaux and working at his thesis. He had experienced social and political chaos during his most impressionable formative years and had been forced to forge a personal identity for himself; he had moved from orthodox Judaism to rationalist philosophy at a time when the public scene, far from giving him secure anchorage, was itself subject to rapid transformations.

After the Boulanger crisis, the moderate Opportunists tended to form temporary alliances with the Right, which was now somewhat tamed since Pope Leo XIII had enjoined the faithful to rally to the Republic and to give up their monarchist allegiances. This made for a greater degree of political stability. But the moderates had another reason for turning toward the Right, one that pointed to new crises to come. The labor movement slowly revived in the nineties and the moderates saw in this revival a new threat to established order. In 1893, the year the *Division of Labor* was published, a number of socialist deputies, among them Durkheim's friend Jean Jaurès, were for the first time elected to parliament.

Although the times were now more peaceful, the social order continued to be unstable. In 1892, the Panama Scandal broke. It was revealed that agents of the Panama Company, in an effort to mobilize new capital for a project that had been undertaken by one of France's national heroes, Ferdinand de Lesseps, had bribed enough politicians and journalists to have parliament approve the issuance of a lottery loan. Although the court procedure that dealt with this affair was almost a complete whitewash, the public's confidence in its political leaders was badly weakened. The provinces, in particular, began to look at Paris as the seat of iniquities and corruption. Moreover, since the two agents who had bribed most of the politicians involved happened to have been Jewish, anti-Semitic tendencies were given a new impetus.

A few years later, in 1896, the Dreyfus affair broke out, and the short breathing spell the Third Republic had enjoyed was over. Two years earlier, a French staff officer, Major Charles Esterhazy, started selling information to the German Embassy. In the search for the culprit, counterintelligence accused another staff officer, Captain Alfred Dreyfus, a Jew. They might have abandoned the accusation had not a professional anti-Semite, the journalist Edouard Drumond, learned of the affair and raised a public outcry. Dreyfus was court-martialed and sent to Devil's Island for life. Soon after, a new head of the counterintelligence, Colonel Picquart, reexamined the files and concluded that Dreyfus was innocent, but his superiors refused to reopen the case, and Picquart was exiled to Tunisia. In the meantime a few newspapers, notably Clemenceau's, had gotten hold of the case and proclaimed Dreyfus' innocence. Durkheim was among the first to sign a public appeal in Dreyfus' behalf.

By 1898 almost the entire educated elite of France was committted to one side or the other. The Dreyfus affair shook French society to its very foundations. It pitted the liberal anticlerical defenders of the Republic against the Church and the army, the left-wing intellectuals against the nationalists, the Sorbonne against the traditionalist judiciary, and the local school teacher against the resident priest. Finally the defenders of Dreyfus won their case, and the Republic survived. But the days of opportunism were now over. The polarization of political forces that the affair had brought in its wake led to a much more militantly anticlerical regime, manned in the main by the Radical party of Clemenceau and his successors. The renovated Republic, now often called the Radical Republic (or, because so often its leaders were former university teachers, the Republic of Professors), remained in power until World War I. But France continued to be torn politically, as well as ideologically, between the Right and the Left, between the spiritual heirs of the *ancien régime* and the inheritors of the tradition of the French Revolution.

"The Third Republic," the historian Gordon Wright has written, "was created by the aristocracy, administered by the upper bourgeoisie, operated by the lower bourgeoisie, and dominated by the peasantry."[48] In the early years of the Third Republic its political and administrative elite was drawn for the most part from the upper middle classes—men who had held the reins of power in the Orléanist regime of Louis Philippe, although many had later rallied to Napoleon III. But this directing *haute* and *grande bourgeoisie* was joined by the lesser bourgeoisie, which began to establish roots in the new institutional structure of the Third Republic. Now the *petite* and even the *très petite bourgeoisie* demanded its share of recognition and power. These "little Frenchmen"—shopkeepers, white-collar employees, school teachers, petty civil servants in both Paris and the provinces—tended to be anticlerical in their political orientation, positivist in their general philosophy, and egalitarian in their moral views. They had provided the basis for the assault on the privileged position of the Church, especially in the crucial area of education, during the Opportunist Republic, and even more pronouncedly during the years after the Dreyfus affair. This lesser bourgeoisie manned the ranks of the Radical movement. Its greatest strength was in local politics where radical school teachers and local Freemasons became ward heelers, town councillors, and mayors, as well as members of the electoral committees that chose candidates for parliament. Its intellectual and ideological armature, however, was mainly provided by the Sorbonne, where Durkheim had now become significant spokesman for the forces of political liberalism.

The changes in the social and political structure of France were accompanied by major changes in its economic affairs. While in 1870 a majority of Frenchmen made their living in agriculture, by 1914 the agricultural population had dropped to 44 percent. In 1870 only 23 percent of the population were industrial workers or artisans; by 1914 this figure rose to 39 percent. Although France still had many more small workshops and artisan enterprises around the turn of the century than England or Germany, modern industrial workers

[48] This section relies mainly on Gordon Wright's fine *France in Modern Times* (New York, Rand McNally, 1960). This particular quotation can be found on p. 354.

now far outnumbered craftsmen and artisans. Yet despite this, urban workers remained the truly forgotten men in the early period of the Third Republic. In 1884, trade unions were legalized and somewhat later a few modern measures of social legislation were passed. But in its social policies France still lagged behind all other industrial nations in Europe. The *petite bourgeoisie,* which together with the *grande* manned the positions of power in the state, was not much concerned with working-class problems. Understandably, there grew among the workers a syndicalist and antiparliamentary movement which stressed that the workers could only rely on their own strength if they wished to gain ascendancy in society. At the same time, a new socialist movement arose, but it was initially split among a variety of more or less reformist organizations, which sent deputies to parliament and played the parliamentary game. It was not until 1905 that the socialist movements united under the leadership of Jean Jaurès. Until then the Jaurèsian wing collaborated with the Radicals in the defense of the Republic and the movement led by Guesde adhered to a strict Marxist position of noncollaboration with bourgeois parties. Even after the socialist movement was formally unified, the working class until World War I was splintered among the collaborationists, the Marxists, and the fairly influential syndicalists. It therefore had much less of an impact on political affairs than it might otherwise have had. The Third Republic continued to be operated by the middle class, and despite pious proclamations to the contrary, it remained devoted to the furtherance of middle-class aims and interests.

The economic scene was for them a source of great satisfaction. France was apparently prospering under what came to be known as *la belle époque.* A relatively slack period from the seventies to the nineties was followed by a period of comparatively rapid growth that lasted till the World War. But rising production and trade figures only concealed that France was losing out to its major competitors on the markets of the world. Its failure to compete successfully with the new and more dynamic industrial nations may be explained, at least in part, by the lack of an aggressive entrepreneurial spirit. France's industry continued to be dominated by family firms, the heads of which were more concerned with handing over intact the family heritage to the next generation than taking a possible risk through aggressive expansion. While private enterprises continued to adhere to what the economic historian David Landes has called a "genteel pattern of entrepreneurship," the government, dominated by personnel who were not very knowledgeable or interested in economic affairs, was not moved to use governmental intervention as a spur to economic growth.

Economically and socially the *belle époque* of the Third Republic presented to those unaware of underlying dangers a picture of a stolid, solid, and unexciting regime. But it was otherwise in the world of the intellect. In the first two decades of the Third Republic, the intellectual life was dominated by the scientific and positivist spirit of two key representatives, Hippolyte Taine and Ernest Renan. Emile Littré, who had purified the Comtean heritage and shorn it of its fantastic trappings, was also a guiding spirit in the early years of the Republic. In literature, Emile Zola, a central figure in the Dreyfus affair and the dominant French novelist of the period, represented this positivist and scientific tradition. But the whole trend was challenged after the turn of the century by a new antiscientific and antirationalist school, whose fountainhead was the great philosopher, Henri Bergson. This prophet of the *élan vital,* the creative life force, attacked positivist thought and the determinism it brought in its wake, opening the way for a vitalistic and voluntaristic countertrend. In poetry, the symbolists Verlaine and Mallarmé, as well as their successors, rebelled against what they considered to be the desiccating influence of the spirit of science and advocated the cultivation of a new and refined private sensibility. In political thought, Georges Sorel preached the primacy of the deed over the ratiocination of the intellectuals, and the prominent novelist Maurice Barrès defended the claims of "integral nationalism" against those intellectuals who, he said, had lost contact with the life-giving soil of *la patrie*. At the turn of the century, the forces of science and rationalism seemed to be fighting a rear-guard battle in practically all fields of intellectual and artistic endeavor. Yet there was one exception, the educational system. Here the scientific spirit was solidly entrenched. Around 1900 the Sorbonne, where Durkheim had become a major figure, developed into the main redoubt from which the defenders of science and liberalism waged their war against the antiscientific reaction.

DURKHEIM'S BACKGROUND

Little is known about Durkheim's background or about his family, but information is available about the Jewish community in eastern France where Durkheim was born and raised. The Jews who lived in that part of the country belonged to the Ashkenazi branch of Judaism; they were much different from the Spanish and Portuguese Jews of the Sephardic branch, who had fled from religious persecution in the sixteenth century and had settled in southwestern France, especially in Bordeaux and Bayonne. The Ashkenazi of Alsace and Lorraine had drifted into the region from Germany since the sixteenth century; they spoke almost exclusively Yiddish and Hebrew and were almost totally ignorant of French even into the Revolutionary era. In contrast, the Sephardim, who originally spoke Spanish and Portuguese, had become fluent in the French language. What there was of Jewish writing in French on general subjects before the Revolution came almost exclusively from the Sephardim. Moreover, though both communities had separate communal authorities, the Sephardim never acquired civil jurisdiction over their members, limiting themselves to religious and charitable functions; the Ashkenazi on the other hand had their own courts of law and generally attempted to regulate their own affairs with only minimal interference by royal authority.[49]

Even before the emancipation acts of the Revolution gave Jews French citizenship, the Sephardim had moved a considerable way toward assimilation, whereas the Ashkenazi community was largely insulated from, and encapsulated within, the larger French society. Although the Revolution put an end to Jewish self-government, the differences between Sephardic and Ashkenazi communities persisted throughout the nineteenth century.

The Jews of eastern France had been emancipated for more than two generations at the time of Durkheim's youth, but they still maintained a cultural identity, which had long been shed by their Sephardic brethren. Although these eastern Jewish communities had begun to show many signs of breaking up in the middle of the century, they still had many of the characteristics of the central European Jewish world where internal affairs were largely under the sway of appointed elders (*parnassim*) or rabbis, and where "mechanical solidarity" had not yet fully given way to the "organic solidarity" of the surrounding secular society.

Durkheim, it will be recalled, was the son of a rabbi; his more remote ancestors had likewise been rabbis. His family must therefore have belonged to the pillars of the local Jewish community and must have had a particular stake in maintaining the communal patterns that insured them at least a high measure of communal prestige if not the powers that their forebears had once enjoyed. Through them Durkheim belonged to the elite of the community. His break with the Jewish tradition of his father consequently must have been a traumatic and decisive event in his life—a decision that went to the very roots of his personal and cultural identity. A Sephardic boy could have moved by almost imperceptible steps into the world of French secular culture; an Ashkenazi boy like Durkheim could not.

It has been said that in modern societies romantic love performs the vital function of emancipating sons from exclusive ties to their mothers by providing another object for their passionate attachment. A similar mechanism is likely to have been at play in Durkheim's development. His intense involvement with secular French society and with the *nation française* allowed him to cut his umbilical ties to the religious community he was so deeply involved in during his early formative years. French republican and secular society became for him a passionate object of love, replacing his attachment to the religious community of his native home. As he moved from the mechanical solidarity of the Jewish world of Epinal to the organic solidarity of the modern world of Paris, he experienced the resultant change as a true emancipation. Whereas many German theorists could never fully make their peace with

[49] On the condition of French Jewry before the Revolution cf. Arthur Hertzberg, *The French Enlightenment and the Jews* (New York, Columbia University Press, 1968).

modern society and continued to look back with nostalgia to the *Gemeinschaft* of the rural past, Durkheim was free of such conceits.

Durkheim's search for a new secular base for civic morality may be seen, in the Freudian sense, as being overdetermined. He responded to the public need for a basis of common beliefs and values in a largely secularized and partly anomic society, but he also seemed impelled to fashion a secular morality to replace the religious values with which he himself had been brought up.

The curiously abstract character of Durkheim's intense "religious" devotion to French society may also be explained in terms of his background. In most French patriotic writings there is evidence of an attachment to particular localities or regions, to particular historic or linguistic traditions. It is not so with Durkheim. One encounters in his writings a highly abstract and generalized attachment to *la patrie,* an intellectualized relation to his country that may have had its source in his origins. When this son of a rabbi came to Paris and began to develop into one of the guiding spirits of the Republic, he severed himself from any community or region. His loyalty went to the France of the emancipation, which for him was the prototype of *the* modern society. His attachment was not mediated through tradition and history but was direct and immediate.[50]

This is not to say that Durkheim ever repudiated his background. Most French Jews in his days were still torn, to use Hannah Arendt's telling phrase, between the roles of pariahs and parvenus;[51] Durkheim assumed neither of these. While he proudly assumed front rank among the intellectual elite of his nation, he never denied his origins. And when, in the last phase of his life, he turned to the analysis of the communal sources of religion, he put to creative uses the memory of the religious community in which he had once been so deeply involved.[52]

GATHERING DISCIPLES AND FINDING AN AUDIENCE

Durkheim must truly be considered one of the founders of modern sociology: he made it a legitimate academic enterprise. But this could only be done after the rough outlines of the field had been mapped out by the founding fathers—the men who were discussed in the previous chapters—Comte, Marx, and Spencer.

This distinction between the founding fathers and their modern successors

[50] An additional factor to be considered here is the hostility that persons born in Alsace and Lorraine often encountered in French nationalist circles who judged them to be too close to German culture. Durkheim's ardent patriotism may in part have been stimulated by an unconscious desire to disprove such accusations.

[51] Hannah Arendt, *The Origins of Totalitarianism,* new ed. (New York, Harcourt Brace Jovanovich, 1960), Chapter 3.

[52] Cf. Leon Apt, "Emile Durkheim and French Social Thought," paper read at the 1967 American Historical Association meeting in Toronto.

is derived from Robert K. Merton. The first, he writes, "initiated and defended the claim of sociology to intellectual legitimacy." Once the claim was heard, the true founders of modern sociology "pressed [this] claim to institutional legitimacy, by addressing themselves to those institutionalized status-judges of the intellect: the universities."[53] Comte and Spencer had spent much of their energies in convincing the public that the new science deserved a hearing among the educated. Their successors, though still continuing this struggle, faced the additional task of giving sociology an institutionalized stronghold within the confines of the academy.

The patterns differed somewhat in different countries, but in general, before the days of Durkheim, Simmel, or Weber, "sociology was variously regarded by the faculties as an illegitimate upstart, lacking warrant for a recognized place in the collegial family, or sometimes as an institutional competitor."[54] In an effort to break down this pattern of exclusion, the founders of modern sociology employed a number of stratagems that varied in detail yet all had a similar purpose: academic legitimacy. They were determined to show that sociology could claim an academic territory not yet preempted by other disciplines.

Simmel's effort to delimit the field by stressing the notion of a geometry of social interaction was one response to this need; Durkheim's polemical thrust against psychologistic interpretation of social behavior was another. In fact, a major part of Durkheim's work can be understood as a self-conscious effort to demonstrate to the general public, but above all to his university colleagues, that sociology dealt with a vitally important subject matter not previously considered by other disciplines, which should be recognized and accepted as the equal of older disciplines in the social sciences within the walls of academe.

Durkheim tried to make sociology legitimate not only through intellectual argument but through the tactic of organization. Although deeply convinced of the power of ideas, he was also aware that ideas needed an organizational correlative to prevail within the framework of a university, which serves the mind from behind a bulwark of well-organized and institutionally encrusted academic disciplines.

Soon after having published *Suicide,* and having noted that sociology, practically unknown ten years earlier, was now "in fashion," Durkheim conceived the idea of creating a journal of sociology around which he would gather the defenders of the new discipline. They could constitute a little band of zealots ready through their united efforts to take on those who still resisted its claims.

The group of sociologists Durkheim brought together in 1898, and who were to stay together and contribute to the *Année Sociologique* until the First

[53] Robert K. Merton, "Social Conflict over Styles of Sociological Work," *Transactions of the Fourth World Congress of Sociology,* III (1959), pp. 211–44. [54] *Ibid.*

World War, was probably the most brilliant ever gathered in the history of the discipline. Initially a loose grouping of collaborators, it soon developed into a closely knit school—so closely knit, in fact, that one of its members, Georges Davy, referred to it as *"une petite société sui generis, le clan de l'Année Sociologique."* The other two schools which have appeared so far in sociology included the Chicago School, created by Albion Small, and composed of such major figures as Robert Park, William I. Thomas, and Ellsworth Faris; it was much less unified in its general approach. The Polish school, founded by Florian Znaniecki, was much more restricted in its scope.

To stress the unity of the *Année Sociologique* and the school it helped found is not to suggest that Durkheim ruled it with an authoritarian hand. He was a *primus inter pares,* recognized by all as the most gifted among them and drawing considerable authority from this recognition. Durkheim did not attempt to impose a gray conformism among the collaborators of the *Année.* Nevertheless, this was not an eclectic assembly of papers, written from different theoretical points of departure or with different methodological premises, such as the modern reader finds in most scientific journals. It had a point of view, a purpose, and a mission. But its pages were open to a variety of collaborators who, although committed to its overall approach, differed in greater or lesser degree from the views of the founder. Moreover, it would be a mistake to see the *Année* as simply a mouthpiece through which Durkheim attempted to impose his personal views on the intellectual scene. Although he did perhaps not learn as much from his disciples as they learned from him, a reciprocity of influence, rather than a unilateral imposition of Durkheim's will, characterized the collaboration.[55]

The list of even the major collaborators whom Durkheim gathered around the *Année* is too long to reproduce here. It may suffice to say that French anthropology attained its world-wide reputation mainly through the efforts of such disciples of Durkheim as Henri Hubert, Marcel Mauss, and, although he differed from Durkheim in many particulars, Lucien Lévy-Bruhl. French economic sociology was almost single-handedly founded by François Simiand. The sociology of law owed much of its influence in French law schools to Henri Lévy-Bruhl, Georges Davy, and Paul Fauconnet. Célestin Bouglé, one-time co-editor of the *Année,* made significant contributions to general sociology as well as to the history of socialist doctrines. (It may be remarked in passing, to indicate lines of continuity, that the last two were both teachers of the present writer at the Sorbonne in the thirties.) These few names will indicate the quality of the extraordinary galaxy of men whom Durkheim succeeded in converting to his theoretical angle of vision.

While highly successful in attaching to himself brilliant younger scholars,

[55] Cf. Robert Bierstedt, *Emile Durkheim* (London, Weidenfeld and Nicholson, 1966), pp. 21–22, and Terry Clark, "The Structure and Functions of a Research Institute: the *Année Sociologique,*" *European Journal of Sociology,* IX (1968), pp. 72–91.

Durkheim was perhaps even more successful in using the medium of the *Année* as a vehicle to "infiltrate" sociological ideas and approaches into other, older fields of scholarship. Within a relatively short time, the Durkheimians managed to exert such a marked influence on French historiography, French social psychology, and French linguistics that these fields have never been the same since. The shock of recognition brought about by Durkheim and his followers among some of their most eminent colleagues in other disciplines helped transform them fundamentally. French history, for example, underwent a profound change as a result of the emphasis on social factors that characterizes the work of such eminent French historians as Henri Berr, Lucien Febvre, Marc Bloch, and, in our days, Ferdinand Braudel.

As has been noted earlier, each issue of the *Année* contained, in addition to the original contributions by Durkheim and others, a great number of critical reviews of books and articles in the social sciences that had appeared in the preceding year in France and abroad. The fifth volume, for example, contained no fewer than 477 such reviews covering general sociology, religious sociology, juridical and moral sociology, criminal sociology and moral statistics, economic sociology, and social morphology, as well as more than forty sub-categories of these fields. It is probably correct to say that these detailed critical reviews, written on a high level of competence and scholarship, were at least as responsible in welding together the group of the *Année* and in carrying its message as were the original contributions. They helped the collaborators to define their own enterprise through critical assessment of the work carried on elsewhere; they also brought the message of the Durkheimian approach to as yet unconvinced outsiders who, given the high quality of the reviews, could not help but listen to this new voice.

The *Année* stirred up an intellectual excitement in French academic circles that is difficult to recapture for the contemporary reader. It is hard to conceive, say, of American historians waiting anxiously for the appearance of the next issue of the *American Sociological Review* or the *American Journal of Sociology*. But contemporaries testified that each issue of the *Année* was indeed an intellectual event for historians or social psychologists, as well as for sociologists. Within a few years Durkheim had created in the *Année* and in the group of men who wrote for it a potent intellectual instrument in the good fight for sociology.

The *Année* was an extraordinary undertaking, and it probably could not have flourished had it not been for an extraordinary publisher, Félix Alcan. Alcan, like Durkheim, was a former student at the *Ecole Normale* and, like him, was imbued with an ardent love for the Republic. Consequently, his publishing program leaned heavily toward those intellectuals and academic men who were willing to make a contribution to republican civic reconstruction. More particularly, Alcan became the key publisher of the new scientific and democratic elite that began to fill the major chairs at the reconstructed

Sorbonne. He published not only Durkheim's *Année,* but also Xavier Léon's *Revue de Métaphysique et de Morale,* a journal devoted to the creation of a republican civic morality so near to Durkheim's heart and one in which he often published. All of Durkheim's major works, as well as those of Lucien Lévy-Bruhl or of social historians like Henri Berr, were published by Alcan. This publishing house became the "rallying ground of sociological neo-positivism," and Alcan used the prestige of his house and its credit "to spread among the public, by books and reviews, by recommendations, conversations, confidences and references, the ideas, methods and doctrines of the most advanced historians and philosophers.[56] Its history, which it is hoped will be written one day, will furnish many clues to an understanding of the rapid spreading of Durkheimian ideas under the Third Republic.

But there were still other reasons for the success of Durkheim's teachings. As his collaborators began to assume major academic positions at the Sorbonne and in provincial *lycées* and universities, as they took over key positions in the Ministry of Education as well as seats of power in primary and secondary school systems, the *Année* group permeated the entire educational establishment of the Third Republic. In this respect they were similar to the Fabians, whose ideas pervaded the British Civil Service.

PATTERNS OF INFLUENCE

It will be remembered that the building and strengthening of a public school system on both the primary and the secondary level had been the major accomplishment of the early period of the Third Republic. Later on, in the years immediately following the Dreyfus affair, the anticlerical ministries of Waldeck-Rousseau and Combes further weakened Catholic education by evicting most religious orders who had carried the main burden of teaching in Catholic schools. When Church and state were fully separated early in the twentieth century, the number of children in Catholic schools rapidly fell by more than a third on the primary level and by a quarter on the secondary level. This meant that the Republic faced a major task in the training of lay teachers to staff the newly opened public schools. It also had to elaborate very swiftly an ideology, a civic morality, which could take the place religious instruction had occupied in the Catholic schools.

[56] Hubert Bourgin, *De Jaurès à Léon Blum* (Paris, Fayard, 1938), pp. 236–37. This book is a most valuable source for an understanding of the intellectual and political milieu of Durkheim's time, despite the reactionary and anti-Semitic bias of its author. Bourgin had been a socialist in his youth and contributed to the *Année* in the fields of economic sociology and the history of socialist thought. We are indebted to him for some fine studies of, among others, Charles Fourier. During the First World War he became a superpatriot, and he moved to the extreme right in the interwar years. He ended up as a Nazi collaborator during the Second World War. Many of his pen portraits in the above book are drawn with hatred and venom. But he remained highly respectful of Durkheim and there is hence no reason to disregard his testimony when it comes to Durkheim and his school.

Durkheim took this as a major opportunity to apply his theories. It will be recalled that the man who was Durkheim's original patron—who had obtained for him a position at the University of Bordeaux and sponsored his trip to Germany to survey its system of philosophical and moral instruction—was the philosopher Louis Liard, who in 1884 had become Director of Higher Education at the Ministry of Public Education. Liard, an ardent Republican and a firm believer in the scientific study of social life, early recognized a kindred spirit in the young Durkheim. He saw that Durkheim was animated, as he was himself, by the belief that only a new social science could provide the basis for the moral reconstruction of the Third Republic. Liard, who throughout Durkheim's lifetime occupied key administrative positions in the French educational system, proved a faithful ally and supporter of Durkheim and his disciples. Henri Massis and Guillaume de Tarde, acute observers, but reactionary critics of the trends of the time, wrote in 1910 about Durkheim and Liard, who by then had become vice-rector of the University of Paris: "He made [Durkheim] a sort of overall prefect of studies. He [Liard] gave him all his confidence and had him appointed first to the Council of the University of Paris, and then to the Consultative Committee. This allowed Monsieur Durkheim to oversee all the appointments to positions in higher education. Charged with the dignity of the university, Durkheim is the regent of the Sorbonne, he is the all-powerful master."[57] This account exaggerates Durkheim's importance, of course, but as the French say in their fashion, as we in ours, *il n'y a pas de fume sans feu.* Although not the dictator he was pictured to be, under Liard, Durkheim had a powerful influence on the centrally run French secondary system of education.

On the primary level of education, Durkheim had an even greater impact. The Director of Primary Education, Paul Lapie, was a collaborator of the *Année,* whereas Liard was in sympathy with the group but never belonged to it. Lapie succeeded in introducing sociology in the *écoles normales* in which the future primary school teachers were being trained. It is no exaggeration to say that by 1914 Durkheimian doctrine had become the standard fare of courses in civic morality in primary schools.

The Durkheimian spirit of civic morality had conquered the primary schools, and both the Catholic Right and the Marxist Left felt threatened since they feared that their potential sources of recruitment might now dry up. All this helps us understand the feelings of the Catholic sociologist Jean Izoulet when he wrote: "The obligation to teach the sociology of Monsieur Durkheim in the two hundred *normal schools* of France is the most serious national peril which our country has known for a long time."[58] The brilliant

[57] Agathon, *L'Esprit de la nouvelle Sorbonne* (Paris, Mercure de France, 1911), p. 98. Agathon was a pen name used by Massis and de Tarde.

[58] Quoted in Célestin Bouglé, *Bilan de la sociologie francaise* (Paris, Alcan, 1935), p. 168.

young Marxist philosopher Paul Nizan had similar reactions when he wrote that

> it looks indeed as if the founder of French sociology had written the *Division of Labor* in order to allow obscure administrators to put together a course of instruction for primary teachers. The introduction of sociology into normal schools consecrated the administrative victory of official morality. . . . In the name of [Durkheim's] science, primary teachers teach children to respect *la patrie française,* to justify class collaboration, to accept everything, to commune in the cult of the flag and bourgeois democracy. . . . The success of Durkheim came precisely from the effects of the moral propaganda that he had been able to set up.[59]

As in primary and secondary instruction, Durkheim also exercised a powerful influence in the university itself. This was made possible because the whole university system was in the process of reorganization around the turn of the century. Although stripped of its medieval character during the Revolution, it only assumed eminence in the scholarly world under the Third Republic. In the 1880's and 1890's the separate faculties and the university as a whole were given legal status and provided for the first time with an independent budget. Only in 1896 were the united faculties allowed to assume the name of university.[60] The whole curriculum of the Sorbonne, especially the humanities and the social sciences that had been dominated by a sluggish and dilettantish style of teaching and research, was revamped at the turn of the century in a scientific spirit. Influenced in part by German models, history, under the impact of Charles Seignobos and Ernest Lavisse, and literary scholarship, under Gustave Lanson and others, were now taught according to the canons of scientific method. Between 1870 and 1895, the budget for higher education was increased threefold.[61]

The *Ecole Normale Supérieure* was also reorganized in 1904. It was shorn of much of its autonomy and all its students from then on had to take their courses at the Sorbonne. Moreover, the spirit of elegant superficiality from which Durkheim had suffered so much during his days, was definitely banished.

The new Sorbonne became the bulwark of liberalism and anticlericalism.

[59] Paul Nizan, *Les Chiens de garde* (Paris, Maspero, 1967), pp. 97–98. Cf. also pp. 144–50 where Nizan quotes a number of writers all testifying to the influence of Durkheim on the French school system. Cf. also Albert Thibaudet, *La République des professeurs* (Paris, Grasset, 1927), p. 222. [60] Pierre Leguay, *La Sorbonne* (Paris, Grasset, 1910), p. 12.

[61] Terry Clark, "Emile Durkheim and the Institutionalization of Sociology in the French University System," *European Journal of Sociology,* IX (1968), pp. 37–71. This paper, which I read only after this chapter was substantially completed, contains a wealth of detailed factual information and valuable bibliographical indications. Professor Clark is soon to publish a full-scale sociological history of French sociology, which contains a great deal of information on Durkheim and his school.

While the schools of law and medicine were attended mainly by sons of the politically conservative bourgeoisie who could afford the high cost of these studies, the Sorbonne and the *Ecole Normale,* which charged no tuition, attracted some of the *petite bourgeoisie*. Eight out of ten students from the *Ecole Normale* studied there on government fellowships. Normal schools for primary teachers were even more widely open to the sons of the lower strata. Teachers in the Third Republic who were trained in these schools were typically left of center in their political allegiances. It is understandable, therefore, that the Sorbonne, the *Ecole Normale Supérieure* and the normal schools were the mainstays of Dreyfusard agitation during the affair and that the schools of law and medicine remained for the most part in the anti-Dreyfusard camp.

During the years 1890 to 1914 the Sorbonne was the center of the intellectual defense of democratic and rationalist values, and many of its key professors, with Durkheim in the forefront, were the intellectual spokesmen for these liberal trends. Durkheim made the most of the opportunity. He sat in a number of administrative commissions and councils; he became the intermediary between top officials in the Ministry of Education and in the university bureaucracy; he placed a good number of his friends in strategic positions both in administration and in the educational system. He had a key hand in filling vacant chairs in the social sciences both at the Sorbonne and in the provinces.

Durkheim was deeply convinced that the social scientist had the duty, in addition to his strictly scientific work, to intervene on the public scene. "Nothing is so vain and sterile," he wrote, "as that scientific puritanism which, under the pretext that science is not fully established, counsels abstention and recommends to men that they stand by as indifferent witnesses, or at least resigned ones, at the march of events."[62] And he practiced what he preached. As a consequence, he was involved with men from various walks of life, all of whom, he hoped, might be of help in furthering the great work of moral reconstruction on which he was embarked. Far from limiting himself to an audience of colleagues, Durkheim endeavored to spread his message widely and as a result he developed a complicated set of associates and audiences. Among these were high officials in the Ministry of Education and at the university, through whom Durkheim hoped to spread his message into all the reaches of the French educational system. Though Durkheim published mainly in his *Année,* he also wrote some seventy-five articles in other magazines and journals in order to reach a broader audience.

In the pursuit of this task he was by no means averse to active participation in the social life of the capital, provided that this afforded him another occasion to work for his moral goals. He was not the austere and distant man who never seemed to have left his scholar's quarters—an image that has been conveyed by many of his commentators. He participated actively in the rounds

[62] Emile Durkheim, *Education and Sociology* (New York, The Free Press, 1956), p. 104.

of social life, meeting politicians, industrialists, journalists, even military men in various salons.[63] They afforded him another occasion to spread his ideas. Hubert Bourgin has left us a fine description of Durkheim as a guest in these salons:

> One found the master, in evening dress . . . and enhanced by a dignity respected by all, relaxed and friendly, at those great half-*mondain,* half-academic gatherings, at Gustave Lanson, at Henri Berr, above all at the house of Xavier Léon, the director of the *Revue de Métaphysique et de Morale.* Léon assembled in his home everyone from the Sorbonne, the *Collège de France,* among the leaders of philosophy, sociology, history, mathematics, the natural sciences, who accepted an invitation. This was always flattering since it had the value of an attestation. His was a place for get-togethers, negotiations and the like, the object of which was almost always of a scientific or university nature. Sometimes conversations dealt more with spiritual matters, sometimes with temporal and political affairs. Politics was represented by great university figures who had become politicians, and by others who wished to become politicians. . . . In the great salon one would meet Henri Poincaré . . . Painlevé, Emile Borel, Jean Perrin, Gustave Lanson, Lévy-Bruhl, and generation after generation of professors, mostly philosophers, in the beginning of their career. . . . In this crowd, Durkheim . . . passed from one to the other, stopped to speak, said a few words, and, without affectation, continued his mission.[64]

Durkheim seems to have been acutely aware that his active participation in the university and in the educational affairs of the Third Republic brought with it the danger that his sociological work would be overshadowed by political commitments. Although he was known as a man of the Left, he refused throughout his life to commit himself to a particular political party. Some of the collaborators of the *Année* became militants in the Socialist or in the Radical Socialist Party. Durkheim himself never adhered to either, although he had close ties with both.

However, Durkheim and some of his sociologist friends became somewhat involved in an intellectual movement, *solidarism,* which was first started around the turn of the century by Radical Socialists, republicans of the Left who were neither particularly radical nor particularly socialist. Some of them, urgently in quest of an ideology to distinguish them from the Socialists and from the more moderate republicans, embraced the so-called solidarist philosophy that had been founded somewhat earlier by the philosopher Alfred Fouillé. Solidarism was a kind of welfare-state philosophy in French garb, a vague and elastic doctrine that stressed the need for solidarity among all the citizens of the Republic; it had a social welfare approach rather similar to that practiced at the time by the Lloyd George liberals in England and taught by the

[63] Leguay, *op. cit.,* p. 175. [64] Bourgin, *op. cit.,* pp. 223–24.

"socialists of the chair" in Germany. Quite popular for a few years, solidarism was especially listened to by teachers from some 100,000 elementary schools, as well as around the Sorbonne. The main lines of the doctrine were summarized in a speech by its major propagandist, the Radical Socialist politician Léon Bourgeois, entitled, "The politics of those who think about other men."[65]

Solidarité was launched among intellectuals by means of a series of conferences. The first of these was the *Congrès International de l'Education Sociale* held in Paris under government auspices upon the occasion of the *Exposition Universelle* in 1900. Among the main speakers were leading Radical Socialist politicians, as well as such eminent spokesmen of the new Sorbonne as the historian Charles Seignobos, the republican educator Ferdinand Buisson, and the economist Charles Gide. Emile Durkheim was among the featured speakers. The work of the Congress was followed up by a series of lectures by Gide, Bourgeois, and Buisson among others, under the sponsorship of the newly founded and solidarist-inspired *Ecole des Hautes Etudes Sociales.* The president of the school was Durkheim's old teacher Emile Boutroux, and its social science department was staffed by leading republican historians and philosophers including Georges Weill and Gabriel Séailles. Emile Durkheim himself, as well as such Durkheimians as Célestin Bouglé, lectured there regularly.[66]

Durkheim was in sympathy with much of the solidarist doctrine, but he never wished to tie himself directly to its ideology. This was so not only because he did not want to compromise his sociology through a direct political engagement, but because he was drawn to Jaurèsian socialism as much as he was to the many Radical Socialist circles in which the solidarist doctrine found its major exponents. Jaurès was his close personal friend since they had been students together. Moreover, Durkheim, who had been instrumental in moving Jaurès away from his initial allegiance to liberal Radicalism, often expressed his sympathy for the largely non-Marxist socialism of Jaurès. However, repelled by the class character of French socialism and by its stress on class conflict, he never became a socialist himself but "stayed all his life in a *juste milieu;* he sympathized . . . with the socialists, with Jaurès, with socialism. He never gave himself to it."[67] Carefully poised between Radical Socialist solidarism and the Jaurèsian wing of the Socialists, Durkheim adhered to neither while keeping excellent relations with both. He endeavored to recruit as many of their adherents as he could to the sociological view of things and to his continued emphasis on the need for a new science of morality as the basis of civic unity.

[65] Quoted in *Republican Ideas,* p. 170. This book has an excellent chapter on Solidarism. See also Book V, Chapter 3 of Charles Gide and Charles Rist, *A History of Economic Doctrines* (Boston and New York, Heath, n.d.).

[66] Scott, *op. cit.,* p. 181, and Leguay, *op. cit.,* pp. 174–75.

[67] Marcel Mauss, "Introduction" to Emile Durkheim, *Socialism and Saint-Simon,* ed. by Alvin Gouldner (Yellow Springs, Ohio, Antioch Press, 1958).

IN SUMMARY

Durkheim was a man of character, like the men described by Ralph Waldo Emerson, "who are the conscience of the society to which they belong." In contrast to those who, in Emerson's words, "consider life as it is reflected in opinions, events, and circumstances," Durkheim attempted to mold events in order to put his cherished principles into practice.

Throughout his life Durkheim was passionately engaged in the moral issues of his time; he saw it as his life task to contribute to the moral regeneration of the French nation to which he was so deeply attached. But he refused to take short cuts in reaching his goals. He imposed upon himself a self-denying ordinance when it came to immediate political activity. According to his austere code of ethics, a social scientist could claim the mandate to intervene in the affairs of society only when his scientific investigation had brought results that warranted public trust. He wanted to build a social science that could serve as the foundation for public action, but, except in the sphere of education, he was not convinced that investigation had already progressed far enough to apply sociological findings in detailed legislation.

However, he made a number of proposals for reforms, among them, the gradual abolition of the right of inheritance as a means for widening the channels of opportunity; the correction of what he termed "abnormal" aspects of the division of labor; and the reconstruction of professional associations as intermediaries between the individual and his society. But in all these instances he put forward what he meant as tentative suggestions rather than definite "scientific" conclusions in the grand manner of a Comte or a Spencer or a Marx.

In Durkheim's case, just as in that of Marx, it is necessary to separate analytically those elements in his work that are value-laden and ideological from those that are not. Even those who remain cool to many of his moral passions have been permanently enriched by his scientific mode of analysis. Durkheim's rage for order and unity in the body social may have led to a conservative bias in some of his writings and to an attendant disregard for the creative functions of conflict. No doubt the fact that Durkheim was so deeply entrenched in the academic establishment and was so passionately bound to the established ideas of the Third Republic, while struggling against reactionary trends, made it virtually impossible for him to transcend, even in theory, the limits of the contemporary reality. His allegiance to the existing state of affairs may have prevented him from being fully attuned to the forces of novelty that were slowly sprouting.[68]

[68] For a detailed critical discussion of Durkheim's conservative bias, see my "Durkheim's Conservatism" in my *Continuities in the Study of Social Conflict* (New York, The Free Press, 1967).

Despite these limitations, Durkheim's work was that of a master. By providing the essential principles of structural and functional analysis in sociology, by furnishing a highly pertinent critique of psychologistic methods in the study of society, by introducing such key concepts as anomie, social integration, and organic solidarity, Durkheim made a contribution to modern sociology that can be compared only to that of his great German contemporary, Max Weber. Even when the objects of his moral passion have faded, the scientific work that grew out of his concerns survives and produces an echo in the work of many sociologists who may feel impelled to follow a quite different normative path.

The achievements of sons are held to be a tribute to their fathers. Emile Durkheim, the man whose approach stimulated Maurice Halbwachs to write his pathbreaking work on *The Social Framework of Memory,* whose method is at the root of Marcel Granet's work on *La Pensée chinoise,* whose work inspired a renaissance in the study of comparative religion associated with the names of Jane Harrison and Francis Cornford, and whose influence in our day has been so powerful on the new anthropology of Claude Lévi-Strauss and the comparative mythology of Georges Dumézil, has been a most successful father of ideas in France and in England.[69] In the United States, his ideas, filtered through the work of Talcott Parsons and Robert K. Merton, have come to be the common fare in the social sciences. He is, if not the father, then the grandfather of us all.

69 For a general survey of the work and influence of Durkheim's school, cf. Célestin Bouglé, *op. cit.*

Georg Simmel

1858-1918

THE WORK

Simmel's approach to sociology can best be understood as a self-conscious attempt to reject the organicist theories of Comte and Spencer, as well as the historical description of unique events that was cherished in his native Germany. He advanced, instead, the conception that society consists of a web of patterned interactions, and that it is the task of sociology to study the forms of these interactions as they occur and reoccur in diverse historical periods and cultural settings.

When Simmel turned his attention to sociology, the field was most often characterized by the organicist approach so prominent in the works of Comte in France, of Spencer in England, and of Schäffle in Germany. This view stressed the fundamental continuity between nature and society. Social process, it will be recalled, was conceived as qualitatively similar to, although more complex than, biological process. Life was seen as a great chain of being, stretching from the simplest natural phenomenon to the most highly differentiated social organism. For this reason, although the methods developed in the natural sciences had to be adapted to the particular tasks of the social sciences, such methods were considered essentially similar to those appropriate to the study of man in society. Sociology was regarded as the master science through which one could discover the laws governing all social developments.

The organicist view of social life was vigorously opposed in the tradition of German scholarship as represented in the school of idealistic philosophy. The German tradition viewed *Naturwissenschaft* (natural science) and *Geisteswissenschaft* (moral or human science) as qualitatively different. In this tradition, natural laws would have no place in the study of human culture, which represented the realm of freedom. The method considered appropriate for the study of human phenomena was *idiographic,* that is, concerned with unique events, rather than *nomothetic,* the method concerned with establishing general laws. It was believed that the student of human affairs could only describe and record the unique events of human history and that any attempt to establish regularities in the sphere of human culture would collapse because of the autonomy of the human spirit. *Natur* and *Kultur* were essentially different realms of being.

Moreover, the proponents of the German tradition argued, sociology had no real object of study: the term *society* was but a rough label, convenient for certain purposes but devoid of substance or reality. They asserted that there is no society outside or in addition to the individuals who compose it. Once these individuals and their historically located actions are investigated, nothing remains by way of subject matter for a science of society. Human freedom, the uniqueness and irreversibility of historical events, the fundamental disjunction between *Natur* and *Geist* (nature and spirit), all combined to make attempts at founding a science of sociology a quixotic—even a scandalous—enterprise. Far from being queen of the sciences, sociology was not a science at all.

Simmel rejected both the organicist and the idealist schools. He did not see society as a thing or an organism in the manner of Comte or Spencer, nor merely as a convenient label for something that did not have "real" existence. In his view, society consists of an intricate web of multiple relations between individuals who are in constant interaction with one another: "*Society* is merely the name for a number of individuals, connected by interaction."[1] The larger superindividual structures—the state, the clan, the family, the city, or the trade union—are only crystallizations of this interaction, even though they may attain autonomy and permanency and confront the individual as if they were alien powers. The major field of study for the student of society is, therefore, *sociation,* that is, the particular patterns and forms in which men associate and interact with one another.

Simmel argued that the grandiose claims of those who wish to make sociology the master science of everything human are self-defeating. Nothing can be gained by throwing together all phenomena heretofore studied by jurisprudence and philology, by political science and psychology, and labeling them *sociology. Qui trop embrasse, mal étreint.* By trying to embrace all phenomena that are in any way connected with human life one pursues a will-o'-the-wisp. There can be no such totalistic social science, just as there is no "total" science of all matter. Science must study *dimensions or aspects of phenomena rather than global totalities.* The legitimate subject matter of sociology lies in the description and analysis of particular forms of human interaction and their crystallization in group characteristics: "Sociology asks what happens to men and by what rules they behave, not insofar as they unfold their understandable individual existences in their totalities, but insofar as they form groups and are determined by their group existence because of interaction."[2] Although all human behavior is behavior of individuals, much of it can be explained in terms of the individual's group affiliation, as well as the constraints imposed upon him by particular forms of interaction.

Although Simmel considered the larger institutionalized structures a legitimate field of sociological inquiry, he preferred to restrict most of his work

[1] *The Sociology of Georg Simmel,* ed. and trans. by Kurt H. Wolff (New York, The Free Press, 1950), p. 10. [2] *Ibid.,* p. 11.

to an investigation of what he called "interactions among the atoms of society."[3] He limited his concern, in the main, to those fundamental patterns of interaction among individuals that underlie the larger social formations (what is today described as "microsociology"). The method he advocated and practiced was to focus attention upon the perennial and limited number of forms such interaction might take.

FORMAL SOCIOLOGY

Sociology, as conceived by Simmel, did not pretend to usurp the subject matter of economics, ethics, psychology, or historiography; rather, it concentrated on the forms of interaction that underlie political, economic, religious, and sexual behavior. In Simmel's perspective a host of otherwise distinct human phenomena might be properly understood by reference to the same formal concept. To be sure, the student of warfare and the student of marriage investigate qualitatively different subject matters, yet the sociologist can discern essentially similar interactive forms in martial conflict and in marital conflict. Although there is little similarity between the behavior displayed at the court of Louis XIV and that displayed in the main offices of an American corporation, a study of the forms of subordination and superordination in each will reveal underlying patterns common to both. On a concrete and descriptive level, there would seem little connection between the early psychoanalytic movement in Vienna and the early Communist movement, but attention to typical forms of interaction among the members of these groups reveals that both are importantly shaped by the fact that they have the structural features of the sect. Sectarians are characterized in their conduct by the belief that they share an esoteric knowledge with their fellow sectarians and are hence removed from the world of the vulgar. This leads to intense and exclusive involvements of the sectarians with one another and concomitant withdrawal from "outside" affairs.

Simmel's insistence on the forms of social interaction as the domain peculiar to sociological inquiry was his decisive response to those historians and other representatives of the humanities who denied that a science of society could ever come to grips with the novelty, the irreversibility, and the uniqueness of historical phenomena. Simmel agreed that particular historical events are unique: the murder of Caesar, the accession of Henry VIII, the defeat of Napoleon at Waterloo are all events located at a particular moment in time and having a nonrecurrent significance. Yet, if one looks at history through the peculiar lenses of the sociologist, one need not concern himself with the uniqueness of these events but, rather, with their underlying uniformities. The sociologist does not contribute to knowledge about the individual actions of a

[3] *Ibid.*, p. 10.

King John, or a King Louis, or a King Henry, but he can illuminate the ways in which all of them were constrained in their actions by the institution of kingship. The sociologist is concerned with *King* John, not with King *John.* On a more abstract level, he may not even be concerned with the institution of kingship, but rather with the processes of conflict and cooperation, of subordination and superordination, of centralization and decentralization, which constitute the building blocks for the larger institutional structure. In this way, Simmel wanted to develop a geometry of social life: "Geometric abstraction investigates only the spatial forms of bodies, although empirically these forms are given merely as the forms of some material content. Similarly, if society is conceived as interaction among individuals, the description of the forms of this interaction is the task of the science of society in its strictest and most essential sense."[4]

Simmel's insistence on abstracting from concrete content and concentrating on the forms of social life has led to the labeling of his approach as *formal* sociology. However, his distinction between the form and the content of social phenomena is not always as clear as we should like. He gave variant definitions of these concepts, and his treatment of particular topics reveals some obvious inconsistencies. The essence of his thought, nevertheless, is clear. Formal sociology isolates form from the heterogeneity of content of human sociation. It attempts to show that however diverse the *interests* and *purposes* that give rise to specific associations among men, the social *forms* of interaction in which these interests and purposes are realized may be identical. For example, both war and profit-making involve cooperation. Inversely, identical interests and purposes may crystallize into different forms. Economic interests may be realized in competition as well as in planned cooperation, and aggressive drives may be satisfied in various forms of conflict from gang warfare to legal battles.

In formal analysis, certain features of concrete phenomena, which are not readily observable unless such a perspective is applied to them, are extracted from reality. Once this has been successfully accomplished, it becomes possible to compare phenomena that may be radically different in concrete content yet essentially similar in structural arrangement. For example, leader-follower relations may be seen to be structurally the same both in deviant juvenile gangs and in conformist scout troops. On this point Simmel is often misunderstood: he was not asserting that forms have a separate and distinct existence, but that they inhere in content and can have no independent reality. Simmel's was far from a Platonic view of essences. He stressed that concrete phenomena could be studied from a variety of perspectives and that analysis of the limited number of forms which could be extracted from the bewildering multiplicity of

[4] *Ibid.*, pp. 21–22.

social contents might contribute insights into social life denied those who limit themselves to descriptions of the concrete.

The term *form* was perhaps not a very happy choice since it is freighted with a great deal of philosophical ballast, some of it of a rather dubious nature. It may have frightened away certain modern sociologists intent on exorcising any metaphysical ghosts that might interfere with the building of a scientific sociology. Had Simmel used the term *social structure*—which, in a sense, is quite close to his use of *form*—he would have probably encountered less resistance. Such modern sociological terms as *status, role, norms,* and *expectations* as elements of social structure are close to the formal conceptualizations that Simmel employed.

Furthermore, much of the building of modern sociological theory proceeds precisely with the help of the perspective that Simmel has advocated. For example, in a reanalysis of some of the data of *The American Soldier,*[5] Merton and Rossi, when explaining the behavior of "green" troops and their relationships with seasoned troops in different structural contexts, use this [illegible]erspective to account more generally for social situations in which newcomers [illegible]volved in interaction with oldtimers. By [illegible]tracting from the concrete
[illegible] life, they expl[illegible] of the behavior of new-
[illegible] terms of their relation to
[illegible]ltimer relationship, or the
[illegible] as a particular form that
[illegible]ne various concrete social
[illegible]bstraction from concrete
[illegible]possible.

[illegible] never pure: every social
[illegible]s. Cooperation and con-
[illegible]d distance all may be
[illegible] structure. In concrete
[illegible]f forms leads to their
[illegible]an ever be realized in
[illegible] there is no "pure" co-
[illegible]relationships never to
[illegible]zations about aspects
[illegible] as to bring out con-
[illegible]t factually actualized
[illegible]baroque" style, even

[illegible] Rossi, "Contributions to the Theory of Reference Group Be-[illegible] Merton, *Social Theory and Social Structure* (New York, The Free Press, 1957), pp. 225–80.

[6] F. H. Tenbruck, "Formal Sociology," in Lewis A. Coser, ed., *Georg Simmel* (Englewood Cliffs, New Jersey, Prentice-Hall, 1965), p. 84.

though no known work of architecture exhibits all the elements of either style in all their purity; so too the sociologist may construct a "pure" form of social conflict even though no empirically known process fully embodies it. Just as Weber's ideal-type may be used as a measuring rod to help calculate the distance between a concrete phenomenon and the type, a Simmelian form—say, the typical combination of nearness and distance that marks the relation of "the stranger" from the surrounding world—may help gauge the degree of "strangerness" inherent in the specific historical circumstances of, for example, the ghetto Jews or other pariah peoples.

SOCIAL TYPES

Simmel constructed a gallery of social types to complement his inventory of social forms. Along with "the stranger," he describes in great phenomenological detail such diverse types as "the mediator," "the poor," "the adventurer," "the man in the middle," and "the renegade." Simmel conceives of each particular social type as being cast by the specifiable reactions and expectations of others. The type becomes what he is through his relations with others who assign him a particular position and expect him to behave in specific ways. His characteristics are seen as attributes of the social structure.

For example, "the stranger," in Simmel's terminology, is not just a wanderer "who comes today and goes tomorrow," having no specific structural position. On the contrary, he is a "person who comes today and stays tomorrow. . . . He is fixed within a particular spatial group . . . but his position . . . is determined . . . by the fact that he does not belong to it from the beginning," and that he may leave again.[7] The stranger is "an element of the group itself" while not being fully part of it. He therefore is assigned a role that no other members of the group can play. By virtue of his partial involvement in group affairs he can attain an objectivity that other members cannot reach. "He is not radically committed to the unique ingredients and peculiar tendencies of the group, and therefore approaches them with the specific attitude of 'objectivity.'" Moreover, being distant and near at the same time, the stranger will often be called on as a confidant. Confidences that must be withheld from more closely related persons can be given to him just because with him they are not likely to have consequences. In similar ways, the stranger may be a better judge between conflicting parties than full members of the group since he is not tied to either of the contenders. Not being "bound by commitments which could prejudice his perception, understanding, and evaluation of the given," he is the ideal intermediary in the traffic of goods as well as in the traffic of emotions.

[7] "The Stranger" in *The Sociology of Georg Simmel,* pp. 402–08.

Similarly, the poor[8] as a social type emerge only when society recognizes poverty as a special status and assigns specific persons requiring assistance to that category. In Simmel's view,

> the fact that someone is poor does not mean that he belongs to the specific social category of the 'poor.' . . . It is only from the moment that [the poor] are assisted . . . that they become part of a group characterized by poverty. This group does not remain united by interaction among its members, but by the collective attitude which society as a whole adopts toward it. . . . Poverty cannot be defined in itself as a quantitative state, but only in terms of the social reaction resulting from a specific situation. . . . Poverty is a unique sociological phenomenon: a number of individuals who, out of a purely individual fate, occupy a specific organic position within the whole; but this position is not determined by this fate and condition, but rather by the fact that others . . . attempt to correct this condition.

Once the poor accept assistance, they are removed from the preconditions of their previous status, they are declassified, and their private trouble now becomes a public issue. The poor come to be viewed not by what they do—the criteria ordinarily used in social categorization—but by virtue of what is done to them. Society creates the social type of the poor and assigns them a peculiar status that is marked only by negative attributes, by what the status-holders do *not* have.

The stranger and the poor, as well as Simmel's other types, are assigned their position by virtue of specific interactive relations. They are societal creations and must act out their assigned roles. They resemble the character in one of Randall Jarrell's academic novels who "had never been what intellectuals consider an intellectual but other people had thought him one, and he had had to suffer the consequences of their mistake."[9]

THE DIALECTICAL METHOD IN SIMMEL'S SOCIOLOGY

Simmel's sociology is always informed by a dialectical approach, bringing out the dynamic interconnectedness and the conflicts between the social units he analyzes. Throughout his work he stresses both the connections and the tensions between the individual and society. He sees individuals as products of society, as links in the social process; yet "the total content of life, even though it may be fully accounted for in terms of social antecedents and interactions, must yet be looked at at the same time under the aspect of singularity,

[8] "The Poor" trans. by Claire Jacobson in *Social Problems,* XIII, 2 (Fall, 1965), pp. 118–39. Cf. also my "The Sociology of Poverty" immediately following.

[9] Randell Jarrell, *Pictures from an Institution* (New York, Alfred A. Knopf, 1954), p. 110.

as oriented toward the experience of the individual."[10] According to Simmel, the socialized individual always remains in a dual relation with society: he is incorporated within it and yet stands against it. The individual is, at the same time, within society and outside it; he exists for society as well as for himself: "[Social man] is not partially social and partially individual; rather, his existence is shaped by a fundamental unity, which cannot be accounted for in any other way than through the synthesis or coincidence of two logically contradictory determinations: man is both social link and being for himself, both product of society and life from an autonomous center."[11] The individual is determined at the same time as he is determining; he is acted upon at the same time as he is self-actuating.

The insistence on the pervasive dialectic of the relation between individual and society informs all of Simmel's sociological thought. Incorporation into the network of social relations is the inevitable fate of human life, but it is also an obstacle to self-actualization; society allows, and also impedes, the emergence of individuality and autonomy. The forms of social life impress themselves upon each individual and allow him to become specifically human. At the same time, they imprison and stultify the human personality by repressing the free play of spontaneity. Only in and through institutional forms can man attain freedom, yet his freedom is forever endangered by these very institutional forms.

To Simmel, sociation always involves harmony *and* conflict, attraction *and* repulsion, love *and* hatred. He saw human relations as characterized by ambivalence; precisely those who are connected in intimate relations are likely to harbor for one another not only positive but also negative sentiments. Erotic relations, for example, "strike us as woven together of love and respect, or disrespect . . . of love and an urge to dominate or the need for dependence. . . . What the observer or the participant himself thus divides into two intermingling trends may in reality be only one."[12]

An entirely harmonious group, Simmel argued, could not exist empirically. It would not partake of any kind of life process; it would be incapable of change and development. Moreover, Simmel stressed, it is naive to view as negative those forces that result in conflict and as positive those that make for consensus. Without, for example, "safety valves" allowing participants "to blow off steam," many social relations could not endure. Sociation is always the result of both categories of interaction; both are positive ingredients, structuring all relationships and giving them enduring form.

Simmel differentiated sharply between social appearances and social realities. Although a given conflictive relationship might have been considered

[10] Georg Simmel, *Soziologie* (Leipzig, Duncker und Humblot, 1908), p. 40. [11] *Ibid.*, p. 41.

[12] Georg Simmel, *Conflict and the Web of Group Affiliations*, translated by Kurt H. Wolff and Reinhard Bendix (New York, The Free Press, 1956), pp. 22–23.

wholly negative by participants or by outside observers, it nevertheless showed, upon analysis, to have latent positive aspects. Only a withdrawal from a relationship could be considered wholly negative; a conflictive relationship, though possibly painful for one or more participants, ties them to the social fabric through mutual involvement even in the face of dissensus. It is essential to recognize, Simmel argued, that social conflict necessarily involves reciprocal action and therefore is based on reciprocity rather than unilateral imposition. Conflict can serve as an outlet for negative attitudes and feelings, making further relationships possible; it can also lead to a strengthening of the position of one or more parties to the relationship, thereby increasing the individual's dignity and self-esteem. Because conflict can strengthen existing bonds or establish new ones, it can be considered a creative, rather than a destructive, force.

Simmel never dreamed of a frictionless social universe, of a society from which clashes and contentions among individuals and groups would be forever banned. For him, conflict is the very essence of social life, an ineradicable component of social living. The good society is not conflict-free; it is, on the contrary, "sewn together" by a variety of crisscrossing conflicts among its component parts.[13] Peace and feud, conflict and order are correlative. Both the cementing and the breaking of custom constitute part of the eternal dialectic of social life. It would therefore be a mistake to distinguish a sociology of order from one of disorder, a model of harmony from one of conflict. These are not distinct realities but only differing formal aspects of one reality.

Throughout his work Simmel considered the individual's social actions not in themselves but in relation to actions of other individuals and to particular structures or processes. In his famous chapter on "Superordination and Subordination," he shows that domination does not lie in the unilateral imposition of the superordinate's will upon the subordinate but that it involves reciprocal action. What appears to be the exercise of absolute power by some and the acquiescence by others is deceptive. Power "conceals an interaction, an exchange . . . which transforms the pure one-sidedness of superordination and subordination into a *sociological* form."[14] Thus, the superordinate's action cannot be understood without reference to the subordinate, and vice versa. The action of one can only be analyzed by reference to the action of others, since the two are part of a system of interaction that constrains both. Attempts at analyzing social action without such reference would have been rejected by Simmel as examples of what he called *the fallacy of separateness.*

Moreover, he does not rest his case after demonstrating that, contrary to first appearance, domination is a form of interaction. He proceeds to show in

[13] Cf. Lewis A. Coser, *The Functions of Social Conflict* (New York, The Free Press, 1956).
[14] *The Sociology of Georg Simmel,* p. 186.

considerable detail the particular ways in which various types of group structure are associated with different forms of subordination and superordination—distinguishing, for example, between levelling and gradation. If a number of individuals are equally subject to one individual, he argued, they are themselves equal. Such levelling, or "negative democratization" to use Karl Mannheim's term, favors and is favored by despotic rulers. Despots try to level their subjects and, conversely, highly developed levelling easily leads to despotism. On the other hand, strong intermediate gradations among a ruler's subjects tend to cushion his impact and weaken his hold over them. Although intermediate powers may increase inequalities in the subject population, they shield the individual from the direct powers of the ruler. A pyramidal form of social gradation, whether it develops under the plan of the ruler or results from the usurpation of some of his power by subordinates, gives every one of its elements a position both lower and higher than the next rungs in the hierarchy. In this way, each level—except the very highest and the very lowest—is subordinate to the authorities above and, at the same time, is superordinate to the rungs beneath. Dependence on some persons is compensated by authority over others.

THE SIGNIFICANCE OF NUMBERS FOR SOCIAL LIFE

Simmel's emphasis on the structural determinants of social action is perhaps best exemplified in his seminal essay, "Quantitative Aspects of the Group."[15] Here he comes nearest to realizing his goal of writing a grammar of social life by considering one of the most abstract characteristics of a group: the mere number of its participants. He examines forms of group process and structural arrangement insofar as these derive from sheer quantitative relationships.

A dyadic relationship differs qualitatively from all other types of groups in that each of the two participants is confronted by only one other and not by a collectivity. Because this type of group depends only on two participants, the withdrawal of one would destroy the whole: "A dyad depends on each of its two elements alone—in its death though not in its life: for its life it needs *both,* but for its death, only one."[16]

Hence the dyad does not attain that superpersonal life which, in all other groups, creates among its members a sense of constraint. Yet the very lack of superpersonal structure also entails intense absorption of the participants in their dyadic relationship. The dependence of the whole on each partner is obvious; in all other groups duties and responsibilities can be delegated, but not in the dyad, where each participant is immediately and directly responsible for any collective action. Because each partner in the dyad deals with only one

[15] *Ibid.,* pp. 87–177. [16] *Ibid.,* p. 124.

other individual, who forms a unit with him, neither of the two can deny responsibility by shifting it to the group; neither can hold the group responsible for what he has done or failed to do.

When a dyad is transformed into a triad, the apparently insignificant fact that one member has been added actually brings about a major qualitative change. In the triad, as in all associations involving more than two persons, the individual participant is confronted with the possibility of being outvoted by a majority.

The triad is the simplest structure in which the group as a whole can achieve domination over its component members; it provides a social framework that allows the constraining of individual participants for collective purposes. The dyad relies on immediate reciprocity, but the triad can impose its will upon one member through the formation of a coalition between the two others. Thus, the triad exhibits in its simplest form the sociological drama that informs all social life: the dialectic of freedom and constraint, of autonomy and heteronomy.

When a third member enters a dyadic group, various processes become possible where previously they could not take place. Simmel singled out three such processes, although others have since been identified.[17] A third member may play the role of mediator vis-à-vis the other two, helping, through his own impartiality, to moderate passions that threaten to tear the group apart. He may, alternately, act as a *tertius gaudens* (the third who rejoices), seeking to turn to his own advantage a disagreement between the other two. Finally, through a strategy of *divide et impera* (divide and rule), he may intentionally create conflicts between the other two in order to attain a dominant position or other gains.

This brief outline of three types of strategy open to the third participant can hardly exhaust the richness of Simmel's thought in this analysis. He offers a great variety of examples, deliberately comparing intimate human involvements, such as the competition of two men for one woman, with such large-scale events as the European balance of power and the formation of coalitions among political parties. He compares the strategy of a mother-in-law who confronts a newly married couple with the ways in which Rome, after subjugating Greece, dealt with Athens and Sparta.

It is a virtuoso performance, one of the more persuasive demonstrations of the power of sociological analysis. Simmel reveals the sterility of total psychological reductionism by demonstrating how the apparently peripheral fact that a third member has been added to a group of two opens up possibilities for actions and processes that could not otherwise have come into existence. He uncovers the new properties that emerge from the forms of association among individuals, properties that cannot be derived from characteristics of

[17] Cf. Theodore Caplow, *Two Against One: Coalitions in Triads* (Englewood Cliffs, New Jersey, Prentice-Hall, 1969), esp. Chapter 2, "In Praise of Georg Simmel."

the individuals involved. The triad provides new avenues of social action while at the same time it restricts other opportunities, such as the expression of individuality, which were available in the dyadic group.

Simmel does not restrict his analysis of numbers to the dyad and triad. Although it is not possible to demonstrate that each addition of new members would produce a distinct sociological entity, he shows that there is a crucial difference between small groups and larger ones.

In small groups, members typically have a chance to interact directly with one another; once the group exceeds a relatively limited size, such interaction must be mediated through formal arrangements. In order to come to grips with the increasing complexity of relationships among large numbers of individuals, the group must create special organs to help the patterning of interactions among its members. Thus, no large group can function without the creation of offices, the differentiation of status positions, and the delegation of tasks and responsibilities. This is the reason larger groups become societies of unequals: in order to maintain themselves, they must be structurally differentiated. But this means that the larger group "gains its unity, which finds expression in the group organs and political notions and ideals, only at the price of a great distance between all of these structures and the individual."[18]

The smaller the group, the greater the involvement of its members, for interaction among a few tends to be more intense than interaction among many, if only because of the greater frequency of contact. Inversely, the larger the group, the weaker the participation of its members; chances are high that they will be involved with only a segment of their personalities instead of as whole human beings. The larger group demands less of its members, and also creates "objective" structures that confront individuals with superpersonal powers: "For it is this large number which paralyzes the individual element and which causes the general element to emerge at such a distance from it that it seems that it could exist by itself, without any individuals, to whom in fact it often enough is antagonistic."[19]

Although through its formal arrangement the larger group confronts the individual with a distant and alien power, it liberates him from close control and scrutiny precisely because it creates greater distance among its members. In the dyad, the immediacy of the *we* is not yet marred by the intrusion of structural constraints, and, it will be remembered, in the triad two members may constrain the third and force their will upon him. In the small group, however, the coalitions and majorities that act to constrain individual action are mitigated by the immediacy of participation. In the large group, the differentiated organs constrain the individual through their "objective" powers, even though they allow freedom from the group through segmental rather than total involvement.

[18] *The Sociology of Georg Simmel, op. cit.*, p. 96. [19] *Ibid.*

Simmel's discussion of the differences between small and large groups—between the intensity of involvement among individuals in the primary group and the distance, aloofness, and segmentation of individuals in larger groups—reveals his general dialectical approach to the relation between individual freedom and group structure. His minute sociological analysis is part of his general philosophical view of the drift of modern history. Like Durkheim, Simmel theorizes about types and properties of group relations and social solidarities as part of a more general endeavor to assess and evaluate the major trends of historical development and to elaborate a diagnosis of his time.

SIMMEL'S AMBIVALENT VIEW OF MODERN CULTURE

Perhaps nothing so clearly reveals Simmel's profound ambivalence toward contemporary culture and society as his view of the drift of modern history. This view is a compound of the apparently contradictory assessments of liberal progressivism and cultural pessimism, as revealed in the writings of Herbert Spencer and as reflected in German idealism since the days of Schiller or Nietzsche.

The trend of modern history appears to Simmel as a progressive liberation of the individual from the bonds of exclusive attachment and personal dependencies in spite of the increasing domination of man by cultural products of his own creation. In premodern societies, Simmel argued, man typically lived in a very limited number of relatively small social circles. Such circles, whether kinship groups or guilds, towns or villages, tightly surrounded the individual and held him firmly in their grip. The total personality of the individual was immersed in this group life. Thus, medieval organizational forms "occupied the whole man; they did not only serve an objectively determined purpose, but were rather a form of unification englobing the total person of those who had gathered together in the pursuit of that purpose."[20] Associations in premodern societies were not functionally specific or limited to clearly articulated purposes; they bound the individual through undifferentiated dependencies and loyalties. Moreover, subordination in premodern society typically involved domination over the entire personality of the subordinate. The lord of the manor was not only the political overlord of the serf; he dominated the total person of the serf—economically, juridically, and socially. Dependence, therefore, was all encompassing.

In such premodern societies, the individuals were organized, as it were, in a number of linked concentric circles. A man could be a member of a guild, which in turn was part of a wider confederation of guilds. A burgher may have been a citizen of a particular town and this town may have belonged to a federation of towns, such as the *Hanse*. An individual could not directly join a larger social circle but could become involved in it by virtue of member-

[20] *Soziologie,* p. 419.

ship in a smaller one. A primitive tribe does not consist of individual members but of clans, lineages, or other groupings in which individuals participate directly.

The principle of organization in the modern world is fundamentally different: an individual is a member of many well-defined circles, no one of which involves and controls his total personality. "The number of different circles in which individuals move, is one of the indices of cultural development."[21] Modern man's family involvements are separated from his occupational and religious activities. This means that each individual occupies a distinct position in the intersection of many circles. The greater the number of possible combinations of membership, the more each individual tends toward a unique location in the social sphere. Although he may share membership with other individuals in one or several circles, he is less likely to be located at exactly the same intersection as anyone else.

Human personality is transformed when membership in a single circle or in a few of them is replaced by a social position at the intersection of a great number of such circles. The personality is now highly segmented through such multiple participation. In premodern societies, for example, locality or kinship determined religious affiliation; one could not coexist with men who did not share his religious beliefs, for the religious community coincided with the territorial or kinship community. In the modern world, in contrast, these allegiances are separated. A man need not share the religious beliefs of his neighbors, although he may be tied to them by other bonds. It does not follow, however, that religion loses its force; it only becomes more specific. Religious concerns are differentiated from other concerns and hence become more individualized; they do not necessarily overlap with a person's kinship or neighborhood ties.

Multifaceted involvement in a variety of circles contributes to increased self-consciousness. As the individual escapes the domination of the small circle that imprisons his personality within its confines, he becomes conscious of a sense of liberation. The segmentation of group involvement brings about a sense of uniqueness and of freedom. The intersection of social circles is the precondition for the emergence of individualism. Not only do men become more unlike one another; they are also afforded the opportunity to move without effort in different social contexts.

The forms of subordination and superordination also assume a novel character in the modern world. No longer can the individual be totally dominated by others; whatever domination continues to exist is functionally specific and limited to a particular time and place. As compared with the lord of the manor, the modern employer cannot dominate the entire personalities of the workers in his factory; his power over them is limited to a specifically economic context and a specified number of hours. Once the workers leave

[21] *Ibid.*, p. 411.

the factory gates, they are "free" to take part in other types of social relations in other social circles. Although they may be subordinate in some of these relations, they may well be superordinate in others, thus compensating for their inferiority in one area by superiority in another.

It should be clear that Simmel, in his original manner, is retracing the liberal view of historical patterns that could be found in such otherwise diverse thinkers as Spencer and Durkheim. Differentiation, in this view, involves a shift from homogeneity to heterogeneity, from uniformity to individualization, from absorption in the predictable routines of a small world of tradition to participation in a wider world of multifaceted involvements and open possibilities. The drift of western history leads from status to contract, from mechanical solidarity to organic solidarity, from societies in which custom is so rigid that it militates against individuality to those in which the multiplicity of involvements and contacts allows the emergence of uniqueness and individual autonomy.

This is only one of the two perspectives Simmel used to consider the past and present cultural situation. His other view owes more to Marx and to German cultural pessimism than to the optimism of British and French progressive thought. From this perspective, Simmel writes of the ineradicable dualism inherent in the relation between individuals and objective cultural values. An individual can attain cultivation only by appropriating the cultural values that surround him. But these values threaten to engulf and to subjugate the individual. More specifically, the division of labor, while it is the origin of a differentiated cultural life, in its way also subjugates and enslaves the individual.

The human mind creates a variety of products that have an existence independent of their creator as well as of those who receive or reject them. The individual is perpetually confronted with a world of cultural objects, from religion to morality, from customs to science, which, although internalized, remain alien powers. They attain a fixed and coagulated form and tend to appear as "otherness" to the individual. Hence, there is a perennial contradiction "between subjective life, which is restless but limited and time-bound, and its contents which, once created, are . . . timelessly valid."[22]

The individual needs art and science and religion and law in order to attain autonomy and to realize his own purposes. He needs to internalize these cultural values, making them part of himself. Individual excellence can be attained only through absorption of external values. And yet the fetishistic character that Marx attributed to the economic realm in the epoch of commodity production constitutes only a special case of the general fate of cultural contents. These contents are, particularly in more developed cultural epochs, involved in a peculiar paradox: they have been created by people and they

[22] Georg Simmel, "Der Begriff und die Tragödie der Kultur," in *Philosophische Kultur* (Potsdam, Gustav Kiepenheuer Verlag, 1923), p. 236.

were intended for people, but they attain an objective form and follow an immanent logic of development, becoming alienated from their origin as well as from their purpose.[23]

In passages that may express more pathos than analytical understanding, Simmel sees modern man as surrounded by a world of objects that constrain and dominate his needs and desires. Technology creates "unnecessary" products to fill "artificial" wants; science creates "unnecessary" knowledge, that is, knowledge that is of no particular value but is simply the by-product of the autonomous expansion of scientific activities.

As a result of these trends, modern man finds himself in a deeply problematical situation: he is surrounded by a multiplicity of cultural elements, which, although they are not meaningless to him, are not fundamentally meaningful either. They oppress the individual because he cannot fully assimilate them. But he cannot reject them because they belong at least potentially to the sphere of his own cultural development.[24] "The cultural objects become more and more linked to each other in a self-contained world which has increasingly fewer contacts with the subjective psyche and its desires and sensibilities."[25] Simmel, like Marx, exemplifies this process by reference to the division of labor. Once this division is highly developed, "the perfection of the product is attained at the cost of the development of the producer. The increase in physical and psychical energies and skills which accompanies one-sided activities hardly benefits the total personality; in fact it often leads to atrophy because it sucks away those forces that are necessary for the harmonious development of the full personality."[26] The division of labor severs the creator from the creation so that the latter attains an autonomy of its own. This process of reification of the cultural products, accentuated, though not originated, by the division of labor, causes increasing alienation between the person and his products. Unlike the artist, the producer can no longer find himself within his product; he loses himself in it.

The cultural universe is made by men, yet each individual perceives it as a world he never made. Thus, progress in the development of objective cultural products leads to an increasing impoverishment of the creating individuals. The producers and consumers of objective culture tend to atrophy in their individual capacities even though they depend on it for their own cultivation.

Although committed in one facet of his *Weltanschauung* to the progressive liberal vision of those French and English thinkers who influenced him deeply, Simmel is equally bound to a tragic vision of culture. He combines in an original, though not fully resolved, way the uncomplicated evolutionary faith in the perfectibility of man of a Condorcet with the metaphysical pathos of a

[23] *Ibid.*, p. 260. [24] *Ibid.*, p. 264.
[25] Georg Simmel, *Philosophie des Geldes* (Leipzig, Duncker und Humblot, 1900), p. 492.
[26] *Ibid.*, p. 484.

Schiller or a Nietzsche. Unable to relinquish the vision of a progressive liberation of the individual from the bonds of tradition and subjugation, Simmel yet foretells, with a sense of impending doom, "a cage of the future" (to use Max Weber's term), in which individuals will be frozen into social functions and in which the price of the objective perfection of the world will be the atrophy of the human soul.[27]

A NOTE ON THE PHILOSOPHY OF MONEY

Simmel's *The Philosophy of Money* is a much neglected classic. While most of his sociological work has now been translated into English, we still lack a translation of this seminal work. One possible reason for its neglect is the title, which could have led many to infer that this is one of Simmel's metaphysical works. An early interpreter of Simmel in this country, Nicholas Spykman, took just that view.[28] Although this large book does contain certain important philosophical ideas, it is mainly a contribution to cultural sociology and to the analysis of the wider social implications of economic affairs.

Economic exchange, Simmel argues, can best be understood as a form of social interaction. When monetary transactions replace earlier forms of barter, significant changes occur in the forms of interaction between social actors. Money is subject to precise division and manipulation and permits exact measurement of equivalents. It is impersonal in a manner in which objects of barter, like crafted gongs and collected shells, can never be. It thus helps promote rational calculation in human affairs and furthers the rationalization that is characteristic of modern society. When money becomes the prevalent link between people, it replaces personal ties anchored in diffuse feelings by impersonal relations that are limited to a specific purpose. Consequently, abstract calculation invades areas of social life, such as kinship relations or the realm of esthetic appreciation, which were previously the domain of qualitative rather than quantitative appraisals.

Just because money makes it possible to limit a transaction to the purpose at hand, it helps increase personal freedom and fosters social differentiation; money displaces "natural" groupings by voluntary associations, which are set up for specific rational purposes. Wherever the cash nexus penetrates, it dissolves bonds based on the ties of blood or kinship or loyalty. Money in the modern world is more than a standard of value and a means of exchange. Over and above its economic functions, it symbolizes and embodies the modern spirit of rationality, of calculability, of impersonality. Money levels qualitative

[27] This section follows in the main the pertinent pages of my introduction to Lewis A. Coser, ed., *Georg Simmel*. For a survey of Simmel's general philosophy, not touched upon here, see Rudolph H. Weingartner, *Experience and Culture* (Middletown, Connecticut, Wesleyan University Press, 1962).

[28] Nicholas J. Spykman, *The Social Theory of Georg Simmel,* new ed. (New York, Atherton, 1966).

differences between things as well as between people; it is the major mechanism that paves the way from *Gemeinschaft* to *Gesellschaft.* Under its aegis, the modern spirit of calculation and abstraction has prevailed over an older world view that accorded primacy to feelings and imagination.

The Philosophy of Money elaborates on various themes Simmel discussed in other works, some of which have already been taken up in the preceding pages. However, because this work gives a fuller treatment of these themes than do his other writings, it is indispensable for an understanding of his cultural analyses and his cultural criticism.

THE MAN

Georg Simmel was born on March 1, 1858, in the very heart of Berlin, the corner of Leipzigerstrasse and Friedrichstrasse. This was a curious birthplace—it would correspond to Times Square in New York—but it seems symbolically fitting for a man who throughout his life lived in the intersections of many movements, intensely affected by the cross-currents of intellectual traffic and by a multiplicity of moral directions. Simmel was a modern urban man, without roots in traditional folk culture. Upon reading Simmel's first book, F. Toennies wrote to a friend: "The book is shrewd but it has the flavor of the metropolis."[29] Like "the stranger" he described in his brilliant essay of the same name, he was near and far at the same time, a "potential wanderer; although he [had] not moved on, he [had] not quite overcome the freedom of coming and going." One of the major theorists to emerge in German philosophy and social science around the turn of the century, he remains atypical, a perturbing and fascinating figure to his more organically rooted contemporaries.

Simmel was the youngest of seven children. His father, a prosperous Jewish businessman who had converted to Christianity, died when Simmel was still young. A friend of the family, the owner of a music publishing house, was appointed the boy's guardian. Simmel's relation to his domineering mother was rather distant; he seems not to have had any roots in a secure family environment, and a sense of marginality and insecurity came early to the young Simmel.

After graduating from *Gymnasium,* Simmel studied history and philosophy at the University of Berlin with some of the most important academic figures of the day: the historians Mommsen, Treitschke, Sybel and Droysen, the philosophers Harms and Zeller, the art historian Hermann Grimm, the anthropologists Lazarus and Steinthal (who were the founders of *Voelkerpsychologie*), and the psychologist Bastian. By the time he received his doctor-

[29] Ferdinand Toennies and Friedrich Paulsen, *Briefwechsel, 1876–1908* (Kiel, Ferdinand Hirt, 1961), p. 290.

ate in philosophy in 1881 (his thesis was entitled "The Nature of Matter According to Kant's Physical Monadology"), Simmel was familiar with a vast field of knowledge extending from history to philosophy and from psychology to the social sciences. This catholicity of tastes and interests marked his entire subsequent career.

Deeply tied to the intellectual milieu of Berlin, both inside and outside the university, Simmel did not follow the example of most German academic men who typically moved from one university to another both during their studies and after; instead, he decided to stay at the University of Berlin, where he became a *Privatdozent* (an unpaid lecturer dependent on student fees) in 1885. His courses ranged from logic and the history of philosophy to ethics, social psychology, and sociology. He lectured on Kant, Schopenhauer, Darwin, and Nietzsche, among many others. Often during a single academic year he would survey new trends in sociology as well as in metaphysics. He was a very popular lecturer and his lectures soon became leading intellectual events, not only for students but for the cultural elite of Berlin. In spite of the fascination he called forth, however, his academic career turned out to be unfortunate, even tragic.

THE ACADEMIC OUTSIDER

For fifteen years Simmel remained a *Privatdozent.* In 1901, when he was forty-three, the academic authorities finally consented to grant him the rank of *Ausserordentlicher Professor,* a purely honorary title that still did not allow him to take part in the affairs of the academic community and failed to remove the stigma of the outsider. Simmel was by now a man of great eminence, whose fame had spread to other European countries as well as to the United States. He was the author of six books and more than seventy articles, many of which had been translated into English, French, Italian, Polish, and Russian. Yet, whenever Simmel attempted to gain an academic promotion, he was rebuffed. Whenever a senior position became vacant at one of the German universities, Simmel competed for it. Although his applications were supported by the recommendations of leading scholars, Max Weber among others, they did not meet with success.

The anti-Semitism that disfigured much of prewar academic life in Germany was one cause of the shabby treatment Simmel received from the academic powers, but it was not the only cause. The breadth of Simmel's knowledge and interests and his refusal to be restricted by any of the existing disciplinary boundaries perturbed many of the more settled spirits in the academic community. His originality, his sparkling intellect, and his ability to move with apparent effortlessness from one topic to another affronted colleagues and superiors who felt that only sustained application to specific problems suited the academic calling. How could one deal, they asked, with a man who in one semester would offer a profound course on Kantian epistemology and, in the next, publish essays on the sociology of smell, on the sociology of the meal, or on the sociology of coquetry and fashions?

Despite all the rebuffs Simmel received from his academic peers, it would be a mistake to see in him an embittered outsider. He played an active part in the intellectual and cultural life of the capital, frequenting many fashionable salons and participating in various cultural circles. He attended the meetings of philosophers and sociologists and was a co-founder, with Weber and Toennies, of the German Society for Sociology. He made many friends in the world of arts and letters; the two leading poets of Germany, Rainer Maria Rilke and Stefan George, were his personal friends. He enjoyed the active give-and-take of conversation with artists and art critics, with top-level journalists and writers. Very much a man about town, Simmel stood in the intersection of many intellectual circles, addressed himself to a variety of audiences, and enjoyed the freedom from constraints that comes from such an interstitial position.

His sense of relative ease must also have been enhanced by the fact that he was free of financial worry. His guardian had left him a considerable fortune so that he was not beset by financial concerns as were so many *Privatdozenten* and *Ausserordentliche Professoren* in the prewar German university. In the Berlin years Simmel and his wife Gertrud, whom he had married in 1890, lived a comfortable and fairly sheltered bourgeois life. His wife was a philosopher in her own right who published, under the pseudonym Marie-Luise Enckendorf, on such diverse topics as the philosophy of religion and of sexuality; she made his home a stage for cultivated gatherings where the sociability about which Simmel wrote so perceptively found a perfect setting.

Although Simmel suffered the rebuff of academic selection committees, he enjoyed the support and friendship of many eminent academic men. Max Weber, Heinrich Rickert, Edmund Husserl, and Adolf von Harnack attempted repeatedly to provide for him the academic recognition he so amply deserved. Simmel undoubtedly was gratified that these renowned academicians for whom he had the highest regard recognized his eminence.

A VIRTUOSO ON THE PLATFORM

Although many of his peers and elders, especially those of secondary rank, felt threatened and unsettled by Simmel's erratic brilliance, his students and the wider, nonacademic audience he attracted to his lectures were enthralled by him. Simmel was somewhat of a showman. Many of his contemporaries who left an account of his lectures have stressed that it seemed to them that Simmel was thinking creatively in the very process of lecturing. He was a virtuoso on the platform, punctuating the air with abrupt gestures and stabs, dramatically halting, and then releasing a torrent of dazzling ideas. What the great German critic Walter Benjamin once said of Marcel Proust, that his "most accurate, most convincing insights fasten on their objects as insects fasten on leaves" applies equally well to Simmel.[30] Emil Ludwig describes him well, though with a touch of characteristic vulgarity, when he writes: "Simmel investigated, when he lectured, like a perfect dentist. With the most delicate probe (which he sharpened himself) he penetrated into the cavity of things. With the greatest deliberation he seized the nerve of the root; slowly he pulled it out. Now we students could crowd around the table in order to see the delicate being curled around the probe."[31] George Santayana, then still experimenting with New England terseness, was given to less fancy modes of expression; but when he wrote to William James that he had "discovered a Privatdozent, Dr. Simmel, whose lectures interest me very much,"[32] he undoubtedly wished to convey in this sober fashion a fascination equal to that experienced by Ludwig.

In view of Simmel's enormous success as a lecturer, it must have been especially galling to him that when he finally achieved his academic goal, a full professorship at the University of Strasbourg, he was deprived of practically every opportunity to lecture to students.[33] He arrived at Strasbourg, a provincial university on the borderline between Germany and France, in 1914, just before all regular university activities were interrupted by the outbreak of the war. Most lecture halls were converted into military hospitals. A man as alive to the incongruities in man's destiny as Simmel could not have failed to smile wryly on this crowning irony. His last effort to secure a chair at Heidelberg, where the death of Wilhelm Windelband and Emil Lask had created two vacancies in 1915, proved as unsuccessful as previous attempts. Shortly before the end of the war, on September 28, 1918, Simmel died of cancer of the liver.

SIMMEL'S WRITING CAREER

In contrast to all the other sociologists discussed so far, Simmel's interest in current affairs and in social and political issues was minimal. Occasionally he would comment in newspaper articles on questions of the day—social medicine, the position of women, or criminal insanity—but such topical concerns were clearly peripheral to him. There is one major exception, however. With

[30] Walter Benjamin, *Illuminations* (New York, Schocken Books, 1969), p. 208.

[31] Quoted in Rudolph H. Weingartner, *Experience and Culture,* p. 7, from Kurt Gassen and Michael Landmann, eds., *Buch des Dankes an Georg Simmel* (Berlin, Duncker und Humblot, 1958). This work is a major source of testimonies on Simmel's impact on his listeners.

[32] Quoted in Weingartner, *op. cit.,* p. 4.

[33] The average age for promotion to full professorship was forty, and Simmel was already fifty-six years old at that time. See Christian R. Ferber, *Die Entwicklung des Lehrerkörpers der deutschen Universitäten* (Göttingen, Vandenhoeck und Ruprecht, 1956), p. 132.

the outbreak of the war Simmel threw himself into war propaganda with passionate intensity. "I love Germany," he wrote then, "and therefore want it to live—to hell with all 'objective' justification of this will in terms of culture, ethics, history, or God knows what else."[34] Some of Simmel's wartime writings are rather painful to read, exuding a kind of superpatriotism so alien to his previous detached stance. They represent a desperate effort by a man who had always regarded himself as a "stranger" in the land to become immersed in the patriotic community. His young friend Ernst Bloch told him: "You avoided decision throughout your life—*Tertium datur*—now you find the absolute in the trenches."[35] Throughout his career Simmel had managed to preserve a distance that enabled him to view events with cool rationality; in the last years of his life he succumbed to the desire for nearness and communion. Perhaps it was a failure of nerve.

Simmel was a most prolific writer. More than two hundred of his articles appeared in a great variety of journals, newspapers, and magazines during his lifetime, and several more were published posthumously. He wrote fifteen major works in the fields of philosophy, ethics, sociology, and cultural criticism, and another five or six less significant works. After his dissertation, his first publication, entitled *On Social Differentiation* (1890), was devoted to sociological problems, but for a number of years thereafter he published mainly in the field of ethics and the philosophy of history, returning to sociology only at a later date. His two major early works, *The Problems of the Philosophy of History* and the two volumes of the *Introduction to the Science of Ethics,* were published in 1892–93; these were followed in 1900 by his seminal work, *The Philosophy of Money,* a book on the borderline between philosophy and sociology. After several smaller volumes on religion, on Kant and Goethe, and on Nietzsche and Schopenhauer, Simmel produced his major sociological work, *Sociology: Investigations on the Forms of Sociation,* in 1908. Much of its content had already been published previously in journal articles. He then turned away from sociological questions for almost a decade, but he returned to them in the small volume published in 1917, *Fundamental Questions of Sociology*. His other books in the last period of his life dealt with cultural criticism (*Philosophische Kultur,* 1911), with literary and art criticism (*Goethe,* 1913, and *Rembrandt,* 1916), and with the history of philosophy (*Hauptprobleme der Philosophie,* 1910). His last publication, *Lebensanschauung* (1918), set forth the vitalistic philosophy he had elaborated toward the end of his life.

Because he was unable to develop a consistent sociological or philosophical system, it is not altogether surprising that Simmel did not succeed in creating a "school" or that he left few direct disciples. With his accustomed lucidity and self-consciousness, he noted in his diary shortly before his death: "I know that I shall die without intellectual heirs, and that is as it should be.

[34] Quoted in *The Sociology of Georg Simmel,* p. xxi.
[35] Quoted in Gassen and Landmann, eds., *op. cit.,* p. 13.

My legacy will be, as it were, in cash, distributed to many heirs, each transforming his part into use conformed to *his* nature: a use which will reveal no longer its indebtedness to this heritage."[36] This is indeed what happened. Simmel's influence on the further development of both philosophy and sociology, whether acknowledged or not, has been diffuse yet pervasive, even during those periods when his fame seemed to have been eclipsed. Robert K. Merton once called him "that man of innumerable seminal ideas"[37] and Ortega y Gasset compared him to a kind of philosophical squirrel, jumping from one nut to the other, scarcely bothering to nibble much at any of them, mainly concerned with performing his splendid exercises as he leaped from branch to branch, and rejoicing in the sheer gracefulness of his acrobatic leaps. Simmel attracted generation after generation of enthralled listeners, but hardly anyone who would call himself a disciple.

Among Americans who sat at his feet was Robert Park. No one who reads Park's work can overlook Simmel's profound impact. Continentals who derived major inspiration from his lectures include such dissimilar figures as the Marxist philosophers Georg Lukacs and Ernst Bloch, the existentialist philosopher-theologian Martin Buber, the philosopher-sociologist Max Scheler, and the social historian Bernhard Groethuysen. German sociologists Karl Mannheim, Alfred Vierkandt, Hans Freyer and Leopold von Wiese also were influenced by Simmel's work. Theodor Adorno, Max Horkheimer, and the other representatives of the Frankfort school of neo-Marxist sociology owe him a great deal, especially in their criticism of mass culture and mass society. Modern German philosophers from Nicolai Hartmann to Martin Heidegger were also indebted to him. It is not an exaggeration to state that hardly a German intellectual from the 1890's to World War I and after managed to escape the powerful thrusts of Simmel's rhetorical and dialectical skills.[38]

[36] Quoted in Coser, *Georg Simmel*, p. 24. [37] Merton, *op. cit.*, p. 404.

[38] As there is no full biography of Simmel, this section had to be pieced together from a variety of sources. In addition to the books already mentioned, see Kurt H. Wolff's "Introduction" to *The Sociology of Georg Simmel;* Michael Landmann's "Einleitung" to Georg Simmel, *Das Individuelle Gesetz* (Frankfurt, Suhrkamp, 1968); several contributions to Kurt H. Wolff, ed., *Georg Simmel, 1858–1918* (Columbus, Ohio, Ohio State University Press, 1959); the biographical section of Nicholas Spykman, *The Social Theory of Georg Simmel* (Chicago, University of Chicago Press, 1925); the "Einleitung" in Michael Landmann, ed., *Georg Simmel—Bruecke und Tor* (Stuttgart, Koehler, 1957); Michael Landmann, "Bausteine zur Biographie," in *Buch des Dankes*.

THE INTELLECTUAL CONTEXT

To trace all the influences that helped fashion Georg Simmel's catholic mind would involve writing a history of western thought, for scarcely a doctrine or set of ideas escaped Simmel's interest at one point or another in his career. Thinkers as divergent as Husserl and Marx, Max Weber and Schopenhauer left their traces in Simmel's work. Such influences, however, are often difficult to ascertain since Simmel, perhaps with a trace of coquetry, disdained footnotes, thus indicating in yet another minor way his departure from the wont of the academy. Moreover, as he explained in his *Introduction to Philosophy,* he saw in philosophical systems only reflections of the "personal attitude" of their originators and cared much less about the system than about the attitude. Yet, at the risk of being somewhat schematic, one can say that Simmel's thought progressed through three distinct, though overlapping, phases. He started his career under the influence of French and English positivistic thought and Darwinian and Spencerian evolutionism. In his middle period, when he wrote his most important sociological work, he turned to Kant and the neo-Kantians. In the last few years of his life he attempted to construct a pan-vitalist philosophy with building blocks acquired from Henri Bergson as well as from Nietzsche.

IN THE FOOTSTEPS OF DARWIN AND SPENCER

In Simmel's work of the nineties, more particularly in *On Social Differentiation* and in the *Introduction to the Science of Ethics,* the twin influences of Spencer and Darwin are unmistakably present. The notion of differentiation itself, although of course found in other thinkers, was most probably derived from Spencer's evolutionary conceptions. Differentiation, Simmel argued here, has the evolutionary advantage of saving energy in the relation between the organism and the environment.[39]

Simmel did not accept all evolutionary theory. He remained sceptical of the then current attempts to use Darwin's doctrines to buttress specific political claims, whether of the left or the right. Even in his early writings he emphasized that the notion of the struggle for existence should not be construed to mean that individuals and species were engaged in incessant battles for dominance. Nevertheless, one finds in these early writings a number of Spencerian or Darwinian modes of reasoning applied to issues of the day. Simmel argued, for example, that marriages engaged in for the sake of money lead to genetic mixtures, which "biology has recognized as the cause of direct and

[39] Georg Simmel, *Ueber Sociale Differenzierung* (Leipzig, Duncker und Humblot, 1890), Chapter 6.

deleterious racial degeneration."[40] In this early period Simmel maintained that criminal dispositions were hereditary, and he even protested against the preservation of the weak who will transmit their inferiority to future generations.[41]

Although never a believer in an unalloyed doctrine of evolutionary progress, in this early period Simmel came close to a Spencerian belief in the progressive development of mankind from primitive immersion in the group to autonomous individual growth in modern society. These notions were reinforced by the ethnological theories propounded in Germany by Simmel's former teacher Adolf Bastian. According to him, all primitive groups independently and automatically pass through the same stages of group consciousness and development. This type of evolutionism or "parallelism" of development became the dominant ethnological doctrine in Germany in the second half of the nineteenth century; especially under the influence of one of its popularizers, Julius Lippert, Simmel was partly converted to this optimistic and comforting belief in future perfectibility. In this period he compared the moral rawness, the cruelty, and the destructive desires of primitives to similar tendencies among young children, expressing the belief that just as children overcome these brutish traits in the process of growth, so the human race would increasingly grow out of such infantile disorders.[42]

THE KANTIAN INFLUENCE

In a more general sense Simmel probably derived much of his sociological method of focusing analysis on interaction, functional relations, and reciprocal dependencies from his reading of Darwin and Spencer as well as from their German disciples and popularizers. Darwinian and Spencerian notions were, however, pushed into the background of Simmel's work as, in his mature period, he came increasingly under the influence of Kant's teaching, more particularly Kant's theory of knowledge. The guiding theme of Kant's critical philosophy of knowledge, it will be recalled, is the notion that the realm of nature, the sensible world, is organized by the human understanding in accordance with certain a priori principles of knowledge. Repudiating the empiricism of Hume, Kant argued that man could never attain immediate knowledge of things in themselves, but only a knowledge that was mediated through certain fundamental mental categories, such as time and space.

When Simmel came to reflect on the character of historical knowledge, especially in his *Problems of the Philosophy of History,* he abandoned what-

40 *Philosophie des Geldes,* p. 420.

41 Cf. Paul Honigsheim, "The Time and Thought of the Young Simmel," in Kurt H. Wolff, ed., *Georg Simmel,* pp. 167–74. Georg Simmel, *Einfuehrung in die Moralwissenschaft* (Berlin, Wilhelm Hertz, 1892), I, pp. 116–18.

42 Cf. Paul Honigsheim, "A Note on Georg Simmel's Anthropological Interests," in Wolff, ed., *Georg Simmel,* pp. 175–79. Georg Simmel, *Einfuehrung in die Moralwissenschaft,* I, pp. 379–80.

ever uncritical empiricism he had earlier advocated and, in agreement with Kant, maintained that mere concrete experience is chaotic and unintelligible. If we ask ourselves how knowledge is possible within a given field of experience we find that the mind creates that knowledge through it own activity.[43] Knowledge becomes usable only when it is being filtered through a categorical apparatus. Thus historical knowledge to Simmel, like the knowledge of nature to Kant, is a product of selecting, categorizing, and constructive thinking. It is never given; it has to be created. Historiography, therefore, can never limit itself to the gathering of facts. It is not a simple enumeration of all that has happened at a particular moment in time, but rather involves a perception of the object of knowledge in terms of the problems and categories of the inquiring mind.[44]

The Kantian approach that served Simmel so well in his attempt to construct a philosophy of history was also prominent in his sociological writings. The sharp separation between form and content, which is central to his sociology, is clearly Kantian in origin, as is his insistence that "abstractions alone produce science out of the complexity or the unity of reality."[45] When Simmel asked himself in his famous essay "How is society possible?"[46] he used Kant's "How is nature possible?" as a point of departure.

This is not to say that Simmel simply applied Kantian principles to the field of sociology in the manner of certain of the neo-Kantians. He was aware that sociological inquiry presented problems that natural science, the area Kant was mainly concerned with, did not have to face. He argued, for example, that Kant's nature comes into being only through the observing mind, which synthesizes incoherent and unstructured world fragments, while the notion of societal connection is immediately given for individuals who form part of a society.[47] It remains true, nevertheless, that Simmel's attempt to build a geometry of social life, a purely formal sociology, could have originated only in a mind deeply steeped in Kantian philosophy. Just as Kant had taught that all experience of nature is shaped by a priori formal categories, Simmel now attempted to show that the ever-changing content of social life could be profitably investigated only through analysis of those enduring social forms or categories in which widely divergent contents were crystallized and captured.

[43] Cf. Maurice Mandelbaum, "Simmel," in *The Problem of Historical Knowledge* (New York, Harper Torchbooks, 1967).

[44] Cf. *ibid.*, and Ernst Troeltsch, "Simmel," in *Der Historismus und seine Probleme* (Tuebingen, J. C. B. Mohr, 1922), pp. 572–96.

[45] Wolff, ed., *Georg Simmel*, p. 316. [46] *Ibid.*, p. 337 ff. [47] *Ibid.*, p. 338.

THE FINAL PHASE: VITALISTIC PHILOSOPHY

The distinction between form and content continued to be crucial for Simmel during the last period of his life. While in his Kantian period his analytical attention had been mainly directed to the relatively enduring forms that channeled and directed individuals' purposes and energies in society, he now shifted, under the influence of Bergson and Nietzsche, to a celebration of the ever renewing stream of vital energy, which, he argued, underlay any formal arrangements. Especially in his last book, *Lebensanschauung,* which he wrote in the shadow of death, Simmel indulged in a kind of lyrical exaltation of life and its continuous flow of vital energy. It was his belief that life ultimately overflows the banks of form to create "more-life and more-than-life."

This outline of the three stages in Simmel's thought must not be taken too literally. The periods overlap. The first line of his *Soziologie,* perhaps the most Kantian of his works, opens with the Baconian-Spencerian sentence: "Knowledge of truth is a weapon in the struggle for existence—as much in the struggle with nature as with other men."[48] Certain vitalistic statements can already be found in writings considerably earlier than *Lebensanschauung.* But Paul Honigsheim is basically correct when he writes that Simmel started in an "unofficial Berlin Culture" of positivism and evolutionism and "ended close to the antirationalistic movements and in friendship with [the antirationalist poet] Stefan George, to whom he dedicated one of his last books."[49] Further clues to this development can be derived from an understanding of the social context in which Simmel moved.

THE SOCIAL CONTEXT

THE GENERAL SCENE

Simmel came of age in the early years of the unified German Reich, which Bismarck, the "Iron Chancellor" under Kaiser Wilhelm I, created after the successful war of 1870 against France. Thereafter, the Reich and its capital developed at a feverish pace. Until then a rather quiet provincial backwater, Berlin suddenly became a world city. It had only 400,000 inhabitants in 1848; by 1914 it had four million. Other major German cities—Hamburg, Köln, Munich, Leipzig, and Frankfort—also developed rapidly. While four fifths of the German population still lived in rural areas in 1830, this fraction decreased to one fifth by 1895.

Economic development proceeded at an even greater tempo than urbani-

[48] *Ibid.,* p. 310. [49] *Ibid.,* p. 169.

zation. From 1871 to 1874, no fewer than 857 new corporations, with a capital of over four billion marks, appeared on the business scene. An extended centralized banking system emerged at the same time. Captains of banking in Berlin, ensconced in their brand new marble palaces, began to dominate the new corporations that were springing up all over Germany. German industry had been a latecomer compared to that of England and France, but it now made up for its delayed emergence by an enormously rapid development. German industrial production surpassed France in the seventies and reached English production records by 1900; at the eve of World War I, it only lagged behind the United States. In 1875, Germany produced 34 million tons of coal; twenty years later, production rose to 74 million tons and then doubled to 150 million by 1910. Germany was becoming a heavily industrialized country within record time.

Although the last quarter of the ninteenth century saw the triumphant emergence of German capitalism, there were no basic changes in the sphere of politics. The new men of finance and industry entered the economic scene with confident strides. Self-satisfied, brutally ambitious and willful, these men felt that the new Germany was theirs, that they who had built its economic groundwork would have to be recognized as the pivots of the new order. Yet despite their new power in the market place, these masters of finance, industry, and trade were not a telling force in the political area. The army, foreign policy, the higher civil service continued to be controlled by the Junkers, an East-Elbian agrarian petty aristocracy, and the older elites, who had traditionally run the affairs of the old Prussia. Parliament, in which the new capitalist class was amply represented, had only a limited influence; in the chancelry and the Emperor's court the men who set the tone and determined affairs came from agrarian and pre-capitalist strata. Germany had a capitalist economy run by a political system that was semi-feudal. The bourgeoisie by and large accepted is political tutelage as long as it was left free to expand economically and to reap its profits unperturbed. The major middle-class parties had made their peace with Bismarck, and most of the once fiercely democratic liberals had now become National Liberals, supporters of the status quo. Only the rapidly growing Social Democrats and the Catholic Center party, as well as a saving remnant of old-fashioned liberals, resisted incorporation into the Bismarckian system.

The new working class created by industrialization swelled the ranks of the Social Democratic party, despite persecutions by the government and attempts to outlaw it completely. Bismarck tried to buy off the workers and to domesticate them through a variety of advanced welfare and social security measures. However, they remained basically antagonistic to a political system that excluded them from citizens' rights or limited their political powers—a system, as in Prussia, in which the vote of a middle-class person counted for considerably more than that of a workman. Since middle-class liberals were very weak, the party of the working class assumed the main burden of fighting for those democratic demands that in France or in England had long been realized as part of the program of the established middle-class parties.

Germany's curious combination of modernity in economic affairs and backwardness in social and political matters had important political effects. As Ralf Dahrendorf has written,

> Representative government was the indispensable instrument for a bourgeoisie advancing a claim of power. Only by equal representation could it hope to make its voice heard. . . . But the German bourgeoisie did not advance a claim to political power. Rather, it permitted the authoritarian state to survive industrialization: a state resting on the assumption that certain individuals, by virtue of very special insight guided by the "well understood interests" of their subjects, are called upon to make all political decisions.[50]

After the new Kaiser, Wilhelm II, dismissed the aging Bismarck in 1890, he continued the general policies but did not have the subtlety and finesse that had characterized Bismarck's rule. The Kaiser soon embarked on a course of foreign expansion and a program of armaments that made Germany a major threat to the older imperialist nations, leading in due course to their alliance against the power-hungry newcomer, who clamored for a larger place in the sun.

The intellectual life of the period flourished. German scholarship was unsurpassed. In poetry, such major figures as Detlev von Liliencron, Richard Dehmel, and, somewhat later, Rainer Maria Rilke, and Stefan George led to a poetic renaissance. Naturalism, especially in the plays of Gerhart Hauptmann, presented sharply drawn critical portraits of the age and indicted the gross self-satisfaction of the middle class in the face of proletarian misery. Impressionistic painting, though dependent on the Paris school, still produced some masters such as Max Liebermann. Yet—and this is of utmost importance for an understanding of the period—"The spirit and the state," as Golo Mann has phrased it, "lived separated from each other."[51] The world of intellect was impotent politically, even though it flourished as it had not done since the classical age. In contradistinction to the France of the Third Republic, German artists and intellectuals were unconcerned with their roles as citizens or with things political and withdrew into their study. By and large they were content

[50] Ralf Dahrendorf, "The New Germanies—Restoration, Revolution, Reconstruction," *Encounter,* XXII, 4 (April, 1964), p. 50.

[51] Golo Mann, *Deutsche Geschichte des 19. und 20. Jahrhunderts* (Frankfort, S. Fischer, 1958), p. 548. I have used this fine work by the historian-son of Thomas Mann throughout this section. Cf. also Arthur Rosenberg, *The Birth of the German Republic* (New York, Oxford University Press, 1931).

to remain, as in earlier periods of German history, compliant subjects rather than political activists.

Among intellectuals, university professors had the place of honor. In liberal societies, such as those of France and England, intellectuals not attached to academia had been actively engaged since the eighteenth century in the market place of ideas and had assumed key roles as critical analysts, ideological spokesmen, and gadflies to the men of power. They had become indispensable guides for the middle classes on questions of taste as well as in matters moral and political. It was not so in Germany, which serves to underscore that country's political and social backwardness. The apathetic middle class cared little for the free play of ideas but stood in awe of the disciplined, ordered, specialized learning of university professors. German professors continued to occupy a high social station and enjoyed commensurate financial remuneration. Those at the bottom of the university hierarchy, the *Privatdozenten,* often lived near starvation level, but the holders of regular chairs were free of financial worries. "Their existences were alike hardworking and jovial. Beer and wine drinking, Alpine vacations and pilgrimages to Italy, found their proper place in lives that were to seem in retrospect both cheerful and productive."[52]

Securely ensconced in their prestigious positions, German professors tended to be satisfied with things as they were and to avoid involvement in critical political thought. Some of them, especially the "socialists of the chair" under the leadership of Schmoller and his *Verein fuer Sozialpolitik,* proclaimed their loyalty to the Reich but urged the government to become more actively involved in social affairs and to initiate reforms to mitigate social injustices. Most professors, however, avoided even such limited critical activities. Historians like Treitschke glorified the Prussian state and celebrated the glory of the Fatherland; others devoted themselves to the minutiae of scholarship. As Golo Mann has written, "To serve the true and the beautiful, to delve into the beginnings of man's history or into the secret recesses of the human soul—these matters appeared immeasurably more important than the political crisis over Morocco or the elections to the Reichstag."[53] When a few Young Turks with Social-Democratic sympathies indicated that they might disturb the self-satisfied quiescence of the academic club, they were relegated to provincial universities, as was the sociologist Werner Sombart, or not given any appointment at all, as happened to his colleague Robert Michels. Because Jews seemed to be at least potential perturbers of the intellectual peace, they were admitted to professorships with reluctance, only after spending some of their most productive schol-

[52] H. Stuart Hughes, *Consciousness and Society* (New York, Vintage Books, 1961), p. 45.

[53] Mann, *op. cit.,* p. 550. Fritz K. Ringer's *The Decline of the German Mandarins* (Cambridge, Massachusetts, Harvard University Press, 1969), is an indispensable study of the politics and social role of German academics.

arly years in marginal academic positions while their loyalty was tested.[54] The university, though not a closed corporation, was encased in a semi-porous membrane that allowed passage into its inner professorial system only to those who had shown that they would help uphold its *Kaisertreu* and conservative standards.

The professoriat dominated intellectual life, yet in all the larger cities, and in Berlin especially, there also grew up an unattached intelligentsia, more sprightly, more lively, and more irreverent than its university counterpart, but still detached from political and social involvement. In this milieu critical journalists, playwrights, writers, and bohemian artists lived in partially overlapping circles, exchanging ideas with more daring than ever occurred within the academy. In Berlin's unofficial "counterculture," for example, one could find adherents of materialism and social Darwinism, which were still shunned by the official university, as well as propagandists for the realistic novels and dramas of Zola, Ibsen, Strindberg or Björnson. But also in this unofficial counterculture there grew an antirationalistic and often estheticizing reaction against what was conceived as the crass materialism of the age. Here, Nietzsche's attacks against bourgeois decadence and, somewhat later, Stefan George's glorification of intellectual elites found willing listeners and followers.[55]

As a whole, this counterculture was more politically alive than the culture of the university; socialist ideas, for example, found some sympathetic ears among many of the members. Nevertheless, it was almost wholly removed from political influence. Some members might advocate various unpopular causes from feminism and sexual emancipation to humane reforms of criminal laws, but by and large they felt powerless to sway poltical currents and were unwilling to become active participants in the political process. For the most part, they either retired to the sidelines with an elitist political stance or withdrew into estheticism. Whereas professors were detached social conformists, the unattached intellectuals tended to be equally detached social and cultural critics.

Georg Simmel, as shall be seen, participated in both the university culture and in the Berlin counterculture. Marginal to both of them, he acquired in this perilous social position the intellectual distance that enabled him to exercise his analytical skills, unhampered by institutional pieties.

[54] In 1909–10, almost 12 percent of the instructors but only 3 percent of the full professors at German universities were Jewish. Cf. Ringer, *op. cit.*, p. 136. Cf. Arthur Mitzman, "Sociology and Disenchantment in Imperial Germany," Ph.D. dissertation (Brandeis University, 1963).

[55] Cf. Honigsheim, *op. cit.* On Stefan George and other representatives of "counterculture," see Peter Gay, *Weimar Culture* (New York, Harper & Row, 1968).

SIMMEL'S TWIN AUDIENCES

Simmel was almost completely disengaged from the affairs of the day. In this he differed sharply from Durkheim who, it will be remembered, endeavored throughout his life to lay the groundwork for an objective study of society. Durkheim was detached from ideological preoccupations and political passions, but at the same time was an intensely engaged political moralist. The contrapuntal relation between detachment and engagement marks Durkheim's work and his life. In contrast, Simmel seems never to have been tempted by involvement in social and political life, execept for the war years. His objectivity—his thorough familiarity with the problems of distance—was facilitated by the fact that he lived wholly detached at the intersection of a variety of circles, never fully part of any and forever maginal to all.

Although bent on an academic career from his student days on, Simmel cultivated relations not only with his academic peers and superiors, but with the members of the Berlin nonacademic counterculture. Fairly early he appeared to be bored with the rigid standards of scholarship and life style that prevailed at Berlin University, which was then nicknamed the "First Guards Regiment of Learning."[56] He was temperamentally attracted by the world of literary reviews, of semibohemian salons, and the lively give-and-take of freewheeling discussion that prevailed in nonacademic circles. Yet at the same time he wanted to be more than a fashionable Berlin essayist, raconteur, and man-about-town; he aspired to make his mark in the world of scholarship. This attempt to live up to the standards of two dissimilar audiences helps to explain, at least in part, Simmel's distinctive style. Generally it has been assumed that the characteristics of this style could be accounted for by his personal characteristics. Although this may partly be so, significant insights can be gained into what may at first appear to be a purely psychological problem if we consider the social role Simmel played within the academic structure, in the Berlin counterculture, and in the general intellectual community.

Contemporaries of Georg Simmel often remarked upon special characteristics of his style that strikingly distinguished his work from that of other major sociologists. They stressed the brittle elegance and dazzling brilliance of his writings, but also noted the lack of systematic exposition and the almost studied disorderliness of his method.

More recently, Kurt H. Wolff observed that "Simmel often appears as though in the midst of writing he were overwhelmed by an idea, by an avalanche of ideas, and as if he incorporated them without interrupting himself, digesting and assimilating only to the extent granted him by the onrush."[57]

[56] Friedrich Meinecke, *Strassburg/Freiburg/Berlin 1901–1919: Erinnerungen* (Stuttgart, Koehler, 1946), p. 145. [57] *The Sociology of Georg Simmel*, p. xix.

These peculiarities of Simmel's style can be explained in part by his peculiar academic career. It will be recalled that Simmel was treated most shabbily by Berlin University and the German academy generally. Even when he was already considered one of the leading intellects of his time, he failed to gain academic recognition. As a *Privatdozent* and later as an *Ausserordentlicher Professor* he was denied full standing within the university and was never given the occasion to participate in academic decision-making as a regular member of the faculty. He maintained an auxiliary and marginal status.

As we have briefly noted, anti-Semitism, as well as academic jealousies, clearly played a part in Simmel's rejection.[58] A leading historian, Dietrich Schaefer, when asked to evaluate Simmel's qualifications for a chair at Heidelberg, wrote to the *Kultusministerium* of the state of Baden: "He is . . . a dyed-in-the-wool Israelite, in his outward appearance, in his bearing, and in his manner of thinking. . . . He spices his words with clever sayings. And the audience he recruits is composed accordingly. The ladies constitute a very large portion. . . . For the rest, there [appears at his lectures] an extraordinarily numerous contingent of the oriental world."[59] In addition to the anti-Semitic venom, Schaefer here draws attention to two other alleged failings: Simmel's success at attracting extra-academic and low-status listeners to his lectures, and his "cleverness."

Many of his colleagues felt that Simmel was much too clever and that his highly critical faculties predisposed him to "destructive" rather than "constructive" activities. Letters and autobiographies of German academics of the period contain repeatedly condescending remarks about Simmel's cleverness, his rootlessness, his lack of constructive intellectual discipline. To give one example, Friedrich Meinecke notes condescendingly in his *Erinnerungen* that Simmel, paying him a visit, made a few "sparkling" remarks, and, when offered a chair, instead of being seated launched on a "philosophy of chairs and of offering chairs."[60]

It may be argued that Simmel's inferior academic status was a consequence of his particular style of work. But even if it can be shown that Simmel's style in his earlier writings often called forth unfavorable judgments from his professional status superiors, one must still ask why he persisted in publishing works that proved to be similar in style to his earlier contributions. Why did he not attempt to conform more closely to the expectations of the senior members of the academy? Why did he accentuate those characteristics that they could be expected to disapprove?

To live up to the expectations of colleagues and superiors within the

[58] Cf. Marianne Weber, *Max Weber, Ein Lebensbild* (Tuebingen, J. C. B. Mohr, 1926), p. 361. See also Simmel's letters to Weber in *Buch des Dankes,* pp. 127 ff.

[59] For the full text see, *The American Journal of Sociology,* LXIII, 6 (May, 1958), pp. 641–42.

[60] Meinecke, *op. cit.,* pp. 102–03.

faculty—in other words, to play the rules of the academic game—is a typical pressure exerted upon incumbents of junior-status positions. These rules require, among other things, intellectual discipline, the observance of fixed standards of scholarship, respect for the boundaries of the various specialized fields, and attention to the contributions of senior men.[61] Those who attempt purely creative work are likely to be considered "unrealiable outsiders," and hence are to be mistrusted. As Plessner has argued: "Only those who are capable of developing the new out of the old fit into the framework of scholarship."[62] Any reader of Simmel will be well aware that his work hardly lives up to these norms. It should therefore not be surprising that quite early in his career he encountered powerful opposition among representative academic role-partners.

But if Simmel did not conform to these expectations, although surely desiring to be accepted in the academy, we are led to inquire whether the academic structure itself did not offer him opportunities for an alternative type of behavior. The concept of *role-set,* introduced by Robert K. Merton, may serve us well here: a social status, Merton argues, involves not a single associated role but an array of associated roles. Merton calls attention to the fact that role-partners who are located differently in the social structure tend to have differing expectations as to the behavior of a person occupying a particular status.[63] This would seem to apply to the position of university instructor at Simmel's time. This position may entail, for those so inclined, a set of roles differing rather pronouncedly from the role of the pure scholar. The German university teacher was expected to contribute to ongoing scholarship, and thus address himself to his colleagues, but he was also expected to lecture to students. Many preferred to keep their lecture work at a minimum or to restrict it to small seminars with selected students. Others, among them Simmel, gave considerable emphasis to their activity as lecturers. Academic colleagues and superiors, however, were often rather ambivalent toward members of the faculty who spent what they considered excessive time in lecturing. What Logan Wilson has said about the American academy, where lecturing is a much more important and highly prized activity than in the German university, applies all the more to the latter: "The chief acclaim of the teacher comes from below, which source is not important as a means of raising one's status. The acclaim from one's peers is frequently of the sort that decries too much attention to teaching, and belittles the popular teacher as a mere showman."[64]

While the popular teacher may incur the displeasure of peers, he may

[61] See Helmuth Plessner, "Zur Soziologie der modernen Forschung," in Max Scheler, ed., *Versuche zu einer Soziologie des Wissens* (Munich, Duncker und Humblot, 1924), pp. 407–25; Logan Wilson, *The Academic Man* (New York, Oxford University Press, 1942).

[62] Plessner, *op. cit.,* p. 422.

[63] Merton, *op. cit.,* pp. 369 ff. Merton defines role-set as "that complement of role relationships which persons have by virtue of occupying a particular social status." [64] Wilson, *op. cit.,* p. 192.

gain the approval of other role-partners—his lecture public or audience.[65] In effect, he lives up to expectations distinct from those of his peers and superiors, which presents a major structural basis for the possible disturbance of a stable role-set among university teachers who have the ability to be popular. The audience does not necessarily judge the lecturer for his systematic gathering of evidence and his disciplined pursuit of painstaking research, but rather for the brilliance of his performance, the novelty of his ideas, and the ability to fascinate.

All contemporary accounts agree that Simmel lived up to such expectations superlatively. He was considered one of the most brilliant, if not the most brilliant, lecturer of his time. He attracted students from the most varied disciplines; foreign visitors; unattached intellectuals from the world of publishing, journalism, and the arts; and a goodly number of members of "society" in search of intellectual stimulation. It is no exaggeration to say that many of Simmel's lectures were public events and were often described as such in the newspapers.[66]

His style of delivery seems to have enthralled his audience. A contemporary writes:

> One could observe how the process of thought took possession of the whole man, how the haggard figure on the lecture platform became the medium of an intellectual process the passion of which was expressed not in words only, but also in gestures, movements, actions. When Simmel wanted to convey to the audience the core of an idea, he not only formulated it, he so-to-speak picked it up with his hands, his fingers opening and closing; his whole body turned and vibrated under the raised hand. . . . His intensity of speech indicated a supreme tension of thought; he talked abstractly, but this abstract thought sprang from live concern, so that it came to life in the listener.[67]

Another contemporary observer writes in a similar vein:

> He "thinks aloud," somebody said of him. One could add: He thinks visibly, one imagines seeing how a thought occurs to him. . . . One can see how his brain operates, how he joins ideas like a carpenter joins wood. . . . One is led to participate in the construction. One doesn't really listen, one participates in the thought process.[68]

Do we not have here some warrant to assume that, hurt and rebuffed as

[65] Cf. Florian Znaniecki, *The Social Role of the Man of Knowledge* (New York, Columbia University Press, 1940).

[66] See, e.g., Emil Ludwig, "Simmel auf dem Katheder," *Die Schaubuehne,* X (April, 1914), pp. 411–13; Theodor Tagger, "Georg Simmel," *Die Zukunft,* LXXXIX (October, 1914), pp. 36–41; Paul Fechter, *Menschen und Zeiten* (Gütersloh, Berdelsmann, 1948), pp. 52–56.

[67] Fechter, *op. cit.,* pp. 52–56. [68] Tagger, *op. cit.*

he may have been by the lack of recognition within the academy, Simmel came to rely increasingly on the approval of his lecture audience and hence to accentuate in his written style, as well as in his oral delivery, those characteristics that brought applause? It is interesting to note in this connection that although his contemporaries have indicated that Simmel's audience gained the impression he was "thinking aloud" while he lectured and that they—the listeners—imagined they were assisting him, he was in actual fact apt to give some lectures several times with virtually no changes.[69] It would seem that Simmel cared so much for audience reaction that at times, like Churchill in a later day, he deliberately gave the impression before his audience that he was struggling with his ideas when he had worked out his thoughts long before.

Not only Simmel's lectures but the bulk of his writings also exhibited the characteristics that his lecture audiences prized. The unmatched brilliance of some of his essays is clearly related to the brilliance of his oral delivery; in fact, many of his essays, if not most, were first presented in lecture form.

In his published papers, Simmel addressed himself much more frequently to the nonacademic audience, and more particularly to the members of Berlin's counterculture. The bibliography compiled by Rosenthal and Oberlaender[70] reveals that, of the 180 articles published in his lifetime in various journals, newspapers, and reviews, only 64 were published in scholarly journals, and 116 appeared in nonscholarly publications destined for a wider cultivated public, such as liberal newspapers, art magazines, and literary monthlies.[71]

This tells about his reading public, but it does not give sufficient evidence to support the claim that the academy's negative sanctions pushed him to seek approval elsewhere. His nonacademic orientation, after all, could be an index of his secondary interest in the academy.

Simmel's development was part of a social process in which he addressed himself to two publics—his scholarly colleagues on the one hand, and his eager, nonspecialized listeners on the other. His success with the latter met with further negative sanctions from his colleagues and induced him to seek further success with that nonacademic audience. This can be shown by following Simmel's development over time. Since his published articles are on record, a simple comparison of their publications in various reviews and papers by dates of appearance will reveal the sequence of his dual orientations.[72]

While Simmel was still a *Privatdozent,* his hopes of being accepted in the academy must have been higher than later, when recognition was not forth-

[69] Fechter, *op. cit.*

[70] Erich Rosenthal and Kurt Oberlaender, "Books, Papers, and Essays by Georg Simmel," *American Journal of Sociology,* XL (November, 1945), pp. 238–47.

[71] Kurt Wolff's supplementary bibliography lists an additional twenty contributions to nonscholarly journals and only two to scholarly journals, pp. liv–lv.

[72] It would be possible to show that what holds true for Simmel's published papers in the periodical press also applies to his books. But this would involve a somewhat complex content analysis, which cannot be undertaken at this time. Yet even a cursory glance at the bibliography will show that Simmel's more systematic and scholarly work was mainly published in the earlier stages of his career.

coming. A comparison between the periodical writings published before the turn of the century (during the time he served as a *Privatdozent*) and those published later shows that in the earlier period one half of his writings appeared in scholarly journals, as against only a little over a quarter in the later period.

PERIOD OF PUBLICATION OF SIMMEL'S PAPERS BY TYPE OF JOURNAL

	Before 1900		*After 1900*		
JOURNAL TYPE	NO.	PERCENT	NO.	PERCENT	TOTAL NO.
Scholarly	31	50	33	28	64
Nonscholarly	31	50	85	72	116
Total	62	100	118	100	180

At the start of his career Simmel apparently communicated with both scholarly and nonscholarly audiences; later he tended to publish more and more in nonscholarly publications. Although it is not possible to prove, there are many indications that his lecture audience was composed of the same type of people, often perhaps the very same people, whom he addressed in the many nonscholarly journals for which he wrote. In later years, while he was not unmindful of the academy, he did not strive to live up to its expectations; the nonacademic audience, therefore, loomed larger for him.

It might be, of course, that, as Simmel became progressively better known and esteemed by other than the academic audience, publishers of lay periodicals increasingly prevailed upon him to publish with them. In short, it may have been a case not only of Simmel's initiative in searching out another audience but also of a greater interest by the agents of that audience in what he had to say. This could be construed as an interactive process between Simmel and the lay audience, with the publishers acting as intermediaries.

It is at least plausible that Simmel's self-image must have been molded to a large extent by the particular audience that rewarded him and his intellectual production was influenced by the saliency of the demands that his nonacademic role-partners made on him. The pressures exerted on his role-set by these role-partners led to appropriate modifications of self-definitions and to appropriate role behavior. His auxiliary status in the academy caused him to find a supportive audience at the margin of the academy, and the attempt to live up to their expectations, which he had provoked, involved him in a further process of alienation from the demands of the academy. As in the case of "The Stranger," of whom he wrote so perceptively and so movingly,[73] his re-

[73] *The Sociology of Georg Simmel,* pp. 402–08.

lations to the academy were a compound of nearness and remoteness. He was inorganically appended to the academy, yet he was an organic member of the group. He could afford to maintain such a difficult marginal role because he found support and encouragement among his nonacademic listeners. It is interesting to note that Simmel had no disciples in the academy, though he exerted some influence, whereas he had many followers among the literary intelligentsia.

Simmel, the marginal man, the stranger, presented his academic peers not with a methodical, painstakingly elaborate system, but with a series of often disorderly insights, testifying to amazing powers of perception. Yet Simmel's quest for originality stemmed in part from his self-image as a scholar. The academy does not, of course, prize purely routine work; it requires that its members contribute original results[74]—such results to be achieved, however, through academically approved means, within the academic rules of the game. Simmel conformed to the goals of the academy, but he rejected the norms governing the ways and means for their attainment.[75] His innovation can be accounted for, at least in part, by the contradictory pressures exerted by the social structure of the academy. That structure led him to engage in nonconformist behavior and, at the same sime, to the development and cultivation of originality.[76]

Motivated to live up to the demands of a largely nonacademic lecture audience despite his craving for the approval of academic friends such as Max Weber, Rickert, or Husserl and the admiration of younger academic men like Max Scheler or Ernst Bloch, Simmel was perilously poised between the two circles and, like a great juggler, always had a number of balls in the air. His complicated playing of diverse roles in front of so variegated a set of role-partners gave a game-like quality to his life and to his work. Forced by his audience to be a performer-lecturer continuously displaying wit and brilliance, he sometimes gave the impression that behind the show business mask lurked a basic sadness, such as one notices in Rouault's poignant portraits of clowns and other circus performers.

Robert A. Nisbet has remarked that the notion of "brilliance" is a peculiarly modern one. "What profundity is to the philosopher," he remarks,

> what depth and thoroughness are to the scholar, brilliance is to the intellectual, especially to the modern intellectual. . . . It is surely no exaggeration

[74] Cf. Robert K. Merton, "Priorities in Scientific Discovery," presidential address read at the annual meeting of the American Sociological Society, August, 1957, *American Sociological Review,* XXII (December, 1957), p. 6.

[75] See Merton's "Social Structure and Anomie," in *Social Theory and Social Structure,* especially pp. 140–41.

[76] This section is based on my earlier, "Georg Simmel's Style of Work: A Contribution to the Sociology of the Sociologist," *The American Journal of Sociology,* LXIII, 6 (May, 1958), pp. 635–41.

> to suggest that today's intellectual would cheerfully forego all praise in terms of mastery, depth, substance, and accuracy if he could be assured of his share of attributed brilliance. And craving it he typically adapts his style of work to its properties: the searching and sealing insight, the flashing riposte, etc.[77]

One might add that such brilliant performance as that of Simmel can only be staged at a time when intellectuals have both the freedom and the burden of moving in a variety of groups, without organic connection to any of them. The price they pay is likely to be high, as it undoubtedly was for Simmel. Today, few would be willing to pay such a price, preferring a condition less torn by conflict and contrary pulls of loyalties and commitments. But then, perhaps for this very reason, it is not given to most of us to develop as acute analytic skills as those that distinguished Georg Simmel.

IN SUMMARY

Despite the unsystematic and often willfully paradoxical character of Simmel's work, it is possible to sift and order it in such a way that a consistent approach to the field of sociology emerges. In fact, it would appear that Simmel's sociological method and his program of study may be set alongside the work of Durkheim in its scholarly importance. Durkheim focused attention on the social structure—the larger institutional structures, religious and educational, and on the overall values that bind societies together and create bonds between individuals. In contrast, Simmel's was in the main a microsociological enterprise; his principal concern was with social process. He illuminates the intricate patterns in which individual actors interact with one another and through which interaction help structure and re-structure the social world. His formal sociology, the geometry of social space, provided a preliminary map, which allowed later investigators to locate and often even to predict the moves of social actors who are caught in webs of group relations at the same time as they attempt to transcend them.

Present-day sociology possesses technological means and a conceptual apparatus far superior to that available in Simmel's day. But only fools would contend that he is therefore *dépassé*. Whether we read him directly or see his ideas filtered through the minds of Robert Park, Louis Wirth, Everett C. Hughes, Theodore Caplow, Theodore Mills, and Robert K. Merton,[78] he continues to stimulate the sociological imagination as powerfully as Durkheim or Max Weber.

[77] Robert A. Nisbet, "What is an Intellectual?" in *Commentary,* XL, 6 (December, 1965), pp. 93–101.

[78] Cf. Caplow, *op. cit.,* and Theodore Mills, "Some Hypotheses on Small Groups from Simmel," in Lewis A. Coser, ed., *Georg Simmel.*

Max Weber

1864-1920

THE WORK

Max Weber conceived of sociology as a comprehensive science of social action.[1] In his analytical focus on individual human actors he differed from many of his predecessors whose sociology was conceived in social-structural terms. Spencer concentrated on the evolution of the *body social* as analogous to an organism. Durkheim's central concern was with institutional arrangements that maintain the *cohesion* of social structures. Marx's vision of society was informed by his preoccupation with the conflicts between *social classes* within changing social structures and productive relations. In contrast, Weber's primary focus was on the subjective meanings that human actors attach to their actions in their mutual orientations within specific social-historical contexts. Behavior devoid of such meaning, Weber argued, falls outside the purview of sociology.

Four major types of social action are distinguished in Weber's sociology. Men may engage in purposeful or goal-oriented rational action (*zweckrational*); their rational action may be value-oriented (*wertrational*); they may act from emotional or affective motivations; or, finally, they may engage in traditionl action. Purposeful rationality, in which both goal and means are rationally chosen, is exemplified by the engineer who builds a bridge by the most efficient technique of relating means to ends. Value-oriented rationality is characterized by striving for a substantive goal, which in itself may not be rational—say, the attainment of salvation—but which is nonetheless pursued with rational means—for example, ascetic self-denial in the pursuit of holiness. Affective action is anchored in the emotional state of the actor rather than in the rational weighing of means and ends, as in the case of participants in the religious services of a fundamentalist sect. Finally, traditional action is guided

[1] I take this formulation from Raymond Aron's essay on Max Weber in his *Main Currents in Sociological Thought* (New York, Basic Books, 1967), Vol. 2, p. 181. This section owes a great deal to this volume as well as to Aron's earlier *German Sociology* (New York, The Free Press, 1964). Talcott Parsons' interpretations of Weber have been equally indispensable to me. Cf. especially his *The Structure of Social Action* (New York, The Free Press, 1949) and his "Introduction" to Max Weber, *The Theory of Social and Economic Organization* (New York, The Free Press, 1947). Julien Freund's *The Sociology of Max Weber* (New York, Pantheon, 1968) and Reinhard Bendix's *Max Weber, An Intellectual Portrait* (Garden City, N.Y., Doubleday, 1960) have also been most helpful, as has been the "Introduction" by Hans Gerth and C. Wright Mills to their edition of *From Max Weber: Essays in Sociology* (New York, Oxford University Press, 1946).

by customary habits of thought, by reliance on "the eternal yesterday"; the behavior of members of an Orthodox Jewish congregation might serve as an example for such action.

This classification of types of action serves Weber in two ways. It permits him to make systematic typological distinctions, as for example between types of authority, and also provides a basis for his investigation of the course of Western historical development. Raymond Aron rightly sees Weber's work as "The paradigm of a sociology which is both historical and systematic."[2]

Weber was primarily concerned with modern Western society, in which, as he saw it, behavior had come to be dominated increasingly by goal-oriented rationality, whereas in earlier periods it tended to be motivated by tradition, affect, or value-oriented rationality. His studies of non-Western societies were primarily designed to highlight this distinctive Western development. Karl Mannheim puts the matter well when he writes, "Max Weber's whole work is in the last analysis directed toward the question 'Which social factors have brought about the rationalization of Western civilization?' "[3] In modern society, Weber argued, whether in the sphere of politics or economics, in the realm of the law and even in interpersonal relationships, the efficient application of means to ends has become predominant and has replaced other springs of social action.

Earlier theorists had attempted to conceive of major historical or evolutionary tendencies of Western society in structural terms: for example, Toennies' conception involved a drift from *Gemeinschaft* (community) to *Gesellschaft* (purposive association); Maine's, a shift from status to contract; and Durkheim's, a move from mechanical to organic solidarity. Weber responded to similar concerns by proposing that the basic distinguishing marks of modern Western man were best viewed in terms of characteristic shifts in human action that are associated with characteristic shifts in the social and historical situation. Unwilling to commit himself either to a "materialistic" or an "idealistic" interpretation of history, Weber's ultimate unit of analysis remained the concrete acting person.

> Interpretative sociology considers the individual and his action as the basic unit, as its "atom." . . . The individual is . . . the upper limit and the sole carrier of meaningful conduct. . . . Such concepts as "state," "association," "feudalism," and the like, designate certain categories of human interaction. Hence it is the task of sociology to reduce these concepts to "understandable" action, that is without exception, to the actions of participating individual men.[4]

[2] *German Sociology*, p. 67.
[3] Karl Mannheim, *Man and Society in an Age of Reconstruction* (New York, Harcourt Brace Jovanovich, 1951), p. 52. [4] Gerth and Mills, eds., *op. cit.*, p. 55.

Weber's focus on the mutual orientation of social actors and on the "understandable" motives of their actions was anchored in methodological considerations, which account for much of the distinctiveness of his approach.

NATURAL SCIENCE, SOCIAL SCIENCE, AND VALUE RELEVANCE

Weber rejected both the positivist contention that the cognitive aims of the natural and the social sciences were basically the same and the opposing German historicist doctrine that in the realm of *Kultur* and *Geist* (that is, in the domain of history) it is impossible to make legitimate generalizations because human actions are not subject to the regularities that govern the world of nature. Against the historicists Weber argued that the method of science, whether its subject matter be things or men, always proceeds by abstraction and generalization. Against the positivists, he took the stand that man, in contrast to things, could be understood not only in external manifestations, that is, in behavior, but also in the underlying motivations. And against both these approaches Weber emphasized the value-bound problem choices of the investigator and the value-neutral methods of social research.

According to Weber, differences between the natural sciences and the social sciences arise from differences in the cognitive intentions of the investigator, not from the alleged inapplicability of scientific and generalizing methods to the subject matter of human action. What distinguishes the natural and social sciences is not an inherent difference in methods of investigation, but rather the differing interests and aims of the scientist. Both types of science involve abstraction. The richness of the world of facts, both in nature and in history, is such that a total explanation in either realm is doomed to fail. Even in physics it is impossible to predict future events in all their concrete detail. No one, for example, can calculate in advance the dispersion of the fragments of an exploding shell. Prediction becomes possible only within a system of conceptualizations that excludes concern for those concrete facts not caught in the net of abstractions. Both the natural and the social sciences must abstract from the manifold aspects of reality; they always involve selection.

The natural scientist is primarily interested in those aspects of natural events that can be formulated in terms of abstract laws. While the social scientist may wish to search for such lawful abstract generalizations in human behavior, he is also interested in particular qualities of human actors and in the meaning they ascribe to their actions. Any scientific method must make a selection from the infinite variety of empirical reality. When the social scientist adopts a generalizing method, he abstracts from random and unique aspects of the reality he considers; concrete individual actions are conceived as "cases" or "instances," which are subsumed under theoretical generalizations. The individualizing approach, in contrast, neglects generic elements and concentrates attention on particular features of phenomena or concrete historical actors. Both methods are defensible, provided neither is alleged to encompass phenomena in their totality. Neither method is privileged or inherently superior to the other.

What particular problem attracts a scholar, and what level of explanation is sought, depends, Weber argues, on the values and interests of the investigator. The choice of problems is always "value relevant." "There is no absolutely 'objective' scientific analysis of culture or . . . of 'social phenomena' independent of special and 'one-sided' viewpoints according to which—expressly or tacitly, consciously or unconsciously—they are selected, analyzed and organized for expository purposes."[5] What is considered "worthy to be known" depends upon the perspective of the inquiring scholar. Hence there is no insurmountable chasm between the procedures of the natural and the social scientist, but they differ in their cognitive intentions and explanatory projects.

When the objection is raised that rational knowledge of causal sequences may be attained in the world of nature, but that the human world is not susceptible to rational explanation because of its unpredictability and irrationality, Weber counters by turning the tables. Our knowledge of nature must always be, as it were, from the outside. We can only observe external courses of events and record their uniformities. But in regard to human action, we can do more than write protocols of recurrent sequences of events; we can attempt to impute motives by interpreting men's actions and words. With this method, he of course opposes the positivists as well. "Social facts are in the last resort *intelligible* facts." We can understand (*verstehen*) human action by penetrating to the subjective meanings that actors attach to their own behavior and to the behavior of others. A sociology of the chicken yard can only account for regularities of behavior—in other words, for a pecking order. A sociology of human groups has the inestimable advantage of having access to the subjective aspects of action, to the realm of meaning and motivation. Hence Weber's definition of sociology as "that science which aims at the *interpretative understanding* (*Verstehen*) of social behavior in order to gain an explanation of its causes, its course, and its effects."[6]

The notion of interpretative understanding did not originate with Weber. It was first advanced by the historian Droysen and was used extensively by such scholars as Dilthey. But for them the method was meant to extol intuition over rational-causal explanation. Weber, in contrast, saw in it only a preliminary step in the establishment of causal relationships. The grasping of subjective meaning of an activity, Weber argued, is facilitated through empathy (*Einfuehlung*) and a reliving (*Nacherleben*) of the experience to be analyzed. But any interpretative explanation (*verstehende Erklaerung*) must

[5] Edward Shils and Henry Finch, eds., *Max Weber on the Methodology of the Social Sciences* (New York, The Free Press, 1949), p. 72.

[6] Max Weber, *Basic Concepts in Sociology* (New York, The Citadel Press, 1964), p. 29.

become a causal explanation if it is to reach the dignity of a scientific proposition. *Verstehen* and causal explanation are correlative rather than opposed principles of method in the social sciences. Immediate intuitions of meaning can be transformed into valid knowledge only if they can be incorporated into theoretical structures that aim at causal explanation.

Against the objection that this manner of interpretation is subject to the danger of contamination from the values held by the scientific investigator, Weber countered that interpretations can be submitted to the test of evidence. This, he argued, is to be distinguished from the fact that the choice of subject matter—as distinct from the choice of interpretation—stems from the investigator's value orientation, which may be the case with the natural scientist as well.

Weber insisted that a value element inevitably entered into the selection of the problem an investigator chooses to attack. There are no intrinsically scientific criteria for the selection of topics; here every man must follow his own demon, his own moral stance, but this in no way invalidates the objectivity of the social sciences. The question of whether a statement is true or false is logically distinct from that of its relevance to values. *Wertbeziehung* (value relevance) touches upon the selection of the problem, not upon the interpretation of phenomena. As Parsons put it, "Once a phenomenon is descriptively given, the establishment of casual relations between it and either its antecedents or its consequences is possible only through the application, explicitly or implicitly, of a formal schema of proof that is independent of any value system, except the value of scientific proof."[7] Hence, the relativity of value orientations leading to different cognitive choices has nothing to do with questions of scientific validity. What are relativized in this view are not the findings but the problems.

Value relevance must be distinguished from value-neutrality, since they refer to two different orders of ideas. In the first place, ethical neutrality implies that once the social scientist has chosen his problem in terms of its relevance to his values, he must hold values—his own or those of others—in abeyance while he follows the guidelines his data reveal. He cannot impose his values on the data and he is compelled to pursue his line of inquiry whether or not the results turn out to be inimical to what he holds dear. A geneticist of liberal persuasion, for example, should not abandon his line of inquiry if his findings suggest that differences in intelligence are associated with biological traits. Value neutrality, in this first meaning of the term, refers to the normative injunction that men of science should be governed by the ethos of science in their role as scientists, but emphatically not in their role as citizens.

In addition, value neutrality refers no less importantly to another order of considerations: the disjunction between the world of facts and the world of

[7] Talcott Parsons, *The Structure of Social Action* (New York, The Free Press, 1958), p. 594.

values, the impossibility of deriving "ought statements" from "is statements." An empirical science, Weber contended, can never advise anyone what he *should* do, though it may help him to clarify for himself what he can or wants to do.

> The scientific treatment of value judgments may not only understand and empatically analyze the desired ends and the ideals which underline them; it can also "judge" them critically. This criticism can . . . be no more than a formal logical judgment of historically given value judgments and ideas, a testing of the ideals according to the postulate of the internal *consistency* of the desired end. . . . It can assist [the acting person] in becoming aware of the ultimate standards of value which he does not make explicit to himself, or which he must presuppose in order to be logical. . . . As to whether the person expressing these value judgments *should* adhere to these ultimate standards is his personal affair; it involves will and conscience, not empirical knowledge.[8]

Weber was fundamentally at odds with those who argued for a morality based on science. In this respect he was as opposed to Durkheim as he would be to those psychoanalysts today who claim they have a scientific warranty to counsel "adjustment" or "self-actualization," as the case may be, to their patients.

The scientist *qua* scientist can evaluate the probable consequences of courses of action, Weber believed, but he cannot make value judgments. Weber had an austere view of science. "Science today," he wrote, "is a 'vocation' organized in special disciplines in the service of self-clarification and knowledge of interrelated facts. It is not the gift of grace of seers and prophets dispensing sacred values and revelations, nor does it partake of the contemplation of sages and philosophers about the meaning of the universe."[9] The realm of moral values, Weber believed, was a realm of warring gods demanding allegiance to contradictory ethical notions. The scientist *qua* scientist, therefore, could have no answer to the Tolstoian question, "What shall we do?" "Academic prophecy . . . will create only fanatical sects," Weber believed, "but never a genuine community."[10] The scientist should not hanker after leadership over men; he finds dignity and fulfillment in the quest for truth. When Weber was once asked why he undertook his wide-ranging studies, he replied: "I wish to know how much I can take."

[8] Shils and Finch, eds., *op. cit.*, p. 54. [9] Gerth and Mills, eds., *op. cit.*, p. 152. [10] *Ibid.*, p. 155.

THE IDEAL TYPE

In his effort to escape from the individualizing and particularizing approach of German *Geisteswissenschaft* and historicism, Weber developed a key conceptual tool, the notion of the *ideal type*. It will be recalled that Weber argued that no scientific system is ever capable of reproducing all concrete reality, nor can any conceptual apparatus ever do full justice to the infinite diversity of particular phenomena. All science involves selection as well as abstraction. Yet the social scientist can easily be caught in a dilemma when he chooses his conceptual apparatus. When his concepts are very general—as when he attempts to explain capitalism or Protestantism by subsuming them under the general concepts of economics or religion—he is likely to leave out what is most distinctive to them. When, on the other hand, he uses the traditional conceptualizations of the historian and particularizes the phenomenon under discussion, he allows no room for comparison with related phenomena. The notion of the *ideal type* was meant to provide escape from this dilemma.

An *ideal type* is an analytical construct that serves the investigator as a measuring rod to ascertain similarities as well as deviations in concrete cases. It provides the basic method for comparative study. "An ideal type is formed by the one-sided accentuation of one or more points of view and by the synthesis of a great many diffuse, discrete, more or less present and occasionally absent *concrete individual* phenomena, which are arranged according to those one-sidedly emphasized viewpoints into a unified *analytical* construct."[11] An *ideal type* is not meant to refer to moral ideals. There can be an *ideal type* of a brothel or of a chapel. Nor did Weber mean to refer to statistical averages. Average Protestants in a given region or at a given time may be quite different from ideal typical Protestants. The *ideal type* involves an accentuation of typical courses of conduct. Many of Weber's *ideal types* refer to collectivities rather than to the social actions of individuals, but social relationships within collectivities are always built upon the probability that component actors will engage in expected social actions. An *ideal type* never corresponds to concrete reality but always moves at least one step away from it. It is constructed out of certain elements of reality and forms a logically precise and coherent whole, which can never be found as such in that reality. There has never been a full empirical embodiment of the Protestant Ethic, of the "charismatic leader," or of the "exemplary prophet."

Ideal types enable one to construct hypotheses linking them with the conditions that brought the phenomenon or event into prominence, or with consequences that follow from its emergence. If we wish to study the religious roots of modern capitalism, it may be advisable to construct an *ideal type* of

[11] Shils and Finch, eds., *op. cit.*, p. 90.

Protestant, based on the distinct features of sectarians as these emerged during the Reformation. We shall then be in a position to determine empirically whether the concrete conduct of Protestants in, say, seventeenth-century England did in fact approximate the type and in what specific aspects it failed to do so. This type will further allow us to distinguish between the conduct of men who adhered to Catholic or Protestant religious bodies. We can then proceed to correlations and causal imputations as to the connections between the emergence of Protestantism and that of modern capitalism—both being conceived in ideal typical terms. As Julien Freund puts it, "Being unreal, the ideal type has the merit of offering us a conceptual device with which we can measure real development and clarify the most important elements of empirical reality."[12]

Weber's three kinds of *ideal types* are distinguished by their levels of abstraction. First are the *ideal types* rooted in historical particularities, such as the "western city," "the Protestant Ethic," or "modern capitalism," which refer to phenomena that appear only in specific historical periods and in particular cultural areas. A second kind involves abstract elements of social reality—such concepts as "bureaucracy" or "feudalism"—that may be found in a variety of historical and cultural contexts. Finally, there is a third kind of *ideal type,* which Raymond Aron calls "rationalizing reconstructions of a particular kind of behavior."[13] According to Weber, all propositions in economic theory, for example, fall into this category. They all refer to the ways in which men would behave were they actuated by purely economic motives, were they purely economic men.

CAUSALITY AND PROBABILITY

It is sometimes argued that, in tune with the German idealistic tradition, Weber rejected the notion of causality in human affairs.[14] This is emphatically not the case. Weber firmly believed in both historical and sociological causality, but—and this may have given rise to misunderstandings—he expressed causality in terms of probability. Such stress on chance or probability, however, has nothing to do with an insistence on free will or the unpredictability of human behavior. Weber argued, for example, that human action was truly unpredictable only in the case of the insane, and that "we associate the highest measure of an empirical 'feeling of freedom' with those actions which we are conscious of performing rationally."[15] This sense of subjective freedom, far from being rooted in unpredictability and irrationality, arises precisely in those situations that can be rationally predicted and mastered. Hence, Weber's notion of prob-

[12] Freund, *op. cit.,* p. 69. [13] *Main Currents,* p. 204.

[14] Cf., for example, the treatment of Weber in Friedrich Jonas, *Geschichte der Soziologie* (Reinbeck bei Hamburg, Rowohlt, 1969), Vol. 4, p. 43 and *passim.*

[15] Shils and Finch, eds., *op. cit.,* p. 24.

ability or chance is not based in some kind of metaphysics of free will but derives from his recognition of the extreme difficulties in making entirely exhaustive causal imputations. Objective empirical certainty in social research seemed to him hardly ever attainable. The best one can do, he concluded, is to follow a variety of causal chains that have helped determine the object under study.

When Weber uses the notion of probability in his definitional statements—for example, in defining a relationship as existing "in so far as there is a probability that" a certain norm of behavior will be adhered to—he responds to similar considerations. Probability is here taken to mean that in all likelihood men involved in a certain context will orient their behavior in terms of normative expectations. But this is always probable and never certain because it can also be assumed that for some actors the chains of causality peculiar to their unique social relationships will lead to departure from the expected probability.

It is convenient to distinguish two directions in Weber's view of causality—historical and sociological. "Historical causality determines the unique circumstances that have given rise to an event. Sociological causality assumes the establishment of a regular relationship between two phenomena, which need not take the form 'A makes B inevitable,' but may take the form 'A is more or less favorable to B.'"[16] The quest for historical causality asks the question: What are the causes of the Bolshevik revolution? The search for sociological causality involves questioning the economic, the demographic, or the specifically social causes of all revolutions or of particular *ideal types* of revolutions.

The quest for historical causes, Weber pointed out, was facilitated by what has been called mental experiments. When we learn that two shots fired in Berlin in 1848 started the revolution of 1848, we must ask whether the revolution would have taken place had these shots not been fired. If we conclude that it would have started in any case, we can rule out these shots as causes of the subsequent revolutionary development. When we ask whether the Battle of Marathon was a major causal event for the subsequent history of Hellenic civilization, we must perform the mental experiment of envisaging Greece dominated by the Persians. Such an experiment will convince us that had the Athenians lost the battle, a Persian Greece would have been a basically different society. We can then conclude as to the probability that the outcome of the Battle of Marathon, by guaranteeing the independence of the city-states, was indeed a major causal factor in the subsequent development of Greek civilization.

> The assessment of the historical significance of an historical fact will begin with the posing of the following question: In the event of the exclusion

[16] *Main Currents,* p. 193.

> of that fact from the complex of the factors which are taken into account as co-determinants, or in the event of its modification in a certain direction, could the course of events, in accordance with general empirical rules, have taken a direction in any way different in any features which would be *decisive* for our interest?[17]

To determine sociological causality, Weber argues, also requires operating within a probabilistic framework. This type of generalization attempts to establish, for example, that the emergence of capitalism required a certain type of personality largely shaped by the preachments of Calvinist divines. The proof of the proposition comes when, either through mental experiment or through comparative study in other cultures, it is established that modern capitalism could probably not develop without such personalities; therefore, Calvinism must be considered *a* cause, though emphatically not *the* cause, of the rise of capitalism.

This example calls attention to the fact that Weber's methodological reflections served as a tool in his substantive investigations. Yet he was not concerned with methodology for its own sake and, like many another scientist, he did not always follow his own methodological guidelines. Contrary to his nominalistic stress on the acting person as the unit of analysis, he advanced a theory of stratification based largely on structural explanations rather than on a subjective theory of class distinctions.

When explaining the decline of the Roman Empire, he focused on structural changes in Roman agriculture. More importantly still, Weber's life-long preoccupation with the increase of rationality in the modern world was to a considerable extent based on structural considerations, as witness his stress on the separation of the household from the business enterprise as a harbinger of economic rationalization. In all these instances, Weber also provides illustrations pointing to changing motivations of historical actors, yet on balance, structure seems more important than motivation.

Though a number of other examples could be cited where Weber did not apply his methodological injunctions, many more instances in his work reveal that he put his methods to brilliant use in his substantive analysis.

TYPES OF AUTHORITY

Weber's discussion of authority relations—why men claim authority, and feel they have a legitimate right to expect willing obedience to their command—illustrates his use of the *ideal type* as an analytical tool and his classification of types of social action.

Weber distinguished three main modes of claiming legitimacy. Authority

[17] Shils and Finch, eds., *op. cit.*, p. 180.

may be based on rational grounds and anchored in impersonal rules that have been legally enacted or contractually established. This type is *rational-legal authority,* which has increasingly come to characterize hierarchical relations in modern society. *Traditional authority,* on the other hand, which predominates in pre-modern societies, is based on belief in the sanctity of tradition, of "the eternal yesterday." It is not codified in impersonal rules but inheres in particular persons who may either inherit it or be invested with it by a higher authority. *Charismatic authority,* finally, rests on the appeal of leaders who claim allegiance because of their extraordinary virtuosity, whether ethical, heroic, or religious.

It should be kept in mind that here, as elsewhere in his work, Weber was describing pure types; he was aware that in empirical reality mixtures will be found in the legitimation of authority. Although Hitler's domination was based to a considerable extent on his charisma, elements of rational-legal authority remained in the structure of German law, and references to Germanic Volk tradition formed a major element in the appeals of National Socialism.

This typology of various forms of authority relations is important on several counts. Its sociological contribution rests more especially on the fact that Weber, in contrast to many political theorists, conceives of authority in all its manifestations as characteristic of the relation between leaders and followers, rather than as an attribute of the leader alone. Although his notion of charisma may lack rigorous definition, its importance lies in Weber's development of the idea that the leader derives his role from the belief his followers have about his mission.

THE FUNCTION OF IDEAS

Weber's concern with the meaning actors impute to relationships did not limit him to the study of types of social action. Rather, he used the typology of forms of social action to understand the drift of historical change. It will be remembered that the problems posed by modern civilization were foremost in his mind, and in this connection he conceived the shift from traditional to rational action as crucial. He showed that rational action within a system of rational-legal authority is at the heart of the modern rationalized economy, that is, of the capitalist system. Only within the framework of a rationalized economy can active individuals weigh utility and costs in a rational manner. Weber maintained that the rationalization of economic action can only be realized when traditional notions about just prices or just wages are discarded and a positive ethical sanction is provided for acquisitive activities aimed at maximizing the self-interests of the actor. Such ethical sanction, Weber argued, was provided by the Protestant Ethic, which broke the hold of traditionalism in the realm of economic behavior even while it fostered a spirit of rigorous self-discipline, encouraging men to apply themselves rationally and methodically to the specific tasks they were "called" to perform within the occupational world.

Weber's emphasis on the influence of religious ideas in the emergence of modern capitalism forced him into a running dialogue with the ghost of Karl Marx. He was most respectful of Marx's contributions, yet believed, in tune with his own methodology, that Marx had unduly emphasized one particular causal chain, the one leading from the economic infrastructure to the cultural superstructure. Weber argued that Marx had presented an overly simplified scheme that could not adequately take into account the tangled web of causative influences linking the economy and the social structure to cultural products and human action. Weber refused to see in ideas simple reflections of material interests. He contended instead that developments in the intellectual, psychic, scientific, political, and religious spheres have relative autonomy even though they all mutually influence one another. There is no preestablished harmony between the content of an idea and the material interests of those who become its champion, but an "elective affinity" may arise between the two. Weber's examples are many. In the seventeenth century, such an elective affinity developed between the ideas of the Calvinist divines and the concerns of certain bourgeois or petty-bourgeois strata, whether in England, Scotland or the Lowlands. Confucian ethics did not "express the needs" of the Chinese literati, but these men became the main carriers of Confucian ideas in so far as these were congenial to their life-styles. Or again: landowning warrior classes have an aversion to any form of emotional religiosity and to religions preaching salvation; instead, they are drawn to religious systems in which the gods are conceived as powerful, passionate beings who clash among themselves and are subject to cajolery through sacrifice or to coercion through magical manipulation. Peasants are attracted to nature worship while urban bourgeois strata incline toward Christian piety.

Fascinated as he was by the dynamics of social change, Weber endeavored to create a more flexible interpretative system than Marx had provided. He attempted to show that the relations between systems of ideas and social structures were multiform and varied and that causal connections went in both directions, rather than from infrastructure to superstructure alone. Weber's modification and refinement of the Marxian scheme is likewise evident in his theory of stratification.

CLASS, STATUS, AND POWER

Weber differed only marginally from Marx when he defined as a class a category of men who 1) "have in common a specific causal component of their life chances in so far as 2) this component is represented exclusively by economic interests in the possession of goods and opportunities for income, and

3) it is represented under the conditions of the commodity or labor market."[18] He even was fairly close to Marx's view, though not necessarily to those of latter-day Marxists, when he stated that class position does not necessarily lead to class-determined economic or political action. He argued that communal class action will emerge only if and when the "connections between the causes and the consequences of the 'class situation'" become *transparent;*[19] Marx would have said when a class becomes conscious of its interests, that is, of its relation, as a class, to other classes. Yet Weber's theory of stratification differs from that of Marx in that he introduced an additional structural category, that of "status group."

Classification of men into such groups is based on their consumption patterns rather than on their place in the market or in the process of production. Weber thought Marx had overlooked the relevance of such categorization because of his exclusive attention to the productive sphere. In contrast to classes, which may or may not be communal groupings, status groups are normally communities, which are held together by notions of proper life-styles and by the social esteem and honor accorded to them by others. Linked with this are expectations of restrictions on social intercourse with those not belonging to the circle and assumed social distance toward inferiors. In this typology we again find Weber's sociological notion of a social category as dependent on the definition that others give to social relationships. A status group can exist only to the extent that others accord its members prestige or degrading, which removes them from the rest of social actors and establishes the necessary social distance between "them" and "us."

Empirically there are fairly high correlations between standing in the class and in the status order. Especially in capitalist society, the economically ascendant class will, in the course of time, also acquire high status; yet in principle, propertied and propertyless people may belong to the same status group. At certain times, an economically weak element, such as the East Elbian Junkers, may exercise considerable influence and power because of its preeminent status. Generally, as much post-Weberian analysis of American politics has shown, political behavior may at times be influenced by men who are fearful of losing their status or who bridle at not having been accorded a status they think is their due; such influence may be as powerful as class-determined modes of political behavior.

In Weber's view every society is divided into groupings and strata with distinctive life-styles and views of the world, just as it is divided into distinctive classes. While at times status as well as class groupings may conflict, at others their members may accept fairly stable patterns of subordination and superordination.

[18] Gerth and Mills, eds., *op. cit.*, p. 181.
[19] *Ibid.*, p. 184.

With this twofold classification of social stratification, Weber lays the groundwork for an understanding of pluralistic forms of social conflict in modern society and helps to explain why only in rare cases are such societies polarized into the opposing camps of the "haves" and the "have-nots." He has done much to explain why Marx's exclusively class-centered scheme failed to predict correctly the shape of things to come in modern pluralistic societies.

In regard to the analysis of power in society, Weber again introduces a pluralistic notion. Although he agrees with Marx in crucial respects, he refines and extends Marx's analytical scheme. For Marx, power is always rooted, even if only in the "last analysis," in economic relations. Those who own the means of production exercise political power either directly or indirectly. Weber agreed that quite often, especially in the modern capitalist world, economic power is the predominant form. But he objects that "the emergence of economic power may be the consequence of power existing on other grounds."[20] For example, men who are able to command large-scale bureaucratic organizations may wield a great deal of economic power even though they are only salaried employees.

Weber understands by power: the chance of a man, or a number of men "to realize their own will in communal action, even against the resistance of others."[21] He shows that the basis from which such power can be exercised may vary considerably according to the social context, that is, historical and structural circumstance. Hence, where the source of power is located becomes for Weber an empirical question, one that cannot be answered by what he considers Marx's dogmatic emphasis on one specific source. Moreover, Weber argues, men do not only strive for power to enrich themselves. "Power, including economic power, may be valued 'for its own sake.' Very frequently the striving for power is also conditioned by the social 'honor' it entails."[22]

BUREAUCRACY

Weber's interest in the nature of power and authority, as well as his pervasive preoccupation with modern trends of rationalization, led him to concern himself with the operation of modern large-scale enterprises in the political, administrative, and economic realm. Bureaucratic coordination of activities, he argued, is the distinctive mark of the modern era. Bureaucracies are organized according to rational principles. Offices are ranked in a hierarchical order and their operations are characterized by impersonal rules. Incumbents are governed by methodical allocation of areas of jurisdiction and delimited spheres of duty. Appointments are made according to specialized qualifications rather than ascriptive criteria. This bureaucratic coordination of the actions of large

[20] *Ibid.*, p. 180. [21] *Ibid.* [22] *Ibid.*

numbers of people has become the dominant structural feature of modern forms of organization. Only through this organizational device has large-scale planning, both for the modern state and the modern economy, become possible. Only through it could heads of states mobilize and centralize resources of political power, which in feudal times, for example, had been dispersed in a variety of centers. Only with its aid could economic resources be mobilized, which lay fallow in pre-modern times. Bureaucratic organization is to Weber the privileged instrumentality that has shaped the modern polity, the modern economy, the modern technology. Bureaucratic types of organization are technically superior to all other forms of administration, much as machine production is superior to handicraft methods.[23]

Yet Weber also noted the dysfunctions of bureaucracy. Its major advantage, the calculability of results, also makes it unwieldy and even stultifying in dealing with individual cases. Thus modern rationalized and bureaucratized systems of law have become incapable of dealing with individual particularities, to which earlier types of justice were well suited. The "modern judge," Weber stated in writing on the legal system of Continental Europe, "is a vending machine into which the pleadings are inserted together with the fee and which then disgorges the judgment together with the reasons mechanically derived from the Code."[24]

Weber argued that the bureaucratization of the modern world has led to its depersonalization.

> [The calculability of decision-making] and with it its appropriateness for capitalism . . . [is] the more fully realized the more bureaucracy "depersonalizes" itself, i.e., the more completely it succeeds in achieving the exclusion of love, hatred, and every purely personal, especially irrational and incalculable, feeling from the execution of official tasks. In the place of the old-type ruler who is moved by sympathy, favor, grace, and gratitude, modern culture requires for its sustaining external apparatus the emotionally detached, and hence rigorously "professional" expert.[25]

Further bureaucratization and rationalization seemed to Weber an almost inescapable fate.

> Imagine the consequences of that comprehensive bureaucratization and rationalization which already today we see approaching. Already now . . . in all economic enterprises run on modern lines, rational calculation is manifest at every stage. By it, the performance of each individual worker is mathematically measured, each man becomes a little cog in the machine and, aware of this, his one preoccupation is whether he can become a bigger cog. . . . It is apparent that today we are proceeding towards an evolution which

[23] Bendix, *op. cit.*, p. 421. [24] Quoted in *ibid.* [25] *Ibid.*, pp. 421–22.

> resembles [the ancient kingdom of Egypt] in every detail, except that it is built on other foundations, on technically more perfect, more rationalized, and therefore much more mechanized foundations. The problem which besets us now is not: how can this evolution be changed?—for that is impossible, but: what will come of it?[26]

Weber's views about the inescapable rationalization and bureaucratization of the world have obvious similarities to Marx's notion of alienation. Both men agree that modern methods of organization have tremendously increased the effectiveness and efficiency of production and organization and have allowed an unprecedented domination of man over the world of nature. They also agree that the new world of rationalized efficiency has turned into a monster that threatens to dehumanize its creators. But Weber disagrees with Marx when the latter sees alienation as only a transitional stage on the road to man's true emancipation. Weber does not believe in the future leap from the realm of necessity into the world of freedom. Even though he would permit himself upon occasion the hope that some charismatic leader might arise to deliver mankind from the curse of its own creation, he thought it more probable that the future would be an "iron cage" rather than a Garden of Eden.

There is yet another respect in which Weber differed from, or rather enlarged upon, Marx. In accord with his focus on the sphere of economic production, Marx had documented in great detail how the capitalist industrial organization led to the expropriation of the worker from the means of production; how the modern industrial worker, in contrast to the artisan of the handicraft era, did not own his own tools and was hence forced to sell his labor to those who controlled him. Agreeing with most of this analysis, Weber countered with the observation that such expropriation from the means of work was an inescapable result of any system of rationalized and centrally coordinated production, rather than being a consequence of capitalism as such. Such expropriation would characterize a socialist system of production just as much as it would the capitalist form. Moreover, Weber argued, Marx's nearly exclusive concern with the productive sphere led him to overlook the possibility that the expropriation of the workers from the means of production was only a special case of a more general phenomenon in modern society where scientists are expropriated from the means of research, administrators from the means of administration, and warriors from the means of violence. He further contended that in all relevant spheres of modern society men could no longer engage in socially significant action unless they joined a large-scale organization in which they were allocated specific tasks and to which they were admitted only upon

[26] Quoted in J. P. Mayer, *Max Weber and German Politics*, 2nd ed. (London, Faber and Faber, 1956), pp. 126–27.

condition that they sacrificed their personal desires and predilections to the impersonal goals and procedures that governed the whole.

RATIONALIZATION AND DISENCHANTMENT

The world of modernity, Weber stressed over and over again, has been deserted by the gods. Man has chased them away and has rationalized and made calculable and predictable what in an earlier age had seemed governed by chance, but also by feeling, passion, and commitment, by personal appeal and personal fealty, by grace and by the ethics of charismatic heroes.

Weber attempted to document this development in a variety of institutional areas. His studies in the sociology of religion were meant to trace the complicated and tortuous ways in which the gradual "rationalization of religious life" had led to the displacement of magical procedure by *wertrational* systematizations of man's relation to the divine. He attempted to show how prophets with their charismatic appeals had undermined priestly powers based on tradition; how with the emergence of "book religion" the final systematization and rationalization of the religious sphere had set in, which found its culmination in the Protestant Ethic.

In the sphere of law, Weber documented a similar course from a "Kadi Justiz," the personalized dispensing of justice by wise leaders or elders, to the codified, rationalized, and impersonal justice of the modern world. He traced the development of political authority from kings endowed with hereditary charisma and thaumaturgical powers, to cool heads of state, ruling within the strict limits of legal prescriptions and rationally enacted law. Even so private an area of experience as music, Weber contended, was not exempt from the rationalizing tendencies of Western society. In his writings on the sociology of music Weber contrasted the concise notations and the well-tempered scale of modern music—the rigorous standardization and coordination that governs a modern symphony orchestra—with the spontaneity and inventiveness of the musical systems of Asia or of nonliterate tribes.

In his methodological writings, as we have seen, Weber strenuously objected to any interpretation of human history that subjected such history to an ineluctable driving force. He argued that society must be considered as a delicate balance of multiple opposing forces, so that a war, a revolution, or even an heroic leader might succeed in throwing the total balance in favor of a particular outcome. This is why he almost always made his statements in probabilistic terms. Nevertheless, when it came to the trends toward rationalization and bureaucratization of modern society, Weber tended to throw much of his usual analytic caution to the winds and to assert that the chances were very great indeed that mankind would in the future be imprisoned in an iron cage of its own making. In this respect, his message is thus fundamentally at variance with that of most of his nineteenth-century forebears. He is not a prophet of glad tidings to come but a harbinger of doom and disaster.

It would be pointless to attempt to summarize a work that is as amazing in its diversity as it is overwhelming in its breadth. It suffices to state explicitly what must already be apparent: Weber's work is a crucial landmark in the history of the social sciences.

There is a pre-Weberian and a post-Weberian sociology. All contemporary or near-contemporary sociology shows the impact of his genius. Even those who cannot share his pessimistic prognosis or his somewhat romantic beliefs in the saving grace of charismatic heroes can profit from the fruits of his powerful analytical labors.

THE MAN

Max Weber[27] was continually beset by psychic torment. It is impossible to understand his work without reference to the inner conflicts that attended his intellectual production. But it would be inadvisable to focus here on all the details of Weber's psychic turmoils. The commentator should discriminate; otherwise he will succumb to what Hegel once called the "psychology of the valet," the detailed analysis of small human particularities that do not touch upon a man's historical and intellectual significance.

Weber's inner tensions stemmed largely from the tangled web of his relations with his family, as well as from his attempts to escape from the stultifying political atmosphere of the Kaiser's Germany in which he lived and worked. His ambivalence toward authority in his personal life and his fascination with the topic in his writings, his double concern with rationality and with the ethic of responsibility, his attraction to innerworldly asceticism and his partial identification with the heroic life-styles of charismatic leaders—these and many other themes in his work have their source in his biography.

[27] The main information for this section comes from three major works: Marianne Weber's *Max Weber: Ein Lebensbild* (Tuebingen, J. C. B. Mohr, 1926) is a basic source for all later biographies; Eduard Baumgarten's *Max Weber: Werk und Person* (Tuebingen, J. C. B. Mohr, 1964) is a valuable account by a member of the Weber family circle who is in possession of private letters and other unpublished documents. He throws new light on a number of facets of Weber's life not sufficiently revealed by Marianne Weber; Arthur Mitzman's *The Iron Cage: An Historical Interpretation of Max Weber* (New York, Alfred A. Knopf, 1970) is a brilliant evaluation of Weber's work in terms of the social and political structure of his Germany and of the family relationships that were responsible for many of his torments.

From Max Weber: Essays in Sociology, contains a fine Introduction that provides the best short biography available. Wolfgang J. Mommsen's monumental *Max Weber und die deutsche Politik* (Tuebingen, J. C. B. Mohr, 1959) is indispensable for the consideration of Weber's relationship to the German political scene. This matter is also treated, although much more superficially, in J. P. Mayer's *Max Weber and German Politics.* Paul Honigsheim's recently translated *On Max Weber* (New York, The Free Press, 1968) is a prime source on Weber's Heidelberg circle.

IN THE FATHER'S HOUSE

Max Weber was born on April 21, 1864, the eldest of seven children of Max Weber and his wife Helene. Both parents descended from a line of Protestants, who had been refugees from Catholic persecution in the past but had later become successful entrepreneurs. Weber's paternal grandfather had been a prosperous linen dealer in Bielefeld, where the family had settled after being driven from Catholic Salzburg because of their Protestant convictions. While one of his sons took over and expanded the family business, another, Weber's father, worked for a while in the city government of Berlin and later as a magistrate in Erfurt (where Max was born) but then embarked upon a political career in the capital. In Berlin he was first a city councillor and later a member of the Prussian House of Deputies and of the German Reichstag. He was an important member of the National Liberal Party, the party of those liberals who had made their peace with Bismarck and now supported most of his policies. Very much a part of the political "establishment," the older Weber lived a self-satisfied, pleasure-loving, and shallow life. He was a fairly typical German bourgeois politician, at home in the wheeling and dealing of political affairs and not given to engage in any "idealistic" ventures that might undercut his solid anchoring with the established powers.

Weber's mother, Helene Fallenstein, came from a similar background but was made of wholly different cloth. Her father, who descended from a line of school teachers, had been a teacher himself, a translator, and romantic intellectual. After having fought in the war of liberation against Napoleon, he settled down to the rather prosaic life of a Prussian civil servant. When his first wife died, he married Emilie Souchay, the daughter of a prosperous merchant in Frankfurt. His financial position now assured, he retired to live in Heidelberg where he endeavored to be a kind of patron of the resident academic community. The Souchays descended from Huguenot emigrants who had been driven from their native France after Louis XIV had outlawed French Protestantism. They became very wealthy in Germany but continued the cultivation of an intense Calvinist religiosity.

The young Weber grew up in a cultured bourgeois household. Not only leading politicians but leading academic men were among its frequent house guests. Here Weber met, at an early age, historians Treitschke, Sybel, Dilthey and Mommsen. But his parents' marriage, though at first a seemingly happy one, was soon to show signs of increasing tension, which could hardly be hidden from the children. Weber's mother, with her strong religious commitments and her ingrained Calvinist sense of duty, had little in common with a husband whose personal ethic was hedonistic rather than Protestant.

Max Weber was precocious, yet sickly, shy, and withdrawn. His teachers complained about his lack of respect for their authority and his lack of discipline. But he was an avid reader. At the age of fourteen, he wrote letters studded with references to Homer, Virgil, Cicero, and Livy, and he had an extended knowledge of Goethe, Spinoza, Kant, and Schopenhauer before he entered university studies.

The parental household was ruled with a strong authoritarian hand by his father, who may perhaps have compensated for his flexibility in things political by being an inflexible disciplinarian at home. Although his mother made efforts to draw Max to her side and to cultivate in him the Christian piety she prized so highly, Max tended in his youth to identify with his father rather than with her. This identification may explain why the previously withdrawn and encapsulated young Weber suddenly became very much "one of the boys" when he went to the University of Heidelberg at eighteen. He joined his father's duelling fraternity and chose as his major study his father's field of law. He became as active in duelling as in drinking bouts, and the enormous quantities of beer consumed with his fraternity brothers soon transformed the thin and sickly looking young man into a heavy-set Germanic boozer proudly displaying his fencing scars.

These distractions did not keep Weber from his studies. Apart from his work in law, he attended Knies' lectures in economics and studied medieval history with Erdmannsdoerffer and philosophy with Kuno Fischer. Immanuel Bekker introduced him to Roman law and Roman institutions. In addition, Weber read a great deal in theology in the company of his elder cousin, the theologian Otto Baumgarten. After three terms, Weber left Heidelberg for military service in Strasbourg. Here he came under the influence of his uncle, the historian Hermann Baumgarten, and his wife Ida, Helene Weber's sister.

The Baumgartens soon became a second set of parents for Weber. Their influence on his development proved decisive. Hermann Baumgarten had been a liberal comrade-in-arms of his father, but, unlike him, had never made peace with the Bismarckian Reich and still adhered to the unalloyed liberalism of his youth. He refused the compromises that had advanced the political career of Weber's father. Baumgarten was content with a maverick role as an unreconciled 1848 liberal, one who was basically at odds with the dominant tendencies of the day and preferred the role of a German Jeremiah. His wife Ida was in many ways like her sister, Weber's mother, sharing her deep Calvinist piety and a thorough devotion to religious principles. She differed from her, however, in being forceful, even dominant, rather than withdrawn.

Unlike his father, who treated young Weber with patronizing authoritarianism, the uncle regarded the nephew as an intellectual peer. From the Strasbourg days to the time of Baumgarten's death in 1893, as Weber's letters eloquently testify, the uncle was his main mentor and confidant in matters political and intellectual. The influence of his aunt was equally strong. Contrary to his mother, who had not succeeded in stirring his interests in religion, his aunt led him to immerse himself in religious reading, especially in her favorite theologian, the New England divine William Ellery Channing. More generally, Weber was greatly impressed with Ida's forceful personality, the uncompromising religious standards with which she ran her household, and her deep sense of social responsibility which led her to spend a great deal of her time in charitable work. He came to appreciate the values and orientations of his mother when seeing them put into action by her sister. It is most probably in the Strasbourg period that Weber acquired his lifelong sense of awe for the Protestant virtues, even though he was unable to share the Christian belief on which they were based. He never lost respect for men who not only believed as Channing did but who actually lived his moral philosophy.

In the Strasbourg days, Weber partly freed himself from the model of a father whom he came to see as an amoral hedonist. He now tended to identify, though never fully, with the moral sternness represented in different, and even partly contradictory, ways by his uncle and aunt. He was to live with the strain created by these identifications for a long period to come.

Weber's first love was his cousin, the Baumgartens' daughter Emmy. His engagement to her lasted for six years, throughout which time the relationship was tension-ridden and brittle. Emmy was in frail health both physically and mentally. After years of agonizing doubts and guilt feelings, Weber finally broke the engagement to Emmy, who had been confined to a sanitarium for much of that time.

In the fall of 1884, his military service over, Weber returned to his parents' home to study at the University of Berlin. His parents wanted him back not only to control his rather free-wheeling ways but also to remove him from the influence of the Baumgartens. For the next eight years of his life, interrupted only by a term at the University of Goettingen and short periods of further military training, Weber stayed at his parents' house, first as a student, later as a junior barrister in Berlin courts, and finally as a *Dozent* at the University of Berlin. In those years Weber was financially dependent on a father he increasingly disliked. He had developed a greater understanding of his mother's personality and her religious values during his stay in the household of her sister, and he came to resent his father's bullying behavior toward her.

THE EARLY ACADEMIC CAREER

As a student at Berlin, Weber developed a strong antipathy for Treitschke's patriotic blustering and ranting but grew to appreciate men of sober scholarship, like his thesis advisor Jakob Goldschmidt and the historian Mommsen, with whom he studied Roman law. Weber had so close a relation with this teacher that at the defense of his Ph.D. thesis on the *History of Commercial Societies in the Middle Ages,* in 1889, Mommsen said to him: "When I come to die, there is no one better to whom I should like to say this: Son, the spear is too heavy for my hand, carry it on."

In the Berlin years Weber was enormously productive. His frantic work pace was perhaps a means for diverting his increasingly antagonistic feelings toward a father on whom he was still wholly dependent. His Ph.D. thesis, rated *summa cum laude,* was followed in 1891 by an important work on *Roman Agrarian History,* which served as his *Habilitationsschrift,* a post-doctoral thesis necessary for a university teaching position. There followed several studies on the condition of East-Elbian agricultural workers for the *Verein fuer Sozialpolitik* and for the *Evangelisch-soziale Verein.* The major one of these East-Elbian studies ran to almost nine hundred pages and was written in about a year, during which time Weber was replacing his former teacher Goldschmidt as a lecturer at the University of Berlin and also holding a full-time job at the bar. In these years Weber submitted himself to a rigid and ascetic discipline, regulating his life by the clock and dividing his daily routine into component parts with monkish rigidity.

Release from this psychic ordeal finally seemed to come in 1893, when he married Marianne Schnitger, the twenty-two-year-old daughter of a physician (a cousin on his father's side), and was appointed to a chair in economics at the University of Freiburg. From then on, Marianne and Max Weber enjoyed a very intense intellectual and moral companionship—theirs was, as the Germans say, a *Musterehe*—yet, it appears that the marriage was never consummated. Sexual fulfillment came to Weber only in his late forties, shortly before World War I, in an extramarital affair.[28]

Weber's inaugural address of 1895 on *The National State and Economic Policy,* which combined intense nationalism and superb scholarship, brought him to the attention of a wider scholarly and political world than he had been able to reach with his previous specialized studies. His new renown led to his being called to Heidelberg in 1896 to succeed his former teacher Knies as professor of economics. In Heidelberg, Weber not only reestablished contacts with his other former teachers, Bekker, Erdmannsdoerffer and Kuno Fischer, but found new friends and colleagues, such as the legal scholar Georg Jellinek and the theologian Ernst Troeltsch. The Weber home soon became a gathering ground for the flower of Heidelberg's academic intellectuals, and Weber, though still quite young, came to be seen as the central figure in an extended network of colleagues and like-minded scholars.

In addition to his scholarly concerns, Weber also pursued his political interests, playing an increasing role in Christian-Social political circles and publishing a variety of papers and memoranda on issues of the day. He was settling down to an active and creative participation in the worlds of both scholarship and politics, and he seemed destined to become a major figure in German intellectual life.

All at once, this promising career seemed to come to an end. In July 1897,

[28] Cf. Mitzman, *op. cit.* Mitzman bases his finding on Eduard Baumgarten, who is in possession of much of the unpublished family correspondence and gave Mitzman access to these data.

his parents visited Heidelberg. His father had insisted upon accompanying his wife, who would have preferred to spend a few weeks with her children without him. On that occasion, father and son clashed violently: the son accused his father of treating his mother tyrannically and brutally, and ended by telling the old man to leave his house. The father died only about a month later. Shortly thereafter Max Weber suffered a complete breakdown and did not recover for more than five years.

Weber's unresolved difficulties of identification, his inner conflicts regarding the values of father and mother, aunt and uncle, may partly account for the breakdown. Additional sources of tension and guilt may have arisen from his broken engagement with a mentally burdened cousin and his marriage to yet another cousin, who had previously been courted by a close friend of Weber's from whom he had snatched her away. Chronic overwork, in itself probably a means for escaping inner tensions, may have played its part, as may his impotence with his new wife (which in turn may have been related to his other conflicts). A detailed self-analysis, which Weber prepared for an attending physician, has been lost, so it is unlikely that the concrete causes for Weber's breakdown will ever be fully clarified.

During the next few years, Weber found himself unable to work. Often he could not even concentrate long enough to read. He traveled a great deal, especially to Switzerland and Italy. At times he seemed to be recovering, but another relapse would soon follow. When it seemed unlikely that he would ever again be able to lecture to students, he resigned from his chair at Heidelberg. He spent some time in a sanitarium and was treated by a number of specialists, but all seemed to no avail. Then almost unexpectedly, in 1903, his intellectual forces were gradually restored. He managed in that year to join with Werner Sombart and Edgar Jaffé in the editorship of the *Archiv fuer Sozialwissenschaft,* which became the leading German social science journal; his editorial duties allowed him to reestablish the contacts with friends and academic colleagues he had lost during the years of his illness.

In 1904, his former colleague from Goettingen, Hugo Muensterberg, now at Harvard, invited him to read a paper before a Congress of Arts and Sciences in St. Louis. The lecture he delivered there, on the social structure of Germany, was the first he had given in six and a half years. Weber subsequently traveled through America for over three months and was deeply impressed with the characteristics of American civilization. The roots of many later conceptions on the part played by the Protestant sects in the emergence of capitalism, on the organization of political machines, on bureaucracy, and even on the role of the Presidency in the American political structure can be traced to his stay in America.

THE YEARS OF MASTERY

Upon his return to Heidelberg, Weber resumed a full writing career, but he returned to teaching only in the last few years of his life. His intellectual output was now again astonishing. His methodological writings, the most important of which are translated in *Max Weber on the Methodology of the Social Sciences,* date from these years. *The Protestant Ethic* was published in 1905. There followed in 1906 several important studies on the political developments in Russia after the revolution of 1905. In 1908 and 1909 he did a major empirical study in the social psychology of industrial work and of factory workers. In these years he also participated actively in academic conventions and spoke at political meetings. In 1910 he became the co-founder, with Toennies and Simmel, of the German Sociological Society. He remained its secretary for several years and decisively influenced its initial program of study.

Before World War I, Weber's home in Heidelberg became the center for richly stimulating and varied intellectual gatherings. The Webers for a time shared their house with Ernst Troeltsch. Sociologists Simmel, Michels, and Sombart, and among the younger generation, Paul Honigsheim and Kurt Loewenstein, were frequent visitors, as were the philosophers Emil Lask, Wilhelm Windelband, and Heinrich Rickert, the literary critic and historian Friedrich Gundolf, and the psychiatrist-philosopher Karl Jaspers. Young radical philosophers like Ernst Bloch and Georg Lukacs were to join the circle shortly before the war.

When the World War broke out, Weber, in accord with his nationalist convictions, volunteered for service. As a reserve officer, he was commissioned to establish and run nine military hospitals in the Heidelberg area. He retired from this position in the fall of 1915.

After having said initially that, "In spite of all, this is a great and wonderful war," Weber lost his illusions. He now devoted much of his time to writing memoranda and to seeking to influence government officials, as a kind of self-appointed prophet of doom. He attacked the conduct of the war and the ineptitudes of Germany's leadership. He was particularly enraged by the increasing reliance on submarine warfare, which, he prophesied, would bring America into the war and lead to eventual defeat. He was not a principled enemy of the war, yet he urged limited war aims and restraints on the industrialists and the Junker forces of the Right, whose imperialist ambitions were wide ranging. He advocated the extension of peace feelers, especially in the direction of the English.

The established powers never availed themselves of Weber's advice and he was driven to a paroxysm of loathing and despair about the current German leadership. Articles urging a change in the whole political structure of Germany, the development of responsible parliamentary government, restrictions on the powers of the Kaiser and the Chancellor led the government to consider prosecuting him for the crime of *lèse majesté.* The reliable nationalist of yesterday seemed to come perilously close to the *Vaterlandslosen Gesellen,* the enemies of the fatherland, on the pacifist and "defeatist" Left.

When the sailors mutinied at Kiel on November 3, 1918, and gave the signal for the German revolution, Weber's first reaction was negative. He called the revolution a bloody carnival. But he soon rallied to it and attempted to develop the basis for a liberal German polity.

Earlier in 1918 Weber had for the first time in many years lectured for a full semester at the University of Vienna; a year later he accepted a call to the University of Munich where he began to lecture in the middle of the year. His well-known lectures, *Science as a Vocation* and *Politics as a Vocation,* were first delivered to an audience of students at Munich in 1919, and bear all the marks of his attempt to define his major political and intellectual orientation in a time of revolutionary upheaval.

In the last three years of his life, 1918–20, Weber developed an astounding political activity. He wrote a number of major newspaper articles, memoranda, and papers on the politics of the hour. He was a founding member of and active campaigner for the newly organized Deutsche Demokratische Partei; he served as an adviser to the German delegation to the Versailles peace conference; he had an active hand in the preliminary work of writing a new German constitution; he addressed student assemblies and academic groups alike and endeavored, in the revolutionary turmoil of these days, to define a rational-democratic orientation, opposed alike to the right-wing excesses of the enemies of the Republic and the revolutionary chiliasm of some of his young friends on the Left. He attempted to establish close contacts with the Social Democratic movement, but the man who had committed the sacrilege of calling the revolution a bloody carnival never managed to overcome the opposition of most left-wing politicians. As a result, proposals to have him join the government or to make him a candidate for the Presidency of the Republic came to naught. Party bureaucrats could only be suspicious of a man who, though he had shifted from monarchist to republican loyalties, continued to be highly critical of party machines and openly hankered for some decisive charismatic breakthrough that would put an end to the reign of mediocrities.

During the war years, Weber put the finishing touches to his work on the sociology of religion. *The Religion of China* and *The Religion of India* were published in 1916, and *Ancient Judaism* appeared a year later.[29] During this period, and in the immediate postwar years, Weber also worked on his *magnum opus, Wirtschaft und Gesellschaft* (*Economy and Society*). Although he was not able to complete this work, what he finished was published post-

[29] I list these works for convenience by the titles given to them in Hans Gerth's English translations. They are all published by The Free Press.

humously, as were his last series of lectures at Munich, entitled *General Economic History*.

AN EXEMPLARY MORALIST

Early in June 1920, Weber developed a high fever, and at first it was thought that he suffered from the flu. The illness was later diagnosed as pneumonia, but it was too late. He died on June 14th.

The last fevered words of the man whose physical appearance was once compared by a contemporary to that of Albrecht Dürer's gaunt knights, were: "The Truth is the Truth." Weber indeed had much in common with those Germanic cultural heroes who battled for what they considered justice and truth, unconcerned with what lesser souls might consider the demands of expediency. He was a man in the tradition of Luther's "Here I stand, I can do no other," even though at times it would almost appear to his contemporaries that he had more in common with Don Quixote.

In all circumstances Weber remained fiercely independent in his political stand, refusing to bend to any ideological line. He was the man who advocated after the lost war that the first Polish official to set foot in the city of Danzig should be shot, thus appearing to support the politics of the right; he was also the man who pressed for the execution of the right-wing assassin of Kurt Eisner, the socialist leader of Bavaria's revolutionary government. He was the man who hated Ludendorff, the detested head of the general staff, yet toyed with the idea of defending him after the war against what he considered unjust accusations and even attempted to convert him to his version of plebiscitarian democracy.

Wherever he perceived an injustice, Weber entered the arena like a wrathful prophet castigating his fellows for their moral sloth, their lack of conviction, their sluggish sense of justice. When the academic powers refused to recognize the merit of a Sombart or a Simmel or a Michels, Weber rose passionately to their defense, even risking old friendships, when he felt that certain of his colleagues were moved by expediency in refusing professorships to Jews or political radicals. When Russians, Poles, and Eastern Jewish students were shunned by respectable German professors, Weber gathered them around himself and invited them to his home. When, during the war, pacifists and political radicals like the poet Ernst Toller were being persecuted, he asked them to his famous Sunday open house. Later, when Toller was arrested, Weber testified for him in a military court and succeeded in having him released. When anti-Semitic, right-wing students in Munich insulted a Jewish student, Weber got hold of their leader and insisted that he apologize immediately. When a friend of his, Frieda Gross, had a love affair with a Swiss anarchist and was threatened with losing the custody of her children, Weber fought in the courts for over a year to defend her maternal rights. When

Ernst Troeltsch refused during the war, in his capacity as administrator of a military hospital, to permit French prisoners to be visited by Germans, Weber denounced this as a "wretched case of chauvinism" and broke off relations with his old friend.

Always and everywhere, Weber followed only the call of his own demon, refusing to be bridled by political expediency. He was first and foremost his own man. Although he repeatedly entered the political arena, he was not truly a political man—if we define such a man (as Weber himself did) as one who is able to make compromises in the pursuit of his aims. Weber has written that the true politician feels "passionate devotion to a 'cause,' to the god or demon who is overlord."[30] This passion he possessed in full measure; but the concomitant sense of "distance to things and men" did not characterize his political actions, although it is very much in evidence in his scholarly work. As a result, Weber found himself isolated in his political activities. He never qualified as "a good party man."[31] His open nationalism of the Freiburg days antagonized his old-fashioned liberal friends, while his attacks on the Prussian Junkers made him the *bête noire* of the conservatives. His dire prophecy that socialism would hasten the trend toward bureaucratization, rather than bring the promised freedom from necessity, alienated him from the Social Democrats despite his sympathy for the labor unions and his admiration for the sober virtues of skilled German workmen. His passionate attacks against Kaiser Wilhelm and his entourage, his violent outbursts against the leadership in the war effort, endeared him to the pacifist and radical Left, whose trust he yet failed to gain after he characterized the revolution as a bloody carnival.

How could Weber, the exponent of "disenchantment" and "the ethic of responsibility," the German patriot and life-long admirer of the innerworldly asceticism of the Protestant Ethic feel himself drawn to rebels and outcasts? Why could the dispassionate and disciplined author of *Science as a Vocation* not hide his sympathies for passionate bohemians or Tolstoyan mystics? These questions become clearer after examining the context of his Germany and considering more fully his involvement in its politics.

THE INTELLECTUAL CONTEXT

Weber's mind was amazingly catholic and the influences on his thought were many and diverse. He was not a philosopher, yet he was familiar with most of the classical philosophical systems by the time he was a university student. He was not a theologian, but his work offers evidence of his extensive reading in theology. An economic historian, he read practically everything that was written in this field and in the field of economic theory as well. He had a

[30] Gerth and Mills, eds., *op. cit.*, p. 115. [31] *Ibid.*

first rate legal mind and was thoroughly versed in the history and philosophy of law. He had an encyclopedic knowledge of ancient and modern history as well as of the history of oriental societies. He was naturally immersed in all the important sociological works of the day, and he seems even to have been familiar with the then still fairly unknown writings of Sigmund Freud. Weber was one of the last polyhistors.

Among the many intellectual forces that affected Weber's thought, a few lines of influence stand out that link him to some of his contemporaries and near contemporaries. Weber's overall approach to the social sciences was significantly affected by the methodological discussions on the differences between the sciences of nature and of men; these discussions started in Germany in the generation of Kant, were further extended with Hegel and the romantics and were revived in the last decades of the nineteenth century.

WEBER AND THE INHERITANCE OF IDEALISM

Ever since Kant, the German idealistic tradition had established a radical disjunction between the world of man and of nature. Kant taught that man participated in the phenomenal world as an object, as a physical body, but that the distinctive aspect of man was not his body but his spirit. As a spiritual being, man was seen to participate in the domain of ideas as a free subject, even though he was a determined object as a physical body. "Hence," Talcott Parsons states, "the Kantian scheme favored the reduction of all phenomenal aspects of man, especially the biological, to a 'materialistic' basis, and produced a radical hiatus between this and the spiritual life."[32]

This Kantian disjunction informed, in a variety of ways, all German philosophy down to the days of Weber. It claimed that man as an active, purposive, and free actor in the realm of culture and history could not be dealt with by the analytical and generalizing methods appropriate for the investigation of nature. His mind and its creations are not subject to natural laws. The methods of analysis applicable to the sciences of man must be particularizing rather than generalizing; they must limit themselves to the empathic apprehending of the springs of action of individual historical actors or to efforts to grasp intuitively total cultural wholes (*Gestalten*). Any attempt to break down such totalities by "atomistic" analyses, or to subsume under generalizing categories or laws the activities of individual actors within unique constellations, was considered illegitimate. To quote Parsons again: "Since the general analytical level of scientific comprehension is *a priori* excluded, things human can be understood only in terms of the concrete individuality of the specific historical case."[33]

[32] *The Structure of Social Action*, p. 474. [33] *Ibid.*, p. 477.

Weber's work grows out of this German tradition, even though he broke with many, if not most, of its main tenets. Three major figures among his contemporaries had an impact on his thinking: the philosophers Wilhelm Windelband (1848–1915) and Heinrich Rickert (1863–1936), key representatives of the so-called Marburg or South-Western school of neo-Kantianism, and the philosopher and cultural historian Wilhelm Dilthey (1833–1911), who taught at Berlin. These men influenced Weber by transmitting to him some of the classical Kantian doctrines in modern dress and by giving him the occasion to fashion his own methodology partly in agreement and partly in opposition to their teachings. Dilthey as well as the neo-Kantians were intent upon combatting naturalism and materialism in the sciences of men and defending the distinctiveness of these sciences in the face of what they considered the positivistic heresy. Yet they differed in their approaches and proposed solutions.

Dilthey's ambition throughout his long life was to write a critique of historical reason, which would do for history what Kant had done for the epistemology of the natural sciences and for ethics. He never realized this ambition, but he left a mass of, often contradictory, fragments. Dilthey opposed positivism by constructing the outlines of an approach to the data of human culture and human history, which, though meant to be scientific, was wholly at variance with the approach of the natural sciences. Knowledge of the world of man, Dilthey claimed, could only be attained through an internal process, through experience (*erleben*) and understanding (*verstehen*), rather than through merely external knowledge. Since human actors and their cultural creations are endowed with meaning, the humanistic scholar must be concerned with understanding these meanings, and the only way in which he can accomplish this is through re-experiencing (*Nacherleben*) the meanings carried by historical actors or cultural objects. A major tool for this enterprise, Dilthey asserted, would be a novel type of psychology, for here the old analytical and atomizing psychology would be of no avail. What was needed was a synthesizing and descriptive psychology that could grasp the totality of the subject's experiences by empathic understanding. The natural sciences (*Naturwissenschaften*) can do no more than explain (*erklaeren*) observed events by relating them to natural laws. In the humanistic disciplines, the *Geisteswissenschaften,* knowledge is not external but internal. Men are intelligible to us in their uniqueness and individuality.[34]

Although the neo-Kantians Rickert and Windelband had much in common

[34] On Dilthey cf. H. A. Hodges, *Wilhelm Dilthey* (London, Trubner, 1944), as well as the same author's *The Philosophy of Dilthey* (London, Routledge, 1952), and his short article on Dilthey in *The International Encyclopedia of the Social Sciences* (New York, Macmillan, 1968). I have also borrowed from H. Stuart Hughes' treatment of Dilthey in his *Consciousness and Society* (New York, Vintage Books, 1961), and from Fritz K. Ringer's remarks on Dilthey in his *The Decline of the German Mandarins* (Cambridge, Harvard University Press, 1969).

with Dilthey's attempt to distinguish the procedures appropriate to the study of man from those used in the natural sciences, they differed from him both in their analytical focus and in their specific doctrine. They did not accept his *Naturwissenschaft-Geisteswissenschaft* dichotomy and argued that the distinctions to be drawn had to be in terms of method rather than of subject matter. Since certain aspects of human behavior could be studied by the methods of the natural sciences used in traditional psychology, the whole domain of human activities could not be claimed by the *Geisteswissenschaften*. The real distinctions to be made, Rickert and Windelband taught, hinge on the differences between individualizing and generalizing thought. There exist two radically opposed scientific approaches: the *nomothetic* sciences that aim at establishing universal laws and uniformities, and the *idiographic* sciences, above all history or *Kulturwissenschaft,* that only give descriptive accounts of particular historical constellations or individual historical actors. In the domain of history, they argued, generalizing thought is inapplicable.

In his treatment of historical knowledge, Rickert, in tune with the Kantian heritage, insisted that the act of knowing transforms the object of knowledge. "Such a transformation is always determined by the theoretical purpose (*Erkenntniszweck*) which lies behind the attempt to gain knowledge."[35] Historical knowledge is characterized by an interest in the particular rather than the general; it attempts to grasp concreteness and individuality.

Even if it is granted that historical knowledge aims at the understanding of historical individuals rather than general laws, one may still ask why the historian chooses one individual rather than another as his object of research. Here Rickert introduces the notion of value-relevance (*Wertbeziehung*), which, however, he defines differently than Weber was to do later. According to Rickert, what makes an actor a historical individual is not the fact that a particular scholar values him, but rather his relevance to universally acknowledged cultural values. Rickert emphasized, as Weber did after him, that historians are selective when they proceed to attack a historical problem; they choose to seek understanding of one aspect of history rather than another. But in contrast to Weber, who took it as an irreducible fact that the investigator's own values influence these choices, Rickert believed there existed a normal consciousness of cultural values shared by all mankind. He attempted to shield himself from accusations of cultural relativism by asserting that primary historical objects are those historical individuals in whom generally acknowledged cultural values are uniquely embodied.

Weber owed much of his notion of *verstehen* to Dilthey, as well as to his close personal friend, the psychiatrist-philosopher Karl Jaspers, who made much of the distinction between explanation and understanding. Jaspers argued that

[35] The quotation is from Maurice Mandelbaum's *The Problem of Historical Knowledge* (New York, Harper & Row, 1967), p. 121. I have profited much from Mandelbaum's fine essay on Rickert in this volume. Cf. also H. Stuart Hughes, *op. cit.*

we can explain a falling rock in terms of physical laws, but that the relation between, say, a childhood experience and a later neurosis could only be grasped through empathic understanding of the working of the psyche. But Weber stripped these notions of the implication that intuitive knowledge and causal knowledge were irreconcilable. He emphasized, to the contrary, that *verstehen* should only be the first step in a process of causal imputation. Weber learned much from the neo-Kantian concept of value-relevance, but he divorced it from its metaphysical underpinnings in the notion of universally acknowledged values. He remained cognizant of the distinctions between *Naturwissenschaft* and *Geistes-* or *Kulturwissenschaft* but kept insisting that these distinctions hinged on the cognitive purposes of the investigator, not on principled differences in method or subject matter. All in all, he attempted to direct the German idealistic position into a closer relation with the positivist tradition of empirical verification and causal imputation. But he still retained what seemed to him the distinctive achievements of the German tradition: the emphasis on the search for subjective meanings that impel the action of historical actors.

WEBER AND GERMAN HISTORICISM AND SOCIOLOGY

In regard to Weber's substantive concerns, the men who made a profound impression were the economic historians and historicist economists Wilhelm Roscher and Karl Knies, and among the younger generation Gustav Schmoller, Adolph Wagner and Lujo Brentano and their associates. Knies had been Weber's teacher; with most of the others Weber had continued contact through his involvement in the *Verein fuer Sozialpolitik* in which many of them played leading roles.

The so-called "older" branch of the historical school of economics, which dated back to the middle of the nineteenth century, and the "younger" branch founded by Schmoller in the 1870's differed in many respects, but what united all major exponents was the rejection of classical economics. They objected to the notion that economic laws applicable under any conditions could be deduced from a few axiomatic propositions; they urged instead that the economic life of a nation could only be understood in terms of its particular cultural and historical development. Rather than reasoning deductively from the assumed behavior of some imaginary "economic man," they urged that economics had to be an inductive science of the concrete economic behavior of particular men in particular social contexts. This accounts for their institutional emphasis and their insistence on the importance of the noneconomic matrix of economic life.

When Schmoller, Wagner, and Brentano founded the *Verein fuer Sozialpolitik* in 1872, they broadened their interests and moved from purely scholarly concerns to questions of public policy. The *Verein* served as a vehicle for molding public opinion and urging the administration to take a greater interest in social issues and in social reform. The leaders of the *Verein,* who soon came to be known as "Socialists of the Chair," urged the adoption of improved social insurance schemes, better factory inspection, limited programs for public works, and state ownership of all railroads. They argued that only an active policy of reform would prevent the further rise of the Socialist movement and that state planning, rather than unbridled laissez faire, was to the interest of the nation and the state. Some members of the group differed politically—Schmoller, for example, was a "state socialist," while Brentano was much more of an old-time liberal. But they all had in common the concern with an "ethically oriented" social and economic policy that would reduce some of the glaring inequities of modern industrial society and help reintegrate the alienated working class.[36]

Weber took much of his approach in economic history and sociology from the historicist school, even though he was by no means as hostile to classical economics as they were. Against them he argued that generalized theoretical categories were as necessary in the social sciences as in the natural sciences, and that the historicists' atheoretical position threatened to bog them down in the futile gathering of a multitude of historical facts. Yet he agreed with them in insisting that economic behavior must be conceptualized within a social and institutional context.

Weber's major disagreement with the members of the *Verein fuer Sozialpolitik,* however, lay on another plane. He objected strenuously to their failure to discriminate between facts and values. For example, despite the fact that Knies was Weber's teacher and had a profound influence on his thought, nonetheless he was at variant with some of Knies' notions, for example, his romantic idea of "folk soul." Such concepts, Weber wrote in his essay on Roscher and Knies, were only a "metaphysically paler version of Roscher's pious belief that the 'souls' . . . of peoples originate directly from the hand of God."[37] Weber was even more critical of the younger members of the school grouped around Schmoller. He objected that their glorification of the national state and of the house of Hohenzollern vitiated their scientific work and, wittingly or unwittingly, made them partisans of the existing state instead of disinterested scholars. He shared their concern with social policy, and he conducted some of his own investigations within the framework of the *Verein,* but he chided them repeatedly for their neglect of a principle that seemed of overriding importance to him: the principle of value neutrality.

Among contemporary sociologists, Simmel and Toennies influenced Weber most. In the preface to *Wirtschaft und Gesellschaft,* he specifically drew atten-to the "fine work" of Toennies, the author of *Gemeinschaft und Gesellschaft,*[38]

[36] On the German school of historical economics, cf. Ben B. Seligman, *Main Currents in Modern Economics* (New York, The Free Press, 1962), and Fritz Ringer's *The Decline of the German Mandarins.* [37] Quoted in H. Stuart Hughes, *op. cit.,* p. 303.

[38] *The Theory of Social and Economic Organization,* p. 88.

from whom he directly borrowed the distinction between communal and associative relationships (*Vergemeinschaftung* and *Vergesellschaftung*). The influence of Simmel, who was Weber's close personal friend, is easily traced. Simmel's social "forms," for example, have a great deal in common with Weber's ideal types. Weber's insistence on the crucial importance of money in the emergence of rationalized economic systems owes much to Simmel's *Philosophy of Money*. Weber's methodological reflections on the function of the quest for meaning in historical and sociological research were stimulated in part by Simmel's early work on *The Problems of the Philosophy of History*. In this last respect, however, he differed very significantly from Simmel in that, to quote him directly, he drew "a sharp distinction between subjectively intended and objectively valid 'meanings'; two different things which Simmel not only fails to distinguish but often deliberately treats as belonging together."[39]

TWO CRUCIAL INFLUENCES: NIETZSCHE AND MARX

A fuller account than can be given here would also probe into the reciprocal influences between Weber and the social and economic historian Werner Sombart, the church historian and social historian Ernst Troeltsch, the sociologist Robert Michels, the legal scholar Georg Jellinek, and many other close friends and associates with whom Weber often talked for hours in his Heidelberg study and elsewhere, and with whom he was associated either in the editing of the *Archiv fuer Sozialwissenschaft,* as a member of the *Verein fuer Sozialpolitik,* or in his capacity as the first secretary of the German Society for Sociology. This discussion will concentrate on Weber's lifelong involvement with two most divergent intellectual giants of the past: Friedrich Nietzsche and Karl Marx.

The influence both these writers had on Weber is especially apparent in his sociology of ideas and interests. "Not ideas, but material and ideal interests," wrote Weber, "directly govern men's conduct. Yet very frequently the 'world images' that have been created by 'ideas' have, like switchmen, determined the tracks along which action has been pushed by the dynamic of interests."[40] As this quotation makes clear, Weber, while insisting on a greater relevance of ideas than either Nietzsche or Marx would grant, was affected by Marx's notion that ideas were expressions of public interests and served as weapons in the struggle of classes and parties. He was also highly sensitive to the Nietzschean analysis of the psychological mechanisms by which ideas became rationalizations utilized in the service of private aspirations for power and mastery. Weber was especially impressed, as was Max Scheler at almost the same time, with the Nietzschean notion of *Ressentiment* as an expression of

[39] *Ibid.* [40] *From Max Weber,* p. 280.

the repressed envy and hatred of socially disadvantaged groups.[41] Objecting to both Marx and Nietzsche, Weber claimed that ideas are not mere reflections of psychic or social interests and argued that with both these men the analysis of ideas often turned into crude debunking. Yet no reader of Weber can fail to note his debt to them in his sociology of ideas.

Nor should it be difficult to see that such notions as "disenchantment," "charisma" and the like, though not directly traceable to Nietzsche, were elaborated by Weber with the assistance of powerful stimulation from the author of *Beyond Good and Evil.* A good deal of Weber's personal ethic of heroic stoicism was also inspired by Nietzsche. There was much of *Zarathustra* in Max Weber.

Reference has already been made to the fact that much of Weber's work, not only his sociology of ideas, can best be understood as a continued interchange of ideas with Karl Marx. His theories of stratification and of economic behavior, for example, have their roots in Marxian economics and sociology. More generally, Weber admired Marx's hard-headed and matter-of-fact scholarship, his contempt for the cloudy "idealistic" mystifications of the German philosophical tradition. He saw in him a kindred spirit who refused to think in terms of a disembodied *Kultur, Geist,* and *Volk* but focused his attention on the actions of concrete human actors. Even when he criticized what he came to regard as Marx's overly simplified economic interpretation of history, he always remained respectful of Marx's intellectual eminence.

Weber once said to one of his Munich students, "The honesty of a contemporary scholar, and above all of a contemporary philosopher, can be easily ascertained in terms of his position vis-à-vis Nietzsche and Marx. Those who do not admit that they could not do major parts of their own work without the contributions made by these two men, deceive themselves as well as others. The world in which we live intellectually has been shaped to a large extent by Marx and Nietzsche."[42] Weber did not deceive himself or his students. A large part of his own work stands under the shadow of these two figures.

THE SOCIAL CONTEXT

Weber, like Simmel, struggled to find a vantage point from which he could analyze society with a maximum of objectivity, but they differed in the strategy they pursued, which was largely determined by their dissimilar existential situation. Simmel attempted to withdraw as much as possible from the political and social struggles of the day and reached objectivity by taking

[41] Max Scheler, *Ressentiment,* transl. by Wolfgang Holdheim, ed., and with an introduction by Lewis A. Coser (New York, The Free Press, 1961).

[42] Baumgarten, *op. cit.,* pp. 554–55.

advantage of his double marginality, as a Jew and as an outsider in the university. Weber, the son of Protestant "insiders," attained similar goals by actively involving and immersing himself in the issues and policies of his day. Much like the "innerworldly ascetics" of early Calvinism about whom he wrote with such awe and admiration, Weber gained intellectual autonomy by plunging into the struggles of the social and political world rather than by "otherworldly" withdrawal from its turmoils.

Some of the roots of such variant strategies may be found in the dissimilar family backgrounds of Simmel and Weber. Simmel, it will be recalled, lost his father at an early age and had rather cool relations with his mother. He never experienced a close and emotionally rich involvement with members of his immediate family, but seems to have been an outsider at a fairly early age. In contrast, Weber was deeply enmeshed in his family relationships, tied by multiple bonds of emotion and identification not only to his father and mother but to other kinsmen, particularly his Strasbourg relatives. Pulled in different directions by differing claims of loyalty, the young Weber did not withdraw, as Simmel had done, but rather attempted to clarify his emotions and sort out his commitments by viewing his relationships with detached concern.[43] Such a strategy, however, took a serious toll of his psychic energies; it finally led to his breakdown when repressed antagonisms burst out in that final confrontation between father and son shortly before the father's death.

Weber pursued a similar course in his involvement on a political scene, where repressive and antagonistic forces were at least as pronounced as those that he had found at home. Here also he gained detachment through immersion. He became master of the forces that impinged upon him by striving for unillusioned analytical clarity. In this he was helped by his affiliation with the academy, which provided a haven for scholarly detachment, even though many of its members failed to live up to the ideal of objectivity.

THE FAMILY NETWORK

"The bonds of kinship," writes his biographer, Eduard Baumgarten, "within which the young and growing Max Weber developed his capacities of empathy and self-protection, formed an unusually close net. Throughout his life he remained truly within the net and yet learned, even as a child, to escape from its narrow meshes into the wider world of adventure and wonder."[44]

It will be remembered that the young Weber attempted to escape from the contradictory pulls of father and mother by withdrawing into the world of

[43] The notion of detached concern originated in the work of Robert K. Merton and some of his students, particularly Renée Fox. Cf. Robert K. Merton, George G. Reader, and Patricia Kendall, eds., *The Student Physician* (Cambridge, Mass., Harvard University Press, 1957).

[44] Baumgarten, *op. cit.,* p. 627.

study. He developed a general rebelliousness against authority figures other than his father, mainly his teachers. Somewhat later, as a student, he attempted to overcome his tensions by identifying with paternal authority and by adopting life styles, such as drinking bouts and dueling, which were peculiar to the culture shared by his father. That these attempts at identification with the father were superficial is attested to by the fact that when Weber moved to Strasbourg, he quickly came to identify with his aunt's active Christian piety, as well as his uncle's stern, uncompromising, and principled liberalism. The oppressive family triangle was now enlarged for Weber by the addition of these two significant people. Though he was to return to a partial identification with his father at a later time, he had now acquired a new perspective about the values and the personality of his mother through her more forceful and dominant sister, and gained new insight about the self-satisfied and compromise-prone authoritarianism of his father through his contact with his uncle. This led Weber to reject much of the paternal image and to gain new understanding and love for his mother. He now had in the person of his uncle, a supportive high-status friend on whom he could rely in his struggle against the authority and the authoritarianism of his father.[45]

During the years when he was totally dependent on his father, Weber came increasingly to detest him and moved closer to his mother. There are indications that she now openly told the son of the indignities she suffered from her husband. Following his marriage and academic appointments to Freiburg and later to Heidelberg, he seemed at first able to look at his parents' situation with the detachment that comes from autonomy. Yet, his mother's complaints about the brutal and authoritarian treatment she received continued to preoccupy the son and led to the final rupture. The feelings of guilt he incurred when his father died soon afterwards are likely to have contributed to Weber's subsequent breakdown. He had tried to stand above the battle between his parents and take the side of his mother in a covert manner but he failed. This inability to remain neutral, he must have felt, had thus precipitated a catastrophe.

One may assume from the relative emotional balance Weber later achieved that, during the course of his illness, he slowly arrived at an inner clarification of his confused tangle of personal relations and emotions, of family identifications and loyalties. Throughout the rest of his life he was by no means what modern conceit would call a "well-adjusted" man. Erratic outbursts and passionately intense eruptions would often punctuate more calm stretches of his life course, but on the whole he managed to keep in balance the contradictory urges in his personality. As his work shows, he would pass from admiration for the ascetic self-restraints of Calvinism to a greater appreciation of the charismatic virtues of aristocratic heroism. Usually, however, he would keep

[45] Cf. Morris Freilich, "The Natural Triad in Kinship and Complex Systems," *American Sociological Review*, XXIX, 4 (August, 1964), pp. 530 ff.

these variant personal preferences in check through a severe self-denying ordinance that enjoined him to be value-neutral in his scholarly work.

After his recovery, Weber remained very close to his mother, who fully discussed her problems with him and who considered him, so she said, like a "sister." His relationship with his wife, marred though it must have been by his incapacity to consummate the marriage, was nevertheless marked by full trust and devotion on both sides. Furthermore, Weber remained deeply attached to his brothers and sisters, as well as to a number of other relatives. The intensity of these family relationships is revealed in the many long and personal letters exchanged between Weber and his kin, only a few of which have as yet been published. A contemporary American reader may find it hard to understand how people could spend so much energy discussing the ethical criteria of their own conduct and that of others, questioning who was right and who was wrong. This endless weighing of the motives and consequences of moral action must be understood in terms of a Lutheran and Kantian culture of moral duty—one that is fairly alien to contemporary English-American civilization, which often appears to be governed by an ethic of compromise and expediency. The Lutheran culture of Weber's day was still haunted by the words of Matthew (XIX:21), "If thou wilt be perfect. . . ."

Weber's devotion to his mother was probably "overdetermined." Apart from oedipal themes, one must consider that Weber was the oldest son. In the German upper-class tradition—witness for example Thomas Mann's *Buddenbrooks*—the oldest son is expected to continue the paternal tradition and to walk in the father's footsteps; he must protect the members of his family, including his mother. Thus, what prompted Weber to shield his mother from his father was not only a sense of justice, combined with an oedipal attachment and respect for her values; it was his culturally legitimized self-image as a dutiful German bourgeois son.

Weber's conviction that as the oldest son he had to assume family leadership is evidenced by his desire to act as a guide and counsel to his younger siblings and to other relatives. He was concerned with all their personal, marital, and professional problems, while still attempting to retain an impartiality that characterizes the truly wise counsellor.

THE PUBLIC SCENE

Weber's conduct on the public scene has a remarkable resemblance to his behavior in the private sphere. Here also he made no attempts to withdraw, in the manner of Simmel, but rather immersed himself deeply in public matters, striving at the same time to maximize his objective understanding. Just as in the case of his relation with his family, his efforts toward detachment and objectivity were never fully successful. In fact, he was often subject to contradictory pulls, which he tried to keep in some balance by simultaneous emphasis on his two roles: as a political actor and as a value-neutral observer.

Weber's Germany had a highly developed industrial economy, with a political structure dominated by the semifeudal values of Prussian conservatism.[46] Its political system was "a combination of a patriarchal type of authoritarianism with a highly developed formal legalism."[47] Rigidly trained civil servants, deeply devoted to the Kantian notion of duty and imbued with a strong sense of prerogative and authority, ran the affairs of the country in close collaboration with an officer corps composed of East-Elbian Junkers or of men who aped their lifestyles. The middle classes prospered economically while being politically subservient. The working class was excluded from political decision-making, though at times it was indulged economically through social welfare measures. The intellectual elite among the university professors cultivated what Ringer, a modern American historian of ideas, has called a "mandarin" style of life. They flaunted their devotion to the world of ideas, resented the "materialistic" interests of the new industrial class society, and cultivated their status-honor. Most of them refused to immerse themselves in what they considered "dirty politics." Uninvolved in the struggles of the hour, they in fact supported the Wilhelminian *status quo*.[48]

Weber differed from the majority of his colleagues in the university by having intense political interests. Like most of them he was a passionate German nationalist, but unlike them he was deeply dissatisfied with Prussian conservatism rather than with the alleged "materialism" of the new industrial society. He resented the continued political dominance of the Junkers and civil servants, not out of commitment to democratic values as such, but because he feared that such continued dominance would be injurious to the German national mission. His lifelong preoccupation with social reform was not solely motivated by concern for the fate of the working class in industrial society. It was at least co-determined by his belief that the German national mission would be impaired if the country were internally torn and if the working class were to remain permanently alienated from the rest of society.

Although Weber's early writings on the agricultural situation of East Elbia display, as Mitzman, a contemporary biographer of Max Weber, has shown, a number of internal inconsistencies, they are informed as a whole by his feeling that continued Junker dominance in the East would undermine the power of the German nation and would lead to economic decadence and to the enlarged influence of culturally unassimilable Poles. He opposed the Junkers not so much because they were "undemocratic" but because they stood in the way of the political and economic development of Germany as a powerful

[46] Talcott Parsons, *Essays in Sociological Theory,* rev. ed. (New York, The Free Press, 1954), pp. 104 ff. [47] *Ibid.,* p. 109.

[48] For a more complete description of Germany's political and social scene during this time, see the preceding chapter on Simmel.

industrial country. The Junkers were to him upholders of patriarchal and feudalistic traditions, which hampered the emergence of a truly modern bourgeois polity. Weber hoped for the growth of a "class-conscious bourgeoisie" ready and eager to take the reins from an antiquated, semifeudal stratum and from rule-obsessed, uncreative, and hide-bound civil servants. As distinct from most of his colleagues who still hankered after a romanticized pre-industrial age in which the *Volk*, not economic interest groups, dominated the arena, Weber stood resolutely on the side of modernity and against those who whined and complained about the demise of the good old days.

Nevertheless Weber also differed profoundly from those liberals who professed to see in modernity the evidence of unalloyed progress. He showed in exhaustive detail the advantages of the rational, methodical ethic of work, which lay at the root of the spirit of capitalism, and, more particularly, the economic miracle that rational capitalism had made possible. But he also pointed out that a deadening of initiative and creativity was likely to follow from further extending the scope of rational-legal bureaucratic modes of administration on which state and economy must rest in the modern age.

Weber was convinced that increasing rationalization and bureaucratization was unavoidable, but this was precisely why he tried to avoid the domination (*Herrschaft*) of the bureaucracy. When in his last years he became the resolute champion of a political reorganization in which Parliament would no longer play its subservient role of the past, he was not so much expressing a principled commitment to democratic ideas but rather the hope that Parliament would be able to control the spread of bureaucratization. His stand for a mass democracy led by powerful leading figures, a vision similar in many ways to that of General de Gaulle in our day, was mainly rooted in his concern for the maintenance of a strong modern national state—one that would not be held back by Junker dominance or allowed to ossify under continued rule by Prussian civil servants.

These are some of the preoccupations that characterize Weber's overall political thought. His concrete political stance, however, changed considerably over time. When he voted for the first time, he chose the Conservatives, and he belonged for a few years to the reactionary and jingoistic *Alldeutscher Verband*. At the time of his famous Freiburg Inaugural Address on "The National State and Economic Policy," in which he urged his listeners to be guided by one standard only, "the permanent power-political interests of the nation," he had already lost hope in the Conservatives and had come to see them as tools of the interests of the Junkers. He now opted for a kind of liberal imperialism through which the powers of the new industrial nation would be mobilized to enable Germany to assume a stronger and more dominant role on the world scene. A few years later he was deeply involved with the Christian-Social movement, led by his close friend Friedrich Naumann, which attempted to battle for social reform and liberalism at home and for resolute and assertive national politics abroad.

During the war, Weber's hatred of the incompetence of the nation's leadership—his despairing vision that the civil servants, the Junkers, the Court, and the army would lose the war and ruin Germany's world chances forever—brought him closer to the radical opponents of the war. After the war, he attempted to come nearer to the leadership of the now dominant Social Democrats, and even was sympathetic with such ultra-leftists as Ernst Toller. He took a leading hand in the creation of the German Democratic Party, the bourgeois liberal allies of the Social Democrats. This party was meant to represent those middle-class forces that accepted the new regime and were willing to lay the foundation of a popular democracy opposed alike to traditionalistic conservatism of the right and to the revolutionary chiliasm of the left.

Yet, although susceptible to the attractions of various ideological commitments and subject to the contrary pull of differing loyalties, Weber managed to maintain a measure of political and intellectual distance by never fully succumbing to the blandishments of any of them. He was never a party man even when he descended into the political arena, but he never played the role of bystander, which Simmel had chosen for himself. Despite his passionate concern for political issues, he remained largely detached from partisan passions. He was to some extent above the battle even while he was engaged in a political struggle—a stance that became feasible because his major roots were in the academy and not in the political market place. As an academic man, Weber could cultivate a value-neutral analysis of political and social trends in which he himself participated. Here he could analyze political commitments, whether his own or others, *sine ira et studio*. In this way he achieved a distance from them that in many ways resembled the relative distance he had come to gain within his web of kinship. By splitting himself, so to speak, into a politically active and an observant self, he tried, though not without a great deal of struggle, to do justice to both his active and contemplative temperaments and to reach intellectual mastery in the face of conflicting commitments.

THE ACADEMIC MAN

Weber's academic position allowed him to escape through value-neutral analysis from the Babel of discordant voices that characterized the public scene, and to proceed to that "ideological demystification," to use Ernst Topitsch's phrase, which characterizes much of his contribution to sociology.[49]

49 *Verhandlungen des 15ten Deutschen Soziologentages* (Tuebingen, J. C. B. Mohr-Siebeck, 1965), pp. 19 ff.

In contrast to Simmel, an academic outsider, Weber was very much part of the academic scene, which, however, he criticized most sharply from the inside. While Simmel's advancement in the university hierarchy had been severely impeded—he became a full professor only at the end of his life and then only in a minor university—Weber very early was made a full professor in prestigious Freiburg University. At the age of thirty-two he was called to one of the most renowned chairs at the University of Heidelberg, which was second only to Berlin. He did not have to struggle for recognition: very early in his career his contributions were judged to be of the first order, and he quickly attracted the attention of major academic figures both among his elders and his peers. His sharp polemics and uncompromising stands in the sphere of scholarship brought him many enemies, to be sure. His political interventions seemed to many mandarin academics *infra dignitatum*. Yet there were only few who, whether agreeing with him or not, failed to recognize his talent. Both before his breakdown and after, Weber was an outstanding member of the academy.

This general consensus about the high quality of his accomplishments was by no means limited to the small circle of men who by then called themselves sociologists. In leafing through Weber's pages and notes, one is impressed with the range of men with whom he engaged in intellectual exchanges and realizes the widespread net of relationships Weber established within the academy and across its various disciplinary boundaries. His academic role-set, that is, those people to whom he related by virtue of his role in the university, was varied and complicated because his contributions touched upon the concerns of economists and philosophers, of legal scholars and of historians.

Because of this great variety of role-partners Weber was able to attain a measure of detachment more readily than men who are bound only to one scholarly audience or disciplinary circle. What Rose Laub Coser has remarked in regard to the mature individual generally seems to apply particularly to men like Weber who manage to convert a complicated and sometimes conflicting role-set into a special resource for objectivity and creativeness. "The ability to use inner resources," she writes,

> that were developed through successive resolutions of conflicts with the expectations of various role-partners is the sociological counterpart to what Freud has called sublimation. It is the ability of the individual with a strong ego to make use of the accumulated resources developed in manifold patterned role relationships . . . in the performance of his various roles. Role relationships, rather than being a source of constraints as some will have it, provide the opportunity for socially creative behavior.[50]

[50] Rose Laub Coser, "Role Distance, Sociological Ambivalence and Transitional Status Systems," *The American Journal of Sociology,* LXXVII, 2 (September, 1966), pp. 173–87.

Weber's involvement with many scholarly circles and audiences, his many contacts with students and colleagues, were both the reason for and the result of his amazing creativity in various fields of traditional scholarship. His membership in many circles allowed him to gain intellectual autonomy.

Weber's predominant orientation toward an academic audience is illustrated by the fact that almost all his work appeared in scholarly publications rather than in books accessible to a wider circle of readers. Most of his contributions that are known to American readers in their translation in book form appeared first in academic journals. (His *summa, Wirtschaft und Gesellschaft,* was to be presented in a huge volume, but he never completed it.) This orientation toward an academic audience helps to explain the complicated and involuted style of most of his writings. The labored exposition, the qualifications, the sentences within sentences, and the long footnotes are the result of his painstaking effort to attain the maximum of precision and clarity and to indicate to his academic audience that he eschewed all striving for "effect."

Clearly, the heavy style of Weber's academic writing is not due to any congenital inability to write simply, for when he addressed other audiences he wrote and spoke quite differently. His great public lectures, those on *Politics as a Vocation* and on *Science as a Vocation,* for example, are written in a clear and muscular style—a limpid prose that reminds one of a Nietzsche or a Heine. His memoranda to policy-makers and his articles in the general press, while sometimes lacking the passionate intensity of his public address, are likewise models of clear, economical, and forceful exposition.

What was true of Weber's general writing style was also true of his vocabulary. It too was attuned to the audience he happened to address. When he wished to reach the ear of political decision-makers, Weber used a language they would understand. He thought it futile to speak to them in terms of an absolutist ethic that could be espoused by prophets and revolutionaries but not by practicing political men. A political audience, Weber believed, required a political vocabulary focused on the pursuit of interests. An academic public, on the other hand, was an audience of men committed, at least in principle, to the search for truth rather than the pursuit of ideal or material interests. Therefore, what this audience required was illusionless clarity and utmost self-awareness. In this circle, he thought, it should be axiomatic that the unexamined life is not worth living. Rational clarification, as well as uncompromising and unsparing analysis, alone suited such an audience.

His very high estimate of the academic calling also helps explain Weber's intensely critical attitude toward those professors who failed to achieve scientific detachment or did not even strive for it. He was passionately devoted to an ethos of science, which precludes the mixing of science and values; he believed strongly that only through an exclusion of values from scientific discourse would it be possible to safeguard the scholarly enterprise. Only value-neutrality could rescue it from the chaos of clashing and contending voices that raged in society at large and seemed to make reasoned dialogue all but impossible. Even though, and perhaps just because, he was committed to a set of political and moral values, Weber was convinced that objectivity could be safeguarded only if it were given permanent sanctuary within an academy. Here, scholars, though concerned with different problems chosen in terms of differing values, would be pledged in common to the civilization of rational dialogue and the pursuit of an ever elusive truth.

In his scholarly work, in his family life or in his political activities, Weber always sought to attain a balance of detachment and concern. He felt that a scholar who lacked detachment when he spoke from his academic chair abused his privilege and became a mystagogue and misleader of youth. At the same time he believed that those who cultivated pure detachment from the affairs of the day were, either wittingly or unwittingly, contemptible toadies of political and academic powers. For want of "civil courage," they turned into instruments used for the obscurantist designs of civil servants and academic bureaucrats.

Weber was not always able to avoid the divergent pulls that this complicated position brought forth—a fact that helps account for some of his contradictory, or apparently contradictory, statements. The Weber who said that social thought is always bound to "the permanent power-political interests of the nation," also replied, though at a later date, to someone who had claimed that one ought to love the state: "What, I should even love the monster?"[51]

Quite apart from the evolution of his political ideas, Weber attempted, especially after the years of his illness, to keep his political concern balanced by his commitment to the ethos of scientific detachment. Once we realize that, many, though not all, of the apparent contradictions dissolve. He might have said in the last period of his life that the realities of the national state within a universe of other contending states are stark facts. No amount of moralizing can wish away the contentions for national power on the world scene. A realistic assessment of political necessities and compulsions is required for any responsible political actor if he is to be at all effective. The scholar, while not endorsing the aims of the politician and statesman, is in a position to clarify typical courses of action in the political domain, to "understand" them and to assess the probable consequences of given courses of action. All this does not prevent him, as he contemplates the bloody course of history, from pronouncing the moral judgment that the whole world of power and of politics is the domain of the devil.

[51] Karl Jaspers, *Max Weber, Politiker, Forscher, Philosoph* (Munich, R. Piper, 1958), p. 8.

IN SUMMARY

Weber achieved his lucid vision only at the price of never-ending struggle. He plunged into depths few men have ever probed. His involvements were many, and he emerged from the battles often bruised, sometimes battered. But he brought forth from these forays insights into the nature of man and his society that will provide abundant riches for many generations of scholars and political men alike. His *detached concern* for the trials, the tragedies, and the occasional successes of social action made him an as yet unsurpassed master of the art and science of social analysis.

Thorstein Veblen

1857-1929

THE WORK

There are at least three Thorstein Veblens: first, the seriously unserious, reverently irreverent, amoral moralist[1] whose iconoclastic assault on the received pieties of America place him in the front ranks of social critics. Second, there is the economist whose institutional economics and meticulous anatomy of American high finance and business enterprise have earned him several generations of distinguished followers and a permanent niche among the greats of political economy. Finally, there is the sociologist to whom we owe theories of socially induced motivations, of the social determinants of knowledge, and of social change. This account will be concerned mainly with the third Veblen.

It is difficult to summarize the major aspects of Veblen's thought not only because he wrote in a complicated, illusive, and polysyllabic style, but also because he lacked a systematic exposition and deliberately attempted to pass on his highly charged value judgments as statements of fact.

In a writer like Marx it is relatively easy to distinguish analysis from prophecy, and normative from scientific judgment; not so with Veblen. Although he used to repeat to his students, "We are interested in what is, not in what ought to be,"[2] even the casual reader will soon discover that behind the scientific stance were hidden strong moral impulses. For example, it is hard to take him seriously when he insists that he uses the term "waste" in a neutral sense, and that "it is not to be taken in an odious sense, as implying an illegitimate expenditure of human products or of human life."[3] Nor is his use of what Kenneth Burke has termed a perspective through incongruity, innocent of moral connotations, as when he compares the livery of servants with the vestments of the priest, "a body servant, constructively in attendance upon the person of the divinity whose livery he wears."[4] When Veblen deliber-

[1] I borrow the first two terms from Daniel Aaron's "Thorstein Veblen: Moralist and Rhetorician," in his *Men of Good Hope* (New York, Oxford University Press, 1951). The third term comes from Morton G. White's *Social Thought in America* (New York, The Viking Press, 1952), Chapter 6.

[2] Cited in Joseph Dorfman, *Thorstein Veblen and His America* (New York, The Viking Press, 1934), p. 247.

[3] Thorstein Veblen, *The Theory of the Leisure Class* (New York, Modern Library, 1934), p. 97.

[4] *Ibid.*, p. 183.

ately links words with respectable and dishonorable meanings such as "trained incapacity," "business sabotage," "blameless cupidity," "conscientious withholding of efficiency," "collusive sobriety" or "sagacious restriction of output," he uses these balanced opposites to pass moral judgment under the protective coloration of detached description.[5] Veblen belonged to the company of Swift as well as to that of Marx.

These are some of the difficulties in attempting to separate the substantive content of Veblen's thought from its ethical husk. But the obstacles are not insurmountable, although, incidentally, Veblen himself would hardly have approved of the enterprise.

THE GENERAL APPROACH

Veblen's point of departure was a critical dissection of the doctrines of the classic economists in the light of evolutionary and sociological reasoning. He objected to the notion that the "laws" they had constructed were timeless generalizations and contended instead that the economic behavior of men, like any other human activity, had to be analyzed in terms of the social context in which it was imbedded. He further objected to the deriving of economic behavior from alleged utilitarian and hedonistic propensities generic to mankind. The categories of the classical economists, he argued, could be applied only to special historical circumstances and in very restricted contexts. Thus, primitive economic behavior could not be understood in terms of Ricardian notions. "A gang of Aleutian Islanders," Veblen wrote derisively, "slashing about in the wrack and surf with rakes and magical incantations for the capture of shell-fish are held, in point of taxonomic reality, to be engaged in a feat of hedonistic equilibration in rent, wages, and interest."[6]

> "The hedonistic conception of man," Veblen argued bitingly, "is that of a lightning calculator of pleasures and pains, who oscillates like a homogenous globule of desire of happiness under the impulse of stimuli that shift him about the area, but leave him intact. He has neither antecedent nor consequence. He is an isolated, definitive human datum. . . . Self-imposed in elemental space, he spins symmetrically about his own spiritual axis. . . . The hedonistic man is not a prime mover. He is not the seat of a process of living."[7]

In contrast to an obsolete economics that centers attention upon alleged transhistorical laws and utilitarian or hedonistic calculations, Veblen urged a new economics that is historical, or, to use his own terminology, evolutionary, and that is based on an activistic conception of man. "It is the characteristic

[5] Cf. Aaron, *op. cit.*, pp. 258 ff.

[6] *The Portable Veblen*, ed. and with an introduction by Max Lerner (New York, The Viking Press, 1948), p. 20. I use this easily available volume throughout this chapter. [7] *Ibid.*, p. 232.

of man to do something. . . . He is not simply a bundle of desires that are to be saturated . . . but rather a coherent structure of propensities and habits which seek realization and expression in an unfolding activity."[8] The economic life history of the individual "is a cumulative process of adaptations of means to ends." What is true of the individual is true of the community. It too is continually engaged in an active process of adaptation of economic means to economic ends. "Evolutionary economics must be the theory of a process of cultural growth as determined by the economic interest, a theory of a cumulative sequence of economic institutions stated in terms of the process itself."[9]

Veblen conceived of the evolution of mankind in Spencerian or Darwinian fashion as a process of selective adaptation to the environment. According to him, there was no goal to historical evolution as the Hegelians and Marxists had claimed, but rather "a scheme of blindly cumulative causation, in which there is no trend, no final term, no consummation."[10]

Human evolution, Veblen argued, involved above all the invention and use of ever more effective technologies. "The process of cumulative change that is to be accounted for is the sequence of change in the methods of doing things—the methods of dealing with the material means of life."[11] Hence, "the state of the industrial arts" ultimately determined the state of adaptation of man to his natural environment. Technology, moreover, likewise determined man's adjustment to his social environment.

A man's position in the technological and economic sphere, Veblen argued, determines his outlook and his habits of thought. Similarly, habits and customs, ways of acting and ways of thinking grow within communities as they are engaged in their struggle to wrest a livelihood from nature. Such habits and customs in their turn crystallize over time into institutional molds into which communities attempt to press their component members. Institutions are clusters of habits and customs that are sanctioned by the community. An institution "is of the nature of a usage which has become axiomatic and indispensable by habituation and general acceptance."[12] The evolution of human societies, contended Veblen, must be seen as "a process of natural selection of institutions."[13] "Institutions are not only themselves the result of a selective and adaptive process which shapes the prevailing or dominant types of spiritual attitude and aptitudes; they are at the same time special methods of life and human relations."[14]

Hence, the scheme of man's social evolution is to Veblen essentially a pattern of institutional change rooted in the development of the industrial arts.

[8] *Ibid.*, p. 233. [9] *Ibid.*, p. 236.

[10] Thorstein Veblen, *The Place of Science in Modern Civilization* (New York, W. B. Huebsch, 1919), p. 436.

[11] Quoted in L. E. Dobriansky, *Veblenism: A New Critique* (Washington, D.C., Public Affairs Press, 1957), p. 159.

[12] Thorstein Veblen, *Absentee Ownership* (New York, The Viking Press, 1938), p. 101.

[13] *The Theory of the Leisure Class*, p. 188. [14] *Ibid.*

Four main stages of evolution are distinguished: the peaceful savage economy of neolithic times; the predatory barbarian economy in which the institutions of warfare, property, masculine prowess and the leisure class originated; the premodern period of handicraft economy; and finally the modern era dominated by the machine. Much of this, especially the distinction between savagery and barbarism, was based on conjectural history. But Veblen accepted it, despite his often caustic remarks about such history. When a student once asked him what he considered the difference between real and conjectural history, he answered that the relation was about the same as that between a real horse and a sawhorse.[15]

Veblen's theory of evolutionary stages may well be relegated to the museum of antiquities, but his more general theory of technological determination, though often blended with one or another form of Marxism, has continued to exert influence among contemporary social scientists. Much current work in anthropology is still informed by his view—for example, that "A study of . . . primitive cultures . . . shows a close correlation between the material (industrial and pecuniary) life of any given people and their civic, domestic, and religious scheme of life; the myths and the religious cult reflect the character of these other—especially the economic and domestic—institutions in a peculiarly naive and truthful manner."[16] The main thrust of Veblen's work, however, does not come in his anthropological studies but rather in his discussion of contemporary or near-contemporary society. Here his distinction between industrial and pecuniary types of employment is crucial.

Veblen's central idea in regard to the modern capitalist world is that it is based on an irremediable opposition between business and industry, ownership and technology, pecuniary and industrial employment—between those who make goods and those who make money, between workmanship and salesmanship. This distinction served Veblen as a major weapon in his attack against the prevailing scheme of things in America, and against prevailing evolutionary doctrine. His fellow evolutionists, men like his former teacher Sumner, argued that the leading industrialists and men of finance, having shown in the competitive struggle that they were "the fittest," had to be regarded as the flowers of modern civilization. Veblen argued that, far from being the fittest agents of evolutionary advancement, men engaged in pecuniary activities were parasites growing fat on the technological leadership and innovation of other men. "The leisure class lives by the industrial community rather than in it."[17] The "captains of industry" made no industrial contribution and therefore had no progressive function in the evolutionary process; rather, they retarded and distorted it.

Veblen adapted the Spencerian distinction between militant and industrial societies to his own uses. Whereas Spencer had argued that businessmen were

[15] Cited in Dorfman, *op. cit.*, p. 248. [16] *Ibid.*, p. 298.
[17] *The Theory of the Leisure Class*, p. 246.

engaged in a peaceful way of life, which stood in opposition to that of the militant warrior, Veblen insisted that the "captains of industry" were only pursuing the predatory ways of their militant forebears under new circumstances. American robber barons were as eager to exploit the underlying population as had been their medieval ancestors. The price system in which businessmen and speculators were involved only hampered and impeded the system of industrial arts and so delayed the forward course of mankind's evolutionary advancement. The differential income businessmen derive from their position in the price system is far from a reward for creative entrepreneurship but rather a ransom exacted from the underlying productive population. The institution of absentee ownership, the foundation of the modern price system, creates perpetual crises and competitive anarchy leading to the "sabotage" rather than the advancement of production.

In tune with his overall theory of technological determinants of thought, Veblen argued that positions in the spheres of industrial or of pecuniary employment respectively fostered radically different casts of mind or habits of thought. Those in pecuniary employment were inclined toward an "animistic bent," that is, they thought in magical categories. Those involved in industrial employment, on the other hand, were impelled to think in rational, matter-of-fact terms. Magical and animistic types of reasoning are at variance with the requirements of modern industrial societies; such reasoning is partly a survival from earlier barbaric conditions of life and partly a response to the existential conditions of those who continue to depend on luck in their speculative manipulations. Modern industry depends on rationality and, in turn, fosters it. "In the modern industrial communities, industry is, to a constantly increasing extent, being organized in a comprehensive system of organs and functions mutually conditioning one another; and therefore freedom from all bias in the causal apprehension of phenomena grows constantly more requisite to efficiency on the part of men concerned in industry."[18]

Veblen believed that the major disciplining agent in the modern world was the machine process of production. "The machine technology," he reasoned, "rests on a knowledge of impersonal, material cause and effect. . . . Within the range of this machine-guided work, and within the range of modern life so far as it is guided by the machine process, the cause of things is given mechanically, impersonally, and the resultant discipline is a discipline in the handling of impersonal facts for mechanical effect. It inculcates thinking in terms of opaque, impersonal cause and effect, to the neglect of those norms of validity that rest on usage and on the conventional standards handed down by usage."[19] This being the case, Veblen argued further, the future evolution of mankind depended on those whose minds had been disciplined by involvement in the industrial arts and in the machine process. Further evolutionary advances could be expected only if the habits inculcated by the disciplinary

[18] *Ibid.*, p. 283. [19] *The Portable Veblen*, p. 338.

effects of the machine prevailed over the predatory life-styles and the magical and animistic casts of thought of those involved in pecuniary employment.

THE ANATOMY OF COMPETITION

Veblen's work is especially noteworthy when he analyzes and dissects the habits of thought and modes of conduct that underlie competitive relations between social actors. He advanced a sophisticated theory of the social sources of competitiveness in human affairs. Self-esteem, he argued, is only a reflection of the esteem accorded by one's fellows. Consequently, when such esteem is not forthcoming because a person has failed to excel in prized competitive endeavors, he suffers from a loss of self-esteem. The drive for ever-renewed exertion in a competitive culture is therefore rooted in the fear of loss of self-esteem.

> Those members of the community who fall short of [a] somewhat indefinite, normal degree of prowess or of property suffer in the esteem of their fellow-men; and consequently they also suffer in their own esteem, since the usual basis of self-respect is the respect accorded by one's neighbors. Only individuals with an aberrant temperament can in the long run retain their self-esteem in the face of the disesteem of their fellows. . . . So soon as the possession of property becomes the basis of popular esteem, it becomes also a requisite to that complacency which we call self-respect.[20]

In a competitive culture, where men judge their worth in comparison with that of their fellows, they are bound to a perpetually revolving Ixion's wheel because they constantly aspire to outdo their neighbors.

> As fast as a person makes new acquisitions, and becomes accustomed to the new standard of wealth, the new standard forthwith ceases to afford appreciably greater satisfaction than the earlier standard did . . . the end sought by accumulation is to rank high in comparison with the rest of the community in point of pecuniary strength. So long as the comparison is distinctly unfavorable to himself, the normal, average individual will live in chronic dissatisfaction with his present lot; and when he has reached what may be called the normal pecuniary standard of the community, or of his class in the community, this chronic dissatisfaction will give place to a restless straining to place a wider and ever widening pecuniary interval between himself and the average standard.[21]

Veblen is at his best when he analyzes the various means by which men attempt to symbolize their high standing in the continuous struggle for com-

[20] *The Theory of the Leisure Class*, pp. 30–31. [21] *Ibid.*, p. 31.

petitive advantage. Conspicuous consumption, conspicuous leisure, conspicuous display of symbols of high standing are to Veblen some of the means by which men attempt to excel their neighbors and so attain heightened self-evaluation. "High-bred manners and ways of living are items of conformity to the norm of conspicuous leisure and conspicuous consumption. . . . Conspicuous consumption of valuable goods is a means of reputability to the gentlemen of leisure."[22] "With the inheritance of gentility goes the inheritance of obligatory leisure."[23] Conspicuous consumption or conspicuous leisure need not necessarily be engaged in directly by those in search of heightened competitive standing. Rather, such characteristic life-styles may be displayed by persons who are dependent on the head of a household—his wife and servants, for example—to enhance the status of the master. In the modern world, the head of the middle-class household has been forced by economic circumstances to gain a livelihood in an occupation, "but the middle-class wife still carries on the business of vicarious leisure, for the good name of the household and its master."[24] The liveried servant displays his multi-colored coat of servitude not to improve his own image but rather to symbolize that of his master.

In the aristocratic age, "the age of barbarism," such characteristically "wasteful" styles of competitive display were limited to the leisure class, the top of the social pyramid. Now, Veblen contended, they tend to permeate the whole social structure. Each class copies the life-styles of its superordinates to the extent of its ability. "The result is that the members of each stratum accept as their ideal of decency the scheme of life invoked in the next higher stratum, and bend their energies to live up to that ideal."[25] "The canon of reputability" must adapt itself to the economic circumstances and the traditions of each particular class,[26] but it permeates all society to greater or less degrees. Though originating among the leisure class, it characterizes the total culture and shapes its characteristic life-style. This is why even the poor, though they are physically better off in modern society than their forebears were in their time, suffer more. "The existing system has not made . . . the industrious poor poorer as measured absolutely . . . but it does tend to make them relatively poorer, in their own eyes . . . and . . . that is what seems to count."[27] Clearly, Veblen, like others before and after him, had in effect come upon the idea of "relative deprivation."

In Veblen's opinion the simplistic notions of human motivation on which classical economics rest cannot serve to explain the springs of action of man in modern pecuniary civilization. It is not the propensity to save or to truck and barter that animates man in the modern world, but the propensity to excel his neighbor. The struggle for competitive standing becomes a basic datum if one is to understand the institutional framework of modern economic behavior.

[22] *Ibid.*, p. 75. [23] *Ibid.*, p. 76. [24] *Ibid.*, p. 81. [25] *Ibid.*, p. 84. [26] *Ibid.*, p. 105.
[27] *The Place of Science*, p. 392.

SOCIOLOGY OF KNOWLEDGE

Throughout his writings Veblen emphasized the ways in which habits of thought are an outcome of habits of life and stressed the dependence of thought styles on the organization of the community. "The scheme of thought or of knowledge," he wrote, "is in good part a reverberation of the schemes of life."[28]

In his anthropological writings, Veblen makes a sharp distinction between peaceable agricultural communities in the age of savagery and the predatory life of pastoral people. He relates their different life-styles to characteristically different religious orientations. In agricultural societies one is likely to find a polytheistic theology as a replica of the various powers of nature. "The relation of the deities to mankind is likely to be that of consanguinity, and as if to emphasize the peaceable noncoercive character of the divine order of things, the deities are in the main very apt to be females. The matter of interests dealt with in the cosmological theories are chiefly matters of the livelihood of the people."[29] By contrast, predatory cultures, with their more centralized authority-structures and their warrior chiefs, will tend to have monotheistic religious systems, and there will be an emphasis on the arbitrary schemes of divine government. "Such a people will adopt male deities, in the main, and will impute to them a coercive, imperious, arbitrary animus and a degree of princely dignity."[30]

Veblen distinguishes between earlier stages of human evolution, when whole communities exhibited characteristic habits of thoughts, and later stages, when human societies have differentiated into distinct strata, with distinct occupational roles emerging. Here different habits of thought exist side by side and are associated with location in the class and occupational structure. "The pecuniary employments call into action chiefly [the invidious] aptitudes and propensities, and act selectively to conserve them in the population. The industrial employments, on the other hand, chiefly exercise the [noninvidious or economical attitudes], and act to conserve them."[31] Pecuniary employments foster magical beliefs in luck; the industrial arts foster rationality.

Veblen argues that habits of thought, which arise in tune with a man's position in the social and occupational order, find their reflection in types of knowledge as well as in behavior. "The scheme of life which men perforce adopt under the exigencies of an industrial situation shapes their habit of thought on the side of their behavior. . . . Each individual is but a single complex of habits of thought, and the same psychical mechanism that expresses itself in one direction as conduct expresses itself in another direction as knowledge."[32]

[28] *Ibid.*, p. 105. [29] *Ibid.*, p. 47. [30] *Ibid.*, p. 48.
[31] *The Theory of the Leisure Class*, p. 239. [32] *The Place of Science*, p. 105.

These are, of course, fairly general statements, and Veblen never attempted to verify them in a systematic manner. Yet throughout his work he provides telling illustrations. For example, Veblen had a very keen eye for instances of maladaptation—of dysfunctions as the modern sociologist would call them—that arise from a lack of congruity between habits of thought and occupational or technological settings. His notion of "trained incapacity" indicates one such instance of maladaptation. This applies to a person who has been so thoroughly trained for one occupational setting that he finds it impossible to operate effectively in a different situation; the very effectiveness of his training in the past leads to inappropriate behavior in the present.

Veblen not only stressed how habits of thought arise from social and occupational placement, but he also advanced a theory of the social determinants of cognitive interests. He accounted for the tendency of the leisure class to be drawn to classical studies, law, and politics, rather than to the natural sciences because of the pragmatic interests of its members. "The interest with which [a] discipline is approached is therefore not commonly the intellectual or cognitive interest simply. It is largely the practical interest of the exigencies of that relation of mastery in which the members of the class are placed."[33] For Veblen, science and scientific attitudes are rooted in material exigencies; only those members of the community who are engaged in the industrial arts are in tune with such exigencies and hence are drawn to the study of the sciences.

These examples suggest that Veblen was already engaged in an analysis of what are in effect the latent functions of a wide range of types of conduct and habits of thought. Robert K. Merton drew upon Veblen as well as on a long line of previous theorists when he formulated the notions of latent and manifest functions. Merton also pointed out that Veblen's gift for seeing paradoxical, ironic, and satiric aspects of social life predisposed him to pay attention to latent functions.[34]

FUNCTIONAL ANALYSIS

When Veblen describes the various manifestations of the pattern of conspicuous consumption, he is always at pains to ferret out their latent functions. Manifestly, candles are meant to provide light and automobiles are means of transportation. But under the pecuniary scheme they serve the latent function of indicating and enhancing status. Candle light at dinner indicates that the host makes claims to a style of gracious living that is peculiar to the upper class; one drives a Cadillac to indicate that he belongs to a stratum superior to that of Chevrolet owners; one serves caviar to symbolize a refinement of the palate that is the mark of a gentleman. Patterns of consumption, and pat-

[33] *The Theory of the Leisure Class*, pp. 382 ff.

[34] Robert K. Merton, *Social Theory and Social Structure* (New York, The Free Press, 1968), esp. the chapter on "Manifest and Latent Functions."

terns of conduct generally, must never be explained in terms of manifest functions alone but must be seen as having the latent function of enhancing status.[35] In some cases, indeed, no manifest function may be served at all and the pattern can be explained only by status enhancement. The Chinese mandarin, when asked why he cultivates long fingernails, might answer that "this is the custom"; the analyst, however, will conclude that the man who cultivates long fingernails cannot possibly work with his hands and must therefore occupy an honorific position.

One last example will suffice. When Veblen spoke of the prevalence among journeyman printers of dram-drinking, "treating," and smoking in public places, a pattern apparently quite marked in his day, he gave a functional explanation in terms of the conditions of life of such men. The members of this occupation, he explained, have a higher rate of geographic and employment mobility than most others. As a consequence, "these men are constantly thrown in contact with new groups of acquaintances, with whom the relations established are transient or ephemeral, but whose good opinion is valued none the less for the time being."[36] Hence, a journeyman's ability to consume in an ostentatious manner in company and to treat his fellows may be conceived as serving to establish quick contact and to enhance his status in their eyes. The capacity to "give" to others elicits deference and admiration in a transient environment where other symbolizations of status, such as high standing in the residential neighborhood, are not available.

THE THEORY OF SOCIAL CHANGE

Veblen's theory of social change is essentially a technological theory of history. He believed that in the last analysis the "state of the industrial arts," that is, the technology available to a society, determines the character of its culture. Invention was the mother of necessity. Yet this influence of technology, while crucial, was to Veblen by no means immediate and direct. A new technology does not automatically bring forth new systems of laws, new moral attitudes, or new types of education. Rather, it challenges old institutions and evokes their resistance. "Institutions are products of the past process, are adapted to past circumstances, and are therefore never in full accord with the requirements of the present."[37] Those who have a "vested interest" in the old order will bend every effort to maintain old institutions even when they are no longer in tune with technological developments. The characteristic attitude of those advocates of the status quo "may be summed up in the maxim: 'Whatever is, is right;' whereas the law of natural selection, as applied to human institutions, gives the axiom: 'Whatever is, is wrong.' "[38] In the end, Veblen

[35] *Ibid.*, pp. 123 ff. [36] *The Theory of the Leisure Class*, p. 90. [37] *Ibid.*, p. 191.
[38] *Ibid.*, p. 207.

believed, a new technology erodes vested ideas, overcomes vested interests, and reshapes institutions in accord with its own needs. But this process may take considerable time, and in that time lag—when, for example, an industrial society is still governed by legal and moral rules dating from the handicraft era—society suffers from the waste that is brought about by the lack of correspondence between its institutions and its technology.

In periods of transition between an old order and one about to be born, social conflicts are likely to be accentuated. In contrast to Marx, Veblen did not conceive of the class struggle as the motor of history. He saw as the shaping force of history the clash between advancing technology and retarding institutions. Only during periods when this clash was particularly acute did he expect an exacerbation of class antagonisms between those engaged in the pecuniary employments, who had vested interest in things as they were, and those in industrial employments who were in tune with the technological demands of the hour.

Although he was beholden to a general evolutionary doctrine, Veblen did not believe in unilinear evolution. He was acutely aware of what later theorists called "the skipping of evolutionary stages"; hence, he focused attention on "the advantage of borrowing the technological arts rather than developing them by home growth."[39] When technologies are borrowed from another society, Veblen argued, they "do not carry over the fringe of other cultural elements that have grown up about them in the course of their development and use."[40] Technological elements can therefore be acquired ready-made and they do not carry the institutional ballast with which they were freighted in the country of origin. Thus the Germans took over British machine technology "without the fault of its qualities."[41] While in England older institutions still hampered and impeded this technology, and older and newer technological techniques and processes existed side by side, the Germans took over the more advanced technologies and applied them to the fullest in an environment unimpeded by vested interests. These observations seem especially pertinent today in the light of the problems faced by developing societies.

While borrowing may help to accelerate the evolutionary growth of the borrowing country, it leads to relative decline in the competitive position of the country of origin. This is "the penalty of taking the lead." An industrial system like that of England, which "has been long engaged in a course of improvement, extension, innovation and specialization, will in the past have committed itself . . . to what was at the time an adequate scale of appliances and schedule of processes."[42] But such established equipment will be out of date as the industrial process proceeds. Hence, obsolescent technologies are likely to exist alongside new equipment. There will be improvements, adapta-

[39] *The Portable Veblen,* p. 365. [40] *Ibid.* [41] *Ibid.,* p. 367. [42] *Ibid.,* p. 373.

tions, and repairs but also a "fatal reluctance or inability to overcome this all-pervading depreciation by obsolescence."[43] The railroads of Great Britain, for example, were built with too narrow a gauge and the "terminal facilities, tracks, shunting facilities, and all the means of handling freight . . . are all adapted to the bobtailed car."[44] From the point of view of the community at large all this equipment should be discarded, but since it is still profitable the captains of the railroad industry have a vested interest in maintaining it, thereby contributing to the industrial decadence of England. "All this does not mean that the British have sinned against the canons of technology. It is only that they are paying the penalty for having been thrown into the lead and so having shown the way."[45]

Veblen wrote this when England was governed by Lloyd George, and Germany was ruled by the Kaiser. But fifty years later, the England of Prime Minister Edward Heath and the Germany of Chancellor Willy Brandt still seem subject to the same forces; and the contemporary development of Japan furnishes even stronger evidence for Veblen's far-reaching prescience.

The preceding pages have not touched upon a number of Veblenian notions, in particular his theory of "instincts." This omission is deliberate. "The instinct of workmanship," "the parental bent," or "the instinct of idle curiosity"—concepts Veblen used to "explain" the concern for a job well done, the solicitude for one's offspring, and the motive force for scientific curiosity respectively—are vague and unsatisfactory. Veblen introduced them as a kind of deus ex machina when he wished to defend a practice or behavior pattern he liked to see maintained, even though his "instincts" are not meant to denote unchangeable biological impulses but rather prepotent propensities subject to cultural conditioning and modification. Veblen, like all instinct theorists, was prone to infer the operation of instincts from observed behavior—which these instincts were then supposed to explain. This device has little scientific utility.

What is likely to endure in Veblen's sociological work is not the theory of instincts but his theory of the socially induced motivations for competitive behavior, his acute ferreting out of latent functions, and certain elements of his technological interpretation of history and of his theory of the lag between technological and institutional development. It is likely that analysts of the process of "modernization" will still be making use of his notions about the "advantage of borrowing" and the "penalty of taking the lead" when his doctrine of instinct will long have been forgotten.

[43] *Ibid.*, p. 375. [44] *Ibid.*, p. 374. [45] *Ibid.*, p. 375.

THE MAN

Veblen drew a fine self-portrait in an essay entitled, "The Intellectual Preeminence of Jews in Modern Europe," which he wrote toward the end of his career. He says there that the Jewish man of ideas is saved from being intellectually passive "at the cost of losing his secure place in the scheme of conventions into which he has been born and . . . of finding no similarly secure place in the scheme of gentile conventions into which he is thrown." As a consequence, "he becomes a disturber of the intellectual peace, but at the cost of becoming an intellectual wayfaring man, a wanderer in the intellectual no-man's-land, seeking another place to rest, farther along the road, somewhere over the horizon. [Such Jews] are neither a complaisant nor a contented lot, these aliens of the uneasy feet."[46] Nothing could better characterize Veblen's own life. Intentionally or not, he summed up in this passage the price and the glory of his career.

A MARGINAL NORWEGIAN

Thorstein Veblen was born on a frontier farm in Wisconsin on July 30, 1857.[47] He was a son of the Middle Border that produced in his generation Lester Ward, Frederick Jackson Turner, Vernon Parrington, and Charles Beard, all men who, like himself, were to mount an assault against the received wisdom of the intellectual establishment of the East. But unlike these other men, Veblen was almost as much a stranger to the culture of the Midwest as he was to that of the East.

Veblen was the sixth of twelve children of Norwegian immigrants, his parents, Thomas Anderson Veblen and Kari Bunde Veblen, having come to America ten years before his birth. They were of old Norwegian peasant stock, but had had a very hard time as children of tenant farmers in the old country. Veblen's paternal grandfather had been tricked out of his right to the family farm and had fallen from the honored status of farm owner to that of a despised tenant. His mother's father had likewise been forced to sell his farm in order to meet lawyers' fees and, crushed by this loss, had died still a young man, leaving Veblen's mother an orphan at the age of five.

After Veblen's parents emigrated to America to settle first in Wisconsin and then in Minnesota, they encountered obstacles similar to those faced by

[46] *The Portable Veblen*, p. 475.

[47] This account of Veblen's life is based almost entirely on Joseph Dorfman's monumental and definitive *Thorstein Veblen and His America*. I have also profited from David Riesman's *Thorstein Veblen* (New York, Scribner's, 1953), even though I was not persuaded by many of Riesman's psychoanalytic explanations of Veblen's personality. Cf. also R. L. Duffus' delightful memoir on Veblen's Stanford days, *The Innocents at Cedro* (New York, Macmillan, 1944).

their parents in Norway. Land speculators drove them off their first land claim; in their second venture they were forced to sell half their land in order to pay usurious interest rates. Hatred of tricksters, speculators, and shyster lawyers ran deep in the family tradition and found characteristic expression in much of Veblen's later writing.

Despite such obstacles, the Veblens managed through hard work, thrift, and single-minded devotion to the agricultural task at hand to acquire a self-sufficient farmstead in Manitowoc, Wisconsin, where Thorstein was born. When he was eight years old, the family moved to a larger farm on the prairie lands of Wheeling Township in Minnesota. There his father became a leading farmer in the homogeneous Norwegian community, which, like other Norwegian farming communities, lived in almost complete isolation from the surrounding world. Norwegian immigrants seldom met Yankees, except for business reasons or at political conventions. Frugal, hard-working and somewhat dour men piously following the prescriptions of their Lutheran religion, they had contempt for the loose ways of the Yankees and saw in them the representatives of a shallow, pleasure-loving, impious civilization. To the Norwegians, the Yankees seemed to be speculators, wheelers and dealers all, men who couldn't be trusted, and whose ways were not only foreign but abhorrent. These sentiments also later found their way into Veblen's writings.

Although Veblen's parents were deeply rooted in the Norwegian community and its traditional ways, they were nevertheless atypical. Their piousness notwithstanding, they refused to take part in sectarian quarrels over questions of theology or church government, which tended to split these communities. Thomas Veblen minded his own affairs and was respected in the community as a man of judgment and intelligence who, however, showed an unusual independence of conduct.

The son, quite early, took after the father. Children and elders alike were impressed by his precocious intelligence but found his almost compulsively independent ways unsettling. In his early youth, he had fist fights with the boys, teased the girls, and pestered the older people. In his adolescent years, he sublimated aggression into sarcasm, corrosive wit, and scepticism. When the time came for his confirmation, he submitted to the rite but made it clear that he had already lost the faith. All in all, Veblen was as maladjusted in the Norwegian community and as alien to its life styles as he was later to be in the American milieu.

A MARGINAL STUDENT

It is hard to say what would have become of him had he stayed in the Norwegian settlement. As it was, his father, now relatively well-to-do, decided that the road to self-improvement was through education. He would not exploit his children on the farm, as was the wont throughout the community, but he sent them to the higher institutions of learning of alien America. In

1874, when he found that the local preacher considered his son Thorstein a suitable candidate for the ministry, he decided that the boy should enter nearby Carleton College. Thorstein himself was not consulted. He was summoned from the field and placed in the family buggy with his baggage already packed. The first he learned that he was to enter Carleton was when he arrived there; then he was told that he was to live in a log cabin his father had built for his children on the edge of the campus. For seventeen years, Thorstein Veblen had lived in a cultural enclave, speaking little or no English; now he was suddenly being projected into the surrounding American culture from which he had been almost completely insulated.

Carleton College had been founded just a few years before Veblen's arrival by Congregationalists who attempted to build on the prairies of Minnesota a replica of New England gentility. It was a thoroughly Christian and earnestly evangelical school where intemperance, profanity, and the use of tobacco were strictly forbidden, as was "all Sabbath and evening association between the sexes, except by special permission." In teaching, the classics, moral philosophy, and religion were stressed and the natural sciences were slighted. English literature was taught during one quarter of the senior year only, and American history was not taught at all. The really important courses were those in moral philosophy. The reigning doctrine was Scottish Common Sense, as first expounded by Thomas Reid and developed by Sir William Hamilton. This safe philosophy cast no doubts upon the literal interpretation of the Bible and religious orthodoxy and was meant to counter the scepticism of Hume and his school. Reid taught that fundamental and self-evident truths were enshrined in the common sense of mankind and that "anything manifestly contrary to them is what we call absurd."

Quite predictably Veblen, already a village sceptic at home, took badly to the spirit of Carleton. He spent six years there, but the education he acquired stemmed in the main from his voracious independent reading rather than from his teachers. The only faculty man who seems to have impressed him was John Bates Clark, in later years a major figure in economics at Columbia, but at that time a professor of odds and ends who taught everything from English composition and moral philosophy to political economy. Clark, whose melioristic and mildly socialist ideas appealed to Veblen, was probably the only teacher who liked this youth with a "mind clothed in sardonic humour," as a faculty member described it. That Norwegian bull in the genteel china shop of New England culture disturbed his elders no end. Refusing to take seriously all the pieties he was supposed to absorb, he defended himself by mordant wit, corrosive satire, and just plain cussedness.

The dignitaries of Carlton were undoubtedly relieved when Veblen graduated in 1880. Although he is probably Carleton's most famous alumnus, to this day there is no hall or building named in his honor—not even a plaque commemorating him on campus. Veblen, in his turn, was glad his Carleton days were over. While he had fun delivering a "Plea for Cannibalism" before the faculty and students earnestly concerned with the conversion of the heathen, or pronouncing an "Apology for a Toper" before scandalized teetotalers, such prankishness was really only a desperate defense against his repugnant surroundings. He left Carleton with a fine, mainly self-acquired, education, and with an enduring love of his fellow student, Ellen Rolfe, the niece of the president, whom he was to marry a few years later.

A MARGINAL ACADEMIC

After his graduation, Veblen tried his hand teaching at Monona Academy in Madison, Wisconsin, but the atmosphere at this Norwegian school proved as oppressive as that of Carleton. Rent by theological disputes over predestination, election, and strong church authority, subjects totally uncongenial to Veblen, the school closed permanently at the end of the year. When one of his brothers, Andrew, father of the famous mathematician Oswald Veblen, decided to study mathematics at Johns Hopkins, Thorstein accompanied him to Baltimore, expecting to study philosophy. Thus began what Bernard Rosenberg has called "a torturous apprenticeship in academic maladaptation."[48]

When Veblen came East, his thoughts had already been shaped by the agrarian unrest and radicalism that had swept over the Midwest soon after the end of the Civil War. Moreover, when a German exile of the 1848 revolution had opened his library to him, Veblen became acquainted with Kant, Mill, Hume, Rousseau, Spencer, Huxley, and Tyndall—great intellects who had not been discussed in the lecture halls of Carleton. Egalitarian and radical in his outlook, Veblen once again felt alien in the leisurely culture of the South that prevailed in Baltimore and at Johns Hopkins. Lonely, homesick, and short of money, he was moreover intellectually ill-disposed toward the philosophy offerings of that school. He took three courses with George S. Morris but was not impressed by this Hegelian philosopher, who felt that conventional manners and morals might find an even better defender in Hegel than in prevailing Scottish Common Sense. Veblen attended a course in political economy with a young man, Richard T. Ely, who was to become one of the main representatives of the new reform-oriented economics. But neither man cared for the other. To judge from Veblen's later writings, the only man to have made some impact on him was a temporary lecturer in logic named Charles Sanders Peirce, who had already written a series of papers emphasizing that "the whole function of thought is to produce habits of action."

When Veblen failed to receive a scholarship at Johns Hopkins, he decided to transfer to Yale to study philosophy under its president, the Reverend Noah Porter. At Yale, as almost everywhere else, philosophy was still considered the handmaiden of theology, and Veblen, the agnostic, found himself among divinity students, most of whom were preparing to teach the gospel. As a

[48] Bernard Rosenberg, *The Values of Veblen* (Washington, D.C., Public Affairs Press, 1956), p. 5.

means of defense, Veblen accentuated his sardonic attitudes and distance-creating techniques, and he cultivated an air of complete aloofness and worldly-wise scepticism. Even those whom he managed to befriend later said that they found him trying, though stimulating.

At this time the intellectual atmosphere at Yale was charged by epic battles between its president, Noah Porter, a man still deeply steeped in the pieties of New England transcendentalism, and the sociologist William Graham Sumner, who preached the gospel of Herbert Spencer. Sumner relentlessly fought in the name of science and evolution, of Darwin and Spencer, against the theological features of the school. A month before Veblen left Yale, Sumner was victorious and the whole curriculum of Yale was revamped. Science won over religion.

Veblen found himself attracted to Sumner as he had never been attracted to any of his other teachers. In later years he was to dissect Sumner's conservative economics in class, but, according to Dorfman, Sumner was "the only man for whom he expressed . . . a deep and unqualified admiration."[49] What attracted him was not only Sumner's Spencerian and evolutionary thought, but his independence of mind, his refusal to go along with the crowd, his combative individualism. To be sure, the man who was to write withering attacks on the predacious characteristics of captains of industry was hardly impressed by the views of a teacher who saw in these men the flowers of civilization. Veblen could not accept Sumner's doctrine, but he loved the man and partly modeled himself after his image. He also managed to be on excellent terms with the Reverend Porter, under whom he did most of his work and who supervised his dissertation. Locally he was known as "Porter's chum." Porter esteemed Veblen's superior intelligence even though he must have been made uneasy by Veblen's conspicuous lack of reverence.

Veblen specialized in work on Kant and the post-Kantians, his first academic paper being on Kant's *Critique of Judgment*. He was considered by Porter and some of his other teachers to be a highly intelligent, cultivated, though unconventional, young philosopher. But after he had received his doctorate, it became apparent that nobody was willing to give him an academic position. College teachers, especially those in philosophy, were mainly recruited from the ranks of the divinity school. No faculty wanted a "Norskie," especially one around whom there seemed to hover a cloud of agnosticism or worse. After having spent two and a half years at Yale, Veblen returned home defeated and bitter. He now had a Ph.D. but no source of income or hope for a position.

Back on the farm, Veblen claimed that he was ill and needed special care. His brothers were inclined to believe that he was just plain loafing—a sin not lightly forgiven among Norwegian farm folk. In the meantime, Veblen read everything he could lay his hands on, roamed the woods, indulged in desultory

[49] Dorfman, *op. cit.,* p. 311.

botanical studies, did some hack writing for Eastern papers, and seemed to drift into a life of permanent dilettantism.

In 1888, Veblen married Ellen Rolfe, the daughter of one of the leading families of the Middle West. Her father, a grain-elevator and railroad magnate, was appalled that his daughter was marrying a shiftless atheistic son of Norwegian immigrants. But he made the best of it and allowed the young couple to settle on one of his Iowa farms. Veblen now made a few half-hearted attempts to gain a teaching position, but all these moves proved to be of no avail. In the meantime he and his wife followed news of the radical agrarian movement that swept the Middle West with passionate concern. Together they read Edward Bellamy's socialist utopia, *Looking Backward,* which had just been published. Ellen Rolfe wrote later that "this was the turning point in our lives."[50] In his Iowa retreat, Veblen immersed himself deeply in the study of economics, both the orthodox and the heterodox variety. Looking at the passing scene of agrarian and labor unrest, of increasing radicalization among farmers and workmen alike, he began to feel that economics might provide answers to the crisis. After ten years of frustration and idle drifting, Veblen finally decided to return East to study economics, registering at Cornell in the winter term of 1891.

The professor in charge of economics at Cornell, J. Laurence Laughlin, was sitting in his study when an anemic-looking man wearing a coonskin cap and corduroy trousers entered and announced: "I am Thorstein Veblen." Laughlin became so impressed with Veblen that he secured a special university grant for him, even though all regular fellowships had already been filled. Heartened by this modest encouragement, Veblen now began to get down to the business of serious writing. His first paper in economics, "Some Neglected Points in the Theory of Socialism," adumbrated his later interest. It was an attempt to use Spencerian evolutionary method while arguing against Spencer that without the abolition of private property and free competition the crisis of the current industrial order could not be overcome. Several fairly technical papers for *The Quarterly Journal of Economics* followed in short order. Veblen's mentor, Laughlin, thought so highly of them that he arranged for a fellowship for Veblen at the new University of Chicago, where Laughlin had just been appointed head professor of economics.

The University of Chicago, where Veblen stayed from 1892 to 1906, provided the most congenial academic setting he was ever to find. The aggressive president, William Rainey Harper, had managed in a few years to attract a most distinguished faculty, and Veblen found a number of colleagues with whom he could engage in lively interchange. John Dewey in philosophy, William I. Thomas in sociology, Jacques Loeb in physiology, to name just a few, influenced him deeply and in turn were stimulated by him. Veblen later

[50] *Ibid.*, p. 68.

wrote a venomous portrait of Harper as a prime example of those "captains of erudition" who prostitute genuine scholarship in their drive for competitive standing in the academic world. There was much truth in what Veblen said, but it must be acknowledged that, no matter how autocratic his administration, no matter what questionable methods Harper may have used to extract ever increasing funds from the University's founder, John D. Rockefeller, he attracted a first-rate faculty to Chicago and so made it possible for Veblen to enjoy the company of peers and colleagues that he could genuinely respect.

This is not to say that Veblen's Chicago career was without difficulties. Althought he soon took over the editorship of *The Journal of Political Economy,* which Laughlin had founded soon after their arrival, Veblen was not originally a member of the faculty, but only a tutor. It was not until three years after coming to the University that he was promoted, at the age of 38, to instructor. His promotion to assistant professor had to wait another five years. There were a number of reasons for this academic neglect. Veblen was unorthodox in his thinking, in his teaching, and in his love life.

Veblen now wrote profusely, but his many brilliant contributions to *The Journal of Political Economy* were scarcely of a sort to please the more staid members of his academic audience. They were, in fact, fierce assaults upon prevailing utilitarian and classic doctrine in economics, and upon the custom and use of capitalist enterprise in the United States and elsewhere. Ranging widely over the fields of history, anthropology, sociology, and economics, Veblen proceeded with mordant wit and sarcasm to undermine the received wisdom of economic theory. Whether reviewing books by Sombart or Schmoller, by Marx or Labriola, whether writing a fundamental paper such as the one entitled "Why Is Economics Not an Evolutionary Science?" Veblen was single-minded in his iconoclastic enterprise of demolishing conventional ideas in economics and the social sciences generally.

Veblen's teaching methods were even more unorthodox than his writings. He seemed to make a deliberate effort to discourage students from taking his courses. His lectures were wide ranging, and he usually presented the material in a rambling and unorganized manner. As a result, his audience never quite knew what to expect next. One of his former students describes his teaching thus:

> He would come into the classroom with a half-dozen books under his arm, sit down bashfully behind his desk, and commence mumbling through his whiskers the characteristic economic blasphemies for which he was famous. His inimitable wit played over the field and made what might have been a rather dreary exercise something to chuckle over. Judged by conventional standards, he was the world's worst teacher. He seldom knew at the beginning of the hour what he would say or where he would arrive at its end. . . . I felt that these mumbling lectures were a good deal of a bore

> to him except for the opportunity they afforded him for flashes of wit and irony, and he took little interest in the question of whether his students were reading lessons and doing work in the course or not.[51]

Veblen found the task of evaluating students or grading papers profoundly distasteful and as a consequence usually gave the whole class, as the spirit moved him, either a C or a B. When students tried to pin him down and asked him to say in plain language what he meant by his oracular and illusive pronouncements, he usually brushed them off with a sardonic smile and a witty remark. When pressed hard, he would say: "Well, you know, I really don't think I quite understand it myself."

Despite all these calculated maneuvers to rebuff student interest, Veblen acquired some of his most distinguished followers—among them, Wesley Mitchell, Robert Hoxie, and H. J. Davenport—in the Chicago days. These and a few others learned not to be put off by his manners and quirks and to reach down to the serious core of his teaching. But the bulk of his students couldn't make sense of his lectures, especially when their quest for certainty was met with Veblen's studied elusiveness. Wesley Mitchell has written that Veblen "took a naughty delight in making people squirm." As a result, his classes were large for the first few days, but soon only a handful remained. Students were not an audience that Veblen appreciated.

Veblen was unorthodox in his teaching and in his writing, but what shocked the university administration and many older colleagues profoundly was his unorthodox love life. Women were much attracted to him, and stories about his affairs and escapades soon were bandied around in scandalized faculty gatherings. Mrs. Veblen was much perturbed by these affairs and threatened to leave him. Matters were not made easier by his habit of leaving in his pockets the letters he received from his female admirers. In all these affairs, Veblen was more the pursued than the pursuer. "What is one to do when a woman moves in on you?" he once complained. He remarked, somewhat later, that "the president doesn't approve of my domestic arrangements. Nor do I." Nevertheless, his amatory escapades, even more than his scholarly unorthodoxy and his unconventional teaching, made him an outcast in the university's inner circles and eventually led to his dismissal.

In the Chicago days, Veblen pursued a kind of double-barreled strategy: he would alienate most students and faculty while at the same time building a close intellectual companionship with a chosen group of congenial colleagues. When his first and still most widely read book, *The Theory of the Leisure Class,* was published in 1899, the influence of such Chicago men as Jacques Loeb, Franz Boas, and William I. Thomas could be traced on virtually every page.

The Theory of the Leisure Class helped bring Veblen to the attention of a

[51] *Ibid.*, p. 250.

broader public than he had enjoyed so far. It brought him a circle of admirers who hailed the book as an epoch-making achievement. Lester Ward, the dean of American sociology, praised it highly, as did William D. Howells, the dean of American letters. Veblen was now an intellectual force to be reckoned with. His next book, *The Theory of Business Enterprise* (1904), perhaps his most systematic critique of American business, received a somewhat less enthusiastic response. Conservative critics complained about his destructiveness, his amoralism, and his lack of appreciation for the virtues of free enterprise. Many radicals, appreciative of his critique of capitalism, were nevertheless unhappy about his rejection of Marxism. Others complained about his involuted style and lack of clarity. Yet critics and admirers seemed to agree that Veblenian doctrine was now an established feature on the intellectual scene.

As his fame outside the university grew, his life inside it became well nigh impossible. When Veblen returned from a trip to Europe in 1904, during which he had been accompanied by a female companion who was clearly not his wife, he was asked by the university authorities to sign a paper declaring that he would have no further relations with the woman involved. He replied that he was not in the habit of promising not to do what he was not accustomed to doing. His days at Chicago were now numbered. He made efforts to secure a variety of appointments, among others to the Library of Congress, but all these efforts failed. Finally, Stanford University offered him an Associate Professorship at a relatively high salary, and he joined its staff in 1906.

Veblen stayed at Stanford a little more than three years. His style of life, of morality, and of expression continued to be as unconventional as it had been in Chicago. His wife, who had left him for a time, returned to him in Palo Alto, but the marriage was clearly on the rocks. Matters were not made easier when one of his Chicago admirers wrote him that she wanted to be the mother of a great man's children. Mrs. Veblen left him again. When his amatory adventures could no longer be covered up, the administration forced him to resign in December 1909.

Veblen did not make the close intellectual friends at Stanford that he did at Chicago. The major elements of his "system," if such it can be called, had been set down in the Chicago days. His subsequent books, beginning with *The Instinct of Workmanship* (1914) on which he was working at Stanford, are, with one exception, only elaborations of previous lines of thought. Veblen probably was therefore less eager for intellectual stimulation than he had been earlier. He was as distant and aloof at Stanford as he had been at Chicago, but apparently made less of an effort to gather around himself a chosen few intellectual peers.

After having been forced to resign at Stanford, Veblen applied for a position at various schools. But the known circumstances of his severance from Stanford led every administration that was approached to recoil. Veblen was a marked man. To have offended the academic proprieties twice in a row was just too much. Finally, a former student, H. J. Davenport, came to the rescue and persuaded the president of the University of Missouri to offer Veblen a position in its School of Commerce, of which Davenport was dean. Ellen Rolfe Veblen now secured a divorce and, as a result, the president of Stanford, in a recommendation to make the temporary appointment permanent, wrote to the president of the University of Missouri that he saw no reason why Veblen should not be retained since he had now straightened out his matrimonial affairs. In 1914 Veblen married his second wife, Anne Fessenden Bradley, a divorcee whom he had known at Chicago and Stanford. The new Mrs. Veblen, far less educated than the first, did all his typing, washed all the laundry and sewed all the clothes for her two daughters from an earlier marriage. She seems to have been totally devoted to Veblen, and being a radical like him, she was wholeheartedly in favor of "the movement," forever discussing the virtues of Socialism with the conventional faculty wives. She was also in full agreement with her husband's rather original ideas in regard to household duties. For example, the making of beds was considered a useless ceremonial; the covers were merely turned down over the foot of the bed so that they could be easily drawn up at night. Dishes were washed only when the total supply was exhausted; then they were stacked in a tub, a hose turned on them, and, after the water had been drained off, they were left to dry. Veblen also advocated, though he stopped short of practicing, the making of clothes out of discardable paper.

Although Veblen was coddled and indulged by a number of his former students now on the staff of the University of Missouri, he lacked the wider intellectual companionship he had enjoyed at Chicago and, to a degree, at Stanford. Neither faculty nor students at the University of Missouri were of the quality that Veblen had been accustomed to; as a result, he withdrew even more. As his health grew poorer and he began to feel the weight of years, his courses became even less organized than before, and his contempt for his students deepened. The university authorities were flattered to have attracted a man of his reputation, but they felt he was not contributing fully. As a result, he never got a permanent position and remained a lecturer, whose appointment had to be renewed annually, during the entire seven years of his stay. His Stanford salary had been $3000; at Missouri he was paid under $2000 in his first few years and received only $2400 in 1917, just before he left.

While at Missouri, Veblen completed his third book, *The Instinct of Workmanship,* and soon after the beginning of World War I, he published his *Imperial Germany and the Industrial Revolution,* one of his more important works. Soon after, there followed *An Inquiry into the Nature of the Peace* (1918), a less significant and more ephemeral book. In the same year, he finally published his savage onslaught on the structure and operation of the American university, *The Higher Learning in America,* most of which had been put to paper in the Chicago days. The books that followed were either collections of previously published papers or restatements usually in somewhat more high-flown language, of points he had made before. These books included *The Vested Interests and the Common Man* (1919), *The Place of Science in Modern Civilization* (1919), *The Engineers and the Price System* (1921) and *Absentee Ownership and Business Enterprise in Recent Times* (1923).

A MARGINAL FREE LANCE

In 1917, when questions of war and peace assumed foremost importance in the minds of many American intellectuals, Veblen resolved to move to Washington to be nearer to the center of events. In the fall of 1917 President Wilson had asked Colonel House to bring together an academic study group to discuss the terms of a possible peace settlement. Veblen prepared several memoranda for this inquiry, but his contributions seem not to have been much appreciated. Soon, however, he was given another opportunity to serve the administration. Having been granted a leave of absence from Missouri, he joined the Food Administration as a special investigator. But his time in government service was short and nasty: he was as little concerned with pleasing governmental bureaucrats as he had been with placating their academic counterparts. Veblen was put to work investigating methods for alleviating the manpower shortage in the Midwest, which was impeding the harvest. He suggested that the despised Industrial Workers of the World, the antiwar syndicalist and radical organization that had been persecuted by the government, be used for harvesting. He proposed that members of the I.W.W. be enrolled under officers of their own choice as members of a collective labor force. In this way agricultural productiveness would be enhanced, and the persecution of the I.W.W. would cease. As might be expected, the proposal was received with a combination of hostility and indifference, as was another memorandum that suggested how the shortage of sales personnel in retail establishments could be overcome. The administration need only install a farm-marketing and retail-distribution system under the parcel-post division of the Post Office to avoid the waste resulting from an excessive number of retail outlets. It must be conceded that a man who suggested to the administration that his plans would lead to a reduction of the parasitic population of country towns by nine tenths, and a consequent increase in the available labor supply, was not exactly attuned to the political realities of governmental policy-making. Veblen's sojourn among the Washington bureaucrats ended rather abruptly, having lasted less than five months.

During the war, Veblen's influence among a small group of left-wing intellectuals and progressive academics began to grow. Francis Hackett, the literary editor of *The New Republic,* lost no opportunity to praise his work. Graham Wallas, in a review of *Imperial Germany,* called its author a genius. Max Weber and Werner Sombart had earlier expressed their appreciation of his work. Professor Frederick W. Taussig of Harvard called his *Instinct of Workmanship* a "brilliant and original book, like everything that comes from his pen," and Alvin Johnson spoke of the "sheer intellectual power of the author." Radicals like Floyd Dell wrote that his *The Nature of the Peace* "should result in his being either appointed to the President's War Council, or put in jail for treason."

What Dell wrote in jest proved to be not so far from reality. In view of the obscurity of Veblen's approach, the Postmaster of the City of New York ruled that *Imperial Germany* could not be mailed since it fell under the provisions of the Espionage Act, while the official governmental propaganda agency, the Committee on Public Information, believed it to be excellent war propaganda. Some government bureaus thought the book damaging to America, while others thought it damaging to Germany.

In the fall of 1918, Veblen moved to New York to become an editor of *The Dial,* as well as a key contributor to it. The magazine, which Ralph Waldo Emerson had founded, was now proposing to devote itself to matters of international reconstruction and to the reform of industry and education. Although the masthead included other major figures, John Dewey and Randolph Bourne among them, the magazine was soon referred to as the "Veblenian Dial." For a year or two, and despite personal tragedy—his wife had a psychotic breakdown and had to be removed to a sanitarium—Veblen now experienced for the first time the pleasures of being an intellectual celebrity. Fame, which had eluded him for so long, now came to the man of sixty.

Veblen's articles for *The Dial,* more savage and mordant even than his earlier writing, fitted perfectly the disillusioned mood that gripped the liberal world after the failure of Wilsonianism. Moreover, Veblen, who had up to this point always maintained the mask of the objective observer, now advocated a thoroughgoing revamping of the whole structure of American society. His writings in *The Dial* lacked the precision of his earlier work, but they made up for this by an impassioned rhetoric. Moreover, the man who had always held Marx at a distance, now praised the Russian Revolution. "The Bolshevist scheme of ideas," he wrote, "comes easy to the common man." He felt that salvation from the messy anarchy of predatory capitalism would come through the matter-of-fact expertise of engineers; he called, perhaps somewhat tongue-in-cheek, for a Soviet of Engineers.

These savage onslaughts on the established order gained Veblen many new admirers, while making some of his old friends uncomfortable. Walton Hamilton wrote that Veblen had better return to his work as a "certified economist," while Randolph Bourne and Maxwell Anderson felt that Veblen's ideas were seminal and permeated the whole intellectual atmosphere. The final accolade came when the great curmudgeon of American letters, H. L. Mencken, as conservative in his political views as he was radical in his cultural criticism, honored Veblen with a fierce assault: "In a few months," he wrote, "almost in a few days, he was all over *The Nation, The Dial, The New Republic* and the rest of them, and his books and pamphlets began to pour from the presses. . . . Everyone of intellectual pretensions read his works. . . . There were Veblenists, Veblen clubs, Veblen remedies for all the sorrows of the world. There were even, in Chicago, Veblen girls—perhaps Gibson girls grown middle-aged and despairing." Mencken felt that this Veblen adulation was all so much hokum. He considered Veblen's writing intolerably bad, and his thinking "loose, flabby, cocksure, and preposterous."[52]

Mencken predicted that the Veblen vogue would soon subside. He proved to be correct. The mood of revolt that had followed the failure of Wilsonianism soon subsided. Some leading intellectuals left in despair for exile in Europe, but the majority made their peace with America or drowned their anxieties in the pleasure-seeking whirl of the Jazz Age. Radicals were hounded and persecuted by the notorious Lusk Committee of the New York State Legislature and by the infamous raids of Attorney-General Mitchell Palmer, who led the manhunt against those suspected of sympathy with the Russian Revolution.

Veblen's career at *The Dial* came to an end after one year, when it was turned into a literary magazine. The newly organized New School for Social Research now offered him refuge. It boasted an eminent faculty including Charles Beard, James Harvey Robinson, Wesley Mitchell, Harold Laski, Alexander Goldenweiser, and Horace Kallen, and promised to become the fountainhead of revolutionary departures in American education. Veblen had a fairly comfortable position there. His salary of $6000 was mainly contributed by a former student from the Chicago days who admired him greatly. He again offered his by now-famous course on "Economic Factors in Civilization"; he also worked on articles that continued *The Dial* series and were now published by another radical publication, *The Freeman,* and prepared his last book, *Absentee Ownership.* But he was becoming increasingly tired. He was now in his middle sixties, and age began to make itself felt.

Two ironic incidents from this last period of his life are worth recounting. The editor of a leading Jewish magazine approached Veblen and asked him to write a paper discussing whether Jewish intellectual productivity would be increased if the Jews were given a land of their own and Jewish intellectuals were released from the taboos and restrictions that impeded them in the gentile world. Veblen accepted, and delivered his essay on "The Intellectual Preeminence of the Jews," in which he argued that the intellectual achievement of the Jews was due to their marginal status and persecuted role in an alien world, and that their springs of creativity would dry up should they become a people like any other in their own homeland. Needless to say, the essay was not published by the editor who had commissioned it. It appeared instead in *The Political Science Quarterly* of Columbia University.

[52] *Ibid.,* p. 423.

A few years later, some of Veblen's admirers urged his nomination for the presidency of the American Economic Association. Conservative members of the old school objected. After a long academic wrangle it was decided that he would be nominated, provided that he would consent to become a member of the Association. Veblen refused. "They didn't offer it to me when I needed it," he said.

In the middle twenties, although he had attracted new admirers and disciples, Veblen felt increasingly lonely in New York. He had some desultory contact with the leaders of what was to become the short-lived technocratic movement, but none of this seemed to satisfy him. When meeting with friends or foreign visitors, he often remained silent throughout the encounter. "His protective mechanism of silence had become his master," says Dorfman. He became increasingly helpless in practical matters and relied almost entirely on the protection of his friends. Ellen Rolfe died in May, 1926. In 1927 Veblen decided to return to California in the company of his stepdaughter Becky. He pretended to himself that this was only a temporary visit, but probably knew there would be no return.

Back in Palo Alto, Veblen lived for a year in an old town shack that he still owned from his Stanford days. He later moved into his mountain cabin in the adjacent hills, where he lived in almost total isolation. Eager for conversation, he felt altogether lonely and neglected. Everyone, he thought, had forgotten him. Worried about his financial situation, he tried (and failed) to recoup his investments in the collapsing raisin industry. Absentee ownership did not profit him.

In the summer of 1929, Veblen made plans to return East, but a relative persuaded him that his ill health would not allow this. On August 3, 1929, he died of heart disease.

As the depression struck America in the year of Veblen's death, he was suddenly rediscovered. Some of his admirers and disciples, including Rexford Tugwell, A. A. Berle, Thurman Arnold, and Felix Frankfurter, became leading members of Roosevelt's braintrust or intellectual spokesmen for the New Deal. They all attempted to apply Veblenian doctrine to the social and economic reconstruction, which was now the order of the day. Leading left-wing spokemen and publicists such as Stuart Chase, John Chamberlain, and Max Lerner spread Veblen's message. William Ogburn and Robert Lynd incorporated his thought into the fabric of their sociological investigations. In 1938, when a number of leading intellectuals were queried by the editors of *The New Republic* to name "The Books that Changed [Their] Minds" Veblen's name came first on the list.[53] At the time of his death, the total sales of his ten books was approximately 40,000 copies. Over half of this was represented by *The Theory of the Leisure Class,* the only book by which he was then remembered. Between February 1930 and September 1934, his books sold about

[53] Richard Hofstadter, *The Progressive Historians* (New York, Alfred A. Knopf, 1968), p. 220.

4,000 copies. Today most of them are available in paperback, and *The Theory of the Leisure Class* has become a perennial best-seller in a variety of inexpensive editions. Veblen paid a heavy penalty for having taken the lead twenty years too soon.

THE INTELLECTUAL CONTEXT

At the risk of oversimplification, one can say that Veblen's work stands under the shadow of two ill-assorted figures, Herbert Spencer and Edward Bellamy, while also being strongly influenced by Marx. From Spencer, and of course from Darwin, Veblen derived his evolutionary approach to the social sciences. From Bellamy, probably more than from Marx or other socialist theoreticians, he acquired his critical rejection of what he termed the current anarchy of capitalist production and a vision of a planned and rationally organized society.

THE INFLUENCE OF BELLAMY, MARX, AND EVOLUTIONISM

Veblen and his wife, it will be recalled, read Bellamy's socialist utopia, *Looking Backward,* with growing enthusiasm shortly after its publication. The work was, according to Ellen Rolfe, the turning point in their lives. Veblen probably had read other utopias before. What particularly appealed to him in Bellamy was that, in Dorfman's words, "Unlike most utopians and reformers, Bellamy believed not in fighting . . . the machine process, but in making [it] the means of achieving the socialist state."[54] Veblen found in the book not a plea for a return to arcadian modes of rural existence, but a forward-looking vision that accepted and welcomed the machine. Bellamy urged "the substitution of scientific methods of an organized and unified industrial system for the wasteful struggle of the present competitive plan with its countless warring and mutually destructive undertakings."[55] This goal must have struck a responsive chord in the young Veblen, as is apparent in all of his later writings.

Bellamy's work contained savage onslaughts against a system that periodically created business crises and depressions, disrupted economic life, and created mass unemployment and privation for the bulk of the population. "The daydream of the nineteenth-century producer," he wrote, "was to gain absolute control of the supply of some necessity of life, so that he might keep the public at the verge of starvation, and always command famine prices for what he supplied. . . . This is what was called a system of production [but it seemed in some of its aspects] a great deal more like a system for preventing production."[56] In contrast to this exploitative system, Bellamy put forward a vision

[54] Dorfman, *op. cit.,* p. 68. [55] Quoted in Aaron, *op. cit.,* p. 103.
[56] *Ibid.,* p. 118.

of nationalized industry as "the triumph of common sense." In his utopia, there existed no leisure class of property, no competitive emulation, no chronic depression with idle capital and labor. With a "perfect interworking" of "every wheel and every hand," all industrial processes would interlock and industrial affairs would be run by a vast, disciplined, and highly efficient industrial army.

Bellamy's regimented utopia had certain frightening features, especially when viewed through the lens of our contemporary experience. But in his day, it seemed to provide a way out of anarchy and decay for a public appalled by economic crises and by strife and conflict on the industrial scene. *Looking Backward* sold the fabulous number of 370,000 copies in the first two years after its publication in 1888, and more than a million by 1900. The father of Emily Balch, advocate of pacifism and women's rights, exclaimed after reading it: "It's slavery, but it's worth it." This is a startlingly modern reaction, but it was certainly a minority view at the time.[57] Veblen, it would appear, had no such awareness of the ambiguity inherent in such a fantasy, and he seems to have been among those thousands of Bellamy's readers whose image of the "good society" and whose rejection of present institutional arrangements were shaped in large part by *Looking Backward.*

Veblen's vision of the "good society," although it informed his critique of the present, was only subjacent in his main work. He expressed it openly only in his late essays written for the *Dial* and the *Freeman*. His evolutionism, on the other hand, provides the dominant thread of almost all his published writings.

Spencerian and Darwinian evolutionism served Veblen as a means for what Morton White has termed "the revolt against formalism." In this, Veblen was not alone. A number of leading American intellectuals—John Dewey and Charles Beard, Justice Holmes and James Harvey Robinson—ranged themselves in the 1890's against formalism, that is, excessive reliance on logic, abstraction, deduction, and formalization in the social sciences. They contended that these were "incapable of containing the rich, moving, living current of social life."[58] Although differing in some details, Peirce's and James's pragmatism, Dewey's instrumentalism, Beard's economic determinism, Holmes's legal realism, and Veblen's institutionalism showed a striking philosophical kinship. "They [were] all suspicious of approaches which [were] excessively formal; they all protest[ed] their anxiety to come to grips with reality, their attachment to the moving and vital in social life."[59]

The specific formalistic system of thought against which Veblen reacted was, of course, classical economics with its methodological emphasis on rational behavior and on the "economic man." Veblen strongly objected to the abstractions of the classical economists and their use of the subjunctive conditional as

[57] Cf. Lewis A. Coser and Henry Jacoby, "Utopia Revisited," *Common Cause*, IV, 7 (February, 1951), pp. 370–78. [58] White, *op. cit.*, p. 11. [59] *Ibid.*, p. 6.

in the clause, "if perfect competition prevailed."[60] Such abstraction, Veblen argued, distorted reality and allowed no access to the concrete variety and historical variability of human motives. In contrast to such approaches, Veblen urged viewing man as an engaged, active, and many-sided actor, rather than as a rational calculator of hedonistic satisfactions. Veblen used the evolutionary science of Darwin and Spencer to demolish the ahistorical categories of the classical economists. To him, economics was an evolutionary science—one that viewed men as engaged in an evolutionary struggle with the natural environment for ever more efficient adaptation.

The evolutionist doctrine of Darwin and Spencer provided Veblen with his general method as well as with his overall view of the story of mankind. But while earlier American social evolutionists, such as Veblen's teacher Sumner, had adopted Spencer's laissez faire doctrine along with his evolutionary approach, Veblen rejected the individualistic conclusions of Spencer while retaining his method.

The third major influence on Veblen, besides Bellamy and the evolutionists, was Karl Marx. Although he rejected Marxism, objecting above all to what he called Marx's unscientific Hegelianism and teleological optimism, much of Veblen's economic writing is nevertheless deeply influenced by the Marxian approach. In fact, the parallelisms and similarities between his thought and that of Marx are so striking that European writers have often been moved to deny Veblen's originality and to contend that his thought is simply Marxism in American and technological dress. It should be clear from the chapter on Marx and from the preceding section on Veblen's work that this is not the case. Yet major elements of Veblen's technological explanation of evolution have their roots in Marx's economic interpretation of mankind's history and in the Marxian distinction between economic infrastructure and cultural superstructure. Even Veblen's writing about the thwarting of the instinct of workmanship under capitalism may owe something to the Marxian notion of alienation.

In addition to Engels, Kautsky, Antonio Labriola and other Marxists, as well as the young semi-Marxist Werner Sombart, Veblen was influenced by the German historical school of economics, more particularly by Gustav Schmoller, the leader of the "socialists of the chair." Veblen rejected, as they did, the abstract approach of the classical economists, and saw Schmoller and his colleagues as allies in their common insistence on historical and institutional factors in the development of economic behavior. He did not accept them completely, however; he accused them of remaining stuck in the preparatory stage of description, classification, and observation, and not helping to advance the discovery of uniformities and laws. They provided no causal explanation of economic phenomena, Veblen argued, because, like the Marxist economists, they were

[60] *Ibid.*, p. 25.

still arguing in a pre-Darwinian framework. Despite this rejection, it is apparent that Veblen's institutional economics much resembles the methods of the German historical economics, which, if his book reviews are taken as evidence, Veblen knew exceedingly well.[61]

A variety of other thinkers, in one way or another, left an imprint on Veblen's exceedingly well-furnished mind. He was, for example, intimately familiar with the work of all major economists from Adam Smith to John Stuart Mill, from the Austrian marginalists to Alfred Marshall, and even to the early writings of John Maynard Keynes. He knew the works of most evolutionary anthropologists from Tylor to Morgan. His earlier training had given him a good grounding in philosophy, and he was somewhat of a specialist in the philosophy of Kant. Yet more significant than these influences was the impression left on him by contemporaries with whom he was in personal contact.

THE DEBT TO PRAGMATISM

Veblen's activist conception of man is closely related to the American pragmatism that pervaded the intellectual milieu in which he periodically lived. It will be recalled that he attended Charles Peirce's lectures at Johns Hopkins; John Dewey and George H. Mead were among his colleagues in Chicago. Although there is no evidence that he knew William James personally, his conception of the social source of self-esteem and self-regard evidently owes something to James as well as to Mead and Dewey.

In addition to the pragmatic philosophers among his Chicago colleagues, the physiologist Jacques Loeb must be reckoned among the major influences on Veblen's thought. Loeb's theory of instincts and tropisms, his strictly mechanistic interpretation of biological and psychological phenomena, may have been the source of Veblen's theory of instincts. William I. Thomas, of the Chicago Department of Sociology, and a friend of Veblen's, was himself influenced by Loeb's theory of tropisms; during the time Veblen worked at Chicago, Thomas gave courses on Comparative Institutions of Primitive People, Comparative Technology, and Animism. It seems clear that Veblen was guided and stimulated by Thomas's work in his own anthropological and comparative studies. Finally, Franz Boas, who was the curator of Chicago's Field Museum during part of the time when Veblen served at Chicago "was illustrating . . . the law of conspicuous waste in his ethnological study of the Kwakiutl Indians of British Columbia."[62] Any reader of Boas' work, or of its *haute vulgarisation* in Ruth Benedict's *Patterns of Culture,* will be struck by the resemblance between Boas' description of the competitiveness among the Kwakiutl, where rivals

[61] On the German historical school of economics, cf. Ben B. Seligman, *Main Currents in Modern Economics* (New York, The Free Press, 1962). This book has also a fine chapter on Veblen's economics. [62] Dorfman, *op. cit.,* p. 115.

fight with property only, and Veblen's descriptions of conspicuous consumption and waste in his *The Theory of the Leisure Class.*

There will be an occasion for considering the further impact of Veblen's colleagues in the social context in which he worked.

THE SOCIAL CONTEXT

THE GENERAL SCENE

Veblen grew up and did his most creative work in what has been called the Gilded Age, but was also known as the Age of Protest. It was the age of the Robber Barons who, while fattening on the "underlying population," built, in a few decades, an amazing industrial complex in what had been an essentially agrarian nation. Only half a century after the end of the Civil War, America had won first place among the industrial powers of the world. From the end of the sixties to the turn of the century, the number of factories increased fourfold; the number of factory workers, fivefold; the value of industrial products, sevenfold; and the amount of available capital, ninefold. The annual production of pig iron increased by a factor of sixteen, and steel production, which was insignificant until the sixties, expanded to more than 10,000,000 tons a year.

The men who directed this stupendous industrial expansion were hardheaded, vulgar, and determined nouveaux riches. They were, in Vernon Parrington's estimation, "primitive souls, ruthless, predatory, capable; single-minded men; rogues and rascals often, but never feeble, never hindered by petty scruples, never given to puling or whining—the raw materials of a race of capitalist buccaneers." They worked hard and they played hard. Though some of them still adhered to the austere standards of their puritan ancestors, most were given to a gaudy and vulgar display of their newly acquired riches, often squandering the wealth acquired in the Great Barbecue almost as soon as they had gained it. They built themselves fantastic and tasteless mansions in styles that mixed the architecture of the Taj Mahal and that of Gothic cathedrals. They ransacked the art galleries of Europe to adorn their houses, and they lured the sons of the European aristocracy to America to marry them to their daughters and to adorn their family tree. This was the "leisure class" that Veblen depicted in his savage portrayal.

Oil, steel, and railroad companies dominated the business world, and the Rockefellers, Carnegies, and Vanderbilts who ran them acquired a power that not even the President of the United States enjoyed in the simple agrarian America of the Founding Fathers. But when the power of the industrial and railroad promoters was at its height, it brought with it a powerful reaction. Midwestern farmers were the first to band together into a political crusade against the "sinister interests" and deflationary policies that spelled ruin to the debtor class. In the seventies, the Patrons of Husbandry, or the Grange, became a power on the plains, and began their fiery campaigns against the railroad interests, the grain elevator operators, and the Eastern bankers who victimized the farmers. Soon they were joined by the Greenbackers, who organized the debtors among the farm population against the hard money men from the East, and urged easier credit for the embattled farmers. Under the leadership of a fiery Minnesotan agitator, Ignatius Donnelly, they asked whether the ordinary man "could retain his economic independence, or [whether] he must become the wage slave of the possessors of great wealth."

The troubles of the farmers were multiplied when a five-year drought hit the plains in the late eighties and early nineties, just at the time when Veblen and Ellen Rolfe were reading economics on their Iowa farm. From 1890 to 1894, more than eleven thousand farm mortgages were foreclosed in Kansas alone. Many of the pioneers who had gone West full of hope now returned and scrawled on their wagons, "In God we trusted, in Kansas we busted." When the price of wheat fell below fifty cents a bushel, many Midwestern towns and counties went bankrupt and schools and churches closed their doors.

Meanwhile the leaders of the agrarians were reaching out to try to achieve a united front of reformers. Under the leadership of Donnelly of Minnesota, Tom Watson of Georgia, and James B. Weaver of Iowa, they founded the People's Party of America, or, as it would be better known, the Populist Party in 1892. Its platform proclaimed the common interest of farmers and laborers, urged government ownership and management of the railroads, telephone, and telegraph services, and demanded free and unlimited coinage of silver to increase the monetary supply. It also advocated a graduated income tax, adoption of the initiative and referendum, direct elections of U.S. Senators, and single terms for Presidents and Vice-Presidents. Populists soon controlled several state legislatures. When the Presidential elections of 1896 were in the offing and the Republicans nominated William McKinley, a firm defender of tight money, the gold standard, and financial orthodoxy, the Democrats appropriated major parts of the Populist platform. William Jennings Bryan, their candidate, became the fiery spokesman of the Western debtors and farmers against the creditor and banking interests of the East. His famous "cross of gold" speech delivered at the Democratic convention in Chicago, where Veblen was by then teaching, had an immense repercussion throughout the West and Midwest, with its rhetorical climax: "You shall not press down upon the brow of labor this crown of thorns; you shall not crucify mankind upon a cross of gold." Nevertheless, McKinley won the election.

Industrial unrest was almost as pronounced as the discontent of the farmers. Some of the most bloody and violent strikes in American labor history were fought in those years. Americans who had believed until then that class conflicts were exclusively European affairs were rudely awakened. The

McCormick Harvester strike and the attendant Haymarket riot of 1886, which resulted in the judicial murder of five alleged anarchists, the bloody Homestead strike of 1892, the great Pullman strike of 1894, the fierce industrial warfare among the Colorado miners—these all marked a new age of violence in American labor relations.

Until the nineties socialism had been considered something of an exotic movement that seemed to flourish only among recent immigrants. Now, under the leadership of a genuinely native leader, Eugene Debs, it gained a foothold not only among Jewish garment workers and skilled German craftsmen but among Western miners as well. In 1899, when Veblen published his *Theory of the Leisure Class,* the American Socialist Party was organized and took Chicago for its headquarters.

The last two or three decades of the nineteenth century are marked by a polarization of political and social forces such as America, with the exception of the Civil War itself, had never known before. Until then American politics had been in the main a politics of coalitions—sectional, economic, or political groupings that formed and reformed alliances according to the requirements of the hour. It had been, and it later again became, a kind of Virginia reel in which one changed partners all the time. But in the last decades of the century a sharp cleavage had set in: farm interests were set against financial interests, debtors against creditors, management against labor, the West against the East—these seemed permanent polarities. And what is more, all these conflicts seemed to be coalescing along a single axis. The farmers of the West were in debt to financiers of the East, who held their mortgages. While social conflicts had previously involved a variety of non-zero sum games, it now appeared as if the whole nation was about to be split between interests fundamentally at variance and engaged in a deadly zero-sum struggle for dominance.

This polarization of conflicts accounts in large part for Veblen's tendency to think in terms of polar opposites, to divide all society into basically opposed camps. Although a Midwestern farmer might not have been able to formulate his convictions in just that way, he was, nonetheless, moved to think of the polarization between "captains of industry" and the "underlying population," between "workmanship" and "salesmanship," between "vested interests" and the "industrial arts." "Veblen's distinction between the engineer and the businessman," writes Henry Steele Commager, "might have been made by a Kansas Populist comparing the constructive work of building the transcontinentals with the destructive work of exploiting them—comparing, let us say, the contributions of General Grenville Dodge and Jay Gould."[63]

The dualistic structure of Veblen's thought was rooted in the social dualism that marked the American scene toward the end of the nineteenth century.

[63] Henry Steele Commager, *The American Mind* (New Haven, Yale University Press, 1950), p. 238. I have not thought it necessary to footnote my sources for this subchapter. The facts are easily available in any competent textbook.

A MARGINAL MAN

Even a swift glance at Veblen's life and career makes it abundantly clear that he was a marginal man.

While deeply rooted in the American soil, Veblen shared none of the assumptions of his America. His overall view of American society in the Gilded Age had more than a tinge of the attitude of the country boy who looks with contempt and abhorrence at the world of the city slickers. American society as a whole was to him the whore of Babylon. Although he had emancipated himself from his Norwegian farming background at a very early age, he was still inexorably wedded to certain of its basic assumptions. Hard work, frugality, energetic application to the tasks at hand—these were to Veblen basic virtues, as opposed to the vices of dissipation, speculation, wastefulness, and lack of discipline in American urban civilization. It was as if a late descendant of the age of Benjamin Franklin had been suddenly projected, by the wave of a magic wand, into the age of the Great Gatsby.

Veblen also found himself at odds with his native Norwegian community. Having broken with the institutionalized pieties of his home environment, Veblen early came to see himself, and was seen by others, as maladapted to his immediate environment. Even though he insisted in his later writings that a man's self-esteem was rooted in the esteem given him by his fellows, Veblen flouted this doctrine in practice and attempted to gain self-esteem by attacking the usual customs of the community and calling forth the disapproval of his Norwegian contemporaries. He was encouraged in this respect by his father, who was himself partly at variance with community standards in his insistence on educating his children and thereby facilitating their social mobility. In attempting to set himself apart from the ways of his fellows, Veblen submitted them to corrosive criticism and analysis, trying to gain a vantage point from which he could view their life styles with the detachment of the outsider.

At Carleton College, and in his subsequent career as a graduate student, instructor, and professor, Veblen's marginality was twice compounded. He lived in two worlds, while belonging to neither. He never could adjust to or even make his peace with the genteel culture of American academia, and yet he was sufficiently attracted to it to want to make his mark within it. Acutely conscious of his Norwegian origins, he felt himself a resident alien, a kind of squatter on foreign territory. Veblen even disdained the common strategy of outwardly conforming while inwardly refusing assent. He declined to be bound by the local proprieties and conventions in order to retain his full freedom. He did not want to be co-opted but seems to have been sufficiently tempted by co-optation to feel the subconscious need to flout the mores of the academy, thus making sure that he would not be admitted into the establishment. His continued efforts to shock the academy must also be seen as a sign of his attachment to it; one shocks and attacks only those considered worthy objects of hostility.

Yet Veblen's academic marginality—the repeated rebuffs and slights he suffered—was only partially a result of his psychological ambivalence. In the pre-World War I university, unlike the one that emerged later, the notion of academic freedom was only slightly institutionalized. A number of well-known academic men were fired for their unconventional opinions even though they lived quite conventional personal lives, which Veblen did not. Professors given to radical views, whether Populists, Christian reformers, or Marxists, were often hounded from their chairs, as the careers of E. A. Ross, Richard Ely, and Scott Nearing testify. In our day, as a number of academic novels have pointed out with relish, unconventionality in a few members of the faculty is regarded with a certain admiration so that sometimes those who are otherwise undistinguished may make a career of their idiosyncrasies. In Veblen's day, the university administration and the bulk of professors tended to be so deeply wedded to proprieties that even minor infringements of the academic code might bring a distinguished career to a sudden close. W. I. Thomas, Veblen's colleague at Chicago, a man not given to flamboyant flouting of conventions, was nevertheless fired from the University of Chicago for what, by contemporary standards, would seem a minor indiscretion.

Throughout his academic career, Veblen refused to bend to the requirements of academic administrators. But in contrast to other academic rebels, he seems also to have offended most of his colleagues. He refused to gain support from the faculty club when battling the powers of the administration building. He was as marginal in relation to most of his colleagues as he was to the "captains of erudition."

It has often been overlooked that he was marginal in a generational sense also. Veblen was thirty-four years old when he came to Cornell University to study economics, which most probably contributed to separating him from the bulk of the graduate students. In the Chicago days, the discrepancy between his chronological age and his academic status also separated him from men with whom he might otherwise have had more in common. He became an instructor at the age of thirty-eight and only in his early forties was he promoted to assistant professor. Hence, in a structural sense, he occupied a kind of no-man's-land. Faculty members of his age typically had higher rank than he, and those who shared his rank were typically much younger. Even had he wanted to, he would have found it difficult to associate intimately with most higher-status age mates or with lower-age status equals.

Veblen came to Chicago as a tutor. John Dewey, who was two years younger and had obtained his Ph.D. in the same year, came as head professor of philosophy. Veblen's Johns Hopkins classmate, Elgin Gould, came as a professor of statistics in the department of economics. Things got worse from

Veblen's point of view as others received faster promotions so that the status distance between them and Veblen increased further. His successive failures in attaining rapid promotion increased his relative deprivation as initial discrepancies between his standing and that of his age mates widened over the course of time.

Some of these difficulties might have loomed less large if the University of Chicago had had a collegial type of departmental organization at the time. Some of the discrepancies in Veblen's status might have been alleviated had he had the possibility of participating actively in the running of a more or less democratic department of economics. But the University of Chicago in William Rainey Harper's days was governed in a pronouncedly autocratic manner. Each department was in the charge of a "head professor," who ran it with a minimum of interference from the lower ranks. There was no chance to attenuate rank distinctions in the give-and-take of colleague-oriented departmental decision-making. It might be argued that such autocratic methods could have led to an increase in solidarity of the lower ranks who were all equally deprived of decision-making power through a kind of negative democratization. This may well have been so. But in this case such in-group solidarity would probably have grown at the expense of Veblen; the outsider would have become a scapegoat. This fact also might have contributed to Veblen's withdrawal into the position of a loner who passively contemplated the foibles of his peers and superiors with the amused detachment of an anthropologist watching the natives.

For many men, the academy is a kind of refuge, a haven, which provides shelter from the buffeting of a society with which they feel themselves at variance. Despite his marginality, this was also, to some extent, the case with Veblen. Even though he was so highly critical of the university system that he had intended originally to sub-title his *Higher Learning in America,* "A Study in Utter Depravity," he nevertheless had much stronger and more enduring ties with the academic community than he had with the larger culture and society of his day.

Veblen was as much a stranger in his America as a man born in another country or in another age would have been. It is precisely this position as a stranger that allowed him to perceive characteristics of American life styles and customs to which the settled citizen would not be as easily sensitized. Marginality sharpened his powers of observation. In contrast to those who are so at ease within a scheme of conventions that they are apt not to notice its problematical aspects, the stranger, in Simmel's words, "is the freer man, practically and theoretically. He views his relations to others with less prejudice; he submits them to more general, more objective standards, and he is not confined in his action by custom, piety or precedent." The stranger as a social analyst regards as secular what others consider sacred. His analysis lays bare latent sources of motivation among members of the community that are hidden from those who are rooted in its conventions and who act out their assigned roles with naive unselfconsciousness. The stranger as analyst thereby threatens the world of the uncomplicated believer with massive disenchantment. He is, in Veblen's words, "a disturber of intellectual peace." Such men are not likely to be welcome in the society at large, even though they may find an audience among other discontented spirits.

VEBLEN'S AUDIENCE AND COLLEAGUES

Veblen followed a different path than Simmel who, it will be recalled, turned increasingly to his academic and extra-academic lecture audience when he was rebuffed by superiors and colleagues. Far from making efforts to attract students, Veblen did all he could to put them off and to drive them from his classes. He cultivated a disorganized style of exposition that was bound to antagonize most students, and his bumbling delivery was as apt to alienate listeners as Simmel's brilliant rhetoric was meant to attract them.

Nor did Veblen make it easy for his reading public. His involuted style, his complicated phraseology, his polysyllabic vocabulary, seemed almost calculated to drive readers away. If that was his unconscious intention, he succeeded only too readily. Of all his books, only *The Theory of the Leisure Class* sold relatively well during his lifetime. As Dorfman points out, publishers thought so little of the sales appeal of Veblen's work that, although he had already written many books, he had to pay Macmillan $700 to get *The Nature of the Peace* published.

The men Veblen appears to have written for were the radicals outside the academy and a few choice spirits within it. Dorfman says that upon the publication of *The Theory of the Leisure Class* "Veblen became the god of all the radicals. . . . W. J. Ghent . . . recalls that in the New York circles of intellectual radicals he always found someone ready with a pat quotation. . . . [His] stinging satire was particularly enjoyed."[64] All later books of Veblen were reviewed by radical and socialist publications; even though the less intelligent reviewers felt the need to defend Marxism against Veblen's lack of respect for the founders and their latter-day disciples, almost all perceived that he gave them long-wanted ammunition in their warfare against American capitalist society. Some of them, like Veblen's former student William English Walling, even went so far as to claim that Veblen had furnished the philosophical backbone for the American socialist movement.[65]

Veblen may have been contemptuous of most radicals, as Dorfman implies, but he seems to have valued his radical audience nevertheless. His critique of the fundamental assumptions of American society drew him to the camp of American radicalism, although he had no taste for political agitation and propaganda or for the facile optimism that infused much of the radical move-

[64] Dorfman, *op. cit.*, p. 196. [65] *Ibid.*, p. 237.

ment. Hence, even while he befriended certain radicals, he remained as marginal to the radical movement as he was in all other respects. Veblen liked to attract an audience of radicals, but this was not his intended prime audience. Except for his last period in New York City, he never published in the radical or even the popular press and contributed almost exclusively to academic publications. His major papers appeared in the *Journal of Political Economy,* which he edited, in the *Quarterly Journal of Economics,* in the *American Journal of Sociology* or the *Political Science Quarterly.*

Despite his marginal academic status and his savage onslaughts against the way the university was organized, Veblen's milieu was still the university. He loved the university as the privileged seat for the exercise of "idle curiosity," while arguing that the academy was no longer dedicated to the quest for truth but was actually guided by a "meretricious subservience" to the Philistines and the "captains of erudition." Although he made fun of traditional scholarship and attacked the holy cows of academia, he paid tribute to it by displaying his own erudition and scholarship in all his writings. He wished to be known as a scholar and not as an agitator. He thought "unholy thoughts on holy ground," to quote Daniel Aaron, "and [used] the ritualistic paraphernalia of scholarship . . . for profoundly subversive purposes."[66] But he did use them, and thereby paid tribute to the company of scholars among whom he lived—even if uneasily. Veblen seems to have been convinced that the run of academic men consisted of fools and knaves. But he felt himself drawn to a choice company of colleagues, an elite audience capable of discerning behind his manifold masks, behind his spoofing, debunking, mocking and cynical manner, the desperately serious moralist and the dedicated social analyst. Marginal to almost every institutional activity, Veblen, at least during his days in Chicago, craved the company and the intellectual stimulation of an audience of likeminded colleagues.

In their eagerness to document Veblen's marginality, many commentators seem to have neglected the fact that while he was at the University of Chicago —and this was the most productive period of his life—Veblen was not totally isolated but enjoyed the colleagueship of a number of eminent men from a variety of fields. The impact on his thought of philosophers Dewey and Mead, of sociologists and anthropologists W. I. Thomas and Franz Boas, of physiologist Jacques Loeb, all of whom taught at Chicago, has already been noted. The psychologist C. Lloyd Morgan and the philosopher James H. Tufts, Dewey's co-author in their *Ethics,* also influenced Veblen's train of thought, as had been documented by Dorfman and others. What is more, the influence was reciprocal, as several of Veblen's Chicago colleagues have testified. Tufts has written that when he was groping for some angle from which he could view the ethics of business, "Veblen's treatment, which was an effort to see

[66] Aaron, *op. cit.,* p. 242.

business as actually conducted, . . . seemed to me to throw light that was much needed on the actual practices and theories of business in this century."[67] Jacques Loeb, from whom Veblen borrowed a good deal of his theory of instincts, in turn borrowed Veblen's "instinct of workmanship." "One of the most important instincts," he wrote in his *Comparative Physiology and Psychology of the Brain,* "is usually not even recognized as such, namely the instinct of workmanship." He added in a footnote: "I take this name from Veblen's book *The Theory of the Leisure Class*."[68]

In Chicago, where he completed his "system," Veblen kept continued intellectual contact with a number of colleagues from various disciplines, and was as stimulated by them as they were by him. We can assume that they criticized his writings, checked excessive flights of his imagination, and generally served as friendly censors whenever Veblen was tempted to stray too far from the scholar's path.

A comparison of his later New York writings with those of the Chicago period shows the change in Veblen's style. He no longer had friendly critics among colleagues. In the post-World War years, when his renown spread and he related to a broader audience rather than to close colleagues, he no longer received critical guidance. Charles Beard told his Columbia students that Veblen's was the most original work on the economic basis of the governmental structure. Wesley Mitchell, his former student, called him "an extremely penetrating theorist." Felix Frankfurter admired him. Veblen had finally acquired a measure of fame and an audience, which, although still relatively restricted, was wider by far than that which he had enjoyed earlier. But now he was mainly surrounded by a clique of admiring disciples, and no longer benefited from a relationship of equality with a set of his peers. As a result, his last works exhibit a harshness of tone that was much less evident in his earlier writings. In the New York years he was no longer so much a marginal man as a man operating in a social vacuum, coddled and indulged by friends and admirers, but no longer subject to the invigorating influence of intellectual controversy on which his work had thrived in the Chicago days.

IN SUMMARY

Veblen is not a thinker of the very first rank, compared to some of the giants of social thought discussed in earlier chapters. Yet his seminal mind is likely to stimulate social theory for a long time to come. Even when those aspects of American culture against which he was most venomous have long disappeared, generations of social scientists will profit from the more generalized propositions that can be extracted from his writings, though he often

[67] Dorfman, *op. cit.,* p. 235. [68] *Ibid.,* p. 196.

buried them in concrete argumentation. His implicit use of the notion of relative deprivation, for example, provides a case in point. He was more nearly a sociological Montaigne than a sociological Weber. His place in the ongoing history of social thought will be largely determined retroactively by future generations of scholars.

Veblen's analysis of the social-psychological roots of motivations for competitive life styles will be valuable even on a scene where men no longer compete through conspicuous consumption of luxury items but rather through the conspicuous display of what used to be indicators of deprivation. His attempts to trace modes of thought to the influence of social and occupational position will inspire further research even in an age when the sons of engineers come to believe in action rather than in rationality. Students of modernization and development will have recourse to his writing even when they no longer discuss Germany or Japan but Nigeria or Malaysia. Veblen will also continue to be read by many of those who wish to model themselves after this intensely serious moralist who hid his profound scholarship under the cover of playful cynicism and who seemed to divert his readers while subverting their social order.

Charles Horton Cooley

1864-1929

THE WORK

"Self and society," wrote Cooley, "are twin-born."[1] This emphasis on the organic link and the indissoluble connection between self and society is the theme of most of Cooley's writings and remains the crucial contribution he made to modern social psychology and sociology.

THE LOOKING-GLASS SELF

Building upon the work of William James, Cooley opposed the Cartesian tradition that posited a sharp disjunction between the knowing, thinking subject and the external world. The objects of the social world, Cooley taught, are constitutive parts of the subject's mind and the self. Cooley wished to remove the conceptual barrier that Cartesian thought had erected between the individual and his society and to stress, instead, their interpenetration. "A separate individual," he wrote,

> is an abstraction unknown to experience, and so likewise is society when regarded as something apart from individuals. . . . "Society" and "individuals" do not denote separable phenomena, but are simply collective and distributive aspects of the same thing. . . . When we speak of society, or use any other collective term, we fix our minds upon some general view of the people concerned, while when we speak of individuals we disregard the general aspect and think of them as if they were separate.[2]

Cooley argued that a person's self grows out of a person's commerce with others. "The social origin of his life comes by the pathway of intercourse with other persons."[3] The self, to Cooley, is not first individual and then social; it arises dialectically through communication. One's consciousness of himself is a reflection of the ideas about himself that he attributes to other minds; thus, there can be no isolated selves. "There is no sense of 'I' . . . without its correlative sense of you, or he, or they."[4]

[1] Charles Horton Cooley, *Social Organization* (New York, Schocken, 1962), p. 5.
[2] Charles Horton Cooley, *Human Nature and the Social Order* (New York, Schocken, 1964), pp. 36–37. [3] *Ibid.*, p. 5. [4] *Ibid.*, p. 182.

In his attempt to illustrate the reflected character of the self, Cooley compared it to a looking glass:

Each to each a looking-glass
Reflects the other that doth pass.

"As we see our face, figure, and dress in the glass, and are interested in them because they are ours, and pleased or otherwise with them according as they do or do not answer to what we should like them to be, so in imagination we perceive in another's mind some thought of our appearance, manners, aims, deeds, character, friends, and so on, and are variously affected by it."[5]

The notion of the looking-glass self is composed of three principal elements: "The imagination of our appearance to the other person, the imagination of his judgment of that appearance, and some sort of self-feeling, such as pride or mortification."[6] The self arises in a social process of communicative interchange as it is reflected in a person's consciousness. As George H. Mead put it when discussing Cooley's contribution, "By placing both phases of this social process in the same consciousness, by regarding the self as the ideas entertained by others of the self, and the other as the ideas entertained of him by the self, the action of the others upon the self and of the self upon the others becomes simply the interaction of ideas upon each other within mind."[7]

This somewhat abstract notion can be illustrated by a delightful example which Cooley gave himself when he imagined an encounter between Alice, who has a new hat, and Angela, who just bought a new dress. He argues that we then have,

> 1) The real Alice, known only to her maker. 2) Her idea of herself; e.g. "I [Alice] look well in this hat." 3) Her idea of Angela's idea of her; e.g. "Angela thinks I look well in this hat." 4) Her idea of what Angela thinks she thinks of herself; e.g. "Angela thinks I am proud of my looks in this hat." 5) Angela's idea of what Alice thinks of herself; e.g. "Alice thinks she is stunning in that hat." And of course six analogous phases of Angela and her dress.[8]

"Society," Cooley adds, "is an interweaving and interworking of mental selves. I imagine your mind, and especially what your mind thinks about my mind, and what your mind thinks about what my mind thinks about your mind. I dress my mind before yours and expect that you will dress yours before mine. Whoever cannot or will not perform these feats is not properly in the game."[9] Multiple perspectives are brought into congruence through continued multilateral exchanges of impressions and evaluations between our minds and those of others. Society is internalized in the individual psyche; it becomes part of

[5] *Ibid.*, p. 184. [6] *Ibid.*

[7] George Herbert Mead, "Cooley's Contribution to American Social Thought," in *Human Nature,* p. xxx.

[8] Charles Horton Cooley, *Life and the Student* (New York, Alfred A. Knopf, 1927), pp. 200–01.

[9] *Ibid.*

the individual self through the interaction of many individuals, which links and fuses them into an organic whole.

THE ORGANIC VIEW OF SOCIETY

Cooley's sociology is decidedly holistic. When he speaks of society as an organism, he does not want to make an analogy with biology in the manner of Spencer, but means to stress the systemic interrelations between all social processes. "If . . . we say that society is an organism, we mean . . . that it is a complex of forms of processes each of which is living and growing by interaction with the others, the whole being so unified that what takes place in one part affects all the rest. It is a vast tissue of reciprocal activity."[10]

This organic view of society leads Cooley to his principled objection to the utilitarian individualism that is at the basis of classical economics and Spencerian sociology alike.

> So strong is the individualist tradition in America and England that we hardly permit ourselves to aspire toward an ideal society directly, but think that we must approach it by some distributive formula, like "the greatest good of the greatest number." Such formulas are unsatisfying to human nature. . . . The ideal society must be an organic whole, capable of being conceived directly, and requiring to be so conceived if it is to lay hold upon our imaginations.[11]

"Our life," Cooley reiterated over and over again, "is all one human whole, and if we are to have any real knowledge of it we must see it as such. If we cut it up it dies in the process."[12]

THE PRIMARY GROUP

This emphasis on the wholeness of social life led Cooley to focus his analysis on those human groupings that he conceived to be primary in linking man with his society and in integrating individuals into the social fabric. "By primary groups," he writes,

> I mean those characterized by intimate face-to-face association and cooperation. They are primary in several senses but chiefly in that they are fundamental in forming the social nature and ideals of individuals. The result of intimate association, psychologically, is a certain fusion of individualities in a common whole, so that one's very self, for many purposes at least, is the common life and purpose of the group. Perhaps the simplest way of describing this wholeness is by saying that it is a "we."[13]

[10] Charles Horton Cooley, *Social Process* (Carbondale, Southern Illinois University Press, 1966), p. 28. [11] *Ibid.*, p. 417. [12] *Social Organization*, p. xxi. [13] *Ibid.*, p. 23.

Cooley did not argue, as is sometimes assumed, that the unity of the primary group is based on harmony and love alone. He stressed that it is usually a competitive unit, admitting of self-assertion and passionate contentions. But he held that "these passions are socialized by sympathy, and come, or tend to come, under the discipline of a common spirit. The individual will be ambitious, but the chief object of his ambition will be some desired place in the thought of the others."[14]

The most important groups in which the intimate associations characteristic of primary groups have had a chance to develop to the fullest are the family, the play group of children, and the neighborhood. These, Cooley believed, are practically universal breeding grounds for the emergence of human cooperation and fellowship. In these groups men are drawn away from their individualistic propensity to maximize their own advantage and are permanently linked to their fellows by ties of sympathy and affection. In other forms of association (which are now referred to as secondary groups, though Cooley himself never used that term) men may be related to one another because each derives a private benefit from that interchange or interaction. In such groups the other may be valued only extrinsically as a source of benefits for the self; by contrast the bond in the primary group is based upon an intrinsic valuation of the other as a person, and appreciation of others does not result from anticipation of specific benefits that he or she may be able to confer. The primary group is built upon the diffuse solidarity of its members rather than upon an exchange of specific services or benefits. It is, moreover, a nursery for the development of human warmth and sympathy, which is contrasted to the formal coldness, the impersonality, the emotional distance of other types of relations.

A few examples will help clarify the distinction. A member of a family, say, the mother, may gladly engage in personally unrewarding labor within the family context because she measures her work in terms of her contribution to the whole, the We, of the family. What she would consider scandalous exploitation in outside employment, she finds acceptable within the family, for she views it as a service to the collectivity. Husbands and wives, parents and children, relatives and friends will cheerfully sacrifice self-interest if it interferes with their duties to the primary group of which they are a part. They will view each other on the basis of intrinsic characteristics rather than in instrumental terms. If a student were asked why a certain person was his friend and he replied, "Because he helps me pass my math exams," that reply would be judged most inappropriate: the student confused the primary character of a friendship group with the instrumental purposes that govern other types of associations. The primary group, in other words, is the domain where Hobbesian man holds no sway, where devotion to the whole and to the other as a full person takes precedence over the maximization of self-interest.

[14] *Ibid.*, pp. 23–24.

The notions of the looking-glass self and of the primary group are closely intertwined in Cooley's thought. Sensitivity to the thought of others—responsiveness to their attitudes, values, and judgments that is the mark of the mature man according to Cooley—can be cultivated and fostered only in the close and intimate interactions of the primary group. Hence, this group is the cell in which characteristically human growth takes place. In the primary group the immature and self-centered person is slowly attuned to the needs and desires of others and becomes fitted to the give-and-take of mature social life. The primary group fosters the ability to put oneself into the position of others, drawing the individual out of egotistic isolation by building into him that sensitivity to the clues of others without which social life would be impossible. "In these [primary groups] human nature comes into existence. Man does not have it at birth; he cannot acquire it except through fellowship, and it decays in isolation."[15]

Cooley's social philosophy was grounded in the idea that human progress involves the ever-widening expansion of human sympathy so that primary group ideals would spread from the family to the local community, to the nation, and finally to the world community. His was indeed, as Philip Rieff has said, a "small-town doctrine of human nature."[16] Cooley's social thought, George H. Mead wrote, "was in a sense an account of the American community to which he belonged, and pre-supposed its normal healthful process."[17] His benign optimism, his somewhat romantic idealism, are likely to appear antiquated to modern observers who view the world through lenses ground by harsh historical experiences from which the sage from Ann Arbor was spared. Yet even in sections of his work that seem marred by an overindulgence in soft-minded benevolence, there can be found hard nuggets of solid sociological insight.

Consider, for example, Cooley's discussion of the twin evils of formalism and disorganization. The first, he avers, "is mechanism supreme"; the second, "mechanism going to pieces."[18] "The effect of formalism upon personality is to starve its higher life and leave it the prey of apathy [and] self-complacency. . . ."[19] Disorganization, on the other hand, "appears in the individual as a mind without cogent and abiding allegiance to a whole, and without the larger principles of conduct that flow from such allegiances."[20] The modern sociological reader may hardly notice such passages in Cooley's work since he is familiar with Durkheim's more extended and detailed treatment of "anomic" phenomena. But it should be noted that despite his generally optimistic views, Cooley was nevertheless sensitized to those phenomena of incipient crisis that loomed large in Durkheim's social awareness. In regard to prescribing the cure of modern man's ailments, Cooley often wrote in a strikingly Durk-

[15] *Ibid.*, p. 30. [16] Philip Rieff, "Introduction" to *Human Nature*, p. xvii.
[17] Mead, *op. cit.*, p. xxxvi. [18] *Social Organization*, p. 347. [19] *Ibid.*, p. 343.
[20] *Ibid.*, p. 347.

heimian vein. "The idealization of the state, the impressing of a unitary life upon the hearts of the people by tradition, poetry, music, architecture, national celebrations and memorials, and by a religion and philosophy teaching the individual that he is a member of a glorious whole to which he owes devotion, is in line with human nature, however it may be degraded in use by reactionary aims."[21]

Cooley's renown does not come from having parallelled some of Durkheim's insights but rather from his crucial contribution to the problems of internalization. Perhaps Parsons puts the matter a bit too sharply when he writes: "Durkheim was the theorist of society as an object in the external world; Cooley was the theorist of society as part of the individual self."[22] But in a general sense Parsons is still correct in stressing that for Cooley, as distinct from Durkheim, society was uniquely a mental phenomenon. "The imaginations people have of one another," he wrote, "are the solid facts of society." "Society . . . is a relation among personal ideas."[23]

Later critics, notably George H. Mead, were to criticize Cooley's excessively mentalistic view of the constitution of the self, but none would deny that he should receive credit, along with such major figures as William James, Sigmund Freud, Emile Durkheim, and George H. Mead, for having succeeded in destroying the Cartesian disjunction between mind and the external social world. Cooley elaborated in convincing detail the notion that man and society, the self and the other, are linked in an indissoluble unity so that the quality of one's social life, of one's relations with his fellows, is a constitutive element of his personality.

SOCIOLOGICAL METHOD

In addition to these substantive concerns, Cooley, like W. I. Thomas and George H. Mead, made a crucially important contribution to sociological method. Independently of Max Weber, but at roughly the same time as he, they argued that the study of human actions must be concerned with the meanings human actors attribute to the situation in which they find themselves; hence, the study must go beyond purely behavioral description.

The sociology of a chicken yard, Cooley and his co-thinkers insisted, could only be based on descriptions of the chickens' behavior, since we can never understand the meanings that chickens attach to their activities. But the sociology of human beings can pursue a different strategy, since it can probe beneath protocols of behavior into the subjective meanings of acting individuals. The social sciences, Cooley argued, deprive themselves of a most

[21] *Social Process,* p. 418.

[22] Talcott Parsons, "Cooley and the Problem of Internalization," in Albert J. Reiss, Jr., ed., *Cooley and Social Analysis* (Ann Arbor, University of Michigan Press, 1968), p. 66.

[23] *Human Nature,* pp. 119, 121.

precious tool if by a self-denying ordinance they abstain from examining the motivational structure of human action. Even if it be granted that Cooley's approach to the problem of the imputation of motives is too speculative, his thoughts moved on the right track.

Cooley distinguished between "spatial or material knowledge" and "personal or social knowledge." The latter

> is developed from contact with the minds of other men, through communication, which sets going a process of thought and sentiment similar to theirs and enables us to understand them by sharing their states of mind. . . . It might also be described as sympathetic, or, in its more active form, as dramatic, since it is apt to consist of a visualization of behavior accompanied by imagination of corresponding mental processes.[24]

The difference, Cooley argued, between our knowledge of a horse or a dog and our knowledge of man is rooted in our ability to have a sympathetic understanding of a man's motives and springs of action.

> What you know about a man consists, in part, of flashes of vision as to what he would do in particular situations, how he would look, speak, move; it is by such flashes that you judge whether he is brave or a coward, hasty or deliberate, honest or false, kind or cruel. . . . It also consists in inner sentiments which you yourself feel in some degree when you think of him in these situations, ascribing them to him. . . . Although our knowledge of people is . . . behavioristic, it has no penetration, no distinctively human insight, unless it is sympathetic also.[25]

Cooley's own use of the method of sympathetic understanding was somewhat marred, as George H. Mead, among others, has pointed out, by his excessively mentalistic and introspective emphasis, and by his failure to make needed distinctions between the imputation of meaning all men must make in the course of interaction and the disciplined and controlled imputations of the social scientist. He must nevertheless be reckoned among the pioneers in sociological method. Like Max Weber and his co-thinkers in Germany, Cooley emphasized that the study of the human social world must be centered upon attempts to probe the subjective meanings human actors attribute to their actions, and that such meanings must be studied in part through "understanding" rather than through exclusive reliance on the reporting of behavior.

[24] Charles Horton Cooley, *Sociological Theory and Social Research* (New York, Holt, Rinehart and Winston, 1930), p. 290. [25] *Ibid.*, p. 294.

SOCIAL PROCESS

Cooley had relatively little to say about social structures; in his organic view he conceived of social life as a seamless web and was not sensitive to structural variables. In regard to social process, however, he proved to be an acute observer and analyst.

In Cooley's view society consists of a network of communication between component actors and subgroups; therefore, the process of communication, more particularly its embodiment in public opinion, cements social bonds and insures consensus. Cooley saw public opinion as "an organic process," and not merely as a state of agreement about some question of the day.[26] It is not a "mere aggregate of separate individual judgments, but an organization, a cooperative product of communication and reciprocal influence. It may be as different from the sum of what the individuals could have thought out in separation as a ship built by a hundred men is from a hundred boats each built by one man."[27] In other words, public opinion does not emerge from prior agreement but from reciprocal action of individual opinions upon each other—from the clash of ideas in the process of communication. "It is not at all necessary that there should be agreement; the essential thing is a certain ripeness and stability of thought resulting from attention and discussion."[28] "Mature public opinion," as distinct from "popular impression," emerges from debate. It does not "express the working of an average or commonplace mind. [It is not] some kind of mean between the higher and the lower intelligences making up the group."[29] It is created through the interchange between opposed tendencies of thought. "Communicated differences are the life of opinion, as cross-breeding is of a natural stock."[30] To be sure, when there is no "underlying like-mindedness, sufficient for mutual understanding and influence, among members of the group,"[31] they cannot act together. But given a common frame of reference, public opinion is the product of communicated disagreement refined through debate and intellectual confrontation.

What holds for public opinion holds for other types of interactions. In tune with his emphasis on social process, Cooley conceived social conflict as necessary and ineradicable.

> The more one thinks of it the more he will see that conflict and cooperation are not separable things, but phases of one process which always involves something of both. . . . You can resolve the social order into a great number of cooperative wholes of various sorts, each of which contains conflicting ele-

[26] *Social Process*, p. 318. [27] *Social Organization*, p. 121. [28] *Ibid.*, p. 122.
[29] *Ibid.*, p. 123. [30] *Social Process*, p. 379. [31] *Ibid.*

> ments within itself upon which it is imposing some sort of harmony with a view to conflict with others.[32]

Conflicts, in Cooley's view, are healthy and normal occurrences, provided they proceed from a ground of underlying consensus about basic matters. He was a passionate defender of the virtues of democracy precisely because he saw it as a mode of governance that arrives at moral unity not through the suppression of differences but through their acting out on the forum of public opinion.

INSTITUTIONAL ANALYSIS

Cooley held with Veblen that systems of economic values, more particularly pecuniary values, are institutional in character, that "their immediate source is a social mechanism, whatever their indirect relation to human nature may be."[33] The market is to Cooley an institution just like the church or the school. He therefore argued that it is futile to discuss economic values without reference to their institutional matrix and antecedents. More particularly, he urged that in the study of pecuniary values it would be fruitful to pinpoint the ways in which control by dominant classes shapes institutions such as the market. In agreement with Veblen, and in contradistinction to the classical approach in economics, Cooley urged his students to see that the industrial system is not a self-adjusting mechanism, but a complex of institutions shaped by habit, custom and law, and "administered by a class, which will largely control its operation."[34]

Earlier historians of institutional economics[35] tended to put Cooley's name next to Veblen's as a major contributor to that branch of economic theory. His name no longer looms as large in this field—in fact, he is not even mentioned in the article on institutional economics in the *International Encyclopedia of the Social Sciences.* The reason for this is that he did not go beyond Veblen in his institutional analysis and, although he used an institutional terminology and approach, his contributions to the subject matter consisted mainly of generalities. Cooley will probably rate only a footnote in future histories of economics. But the chances are high indeed that no history of sociological thought will fail to take into account the man to whom we owe the twin notions of the *looking-glass self* and the *primary group.*

[32] *Ibid.*, p. 39. [33] *Ibid.*, p. 295. [34] *Ibid.*, p. 302.

[35] Cf. Paul T. Homan, "Institutional Economics," *Encyclopedia of the Social Sciences* (New York, Macmillan, 1935).

THE MAN

Charles Horton Cooley was born on the edge of the Ann Arbor campus of the University of Michigan, where he was to spend almost all his life.[36] The Cooley family had its roots in New England. They were direct descendants of one Benjamin Cooley, who settled near Springfield, Massachusetts before 1640. Cooley's father, Thomas McIntyre Cooley, came to Michigan from western New York. Having been born into a large family of farmers living in straitened circumstances, Thomas Cooley felt that his only chance for acquiring an education and moving up the social scale was to move west. He settled in Michigan and first embarked on a career as an editor and real estate operator and then as a lawyer. An intensely ambitious, imperious, and energetic man, he managed to rise from obscure beginnings into a prestigious and honored position among Michigan's legal and social elite. He achieved recognition for the high caliber of his legal thinking and was appointed a member of a faculty of three at the newly organized University of Michigan Law School in 1859. In the year of Charles' birth, 1864, the father was elected to the Supreme Court of Michigan. He remained a Supreme Court Justice and professor of law for many years and in addition became well known nationally for a number of legal treatises, and as the first chairman of the Interstate Commerce Commission.

Charles, the fourth of the judge's six children, was born at a time when the family had already acquired considerable standing and lived in comfortable circumstances in Ann Arbor. Somewhat overawed by and alienated from his hard-driving and success-oriented father, young Cooley early developed the withdrawn, passive, and retiring character that was to mark his life-style throughout. For fifteen years he suffered from a variety of ailments, some of them apparently psychosomatic. Shy and a semi-invalid suffering from a speech impediment, he had few playmates and tended to daydreaming and solitary reading. Highly sensitive, he compensated for his insecurity by imagining himself in the role of a great orator and leader of men. The success-strivings that the father enacted in real life, the son dared to repeat only in his imagination. His fondness for strenuous rides on horseback and for carving and carpentering may perhaps be explained in terms of a typical Adlerian attempt to compensate for bodily weakness and social ineptness.

[36] This account of Cooley's life is mainly based on Edward C. Jandy's *Charles Horton Cooley: His Life and His Social Theory* (New York, The Dryden Press, 1942) and on Robert C. Angell, "Introduction," in Albert J. Reiss, Jr., ed., *Cooley and Social Analysis*. Other writings on Cooley by Robert C. Angell, especially his paper on Cooley in the *International Encyclopedia of the Social Sciences* (New York, Macmillan, 1968) have also been helpful. Some valuable additional information was supplied by Cooley's daughter, Mary Cooley, who was kind enough to read a draft of this chapter and to write to Professor Angell (May 14, 1969). Professor Angell relayed her letter to me.

Cooley's college life lasted seven years, having been interrupted by illness, a journey through Europe, and brief periods of work as a draftsman and as a statistician. He graduated in engineering, a subject he did not particularly like, though he also took several courses in history and one each in philosophy and economics. During the college years and after, Cooley continued to read omnivorously. These independent readings, rather than formal courses of instruction, finally led him to decide on his life career.

Having read a good deal of Darwin, Spencer, and the German organicist sociologist Albert Schaeffle, Cooley decided to return to the University of Michigan in 1890 for graduate work in political economy and sociology. He wrote a dissertation entitled "The Theory of Transportation," a pioneering study in human ecology, and was granted a Ph.D. in 1894. Since there was no formal instruction in sociology at Michigan, he was examined on questions that had been forwarded from Columbia by Franklin Giddings.

Cooley's unusually long period of apprenticeship and preparation may be accounted for in part by ill health but also by the fact that he was the son of well-to-do parents, who could afford to let their son take his time in deciding upon a career. Moreover, Cooley suffered from the fact that he stood under the shadow of a famous father. He once wrote to his mother: "I should like as an experiment to get off somewhere where Father was never heard of and see whether anybody would care about me for my own sake."[37] It would seem that Cooley was long torn by an emotional dependence on a father from whom he was basically alienated, while being conscious of the fact that he was under an obligation to embark on a career that would do honor to his family.

Cooley's early work, a paper on the "Social Significance of Street Railways," which he read at a meeting of the American Economic Association in 1890, as well as his aforementioned dissertation, both grew from two years of work in Washington, first for the Interstate Commerce Commission and later for the Bureau of the Census. These were written in the tough-minded and "realistic" tradition of which his father presumably approved. His mature work, which is characterized throughout by a tender-minded, introspective approach more congenial to his fundamental nature, began to take shape only after he started to teach at the University of Michigan and had achieved independence from his father.

Throughout his teaching career at Michigan, which began in 1892, Cooley was concerned with many social problems and issues of the day, but clearly preoccupation with the self—his own self—remained paramount to him. Having managed to assert his independence, Cooley was resolved to turn his shyness and his inability to compete with his father's driving ambition into an asset by devoting himself to work that derived in large part from self-examination and the observation of the behavior of those close to him, more particularly his own children.

[37] Jandy, *op. cit.*, p. 21.

Cooley's marriage in 1890 to Elsie Jones, the daughter of a professor of medicine at the University of Michigan, enabled him to concentrate fully on scholarly work and the contemplative life he prized above all. A highly cultivated woman, Mrs. Cooley differed from her husband in that she was outgoing, energetic, and hence capable of ordering their common lives in such a manner that mundane cares were not to weigh very heavily on her husband. The couple had three children, a boy and two girls, and lived quietly and fairly withdrawn in a house quite close to the campus. The children served Cooley as a kind of domestic laboratory for his study of the genesis and growth of the self. Hence, even when he was not engaged in the observation of his own self but wished to observe others, he did not need to leave the domestic circle.

THE SAGE OF ANN ARBOR

Cooley rose fairly rapidly through the academic ranks. He was made an assistant professor in 1899, an associate professor in 1904, and became a full professor three years later. He had none of the flashiness and brashness that appeals to the mass of students. The lectures that this slight, nervous, and somewhat sickly looking professor delivered with a high-pitched voice lacking resonance often would not go over well with the undergraduates. Yet he appealed to a number of graduate students who were inspired by his probing and searching intellect. Many of the graduate students felt that it was a privilege to sit in his seminars and to watch him develop slowly and haltingly a train of thought that came from the very depths of his being. Cooley was inept at administrative detail, chafed at participating in the social and political life of the faculty, and even found himself wanting when it came to directing the work of students or initiating faculty research projects. Yet, as many of his students have testified, those who managed to gain privileged access in his seminars and classes to the workings of his complicated mind were influenced by his approach throughout their lives.

Cooley's life-style was in tune with a pattern of academic mores that no longer exists. The academic setting was still dominated by a semi-aristocratic code of gentlemanly poise. Having no financial worries and living in an age in which the publish-or-perish philosophy had as yet made few inroads, Cooley could afford to devote himself to a life of unhurried contemplation and leisurely study. His books grew slowly and organically from notes he made over long periods of time. *Human Nature and the Social Order* was published in 1902 and its companion, *Social Organization,* followed seven years later. His third major work, *Social Process,* appeared after an interval of nine years, in 1918. These three books, together with extracts from a journal he kept throughout his life, entitled *Life and the Student* (1927), constitute almost the whole of his intellectual output. His early papers in social ecology and a few other contributions written in later years are available in a posthumous volume, *Sociological Theory and Social Research* (1930).

Cooley's life was extremely uneventful. He shunned controversy and contention; any sort of conflict upset him and cost him sleep. He participated in the formation of the American Sociological Society in 1905 and went to most of its subsequent meetings, but the hustle and bustle of these meetings were hardly to his taste. After having become president of the Society in 1918 he began to enjoy the meetings a bit more, perhaps because, having now attained a measure of success, he was able to overcome his previous insecurity when meeting colleagues. The fact that his books sold well, and that he had by then acquired an enviable reputation both among peers and among the younger generation, probably also led to increasing self-confidence. His biographer notes that "the years from 1918 to nearly the close of his life, were perhaps Cooley's happiest."[38]

Throughout his many years at the University of Michigan, Cooley had relatively little contact with his colleagues. He was a good deal older than the next man in the department, Arthur E. Wood, so that he found little companionship there. The Cooleys entertained rarely and went to few parties. They liked simple, informal contacts. Cooley often took long walks with a few choice companions and also went on camping trips with them to Canada for several years. They enjoyed roughing it and cooking picnic suppers for their wives.[39] Most of the summer season Cooley and his wife would spend at Crystal Lake in Northern Michigan, where he built a cabin near the lake for the family, and went swimming, boating or walking with his wife and children. He was a good amateur botanist and bird watcher. During these summers, especially during the last period of his life, Cooley seems to have attained the serenity and contentment that had eluded the young man for so long. "I am glad of life here," he wrote in his journal, "glad of the air, the food, and the lake, glad of the work of my hands, glad of my family, glad that I can probably come here every summer, glad of my books, my thoughts, my hopes."[40]

Cooley received many calls to join more prestigious departments of sociology; Giddings invited him to Columbia, for example. But he never even considered these offers seriously. He felt bound to Ann Arbor and to a university where his father and the father of his wife had taught, and where he had spent almost all of his student career. He did not want the excitement and competitiveness of a large university such as Columbia.

In the last decade of his life, Cooley became something of a University of Michigan institution. Although he never conformed to the outward trappings of the academic role, was a poor committee man, and possibly an even worse

[38] *Ibid.*, p. 71. [39] Personal communication from Robert C. Angell, March 21, 1969.
[40] Jandy, *op. cit.*, p. 73.

department chairman, he had managed to produce a body of work that reflected most favorably on his university.

Cooley summed up his career better than any commentator can when he wrote: "It is conducive to intellectual achievement in our universities to be known as incapacitated for anything else. One may be thankful for a poor voice and hesitating address, a perturbable and withdrawing disposition, a general appearance of scholarly inefficiency. It will retard his promotion, but he has some chance of doing something in the long run."[41] Ensconced in the congenial setting of a university that was willing to give him a large measure of "idiosyncrasy credit" and to overlook his lack of regard for the ordinary wont and use of the academic man, Cooley used such institutional assets wisely. Protected from interference and cushioned against the impact of the wider world, Cooley managed during his long career to turn his initial weaknesses—his shyness and sensitivity, his withdrawing nature, and his self-centeredness—into assets which allowed him to bring forth works that were the slowly ripened fruits of leisured contemplation and introspective observation.

Late in 1928 Cooley's health began to fail, and the following March his trouble was diagnosed as cancer. He died on May 7, 1929.[42]

THE INTELLECTUAL CONTEXT

From the point of view of the historian of ideas, Talcott Parsons is undoubtedly correct when he writes that "Cooley's major theoretical reference point was the work of William James. . . . It was Cooley, along with Mead, who harvested the fruits of James's innovations in philosophy and psychology."[43] But chronologically the influence of James on Cooley came relatively late, and Cooley's overall approach was shaped before he encountered the work of the great Harvard philosopher.

After a very early infatuation with the works of Macaulay, young Cooley turned his attention to Emerson, Goethe, and Darwin. "From Darwin," writes Cooley, "I got . . . the most satisfactory idea of the general process of nature and of the way to study it, while for companionship and guidance in my efforts to understand the world of men, I resorted to writers of little system but great wisdom, to Emerson, chiefly as a young man, then to Goethe."[44] Emerson's romantic celebration of man's freedom and creativity, his anthropocentric philosophy and transcendental idealism exerted a major influence on Cooley throughout his life. Most of his writings stand under the shadow of

[41] *Life and the Student*, p. 181.
[42] The date of his death given in Jandy, *op. cit.*, is incorrect. I owe this information to Mary Cooley. [43] Parsons in Reiss, ed., *op. cit.*, p. 59. [44] *Sociological Theory*, p. 4.

this New England philosopher who had written: "No object really interests us but man . . . and though we are aware of a perfect law of nature, it has fascination for us only through its relation to him, or as it is rooted in the mind."[45] Next to Emerson, it was Goethe who had great impact on Cooley. (Goethe had been, of course, a major influence on Emerson himself.) What Cooley learned from Goethe was a sense of the organic wholeness and unity of life. "I have often thought," Cooley writes, "that, in endowment, Goethe was almost the ideal sociologist, and that [someone who possessed] . . . his comprehension, his disinterestedness and his sense for organic unity and movement might accomplish almost anything."[46] In several of Cooley's books there are more references to Goethe than to any social scientist.

Cooley was converted early to an evolutionary point of view through his thorough reading of Darwin whom he admired for his sense of the complex interrelationships that governed the world of biological nature. Cooley's holistic philosophy, his stress on interactions and interrelations, and his rejection of all types of atomistic interpretation in the study of man were as deeply influenced by his reading of Darwin as they were by German idealism filtered through New England transcendentalist thought.

However, Cooley had far less enthusiasm for "social Darwinist" evolutionary thinkers, more especially Herbert Spencer. He wrote that "It was [Spencer's] general conception of the progressive organization of life . . . that appealed to me, rather than his more specific views on society, with which I was never in sympathy."[47] Cooley was ready to acknowledge that "Nearly all of us who took up sociology between 1870, say, and 1890, did so at the instigation of Spencer."[48] But what repelled him in Spencer was his "defect of sympathy," his "disregard of personality," his "lack of literary and historical culture," and his dogmatic mode of reasoning. Spencer, the dour nonconformist social philosopher, Cooley complained, "lacked direct and authentic perception of the structure and movement of human life. . . . [He] conceived these phenomena almost wholly by analogy. The organic wholes of the social order are mental facts of much the same nature as personality, and much the same kind of sympathetic imagination is needed to grasp them. This Spencer did not have, and accordingly his conceptions . . . are, in my opinion, not properly sociological at all."[49] It is none too surprising that Cooley, who considered Goethe the ideal sociologist, thought that Spencer, because of his obtuseness in failing to understand the human psyche, was not a real sociologist at all.

It stands to reason, furthermore, that Cooley, the social reformer and progressivist, would find Spencer's uncompromising utilitarian individualism most unappealing, and would be much more favorably disposed to another

[45] Quoted in Michael Moran's article on Emerson in *Encyclopedia of Philosophy* (New York, Macmillan, 1967). [46] *Social Process*, p. 402. [47] *Sociological Theory*, p. 5.
[48] *Ibid.*, p. 263. [49] *Ibid.*, pp. 266–69.

organicist sociologist, Albert Schaeffle, the German author of *Bau und Leben des sozialen Koerpers*. Schaeffle, Cooley believed, was much less given to the Spencer type of analogical reasoning and came much closer to the view that the organic bond which linked the members of a society was essentially psychic in nature.[50]

DEBT TO BALDWIN AND JAMES

In Cooley's distinctive views of the nature of the self and his elaboration of the notion of the looking-glass self, one notes his debt to both the social psychologist James Mark Baldwin and the psychologist and philosopher William James.[51] In the 1890's, when Cooley embarked upon the task of providing a genetic explanation of the origin and growth of personal ideas, he made a careful study of Baldwin and James, and also of such child psychologists as G. Stanley Hall. The experiments and studies Baldwin published under the title *Mental Development in the Child and the Race* (1895) in particular left their mark upon the author of *Human Nature and the Social Order*. Summing up his doctrine, Baldwin wrote:

> I do not see . . . how the personality of [the] child can be expressed in any but social terms; nor how, on the other hand, social terms can get any content of value but from the understanding of the developing individual. This is a circle of definition, of course; and that is just my point. On the one hand, we can get no doctrine of society but by getting the psychology of the "socius" with all his natural history; and on the other hand, we can get no true view of the "socius" at any time without describing the social conditions under which he normally lives, with the history of their action and reaction upon him.[52]

Were it not that Baldwin lacked Cooley's stylistic felicity, one could easily take this passage as having come from Cooley's pen.

Although Cooley borrowed much from Baldwin's case studies and from his general social psychological orientation as well, he owed even more to William James from whom he derived the underpinnings of his general view of the nature of mind and of the self. In opposition to the then current atomistic emphasis in German psychology, James argued that consciousness does not consist of a joining together of bits and pieces of ideas but that it flows like a stream and that every conscious state is a function of the entire psycho-physical context.

[50] Jandy, *op. cit.*, p. 86.

[51] For reference to the antecedents of the notion of the looking-glass self in the works of Adam Smith and Leslie Stephen see Robert K. Merton, *Social Theory and Social Structure*, Enlarged Edition (New York, The Free Press, 1968), p. 19.

[52] Quoted by David W. Noble in his essay on Baldwin in *The Paradox of Progressive Thought* (Minneapolis, University of Minnesota Press, 1958), p. 92.

Mind is cumulative and it is continuously altered. To James, the mind is not a rigidly fixed structure, but is forever expanding and changing in tune with new experiences. When Cooley wrote: "It is by intercourse with others that we expand our inner experience,"[53] he followed directly in the footsteps of James.

In regard to the notion of self, Cooley's debt to James is even more pronounced. James's major innovation was to view not only the "external world" but also the self as an object and to introduce the notion of the pluralism of selves.[54] He began with the distinction between the *I,* the self as knower, and the *Me,* the self as known, as the sum total of everything a man can designate as *mine.* Hence, the *material Me* includes one's body, attire, immediate family, and property. The second constituent of the *Me,* the *social Me,* is built from the recognition a man receives from his mates, so that "a man has as many social selves as there are individuals who recognize him and carry an image of him in their mind."[55] A man may be said to have as many social selves as there are distinct groups of people about whose opinions he cares. The third constituent of the *Me,* James argued, is the *spiritual Me,* the entire array of a person's states of consciousness and psychic faculties. By dissolving the unitary Cartesian subject into a multiplicity of selves, all of which come into being through a variety of transactions with the outside world, and by stressing that these plural selves, no less than the external world, may be seen as objects, James laid the foundation for both Cooley's and Mead's social psychology and, it may be remarked in passing, for much later sociological and social psychological role theory.

Cooley readily acknowledged his indebtedness to both Baldwin and James when he wrote, "This idea that social persons are not mutually exclusive but composed largely of common elements is implied in Professor William James's doctrine of the Social Self and set forth at more length in Professor James Mark Baldwin's *Social and Ethical Interpretations of Mental Development.* . . . I have received much instruction and even more helpful provocation from the latter brilliant and original work. To Professor James my obligation is perhaps still greater."[56] Yet despite his indebtedness to James, Cooley was convinced that the Harvard philosopher's interpretation was still insufficiently sociological. He wrote in his journal,

> Although William James has insight into the social nature of the self, he did not develop this into a really organic conception of the relation of the individual to the social whole. His conceptions are intensely individualistic, or, if you please, mystically social, but not organically or intelligibly so. . . . He saw men as separate individuals, not as . . . members of one another. A

[53] *Human Nature,* p. 104. [54] Cf. Parsons in Reiss, ed., *op. cit.,* p. 59.

[55] Quoted in William D. Phelan, Jr.'s article on James in *International Encyclopedia of the Social Sciences.* I follow this account of James's notion of the self throughout this paragraph.

[56] *Human Nature,* p. 125.

> social, or perhaps, *I should say a sociological, pragmatism remains to be worked out.*[57]

As should be apparent by now, Cooley was more deeply influenced by historians, psychologists, philosophers, and literary men than by sociologists. In addition to the thinkers already mentioned, Thoreau, Pascal, Dante, Thomas à Kempis, Walter Bagehot, and, in relation to the American scene, de Tocqueville and Lord Bryce, seem to have impressed him more than social scientists —for example, the British social evolutionists or Auguste Comte. Among sociologists who were his contemporaries, Gabriel Tarde in France and Lester Ward and Franklin Giddings in America were probably the nearest to his cast of mind. Both Ward and Giddings had been kind and helpful to him in the beginning of his career. He appreciated their work, as he did Tarde's, to the extent that they emphasized the social psychological foundations of society. Cooley, who felt that he "could never really *see* the social life of man unless [he] understood the process of mind with which it was indissolubly bound up,"[58] appreciated Ward's emphasis on the psychic factors in civilization, even if he could not follow Ward in his general philosophy. And while much of Giddings' statistical work probably did not appeal to his Michigan colleague, he did appreciate the Columbia sociologist's stress on the consciousness of kind.

One other element, the notion of progress, linked Cooley to a number of his contemporaries, more particularly to Ward, Small, Sumner, and Giddings. In common with all of them he believed that human nature is plastic and modifiable, that man is teachable; thus, one is warranted to look at man's future with optimism. "We are so happily contrived," he wrote, "that humanity can progress without a change in human nature, through the peculiar constitution we already have."[59] Like Ward, Sumner, Small and many others among his contemporaries, Cooley was "convinced that social change naturally occurs slowly, gradually, continuously, by degrees. (But unlike them he did not employ the notion of stages.)"[60] Also like them he was aware of the reality of rivalry, competition, conflict, and struggle, but he believed that these would be resolved through compromise and selection so that a new synthesis, affording a new basis of cooperation, would emerge from the struggle.[61] Both Ward and Cooley invoke a botanical model, the growth characteristic of the grapevine, when they attempt to illustrate the progress of the human race. The roots of this benign optimism will become clearer after the social context of Cooley's thought is examined.

[57] Jandy, *op. cit.*, p. 110. [58] *Sociological Theory*, p. 8. [59] Quoted in Noble, *op. cit.*, p. 116.
[60] Roscoe C. Hinkle, "Introduction" to *Social Process*, p. xvii. [61] *Ibid.*, p. xxxii.

THE SOCIAL CONTEXT

Dean Inge once remarked that a man who marries the spirit of the age soon finds himself a widower. Cooley tried throughout his career not to fall prey to such conceits. He anchored his work in a body of universal humanistic values transcending his time and place, even though, paradoxical as it may seem, much of his writing is almost quintessentially Midwestern and reflects the thought of American Progressivism around the turn of the century. Cooley's ideas endure because he managed to rise above intellectual trends and fashion, yet it would be hard to understand these ideas without knowing their source.

Cooley may be called a Progressive sociologist in the same sense that Turner, Parrington, and Beard have been called Progressive historians.[62] Like them, he had no part in the day-to-day politics of his time, but took many cues from the intellectual and political ferment of the period from 1890 to 1915, which was stimulated by Populist and Progressive reformers. Progressive thought was formulated by a generation of Midwestern scholars in revolt against what they conceived to be the intellectual formalism that dominated most of the Eastern schools. The Progressive intellectuals wanted to be concretely responsive to the demands of the day, to infuse their work with the vigorous democratic and anti-elitist spirit that characterized the culture of the Middle Border. They wanted to take American scholarship out of the hands of tired Brahmins and the satisfied classes and bring it into a closer connection with the strivings and interests of the common man. Repelled by the pessimistic views of America as propounded by such Eastern elite spokesmen as Henry Adams or his brother Brooks, the Progressives were intent on celebrating the vigor, the hopefulness, the optimistic vision of America's democratic future, which, they sensed, was prevailing in the burgeoning and expanding culture of the Midwest. They wrote of the virtues of democracy and felt that what the American body politic needed was not a restriction of the democratic process, as Eastern elitist thinkers proclaimed, but rather its further expansion.

Writing in an Emersonian vein, Cooley attempted to fuse the idealism of the New England transcendentalists with that faith in the democratic virtues of the common man which he saw embodied in the civilization of the frontier. Grafting the old puritan idea of a perfect commonwealth in the New World, a "City Set on a Hill," onto the realities of small-town Midwestern culture as he knew it, Cooley dreamed of an ideal community where individuals, in perfect communication with one another, would all join together in the common task of maximizing communal benefits. His constant emphasis on the organic

[62] Richard Hofstadter, *The Progressive Historians* (New York, Alfred A. Knopf, 1968).

interdependence of all parts of the social whole and his persistent antagonism to the utilitarian individualism of the British have their roots in an abiding faith in the goodness and integrity of the communty, a faith Cooley shared with his Progressive co-thinkers. His celebration of *primary groups* and his advocacy of spreading the virtues bred in such groups to society at large must be traced to a deeply felt conviction, held by many reformers, that men should all love one another even as they love the members of their immediate family.

Capitalist interests, whether represented by railroad magnates, industrial tycoons, or Eastern bankers, were in conflict with Progressive thought to the extent that such interests seemed to undermine the democratic process and to corrode the sense of communal fellowship and participation. Therefore, Cooley, in tune with his fellow thinkers, called for a variety of measures, which were meant to provide minimal conditions for protecting individuals from the predatory consequences of unbridled laissez faire. He advocated procedures for settling disputes between management and workers, accident and old age insurance, vocational guidance and employment centers, and control of working conditions so as to allow men to identify with their work. Once men were freed from the inhumane, oppressive consequences of laissez faire, once the class system was truly open and opportunity guaranteed to all, everyone would be free to develop into a fully aware citizen of the democratic commonwealth. Through welfare, control, and planning measures, Cooley and his fellow Progressives hoped to build on the plains an enlarged and more diversified replica of those New England townships in which self-reliant farmers, while aware of their own individuality, still acknowledged the claims of their fellows and recognized the common weal.

Cooley and Veblen were contemporaries, and both had roots in Midwestern Populism and Progessivism. Yet there were such great differences in their intellectual styles that one might question their common background. Could there be anything in common between the strident and bitter voice of the Minnesota Norwegian inveighing against the wickedness and waste of capitalist civilization and the gentle moderation of the Michigan sociologist evoking the bliss of the democratic community? Nevertheless, although their voices contrasted considerably, they conveyed variations of a common theme rather than fundamentally differing messages. They shared a trust in the virtues of the common man, a fundamentally democratic and anti-aristocratic outlook, even though one wrote with the outraged indignation of the radical social critic and the other never departed from a balanced and gentlemanly mode of expression. These differences can be understood by comparing the social contexts in which these two men worked.

COOLEY'S ACADEMIC SETTING AND AUDIENCE

In contrast to Veblen, the son of marginal Norwegian farmers, who was precariously perched on the margin of academia, Cooley was the scion of a highly respected upper-class family, and so organically a part of the University of Michigan that he never left it for any length of time. This helps explain the fact that, though both expressed the *Zeitgeist* of Populist and Progressive thought, their personal manner of responding to its call differed markedly.

Cooley was fully aware that his conservative background stood him in good stead when he began to offer the "radical" subject of sociology at the University of Michigan. "I do not know," he wrote, "that sociology was at any time objected to as a 'radical' subject, but if so it was perhaps to my advantage, in this regard, that I was known to come of conservative antecedents, my father having been the first Dean of the Michigan Law School."[63] Given such an impeccable background, Cooley had no trouble at Michigan when expounding the "controversial" theory of evolution and "in treating such topics as the capitalist class, socialism, the labor movement, class control of the press and the like."[64] He stated proudly that he "said precisely what seemed to [him] to be true and that [he] was never conscious of the least pressure to do otherwise."[65] In view of the fairly frequent infringement of academic freedom in many American universities in those years, one may conclude that Cooley's background saved him from interferences that others of his cast of mind suffered. He was himself aware of such pressures on radical thinkers when he wrote: "The head of a department (whatever his own views) will seldom choose a man whose opinions, or whose mode of expressing them, are likely to discredit the department with the general administration. This does not bar radicals, if they are men of tact, but their radicalism seldom survives their success."[66]

The fair and understanding treatment Cooley received from the academic authorities at Michigan confirmed his disposition to adopt a moderate and balanced tone of voice, just as the rebuffs that marked Veblen's academic career reinforced, in all probability, his inherent rebelliousness. Cooley, as has been seen, was by no means an exemplary academic man. He shunned administrative tasks, and was content to let the sociology department be a joint department with economics in order to minimize administrative chores. His private views of the academy were almost as negative as those of the author of *The Higher Learning*. He could write, toward the end of his career, that, "It is a peculiarity of American universities . . . that much of their activity resembles that of aggressive business."[67] He noted about university administra-

[63] *Sociological Theory*, p. 10. [64] *Ibid.* [65] *Ibid.* [66] *Life and the Student*, p. 185.
[67] *Ibid.*, p. 180.

tors that "It is usually possible to make a fair administrator out of a scholar, just as you can make over a touring car into a tolerable truck. The main thing is to suppress all irregular and exhausting excursions of the mind and use the energy thus saved for system and poise. You lower the gear and stiffen the frame."[68] Nevertheless, Cooley always seemed to convey the impression that he had no quarrel with academic arrangements and proprieties in principle, but only shunned them because of personal inadequacies. Cooley's daughter recalls how her father reacted when a student one day wore a wing collar to class and then in the student paper accused everyone who remarked upon his appearance of being conformist. Cooley said that this was silly: one should conform in small and unimportant matters and save non-conforming for big, important things.[69] This is a far cry from Veblen's ostentatious flouting of the use and wont of the academy. While administrators might often have indulged in mild gossip about his neglect of some administrative detail, Cooley never called forth that active hostility Veblen invariably provoked. Cooley's personal life, moreover, was impeccably in tune with genteel standards of conduct; he therefore moved almost effortlessly into the forefront of Michigan's respected professors at a time when Veblen was being driven from one position after another.

The University of Michigan provided for Cooley that protective environment without which he might never have been able to become a productive scholar. His withdrawn nature, his almost pathological shyness, his inability to establish those superficial contacts that lubricate social intercourse—all these factors might have made him into a misanthropic misfit had he not been able to take advantage of the institutional setting and the privileges and immunities granted a respected professor. In Cooley's day, academics were still assumed to be both scholars and gentlemen; idiosyncratic gentlemen-professors were likely to meet with the same tolerance the English displayed until recently in regard to the foibles of members of the aristocracy.

Cooley was aware of the benefits he derived from his affiliation with the academy. Some of his observations seem autobiographical: "A teacher is sustained by a noble institution as a singer's voice by an orchestra,"[70] or: "Institutions and genius are in the nature of things antithetical, and if a man of genius is found living contentedly in a university it is peculiarly creditable to both."[71]

The University of Michigan also furnished Cooley with an audience to test his ideas. He had only a few close friends among the faculty, yet he was not a complete loner. Both Cooley and John Dewey were members of a small group called the Samovar Club, which met to drink hot chocolate and discuss Russian literature.[72] It is not known how close he was to George Herbert Mead

[68] *Ibid.*, p. 184. [69] Information supplied by Mary Cooley. [70] *Life and the Student*, p. 187.
[71] *Ibid.*, p. 184. [72] Information supplied by Mary Cooley.

when the latter taught at Michigan, but apparently he was close enough to have shared ideas with him. It is also likely that the few personal friends in the fields of philosophy, psychology, and history who accompanied Cooley on his weekend trips and Sunday walks exchanged ideas with him. While he had little intimate contact with the younger men who joined the Department of Economics and Sociology in later years, and though he was not a man who craved company or yearned for the liveliness of intellectual give-and-take, yet he found upon occasion that he could profit from the knowledge and critical commentary of colleagues.

Veblen, it will be recalled, deliberately rebuffed his students. In contrast, Cooley always had many students, though he was not considered a "brilliant lecturer." In his early years he had fifty to a hundred and twenty-five in his classes; in later years, after the publication of *Human Nature* had made him better known, he had between a hundred and twenty and a hundred and fifty students in attendance, and sometimes there were as many as four hundred and fifty. Moreover, his seminars for graduate students, where he was not required to give sustained lectures but could quietly display his critical intelligence and mature wisdom, were highly regarded. Among his former students, Walton H. Hamilton (who was also a student of Veblen), Read Bain, and Robert C. Angell have testified to the spell Cooley cast over them.[73]

Cooley was well aware of the importance of an audience of students. "A University teacher," he wrote, "has one great advantage over more solitary scholars, as regards the building of a novel structure of thought, in the fact that he may count on an intelligent audience to welcome, confirm or correct his work during the process of production. I always had such an audience, and have no pleasanter recollections than those of discussions with small groups of ardent students."[74] For Cooley, "A lecture, like any public speaking [was] an adventure."[75] In line with his theories he attempted to establish a lively dialogue with each member of his audience. "If I stand at the classroom door and seek the eye of each student as they come in," he noted, "I get a human sense of them that makes it easier to talk to them. A strange crowd facing you is oppressive."[76] Though shy and withdrawn, Cooley was acutely aware of the benefits a scholar may gain from lecturing to an audience of students. "Under the more intense feeling of his public that one has when preparing to lecture," he wrote, "his manner takes on a colloquial distinctness that it might never get in writing. One feels that every idea must be lucid and every word get across."[77]

Much of Cooley's shyness seems to have been rooted in his fear of not receiving the recognition that was his due. When such recognition was gradu-

[73] Walton H. Hamilton, "Charles Horton Cooley," *Social Forces,* VIII (December, 1930); Read Bain, "Cooley a Great Teacher," *Social Forces,* VIII (December, 1930); and the various writings on Cooley by Robert C. Angell cited earlier. [74] *Sociological Theory,* p. 12.

[75] *Life and the Student,* p. 173. [76] *Ibid.,* pp. 172–73. [77] *Ibid.,* p. 174.

ally forthcoming, the shyness receded, though it never left him entirely. It is instructive in this connection to compare Cooley's various entries in his journal on the meetings of the American Sociological Society, which he attended faithfully for a quarter of a century. After he returned from the first meeting of the Society he had helped to found, he noted: "I have no great expectations for the movement; even doubt whether such an organization is not, to me personally, more hindrance than help. Organizations foster mediocrity."[78] A few years later, returning from meetings in Atlantic City, he wrote. "These things do not tire me so much as they used to: I am more sure of myself."[79] After he had served as president of the Society in 1918, he remarked: "The two days of the meeting were busy, but no more strain than previous meetings when I had less responsibility. . . . It seems, from my recent experience, that when I relieve myself from mental strain and accumulate a certain surplus of life I can be as good a man of the world as another, able to converse, address an audience and the like, all with a not unpleasing individuality."[80] As Cooley became aware of the favorable response of others to his work, he grew more self-assured and the receptive audience of his sociological colleagues and peers gradually helped him build and sustain that sense of self-assurance he seemed to have achieved in his later years. Moreover, in addition to his live audience, Cooley was also sustained by the fact that his books had a steady and expanding sale. Following the World War there was a jump of a hundred percent in the sale of *Social Organization* alone. By 1925, the sale of all three of his books had reached a grand total of more than thirty-three thousand copies. *Social Organization* had a consistent sale of twice that of *Human Nature* and four times that of *Social Process*.[81] All this was evidence to the author that he had reached not only his immediate peers but a younger generation as well, and that there was a favorable response to his messages.

Cooley led a withdrawn and retiring life not because he was unconcerned with his audience but because he was overly "audience conscious." The notion of the looking-glass self has a strongly autobiographical flavor. Acutely concerned with the impressions he made upon others, he tended to seek out only those audiences whose response to him was relatively predictable and could therefore be fitted into his self-conception with ease. He valued structured academic audiences while withdrawing from relatively unstructured encounters. He avoided, by and large, association with ordinary men and had only minimal involvements in social life outside the university community. His fear of the unpredictability of encounters with nonacademics led Cooley to derive his knowledge of the social processes that governed society mainly from books and from introspection rather than from active participation.

This may help to account for his strongly mentalistic interpretation of the

[78] Jandy, *op. cit.*, p. 60. [79] *Ibid.*, p. 61. [80] *Ibid.* [81] *Ibid.*, p. 290.

forms of social interaction. He tended to visualize them essentially as interactions in the mind rather than as belonging, to quote Mead, "to an objective phase of experience which we set off against a psychical phase."[82] Having removed himself, as far as he could, from objective experiences in the give-and-take of social life, Cooley came to see the mind as the theater of all interactions. Robert C. Angell puts it well: "He sought to encompass society in his own mind, believed that others did the same, and made this activity a scientific principle."[83] Mead, a more outgoing and socially involved thinker, argued that in the process of communication there emerged a social world of selves standing on the same level of reality as that of the physical world. To Mead, inner experiences arise out of this social world. Cooley, in his relative isolation, by contrast remained fixated on the processes of his own mind, which he hoped to understand through self-analysis and introspection, thus slighting the claims of objective reality and affirming that "imagination as a whole . . . is the *locus* of society in the widest sense."[84]

COOLEY'S HERITAGE

The notion of the social and reflected nature of the self has become, though usually in its Meadian version rather than in Cooley's, a constituent part of current sociological theory. There is hardly a textbook in sociology or social psychology that does not discuss it. Matters are somewhat different with the notion of the *primary group*.

Although there was a fair amount of critical discussion of the idea of the *primary group* in the thirties, in particular by L. L. Bernard and Ellsworth Faris,[85] it was neglected by and large until the late forties when it was suddenly "rediscovered." Already before this time, Kurt Lewin and his students had conducted highly significant experimental studies on the internal structure of small groups, and Elton Mayo and his followers had highlighted the importance of spontaneously formed primary groups in determining the attitudes and behavior of industrial workers.[86] The real rediscovery of the concept of primary groups may be traced to two widely differing empirical investigators, Samuel Stouffer *et al.* in *The American Soldier*[87] and Paul Lazarsfeld *et al.* in their studies of voting behavior and consumer choices, more especially *The*

[82] Mead, *op. cit.*, p. xxxv. [83] Robert C. Angell, *op. cit.* [84] *Human Nature,* p. 134.

[85] L. L. Bernard, "Conflict Between Primary Group Attitudes and Derivative Group Ideals in Modern Society," *American Journal of Sociology,* XLI, 5 (March, 1936), pp. 611–24. Ellsworth Faris, "The Primary Group: Essence and Accident," in his *Nature of Human Nature* (New York, McGraw-Hill, 1937).

[86] On these and later studies cf. Edward A. Shils, "The Study of Primary Groups," in Daniel Lerner and Harold Lasswell, eds., *The Policy Sciences* (Stanford, California, The Stanford University Press, 1951).

[87] Samuel A. Stouffer *et al., The American Soldier* (Princeton, New Jersey, Princeton University Press, 1949), Vols. I and II.

People's Choice, Voting, and *Personal Influence.*[88] What all these studies have in common is the recognition of the great importance of primary group loyalty. They indicate that the effect of variables in the public sphere—for example, religion, class, residence, age, or the impact of mass media—is mediated through the influence of relations in primary groups. Most of these studies were not initially guided by Cooley's theoretical conceptions; rather, they led to the rediscovery of the concept in what Robert K. Merton has called a "serendipity pattern." That is, they stemmed from the "experience of observing an unanticipated, anomalous and strategic datum which [became] the occasion for . . . expanding an existing theory."[89] Ever since, Cooley's contribution has been put to use self-consciously, be it in the construction and extension of theoretical work, as in theories of reference-group behavior,[90] or in empirical studies, especially in experimental work on small groups.[91]

IN SUMMARY

Cooley's modest and unassuming writings, it has now turned out, have had a far greater impact on the future growth of sociology than the ambitious attempts of some of his contemporaries to build overall theoretical systems. Who reads Ward and Giddings now? Cooley contributed major building blocks to theories of the middle range, and these have endured while the huge Byzantine structures of some other fathers of sociology are now but picturesque ruins.

Cooley was the prototype of what today is often derisively called an "armchair sociologist." It is therefore worthwhile to take note that the fruits of his readings and introspective analysis are still indispensable elements of present-day sociological thinking while the labors of many fact-gatherers are long forgotten. Those sociologists who are not temperamentally congenial to large-scale empirical work can take heart: it *is* possible to advance the frontier of the social sciences sitting in one's armchair. If one holds with Cooley that "sociology makes us more at home in the world of men,"[92] then any disciplined method that is conducive to that end is welcome.

88 Paul Lazarsfeld *et al., The People's Choice* (New York, Columbia University Press, 1948), Second Ed.; Bernard Berelson, Paul Lazarsfeld, and William McPhee, *Voting: A Study of Opinion Formation in a Presidential Campaign* (Chicago, The University of Chicago Press, 1954); Elihu Katz and Paul Lazarsfeld, *Personal Influence* (New York, The Free Press, 1955).

89 Merton, *op. cit.,* p. 158.

90 Cf. Herbert Hyman and Eleanor Singer, eds., *Readings in Reference Group Theory and Research* (New York, The Free Press, 1968).

91 Cf. A. Paul Hare *et al., Small Groups: Studies in Social Interaction,* Rev. Ed. (New York, Alfred A. Knopf, 1965).

92 *Life and the Student,* p. 159.

George Herbert Mead

1863-1931

THE WORK

John Dewey said of George Herbert Mead that he had "the most original mind in philosophy in the America of the last generation."[1] Though this may have been a slight exaggeration, there seems to be consensus among students of philosophy that Mead ranks in the forefront of the exponents of pragmatism in America.

Mead, a very modest man, published relatively little. Dewey has remarked that "while [he] was an original thinker, he had no sense of being original."[2] This may account for the fact that during his lifetime he was not recognized as being on the same level of importance as his teacher William James or of his intimate friend John Dewey. But the posthumous publications of many of his lectures and continued critical interest in his work make it abundantly clear that Mead has a central position in philosophical thought, linking as he did the themes first adumbrated by James and Pierce with the philosophical preoccupations of Dewey, Whitehead, Bergson, and Santayana.

This account is mainly based on Mead's posthumous *Mind, Self and Society*[3] and on some of his earlier papers in social psychology, most of which can now be found in his *Selected Writings*.[4] That is, only one facet of Mead's work will be commented upon here: his contribution to social psychology. His wider philosophical concerns—for example, the nature of time in his *The Philosophy of the Present*,[5] his exposition of pragmatism in *The Philosophy of the Act*,[6] and his history of *Movements of Thought in the Nineteenth Century*[7]—will be dealt with only tangentially.

1 John Dewey, "George Herbert Mead," *The Journal of Philosophy*, XXVIII, 12 (June 4, 1931), p. 310.

2 John Dewey, "Prefatory Remarks," in George H. Mead, *The Philosophy of the Present* (La Salle, Illinois, Open Court, 1959), p. xxxvi.

3 George Herbert Mead, *Mind, Self and Society* (Chicago, The University of Chicago Press, 1934).

4 George Herbert Mead, *Selected Writings*, edited by Andrew Reck (Indianapolis, Indiana, Bobbs-Merrill, 1964).

5 Mead, *The Philosophy of the Present*.

6 George Herbert Mead, *The Philosophy of the Act* (Chicago, The University of Chicago Press, 1938).

7 George Herbert Mead, *Movements of Thought in the Nineteenth Century* (Chicago, The University of Chicago Press, 1936).

THE SELF IN SOCIETY

Social psychology for Mead is the discipline that "studies the activity or behavior of the individual as it lies within the social process. The behavior of an individual can be understood only in terms of the behavior of the whole social group of which he is a member, since his individual acts are involved in larger, social acts which go beyond himself and which implicate the other members of that group."[8] While earlier social psychology had dealt with social experience from the individual psychological standpoint, Mead suggested that individual experience be dealt with "from the standpoint of society, at least from the standpoint of communication as essential to the social order."[9] His social psychology presupposed "an approach to experience from the standpoint of the individual," and was therefore at variance with Watsonian behaviorism, but it undertook "to determine in particular that which belongs to this experience because the individual himself belongs to a social structure, a social order."[10]

Mead argued that there can be no self apart from society, no consciousness of self and no communication. In its turn, society must be understood as a structure that emerges through an ongoing process of communicative social acts, through transactions between persons who are mutually oriented toward each other.[11]

Mead saw in gesture the key mechanism through which social acts are effected. But he sharply separates nonsignificant (unself-conscious) gestures, as found on the animal level, from the *significant* (self-conscious) gestures that characterize most human intercourse. On the animal level, gesture involves an immediate response to a stimulus. The growling advance of dog A is a stimulus to dog B to react by attack or withdrawal, as the case may be. In contrast, at the human level of communication, *significant* gestures come into play. These rest upon "an arousal in the individual himself of the response which he is calling out in the other individual, a taking of the role of the other, a tendency to act as the other person acts."[12] Significant gestures are based on linguistic symbols carrying a content that is more or less the same for different individuals and hence meaning the same thing to them all. Animals do not put themselves in the position of others, predicting, in effect, "He will act in such a way and I will act in this way." They can not be said to

[8] *Mind, Self and Society*, pp. 6–7. [9] *Ibid.*, p. 1. [10] *Ibid.*

[11] The following account owes much to several analyses and expositions of Mead's social thought, more particularly, Tomatsu Shibutani, "George Herbert Mead," in *International Encyclopedia of the Social Sciences* (New York, Macmillan, 1968); Herbert Blumer, "Sociological Implications of the Thought of George Herbert Mead," *American Journal of Sociology*, LXXI, 5 (March, 1966), pp. 535–44; Maurice Natanson, *The Social Dynamics of George H. Mead* (Washington, D.C., Public Affairs Press, 1956); Reck's "Introduction" to *Selected Writings*. I have freely borrowed from all of them. [12] *Mind, Self and Society*, p. 73.

"think." Human thought arises when there are "symbols, vocal gestures generally, which arouse in the individual himself the response which he is calling out in the other, and such that from the point of view of that response he is able to direct his later conduct."[13] Significant gestures involving the use of symbols always presuppose the ability of each participant in a communicative process to visualize his own performance from the standpoint of the others, to take the role of the others. In nonsymbolic interaction human beings, like animals, respond directly to one another. In symbolic interaction, where they use significant gestures, they interpret each other's attitudes and act on the basis of the meaning yielded by such interpretations. As Blumer puts it, "Symbolic interaction involves *interpretation,* or ascertaining the meaning of the actions or remarks of the other person, and *definition,* or conveying indications to another person as to how he is to act."[14] Human communicative processes involve the constant self-conscious adjustment of actors to the conduct of others, a repeated fitting together of lines of action through definitions and redefinitions, interpretations and reinterpretations.

Following William James, Mead argues that consciousness must be understood as a thought-stream arising in the dynamic relationship between a person and his environment, more particularly his social environment. " 'Mental phenomena,' " he reasoned, cannot be reduced "to conditioned reflexes and similar physiological mechanisms,"[15] as the behaviorists would have it, but neither can they be understood in terms of the insulated conception of the Cartesian ego. Experience is not first individual and then social. Each individual is continually involved in a succession of joint enterprises with others, which form and shape his mind. Consciousness is not a given; it is emergent.

THE GENESIS OF THE SELF

Among Mead's most notable achievements is his account of the genesis of consciousness and of the self through the gradually developing ability in childhood to take the role of the other and to visualize his own performance from the point of view of others. In this view, human communication becomes possible only when "the symbol [arouses] in one's self what it arouses in the other individual."[16] Very young children do not yet have the ability to use significant symbols; therefore, when they are at play, their behavior in many ways is similar to that of puppies playing with each other. As children grow older, however, they gradually learn to take the role of others through play. "A child plays at being a mother, at being a teacher, at being a policeman; that is, it is taking different roles."[17] The growing child who playfully assumes these roles thereby cultivates in himself the ability to put himself in the place

[13] *Ibid.* [14] Blumer, *op. cit.,* p. 537. [15] *Mind, Self and Society,* p. 10. [16] *Ibid.,* p. 149.
[17] *Ibid.,* p. 150.

of others who are significant to him. As he matures, he will not only be able to take these roles by acting them out; but he will *conceive* of them by assuming them in his imagination. A crucial landmark in the child's social development is made when, in showing a picture to someone facing him, he will turn the picture away from himself rather than, as he did up to then, hold it toward himself in the belief that his partner can see only what he himself sees.

Child play at the level of simple role-taking is the first stage in the gradual transformation from simple conversations of gestures—a child's running away when chased—to the mature ability to use significant symbols in interaction with many others. Although he has learned to put himself, in imagination, in the position of his partner, the child still does not relate in his mind the roles that several others play with one another outside himself. Thus, he can understand the relation of mother or father with himself, but he cannot understand that his own mother is not his father's mother also. This breakthrough in his conceptualization comes with his ability to play complex organized games, when he will have in his mind all the roles of other players and make assessments about their potential responses to one another. Such games must be distinguished from simple games such as hide-and-seek, which involve only two types of role partners, or playing jacks, in which the actors do not modify each other's play and hence do not have to anticipate the response of the other partner. In hide-and-seek, "everyone, with the exception of the one who is hiding, is a person who is hunting. A child does not require more than the person who is hunted and the one who is hunting."[18] But in a game in which a number of individuals playing different roles are involved, in baseball for example, "the child taking one role must be ready to take the role of everyone else."[19] This differs not only from the two-role game, but also from what Mead calls "play," from those so-called games that do not involve mutual role-taking, such as jacks.

> The fundamental difference between the [complex] game and the play is that in the former the child must have the attitude of all the others involved in that game. The attitudes of the other players which the participant assumes organize into a sort of unit, and it is that organization which controls the response of the individual. . . . Each one of his own acts is determined by his assumption of the acts of the others who are playing the game. What he does is controlled by his being everyone else on that team, at least in so far as those attitudes affect his own particular response. We get then an "other" which is an organization of the attitudes of those involved in the same process.[20]

The difference between play and games resides in the number of participants and in the existence or absence of rules. Play undertaken by one child

[18] *Ibid.*, p. 151. [19] *Ibid.* [20] *Ibid.*, pp. 153–54.

has no rules. Games have rules but differ as to the number of players. Two person games require only simple role-taking; multiple person games require taking the role of the "generalized other," that is, each player's having an idea of the behavior of every other player toward each other and toward himself. With the help of the rules that govern the game, the child develops the ability to take the place of all the other players and to determine their responses. These "rules are the set of responses which a particular attitude calls out."[21] The final stage in the maturation process of the child, Mead argues, occurs when the individual takes the role of the "generalized other"—the attitude of the whole community.

The fully mature individual, according to Mead, does not merely take into account the attitudes of other individuals, of "significant others," toward himself and toward one another; he must also "take their attitudes toward the various phases or aspects of the common social activity . . . in which, as members of an organized society or social group, they are all engaged.[22] As Natanson puts it, "[rules of the game] . . . mark the transition from simple role-taking to participation in roles of a special, standarized order. Through rules the child is introduced to societal compulsion and the abrasive texture of a more nearly adult reality."[23] "Only insofar as he takes the attitudes of the organized social group to which he belongs towards the organized, cooperative social activity or set of such activities in which that group as such is engaged, does he develop a complete self."[24] Hence, the mature self arises when a "generalized other" is internalized so that "the community exercises control over the conduct of its individual members."[25]

Thus, in the Meadian view of the emergence of role-taking capacities, the self that arises gradually through a progressive widening of the scope of human involvement must never be conceived as a mere body. It is rather a social entity emerging in a social process of development from simple conversations of gestures to the process of identification with the "generalized other." "The conscious self," Dewey comments on Mead's conception, "was to him the world of nature first taken up into social relations and then dissolved to form a new self which then went forth to recreate the world of nature and social institutions."[26]

The essence of the self, according to Mead, is its reflexivity. The individual self is individual only because of its relation to others. Through the individual's ability to take in his imagination the attitudes of others, his self becomes an object of his own reflection. The self as both subject and object is the essence of being social. The peculiar individuality of each self is a result of the peculiar combination, never the same for two people, of the attitude of others that form

[21] *Ibid.*, p. 152. [22] *Mind, Self and Society*, p. 155. [23] Natanson, *op. cit.*, p. 13. [24] *Ibid.*
[25] *Ibid.* [26] Dewey, "George Herbert Mead," p. 313.

the generalized other. Hence, although individuality is rooted in sociality, each person makes an individual contribution to the social process.

THE "I" AND THE "ME"

Mead tried to clarify his views of the social foundation of the self and his concomitant belief that "the self does not consist simply in the bare organization of social attitudes," by introducing the distinction between the "I" and the "me." Both "I" and "me" necessarily relate to social experience. But the "I" is "the response of the organism to the attitudes of the others; the 'me' is the organized set of attitudes of others which one assumes. The attitudes of the others constitute the organized 'me,' and then one reacts toward that as an 'I'."[27] As a "me" the person is aware of himself as an object. He reacts or responds to himself in terms of the attitudes others have toward him. His self-appraisal is the result of what he assumes to be the appraisal by others. The "me" is the self as conceived and apprehended in terms of the point of view of significant others and of the community at large. It reflects the laws and the mores, the organized codes and expectations of the community.[28] The "I," in contradistinction, is "the answer which the individual makes to the attitude which others take toward him when he assumes an attitude toward them . . . it gives the sense of freedom, of initiative."[29] What appears in consciousness is always the self as an object, as a "me," but the "me" is not conceivable without an "I" as a unique subject for which the "me" can be an object. The "I" and the "me" are not identical, for the "I" "is something that is never entirely calculable . . . it is always something different from what the situation itself calls for."[30]

"We are," Mead writes, "individuals born into a certain nationality, located at a certain spot geographically, with such and such family relations, and such and such political relations. All of these represent a certain situation which constitutes the 'me'; but this necessarily involves a continued action of the organism toward the 'me.' "[31] Men are born into social structures they did not create, they live in an institutional and social order they never made, and they are constrained by the limitations of languages, codes, customs, and laws. All of these enter into the "me" as constituent elements, yet the "I" always reacts to preformed situations in a unique manner, "just as every monad in the Leibnizian universe mirrors that universe from a different point of view, and thus mirrors a different aspect or perspective of that universe."[32] To Mead, mind is "the individual importation of the social process,"[33] but, at the same time, "the individual . . . is continually reacting back against . . . society."[34]

[27] *Mind, Self and Society*, p. 175. [28] *Ibid.*, p. 197. [29] *Ibid.*, p. 177. [30] *Ibid.*, p. 178.
[31] *Ibid.*, p. 182. [32] *Ibid.*, p. 201, and Natanson, *op. cit.*, p. 17.
[33] *Mind, Self and Society*, p. 186. [34] *Ibid.*, p. 202.

The self as a whole, as it appears in social experience, is a compound of the stabilized reflections of the generalized other in the "me" and the incalculable spontaneity of the "I." This is why the self as a whole is an open self. "If it did not have these two phases there could not be conscious responsibility, and there would be nothing novel in experience."[35] Mead valued personal autonomy, but he saw it emerging from feedback rather than from attempts at insulation from others. Human actors are inevitably enmeshed in a social world, but the mature self transforms this world even as it responds to it.

Mead was somewhat ambiguous in his definition of social acts. Sometimes he makes it appear as if these acts necessarily involve cooperation between the actors. Elsewhere he talks about social acts when referring to competitive and conflictful interaction.[36] At one point he says specifically: "I wish . . . to restrict the social act to the class of acts which involve the cooperation of more than one individual."[37] But in other places he speaks, for example, of fights among animals as social acts. It would seem, on balance, that what he had in mind was not that social acts are restricted to cooperation but only that social action is always based on "an object of common interest to all the individuals involved."[38] In this formulation, conflict and competition, as well as cooperative behavior, may equally be seen as social action as long as they all involve a mutual orientation of actors to one another. It is only in this way that Mead's interpretation of the nature of social acts can be articulated with his often repeated insistence on the crucial functions of social conflicts. To Mead, just as to Simmel, conflict and cooperation are correlative to each other and no society can exist without both.

> A highly developed and organized human society is one in which the individual members are interrelated in a multiplicity of different intricate and complicated ways whereby they all share a number of common interests . . . and yet, on the other hand, are more or less in conflict relative to numerous other interests which they possess only individually, or else share with one another only in small and limited groups.[39]

MEAD AS A PATHSETTER

Mead's work abounds in suggestive leads for the sociology of knowledge. He prepared the ground for consideration of the concrete sociological links between social and thought processes, to the extent that he stressed, along with his pragmatist co-thinkers, the organic process by which every act of thought is linked to human conduct and to interactive relationships, thus rejecting the radical distinction between thinking and acting that had informed

[35] *Ibid.*, p. 178.
[36] Cf. Charles Morris, *Signs, Language and Behavior* (New York, Prentice-Hall, 1946), pp. 42–45.
[37] *Mind, Self and Society*, p. 7. [38] *Ibid.*, p. 46. [39] *Ibid.*, p. 307.

most classical philosophy. When Mead advanced the idea that consciousness is an inner discourse carried on by public means—that is, a private experience made possible by the use of significant social symbols and hence organized from the standpoint of the "generalized other"—he paved the way for detailed investigations linking styles of thought to social structures. Mead provided valuable indications for future inquiries linking individual modes of discourse to the "universe of discourse" of total epochs or of special strata or groupings within a particular society. Insofar as he stressed that thought is in its very nature bound to the social situation in which it arises, he set the stage for efforts to ascertain the relations between a thinker and his audience.

As in the sociology of knowledge, Mead also provided rich leads for future disciplined inquiry in other spheres of sociological inquiry though only through hypotheses and illustrations. His notion of role-taking, that is, of taking the attitudes of others toward oneself, is not to be confused with what modern sociologists call role performance, or living up to the expectations entailed by a specific position. However, it is hardly a subject of dispute that modern role theory from Linton and Parsons to Newcomb and Merton has been enriched by freely borrowing from Mead. Although reference-group theory has gone beyond Mead in considering not only those groups to which a person belongs but also groups to which he aspires or which he takes as a point of reference while not aspiring to be a member, it owes a good deal to

Mead's insistence that individuals always be considered under the angle of their relations to groups of significant others.[40]

More generally, Mead's work has led to the final demise, at least within sociology, of what Simmel once called the "fallacy of separateness," which considers actors without reference to the interactions in which they are variously engaged. For Mead, no monads without windows ever exist in the social world; there is never an I without a Thou, to use Martin Buber's terminology. An ego is inconceivable without an alter, and the self is best visualized as a vivid nodal point in a field of social interaction. This perspective on human action has by now become an essential characteristic of all thinking that wishes to be called sociological. Although Mead was by no means alone in having prepared it, he surely was one of its major sources.

Little need be said in regard to Mead's contributions to the methodology of the social sciences since the essential points have already been made in the previous chapter on Cooley. Mead must be credited alongside Cooley and other pragmatists with having been instrumental in stressing the need for always considering situations from the point of view of the actor. For him, just as for Weber, when the sociologist refers to meaning, it is to the subjective meaning actors impute to their actions.

While Cooley's theories veered perilously close to a subjectivist and solipsis-

[40] Cf. Robert K. Merton, *Social Theory and Social Structure,* Enlarged Ed. (New York, The Free Press, 1968), pp. 292–93.

tic view of society, Mead remained steadfast in his social objectivism. The world of organized social relationships was to him as solidly given in inter-subjective evidence as the physical world. He did not attempt to reconstruct the world through introspection in the manner of Cooley. He took as fundamental datum that an "objective life of society" exists, which it behooves the scientist to study. To Mead society is not a mental phenomenon but belongs to an "objective phase of experience."[41] The extent to which the differences between these two otherwise closely related thinkers can be accounted for by their differing life situations and existential conditions will become clear later in this chapter.

THE MAN

George Herbert Mead was born at South Hadley, Massachusetts, on February 27, 1863. His father, Hiram Mead, was a minister who descended from a long line of New England Puritan farmers and clergymen. His mother, Elizabeth Storrs Billings, like her husband, came from a family background in which intellectual achievement had been highly valued.[42]

When Mead was seven, his father was called to Oberlin College to take the chair of homiletics (the art of preaching) at the newly founded theological seminary. Mead grew up at Oberlin and went to college there. Although he was to revolt against its pious atmosphere, he was decisively influenced by the mixture of New England Puritan ethics and Midwestern progressive ideas that dominated the college.

Oberlin was founded in 1833 by a militant Congregationalist reformer, the Reverend John Jay Shipherd. Its first president, Asa Mahan, preached a somewhat attenuated form of the perfectionist doctrine that later came to full flowering in the communal and sexual experiments of John Humphrey Noyes' *Oneida* utopian community. Oberlin was one of the first American colleges to admit Negroes and, in 1841, it became the first coeducational college to grant a bachelor's degree to women. In the years preceding the Civil War, Oberlin was one of the chief stations on the Underground Railroad that helped thousands of Southern Negro slaves escape to the North and to Canada. Another

[41] George Herbert Mead in Cooley, *Human Nature and the Social Order* (New York, Schocken, 1962), pp. xxxiv–xxxv.

[42] Since biographical material on Mead is extremely meager, I have had to rely on a few sources, none of which provides the detailed information that is available, for example, in the case of Veblen and Cooley. Most helpful were the following: H.C.A.M. (Henry Mead) "Biographical Notes" in *The Philosophy of the Act;* David Wallace, "Reflections on the Education of George Herbert Mead," *American Journal of Sociology,* LXXII, 4 (January, 1967), pp. 396–408; Andrew J. Reck, "Introduction" to *Selected Writings;* Anselm Strauss, "Introduction" to *George Herbert Mead on Social Psychology* (Chicago, The University of Chicago Press, 1964). Most helpful of all was a long interview with Herbert Blumer, Mead's foremost living disciple and interpreter, in which he generously shared with me his great knowledge of Mead as a person and thinker.

major social cause, that of temperance, also owes much to Oberlin. The Anti-Saloon League originated there.

While Oberlin displayed most prominently its Christian social conscience, in its curriculum it resembled the narrowness that characterized the New England sponsored Protestant colleges that had grown up in the Middle West throughout the nineteenth century. Mead's son recalls that his father's education at Oberlin consisted mainly of "the classics, rhetoric and literature, moral philosophy, mathematics, and a smattering of elementary science. . . . Questioning was discouraged, ultimate values being determined by men learned in the dogmas and passed on to the moral philosophers for dissemination." In this respect Oberlin was similar to Carleton College where, it will be recalled, Thorstein Veblen formed his abrasive personality by pitting himself against the narrow theological dogmatism of his teachers. Mead had a like reaction to Oberlin, his robust intellect revolting against the excessive theological fare. The son of many generations of Puritan theologians lost his faith in the dogmas of the church. Nevertheless, he continued to be marked throughout his life by the Christian ethics of brotherhood and the social conscience that he had absorbed at his father's house and at Oberlin.

In 1881 Mead's father died and the family, left with very little, sold their house and moved into rented rooms. The young Mead waited on college tables to earn his board, and his mother taught at the college to make ends meet. (She later became President of Mount Holyoke College.) In 1883 Mead graduated from Oberlin, and for the next half-year taught school amid circumstances that have a curiously contemporary ring. Several teachers had resigned from the school because they were unable to cope with a group of rowdies who terrorized teachers and classmates. Mead discharged the rowdies, but was fired by the board of trustees who believed that every child had a God-given right to be taught.

Having given up an earlier dream of starting a literary paper in New York, Mead lived for the next three years in the Northwest, alternating between tutoring and doing survey work for railroad construction. He was on the team that laid out the first line from Minneapolis to Moose-Jaw, there to connect with the Canadian Pacific. In the winter months, when surveying was impossible, Mead supported himself by tutoring and read omnivorously. During this period he seems to have been somewhat unsettled, not knowing where next to go or what career to take up. These doubts were resolved in the fall of 1887 when he decided to follow his close college friend Henry Castle to Harvard and to pursue further study in philosophy.

At Harvard, Mead worked mainly with Royce and James, and both these teachers left a permanent mark on his life and outlook. Having been liberated from his father's Puritanism and Oberlin's Christian pieties by reading Darwin and other "advanced thinkers," Mead was converted to pragmatic philosophy by James. His contact with James seems to have been fairly intimate since he not only did much of his work with James but also tutored his children.

After the year at Harvard, Mead decided, as was very common in his generation, to go to Germany for advanced studies in philosophy. He first went to Leipzig to study with Wilhelm Wundt, whose conception of the "gesture" profoundly influenced Mead's later work. It was also at Leipzig that he met G. Stanley Hall, the eminent American physiological psychologist, who seems to have stimulated Mead's interest in the subject. Later in 1889, Mead went to Berlin for further studies in both psychology and philosophy. (I have been unable to find a record of whose classes Mead attended at Berlin, but it is possible he may have listened to an already famous lecturer, Georg Simmel, who had begun to teach there a few years earlier.)

On October 1, 1891, Mead married Helen Castle, the sister of his friend Henry Castle, and the young couple left for Ann Arbor where Mead had been appointed instructor in the University of Michigan Department of Philosophy and Psychology. Charles H. Cooley, John Dewey, and James H. Tufts were all then teaching at the university and they all soon became intellectual companions. Mead pursued the investigations in physiological psychology first suggested by Stanley Hall and began to elaborate a physiological theory of emotions that paralleled the teleological theory John Dewey was working on at the time.

The Meads' only son, Henry, was born in Ann Arbor in 1892. A year later Mead accepted John Dewey's invitation to join him at the new University of Chicago where the latter had become head professor in the Department of Philosophy. Mead stayed at the university until his death on April 26, 1931.

MEAD AT CHICAGO

Chicago, which had been only a small log fort in 1833, had become a major city only sixty years later.[43] Crude, raw, full of vigor and energy, it boasted of spectacular advances in industry and commerce within one generation. It was a major meat-packing center, the "Hog Butcher for the World." South Chicago and neighboring Gary, Indiana, became important steel mill centers where the Lake Superior iron ore shipped down to Lake Michigan joined coal from Illinois fields brought in by rail. Among the major users of that steel was the Chicago-based Pullman Company, which built the sleeping cars for the American railroads and was the location of one of America's most famous labor battles.

[43] Cf. Robert E. L. Faris, *Chicago Sociology 1920–1932* (San Francisco, Chandler, 1967), esp. p. 20 ff. for information on Chicago as the setting of the new university and for details about that university. See also Lincoln Steffens, *The Shame of the Cities* (New York, McClure, 1904), esp. p. 163.

Conscious of its phenomenal rise to eminence among American cities, Chicago boasted of its accomplishments. The first steel-framed skyscraper had been built there, the flow of the Chicago River had been reversed, land values had risen with fabulous rapidity, and even the crime rate, partly the result of rapid migration and the attendant disorganization of many slum districts, was spectacular. Soon the city would claim the world championship in organized crime.

The new university, endowed by John D. Rockefeller, opened its pseudo-Gothic doors in 1892 under the presidency of William Rainey Harper. From the beginning it was meant to be another Chicago spectacular. Rainey ruthlessly raided the campuses of Eastern universities and promised those he wanted to attract not only a salary roughly double what they had been earning, but also the prospect of working in a university that would soon be the greatest in the world. He was eminently successful. Within a very few years the University of Chicago ranked among the first in the country. The original faculty boasted no fewer than eight professors who had given up college presidencies to join its ranks. Although ten among the original thirty-one full professors taught theology, thus still continuing the traditional emphasis of American universities upon training men of the cloth, the university soon became a major center of secular learning.

One of President Harper's proudest coups was young John Dewey. Soon after Dewey assumed his duties as head professor, he enticed his friends Tufts and Mead to join him, thus creating a department in which the new pragmatic philosophy could flourish, unhampered by the resistance of traditional philosophers who impeded the growth of the discipline in older universities. "A *real school,* and *real Thought,* Important thought too"—this was the reaction of William James to the group of philosophers gathered around Dewey at Chicago in the early 1900's.[44]

In accord with the reforming activism of its founder, the Philosophy Department did not limit itself solely to academic work but wanted to have a part in solving the manifold social problems of the city. Educational experimentation, settlement houses, industrial education, and general social reform were all very much on the minds of Dewey and his associates. They wished to learn by doing good, and they took their pragmatic philosophy seriously.

Progressive education was Dewey's foremost preoccupation, and Mead, though himself not as active as his friend, joined him in many of his educational ventures. He was not much inclined toward writing, but nevertheless managed to write eight articles on educational matters between the time he joined the faculty and the First World War. He was active from its inception in the experimental school Dewey had founded. He was president of the School of Education's Parents' Association, and also for a time was an editor

[44] Quoted in Richard Hofstadter, *Social Darwinism in American Thought* (Boston, Beacon Press, 1955), p. 135.

of one of the university's major educational journals, *The Elementary School Teacher.* He spoke out as an observer, critic, and advocate of new educational policies, and served as a member, and sometimes as chairman, of a variety of committees dealing with educational affairs.

Mead's concerns for reform were not limited to education. He was associated with Jane Addams' Hull House and its pioneering work in the settlement house movement, as well as being actively involved for many years in the City Club of Chicago, an association of reform-minded businessmen and professionals. For a while he served as president of this club.[45]

All this outside activity did not distract Mead from his teaching duties. A man of exceptional strength, he conveyed, in Dewey's opinion, "a sense of energy, of vigor, of a vigor unified, outgoing and outgiving."[46] And so he gave to his lecture audience the same energetic devotion he displayed in his reform activities. He prepared his lectures with care, and they were always well attended. His delivery was clear and orderly. Although he had great difficulty in writing down his thoughts, he had no similar impediments when it came to oral delivery.

In particular, Mead's course in social psychology attracted many students from other departments, especially from sociology and psychology. Herbert Blumer has said that he always considered it rather curious that the response to Mead's lectures was invariably bimodal. Some students, among them Blumer himself, were deeply impressed by Mead and felt that he changed their whole outlook. Others, by no means less intelligent than the first group, never understood what the course was all about.[47] There were enough men in the first group to spread Mead's renown and to assure him a steady supply of major students, among them, T. V. Smith and Charles Morris in philosophy, and Ellsworth Faris and Herbert Blumer in sociology.

Something of a myth seems to have spread recently, namely, that the members of the Department of Sociology formed a unified Chicago school of social psychology around the person of Mead. This was not the case. For example, although both W. I. Thomas and Robert Park held Mead in high regard, the former pretended not to understand him and the latter claimed not to have read much of his work.[48] While it is easy to conclude retrospectively that Mead should have had a special appeal for sociologists, in fact, the only major link between Mead and the Sociology Department was Ellsworth Faris, Mead's former student now teaching in that department. Mead's ideas, as well as Dewey's, were surely prevalent in sociology at Chicago, and it may even be true that W. I. Thomas gave up his earlier emphasis on instinct in favor of a more social-psychological orientation under the influence of the pragmatic

45 On the connection between the Chicago Philosophy Department under Dewey and progressive education as well as Hull House, see C. Wright Mills, *Sociology and Pragmatism* (New York, Paine-Whitman, 1964), pp. 298–313.

46 Dewey, "George Herbert Mead," p. 309.

47 Blumer, conversation, April 9, 1969.

48 Blumer, conversation; Strauss, *op. cit.*, p. xi.

philosophers. But this is a far cry from the myth of a unified Chicago school of social psychology created by Mead. Park and Burgess included none of Mead's writings in their famous textbook. Mead never saw himself as head of a "school." And it might be noted that the term "social interactionism" was never known at Chicago while Mead lived.

In his early period at Chicago, Mead was overshadowed by the more dynamic and outgoing Dewey. Even after Dewey had left for Columbia because he felt that his educational experiments were not given enough support at Chicago, Mead did not assume the eminent position his friend had occupied in university affairs. One reason for this was the sparsity of his publications.

Mead experienced great difficulty in putting his ideas down in writing. He would spend agonizing hours at his table, sometimes verging on tears when he despaired of giving adequate expression to the rapid flow of his thought. "In consequence," writes Dewey, "he was always dissatisfied with what he had done; always outgrowing his former expressions, and in consequence so reluctant to fix his ideas in the printed word that for many years it was [only] his students and his immediate colleagues who were aware of the tremendous reach and force of his philosophical mind."[49]

Mead's preferred medium was the spoken, not the written, word. He was clearly autobiographical when he wrote: "We do our thinking in the form of conversation, and depend upon the imagery of words for our meanings."[50] "Conversation was his best medium," wrote his student T. V. Smith, "writing was a poor second best. When he wrote 'something'—as he says in one place of another matter—'something was going on—the rising anger of a titan or the adjustment of the earth's internal pressures.' But true of him as of his illustration, what the reader gets is certainly 'not the original experience.' "[51] That experience he was able to convey and articulate only in the flow of verbal exchanges and significant gestures.

Quite apart from the objective fact of his scanty record of publications, Mead himself did not subjectively feel any urge to reach for a public role similar to that of Dewey. A most modest, balanced, and harmonious man, he was not much attracted by the prospect of major recognition and always saw himself as only a relatively minor worker in the vineyard. Blumer remembers that in the twenties, when Bertrand Russell was to give a lecture at Chicago and Mead was to introduce him, Mead, then about sixty, was as nervous as a young instructor about to meet with one of the great minds of his discipline.

Mead's humility and diffidence should not be interpreted as a weakness of character. He was a man of principle and could act decisively when the occasion demanded it. When the then new president of the university, Robert Hutchins, attempted to force the Philosophy Department to add to its staff

[49] Dewey, "George Herbert Mead," p. 311. [50] *Selected Writings,* p. 302.
[51] T. V. Smith, "The Social Philosophy of George Herbert Mead," *American Journal of Sociology,* XXXVII, 3 (November, 1931), p. 369.

Hutchins' friend, the neo-Thomist philosopher Mortimer Adler, and Mead's protests seemed of no avail, he handed in his resignation and prepared to rejoin John Dewey at Columbia. Only his untimely death cut short the preparations for this move.[52]

Toward the end of his life Mead wrote the sentence that might characterize his own life: "The proudest assertion of independent selfhood is but the affirmation of a unique capacity to fill some social role."[53] In his gentle and unassuming way, Mead had no desire to shine in the limelight. He saw himself as an ordinary soldier in the battle for social and intellectual reform and did not aspire to lead the troops. His profound devotion to scientific inquiry was always controlled by his desire to contribute his share to the betterment of mankind. "We determine what the world has been," he wrote just before his death, "by the anxious search for the means of making it better."[54] His son told Dewey that the phrase which he most associated with his father when any social problem was under discussion was: "It ought to be possible to do so and so."[55]

Mead died in the belief that he would be known to posterity, if at all, only as the writer of a few technical articles. He seems to have had no inkling of the fact that the impact of his work would grow from decade to decade so that he may now well be reckoned as one among a handful of American thinkers who have helped to shape the character of modern social science.

THE INTELLECTUAL CONTEXT

Mead was a man of encyclopedic learning with an enormous range and breadth of intellectual interests. He was thoroughly at home in all the subfields of philosophy and its history and also kept himself abreast of developments in the physical and biological as well as in the social sciences. He was familiar with mathematics and mathematical logic, and also had an intense love of music and poetry. Dewey records that

> He knew large parts of Milton by heart, and has been known to repeat it [sic] for two hours without flagging. Wordsworth and Keats and Shakespeare, especially the sonnets, were equally familiar to him. . . . An accurate and almost photographic memory is rarely associated with a mind that assimilates, digests, and reconstructs; in this combination as in so many others, Mr. Mead was so rare that his personality does not lend itself to analysis and classification.[56]

This explains why any account of Mead's intellectual background risks being sketchy and incomplete.

[52] Blumer, conversation. [53] *Selected Writings,* p. 357. [54] Quoted in Smith, *op. cit.,* p. 369.
[55] Dewey, "George Herbert Mead," p. 312. [56] *Ibid.*

Four major strains are prominent in Mead's intellectual make-up. The New England Congregational tradition with its emphasis on autonomous intellectual search and on moral duty to the community; the frontier tradition with its emphasis on doing things, which is so congenial to pragmatic philosophy, even though this philosophy originated among Harvard men; Darwinian evolutionary thinking with its emphasis on change and its insistence that nothing is permanent but process itself; finally, the German idealistic tradition of philosophy from Kant to Schelling with its parallel emphasis on process and transformation and its central concern with the free and responsible subject, the Absolute Self, the transcendental "I," as the creator of the human world.

THE HERITAGE OF PROTESTANTISM AND THE FRONTIER

Mead was part of a whole generation of American thinkers, among them most early sociologists, who were reared in a strict Puritanical atmosphere but who freed themselves from theological moorings, most often under the impact of Darwin's teaching. Like them, Mead remained tied to his Puritan background, even though he transmuted this heritage into a secular concern with social ethics and transformed the Christian emphasis on the brotherhood of men in Christ into a humanitarian quest for pan-human fraternity. It is doubtful that he read much in theology beyond the requirements of Oberlin College, and although the Puritan tradition is not manifestly evident in his writings, one can hardly come away from them without being struck by the fact that this secular philosophy had strong and enduring roots in Puritan Christianity.

EVOLUTIONISM

It is easier to document Mead's indebtedness to the Darwinian tradition. He owed to Darwin not only his liberation from the theological shackles of his youth, but a major impetus in the development of his pragmatic philosophy. In fact, Darwin's theory of biological evolution is the foundation of the pragmatism of Mead and his co-thinkers. This theory views the living organism

as engaged in a continual struggle for control over the environment; it is based on a naturalistic conception of the mind, which is radically at variance with traditional views about the nature of intelligence. Once the Darwinian conceptualization is accepted, the mind can be seen as engaged in an elaborate instrumental process to insure the organism's survival. Thinking can now be considered an activity aimed at grasping the world so that it will be favorable to conduct. "The test of intelligence is found in action."[57] Intelligence is a problem-solving activity. "Truth is . . . synonymous with the solution of the

[57] *Movements of Thought,* p. 345.

problem."[58] Science is "only the evolutionary process grown self-conscious."[59] "The animal is doing the same thing the scientist is doing."[60]

Darwin taught Mead and his associates to think in terms of process instead of fixed forms. "The heart of the problem of evolution," wrote Mead, "is the recognition that the process will determine the form."[61] "The process takes now one form and now another, according to the conditions under which it is going on."[62]

Mead derived many other ideas from his close study of the work of Darwin. His conception of scientific method was closely modeled after Darwin's observational procedures, and some of the roots of Mead's concept of the gesture are to be found in Darwin's *The Expression of Emotion in Man and Animals.* His main debt to evolutionary thought, however, whether in Lamarckian or Darwinian form, was in highlighting the dissolution of fixed structure into changing forms through continued process.

GERMAN IDEALISM

Mead took a related idea from the German idealistic tradition. What struck him in Fichte, Schelling, and Hegel, whom he called "the Romantic Philosophers," and also partly in Kant, was that they generalized and made a philosophical doctrine of the notion of the life process. "The Romantic idealists undertook to identify this process, first of all, with the self-not-self process in experience, and then to identify this self-not-self process with the subject-object process."[63] Pre-Kantian philosophy, Mead wrote, "assumed that the world was there and that human beings later came into it. . . . But, what the Romantic idealists insisted upon is that you cannot have an object without a subject."[64] On the other hand, there can also be no consciousness which is not consciousness of something, so that subject and object are inevitably intertwined. Mead learned from the German tradition the insistence on the interplay between subject and object in the process of knowing and in the construction of the self. "We can see that the self-process of the Romantic idealists —this fusion of the two phases of experience, the self-experience on the one hand and the subject-object experience on the other hand—was one which enabled them to insist not only that the subject involved an object but also that the object involved a subject."[65]

As Mead read the German idealists, they were all centrally preoccupied with the relation of the self to its objects. Fichte, Mead taught, was mainly concerned with the problem in terms of moral experience, while Schelling and Hegel respectively focused attention upon the esthetic experience and the experience of thought. Their common problem was "that of bringing the world

[58] *Selected Writings,* p. 328. [59] *Movements of Thought,* p. 364.

[60] *Ibid.,* p. 346. I have freely borrowed in this paragraph from Reck's "Introduction" to *Selected Writings,* p. xvi. [61] *Movements of Thought,* p. 166. [62] *Ibid.* [63] *Ibid.* [64] *Ibid.,* p. 167.

[65] *Ibid.,* pp. 167–68.

which seems to be independent of the self into the experience of the self."[66] This was particularly evident in Fichte's work. "For the individual the world is always a task to be accomplished. . . . It is a world, a real thing, just to the extent that one constructs it, that one organizes it for one's action."[67] Summing up his view of Romantic philosophy as a philosophy of process and as the background for the development of the theory of evolution, Mead wrote:

> The Romantic philosophy pointed out that the self, while it arises in social experience, also carried [sic] with it the very unit that makes society possible, which makes the world possible. . . . It is the self which organizes the world; but when it has organized it, it has really organized that which is identical with itself, it has organized its own experiences. It has, in one phase of its nature, discovered what it is in another phase.[68]

It need not be stressed that Fichte or Schelling would hardly have approved of this interpretation of their doctrine or that their later followers would have been horrified to learn that their beloved idealist metaphysics had served to lay the groundwork for a scientific philosophy based on Darwin's "horrid materialism." What matters is that this was the message that Mead derived from his reading of their work and integrated into his own views.

Among later German thinkers, Wilhelm Wundt, under whom, it will be remembered, Mead had studied for a semester, influenced him most. This is most readily apparent in Mead's treatment of the notion of gesture. Wundt defined the gesture as that which is to be found in earlier stages of development as a part of a social act and which later becomes a symbol. It is the part of the social act that serves as a stimulus for further acts.[69] To Darwin, gestures expressed the emotions of animals, but Wundt objected that this does not exhaust the functions of gestures. Rather, they are initial and truncated parts of complex acts. Mead often stressed that the formulation of the relation of language to gesture "has been considerably advanced by Wundt," but added that Wundt had not sufficiently emphasized "the value which these truncated acts, these beginnings of inhibited movements, these gestures, have as appropriate stimulations for the conduct of other individuals."[70] Wundt's exclusively psychological emphasis missed the notion of communication. In any case, Mead saw himself as working directly in the Wundtian tradition when he explored the nature of significant gestures.

It has often been observed that Adam Smith's notion of the "impartial spectator" has very strong resemblances to Mead's "generalized other," as well as to Cooley's "looking-glass self." T. V. Smith, one of Mead's students, puts this matter in the right perspective when he writes of Mead:

> I once jocosely taxed him with "having stolen his thunder from Smith." He replied genially that he had come under the influence of Adam Smith

[66] *Ibid.*, p. 87. [67] *Ibid.*, p. 89. [68] *Ibid.*, p. 125. [69] *Mind, Self and Society*, p. 42.
[70] *Selected Writings*, p. 109.

> while studying at Harvard, and had there written a paper on Smith. . . . But whatever he may have borrowed from Smith, his "generalized other" is much richer than what he borrowed. Smith's "man within the breast" is an altruistic guest housed in an egoistic household for purposes of respectability; Mead's "generalized other" is no guest. He is the householder himself.[71]

Among his own contemporaries, Mead seemed to be most impressed, next to the American pragmatists, by the work of the French philosopher Henri Bergson, whose emphasis on the flow of experience appealed to him. To Bergson, wrote Mead approvingly, "Life is a process of continued reconstruction involved in the world as experienced."[72] Mead did not follow Bergson when he gave his vitalistic philosophy an anti-rationalistic and anti-intellectual bent. Bergson failed to see, Mead argued, "that the flow, the freedom, the novelty, the interpenetration, the creativity, upon which he sets such store, are not necessarily limited to the interpenetration in the inner flow of consciousness. They may also be gotten in an objective statement."[73] Mead was never willing to give up his overriding commitment to scientific objectivism, but in formulating his views on the flow and stream of consciousness in its transactions with the world of experience he owed something to Bergson, even as he had earlier been influenced by William James.

THE FELLOWSHIP OF PRAGMATISTS

Many complicated lines of mutual influence link Mead to James, to Baldwin, to Cooley, and, above all, to John Dewey, though only very detailed and specialized inquiry could trace the lines precisely. The notion of the act as social was the root metaphor for Mead as it was for Cooley and Dewey. Dewey has testified that Mead's ideas in social psychology "worked a revolution" in his own thinking,[74] and it is obvious to any informed reader that many passages in Mead can in turn be traced to the influence of Dewey. Charles Morris puts the matter well when he speaks of these two philosophers being engaged in "a natural division of labor at a common task." "Neither stands to the other," he writes, "in the exclusive relation of teacher to student; both . . . were of equal though different intellectual stature; both shared in a mutual give-and-take according to their own particular genius. If Dewey gives range and vision, Mead gave analytical depth and scientific precision."[75]

One is likewise impressed by the close similarities between many of Mead's ideas and those of Cooley and of James. However, though Mead was deeply beholden to James and Cooley for his ideas on the nature of the self, he differed from them in rejecting an introspective and mentalistic account of the self in

[71] Smith, *op. cit.*, pp. 378–79. [72] *Movements of Thought*, p. 292. [73] *Ibid.*, p. 325.
[74] Dewey, "George Herbert Mead," p. 313.
[75] Charles Morris, "Introduction" to *Mind, Self and Society*, p. xi.

favor of a view of the self as emerging in an objective social process. Much of this difference is undoubtedly associated with differences in the social context in which these men lived and worked.

THE SOCIAL CONTEXT

It is useful to juxtapose Mead's career with Cooley's in order to highlight some social roots of the sources of disagreement between these otherwise intimately related thinkers.

Mead's early life was much more deeply marked by a variety of social experiences and involvements than was Cooley's. Cooley wrestled with illness and attempted to overcompensate for his near pathological shyness by flights of imagination. Mead, in contrast, was always active. He waited on tables during his college years and thereafter immersed himself in the drama of the frontier while serving on surveying expeditions. Cooley, the son of an upper-status and independently wealthy member of the elite, could afford a long period of semi-idleness in order "to find himself." Mead, the son of a poorly paid professor of theology who died when Mead was still in college and left his widow and children in straitened circumstances, could not afford such leisure. If he was "to find himself," it was not in the privacy of his study but in the demanding environment of surveying crews, among rough companions who generally knew little about the life of the mind.

At a later stage in their careers, both men went to Europe, but Cooley, partly insulated from European experiences by illness and withdrawal, seemed not to be very deeply marked by this sojourn. Mead, however, involved himself fully not only in German university life but in the social affairs of Germany and other European countries. His wife told her son that when she traveled with her husband

> through, say, France or Germany, [she] could tell all about the difficulties of most fellow-travellers on the train; he, on the other hand, would have some difficulty in placing individuals but could give a clear exposition of the political, social, historical problems of the regions traversed; and he might for good measure discuss the aims and ambition of the outstanding figures of the region.[76]

Cooley taught throughout his life in a quiet and socially insulated university town, socially far removed from the industrial city of Detroit, though geographically quite near. Mead, after his short period at Ann Arbor, taught in Chicago, a city second to none in its newness, roughness, industrial vitality,

[76] Henry Mead in *The Philosophy of the Act,* p. lxxix.

and the extent of its social problems. Cooley could wander about a tree-shaded campus that was an ideal world in itself, protected from outside concerns. When Mead walked across the quadrangles of his university's buildings, the pungent smell of the stockyards of South Chicago and the steel plants of Gary was always in the air. Although there was then no Negro ghetto just beyond the splendor of the Midway, it was hard to forget, even in Mead's day, that the University of Chicago was only a small oasis in a city preoccupied with making things and making money, but hardly devoted to the cultivation of high culture.

It is idle to speculate what Mead's life course would have been had he chosen to live elsewhere than in Chicago. The fact is he decided to stay there, and shared the activist and reforming spirit that Dewey instilled in his Department of Philosophy. Cooley, in his protected environment, could continue to nurture ideas that were still rooted in the agricultural communities of an America that was rapidly disappearing. Mead was confronted by the new urban and industrial America in a manner he could not ignore. He responded to the challenge and took part enthusiastically in the reform movements that radiated from the University of Chicago to the city at large. Unlike the sage of Ann Arbor, the one-time president of Chicago's reforming City Club could not maintain a stance of detached observation, but was deeply immersed in the problems of urban America.

In his manifold reform activities, Mead had to put himself continually in the role of others whose activities within the rules of the game of urban politics, urban education, and urban industrial relations he wished to comprehend. Blumer and others have testified to the fact that Mead was an acute observer of the social scene, and that much of his theoretical scheme was rooted in concrete observation of what went on around him. He seems to have looked on the city of Chicago as a complex ecology of games, to use Norton Long's formulation, and to have felt that one could best learn about the rules governing these games when one became a participant observer. All this is, of course, a far cry from Cooley's insulated situation.

For Cooley, social reality is in the last analysis something that goes on in a man's mind; for Mead, it is an objective and external process. Moreover, Cooley is, on the whole, tender-minded when he describes and analyzes society. Although by no means oblivious to social conflicts and the uglier aspects of competition, he still seems to have regarded all these blemishes as temporary, destined to disappear in the long run as the whole world would increasingly resemble a huge cooperative, an extended primary group. Mead is a less sentimental thinker, while sharing with Cooley and Dewey a belief in progressive improvement and humanitarian advance. In contrast to Cooley, for example, Mead argued that "there is nothing in the history of human society nor in present-day experience which encourages us to look to the primal impulse of neighborliness for . . . cohesive power. The love of one's neighbor cannot be made into a common consuming passion."[77] Mead agreed with the tough-minded Yale sociologist William Graham Sumner, rather than the tender-minded Cooley, when he reasoned that in-group solidarity usually arose from antagonism toward an out-group. Similarly, he, like Durkheim, argued forcefully that respect for the law as law was rooted in "the psychology of punitive justice," in which in-group solidarity is maintained at the price of stigmatization of the criminal transgressor. "The revulsions against criminality reveal themselves in a sense of solidarity with the group, a sense of being a citizen which on the one hand excludes those who have transgressed the laws of the group and on the other hand inhibits tendencies to criminal acts in the citizen himself."[78]

There is no need to draw too sharply the contrasting lines between Cooley and Mead. In a larger sense both participated in the optimistic and hopeful atmosphere that marked the Age of Reform. Their differences are of intellectual style, not of ultimate substance. That Mead himself did not fully resolve his ambiguities in respect to the nature of the social process is perhaps best shown in his attempts to define social acts. He fluctuated in his usage and definition of social acts, sometimes assuming that these are necessarily cooperative, and sometimes holding to the more realistic view that social conflict is as much a social act as is cooperation. There were both tender- and tough-minded strains in Mead, but his location in Chicago and his involvement in its often ugly and unpleasant social struggles were conducive to the predominance of "realistic" views, which found only a much more muted expression in the fruits of Cooley's introspective analyses.

MEAD'S AUDIENCE AND COLLEAGUES

It will be remembered that at the University of Chicago Mead stood for many years under the shadow of the imposing figure of John Dewey. Dewey, who was only four years older than Mead, had become an amazingly productive scholar at a very early period in his life, while Mead produced his first major paper at the age of forty. Dewey published his first book in 1886, when he was only twenty-seven years of age; his next book appeared two years later and two more books followed in 1894. His famous volume on experimental logic was published when he was forty-three. Dewey continued to produce voluminously and his work exhibited a truly impressive range and scope. Mead's contributions, in contrast, were scanty, consisting mainly of articles on philosophical and psychological questions that appeared in specialized journals. He published on educational and social reforms, to be sure, but only occasionally and in a manner that was not likely to attract wide attention.

Dewey was known to the general public as a major figure in educational

[77] *Selected Writings*, pp. 361–62. [78] *Ibid.*, p. 222.

reform as early as the 1890's, but Mead received little public notice except perhaps among local reformers. He never became, and probably had no desire to become, a national spokesman for the cause of liberalism. Mead was not listed in *Who's Who in America* until 1910 (about seven years later than Dewey) and then only because of his full professorship.[79]

All evidence indicates that Dewey and Mead were close friends and companions and that no overt competitiveness clouded their relations. It is interesting to note, however, that Herbert Blumer relates that Mead would sometimes point with a bit of sarcasm to the profuseness of Dewey's output and to his attendant tendency to write sloppily and with lack of precision. Nevertheless, during their long association at Chicago, and even after Dewey moved to Columbia, Mead was content to play second fiddle to Dewey's resounding first violin.

One gains the impression, although it is difficult to prove, that Mead's general tendency to reformulate his ideas continuously, never being content with what he had achieved, may have become more pronounced when he was forced to compare himself with Dewey who had the opposite tendency and, as a consequence, achieved a renown that was denied his younger friend. By taking the prodigiously productive Dewey as a point of reference, Mead might well have increased his inherent writing difficulties.

IN SUMMARY

Not only in his relations with Dewey, but apparently with others among his respected colleagues, Mead never tried to put himself forward. He was proud and happy to have gifted students and highly valued the student audience he invariably attracted. He spent much time encouraging and guiding his students, imparting to them his animated vision. But he was never intent on creating a school around himself. During his lifetime Mead's influence on others can be found only in the effects his teachings and conversations had on students and colleagues; his wider impact came only after the posthumous publication of his work. Insofar as he was influenced by his audience, that influence came in the course of his lectures and in the vivid conversations—as Mead would put it, the "significant gestures"—he had with friends and students, which Mead prized above all. In this respect Mead was like one of those philosophers of old who never wrote at all, but continued to live in the minds of students who had been touched and transformed by their message.

[79] For most of the above, cf. Anselm Strauss, "Introduction" to *George Herbert Mead on Social Psychology*, p. ix.

Robert Ezra Park

1864-1944

THE WORK

Readers who are familiar with the work of the Chicago School of Sociology and its most influential member, Robert E. Park, may wonder why a chapter in a book on sociological theory is devoted to a man most often associated with research rather than theory. The fact is, however, that Park himself, although very much concerned with accurate social reporting and description, saw his major contribution in the development of a set of concepts that would allow systematic classification and analysis of social data.

The contemporary assessment of Robert Park's work roughly coincides with his self-appraisal when he wrote:

> We had in sociology much theory but no working concepts. When a student proposed a topic for a thesis, I invariably found myself asking the question: what is this thing you want to study? What is a gang? What is a public? What is a nationality? . . . etc. I did not see how we could have anything like scientific research unless we had a system of classification and a frame of reference into which we could sort out and describe in general terms the things we were attempting to investigate. Park and Burgess' *Introduction* was a first rough sketch of such a classification and frame of reference. My contribution to sociology has been, therefore, not what I intended, not what my original interest would have indicated, but what I needed to make a systematic exploration of the social work [sic] in which I found myself. The problem I was interested in was always theoretic rather than practical.[1]

Park not only classified, as he modestly says; he searched for relationships between classified variables and thus engaged in theoretically guided research rather than merely descriptive reporting. As Everett Hughes has noted, "[Park] had no desire to form a system, yet he was primarily a systematic sociologist."[2] It is as such that he commands our attention.

[1] Quoted in Howard Odum, *American Sociology* (New York, Longmans, Green, 1951), pp. 132–33.
[2] Everett C. Hughes, "Robert E. Park," in T. Raison, ed., *The Founding Fathers of Social Science* (Harmondsworth, England, Penguin, 1969), p. 169.

COLLECTIVE BEHAVIOR AND SOCIAL CONTROL

Park defined sociology as "the science of collective behavior,"[3] and this definition already suggests that while he was not unmindful of the need for analysis of social structures, he was mainly concerned with the study of more fluid social processes.[4] In Park's view society is best conceived as the product of interactions between component individuals which are controlled by a body of traditions and norms that arise in the process of interaction. Social control is "the central fact and the central problem of society."[5] "Society is everywhere a control organization. Its function is to organize, integrate, and direct the energies resident in the individuals which compose it."[6] Accordingly, sociology is "a point of view and method for investigating the processes by which individuals are inducted into and induced to cooperate in some sort of corporate existence we call society."[7]

Social control refers to the variety of mechanisms by which collective behavior is organized, contained, and channelled. The social process involves forms of antagonism, of conflict and competition, and social control serves to order these processes. Whether it be the more elementary forms of control that arise among members of a crowd, or the more elaborate forms that crystallize into public opinion and the law, social control always operates so as to regulate competition, to compromise conflict, and to harness individuals to the necessary requirements of the social order. Yet social control can never achieve a permanent state of equilibrium in society. The fact that antagonisms are regulated by control mechanisms does not mean that they are eradicated, but only that they have become latent or have been driven into socially accepted channels. "Every society represents an organization of elements more or less antagonistic to each other but united for the moment, at least, by an arrangement which defines the reciprocal relations and respective sphere of action of each. This accommodation, this *modus vivendi,* may be relatively permanent as in a society constituted by castes, or quite transitory as in societies made up of open classes."[8]

For Park, a relatively stable social order is one in which mechanisms of social control have for the time being succeeded in containing antagonistic forces in such a way that an accommodation has been reached between them. But while accommodation may be reached temporarily between specific groups

[3] Robert E. Park and Ernest W. Burgess, *Introduction to the Science of Sociology* (Chicago, The University of Chicago Press, 1921), p. 42.

[4] This subchapter is much in debt to Ralph H. Turner's fine "Introduction" to Ralph H. Turner, ed., *Robert E. Park on Social Control and Collective Behavior* (Chicago, The University of Chicago Press, 1967). [5] *Introduction,* p. 42.

[6] Robert E. Park, *Human Communities* (New York, The Free Press, 1952), p. 157.

[7] *Introduction,* p. 42. [8] *Ibid.,* p. 665.

and individuals, there is, according to Park, every reason to believe that an overall accommodation, at least in modern society, can never be permanent because new groups and individuals are likely to arise and claim their share of scarce values, thus questioning the scheme of things that has arisen from previous accommodations.

FOUR MAJOR SOCIAL PROCESSES

Park distinguished four major social processes: competition, conflict, accommodation, and assimilation. Competition he took to be "a universal phenomenon . . . first clearly conceived and adequately described by the biologists" and "defined in the evolutionary formula 'the struggle for existence.' "[9] "Competition is the elementary universal and fundamental form"[10] of social interaction. It is "interaction without contact:"[11] whether the competition is among members of a plant community struggling for a share of sunlight or among human beings competing for prized goods or values, the individual unit is unaware of its competitors. "It is only when minds meet, only when the meaning that is in one mind is communicated to another mind so that these minds mutually influence one another, that social contact properly speaking, may be said to exist."[12] When this is the case, unconscious competition becomes conscious conflict and "competitors identify one another as rivals or as enemies."[13] Competition is as universal and continuous in human society as it is in the natural order. It assigns persons their position in the division of labor as well as in the ecological order. Conflict, on the other hand, is intermittent and personal. While competition is a struggle for position in the ecological and economic order, "the status of the individual, or a group of individuals, in the social order . . . is determined by rivalry, by war or by subtler forms of conflict."[14] "Competition determines the position of the individual in the [ecological] community, conflict fixes his place in society. Location, position, ecological interdependence—these are the characteristics of the [ecological] community. Status, subordination, and superordination, control—these are the distinctive marks of a society."[15]

Accommodation implies a cessation of conflict, which comes about when the system of allocation of status and power, the relations of superordinates to subordinates, have been temporarily fixed and are controlled through the laws and the mores. "In accommodation the antagonism of the hostile elements is, for the time being, regulated, and conflict disappears as overt action, although it remains latent as a potential force. With a change in the situation, the adjustment that had hitherto successfully held in control the antagonistic forces fails."[16] Accommodation, like social control generally, is fragile and easily up-

[9] *Ibid.*, p. 505. [10] *Ibid.*, p. 507. [11] *Ibid.* [12] *Ibid.* [13] *Ibid.* [14] *Ibid.*, p. 574.
[15] *Ibid.*, pp. 574–75. [16] *Ibid.*, p. 665.

set. To Park, accommodation and social order, far from being "natural," are only temporary adjustments and may at any moment be upset by underlying latent conflicts that press to undermine the previous order of restraint.

In contrast to accommodation, assimilation "is a process of interpenetration and fusion in which persons and groups acquire the memories, sentiments, and attitudes of other persons and groups, and, by sharing their experience and history, are incorporated with them in a common culture."[17] While Park seems to have felt that the other three fundamental social processes operate in a very wide variety of social interactions, he reserves the discussion of assimilation more especially to the sociology of culture and to the process by which ethnic groups or races are slowly incorporated into a wider whole through assuming a common cultural heritage. When assimilation is achieved, this does not mean that individual differences are eradicated or that competition and conflict cease but only that there is enough unity of experience and communality of symbolic orientation so that a "community of purpose and action" can emerge.

SOCIAL DISTANCE

Although Park hoped for the eradication of racial differences through full assimilation in the very long run, he did not think of it as a process that had much relevance to the analyses of race relations in his America. The concept of "social distance," which Park derived from Simmel, seemed to him of much greater importance for an understanding of contemporary race relations. This concept refers to the degree of intimacy that prevails between groups and individuals. "The degree of . . . intimacy measures the influence which each has over the other."[18] The greater the social distance between individuals and groups, the less they influence each other reciprocally. Such terms as race consciousness or class consciousness, Park argues, refer to social distance between groups of people. They "describe a state of mind in which we become . . . conscious of the distances that separate, or seem to separate, us from classes and races whom we do not fully understand."[19] In American race relations in particular, a fixed and conventional social distance assures that the Negro is "all right in his place." As long as he keeps his place and his distance, a great deal of warmth between the subordinate and the superordinate may obtain. The lady of the house may be on the closest terms with her cook, but these relations can be maintained only as long as the cook keeps her "proper distance." Similarly, interpersonal relations between Negroes and whites may be more personal in the South than they are in the North, because the southern white is assured that the Negro will know precisely how to keep the proper distance.

[17] *Ibid.*, p. 735.
[18] Robert E. Park, *Race and Culture* (New York, The Free Press, 1950), p. 257. [19] *Ibid.*

Park thought that what is ordinarily called prejudice "seems . . . to be [the] more or less instinctive and spontaneous disposition to maintain social distance."[20] Prejudice in this sense was to Park by no means pathological; it was a universal human phenomenon. Men, he argued, come into the world with certain predispositions and they acquire others in later life. "A man without prejudices is a man without conviction, and ultimately without character."[21] Friendships and enmities are correlative. "As it seems impossible to conceive of a world without friendship, so it seems improbable, in such a world, that life should go without enmities, for those two things are, in some sense and some degree, correlative, so that the bias with which we view the qualities of our friends makes it difficult if not impossible to do justice to the virtues of our enemies."[22] Prejudice and social distance are therefore ineradicable aspects of human association.

Race prejudice, like caste or class prejudice, is in this view "merely one variety of a species."[23] It can be looked at as "a phenomenon of status."[24] "Every individual we meet inevitably finds a place in our minds in some category already defined."[25] Every person we encounter is categorized and assessed according to his imputed status in the established order of things. And so, in racially divided American society, Negroes are assigned inferior status and they are enjoined to maintain the proper distance toward those who have superordinate status.

Racial prejudice and social distance, Park argued forcefully, must not be confused with racial antagonism and conflict. The former operate when the subordinate accepts his inferior status; the latter arise when he is not longer willing to do so. Writing in 1928, Park penned these prophetic words: "There is probably less racial prejudice in America than elsewhere, but there is more racial conflict and more racial antagonism. There is more conflict because there is more change, more progress. The Negro is rising in America and the measure of the antagonism he encounters is, in some very real sense, the measure of his progress."[26] Race prejudice refers to the normal process of categorizing individuals according to the position they occupy in the traditional order. "Prejudice is not on the whole an aggressive but a conservative force."[27] Racial conflicts and antagonisms, on the other hand, indicate that the traditional order is weakening so that the customary accommodations are no longer effective and social distance in no longer maintained effectively. Racial conflicts are harbingers of change in the racial status order. As previous accommodations break down under the impact of antagonism and conflict, they prepare the way for a new accommodation between contending racial status groups in which the previously inferior group achieves more nearly equal status. Once this has been accomplished, the basis may have been laid for a fusion of the previously distinct groups through racial assimilation and the eradication of social dis-

[20] *Ibid.*, p. 259. [21] *Ibid.*, p. 230. [22] *Ibid.*, p. 231. [23] *Ibid.*, pp. 231–32. [24] *Ibid.*, p. 232. [25] *Ibid.* [26] *Ibid.*, p. 233. [27] *Ibid.*, p. 260.

tance between them. Hawaii's racial situation is a case in point. The race relations cycle from accommodation to conflict to new accommodation and possibly to assimilation is to Park only a special case of the general process of social change.

SOCIAL CHANGE

Park conceived of the process of social change as involving a three-stage sequence, or "natural history," beginning with dissatisfactions and the resulting disturbances and social unrest, leading to mass movements, and ending in new accommodations within a restructured institutional order. Social unrest "represents at once a breaking up of the established routine and a preparation for new collective action."[28] Crowds as agents of unrest were, as Park said in a discussion of the French social psychologist Le Bon, "not merely any group brought together by the accident of some chance excitement."[29] They were "the emancipated masses whose bonds of loyalty to the old order had been broken."[30] The crowd, in Park's view, is an elementary and rudimentary social formation. It "has no tradition. . . . It has therefore neither symbols, ceremonies, rites, nor ritual; it imposes no obligations and creates no loyalties."[31] Yet religious sects and social movements have their origin in the excitement of the crowd. To the extent that leaders emerge from previously amorphous crowds, ephemeral and unreflective actions give way to more stable and permanent forms of organization. The leaders of emerging social movements or religious organizations impose social control on the previously unstructured collective behavior of the crowd, thereby transforming it into an audience. "The crowd does not discuss and hence it does not reflect. It simply 'mills.' "[32] In contrast, "in the public, interaction takes the form of discussion. Individuals tend to act upon one another critically; issues are raised and parties form. Opinions clash and thus modify and moderate one another."[33] When unthinking crowds are transformed into reflective publics, there emerge new social entities that may, if conditions are propitious, make successful claims which break the cake of custom and thus prepare the way for novel accommodations characterizing a new social order.

The notion of "natural history" conceived as a sequence of stages is central not only to Park's account of the rise of social movements but to many other of his analyses as well. He attempted to write a natural history of the press, "not a record of the fortunes of individual newspapers, but an account of the evolution of the newspaper as a social institution."[34] He inspired his student

[28] *Introduction*, p. 866. [29] *Ibid.*, p. 868. [30] *Ibid.* [31] *Ibid.*, p. 790. [32] *Ibid.*, p. 869.

[33] *Ibid.*, and Robert E. Park "aus Watertown, S.D., U.S.A.," *Masse und Publikum* (Bern, Switzerland, Lack und Grunau, 1904), *passim*. (Park's Heidelberg dissertation.)

[34] Robert E. Park, *Society* (New York, The Free Press, 1955), p. 176.

Lyford Edwards to write a natural history of the stages of revolution, with each stage inevitably triggering the emergence of the next. Above all, his urban sociology is anchored in his conceptualization of various stages in the process of invasion and succession through which various groups carve out their ecological niches, their natural areas, in the urban environment.

THE BIOTIC ORDER AND THE SOCIAL ORDER

Taking his point of departure from the Darwinian notion of the "web of life," Park conceived of a biotic order, common to animals and plants, to which he applied the term "community." "The essential characteristics of a community," he writes, "are those of: 1) a population, territorially organized, 2) more or less completely rooted in the soil it occupies, 3) its individual units living in a relationship of mutual interdependence that is symbiotic."[35] "These symbiotic societies are not merely unorganized assemblages of plants and animals which happen to live together in the same habitat. On the contrary, they are interrelated in the most complex manner."[36] Within the limits of a symbiotic community, different individual units of the population are involved in a complex form of competitive cooperation leading to a spatial order in which each individual unit is assigned a niche in the environment commensurate with its ability to impose itself. Competition gives rise to the two main ecological principles, dominance and succession. "In every life-community this dominance is ordinarily the result of struggle among the different species for light."[37] Succession, on the other hand, denotes the various stages, the "orderly sequence of changes, through which a biotic community passes in the course of its development."[38]

Park maintained that the processes characterizing the growth and development of plant and animal communities applied to human communities as well. The spatial location of various groups in the city reflects ecological processes as much as the spatial order of an animal community. But, and this has often been overlooked, Park also argued that while human communities exhibited an ecological or symbiotic order quite similar to that of nonhuman communities, they also participated in a social or moral order that had no counterpart on the nonhuman level. Park studied the ecological order to understand better man's moral order.[39]

The competitive struggle for economic advantage among men had many analogies, Park reasoned, with the impersonal struggle for existence among animals. "The principle of dominance operates in the human as well as in the plant and animal communities. The so-called natural or functional areas of a metropolitan community . . . owe their existence directly to the factor of dominance, and indirectly to competition."[40] Similarly, the territorial succession

[35] *Human Communities,* p. 148. [36] *Ibid.* [37] *Ibid.,* p. 151. [38] *Ibid.,* p. 152.
[39] Cf. Hughes' "Introduction" to *Human Communities,* p. 6. [40] *Human Communities,* p. 151.

of immigrant groups in the "natural areas" of the city can best be conceived in analogy with successions in the development of animal and plant communities. "It has been observed," Park writes, "that immigrant people ordinarily settle first in or near the centers of cities, in the so-called areas of transition. From there they are likely to move by stages . . . from an area of first to areas of second and third settlement, generally in the direction of the periphery of the city and eventually into the suburban area. . . . To these movements, seeing in them the effects of natural tendencies in the life of the urban community, students have applied the term 'succession.' "[41]

Park argued that human groupings, insofar as they participate in biotic communities and form a distinctive ecological order, can be studied through methods borrowed from biologists who investigate nonhuman communities. Yet, if only such methods were used, one could not hope to capture that which is distinctly human, the creation of a moral order. Human societies have a double aspect: they are made up of interdependent individuals competing with each other for economic and territorial dominance and for ecological niches, but who are, at the same time, involved in common collective actions.

> [Societies] are composed of individuals who act independently of one another, who compete and struggle with one another for mere existence, and treat one another, as far as possible, as utilities. On the other hand, it is quite as true that men and women are bound together by affections and common purposes; they do cherish traditions, ambitions, and ideals that are not all their own, and they maintain, in spite of natural impulse to the contrary, a discipline and a moral order that enables them to transcend what we ordinarily call nature, and through their collective action, recreate the world in the image of their collective aspirations and their common will. . . . Society . . . always includes something more than competitive cooperation and its resulting economic interdependence. The existence of a society presupposes a certain amount of solidarity, consensus and common purpose . . . [societies] grow up in the efforts of individuals to act collectively.[42]

In the moral or social order, as distinct from the ecological order, men participate as self-conscious individuals in communication with one another and hence are able to engage in collective action. The social order softens the impact of the competitive struggle for existence through social control and involvement in common tasks.

[41] *Ibid.*, p. 223. [42] *Ibid.*, pp. 180–81.

THE SELF AND THE SOCIAL ROLE

Park's notion of the self is mainly derived from the tradition of William James and his followers, which has been discussed in previous chapters. What is distinctive in his approach, however, is his linking of the notion of the self with that of the social role. Park pointed out that the word *person* in its root-meaning refers to a mask, and that this was "a recognition of the fact that everyone is always and everywhere, more or less consciously, playing a role. We are parents and children, masters and servants, teachers, students and professional men, Gentiles and Jews. It is in these roles that we know ourselves."[43]

Self-conceptions, Park argued, are rooted in the status we occupy and in the roles we play on the social scene. The individual's conceptions of himself are anchored in the division of labor and hence in the status order.

> The conceptions which men form of themselves seem to depend upon their vocations, and in general upon the role that they seek to play in the communities and social groups in which they live, as well as upon the recognition and status which society accords them in these roles. It is status, i.e., recognition by the community, that confers upon the individual the character of a person, since a person is an individual who has status, not necessarily legal, but social.[44]

To Park the self is constituted by the individual's conception of his role, and this role in its turn is built upon the recognition others in society accord the status upon which roles are based. "The individual's conception of himself . . . is based on his status in the social group or groups of which he is a member. The individual whose conception of himself does not conform to his status is an isolated individual. The completely isolated individual, whose conception of himself is in no sense an adequate reflection of his status, is probably insane."[45]

Park's well-known notion of the marginal man emerges directly from his views on self-conceptions as reflections of the status a person has within a group. Marginal men, like American mulattoes, Asiatic mixed bloods, or European Jews, have their anchorage in two distinct groups while not belonging fully to either; as a result, their self-conceptions are likely to be fairly inconsistent and ambivalent. The marginal man "lives in two worlds, in both of which he is more or less of a stranger."[46] Yet this very marginality, Park argues in accord with Simmel and Veblen, brings not only burdens but assets. "Inevitably he becomes, relatively to his cultural milieu, the individual with the wider horizon, the keener intelligence, the more detached and rational view-

[43] *Race and Culture,* p. 249. [44] *Society,* pp. 285–86. [45] *Introduction,* p. 55.
[46] *Race and Culture,* p. 356.

point. The marginal man is always relatively the more civilized human being."[47] "It is in the mind of the marginal man that the moral turmoil which new cultural contacts occasion, manifests itself in the most obvious forms. It is in the mind of the marginal man—where the changes and fusions of culture are going on—that we can best study the processes of civilization and progress."[48]

In his sociology of the marginal man as in the rest of his sociology, Park always focused analytical attention on those processes or situations which foster the emergence of novel forms that upset or render obsolete previous adjustments and accommodations. Durkheim emphasized the constraints that force society into predictable patterns. By contrast, although by no means oblivious to the need for social order, Park sensitizes us to the forces that break through constraints and thereby produce the new.

THE MAN

Robert Ezra Park[49] was born on February 14, 1864 in Harveyville, Pennsylvania. Soon after his birth his family moved to Red Wing, Minnesota, where the young Park grew up on the Mississippi River as the son of a prosperous businessman. Like Veblen, Cooley, and Mead, he is a product of the Middle Border. After his graduation from the local high school and despite the opposition of his father, Park went to the University of Minnesota. After one year there, he transferred to the University of Michigan.

At Ann Arbor, Park was fortunate to find an inspiring teacher, the young John Dewey, and to become a member of a group of like-minded students who discussed the social issues of the day in the spirit of the reforming ideas then spreading all over the Midwest. Dewey introduced Park to a remarkable man, Franklin Ford, who was to have a decisive influence on his subsequent career. Ford had been a newspaperman and had reported in detail on the vagaries of the stock market and the impact of news on that market. He had come to see stock prices as a reflection of public opinion shaped by the news,

[47] *Ibid.*, p. 376. [48] *Ibid.*, p. 356.

[49] Since there is no biography of Robert Park, though I understand that one by Winifred Raushenbush is in preparation, I have been forced to gather materials for this section from a number of sources. Chiefly used were the following: Helen MacGill Hughes, "Robert E. Park," *International Encyclopedia of the Social Sciences* (New York, Macmillan, 1968); Everett C. Hughes, "Robert E. Park," pp. 162–69; Robert E. L. Faris, *Chicago Sociology, 1920–1932* (San Francisco, Chandler; 1967) Ellsworth Faris, "Robert E. Park," *American Sociological Review,* IX, 3 (June, 1944), pp. 322–25; Ernest W. Burgess, "Robert E. Park," *American Journal of Sociology,* XLIX, 5 (March, 1944), p. 478; Ernest W. Burgess, "Social Planning and Race Relations," in *Race Relations: Problems and Theory, Essays in Honor of Robert E. Park,* ed. by J. Masuoka and Preston Valien (Chapel Hill, North Carolina, the University of North Carolina Press, 1961), pp. 17–25; Everett Hughes' prefaces to the three volumes of Park's collected writings noted below; and, above all, Park's "An Autobiographical Note" in his *Race and Culture,* pp. v–ix.

and was therefore led to infer that with more adequate reporting, general public opinion could be made to respond to current events in as accurate a manner as the stock market. Much like some later pollsters and survey analysts, Ford believed that if the changes in public opinion could be gauged with precision, "the historical process would be appreciably stepped up, and progress would go forward steadily, without the interruption and disorder of depression or violence, and at a rapid pace."[50]

Ford and Park planned a new kind of newspaper, to be called *Thought News,* which would register as well as influence movements of public opinion by more accurate presentation of the news. The paper never reached publication, but Park's views on the crucial importance of the news, the media of communication, and the influence of public opinion were largely shaped by his conversations with Franklin Ford.

PARK—A NEWSPAPERMAN AND STUDENT OF PHILOSOPHY

Having been immersed in a progressive atmosphere at the University of Michigan, Park decided upon graduation in 1887 not to go into his father's business but to seek a career in which he could give expression to his reforming concerns. He soon realized, however, that he differed from his Michigan friends by not indulging in utopian dreams and blueprints for reform. Most well-intentioned programs for change, he seemed to believe, were futile since they were based on insufficient knowledge of underlying social realities. Before reform could be implemented, a much greater knowledge was needed of present-day society than was so far available. Intimate acquaintance with social problems was a prerequisite for attempts to resolve them. The one career that seemed to present an opportunity for first-hand observation was newspaper reporting. So Park became a newspaperman.

From 1887 to 1898 Park worked for daily newspapers in Minnesota, Detroit, Denver, New York, and Chicago. He was soon given special assignments to cover the urban scene, often in depth through a series of articles. He wrote on city machines and the corruption they brought in their wake. He described the squalid conditions of the city's immigrant areas and the criminal world that was ensconced there. Constantly on the prowl for news and feature stories on urban affairs, Park came to view the city as a privileged natural laboratory for the study of the new urban man whom industrial society had created. Much of Park's later work and research interests grew organically out of his experiences as a newspaperman.

In 1894 Park married the daughter of a leading Michigan lawyer, Clara Cahill. The couple were to have four children. Four years after his marriage, Park decided that his empirical knowledge of the ways news was being created

50 "An Autobiographical Note," p. vi.

might be broadened by further academic study. He went to Harvard to study philosophy "because [he] hoped to gain insight into the nature and function of the kind of knowledge we call news." In addition, he "wanted to gain a fundamental point of view from which [he] could describe the behavior of society under the influence of news, in the precise and universal language of science."[51]

At Harvard, Park studied psychology with Muensterberg and philosophy with Royce and James. After earning his M.A. in 1899, he decided to go to Germany for further studies. He first went to the University of Berlin where he listened to Georg Simmel and was deeply influenced by him. Except for these courses with Simmel, Park never received any formal instruction in sociology.

While in Berlin, Park came across a treatise on the logic of the social sciences, *Gesellschaft und Einzelwesen* (1899), by the Russian sociologist B. Kistiakowski. "It was the first thing I had found anywhere," he wrote, "that dealt with the problem with which I was concerned in terms in which I had come to think of it." According to Pitirim Sorokin, Kistiakowski expounded in this book a series of views on the characteristic tendencies of modern society that were in many respects similar to those developed by Simmel as well as by Toennies in *Gemeinschaft und Gesellschaft*.[52] Since Kistiakowski had been a student of Wilhelm Windelband, Park went to Strasbourg and later to Heidelberg to study with the neo-Kantian philosopher. He wrote his Ph.D. thesis, entitled *Masse und Publikum,* under Windelband. Returning to Harvard in 1903 he put the finishing touches to his dissertation and served for a year as an assistant in philosophy.

PARK—AN ACTIVIST

Park soon gave up his previous ambition to teach because he felt "sick and tired of the academic world, and wanted to go back into the world of men." He wrote much later that he could "trace [his] interest in sociology to the reading of Goethe's *Faust*." "You remember," he explained, "that Faust was tired of books and wanted to see the world."[53]

William James once read to his class his essay "On a Certain Blindness in Human Beings." This essay greatly impressed Park. "The 'blindness' of which James spoke," writes Park, "is the blindness each of us is likely to have for the meaning of other people's lives. . . . What sociologists most need to know is what goes on behind the faces of men, what it is that makes life for each of us either dull or thrilling."[54] James spoke of the "personal secret" that makes life boring to one person and full of zest to another. Park seems to have con-

[51] *Ibid.*

[52] *Ibid.,* and Pitirim Sorokin, *Contemporary Sociological Theories* (New York, Harper & Row, 1928), p. 492. [53] "An Autobiographical Note," pp. v–vi. [54] *Ibid.,* p. vi.

cluded after listening to James that his own "secret" consisted in his desire to alternate between active involvement in social affairs and detached analysis and social description. Having spent six years in the academy, Park resolved to return to the give-and-take of the social world which had fascinated him during his newspaper career.

The social problems of the Negro seemed to Park at the time to be the most acute in America. His interest in racial issues, which continued to be a prime focus of his concerns throughout his later career, was spurred by having met Booker T. Washington, the President of Tuskegee Institute. Park soon joined forces with Washington and became his informal secretary, accompanying him on his travels. He went along on the research trip to Europe, which resulted in Washington's book, *The Man Farthest Down;* experts agree that this account of the miseries of Europe's underclass was mostly written by Park. Park worked with Washington for nine years and had great respect for him. He once remarked to Ernest Burgess that he learned more from Washington than from any of his teachers.[55] Park seems to have been especially impressed by Washington's consummate skills in the strategy and tactics of social action.

Park met Washington when he was invited to become secretary and press agent of the Congo Reform Association, a group of reformers who wanted to draw public attention to the oppression, corruption, and depravity of the Belgian colonial regime in the Congo. He was about to go to Africa to study the situation at first hand, when Washington invited him to Tuskegee and convinced him that he might best start his studies of Africa in the South. As a result, Park spent seven winters, partly at Tuskegee and partly roaming about the South, "getting acquainted with the life, the customs, and the condition of the Negro people."[56] During those years he also wrote a series of muckraking exposés of the Belgian colonial atrocities in the Congo for *Everybody's Magazine.*

PARK'S ACADEMIC CAREER

In 1914, at the age of fifty, there came another turning point in Park's life: he embarked on an academic career. At the suggestion of W. I. Thomas, he accepted a summer appointment in the Department of Sociology at the University of Chicago to give a course on "The Negro in America" for a fee of $500. Soon afterward he joined the department as a permanent member and continued teaching there until 1936.

Park's success at Chicago was not immediate. When he joined the department, its founder and *spiritus rector,* Albion Small, still dominated it, and Thomas, who had joined the department in 1896, was its most creative and

[55] Burgess, in *Race Relations,* p. 15. [56] "An Autobiographical Note," p. vii.

forceful member. By 1920, however, when the students came back after the war, Small was nearing retirement and Thomas had been forced to resign. Park became the outstanding member of the department.

Stimulating though his lectures were, Park's reputation did not depend on them. He insisted on getting to know each of his students personally and having protracted interviews and sessions with them. Learning about their background and interests in this personal way, Park then helped them map out their field of research and specific research problems. It was a time-consuming procedure, but he loved it.

Park brought his interest in the city into the university. He wrote that he had "actually covered more ground, tramping about in cities in different parts of the world, than any other living man." Out of this he had gained "a conception of the city, the community, the region, not as geographical phenomena merely but as a kind of social organism."[57] It was the study of this organism in all its details that he now urged upon his students. The city of Chicago was to become a great natural laboratory for research on urban man and his natural habitat.

For nine years Park taught at Chicago as a professorial lecturer with the same nominal salary. But being dedicated to his students and having some independent means by inheritance, he offered more courses than he was paid for. One day he received an official document "authorizing Dr. Park to give courses in the winter quarter without salary." The administration had finally discovered what was going on and wished to regularize the irregular. Park's appointment as a full professor came only in 1923, when he was fifty-nine years old.

Park was a colorful man, even in appearance. Leading a sedentary life while at the university, he developed a thickset and pudgy physique. His white hair was long, perhaps because he forgot to pay regular visits to the barber. Living up to the stereotype of the absent-minded professor, he would sometimes appear before his class with shaving soap in his ears and with his clothes in disarray. He would frequently forget where he had placed a book, and it even happened that he came to a convention forgetting to bring a copy of the paper he was scheduled to read. He once continued serenely with his lecture while a student walked to the front of the room and tied his neckwear, which had been dangling loose from his collar.

In the classroom Park had a gruff voice and manner, so he sometimes felt the need to explain that when he spoke rudely he did not mean to offend but that this was just his manner when thinking hard. Nevertheless, tears would sometimes flow when he told a student that his (the student's) ideas were not worth a damn. At times the chairman of the department, Ellsworth Faris,

[57] *Ibid.*, p. viii.

found it advisable to inform incoming graduate students that Park was one of the great scholars in sociology and that they should not be put off by his crustiness, thus depriving themselves of an exceptional opportunity.[58] Once students got to know Park, and discovered the warmhearted and affectionate man behind the gruff mask he liked to present, they became exceptionally devoted to him. Few men have had as many deeply attached and grateful students.

Park was not a very prolific writer. Ellsworth Faris said of him that he would rather "induce men to write ten books than to take time off to write one himself." Apart from his dissertation, he wrote only one book, *The Immigrant Press and Its Control* (1922).[59] His main contributions came in a series of influential articles and introductions to the books of his students, which have now been gathered in the three volumes of his *Collected Papers*.[60] Perhaps his most influential publication was the pathbreaking *Introduction to the Science of Sociology*,[61] which he published, with Ernest Burgess as a junior author, in 1921 and which is by far the most important textbook-reader in the early history of American sociology. One other book that appeared under his name, *Old World Traits Transplanted*,[62] was the result of Park's collaboration with W. I. Thomas, though it was signed by Park and a junior author. This was done because the publishers and sponsors refused to print a book authored by Thomas, who had recently been forced to resign his university position because of what was then judged to be a case of sexual indiscretion.

Park received ample professional recognition during his lifetime. He served as President of the American Sociological Society (1925), a delegate to the Institute of Pacific Relations, a director of the Race Relations Survey on the Pacific Coast, an editor of a series of books on immigration for the Carnegie Corporation, an associate editor of several academic journals, and was a member of the Social Science Research Council and more than a dozen other learned societies. He was also the first President of the Chicago Urban League.

An inveterate traveller, Park, before, during and after his Chicago appointment, roamed all over the world, exploring its racial frontiers and studying its cities. He visited Germany and conferred with its leading sociologists; he spent a whole academic year at the University of Hawaii; he lectured in Peiping and visited India, South Africa and Brazil.

After his retirement from the Chicago faculty, Park, ever ready to share his knowledge with students, moved to Fisk University, where, right through

58 The source for the information in this and the preceding paragraph is Faris, *op. cit.*, pp. 29–30.

59 Robert E. Park, *The Immigrant Press and Its Control* (New York, Harper & Row, 1922).

60 *Race and Culture, Human Communities, Society.* All three volumes were edited by Everett C. Hughes *et al.* 61 *Introduction.*

62 Robert E. Park and Herbert A. Miller, *Old World Traits Transplanted* (New York, Harper & Row, 1921).

his eightieth year, he taught students and directed their research activities. He died at Nashville, Tennessee on February 7, 1944, exactly one week before his eightieth birthday.

Perpetually curious and ever open to novel experience whether on the racial frontier or in the wilderness of cities, Park was above all devoted to training men who would be able to map the social world with precision and objectivity. He was deeply committed to reform and improvement of the human condition, but felt what was needed at that juncture were trained and disciplined observers of the passing scene. Students attracted to the area of race relations were generally strongly disposed to social action against racial discrimination and for Negro civil rights. Park shared their sentiments. But, in Ernest Burgess' words, he "told them flatly that the world was full of crusaders. Their role instead was to be that of the calm, detached scientist who investigates race relations with the same objectivity and detachment with which the zoologist dissects the potato bug."[63]

According to Park, "a sociologist was to be a kind of super-reporter, like the men who write for *Fortune*. He was to report a little more accurately, and in a manner a little more detached than the average . . . the 'Big News.' "[64] But in Park's view the sociologist was no mere gatherer of facts. He gave his students, in Everett Hughes' words, "a perspective in which to see themselves and thus satisfy their curiosity. The perspective was a system of concepts abstract enough to comprehend all forms of interaction of men with one another."[65]

Devoted to the enterprise of studying urban life and culture with the same painstaking meticulousness and attention to detail that anthropologists use when they describe primitive tribes, Park was convinced that no such study was, to use his expression, worth a damn, if it was not guided by an array of concepts that would allow the student to sift the significant from the unessential. To the extent that he managed to convey this sense of the importance of theory to his students, and he was by no means always successful, he made them transcend mere empiricism to become true sociologists.

There is no better testimony to the impact of Park's teaching than the imposing roster of his students. Everett C. Hughes, Herbert Blumer, Stuart Queen, Leonard Cottrell, Edward Reuter, Robert Faris, Louis Wirth, and E. Franklin Frazier all became presidents of the American Sociological Society. Helen McGill Hughes, John Dollard, Robert Redfield, Ernest Hiller, Clifford Shaw, Willard Waller, Walter C. Reckless, Joseph Lohman and many other students of Park became leading social scientists. It is hard to imagine the field of sociology without the contribution of the cohort of gifted men whom Park trained at Chicago. What higher tribute can be paid to a teacher?

[63] Burgess, in *Race Relations,* p. 17. [64] "An Autobiographical Note," p. ix.
[65] "Preface" to *Race and Culture,* p. xiii.

THE INTELLECTUAL CONTEXT

Park's was above all a synthesizing mind, able to put to its own uses many differing and often contradictory strands of ideas. His ability to absorb was considerable, and so he was able to profit from his wide reading by utilizing ideas derived from many thinkers. In attempting to list those men who were most influential in Park's development as a student, one can best be guided by the short intellectual biography that he appended to his dissertation, *Masse und Publikum.*[66]

When discussing his undergraduate days at Michigan, Park mentions only one academic figure, John Dewey. (Franklin Ford, the other major influence on Park in Michigan, was, of course, not an academic man.) It seems certain that Dewey was instrumental in forming the young Park's overall world view: he introduced him to the world of progressive meliorism, democratic enthusiasm, and pragmatic philosophy—all of which formed the trunk onto which Park grafted his later ideas. Although he never wrote specifically on philosophical themes, one can infer from all his writings that he belonged to the general pragmatic movement of ideas described in some detail in previous chapters.

At Harvard, where he went after twelve years as a journalist, Park worked in the main with Josiah Royce and William James. James's theory of the self, which has already been reviewed in connection with Cooley and Mead, so impressed Park that his writings on the subject may be said to be largely instructive variations on the Jamesian theme. What Park derived from Royce's absolute idealism is harder to know, even though he notes that he was "largely influenced" by him as well as by James. He listed various contributions of Royce in the bibliography for his (and Burgess') *Introduction to the Science of Sociology* under the headings of "Social Interaction and Social Consciousness," "Communication and Interaction," and "Imitation and Suggestion"; we may therefore assume that Royce stimulated his thinking in these areas. The third Harvard man listed by Park in his intellectual biography is the psychologist Hugo Muensterberg. Park said that the "point of view" of his dissertation was influenced by Muensterberg, as well as by his thesis director, Windelband. A student of Wundt, Muensterberg had been brought to Harvard at James's invitation as an exponent of the new experimental psychology, but soon his interests changed and he became one of the earliest proponents of applied psychology in America. Muensterberg is mentioned frequently in Park's *Introduction,* and the book includes a selection by Muensterberg on "The Psychology of Subordination and Superordination," which deals with suggestion, imitation, and sympathy in terms of domination and submission.

66 Park, "Lebenslauf," in *Masse und Publikum,* pp. 111–12.

PARK'S DEBT TO GERMAN SOCIAL SCIENCE

Though his study at Michigan and Harvard was undoubtedly important for laying the foundation for Park's general philosophy, it was during his studies in Germany that he formed most of the sociological ideas he later put to use in his teaching and writings. The one semester he spent in Simmel's classroom was probably the most important academic semester in his life. Park's general approach to society as a system of interactions, and his more specific ideas such as those on social conflict, the marginal man, the characteristics of urban dwellers, and social distance, were all stimulated by Simmel. What is more, Park's whole emphasis on sociology as a science concerned with abstracting from multiform reality a set of concepts that allow the establishment of relationships between specified variables is largely conceived in Simmel's spirit. When Park looks at society as collective behavior organized through social control, he translates into American terminology Simmel's distinction between the spontaneous flow of social life and the controls that established forms of interaction exercise by channelling diverse human urges into patterned uniformities. Park's stress on social process as a source of novelty—his rejection of a static structuralism in favor of a processual view—likewise has some of its sources in the work of the great German sociologist. Park cannot be called a disciple of Simmel but he certainly was deeply marked by his spirit. The index to the *Introduction* has no fewer than 43 entries for Simmel, more than for any other name. The book contains ten selections from Simmel, again more than from any other author. Park translated Simmel's sparkling and brilliant observations into a more matter-of-fact idiom and merged the German's erudition with the themes of Midwestern progressive thought.

The only other teacher at Berlin whom Park mentions is the philosopher Friedrich Paulsen. One may doubt that Park was much interested in Paulsen's metaphysics, but it may be that through Paulsen, who was an intimate personal friend of Ferdinand Toennies, Park was introduced to the latter's *Gemeinschaft und Gesellschaft*. This work certainly had an impact on him and formed one of the major underpinnings, together with the writings of Simmel and the German philosopher Oswald Spengler, for his later distinction between the urban civilization of the metropolis and simpler cultures. It is most likely through Park that Robert Redfield, Park's student and son-in-law, learned of Toennies' work, which he put to creative uses in his well-known studies of Mexican folk culture and its transformations.

The influence of Simmel and Toennies on Park's mind was reinforced by his chance encounter with the work of Bogdan A. Kistiakowski,[67] that far

[67] Cf. Georges Gurvitch, "Bogdan A. Kystiakovsky," in *Encyclopedia of the Social Sciences* (New York, Macmillan, 1938). Gurvitch points to Kistiakowski's importance for the sociology of law,

from well-known Russian social scientist referred to previously. This author's *Gesellschaft und Einzelwesen* (*Society and Individuals*, 1899) joined an emphasis on the centrality of "dynamic interaction" in the study of human society, which was derived from Simmel, with a neo-Kantian philosophy of science derived from Rickert and Windelband. The reading of Kistiakowski's book induced Park to go to Strasbourg and later to Heidelberg to study with Windelband.

From Windelband Park derived the distinction between *Geschichte und Naturwissenschaft* (*History and Natural Science*), to quote the title of Windelband's famous inaugural lecture upon becoming rector of the University of Strasbourg. Windelband argued there, as will be recalled from the chapter on Weber, that natural science seeks to formulate laws. It is a nomothetic science, while history, which is concerned with specific and unique events, is an idiographic discipline. Windelband was profoundly sceptical of attempts "to make of history a natural science" and argued that positivist attempts to do so had only led to "a few trivial generalities."[68] It seems characteristic of Park's style of thought that he reproduced a major part of Windelband's argument in his *Introduction* only blithely to proceed on the next page to argue that "sociology . . . seeks to arrive at natural law and generalization in regard to human nature and society, irrespective of time and place."[69] In other words, although he learned from Windelband to distinguish between the idiographic methods of history and the nomothetic methods appropriate for the study of nature, he did not share Windelband's scepticism regarding the possibility of discovering lawful uniformities in the world of man. His whole notion of a "natural history," of a history that disregards specific instances in order to concentrate on "natural" stages and cycles in the evolution of institutions, owes a good deal to the influence of Windelband, even though Windelband would probably have disapproved heartily of the notion.

PARK'S DEBT TO EVOLUTIONISM AND TO CONTINENTAL SOCIAL PSYCHOLOGY

The Darwinian influence on American sociology has already been dealt with in other chapters, and it is obvious that Park too stood generally under the shadow of Darwin's work, especially in regard to his thinking in ecology. There are thirty entries for Darwin in the index of the *Introduction*, and the book contains four selections from his work. The names of other evolutionists, including Ernst Haeckel and Thomas and Julian Huxley, also appear frequently in the indexes of Park's works.

Park refers to Spencer's principle of differentiation in his dissertation, and

while Sorokin, quoted earlier, stresses his views on interaction. Moreover, Gurvitch spells his name with a "y" while Sorokin spells it with an "i." I have followed Sorokin's and Park's usage. [68] Cf. the selection from Windelband's address in *Introduction*, pp. 8–10.

[69] *Ibid.*, p. 11.

there are references to him in other contexts as well as many entries in the index to the *Introduction*. It would not seem, however, that Park owed as much to the social evolutionists as to the biological. By the time he started writing, Spencer's vogue had already receded and Park seems to have been as averse to what was perceived as Spencer's unilinear evolutionism as were most of Park's contemporaries. Park's estimate of Comte appears to have been higher. The first page of the *Introduction* starts with the sentences: "Sociology first gained recognition as an independent science with the publication . . . of Auguste Comte's *Cours de philosophie positive*. Comte did not, to be sure, create sociology. He did give it a name, a program, and a place among sciences." Park did not follow Comte in all the vagaries of his doctrine, but he recognized in him the man who had first ventured to create a natural science of society—an enterprise to which Park wished to contribute his share.

In regard to Park's view of collective behavior of classes and sects, three names, prominently discussed in his dissertation, stand out: Scipio Sighele, the Italian criminologist and author of a book entitled *Psychologie des sectes,* and the French social psychologists Gustave Le Bon and Gabriel Tarde. Several selections by these men are included in the *Introduction,* as well as numerous references to them in the index. Park's perennial interest in crowds, sects, revivals, crazes, fads, and fashions may derive in the first instance from his voracious appetite for anything and everything on the social scene that might prove interesting, but it was also partly aroused, as his dissertation makes clear, by his reading of these men. Everett Hughes recently pointed out that Park was interested in Tarde not only as the author of works on imitation and on the mass and the public, but as a social psychologist who put forward the idea that "all society results from acts of faith," that is, from beliefs and expectations in the probable reaction of those to whom we address our wishes and desires.[70]

Park's Chicago colleagues and other contemporaries are best discussed in the next section where the social context of his work will be analyzed.

THE SOCIAL CONTEXT

Although Park lived into the 1940's, his formative years in the 1880's and 90's were roughly the same as those of Veblen, Cooley, and Mead. All these sociologists were the products of Midwestern progressivism and of the pragmatic revolt against intellectual formalism. In the first part of his career, Park devoted himself primarily to activities he considered paramount for implementing his progressivism. He became a sociologist only in the second part, when he joined the Department of Sociology of the University of Chicago.

[70] Hughes, "Preface" to *Society*.

Park's double career, first as a newspaperman and later as a member of the academy, illustrates the proposition that the audience to which a man addresses himself helps to shape his intellectual output. Each of his careers was marked by a different style of thought.

Throughout his early years, Park was dominated by the idea that more accurate reporting of the news would have beneficial effects on American democracy. He was committed to the belief that better knowledge of facts would greatly improve the quality of life and the democratic process in America. For that reason he threw himself with great ardor into his work as a newspaperman. These idealistic motivations must be underlined to understand Park's choice of an occupation, since the status of a newspaperman, especially one reporting on crime, corruption, and city slums, was not very high in his day. Although muckraking was coming into fashion just then, muckrakers were not likely to gain much repute in the eyes of the pillars of the community. Park's father, a well-to-do businessman who even disapproved of his son's going to college instead of joining the family business, was likely to have been appalled by his son's subsequent career choice. Furthermore, newspaper reporting was at the time a dead-end career; a very short peak period was followed by years of declining opportunity. A reporter either moved out of reporting into editorial work or he was steadily given less rewarding assignments. Park knew this to be the case: "The life of the average newspaperman seemed, at that time, to be about eight years. After that, if he remained in the profession, his value steadily declined."[71] It clearly required an unusual amount of idealism and devotion for the son of a well-to-do family to engage in such a career.

Park resolved to write for a wide public audience. It is significant that he chose to work for newspapers rather than for magazines. He shared John Dewey's faith in the common man and his belief that it was an urgent task to make citizens participate in a more active and informed way in the political process. Park apparently considered mass circulation media preferable to magazines, which, by and large, catered to a more restricted and more highly educated readership.

Much like Lincoln Steffens, but without his subjacent cynicism, Park believed that the public would respond to evidence of malfeasance, corruption, crime, and misery with concerned attention and concerted efforts at reform. That facts would make men free seems to have been his credo. His public may not always have been stirred to the righteous indignation that he wished to call forth, but it was certainly hungry to learn more of the facts, especially the ugly variety, which Park and his fellow muckraking newspaper crusaders poured forth in a steady stream.

Park worked as a newspaperman in a period when the Pulitzers and

[71] *Race and Culture,* p. v.

Hearsts created the modern press for mass circulation. They invented a type of newspaper that appealed to the millions of modern urban dwellers, with their hunger for news, and especially for news that exposed the lives and deeds of the high and mighty. Walter Lippmann once observed that there were two types of newspaper readers: "Those who find their own lives interesting and those who find their own lives dull, and wish to live a more thrilling existence."[72] Since in modern cities there are apparently more men who find their own lives dull, Pulitzer, who "invented muckraking," transformed the staid *New York World* into the most talked-about paper in New York within six short years, and Hearst made the then moribund *San Francisco Examiner* into the most widely read paper on the Pacific Coast.[73]

Park was, of course, aware that the new lords of the press were hardly activated by benevolent motives when they created the modern mass newspaper. Most of them wanted to make a fortune, not remake the democratic process. But Park held nevertheless to an idealistic, not to say idealized, notion of the functions of the press. Even some forty years after he quit working for the press he could still write:

> News performs somewhat the same function for the public that perception does for the individual man; that is to say, it does not so much inform as orient the public, giving each and all notice as to what is going on. . . . The first typical reaction of an individual to the news is likely to repeat it to someone. This makes conversation, arouses further comment, and perhaps starts a discussion. . . . The clash of opinions and sentiments which discussion inevitably invokes usually terminates in some sort of consensus or collective opinion.[74]

As a newspaperman, Park was devoted to what he felt to be the high calling of reporting as much relevant news as he could gather. He saw the fact-gatherer involved in the mission of educating the public, that andience of millions of common men who had to be brought nearer to decision-making power through closer involvement with the realities of the social and political scene. Fact-gathering to Park was not just a private passion; it was a public duty.

During the years Park worked for Booker T. Washington, he gave up regular writing for newspapers but wrote exposés on the abuses of colonialism, more particularly Belgian colonialism, for mass circulation magazines. Though he was now groping for a new profession, he was still thinking of himself as a highly skilled gatherer of facts, a muckraker with a Heidelberg degree. The decisive change in his career came one day in 1911 when Park met W. I. Thomas at Tuskegee. One may speculate as to what Thomas found attractive

[72] Quoted in *Society*, pp. 100–01. [73] *Ibid.*, p. 102. [74] *Ibid.*, p. 79.

in Park. He was most likely impressed by Park's wide knowledge of race relations in general and of the American Negro in particular, but knowledgeable journalists abounded then as they do now. Thomas may have sensed that Park, the student of James and Windelband, was a man who could do more than reporting; he could, given the proper stimulating environment, think conceptually. It is likely that Thomas was impressed by this potential ability in Park and judged him to be useful in his promising department.

The Department of Sociology at Chicago, common misconceptions to the contrary, was by no means only interested in fact-gathering; from the beginning it was groping for conceptual and theoretical formulations that would distinguish the discipline of sociology from applied social work on the one hand and from mere social reporting on the other. In Chicago, Park found a new value climate, and his Chicago colleagues, especially W. I. Thomas, strongly influenced his thinking.[75]

CHICAGO SOCIOLOGY AT THE BEGINNING OF THE CENTURY

The Department came into being when the president of the new University of Chicago invited Albion W. Small, President of Colby College in Maine, to move to the campus as Head Professor of Sociology and to found the first Department of Sociology in America.[76] Small was well trained in German philosophy, history, and political science, and his general outlook was colored by a strong reforming and melioristic bent. This he shared with the second professor of sociology, Charles R. Henderson, a former minister, who was appointed by the president of the university without consulting Small, perhaps to see to it that a proper Christian orientation would not be neglected in the Department. Theological concerns are evident in some of the early M.A. theses. Contemporary students might be amazed to learn that one could receive a sociology degree at Chicago with a thesis entitled "Stages in the Theological Development of Martin Luther." Nowadays one could only get a degree in the area by writing on the psychogenetic stages in his development. But while M.A. theses and Ph.D. dissertations continued to come forth on such religion-oriented topics as "The First Three Years of Paul's Career as a Christian," or "Social Policy of Chicago Churches," there also appeared more and more theses on "Factory Legislation for Women in the United States," "The Garbage Problem in Chicago," and similar topics. The Department was groping to shed some of its theological shell, to move closer to the problems of modern America and to attempts at solving them. In this respect the title

75 The "Preface" to *Introduction* stresses the indebtedness of the editors to Thomas "for the point of view and the scheme of organization" of the book.

76 The following pages are mainly based on Robert E. L. Faris, *Chicago Sociology, op. cit.,* and, in the case of W. I. Thomas, on Morris Janowitz' "Introduction" to Morris Janowitz, ed., *W. I. Thomas on Social Organization and Social Personality* (Chicago, The University of Chicago Press, 1966).

of one (1901) dissertation is revealing: "A Study of the Stock Yards Community at Chicago as a Typical Example of the Bearing of Modern Industry upon Democracy, with Constructive Suggestions."

The growing interest in problems of the city and the wider community, and the humanitarian and reforming concern of the Department, did not, however, result in an atheoretical bias. If anything, Small was inclined somewhat toward abstruse Germanic propensities for system-building and *Methodenstreit,* as the early volumes of *The American Journal of Sociology,* which Small founded and continued to edit for many years, make clear. To cite one instance, the *Journal* early published some of Simmel's major contributions in lucid translation by Small and thus indicated that it was by no means averse to considering highly abstract attempts to define sociology as an academic discipline.

The Department's twin concern in research and in theory was symbolized in the person of W. I. Thomas, who joined it as its fourth and youngest member in 1895 while still working on his doctorate. (The third member of the Department, George Vincent, the son of the founder of Chautauqua and like his father an enthusiastic proponent of popular and general education, made relatively little impact on the Department—although he co-authored a textbook with Small. Vincent left in 1911 to become President of the University of Minnesota, and later President of the Rockefeller Foundation.)

Thomas, an uncommonly vigorous, intellectually adventurous and productive thinker, soon became the most outstanding figure in the Department. Of southern Protestant and rural background, Thomas originally studied English literature and modern languages at the University of Tennessee, but decided, after having received his Ph.D., to go to Germany to study at Goettingen and Berlin. Here he became acquainted with the new field of ethnology and, more particularly, with the "folk psychology" of Lazarus and Steinthal. After returning to the United States to assume a professorship in English at Oberlin, and having been "strongly impressed by Spencer's sociology," he decided to go on leave from Oberlin and to become one of the first graduate students in the Chicago Department in 1893–94. He then gave up his professorship at Oberlin to become an instructor in sociology at Chicago and soon dominated the Department intellectually.

Strongly influenced by the tradition of German folk ethnology of careful reporting and accurate and objective observation, but also having a strong theoretical orientation, he gradually moved from traditional ethnographic research and empirical social psychology to a pronounced interest in the fusion of theory and empirical data in both social psychology and sociology. By the time he published his famous *Source Book for Social Origins* (1908) he had elaborated a theoretical approach, emphasizing the interplay between social organization and the subjective aspects of social reality. This approach was to guide his later masterwork, *The Polish Peasant in Europe and America,* which he published in collaboration with the Polish sociologist Florian Znaniecki in 1918–20. This monumental work is the first great classic in American empirical sociology. It was informed, especially in the lengthy "Methodological Note," by a degree of theoretical sophistication never before attained in a work of social research. Later critics were probably right in pointing out that the theoretical and empirical parts of the book were not as firmly joined as its authors believed. Some of their theoretical conceptualizations, such as the famous basic "Four Wishes," did not stand up well under critical scrutiny.[77] But despite its blemishes the work surely remains an enduring monument to that creative merger of empirical research and theoretical sophistication which even contemporary sociology only attains at rare moments. Thomas and Znaniecki self-consciously rejected the fallacy that any science ever consists in the accumulation of more facts. "A fact by itself," they wrote, "is already an abstraction; we isolate a certain limited aspect of the concrete process of becoming, rejecting, at least provisionally, all its indefinite complexity. The question is only whether we perform this abstraction methodically or not, whether we know what and why we accept and reject, or simply take uncritically the old abstraction of 'common sense.' "[78]

For a detailed discussion of *The Polish Peasant in Europe and America,* see the chapter on Thomas and Znaniecki, beginning on page 511.

UNIVERSITY CAREER

John Dewey is credited with saying that the instincts do not produce the institutions, but rather that the institutions produce the instincts. Whether this proposition is valid in this categorical form or not, it begins to make a good deal of sense when the word "instinct" is replaced by "personality." Park's career seems to testify that institutions help produce personalities. He became in many respects a very different person with a different intellectual outlook after he decided upon an academic career. This is not to say, of course, that there was a disjunction between his earlier and later concerns. That this was emphatically not the case can be seen in even a cursory glance at his academic writings. He continued to be vitally interested in the city, the news, race relations, and other problems of a similar order; in fact, he introduced these topics into the university curriculum and thereby made them respectable. Park did

[77] Everett Hughes writes in a personal communication (September 24, 1969): "When I was a graduate student, Wirth organized a dinner to meet Thomas once when Thomas was passing through Chicago. . . . The older students asked him questions about the four wishes. Thomas asked: 'Now which wishes did we finally use in the introduction to the *Polish Peasant?*' He seemed entirely unconcerned about any defense of them, but did indicate that Znaniecki always insisted on being systematic."

[78] W. I. Thomas and Florian Znaniecki, *The Polish Peasant in Europe and America* (New York, Alfred A. Knopf, 1927), Vol. I, p. 37.

not change his interest in the subject matter, but he altered his framework, his cast of mind, for dealing with it. Before his move into the academy Park had thought concretely; now he thought abstractly and conceptually. This change was already prefigured in his dissertation, his earliest publication addressed to an academic audience.

It will be recalled that Park wrote in an autobiographical fragment that upon coming to Chicago he found himself working on the elaboration of a theoretical system of classifications rather than, as he expected, on purely empirical research problems. "My contribution to sociology has been," he said, "not what I intended, not what my original interest would have indicated, but what I needed to make a systematic exploration of the social work [sic] in which I found myself. The problem I was interested in was always [i.e., always at Chicago, L.A.C.] theoretical rather than practical." The statement indicates that Park was well aware of the ways in which the university environment diverted him from his former interest in reporting and forced him to become, in effect, a sociological theorist. This shift in the focus of his attention and in his style of thought was clearly caused by the new audience of students and academic peers that he encountered when coming to Chicago.

Park himself observed that it was above all the needs of his graduate students that forced him to concern himself with conceptual and theoretical clarification. They often came to him with a rather unsophisticated aim to study "the facts" about some concrete social issue, and he had to explain that before they could study anything in the world of multifarious social phenomena they had to devise for themselves a conceptual framework in which to subsume those facts that were of relevance to what they intended to study. It was the concrete research needs of his students, as well as his own, that forced Park to think abstractly. He could have said about his theories what the great French theoretical physicist Pierre Duhem once said of his doctrine: "It has not been constructed through the sort of meditation that is hostile to concrete detail. It was born and matured in the daily practice of the science."[79]

Many of Park's conceptualizations—those concerning the relation of the ecological order to the social order, or those pertaining to the notions of social distance and prejudice, for example—underwent continuous revision and development in his mind. There are often very considerable differences between early and late formulations, which can be accounted for by the fact that Park rarely set out deliberately to write a theoretical essay. It was rather his custom to think about a conceptual issue in terms of concrete research problems raised by his students in those long sessions when he plotted out their areas of research and helped them devise the theoretical tools they needed for accomplishing their task. His work thus evolved almost literally through an interplay between him and an audience of eager students who stimulated his mind

[79] Quoted in Robert Dubin, *Theory Building* (New York, The Free Press, 1969), title page.

through questions that forced him to respond to them in a creative manner. His student audience led Park, or so it would seem, to develop his ideas in truly pragmatic fashion whenever the reality of research problems presented an obstacle that had to be overcome by creative conceptualization.

Students were not the only audience that pressed Park to conceptualize what had previously been only an array of facts in his mind. The University of Chicago, then as now, was an intellectually demanding place, jealously defending its academic eminence against all comers. Some of the most renowned men in American science and letters taught there. If the Department of Sociology wished to hold its own in the faculty as a whole, it had to validate its existence by more than mere empirical research unguided by theory. The Department had developed because of Small's intelligent realization that the growth of sociology would be inhibited by premature doctrinal closure. The sociology department at Brown under Lester Ward and at Yale under William Graham Sumner had shown the debilitating consequences of concentrating upon the elaboration of the systems of their founders. Small made a crucially important decision when he encouraged the Department's students to venture outside into the complex world of social research. But it was also true that mere fact-gathering would have diminished the stature of the Department in the eyes of powerful neighboring departments and disciplines. When sociologists cast an eye toward the Department of Philosophy, where Dewey and Mead initiated their students into the complexities of the pragmatic theory of truth, or the Department of Political Science, where Charles Merriam and later Harold Lasswell developed a political theory that was to dominate the field for many years, they must have been acutely aware that they had to offer more than mere fact-gathering. Instruction in the art of rummaging around in the laboratory of the city of Chicago for bits and oddments of interesting information was not enough. Representing a discipline that had just barely won academic respectability, they felt the need to underpin their research interests by a more abstract framework of ideas that would gain a measure of recognition from colleagues in other fields. Hence expectations—not always outspoken, to be sure, but implicit in discussions with his colleagues—regarding the focus of sociology may have been almost as powerful in directing Park's thought styles as were the demands of his students. As these two sets of expectations merged in the mind of Park they led him to elaborate the conceptual framework that enabled him to train a plethora of brilliant students and to make a lasting impact, both directly and through them, on the future development of sociology in America.

IN SUMMARY

During the years of his teaching at Chicago and after, Park participated in various social research projects outside the University and served on many social science boards and committees. He was respectfully listened to in the world of foundations and research enterprises. His audience was therefore wider than the university. But the bulk of his publications appeared in scholarly journals or in books primarily oriented toward academic readers. He wrote with an eye for gaining recognition, not only from his Chicago colleagues but also from such men as Cooley at Michigan or Giddings at Columbia, and he occasionally wished to be heard by educational decision-makers. Having started his career with the aim of disseminating the news among a wide public of informed citizens, Park resolved, after having joined the academy, to rely almost exclusively on an academic audience. Whatever the loss to the citizenry, the discipline of sociology can count itself lucky for the change of careers upon which Park resolved after meeting with Thomas at Tuskegee.

Vilfredo Pareto

1848-1923

THE WORK[1]

Toward the end of his life Pareto wrote:

> Driven by the desire to bring an indispensable complement to the studies of political economy and inspired by the example of the natural sciences, I determined to begin my *Treatise,* the sole purpose of which—I say sole and I insist upon the point—is to seek experimental reality, by the application to the social sciences of the methods which have proved themselves in physics, in chemistry, in astronomy, in biology, and in other such sciences.[2]

In this statement Pareto summarized his aim in writing his major sociological work, *The Treatise on General Sociology.*[3]

Pareto's ambition was to construct a system of sociology analogous in its essential features to the generalized physico-chemical system which J. Willard Gibbs formulated in his *Thermodynamics.*[4] A physico-chemical system is an isolated aggregate of individual components such as water and alcohol. The factors characterizing the system are interdependent so that a change in one

[1] This chapter owes a great deal to the interpretations of Pareto's thought by Talcott Parsons and Raymond Aron. It could not have been written without the aid of the following: Talcott Parsons, *The Structure of Social Action* (New York, The Free Press, 1949), Chapters 5 to 7, and Talcott Parsons, "Pareto's Central Analytical Scheme" in James E. Meisel, ed., *Pareto and Mosca* (Englewood Cliffs, New Jersey, Prentice-Hall, 1965), pp. 71–88; Raymond Aron, *Main Currents in Sociological Thought* (New York, Basic Books, 1967), Vol. II, pp. 99–176. I have also profited from S. E. Finer's "Introduction" to S. E. Finer, ed., *Vilfredo Pareto, Sociological Writings* (New York, Praeger, 1966). For a short discussion, see Talcott Parsons, "Vilfredo Pareto," in *The International Encyclopedia of the Social Sciences* (New York, Macmillan, 1968).

[2] Quoted in George C. Homans and Charles P. Curtis, Jr., *An Introduction to Pareto* (New York, Alfred A. Knopf, 1934), p. 291.

[3] Pareto broke up his *Treatise* into 2612 numbered paragraphs. I shall refer to these numbers in all my quotations since this will allow the reader to refer to either the full translation of the *Treatise* edited by Arthur Livingston and entitled *The Mind and Society,* 4 vols. (New York, Harcourt Brace Jovanovich, 1935), or two volumes of selections, which have recently become available: Joseph Lopreato, ed., *Vilfredo Pareto: Selections from His Treatise* (New York, Crowell Collier, 1965), and E. S. Finer, *op. cit.* Finer's selections cover not only the *Treatise* but also other works, and he makes use of new translations by Derick Mirfin rather than using the translation in *The Mind and Society*. The latter work has been reissued under the original title, *Treatise on General Sociology* (New York, Dover, 1963).

[4] Cf. Lawrence J. Henderson, *Pareto's General Sociology* (Cambridge, Harvard University Press, 1935), p. 10 and *passim.*

part of the system leads to adjustive changes in its other parts. Pareto had a similar conception of the social system, in which the "molecules" were individuals with interests, drives, and sentiments "analogous to the mixtures of chemical compounds found in nature."[5] Pareto's general sociology sets forth the concept of social system as a framework for analyzing mutually dependent variations among a number of variables determining human conduct.

The treatise does not attempt to cover all the variables that are part of the social system. Only nonrational aspects of action are considered in any detail. Pareto's interest in sociology arose out of his previous concern with economics and out of his realization that the variables with which economics operated were insufficient to account for much, if not most, of human behavior. The field of economics, he reasoned, especially in its modern form, had limited itself to a single aspect of human action: rational or logical action in pursuit of the acquisition of scarce resources. Pareto turned to sociology when he became convinced that human affairs were largely guided by nonlogical, nonrational actions, which were excluded from consideration by the economists. For this reason he attempts in his *Treatise* to understand the nonrational aspects of human behavior, omitting almost completely the rational aspects which he considered to be treated adequately in his economic writings.

Pareto searched for a rational accounting of the prevalence of human irrationality. He did not intend to discard economic theory, in the manner of Veblen, but rather to supplement its abstractions with sociological and social-psychological concepts that would help toward an understanding of those aspects of human conduct that had proved recalcitrant to economic analysis. It is this analytical distinction between rational and nonrational elements of action and not a classification of concrete behavior that Pareto aimed at: "It is not actions as we find them in the concrete that we are called upon to classify, but the elements constituting them."[6]

LOGICAL AND NONLOGICAL ACTION

Pareto defines logical actions as those "that use means appropriate to ends and which logically link means with ends."[7] This logical conjunction of means with ends must hold not only for the subject performing them, "but [also] from the standpoint of other persons who have a more extensive knowledge."[8] Logical actions are those actions that are both subjectively and objectively logical. Nonlogical action is simply taken to mean all action not falling within Pareto's explicit definition of the logical; it is a residual category.

Pareto follows what he sees as an inductive procedure in developing his conceptual framework for the analysis of the nonlogical element in human action. After considering a wide array of cases in both past and contemporary history, and taking as his evidence many types of ideologies—beliefs and doc-

[5] *Treatise*, 2080. [6] *Ibid.*, 148. [7] *Ibid.*, 150. [8] *Ibid.*

trines that have allegedly moved men to action—Pareto concluded that these nonscientific belief systems and theories were only rarely determinants of action but instead were most frequently the expression of deep-seated sentiments. Pareto argued that although men most often fail to engage in logical action, they have a strong tendency to "logicalize" their behavior, that is, to make it appear as the logical result of a set of ideas. In fact, what accounts for most action is not the set of beliefs that is used to rationalize or "logicalize" it, but rather a pre-existing state of mind, a basic human sentiment. For example, a man has a horror of murder. Therefore, he will not commit murder. He tells himself, however, that "the Gods punish murderers" and imagines that this is why he refrains from murder.[9] If we designate human sentiments, the basic sources of nonlogical action, as A, the theories relating to action as B, and action itself as C, we realize that, although A, B, and C are mutually interrelated, A independently influences B and C far more than B influences C. To think otherwise, Pareto argues, is to fall into the rationalistic fallacy that has been the bane of most previous social theory.

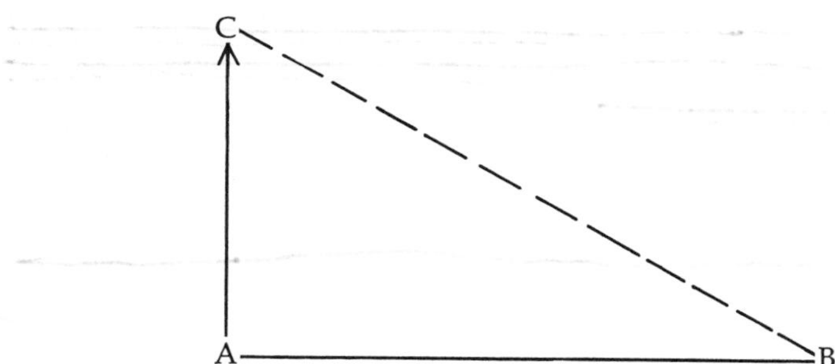

Whereas B and C, nonlogical theories and overt acts respectively, are directly observable, human sentiments or states of mind can only be inferred. Pareto was not prepared to analyze these basic sentiments, but left this task to psychologists. "Nonlogical actions originate chiefly in definite psychic states, sentiments, subconscious feelings, and the like. It is the province of psychology to investigate such psychic states. Here we start with them as data of fact, without going beyond that."[10]

Pareto concentrated his attention on conduct that reflects these psychic states, and, more particularly, the theories and belief systems that serve to justify and rationalize nonlogical action. One of his central concerns is with an exhaustive critique of nonscientific theories associated with action. He submits metaphysical, religious, and moral systems to a destructive analysis and shows to his own satisfaction that all of them, despite their pretensions to the

[9] *Ibid.*, 162. [10] *Ibid.*, 161.

contrary, have nothing at all in common with scientific theories. Notions such as "liberty," "equality," "progress," or "the General Will" are as vacuous as the myths and magical incantations with which savages rationalize their actions. None is verifiable, all are fictions that serve mainly to clothe and make respectable the actions of men. Even though Pareto does not deny that such myths may upon occasion influence conduct, he mainly highlights those instances in which they serve merely as masks. He sees unmasking as one of the main tasks of the social analyst. "We have to see to what extent reality is disfigured in the theories and descriptions of it that one finds in the literature of thought. We have an image in a curved mirror; our problem is to discover the form of the object so altered by refraction."[11] As will become clear later, such unmasking served Pareto's ideological purposes and not only his scientific aims.

RESIDUES AND DERIVATIONS

Pareto's attempt to unmask nonscientific theories and belief systems led him to make a distinction between changing elements accounting for these theories, which he termed *derivations*, and residual, relatively permanent elements, which he termed *residues.* The notion of residues has often been misunderstood as merely a fancy term for instinct and as corresponding to the basic sentiments discussed earlier. Pareto himself brought forth this misunderstanding by occasionally referring to residues as instincts. It seems nevertheless that he conceived of residues as *manifestations* of sentiments or as corresponding to them, rather than as their equivalents.

Residues are intermediary between the sentiments we cannot know directly and the belief systems and acts that can be known and analyzed. Furthermore, residues are related to man's instincts but they do not cover all of them, since we can only discover those instincts that give rise to rationalization in theories while others must remain hidden.[12]

> The element *a* [i.e., the residues] corresponds . . . to certain instincts of man . . . and it is probably because of its correspondence to instincts that it is virtually constant in social phenomena. The element *b* [i.e., the derivations] represents the work of the mind in accounting for *a*. That is why *b* is much more variable, as reflecting the imagination. But if the element *a* corresponds to certain instincts, it is far from reflecting them all. . . . We analyzed specimens of thinking on the look-out for constant elements. We may therefore have found only the instincts that underlay those reasonings. There was no chance of our meeting along that road instincts which were not so logicalized. Unaccounted for still would be simple appetites, tastes, inclinations, and in social relationships that very important class called "interests."[13]

[11] *Ibid.*, 253. [12] Aron, *op. cit.*, p. 120. [13] *Treatise*, 850–51.

A man's appetite or taste for, say, pork chops, does not fall into the category of residues in Pareto's scheme. If, however, a man constructs a theory according to which Chinese cooking is superior to American cooking, then Pareto would be moved to investigate the residues underlying the elaboration of such theoretical justification.[14]

Pareto arrives at his distinctions between residues and derivations by the following procedure: He investigates doctrines that are associated with action, for example, Christian religious doctrine or liberal political theory. From these theories he separates those elements that correspond to the standards of logico-experimental science. Next, he separates the remaining nonscientific elements into constants (residues) and variables (derivations).[15] Derivations only arise when there is reasoning, argument, and ideological justification. When these are present, Paretian analysis looks for the underlying relatively constant elements (residues).

For example, we find in all ages a great variety of verbalizations and doctrines connected with the sexual sphere. These may take the form of pornographic literature or of the denunciation of sexual license. There are strict and permissive theories about proper sexual conduct. Ascetic doctrines condemn what hedonistic doctrines extol. But throughout all these manifold derivations runs a common sexual residue, which remains remarkably stable at all times. Styles, modes, fashions, and ethical theories about the sexual sphere vary immensely, but a uniform sexual nucleus always crops up in a variety of new doctrinal disguises.

A long quotation from the *Treatise* will convey the characteristic flavor of Pareto's analytical procedure, and show at the same time how his political passions override in many instances his scientific intent.

> The weakness of the humanitarian religion does not lie in the logico-experimental deficiencies of its derivations. From that standpoint they are no better and no worse than the derivations of other religions. But some of these contain residues beneficial to individuals and society, whereas the humanitarian religion is sadly lacking in such residues. But how can a religion that has the good of humanity solely at heart . . . be so destitute in residues correlated with social welfare? . . . The principles from which the humanitarian doctrine is logically derived in no way correspond with the facts. They merely express in objective form a subjective sentiment of asceticism. The intent of sincere humanitarians is to do good to society, just as the intent of the child who kills a bird by too much fondling is to do good to the bird. We are not . . . forgetting that humanitarianism has had some socially desirable effects. . . . But . . . humanitarianism is worthless from the logico-experimental point of view. . . . And so for the democratic religion in general. The many varieties of Socialism, Syndicalism, Radicalism, Tolstoyism, pacifism, humanitarianism, Solidarism, and so on, form a sum

[14] Aron, *op. cit.*, p. 121. [15] *The Structure of Social Action*, pp. 199–200.

> that may be said to belong to the democratic religion, much as there was a sum of numberless sects in the early days of the Christian religion. We are now witnessing the rise and dominance of the democratic religion just as the men of the first centuries of our era witnessed the rise of the Christian religion and the beginnings of its dominion. The two phenomena present many significant analogies. To get at their substance we have to brush derivations aside and reach down to residues. The social value of both those two religions lies not in the least in their respective theologies, but in the sentiments that they express. As regards determining the social value of Marxism, to know whether Marx's theory of "surplus value" is false or true is about as important as knowing whether and how baptism eradicates sin in trying to determine the social value of Christianity—and that is of no importance at all."[16]

The message that Pareto hammers home on many a page of the *Treatise* is this: Never take ideas at their face value; do not look at people's mouths but try to probe deeper to the real springs of their actions.

> A politician is inspired to champion the theory of "solidarity" by an ambition to obtain money, power, distinctions. . . . If the politician were to say, "Believe in solidarity because if you do it means money for me," they would get many laughs and few votes. He therefore has to take his stand on principles that are acceptable to his prospective constituents. . . . Oftentimes the person who would persuade others begins by persuading himself; and even if he is moved in the beginning by thoughts of personal advantage, he comes eventually to believe that his real interest is the welfare of others.[17]

Although men have used an infinite number and variety of derivations in order to justify or logicalize their actions, Pareto argues that six classes of residues have remained almost constant throughout the long span of Western history. For this reason he surmises that the major classes of residues correspond closely to certain basic human "instincts" or propensities. The six classes of residues are as follows:

I. Instinct for Combinations.
II. Group Persistences (Persistence of Aggregates).
III. Need of Expressing Sentiments by External Acts (Activity, Self-Expression).
IV. Residues Connected with Sociality.
V. Integrity of the Individual and His Appurtenances.
VI. The Sex Residue.

Pareto intends to show that the same residue can give rise to a great variety of belief systems or derivations, and that men deceive themselves when they believe that they take a given course of action on the basis of a particular

[16] *Treatise,* 1859. [17] *Ibid.,* 854.

theory in which they happen to believe. For example, "A Chinese, a Moslem, a Calvinist, a Catholic, a Kantian, a Hegelian, a Materialist, all refrain from stealing; but each gives a different explanation for his conduct."[18] In view of such variable explanations of a constant characteristic, Pareto concluded that the real cause of the behavior has to be found in the constancy of a residue underlying these different derivations. He reasoned that all these adherents of different schools of thought have in common the need to maintain the integrity of their personality and to preserve their self-regard. Therefore, Class V residues explain their conduct.

Everywhere, and at all times, men believe in the objective reality of gods or spirits, of "progress," "freedom," or "justice." The names and embodiments of these entities change, as do the religious, philosophical, and moral theories that explain these beliefs. But it will always be found that, however expressed, the common belief in such entities is rooted in a stable common element, in this case residue II, the "conservative" tendency to group persistence, to social integration.

Pareto argued repeatedly that it is useless, even a waste of time, to discuss the truth of a doctrine with an adherent to it. Christianity has not been destroyed by arguments disputing the historical reality of Jesus, and Catholic patriotism in France was not hurt by assertions that Joan of Arc was a hysteric.[19] Only a scientific strategy that allows us to trace the multiplicity of belief systems and doctrines to their common source in basic residues can advance science and lead to a measure of enlightenment.

Whether Pareto's explanations amount to more than pseudo-explanations is an open question. I would agree with Raymond Aron who believes that they have much in common with the reasoning of Molière's quack physician who explains the effects of opium by its dormitive powers. As Aron says with characteristic wit, "One does not dare to say [Pareto's] results are false, but perhaps they are not very instructive."[20] Yet before attempting to pass a judgment, one has to realize that Pareto's theory of residues served him not only as a way of explaining theories and belief systems, but also as a means of explaining social movements, social change, and the dynamics of history. Before we turn to this matter, two other Paretian notions, the distinction between types of nonlogical theories, and the distinction between subjective intentions and objective consequences of action need to be examined.

[18] *Ibid.*, 1416. [19] *Ibid.*, 1455–56. [20] *Ibid.*, 173.

TWO TYPES OF NONLOGICAL THEORIES

Commentators often have mistakenly assumed that in Pareto's scheme all nonlogical theories are viewed equally as only reflections or manifestations of underlying propensities. This, however, is not the case. He was careful to distinguish between 1) pseudo-scientific theories and 2) "theories transcending experience."[21]

In the first, Pareto argued, we deal with theories that pretend to scientific status but demonstrably fail to meet the test of scientific evidence. Such theories, he believed, are ultimately anchored in biological needs, drives, and propensities and are directly explainable in terms of the residues underlying them. They are, in fact, rationalizations. When it comes to "theories transcending experience," religious theories, for example, Pareto argued differently. These do not pretend to have scientific status; it is pointless, therefore, to show that they depart from scientific standards. Such theories represent, instead, cultural values and the cultural dimension in human action. They are value-attitudes. When Pareto says that residues are "manifested" in pseudo-scientific theories, he seems to mean that these indicate the presence of such residues, and testify to their power of deception. But when he talks about the manifestation of residues, in theories transcending experience, he seems to mean that they are "manifested" or expressed in symbolic ritual behavior.

Pareto was well aware that scientific method could not in itself determine the ends of human action. "A society determined exclusively by 'reason' does not and cannot exist . . . because the data of the problem that presumably is to be solved by logico-experimental reasoning are entirely unknown."[22] Hence, the ends, as distinct from the means, of human action find expression in "theories transcending experience." To be sure, these can ultimately be traced to the operation of residues, and, in the last analysis, to basic human sentiments; yet Pareto seems to have recognized that the human quest for "meaning" as it manifests itself in "theories transcending experience" must be a basic datum for any analysis of social systems. He did have a powerful tendency to "reduce" such quests to underlying factors, yet he was also eager to point to the indispensability of symbolic elements for maintaining a social system and for directing the goals of human action. Although his tendency to "debunk" informs a good deal of his work, he was by no means oblivious to the central importance of the normative sphere. This may be the reason he has been quoted to say that he hoped his *Treatise* would not be read too widely, since this would help undermine necessary moral values.

[21] This section relies mainly on Talcott Parsons' interpretation. [22] *Treatise,* 2143.

SUBJECTIVE INTENTIONS AND OBJECTIVE CONSEQUENCES

Most of Pareto's concrete analysis in the bulk of the *Treatise* is concerned with the springs of action of individual actors. Coming from economics, a discipline that had paid almost exclusive attention to rational action, he was moved to supplement the economists' system of abstraction with a sociological system emphasizing the nonlogical drives to action. Yet, while focusing most of the time on the actor's motivations, Pareto was also sensitive to the need for analyzing the objective consequences of conduct. Subjective intentions and objective consequences, he stressed, do not always coincide.

Pareto was especially attentive to those instances in which men engage in what they conceive to be logical actions but which the outside observer sees as having no logical end, or, perhaps more importantly, which he finds culminating in consequences other than those that were pursued by the actors. People believe that by means of certain rites and practices they may quell a storm or bring rain. Objectively we know that natural phenomena cannot be produced in this way; yet it may well be that by engaging in such practices the believers experience a euphoric sense of power that makes them better able to withstand the existential trials and tribulations in which they are involved and strengthens the bonds of the social system in which they participate. In this case, a belief system that is patently false still has a high degree of personal or social utility. More generally, "The experimental truth of a theory and its social utility are different things. A theory that is experimentally true may now be advantageous, now detrimental to society; and the same applies to a theory that is experimentally false."[23] "A theory may be in accord with experience and yet be harmful to society, or in disaccord with experience and yet beneficial to society."[24] The assessment of social utility must proceed apart from the investigation of the logical status of theories and of the subjective intentions of individual actors.

THE LIONS AND THE FOXES

In the last part of his *Treatise,* Pareto attempts to show how the distribution of residues in a population is related not only to its belief systems and intellectual life, but also, and most importantly, to the state of the polity and of the economy. Here Pareto deals only with the first two residues, those of "combinations" and of "persistence." Residues of the first type impel men to system making, that is, to elaborate pseudo-logical combinations of ideas. Class I residues lead men to manipulate various elements found in experience. They are at the root of magical practices to control, as the case may be, the weather,

[23] *Ibid.,* 249. [24] Index-Summary IIu in *The Mind and Society.*

the course of a disease, or the love of a maiden. At more complex levels, Class I residues lead people to engage in large-scale financial manipulation—to merge, combine, and recombine enterprises. At still more complex levels, they explain the urge of politicians and statesmen to join and fuse political forces, to make political deals, and to build political empires. Men primarily moved by Class I residues are like Machiavelli's "foxes," capable of experiment, innovation, and departure from common use, but lacking fidelity to principles and to those conservative virtues that insure stability.

The conservative forces of "social inertia" are represented by men in whom the second class of residues (persistence of aggregates) predominate. Such men have powerful feelings of loyalty to family, tribe, city, and nation; they display class solidarity, patriotism, and religious zeal; and they are not afraid of using force when necessary. These are Machiavelli's "lions."

In the world of his day, more particularly in Italy and France, Pareto believed that the foxes were in the ascendancy. The political and economic scene was dominated by political wheelers and dealers, by unscrupulous lawyers and intellectual sophists, by speculators and manipulators of men. Pareto's concern was that if this condition were to remain unchecked, social equilibrium would be fundamentally upset and the social order would totter. Yet he felt that the chances were high that, as had so often happened in the past, men of conservatism and persistence would finally rise, sweep the reign of foxes aside, and make sure that stability could again come into its own. Faith, patriotism, and national honor would once again claim the allegiance of all.

After a certain period of time, the foxes will again infiltrate into the seats of government, for their mental skills and expertise cannot be dispensed with for long. They will slowly undermine the certainties that the lions uphold, and their corrosive intelligence will undermine the uncomplicated faith of the militant lions. As a result, the wheel will come full circle and a new age of deceit and manipulation will dawn.

All belief in progress or evolution was for Pareto so much nonsense. Human society was bound to repeat forever the same cycle from rule by lions to rule by foxes and back again. It is characterized by a continually shifting but ultimately unchanging equilibrium. There is nothing new in history; it is only the record of human folly. Utopia is, literally, nowhere.

THE THEORY OF ELITES AND THE CIRCULATION OF ELITES

It is a basic axiom for Pareto that people are unequal physically, as well as intellectually and morally. In society as a whole, and in any of its particular strata and groupings, some people are more gifted than others. Those who are most capable in any particular grouping are the elite.

> Let us assume that in every branch of human activity each individual is given an index which stands as a sign of his capacity, very much the same

> way grades are given . . . in examinations in school. The highest type of lawyer, for instance, will be given 10. The man who does not get a client will be given 1—reserving zero for the man who is an out-and-out idiot. To the man who has made his millions—honestly or dishonestly as the case may be—we will give 10. To the man who has earned his thousands we will give 6; to such as will just manage to keep out of the poor-house, 1, keeping zero for those who get in. To the woman "in politics" . . . who has managed to infatuate a man of power and play a part in the man's career, we shall give some higher number such as 8 or 9; to the strumpet who merely satisfies the senses of such a man and exerts no influence on public affairs, we shall give zero. To the clever rascal who knows how to fool people and still keep clear of the penitentiary, we shall give 8, 9, or 10, according to the number of geese he has plucked. . . . To the sneak-thief who snatches a piece of silver from a restaurant table and runs away into the arms of a policeman, we shall give 1.[25]

The term elite has no moral or honorific connotations in Pareto's usage. It denotes simply "a class of the people who have the highest indices in their branch of activity."[26] Pareto argues that "It will help if we further divide that [elite] class into two classes: a *governing elite,* comprising individuals who directly or indirectly play some considerable part in government, and a *non-governing* elite, comprising the rest."[27] His main discussion focuses on the governing elite.

There is a basic ambiguity in Pareto's treatment of the notion of the elite. In some passages, as in the one quoted above, it would appear that those occupying elite positions are, by definition, the most qualified. But there are many other passages where Pareto asserts that people are assigned elite positions by virtue of being so labeled. That is, men assigned elite positions may not have the requisite capabilities, while others not so labeled may have them.

> The label "lawyer" is affixed to a man who is supposed to know something about the law and often does, though sometimes again he is an ignoramus. So the governing elite contains individuals who wear labels appropriate to political offices of a certain altitude—ministers, Senators, Deputies . . . and so on—making the apposite exceptions for those who have found their way into that exalted community without possessing qualities corresponding to the labels they wear. . . . Wealth, family, or social connections also help in many other cases to win the label of the elite in general, or of the governing elite in particular, for persons who otherwise hold no claim upon it.[28]

It would seem that Pareto believed that only in perfectly open societies, those with perfect social mobility, would elite position correlate fully with superior capacity. Only under such conditions would the governing elite, for example,

[25] *Treatise,* 2027. [26] *Ibid.,* 2031. [27] *Ibid.,* 2032. [28] *Ibid.,* 2035–36.

consist of the people most capable of governing. The actual social fact is that obstacles such as inherited wealth, family connections, and the like prevent the free circulation of individuals through the ranks of society, so that those wearing an elite label and those possessing highest capacity tend to diverge to greater or lesser degrees.

Given the likelihood of divergencies between ascribed elite position and actual achievement and capacity, Pareto is a passionate advocate of maximum social mobility and of careers open to all. He saw the danger that elite positions that were once occupied by men of real talent would in the course of time be preempted by men devoid of such talent.

> In the beginning, military, religious, and commercial aristocracies and plutocracies . . . must have constituted parts of the governing elite and sometimes made up the whole of it. The victorious warrior, the prosperous merchant, the opulent plutocrat, were men of such parts, each in his own field, as to be superior to the average individual. Under those circumstances the label corresponded to an actual capacity. But as time goes by, considerable, sometimes very considerable, differences arise between the capacity and the label. . . . Aristocracies do not last. . . . History is a graveyard of aristocracies. . . . They decay not in numbers only. They decay also in quality, in the sense that they lose their vigor, that there is a decline in the proportions of the residues which enabled them to win their power and hold it. The governing class is restored not only in numbers, but . . . in quality, by families rising from the lower classes and bringing with them the vigor and the proportions of residues necessary for keeping themselves in power. . . . Potent cause of disturbance in the equilibrium is the accumulation of superior elements in the lower classes and, conversely, of inferior elements in the higher classes.[29]

When governing or nongoverning elites attempt to close themselves to the influx of newer and more capable elements from the underlying population, when the circulation of elites is impeded, social equilibrium is upset and the social order will decay. Pareto argued that if the governing elite does not "find ways to assimilate the exceptional individuals who come to the front in the subject classes,"[30] an imbalance is created in the body politic and the body social until this condition is rectified, either through a new opening of channels of mobility or through violent overthrow of an old ineffectual governing elite by a new one that is capable of governing.

Not only are intelligence and aptitudes unequally distributed among the members of society, but the residues as well. Under ordinary circumstances, the "conservative" residues of Class II preponderate in the masses and thus make them submissive. The governing elite, however, if it is to be effective, must consist of individuals who have a strong mixture of both Class I and Class II elements.

[29] *Ibid.*, 2052–54. [30] *Ibid.*, 2179.

> A predominance of interests that are primarily industrial and commercial enriches the ruling class in individuals who are shrewd, astute, and well-provided with combination instincts; and divests it of individuals of the sturdy impulsive type. . . . One might guess that if cunning, chicanery, combinations were all there was to government, the dominion of the class in which Class I residues by far predominate would last over a very, very long period. . . . But governing is also a matter of force, and as Class I residues grow stronger and Class II residues weaker, the individuals in power become less and less capable of using force, so that an unstable equilibrium results and revolutions occur. . . . The masses, which are strong in Class II residues, carry them upwards into the governing class either by gradual infiltration or in sudden spurts through revolutions.[31]

The ideal governing class contains a judicious mixture of lions and foxes, of men capable of decisive and forceful action and of others who are imaginative, innovative, and unscrupulous. When imperfections in the circulation of governing elites prevent the attainment of such judicious mixtures among the governing, regimes either degenerate into hidebound and ossified bureaucracies incapable of renewal and adaptation, or into weak regimes of squabbling lawyers and rhetoricians incapable of decisive and forceful action. When this happens, the governed will succeed in overthrowing their rulers and new elites will institute a more effective regime.

What applies to political regimes applies to the economic realm as well. In this field, "speculators" are akin to the foxes and "rentiers" to the lions. Speculators and rentiers do not only have different interests but they reflect different temperaments and different residues. Neither is very good at using force, but they both otherwise fall roughly into the same dichotomous classes that explain political fluctuations.

> In the speculator group Class I residues predominate, in the rentier group, Class II residues. . . . The two groups perform functions of differing utility in society. The [speculator] group is primarily responsible for change, for economic and social progress. The [rentier] group, instead, is a powerful element in stability, and in many cases counteracts the dangers attending the adventurous capers of the [speculators]. A society in which the [rentiers] almost exclusively predominate remains stationary and, as it were, crystallized. A society in which [the speculators] predominate lacks stability, lives in a state of shaky equilibrium that may be upset by a slight accident from within or from without.[32]

Like in the governing elite where things work best when both residues of Class I and Class II are represented, so in the economic order maximum effectiveness is attained when both rentiers and speculators are present, each pro-

[31] *Ibid.*, 2227. [32] *Ibid.*, 2235.

viding a balance by checking the excesses of the other. Pareto implies throughout that a judicious mixture in top elites of men with Class I and Class II residues makes for the most stable economic structure, as well as for the most enduring political structure.

SOCIAL UTILITY "OF" AND "FOR" COLLECTIVES

In his efforts to highlight those aspects of a social system that are not amenable to economic investigation and hence require complementary analysis on a specifically sociological plane, Pareto was led to make the key distinction between the maximum utility *of* and the maximum utility *for* a community. The latter is the point where each individual has attained the maximum possible private satisfaction. The former refers to the maximum utility of the group or society as a whole, not of individuals. Only the second type can be treated by the economist; he can consider only the wants of individuals who are dissimilar and whose satisfactions therefore cannot be added up to yield a measure of the maximum utility for the entire group or society. "In pure economics a community cannot be regarded as a person."[33] In contrast, in sociology, Pareto argues, "[A community] can be considered, if not as a person, at least as a unity."[34] The maximum utility to a society can be analyzed sociologically, and may not necessarily coincide with the maximum satisfaction of the wants of its individual members. What is more, there may well exist divergencies between utilities accruing to a total social system and maximum satisfactions of sub-groupings, such as social classes. For example, in regard to an increase in population, the utility *of* the community and the utility *for* the community may well diverge.

> If we think of the utility *of* the community as regards prestige and military power, we will find it advisable to increase population to the fairly high limit beyond which the nation would be diminished and its stock decay. But if we think of the maximum utility *for* the community, we find a limit that is much lower. Then we have to see in what proportions the various social classes profit by the increase in prestige and military power, and in what different proportion they pay for their particular sacrifices.[35]

According to Pareto, the distinction between utility *of* and utility *for* a community is often deliberately obfuscated for manipulative purposes by ruling groups who make it appear as if subject individuals or sub-groups would benefit from certain measures when this is in fact by no means the case.

> The ruling classes oftentimes show a confusion of a problem of maximum utility *of* the community and a problem of maximum utility *for* the com-

[33] *Ibid.*, 2133. [34] *Ibid.* [35] *Ibid.*, 2134.

> munity. They [try] to make the "subject" classes believe that there is an indirect utility which, when properly taken into account, turns the sacrifice required of them into a gain. . . . In reality, in cases such as these, nonlogical impulse can serve to induce the subject classes to forget the maximum of individual utility, and work for the maximum utility *of* the community, or merely *of* the ruling classes.[36]

Or, to give another example, maximum wealth may be considered a prime goal for the society as a whole, but this may not coincide with the satisfaction of some of its members and may create great inequalities and major pockets of poverty in the society. Inversely, a state in which the greatest number of individuals attain the maximum of satisfaction may mark a point of societal decay and national decline.

By making his distinction between the utility *for* and the utility *of* a community, Pareto moved from classical liberal economics, where it was assumed that total benefits for a community simply involved a sum total of the benefits derived by each individual member ("the greatest happiness of the greatest number"), to a sociological point of view in which society is treated as a total unit and sub-groups or individuals are considered from the viewpoint of their contribution to the overall system as well as in terms of their peculiar wants and desires. System needs and individual or sub-group needs are distinguished.

It must be stressed that what is considered to be of maximum utility to society as a whole in fact involves subjective judgments rather than objective assessments. Those who run the affairs of the society, the governing elite, will determine what benefits the society as a whole needs, and they will decide this in terms of their own interests, desires, values, and beliefs.

Pareto's thought converged with that of Durkheim. Both rejected utilitarian and individualistic notions and stressed the need to consider the requirements of social systems, *qua* systems. They diverged, however, insofar as Durkheim believed that system needs could be determined objectively and scientifically, whereas Pareto contended that judgments of such needs derived from the desires and propensities, as well as the values and norms of those who were in command.

SUMMARY AND ASSESSMENT

Although Pareto seems to have believed that his theory of residues and derivations constituted his major contribution to sociological thought, it would seem difficult to concur in his appraisal. Writing from the perspective of an age that has been deeply marked by Freud, contemporary analysts feel by and large that the doctrine of residues and derivations lacks psychological depth. It does not amount to much more than another classification of allegedly basic

[36] *Ibid.*

human drives and propensities, like so many produced in the nineteenth and early twentieth centuries. The alleged explanations turn out, upon inspection, to be tautologies or mere pseudo-explanations; at best they can lead to a classification of character types such as have more recently been advanced by Erich Fromm or David Riesman.

Pareto's enduring importance lies elsewhere. We owe to him the first precise statement of the idea of a social system that can be analyzed in terms of the interrelations and mutual dependencies between constituent parts. We owe to him a theory of the elite and of the circulation of elites, a theory that has continued to inspire concrete investigation into the functions of the upper strata of both governmental and nongovernmental units and that has given major impetus to studies of the origins of and recruitment into such upper strata. The analysis of elites has come to be seen as a vital counterpart of, but emphatically not as a substitute for, analyses of class factors. Theories of stratification would be seriously amiss were they to neglect, say, the ideologies, propensities, and interests of such elite groupings as technocrats, military professionals, or top legal practitioners. Pareto's distinctions between types of nonlogical theories, and between utility *of* and utility *for* the community, have considerable analytical power.

Much of what Pareto wrote is only the fruit of the labors of an embittered, disillusioned, and resentful man who felt that his times had let him down. But many of his ideas can be put to use by those who reject his ideological stance while profiting from his genius.

THE MAN

The Marquis Vilfredo Frederico Damaso Pareto was born in Paris on July 15, 1848.[37] His father, the Marquis Raphael Pareto, came of an old Genovese family that had been ennobled in the eighteenth century. While still a young man, Raphael Pareto had fled Italy and moved to France in the eighteen thirties. Holding republican opinions and adhering to the libertarian cause of Mazzini, he had been persecuted by the House of Savoy, which had annexed Genova in 1815. While in exile, he married a Frenchwoman, Marie Méténier, and all his children, two daughters and the boy Vilfredo, were born in France. In Paris, Raphael Pareto worked as a civil engineer; shortly before the birth of his son he began the necessary formalities to become a naturalized

[37] The information in this subchapter is based on the following: G. H. Bousquet, *Vilfredo Pareto: Sa Vie et son oeuvre* (Paris, Payot, 1928); S. E. Finer, "Biographical Summary," in S. E. Finer, ed., *Vilfredo Pareto: Sociological Writings* (New York, Praeger, 1966); Franz Borkenau, *Pareto* (New York, Wiley, 1936); Werner Stark, "In Search of the True Pareto," in James H. Meisel, ed., *Pareto and Mosca* (Englewood Cliffs, New Jersey, Prentice-Hall, 1965). For a delightful account of Pareto's style of life in his later years, see Manon Michels Einaudi, "Pareto As I Knew Him," *Atlantic Monthly,* CLVI (July–Dec., 1935), pp. 336–46.

French citizen. He decided, however, to return to Italy in 1855, and so his son, although bilingual, was educated in that country.

Pareto received a solid classical education in the very demanding Italian secondary school system and then proceeded to the Turin Polytechnical School to become a civil engineer like his father, who was by then a high-ranking member of the Piedmontese civil service. The five-year course in civil engineering, the first two years of which were devoted to mathematics, deeply influenced Pareto's future intellectual outlook. In 1870 he graduated with a thesis on "The Fundamental Principles of Equilibrium in Solid Bodies." His later interest in equilibrium analysis in economics and sociology is prefigured in this thesis.

PARETO AS BUSINESSMAN AND SPURNED POLITICIAN

After leaving school, Pareto decided to take up a business career. He served for a time as the director of the Rome Railway Company and then became managing director of an iron-products company based in Florence. In these early years of his career, Pareto frequented aristocratic salons and moved in the circles of the high bourgeoisie, but, following in his father's footsteps, he expressed fervently democratic, republican, and even pacifist sentiments. These sentiments were soon to change and the son later violently rejected the ideals that had imbued his father.

In 1876, the free-trading rightist regime that had run Italy fell from power. There followed a long period in which the moderate left parties dominated Italy's political scene; they moved away from free trade, pursued an economic policy of protectionism, and led Italy into military adventures abroad. Pareto soon became a violent opponent of the political regime, the so-called transformism, and attacked it in a series of newspaper blasts. His changed orientation can be accounted for by his principled stand in favor of free trade and against government intervention, as well as the distasteful necessity to make "deals" with influential deputies and government agents in his capacity as company director. In 1882 he ran as an opposition candidate for a Florence constituency but was beaten by the government-supported candidate. Increasingly bitter about the current state of affairs, he now saw in the new ruling elite of Italy a band of corrupt, contemptible, and self-serving careerists who used the levers of government to enrich themselves and to buy political success through economic favors in rigged elections.

Pareto's father died in 1882, and when his mother died a few years later, Pareto decided to change his whole style of life. He gave up his directorship in 1889, married Alessandrina Bakunin, a young, impoverished Russian girl from Venice, and moved from Florence to semiretirement in a villa at Fiesole, where he diverted himself with translations from the classics, read avidly in six or seven languages, and turned to a serious study of economics. No longer encumbered by managerial obligations, Pareto continued his fierce crusade against the government's foreign and domestic policies in the name of free trade and old-fashioned liberalism. Between 1889 and 1893 he wrote no less than 167 articles, mostly violent and vituperative antigovernment polemics, but some of them of a more scholarly cast.

Pareto now turned against the Mazzinian ideals of his father. His democratic faith in the virtues of the people was shattered and he developed that cynical contempt for humanitarianism, republicanism, and progress that was to characterize his views until the end of his days. Like a lover spurned, he turned against the Italian political system that rejected his advice and wallowed, so he felt, in a mire of corruption.

During the years of his semiretirement, Pareto cultivated relations with a number of Italian economists and publicists of liberal persuasion who shared his free trade, Manchesterian principles. Somewhat earlier he had joined the Adam Smith Society in Florence, which was founded by Francesco Ferrara and included in its membership such other liberal economists as De Johannis and Martello.[38] One of its members, Maffeo Pantaleoni, a leading liberal economist, became his close friend and acquainted him with the mathematical equilibrium system in economics then elaborated by Léon Walras, the professor of political economy at Lausanne. From then on, Pareto contributed articles of economic theory, reflecting the Walras viewpoint, to a number of learned journals in Italy and France.

A BELATED ACADEMIC CAREER

In June 1891, Pantaleoni introduced Pareto to Walras with the words, "He is an engineer like you; he is an economist not like you, but wishing to become like you, if you help him."[39] Walras became seriously ill soon after this encounter, and when he was forced to give up his teaching, Pantaleoni persuaded him to propose that Pareto be chosen as his successor. In April 1893 Pareto moved to the University of Lausanne as an "extraordinary professor" of political economy. His appointment was made permanent a year later. He was then in his middle forties.

In Lausanne, Pareto at first continued to write his critical monthly chronicle for the *Giornale degli Economisti,* in which he pursued his anti-interventionist and anti-protectionist critique of the hated Italian government and the wheelers and dealers who remained in the political saddle. But his theoretical work now assumed more importance. His two-volume *Cours d'économie politique,* based on his lectures at the university, appeared only three years after

[38] Vincent J. Tarascio, *Pareto's Methodological Approach to Economics* (Chapel Hill, North Carolina, University of North Carolina Press, 1966), p. 7.

[39] Quoted in Jean-Charles Biaudet, "Pareto à Lausanne," in *Cahiers Vilfredo Pareto,* V (1965), p. 42.

he had arrived there and established him as a major figure in modern economics, a true heir of Walras.

In his early Lausanne period, Pareto still considered himself a man of the liberal left. He provided shelter for many socialist and leftist refugees who had to flee Italy after the 1898 May Riots at Milan, and he passionately took the side of Dreyfus when the Affair broke out in neighboring France. But after 1898, Pareto's views changed sharply and decisively. He gave up hope of a liberal restructuring of Italian economic affairs and turned violently against any form of democratic thought; this almost pathological hatred for the ideas of the left would mar all his subsequent writings. In 1900, he wrote to Pantaleoni that there had once been a time when he wanted to correct the evils of the halt but now he derided their infirmity.[40] He turned away from any reforming endeavors, resolving to comment on the passing scene with the detachment that comes from distance, but also from loathing. Already in 1891 he had written to Walras, "I give up the combat in defense of [liberal] economic theories in Italy. My friends and I get nowhere and lose our time; this time is much more fruitfully devoted to scientific study."[41] Pareto became a cynical, rancorous, utterly disillusioned loner, at variance with all the dominant tendencies of the age, hating all of them without discrimination.

Pareto's misanthropic predisposition and lack of faith in humanity were presumably increased when, after returning from a trip to Paris, he found that his wife had absconded with the cook, taking thirty cases of valuables with her. Being still an Italian citizen, though now living in Switzerland, Pareto could not secure a divorce under canon law. All that could be arranged was a separation of bed and board.

Having acquired a very considerable legacy in 1898 after the death of an uncle, Pareto was financially independent and could order his life in a way that his academic salary would not have allowed him. He built himself a house at Céligny near Lausanne, but in the canton of Geneva where taxes were lower than in Lausanne. Here he was joined by a new companion, Jane Régis, who took care of him and of the vast number of Angora cats he liked to have constantly around him. Leading a somewhat sybaritic existence in his retreat, tasting only the choicest wines and the finest viands, Pareto continued his scientific work. In 1902 he published his *Les Systèmes socialistes,* a detailed analysis and criticism of socialist doctrine and state interventionism. He was still a free-trader, but he now had given up all hope of influencing political events and felt that he could limit himself to pointing out what he considered the logical fallacies and disastrous results of socialist policy. The book seethes with irony and boiling rage, even though its author advertised it as an exercise in scientific analysis.

[40] Quoted in Maurice Allais, "Pareto, Vilfredo—Contributions to Economics," *International Encyclopedia of the Social Sciences.* [41] Quoted in Bousquet, *op. cit.,* p. 19.

Before writing the *Systèmes socialistes,* Pareto had already been struck by the idea that most of human activity was not controlled by rational thought but by sentiments, feelings, superstitions, and other nonlogical determinants. This was why, so he now thought, his long campaign in favor of economic liberalism had failed; rational argument could never move the mass of men who were governed by nonrational beliefs. This new view was first presented in a long article for the *Rivista Italiana di Sociologica* in 1900 and informs much of his writings on socialism. It came to fruition in the *Manual of Political Economy,* which he published in 1906, and was fully elaborated in his monumental million-word *Treatise on General Sociology* (1916), translated into English as *The Mind and Society,* for which he is chiefly remembered among sociologists.

During this last period of his life, Pareto, suffering from a heart disease, lived as a recluse in his Villa Angora. He had retired from regular university teaching in 1907, though he continued to give lectures on sociology there on an irregular basis. Surrounded by his cats, boasting of a cave full of the most renowned wines of all Europe, and of an immense cupboard containing liqueurs from all five continents, Pareto concentrated on his scientific work—and on his hatreds. Suffering from insomnia, he browsed in his encyclopedic library till late at night, after having partaken of the pleasures of the table.

When Mussolini came to power in the last year of Pareto's life, he proclaimed himself a disciple of Pareto and showered him with honors. (Once while living as an exile in Switzerland, Mussolini had registered in two of Pareto's courses at Lausanne, though it is doubtful that he ever attended them with any regularity.) Pareto was made a Senator of the Kingdom of Italy, designated an Italian delegate to the Disarmament Conference at Geneva, and was invited to become a contributor to Mussolini's personal periodical, *Gerarchia.* Pareto welcomed fascism, although with reservations, but he never served for reasons of ill health. In the first years of his rule, Mussolini seemed indeed to implement the program Pareto had advocated for so long. He destroyed liberalism and the workers' movement, but at the same time pursued a liberal economic policy by replacing state management with private enterprise. He decreed, as Borkenau says, "a religious education in dogmas, which he did not himself believe in."[42]

Many fascist spokesmen later claimed that Pareto was one of the chief sources of their ideology. Mussolini characterized Pareto's theory of the elite as "probably the most extraordinary sociological conception of modern times."[43] There is no doubt that the fascists could draw much sustenance from Pareto's writings. Yet, when Mussolini muzzled the universities of Italy and restricted free speech, Pareto protested vehemently. Had Pareto lived it is unlikely that he would have endorsed the complete suppression of liberties during the later

[42] Borkenau, *op. cit.,* p. 18.

[43] Quoted in Stuart Hughes, *Consciousness and Society* (New York, Vintage Books, 1961), p. 272.

stages of Mussolini's regime, or that he would have looked with favor on the state-interventionist course of the fully matured fascist regime.

Pareto saw only the beginning of Mussolini's rule. Early in 1923, when he felt that his end was near, he finally managed to marry Jane Régis by becoming a citizen of the city-state of Fiume, where divorce was legal. He died on August 19, 1923, at the age of seventy-five, after a short illness. He is buried in the cemetery of Céligny, where his tomb carries the simple inscription, "Vilfredo Pareto (1848–1923)." He had been born in 1848, the year of the great liberal revolution, and he died within a year after Mussolini's March on Rome.

THE INTELLECTUAL CONTEXT

Pareto's theoretical ambition may best be understood as an effort to link traditional Italian "Machiavellian" social theory with nineteenth-century positivist thought in its Comtean, Saint-Simonian, or Social Darwinist forms. Underlying this effort was a firm grounding in the classics and in modern mathematics, the two major intellectual traditions that helped shape Pareto's thought from the days of his youth. The classics had been in the foreground of his secondary education, and mathematics and the natural sciences were the major educational fare at the Turin Polytechnical School which he attended. Most of the historical examples, and they are many, that Pareto adduces in the *Treatise* come from the history of Greece and Rome, testifying to the fact that Pareto remained fascinated throughout his life with the classics. At the same time, it is obvious from even a superficial reading of the *Treatise* that its whole methodology, as well as the manner of exposition, are the result of a mind steeped in mathematics. Pareto's twin notions of "system" and "equilibrium" were taken from the natural sciences.

The third major influence on Pareto's thought was modern mathematical economics as it was developed by Léon Walras, his great predecessor at the University of Lausanne.

The first two influences are so pervasive and general throughout his work that they hardly need comment. The third is mainly evident in Pareto's writings in economics.

THE HEIR OF MACHIAVELLI

There are, in addition, some more specific influences on Pareto's sociological thought. Despite his cosmopolitan education and his partly French background, Pareto was thoroughly steeped in Italian intellectual tradition, and this can help explain some of his characteristic approaches to sociology. In the eighteenth century the idea of society as a social order subject to specific laws of its own had already found many exponents in France and Britain but not in Italy. There was very little in Italian social thought that sought to account for the behavior of man by reference to objective social forces. With the exception of the philosopher and jurist Giovanni Vico, the Italian tradition was by and large unreceptive to the idea that society is an objective reality following recognizable laws of its own. The point of departure of the Italian tradition in social thought ever since Machiavelli was not socialized man involved in a web of relations and shaped by institutions, but rather human nature. Men, the Italian thinkers felt, have certain unchanging characteristics, and the social thinker should mainly be concerned with highlighting and scrutinizing human nature so as to understand how it determines conduct under different circumstances. Machiavelli lays down in the *Principe* that men are "ungrateful, fickle, lying, hypocritical, fearful and grasping" creatures. These human traits have to be taken into account by theorists of social action just as an engineer must be aware of the characteristics of his materials when he builds a bridge. To Machiavelli and his successors, rational knowledge does not seek the discovery of social laws regulating stability or change; its aim is to analyze the nature of the materials that go into the social edifice. Moreover, social order is not seen as arising spontaneously from the operation of laws within the body social; it is rather something imposed from above on recalcitrant human nature. Hence, the power some men have over others, the ability of the few to impose their will on the many, is the central theoretical focus of Italian social thought from Machiavelli to the days of Pareto.

Consequently, Italian social thought is mainly concerned with the state rather than with society. The social order is seen as an appendix of the state, or as the area in which individuals or estates vie for dominance and state power. In the Machiavellian tradition, the social analyst is enjoined to cultivate a cool, sceptical ability to penetrate the mainsprings of human nature. If he has this ability he can suggest ways in which powerful and exceptional individuals can learn to utilize men in their endeavors to build a powerful state apparatus that can control the wayward individualistic propensities of the citizens. The notion of the *uomo sociale* is foreign to this tradition. Social integration is brought about, so to speak, from the outside by a *Principe* or by a *Classe scelta,* which constructs a social structure according to rules dictated by its empirical knowledge of human nature and by the forceful imposition of its will on a recalcitrant multitude.[44]

Pareto is first of all a true heir of Machiavelli, even as he supplements the Machiavellian tradition by elements taken from British and French positivism. Like Machiavelli, he wanted to construct a science that would lay bare the springs of human action rooted in man's fundamental nature, a science of power that would explain how the few manage to rule over the many.

[44] For a fine depiction of Italian social thought, on which I lean here, cf. Friedrich Jonas, *Geschichte der Soziologie* (Reinbeck bei Hamburg, Rowohlt, 1969), III, pp. 92 ff.

THE INFLUENCE OF EVOLUTIONISM AND POSITIVISM

In his early writings, Pareto was much attracted by Social Darwinism and by Spencer. When he was writing his *Cours* (1896), he was still in many ways a conventional nineteenth-century liberal, not only opposing state interference and battling for free trade and individual liberty but imbued with a belief in progress. In particular, his chapter on "social evolution" in the *Cours* is Spencerian. Throughout he utilizes Spencer's concept of differentiation, arguing that societies have moved from an undifferentiated homogeneous state to a heterogeneous one, and that there has been a cumulative increase in the degree of social differentiation from the days of the Romans to the present.[45]

When Pareto came to write the *Treatise,* he abandoned his belief in progress in favor of a cyclical Machiavellian theory of history and a belief in the relative constancy of essential human characteristics. He then became critical of Social Darwinians and of Spencer.[46] He admitted that "If it be granted that —apart from temporary oscillations—the institutions of a society are always those best suited to the circumstances in which that society is situated, and that societies not possessing institutions of that kind eventually perish, we get a principle . . . that may well serve to constitute a science." But he argued that initial hopes along these lines had not borne fruit. "Every form of social organization or life has to be explained [in Darwinian theory] by its utility, and to attain that end, arbitrary and imaginary utilities were brought into play. Unwittingly, the theory was just a return to the theory of final causes."[47] He now felt that Social Darwinism had to be considerably modified and that it could explain not "the forms of institutions but merely certain limits that they cannot overpass."[48] The environment does not impose and determine social forms but only sets limits to variations capable of survival. Hence, social behavior could not be explained by environment but required analysis of the characteristics of human actors.

Although Pareto came to reject the twin notions of social evolution and progress, and became highly critical of the Social Darwinian idea that environmental changes could explain changing institutional features, he remained in debt to the Darwinian and Spencerian notion of the mutual interdependence of all social phenomena. He had been prepared for this notion by his study of physical systems, but it seems most likely that he came to view it as applicable to human societies through his reading of Darwin and Spencer. Much like his American contemporaries Cooley and Mead, Pareto derived from his study of Darwin and Spencer a view of the interrelatedness of the various parts of the body social.

[45] Cf. Finer, "Introduction," pp. 16–17. [46] Cf. Bousquet, *op. cit.*, p. 205. [47] *Treatise,* 828.
[48] *Ibid.*

Next to Spencer, it is probably Comte, among sociologists, whom Pareto read most assiduously. There are some thirty entries under his name in the index of the *Treatise*. He had nothing but scorn for Comte's general system. "His sociology," Pareto thought, "is as dogmatic as Bossuet's *Discourse on Universal History*. It is a case of two different religions, but of religions nevertheless."[49] Yet he seems to have been struck by Comte's insistence in his *System of Positive Polity* that sentiments rather than ideas account for social cohesion. Citing at length a passage from the *System* in which Comte speaks about "the universal preponderance of sentiments," Pareto conceded that "If Comte could have rested satisfied with being just a scientist, he might have written an excellent book on the value of religions and taught us many things."[50] But, never one to express gratitude to his forerunners, Pareto then goes on to deride Comte for having become the prophet of a new religion. "Instead of studying the effects of historical or existing forms of worship, he wanted to create a new one. . . . So he gives just another illustration of the harm done to science by the mania for practical application."[51] Nevertheless, Pareto clearly seems to have learned from the Comte of the *Système,* even though he was antagonistic to the prophecies of the religion of humanity and to the optimistic belief in the power of ideas that pervades the *Cours.*

Pareto makes numerous references to Spencer and to Comte in the *Treatise,* but there are none to Saint-Simon—except for some cutting remarks about the Saint-Simonian religion. (Elsewhere Pareto calls Saint-Simon a "buffoon" who put "a scientific veneer on ethico-religious conceptions.")[52] This lack of reference is surprising, since it seems evident that the notion of the circulation of the elite derives from Comte's erstwhile master. Gaetano Mosca, Pareto's great rival, was at pains to point out that Saint-Simon was a brilliant forerunner of his own theories, but no such acknowledgment was forthcoming from Pareto. There are a great many similarities between Pareto's theories and those of the Frenchman who proclaimed that men were born unequal in their faculties, and that society therefore needed to be organized in a hierarchical order where those with the highest capacities would be in command. Pareto's stress on maximum opportunity for social mobility and on the career open to talent is strikingly similar to Saint-Simon's whose last words to his favored disciples were that his life's work was aimed "to afford all members of society the greatest possible opportunity for the development of their faculties."[53]

Not only with Saint-Simon, but with many others Pareto was not very generous in paying intellectual debts. Even Arthur Livingston, his admiring American editor, feels constrained to note this fact in a footnote when he writes:

[49] *Ibid.,* 6. [50] *Ibid.,* 286–88. [51] *Ibid.*

[52] *Les Systèmes socialistes,* 2nd ed., Vol. II, p. 194, as quoted by Frank E. Manuel, *The New World of Henri Saint-Simon* (Cambridge, Harvard University Press, 1956), pp. 3 and 372.

[53] *Ibid.,* p. 302.

In a work of a million words with not a few asides, and containing not a few strictures on great writers of the past and present, a few hundred words more might not have come amiss to describe what Pareto in particular owed, for his general method to Comte, for his theory of derivations to Bentham (some of whose categories Pareto adopts verbatim), for his theory of class-circulation to Gaetano Mosca, for his theory of residues to Frazer and others, and for a number of phrases and items of detail even to Hegel, William James, and many others.[54]

PARETO'S DEBT TO MOSCA AND MARX

Pareto's shabby treatment of men to whom he owed ideas and stimulation is nowhere more apparent than in the case of his contemporary Mosca. The scholarly partisans of Mosca and Pareto still dispute their respective claims, and there is no need for an outsider to attempt any definitive judgments in this respect. It seems indisputable, however, that Mosca anticipated Pareto by many years in outlining the theory of the elite, even though the two men differed considerably in other respects.

In 1884, long before Pareto wrote about the matter, Mosca stated in his book *Teorica dei governi* (*The Ruling Class*), "The ruling class, or those who hold and exercise the public power, will always be a minority, and below them we find a numerous class of persons who do never, in any real sense, participate in government but merely submit to it: they may be called the ruled class."[55] Mosca was only twenty-five when he hit on this *idée maîtresse,* which he elaborated for the rest of his life. He acknowledged his debt to Saint-Simon, who had said that "power in all organized society is split between two orders —one controls the intellectual and moral, the other the material forces. These two powers are exercised by two organized authorities which together form the ruling class."[56] Having been so scrupulous in identifying the source of his inspiration, Mosca was all the more furious to find that Pareto had "appropriated" his favored idea. He became even more outraged when Pareto haughtily dismissed the charge when it was made to him, and even deleted references to Mosca from a new edition of an older work.[57] All this is not to say that Pareto did not go beyond Mosca. Stuart Hughes seems to give a balanced assessment when he writes:

> Mosca's formulation was the first and most general. Yet it was in a characteristically political context—it did no more than hint at the extension of the doctrine to society as a whole. . . . In his first book [Mosca] asserted that each political class rationalized its rules in terms of a convenient "political

[54] *The Mind and Society,* p. 1477. [55] Quoted in Meisel, ed., *op. cit.,* pp. 5–6.
[56] *Ibid.* [57] Cf. Meisel, "Introduction" to *ibid.,* p. 15.

> formula"—liberalism, democracy, and socialism being obvious contemporary examples. Mosca had not pursued this discovery any further. He had not gone on to suggest, as Pareto did, that a political formula was simply one example of a more inclusive category of rationalizations.[58]

When it came to Marx, Pareto was more generous than he could bring himself to be in regard to his contemporary Mosca. He repeatedly acknowledged that Marx was the first to put great stress on the disharmony of class interests, and he wrote in his *Cours:* "The socialists are entirely right in emphasizing the great importance of the 'class struggle,' and in stating that it is the great dominant fact in history. In this respect the works of Marx and Loria deserve the greatest attention."[59] Though he sneered about "the socialist who swears by the Word of Marx and Engels as a treasure-store of all human knowledge,"[60] Pareto was willing to acknowledge that the notion of the class struggle had influenced his view of history in a major way. Marx, the prophet of the classless society, was to Pareto only another purveyor of myth; Marx the tough analyst of the struggles of classes for dominance and power in society was a man close to Pareto's Machiavellian heart.

Pareto's biographer, Bousquet, notes that he was familiar with the social psychology of Tarde and Le Bon, whose writings on the suggestibility and emotionalism of common men appealed to him. He knew the work of Lucien Lévy-Bruhl on the prelogical thought of primitives.[61] He was a life-long admirer of Pierre Bayle (1640–1706) whose sceptical philosophy and subversive criticism of received religions he greatly admired. He was fond of reading Voltaire and other "enlightened" enemies of myth, superstition, and dogma.

All in all, Pareto was a man with deep roots in the sceptical and "debunking" tradition of the Enlightenment, but who nevertheless lacked the eighteenth-century belief in progress and the powers of reason. He wished to make sociology into a positive science in the manner of Comte and Spencer, yet he rejected their belief in progress and evolution, accusing them of having trespassed beyond the limits of science and having created a metaphysics in the name of anti-metaphysics. It was his own ambition to create a science of society devoid of any metaphysical underpinnings and based strictly on logico-experimental principles. He wanted nothing but logical reasoning and factual observations to enter his theoretical system. Yet, he was deflected from his methodological principles by the social and political passions of his time.

[58] Hughes, *op. cit.,* pp. 255–57.
[59] Quoted in Finer, "Introduction," p. 117. See also *The Structure of Social Action,* p. 179.
[60] *Treatise,* 351. [61] Bousquet, *op. cit.,* p. 206.

THE SOCIAL CONTEXT

THE GENERAL SCENE

Pareto left school in 1870. He had been formed by the libertarian ideas of his father and his friends, but when he grew to maturity he soon realized that the Italy of his dreams resembled little the country in which he was now called to assume his adult role.

In 1871, when Rome became the capital of the Kingdom of Italy, the long struggle for Italian liberation and unification had finally come to a victorious end. There was rejoicing in Italy, but also a somewhat melancholy realization that a zestful and exhilarating period of Italian history had come to a close. Benedetto Croce beautifully captured the spirit of the time when he wrote:

> Every close of a period of history brings with it the death of something, however much the end may have been sought and desired . . . and, like all death, it is encompassed by an atmosphere of regret and melancholy. There were now no more youthful strivings and heartburnings after an ideal that was new, lofty, and far removed from realization; no more dreams, boundless as the ocean, shining with beauty and fascination . . . no more trembling hopes, as in 1848 and 1859; no more generous rivalries and renunciations of individual ideas in order to unite in a common purpose; no more understandings, whether tacit or avowed, between republicans and monarchists, Catholics and free-thinkers, ministers and revolutionaries, king and conspirators, all alike being dominated and inspired by devotion to the patriotic cause.[62]

The patriotic fever and exaltation now being over, Italians had to adjust to humdrum and mundane political life. Just as many Frenchmen felt at the same time, "How beautiful the Republic had been under the Empire," so many disillusioned Italians may have felt, "How beautiful a liberated Italy had been under the yoke of foreign oppression."

The unification of Italy, to which generations of Italian patriots had aspired, was now an accomplished fact. But it soon became apparent that underneath the administrative unification were profound differences between the North and South. The North, whether in Piedmont, under the House of Savoy, or in Lombardo-Venetia, under Austrian administration, was fairly developed economically, well administered, and on the road to economic and

[62] Benedetto Croce, *A History of Italy: 1871–1915* (Oxford, The Clarendon Press, 1929), pp. 1–2. In addition to Croce, I have relied in the following pages on Margot Hentze, *Pre-Fascist Italy* (London, George Allen and Unwin, 1939), and René Albrecht-Carrié, *Italy from Napoleon to Mussolini* (New York, Columbia University Press, 1950).

political modernization. But conditions in the South were fundamentally different; it was only on the margin of modern European civilization. Most of the South, especially the Kingdom of the Two Sicilies and the Papal States, had been cruelly exploited by its rulers, and the population lived in degradation and unspeakable poverty. The South was largely rural, and the southern peasantry was overwhelmingly illiterate. Even by 1918 the illiteracy rate in the South was still, depending on the region, between 50 and 70 percent, in contrast to Piedmont where it was 11 percent. Although nominally unified, the South and the North were in fact two dissimilar nations, alien to each other.

The Rightist group that had led the destinies of Italy for a few years after unification, as it had led Piedmont under Cavour and his successors, pursued a policy that might be termed the Piedmontization of Italy. The Right wished to bring to the whole country the enlightened developmental policy that had been successful in the North and to continue the liberal tradition of Cavour that had made Piedmont into a well-governed, modernizing state. The Right imposed a heavy tax burden on the country, gave it a highly centralized administrative structure, favored free trade, balanced the budget, and pursued a cautious foreign policy. It was essentially a government by an enlightened elite of high-minded professionals and members of the middle class. Composed mainly of Piedmontese, Tuscans, and Lombards, this elite hardly veiled its contempt for the backward South. Nor was it concerned that only about two percent of the population had the franchise.

In March 1876 the long reign of the Right came to an end after its defeat in Parliament. Depretis, the leader of the Left, organized an exclusively Left administration and, in order to secure the Left's hold on power, organized new elections. Even by Italy's low standards in such matters, these elections were notorious in terms of the government's intimidating and corrupt practices. Prefects were browbeaten, threatened, or bribed to become the government's electoral agents. Districts favorable to the government were promised post offices, schools, public works, and the like; ones that were unfavorable were told that even their existing government services might be suppressed if they did not step into line. The Left achieved the desired results: it emerged with 408 seats in Parliament against the 90 seats of the Right.

The victory of the Left was not owing to corruption alone. The country was fundamentally tired of the Right, tired of its abstract idealism and its policies of austerity and discipline. Disillusioned and overstrained taxpayers wanted "reparations" for heavy and inequitable taxes, for the meagerness of public works, for excessive administrative centralization, for the absence of public security. The men of the South, who were in the majority on the Left, wanted developmental aid for their neglected area and easier access of southerners to the public trough. Almost everyone believed that the rule of the Left would bring prosperity and enlightened progress.

But it soon became apparent, to quote a contemporary wit, that "the government of the Left is the same as that of the Right, only not so good." Corruption in high places was now perfected into a veritable art. Depretis and his successors were well versed in manipulating the levers of power, but they were incapable of instituting urgently needed reforms. The government promised all sorts of reform but implemented few. The party structure being very weak, rival politicians carved out their personal baronies in Parliament, made deals to enhance their following and power, but rendered orderly governance almost impossible. The Left had no objection to enlarging the electorate. It extended the franchise to some 7 percent of the people in 1882. But a broadened franchise hardly meant enhanced opportunities for popular participation in government; it mainly allowed an increased scale of manipulations, *combinazioni,* and corrupt bargaining. As a consequence, the traditional Italian distrust of the state, especially in the South, was further increased. Little of the Mazzinian patriotic spirit or of Cavour's public-mindedness remained. The bulk of the population saw the state as a gigantic machine sucking the people's wealth through regressive taxation into the coffers of a corrupt ruling clique. And even when deputies secured local benefits for their constituents in exchange for their votes, people did not feel the need to indicate gratitude; they considered it just another deal.

The leaders of the Left held office from 1876 to the First World War. Depretis ruled for ten years, followed by Crispi for another ten years. And, after a short interregnum, Giolitti, the third of the "democratic dictators," held power until the outbreak of the war. These men differed in their personality and their political style, but they all pursued fundamentally similar policies. Unsavory political maneuvers replaced, but were no substitutes for, innovative policies.

Crispi attempted to evade the pressures of domestic tensions by inaugurating a bold policy of colonial expansion. This led to the disastrous war with Ethiopia and to the battle of Adua, where 25,000 "modern" Italians were completely defeated by some 100,000 "primitive" Ethiopians under Menelek, and eventually to the humiliating treaty of Addis Ababa in which Italy recognized the independence of Ethiopia and had to restrict itself to the minor colony of Eritrea. Italy's imperialist ventures were managed with the same consummate inefficiency as her domestic affairs.

The only area in which the successive governments were highly efficient was that of public order. When serious peasant troubles developed in 1894 in Sicily, Crispi put them down ruthlessly with the help of the military. In the next year laws were passed suppressing socialist and anarchist organizations and severely curtailing free speech and assembly. When bread riots broke out in 1898 in various parts of the country and culminated in open conflicts with the troops in Milan in May, martial law was proclaimed by Crispi's successor. Over four hundred members of the civilian population were killed or seriously wounded before order was restored. Heavy sentences by court martial, especially against socialists, ensued and led to large-scale flights of socialist militants to Switzerland and other havens for refugees.

In 1894, the country was treated to a particularly unedifying spectacle. In the midst of a banking crisis, Giolitti had made the managing director of the Banca Romano, Tanlongo, a senator. The Senate refused to confirm the appointment; an investigation resulted in the arrest of Tanlongo and of a number of highly placed and prominent politicians. It was revealed that Tanlongo had issued large sums in duplicate banknotes, that two preceding cabinets had been aware of this, that "loans" had been made to a number of deputies and other officials. Giolitti's government fell, but neither he nor his predecessor Crispi suffered any lasting political injury and Giolitti was soon back in power. His regime became known as *Il ministro della mala vita* (The ministry of the underworld). Under him the franchise was further extended, but as with the previous electoral reforms, this meant no real increase in popular participation but rather a chance for Giolitti, a past master at the art, to display his skills in "making" elections.

Despite misgovernment and corruption, Italy made economic advances in the half-century before the outbreak of the First World War. It developed an important textile industry. Milan came to replace Lyon as the center of silk making. The port of Genoa gradually overtook Marseilles, and an extensive net of railways came to cover the peninsula. Yet, viewed in the perspective of Europe's overall industrial development, Italy remained backward. Her *per capita* income in the nineties amounted to $40, when the corresponding figure for Britain was $155 and for France $130. Italy's exports around the turn of the century were smaller than those of Belgium. And despite all the talk to the contrary, the economic gap between South and North continued to widen. In sections of the South the peasants continued to live in a state of utter destitution. Agrarian reform, the most urgent need of the country, especially of the South, was postponed again and again because no politician in power dared to attack the large landowners who dominated the economic and political scene in rural areas. How were they to "make" elections if they could no longer rely on the agents of the landholding interests? A law for compulsory elementary education was passed in 1877, but it was scarcely enforced. Parliament dreaded the necessary expenses and was apprehensive about the reaction of landowners to the loss of cheap manpower resulting from compulsory education of children old enough to work. Moreover, Parliament feared that an educated electorate might make it difficult to continue its proven methods of manipulating elections. Little was done to improve the harsh and inequitable system of taxation that helped maintain Italy's bloated administrative apparatus.

"From 1878 on," remarked Francesco Crispi with rare candor in 1886, "there have been no political parties in Italy, but only politicians."[63] This

[63] Quoted in Hentze, *op. cit.*, p. 164.

decomposition of the party system and its dissolution into squabbling factions led by temporary leaders in shifting alliances, made long-range planning and even short-term administration most difficult. Only a drastic reform of the whole political system could bring remedy, but no one in the governing elite was willing to sponsor a reform that might undermine his own position. The gradual extension of the franchise simply meant a bolstering of elite positions by new votes and hence it was acceptable; a restructuring of the political process was not.

This lamentable state of political affairs resulted in a turn to pessimism or cynicism among the intellectuals. Until the seventies, the prevailing climate of opinion was a compound of beliefs in social and material progress, in human perfectibility, and in the power of science to usher in the emancipation of mankind. The consensus of ideas favored democracy and rationality, free trade, and the market economy. Prevailing social thought was melioristic and optimistic. After the seventies, the climate of opinion changed. Progress, positivism, and perfectibility all came under increasing attack, and traditional Machiavellian ideas regained the ascendancy. Disenchantment with parliamentary institutions grew rapidly. Free trade and the free market now found few defenders. Employers and their spokesmen, well satisfied by tariff protections and governmental subsidies, and working class representatives battling to extract some social welfare benefits, could not care less about the liberal shibboleths of their forefathers. The last remnants of liberal publicists and economists defending free markets and free trade came to be viewed as anachronistic survivors of a by-gone age. In the pursuit of the mirage of national aggrandizement, the political rulers protected agriculture, thereby raising the cost of living for the underlying population, and conducted disastrous tariff wars with France. They embarked on a heavy program of armaments and on costly colonial wars.[64] When popular desperation led to insurrections, as it did in 1894, 1898, and again in 1904, the government repressed them savagely. When a succession of financial scandals exposed the rot in the political and social structure, the government sat out the ensuing storm and did nothing. No wonder that most of Italy's intellectuals were alienated, distrustful, and pessimistic. A generation that had been imbued with Mazzini's idealistic and romantic belief in freedom and democracy was followed by several generations of disillusioned cynics or decadent irrationalists. Whether in the eroticism and mock heroism of D'Annunzio, in Franciscan or Buddhist mysticism, in theosophy or "futurism," intellectual decadence became a pervasive mark of the time. Only the saving remnant of rational and liberal philosophers around Benedetto Croce and the growing phalanx of Marxist intellectuals around Antonio Labriola upheld libertarian ideals and clung to rational standards. As a whole, Italy's intellectual scene around the turn of the century was as barren as the political scene was

[64] Cf. Finer, *op. cit.*, pp. 3 ff.

corrupt. Pareto was by no means alone in believing that the day of the locust was upon Italy. "That which the palmerworm hath left hath the locust eaten; and that which the locust hath left hath the cankerworm eaten; and that which the cankerworm hath left hath the caterpillar eaten." (Joel 1:4)

On October 28, 1922, Mussolini, promising to end the mess, marched on Rome, and three days later Europe's first fascist regime came to power.

PARETO'S COLLEAGUES AND AUDIENCE

In the early years of his career as a company director and occasional contributor to liberal journals, Pareto was part of a fairly active social network. During his stay in Florence, in particular, he made a number of friends, including Domenico Comparetti, the author of *Virgil in the Middle Ages,* Arthuro Linnacher, a learned classicist, Sidney Sonnino, a leading liberal statesman, and Giustino Fortunato, the biographer of Giordano Bruno. These men formed part of a company of brilliant minds who gathered regularly in the salon of one of Florence's leading hostesses, Emilia Toscanelli-Peruzzi.[65] In this period, one gathers that Pareto, though adhering to Mazzinian beliefs and thus somewhat at variance with the moderate opinions prevailing in this semi-aristocratic milieu, still felt very much at home in Italy.

In the 1880's, when he became convinced that Italy was led to ruin by the ruling Leftist regime, Pareto removed himself deliberately from the circles in which he had lived so far and went into symbolic semi-isolation to a villa in Fiesole. He felt that he was no longer in tune with the main tendencies of the age and that it was his mission to embark upon a crusade against the government's foreign and domestic policies. He now wrote with assiduity for the liberal press, attempting to stem the tide of state interventionism. The vituperative, rancorous, and caustic style that marks his writings from this point on may be traced, at least in part, to his sense of being a man at bay, trying to compensate with invective what he lacked in real power to sway the public at large. Yet the fact that he spent so much energy writing for the public press indicates that he still believed during this period that all was not lost, that there was still a chance to convince the intellectual and political elite of the errors of their ways.

During this period of his life, although removed from the wider circle of which he had once been a part, Pareto formed close personal and intellectual relations with a small group of liberal economists, led by Maffeo Pantaloni, who shared his jaundiced views of the course of Italy under the Left regime. Although he still addressed the wider public, he began in the late eighties and early nineties to write for academic journals, for the restricted audience of those learned in theoretical economics. He seems gradually to have resolved that only

[65] Arthur Livingston, "Biographical Note," *The Mind and Society,* p. xvi.

a relatively select company of *cognoscenti* were worthy readers. He narrowed his public at the same time as he narrowed his social circle.

Pareto's progressive disengagement from Italy and its problems, and from his lay audience, came to a climax with his decision to emigrate permanently to Switzerland, to give up writing much for newspapers, and to devote himself to pure theoretical economics. His appointment to the University of Lausanne at the age of forty-five enabled him, or so he thought, to remove himself completely from the battles of the day. Yet, although he soon came to be admired as one of the leading theoretical economists of Europe and was clearly among the two or three best minds then teaching at Lausanne, Pareto never managed to rely exclusively on an academic audience; he continued, though with much less regularity than previously, to try to convert a wider public to his political views. Had he taught at one of the great universities of Europe, he might have found it easier to take the expectations of his academic colleagues into account. But Lausanne was a provincial backwater, despite the fact that it could boast of some major figures, such as Pareto's predecessor Léon Walras. Soon after his arrival at Lausanne, Pareto began to complain about conditions there. "There is a library here," he wrote in a letter, "where the most recent work in political economy is a work by Mill!"[66] Pareto seems at times to have felt in Lausanne as a Churchill might have felt had he been Prime Minister of Luxembourg.

It was not only the provincial atmosphere that hampered Pareto at Lausanne. He also was largely out of tune with the winds of doctrine that prevailed there. Though Walras and Pareto shared a common concern with the development of mathematical economics, they differed ideologically. Walras had been a firm believer in evolution and social progress and, while he was no longer at the University when Pareto arrived, his spirit was still dominant there. In addition, political economy was then the only social science taught systematically at Lausanne. Social psychology, for example, was considered a marginal field more appreciated in the faculties of medicine and theology than in the faculty of law where political economy was taught. This made for additional difficulties in Pareto's position, especially when he began to conceive of his project to supplement his economic researches by developing sociological theory. Despite the fact that the bulk of the faculty shared Pareto's positivistic ideas, he had few congenial colleagues. Only a few shared his pessimism and jaundiced views of human nature. Moreover, he found himself quite lonely in the faculty of law where he taught among all those professors of law. In 1896 he was elected Dean of the Faculty of Law, but his attempts at reforming the teaching of the social sciences foundered upon the resistance of his colleagues. Nor was he successful in getting approval for his proposal to offer chairs in criminal sociology and penal law to two of his Italian friends. He soon con-

[66] Quoted in Jean-Charles Biaudet, p. 43. Biaudet's paper is my major source on Pareto's Lausanne period. All quotations that follow are from this source.

cluded that cosmopolitans like himself had better not meddle in matters that really belonged to locals, or, as he said, to "Swiss professors and mainly to natives of the Canton de Vaud."

Pareto also encountered difficulties in regard to teaching. He detested lecturing to beginners. This made him feel, he wrote, like becoming a parrot. "There may have been a parrot among my Darwinian ancestors; this would explain my usage of automatic language." Pareto's lectures never consisted of well-ordered presentations, but resembled, says a biographer, "explosions of multiple intuitions." They therefore appealed to specialists rather than to ordinary students. This is probably why only two students wrote theses under his direction that reflected his spirit, Pierre Boven (translator of the *Treatise* into French), *Mathematical Applications in Political Economy*, and Marie Kolabinska, *The Circulation of the Elite in France*.

His lack of success in teaching soon led Pareto to attempt reducing his instructional load. The authorities of the Canton de Vaud, who had jurisdiction in such matters, looked at this with strong misgivings and hesitated to give him the right to hire an assistant to take over some of his teaching. Agreement was only procured after his successor as Dean of the Faculty of Law, one of Pareto's friends, intervened in his favor. The dean's memorandum amusingly reflects the academic balancing act necessary for survival in a small-town university:

> Despite the fact that there may be something legitimate in a certain susceptibility of the government of Vaud in the presence of the bizarre conduct of M. Pareto, and despite the fact that a precedent of that nature may be undesirable, I persist in believing that a major interest of the University and of the Canton speaks in favor of his continuing to belong to the faculty and also in favor of accepting his conditions. . . . It is indeed traditional to relieve a *great* scholar who is about to immortalize his University by *great* works of part or even of the whole of the teaching load.

After this incident, Pareto, while remaining the titular holder of his chair, gave only a one-hour lecture per week in political sociology and history of economic and social doctrines. A few years later, in 1907, he gave up his chair in political economy altogether to become professor of political and social sciences. He now taught only three months per year. Two years later he completely gave up regular teaching and was rarely seen at Lausanne, having retired to his villa in Céligny to live, as he said, "like a snail in its shell."

After 1909, Pareto withdrew from most contact with his colleagues, though he still participated from time to time in academic committees. Some of his personal friends on the faculty continued to visit with him, and friends from other universities, Robert Michels for example, would be his house guests, but his circle shrank from year to year. Most men found it hard to take his violent outbursts and rancorous sallies with equanimity. Even persons who earlier had been among his intimates became targets of Pareto's satirical thrusts. When a friend gently hinted that this seemed inappropriate, Pareto resorted bitterly: "Irony is evidently the weapon of the minority. The majority of men consists of imbeciles and also of scoundrels. One must hence keep them in order through force; and in periods of transition, when this is not possible, there only remains to laugh at the imbeciles and the scoundrels."

During the last period of his life, Pareto's polemics with men who happened to disagree with him often became so violent and vituperative that he embarrassed his few remaining friends. Wrapping himself majestically in the mantle of science, Pareto denied scientific standing to everyone who happened to disagree with his teaching. Like Whistler, of whom Oscar Wilde once said "he spelt art with a capital I," Pareto spelled science that way. Hence, only colleagues who agreed in essentials with his approach, Robert Michels and Georges Sorel in particular, were judged by him to work in a truly scientific spirit.

Pareto wrote his *Treatise* between 1907 and 1912, during a period in which he had in effect almost retired from teaching, cut most of his ties with the University, and given up most of his previous contacts with colleagues. This isolation helps us to understand the disjointed, disorganized and rambling character of the book. While his earlier scholarly works, most of which were the outgrowth of his lectures, were well structured and organized, this last work grew from lonely study when he had little contact with students and peers. Colleagues and friendly critics may have induced Pareto in his earlier works to control his prejudices somewhat. Such contact no longer being available to him, he now gave free rein to his prejudices and passions. More particularly, his venomous derision of democracy and humanitarianism now surpassed all bounds of academic propriety. Moreover, the whole structure of the book is confusing and distracting. Arguments begun on one page peter out, only to reappear many pages later. Very minor points are elaborated in tiresome detail, while major issues that beg to be considered at length are mentioned only in passing. The *Treatise* seems to have been written with no concrete audience in mind to be persuaded by logical argument. Pareto's style reflects his self-absorption. He poured out his ideas indiscriminately and unselectively, gratifying no one but himself. The *Treatise* is a vast *olla podrida,* where flashes of genius stand side by side with petulant observations. Thomas Wolfe was lucky enough to find in Maxwell Perkins an editor who imposed a semblance of order upon his sprawling virgin forest of words. Pareto had no such editor—and he would most probably have refused anybody the right to meddle with his text.

Lacking an audience, having alienated most former colleagues and co-thinkers, Pareto plowed his lonely furrow in his idiosyncratic way. As with Comte before him, his thought became progressively more eccentric the further he removed himself from the centers of intellectual life. Had he had close colleagues, it is likely that they would have drawn his attention to the works of Sigmund Freud, whose major books were all available during the period in which the

Treatise was written. As it was, Pareto ignored Freud completely so that much of what he had to say inevitably appeared anachronistic to his readers. In a like manner, Pareto managed to ignore not only the work of Max Weber, but the whole German tradition of the social sciences. Here again, had he had colleagues, and had he taught in a less provincial university than Lausanne, Pareto would at least have been forced to take notice of this body of work, even though he might have rejected it as insufficiently positivist in orientation. All in all, the self-imposed exile from the world of modernity, the strength of his hatred, and the virulence of his prejudices severely limited the breadth of Pareto's vision and distorted his findings.

It is hardly surprising, therefore, that the *Treatise* had very little impact when it appeared. Though completed in 1912, it appeared only in 1916, in the midst of the World War. Had it been published in English, it might have had a better reception. But the school of Durkheim dominated in France and was unreceptive to Pareto's wholly different approach to sociology, and there was very little of a public for sociology in Italy. Later the fascists claimed Pareto as one of their own, and this may have boosted sales after his death, but the initial sales were as disappointing in Italy as they were in France. Had it not been for the fact that Pareto's name ranked high among economists, one may surmise that the book would have passed almost unnoticed. Even so, his biographer and disciple G. H. Bousquet, writing in 1928, still complained that a "conspiracy of silence" tended to form around Pareto's name. It did not help, of course, that his name came to be tarnished by his flirtation with fascism in the last year of his life.

PARETO'S INFLUENCE IN AMERICA

Pareto came into his own only more than a decade after his death, and then in America. His *magnum opus* first reached the United States in an English version in 1935, and something of a "Pareto vogue" rose in the thirties—only to subside during the war and for many years thereafter. The ground for Pareto's enthusiastic reception in some American quarters had already been prepared earlier when James Harvey Robinson, the father of the "new history," wrote in 1921 that Pareto's theory of residues and derivations "may be ranked by students of a hundred years hence as one of the several great discoveries of our age."[67] Arthur Livingston, the American editor of the *Treatise,* already began to propagandize for Pareto's sociological work in the middle twenties. In 1927, L. J. Henderson, Harvard's brilliant biochemist *cum* social scientist, wrote about the *Treatise*, "This . . . may possibly be the commencement of a new era in the history of thought. . . . One need not hesitate to call this theory

[67] Quoted in Meisel, *op. cit.,* p. 24.

magnificent [and] . . . unique."[68] A few years after writing this encomium Henderson presided over his famous Harvard seminars on Pareto's thought, which were attended by, among others, Talcott Parsons, Robert K. Merton, George Homans, Henry Murray, and Clyde Kluckhohn. All the efforts to interest American social scientists and intellectuals in Pareto proved relatively unsuccessful until the thirties when the name of Pareto suddenly burst upon the wider American intellectual scene.

That the America of the depression proved receptive to Pareto's thought is not surprising. Much like Marxism, which enjoyed a similar vogue at that time, his work appealed to two major strains in the climate of opinion of the thirties: belief in the saving authority of science and loss of belief in the authority of tradition. His positivism appealed in an intellectual climate in which only the claims of science still stood unchallenged, and his debunking stance was congenial to intellectuals whose moorings had been severely shaken ever since the bottom dropped out of the stock market in 1929. Pareto was largely read as a kind of bourgeois answer to Marx, or as a conservative functional equivalent to him. Homans put this well when he wrote, "As a Republican Bostonian who had not rejected his comparatively wealthy family, I felt during the thirties that I was under personal attack, above all from the Marxists. I was ready to believe Pareto because he provided me with a defense."[69]

Pareto's initial defenders in the thirties were largely literary critics and journalists; social scientists soon followed. Bernard De Voto in particular, the literary historian and critic who learned of Pareto from Henderson, did not tire of extolling Pareto in the pages of the *Saturday Review of Literature* and *Harper's*. Even writers for left-of-center publications such as *The New Republic* wrote enthusiastic comments about Pareto. One of *The New Republic*'s contributors, Claude Foreman, thought in 1933 that Pareto's theories "explain not only the Fascist movement in Italy but also the Bolshevik success in Russia."[70]

As to Pareto's academic reception, it is noteworthy that his major impact came at Harvard; other academics, especially Midwesterners, either ignored him or attacked him with vigor. Ellsworth Faris referred to him as "an old man who aspired to be the Machiavelli of the middle classes."[71] William McDougall (then teaching at Duke University) called him the "Karl Marx of Fascism,"[72]

[68] *Ibid.*, p. 23. Henderson, in his turn, was introduced to Pareto by a colleague. William M. Wheeler, whose study of insect societies prompted an interest in instinctual determinants of human society. Cf. Cynthia E. Russett, *The Concepts of Equilibrium in American Social Thought* (New Haven, Conn., Yale University Press, 1966), p. 111.

[69] George C. Homans, *Sentiments and Activities* (New York, The Free Press, 1962), p. 4. Cf. also Barbara Heyl, "The Harvard Pareto Circle," *Journal of the History of the Behavioral Sciences*, IV (1968), pp. 316–34, and Bernard Barber, "Introduction" to *L. J. Henderson on the Social System* (Chicago, The University of Chicago Press, 1970).

[70] Quoted in Homans and Curtis, *op. cit.*, p. 10. [71] Quoted in Meisel, *op. cit.*, p. 14.

[72] *Ibid.*, p. 14.

and pointed to the "out-of-date character of Pareto's thinking and knowledge."[73] Emory Bogardus and Floyd House wrote lengthy refutations in which they attempted to show that what was valid in Pareto had long been said much better by Englishmen and Americans such as Darwin, James and Sumner, and that the rest of his work was no good at all.[74] Perhaps the strong "progressive" tendencies that still survived in Midwestern universities, a pervasive belief in the virtues of the common man, contributed to the rejection by Midwestern academics of Pareto's thought. No such inhibition seemed to have existed at Harvard at the time.

L. J. Henderson, a very strong influence on a number of younger Harvard social scientists in the thirties, had already prepared the ground for Pareto's favorable reception there. In tune with his scientific training and interest, he had placed most stress on Pareto's scientific methodology and, in particular, on his model of a social system and the notion of equilibrium. Bernard De Voto, who had close personal ties with a number of Harvard teachers, made other converts there. The copy of Homans' and Curtis' *An Introduction to Pareto,* which is now at the Stanford University Library, comes from De Voto's library and carries an inscription by Homans, reading: "To Benny who made me a Paretian." For Homans, and also for De Voto, the main importance of the *Treatise* was "that it presents a well-developed theory of nonlogical action."[75] Talcott Parsons, though he was not to become a disciple of Pareto, was yet so deeply marked by Pareto's thought that he wrote in his *Structure of Social Action* (1937): "There is in the *Treatise* nothing essential on either the methodological or the theoretical level which . . . must be discarded."[76] Aspects of Pareto's social system approach, of his methodology, and to a lesser degree of his substantive views were incorporated in Parsons' own theoretical synthesis. Parsons has continued to think of Pareto as one of the most important masters of the social sciences.[77] Not all Harvard social scientists, however, shared Henderson's, Homans', or Parsons' enthusiasm. Among Harvard's historians and economists, only Crane Brinton and Joseph Schumpeter, respectively, were beholden to him. Sorokin, as was his wont, submitted the *Treatise* to a searching critical analysis; and Merton, though he probably developed certain of his own ideas from leads provided by Pareto, was never much attracted by the Italian.

The most crucial impact of Pareto's thought on empirical social science in America came through another Harvard group: the authors of the famous Hawthorne studies carried out by members of the Harvard Business School between 1927 and 1932.[78] In these studies the authors found that workers were neither "economic men" calculating rationally the best way to maximize their

[73] *Ibid.*, p. 27. [74] *Ibid.*, p. 26. [75] Homans and Curtis, *op. cit.*, p. 10.

[76] Parsons, *The Structure of Social Action,* p. 300.

[77] Parsons, "Vilfredo Pareto," in *The International Encyclopedia of the Social Sciences.*

[78] F. J. Roethlisberger and W. J. Dickson, *Management and the Worker* (Cambridge, Massachusetts, Harvard University Press, 1939).

rewards; nor were they simply responding to environmental changes in, for example, the physical conditions of work. These findings were initially a puzzle to the researchers. But they began to make sense after the authors had become acquainted with Pareto's thought at Harvard through Elton Mayo, a member of the Henderson circle. They now concluded that those aspects of the workers' behavior that could not be explained in terms of physiology or economics could be made understandable in terms of Paretian residues. Restrictions of output could be interpreted as manifestations of the work group's sense of solidarity (group persistence); many workers' grievances could be understood as verbalizations of underlying status anxieties and psychological insecurities. More generally, the workers' "logic of sentiment" could be counterposed to management's "logic of cost and efficiency," so that the struggle between them could be understood as being rooted in the clash of sentiments rather than in rational economic antagonisms. All this was, of course, an application of Paretian modes of analysis, even though Pareto himself would have been less rash in concluding that management's conduct was rational. He would have looked for the myths, ideologies, nonscientific theories, and nonlogical beliefs underlying management's conduct as well as that of workers.[79]

IN SUMMARY

The Pareto vogue receded as quickly as it had come into being. Although Parsons continued to hold Pareto's thought in high esteem, his later theoretical work was influenced more deeply by Weber, Durkheim, and Freud. George Homans moved from a preoccupation with nonlogical action to an exchange theory patterned after B. F. Skinner's behavioral psychology and classical economic thought. Among political scientists, Harold Lasswell remained close to Pareto throughout his career. One of the earliest proponents of Pareto in America, he has continued to contribute work which is largely inspired by theories of elite formation and circulation derived from Pareto.[80]

Ever since the publication of C. Wright Mills' *Power Elite* (1959)[81] there has been a revival of interest in Pareto's work in America. Suzanne Keller's *Beyond the Ruling Class,*[82] T. B. Bottomore's *Elites and Society,*[83] as well as S. E. Finer's[84] and Joseph Lopreato's[85] selections from his work testify to this.

[79] Cf. John H. Goldthorpe, "Vilfredo Pareto," in Timothy Raison, *The Founding Fathers of Social Science* (Harmondsworth, England, Penguin Books, 1969), pp. 116–18.

[80] Cf. among many others, Harold D. Lasswell *et al., The Comparative Study of Elites* (Stanford, Stanford University Press, 1952).

[81] C. Wright Mills, *The Power Elite* (New York, Oxford University Press, 1959).

[82] Suzanne Keller, *Beyond the Ruling Class* (New York, Random House, 1963).

[83] T. B. Bottomore, *Elites and Society* (New York, Basic Books, 1964).

[84] Finer, *Vilfredo Pareto.* [85] Lopreato, *Vilfredo Pareto.*

In Europe too there has been a renewal of interest in Pareto, as witness the work of Raymond Aron in France[86] and Jaeggi[87] and Eisermann[88] in Germany.

Now that Pareto's ideological tirades have been largely neutralized by time, his thought is likely to have continued impact on the social sciences.

86 *Main Currents.* 87 Urs Jaeggi, *Die Gesellschaftliche Elite* (Bern, 1960).
88 G. Eisermann, *Vilfredo Paretos System der allgemeinen Soziologie* (Stuttgart, Enke, 1968).

Karl Mannheim

1893-1947

THE WORK

THE SOCIOLOGY OF KNOWLEDGE

Although Karl Mannheim's restless mind made contributions to many areas of sociological inquiry, it is now generally accepted that his sociology of knowledge is the most valuable and enduring part of his work. This branch of sociology studies the relation between thought and society and is concerned with the social or existential conditions of knowledge.

While the nature of the interdependence between knowledge and society is by no means clearly worked out in Mannheim, he was concerned in all phases of his work with considering ideas in relation to the structures in which they are variously embedded. The notion of structure and of interrelation is central to all his thought and guides him in all his writings. Rejecting an atomizing or isolating approach to ideas, he stressed that thinking was an activity that must be related to other social activity within a structural frame. To Mannheim, the sociological viewpoint "seeks from the very beginning to interpret individual activity in all spheres within the context of group experience."[1] Thinking is never a privileged activity free from the effects of group life; therefore, it must be understood and interpreted within its context. No given individual "confronts the world and, in striving for the truth, constructs a world view out of the data of his experience. . . . It is much more correct that knowledge is from the very beginning a co-operative process of group life, in which everyone unfolds his knowledge within a framework of a common fate, a common activity, and the overcoming of common difficulties."[2]

He who goes to Mannheim to learn from him an integrated and consistent way of reasoning on the relation of knowledge to society is bound to be disappointed. Mannheim was a man acutely sensitive to many streams of thought, to many doctrines and perspectives. This accounts for the numerous inconsistencies in his work, which make his readers uneasy but of which he himself was well aware. Toward the end of his life, he wrote to the members of a seminar on the sociology of knowledge:

> If there are contradictions and inconsistencies in my paper this is I think,

[1] Karl Mannheim, *Ideology and Utopia* (New York, Harcourt Brace Jovanovich, 1936), p. 27.
[2] *Ibid.*, p. 26.

> not so much due to the fact that I overlooked them but because I make a point of developing a theme to its end even if it contradicts some other statements. I use this method because I think that in this marginal field of human knowledge we should not conceal inconsistencies, so to speak covering up the wounds, but our duty is to show the sore spots in human thinking at its present stage . . . these inconsistencies are the thorn in the flesh from which we have to start.[3]

What Mannheim said about a particular paper holds true for the entire corpus of his work on the sociology of knowledge. He attempted throughout his life to integrate various perspectives and to emerge with a novel synthesis. But such an integrated system of thought always eluded him. As he said in the letter quoted above: "I want to break through the old epistemology radically but have not succeeded yet fully."[4]

The groping and tentative nature of Mannheim's work makes a succinct exposition of his main ideas extremely difficult. What could be singled out in one place as a characteristic statement is contradicted by assertion elsewhere, often even in the same work. Nor is it possible to distinguish between earlier and later views as one can readily do with, say, Kant's critical and pre-critical phases of thought. Often Mannheim's late formulations are reminiscent of very early ones and sharply contradict formulations arrived at during his middle period.

Mannheim was a pioneer who ventured out on frontiers of knowledge that more cautious thinkers would avoid. He paid the price for this audacity: although he provided brilliant points of departure, approaches, and leads to further investigation, he was unable to gather the full fruits of his endeavors, leaving to his successors the privilege of entering the promised land that he himself could only dimly perceive.

Mannheim distinguished between two ways of dealing with cultural objects or intellectual phenomena. These may be understood, as it were, "from the inside," so that their immanent meanings are disclosed to the investigator; or, and this is the path of sociology of knowledge, they may be understood "from the outside" as a reflection of a societal process in which the thinker is inevitably enmeshed. In this perspective, knowledge is conceived as existentially determined, as *seinsverbunden*.

Mannheim undertook to generalize Marx's programmatic orientation "to inquire into the connection of . . . philosophy with . . . reality,"[5] and to analyze the ways in which systems of ideas depend on the social position—particularly the class positions—of their proponents. Mannheim transformed

[3] Kurt H. Wolff, "The Sociology of Knowledge and Sociological Theory" in Llewellyn Gross, ed., *Symposium on Sociological Theory* (New York, Row, Peterson, 1959), p. 571. [4] *Ibid.*, p. 572.

[5] Karl Marx and Friedrich Engels, *The German Ideology* (New York, International Publishers, 1939), p. 6.

what to Marx had been mainly a tool of polemical attack against his bourgeois adversaries into a general instrument of analysis that could be used as effectively for the study of Marxism as for any other system of thought.

In the Marxian formulation, attention was called to the functions of ideology for the defense of class privileges, and to the distortion and falsification of ideas that derived from the privileged positions of bourgeois thinkers. In contrast to this interpretation of bourgeois ideology, Marx's own ideas were held by the Marxists to be true and unbiased by virtue of their being an expression of a class—the proletariat—that had no privileged interests to defend. Mannheim did not make this distinction between various systems of ideas. He allowed for the probability that all ideas, even "truths," were related to, and hence influenced by, the social and historical situation from which they emerged. The very fact that each thinker is affiliated with particular groups in society—that he occupies a certain status and enacts certain social roles—colors his intellectual outlook. Men "do not confront the objects of the world from the abstract levels of a contemplating mind as such, nor do they do so exclusively as solitary beings. On the contrary, they act with and against one another in diversely organized groups, and while doing so they think with and against each other."[6]

Mannheim defined the sociology of knowledge as a theory of the social or existential conditioning of thought. To him all knowledge and all ideas are "bound to a location," though to different degrees, within the social structure and the historical process. At times a particular group can have fuller access to the understanding of a social phenomenon than other groups, but no group can have total access to it. Ideas are rooted in the differential location in historical time and social structure of their proponents so that thought is inevitably perspectivistic.

In Mannheim's sense,

> perspective . . . is something more than a merely formal determination of thinking. [It] signifies the manner in which one views an object, what one perceives in it, and how one construes it in his thinking. [Perspective] also refers to qualitative elements in the structure of thought, elements which must necessarily be overlooked by a purely formal logic. It is precisely these factors which are responsible for the fact that two persons, even if they apply the same formal-logical rules, may judge the same object very differently.[7]

Like the proverbial seven blind men trying to describe the properties of an elephant, persons viewing a common object from dissimilar angles of vision rooted in their different social location are apt to arrive at different cognitive

[6] *Ideology and Utopia,* p. 3. [7] *Ibid.,* p. 244.

conclusions and different value judgments. Human thought is "situationally relative" (*situations-gebunden*).

The notion of the existential determination of knowledge is the cornerstone of Mannheim's doctrine. Such a determination, Mannheim argues, is established when it can be shown that "the process of knowing does not actually develop historically in accordance with immanent laws, that it does not follow only from the 'nature of things' or from 'pure logical possibilities' and that it is not driven by an 'inner dialectic,'"[8] but that it is influenced decisively by extra-theoretical, that is by existential, factors. The thesis of the existential determination of knowledge is further strengthened, Mannheim argued, when it can be shown that these existential factors "are relevant not only to the genesis of ideas, but that they penetrate into their forms and content and that they decisively determine the scope and the intensity of our experience and observation, i.e. . . . the 'perspective' of the subject."[9]

It is Mannheim's major contention "that not only do fundamental orientations, evaluations, and the content of ideas differ but that the manner of stating a problem, the sort of approach made, and even the categories in which experiences are subsumed, collected, and ordered vary according to the social position of the observer."[10] Mannheim, in other words, moved beyond what he considered the "particular conception of ideology," in which only certain aspects of a statement are scrutinized for the possibility of their being biased, to a total conception in which entire modes of thoughts, their form as well as their contents, are conceived as being bound up with the social position of the proponent. One of Manheim's own examples will help illustrate this:

> When, in the early years of the nineteenth century, an old-style German conservative spoke of "freedom" he meant thereby the right of each estate to live according to its privileges (liberties). If he belonged to the romantic-conservative and Protestant movement he understood by it "inner freedom," i.e., the right of each individual to live according to his own individual personality. . . . When a liberal of the same period used the term "freedom" he was thinking of freedom *from* precisely those privileges which to the old-style conservative appeared to be the very basis of all freedom. . . . In brief, even in the formulations of concepts, the angle of vision is guided by the observer's interests. Thought, namely, is directed in accordance with what a particular social group expects.[11]

Mannheim tended to be elusive in defining the types of relations between social structure and knowledge. He stated that the term "existential determination" did not imply a mechanical cause-effect sequence, and stressed that only empirical investigation would disclose the precise nature of the relation in con-

[8] *Ibid.*, p. 240. [9] *Ibid.* [10] *Ibid.*, p. 130. [11] *Ibid.*, p. 245.

crete cases. Yet, as Merton has shown,[12] he used a variety of terms to point to the connection between thought and social structure. At times he implied that social forces were a direct cause of intellectual products. At other times he attributed the emergence of a particular thought form to the "interests" of the subjects. At yet other times he only claimed that the focus of attention of a subject directs him to certain ideas and not to others. Still again there are passages where he posited a kind of "elective affinity," a "compatibility" or "congruity" between particular social and historical situations and types of intellectual products. Finally, one also finds in Mannheim's work relatively weak formulations of the relations between thought and society. For example, instead of asserting a direct effect of social factors, he only asserts that the emergence of certain sets of ideas has as prerequisite the emergence of certain groups who will become their carrier. Mannheim, in other words, ranges widely when it comes to establishing the connection between "substructure and superstructure," to use Marxian terminology. While he sometimes seems to assert that social forces are necessary and sufficient conditions for the appearance of certain ideas, he is moved at other times to restrict his claim to stressing only facilitating social factors that enable sets of ideas to find expression and to get a hearing.

In the bulk of Mannheim's writings the different social locations of the carriers of ideas are conceived of mainly in terms of class factors. The thought of the *beati possedentes* is contrasted to the thought of the dispossessed; middle-class ideas are contrasted to the ideology of feudal strata; utopian thought rooted in the future orientation of the underprivileged is contrasted to ideological thought expressing a defense of the present order by those who profit from the *status quo*. Yet Mannheim did not limit himself to a program of study inherited from Marxian class analysis. He included a variety of other social factors such as status groups and occupational categories as existential determinants of ideas. For example, in his brilliant depiction of the social roots of German conservative thought in the first decades of the nineteenth century, Mannheim shows that in Prussia, where "the transformation of the feudal society of estates into a class society was still in its early stages," an active response to the French Revolution "came only from those strata in Prussia which their own history and the nature of the social order enabled to be politically effective, the nobility and the bureaucracy."[13] That is, whereas in France an analysis of the social determination of ideas would concentrate on the well-developed class structure of French society, in Germany an analysis of the social roots of ideas would have to focus largely on the status order of estate society.

[12] Robert K. Merton, *Social Theory and Social Structure* (New York, The Free Press, 1957), pp. 498–99. Merton's whole chapter, "Karl Mannheim and the Sociology of Knowledge" was indispensable to me.

[13] Karl Mannheim, "Conservative Thought" in *Essays on Sociology and Social Psychology* (New York, Oxford University Press, 1953), p. 121.

At the present time one is especially attentive to an additional factor to which Mannheim devoted considerable attention, that of generational differences in relation to ideas. In fact, it may be that the comparative neglect in the past of Mannheim's sociology of generations and its "rediscovery" in the present can be considered a prime example of the existential determination of knowledge. Mannheim held that

> The fact of belonging to the same class, and that of belonging to the same generation or age group, have this in common, that both endow the individuals sharing in them with a common location in the social and historical process, and thereby limit them to a specific range of potential experience, predisposing them for a certain characteristic mode of thought and experience, and a characteristic type of historically relevant action.[14]

Furthermore, while youth experiencing the same historical problems may be said to be part of the same actual generation, "those groups within the same actual generation which work up the material of their common existence in different specific ways, constitute separate generation units."[15] Romantic-conservative youth and liberal-rationalistic youth in post-revolutionary France differed in their ideologies but they "were merely two polar forms of the intellectual and social response to an historical stimulus experienced by all in common."[16] They formed different generational units belonging to the same actual generation. In the same way today, hippies and New Left activists might be seen as belonging to different generational units responsive in their differing ways to an historical stimulus experienced by all of them in common. They share a field of vision, yet see it differently.

Mannheim wished it to be understood that his theoretical contributions to the sociology of knowledge fell into two parts: substantive contributions involving "purely empirical investigation through description and structural analysis of the ways in which social relationships, in fact, influence thought," and "epistemological inquiry concerned with the bearing of this interrelationship upon the problem of validity."[17] It would seem that he was considerably more successful in the first endeavor than he was in the second. On epistemological questions regarding the truth value or validity of propositions, Mannheim was frequently muddled and made himself an easy target of criticism. Yet such questions preoccupied him throughout his work on the sociology of knowledge and at times seem to have taken primacy in his mind over empirical investigations.

Mannheim wavered radically when it came to the question of whether the sociology of knowledge is capable of contributing to the establishment of the

[14] Karl Mannheim, "The Problem of Generations" in *Essays on the Sociology of Knowledge* (New York, Oxford University Press, 1952), p. 291. [15] *Ibid.*, p. 304. [16] *Ibid.*

[17] *Ideology and Utopia*, p. 239.

truth value of a proposition. In his middle period he wanted to develop a sociological theory of knowledge, a sociological epistemology, according to which the truth of a statement can be ascertained only through an investigation of the social location of its author. In many incautious statements Mannheim comes perilously close to a universal epistemological relativism which left him defenseless against critics who asserted that such a position was "self-contradictory, for it must presuppose its own absoluteness."[18] Yet in some of his earliest writings dating from 1921 Mannheim gave a radically different solution to the problem of knowledge. He wrote: "The truth or falsity of a proposition or of the entire theoretical sphere can be neither supported nor attacked by means of a sociological or any other genetic explanation. . . . How something came to be . . . is altogether irrelevant for its immanent character of validity."[19] And in his last systematic statement (1936) on the subject—in the end is the beginning—Mannheim returned to the formulation of his youth: "It is, of course, true that in the social sciences, as elsewhere, the ultimate criterion of truth or falsity is to be found in the investigation of the object, and the sociology of knowledge is no substitute for this."[20]

During the middle period of his work on the sociology of knowledge Mannheim asserted programmatically that all thought necessarily has an ideological character. Critics soon pointed out that such a position, in addition to being self-contradictory, would lead to total relativism and nihilism. Stung by such criticism Mannheim made several attempts to save the assertion from the critics. At times he argued in terms of a pragmatic theory of adjustment to the requirements of particular historical situations. In this perspective, a set of ideas is valid if it can be shown that it contributes to the adjustment of a society in a given historical stage, and an opposing set of ideas is invalid if it fails to contribute to such an adjustment. This solution has patent weaknesses. Judgments as to what contributes to adjustment and what does not are not only largely normative, but they are likely, at best, to be *ex post facto* judgments. It may be possible in many cases to decide after the event which ideas contributed to historical adjustments, but it seems impossible to make such evaluations about contemporary ideas.

When pragmatic criteria turned out to be unsatisfactory, Mannheim turned to another solution to the dilemma. Seizing upon a notion first advanced by his teacher Alfred Weber, he now asserted that although all strata and groups produce ideas whose validity is compromised by virtue of the existential position of their upholders, there was one type of people, the "socially unattached intelligentsia" (*die sozial freischwebende Intelligenz*), who is capable of un-

[18] H. Otto Dahlke, "The Sociology of Knowledge" in Barnes, Becker, and Becker, ed., *Contemporary Social Theory* (New York, Appleton, 1940), p. 87.

[19] Quoted from an unpublished manuscript in David Kettler, "Sociology of Knowledge and Moral Philosophy: The Place of Traditional Problems in Mannheim's Thought," *Political Science Quarterly*, LXXXII, 3 (September, 1967), pp. 399–426.

[20] *Ideology and Utopia*, p. 4.

distorted and hence valid thought. Mannheim argued that because intellectuals have cut themselves loose from their original roots and, moreover, engage in a continued dialogue with each other, sloughing off through mutual criticism the remaining traces of their original biases, these intellectuals are able to reach an Olympian detachment from the mundane traces of earthly involvement. It seems fairly obvious that Mannheim here managed to create a kind of *deus ex machina,* which has more affinity with the Marxian myth of the pure and unsullied proletariat or the Hegelian absolute spirit than with empirical realities. Later it will become clear how deeply rooted in Mannheim's own intellectual history was the belief in the redeeming qualities of detached intellectuals. Here it may suffice to note that the belief in a category of people, who by "translation of one perspective into the terms of another" manage to encompass all of them and hence attain truly valid knowledge, is hardly more than a wish fulfilling dream. Even if it be granted that men of ideas often manage to divest themselves from certain biases and prejudices that infect the multitude, one need only point to the numerous "treasons of the clerks" (to use Julien Benda's term) that have marked history to realize that intellectuals are by no means immune from the passions, the temptations, and the corruptions of their time. Individual intellectuals may indeed at times manage to be *au dessus de la mêlée;* intellectuals as a category are not. Education and intellectual endeavors may indeed lead to a measure of critical detachment, but they do not suffice to make intellectuals into pristine custodians of pure reason.

It seems to be the scholarly consensus that Mannheim's attempts to escape the accusation of relativistic nihilism by the routes of the notion of pragmatic adjustment or of the free floating intelligentsia were far from successful. To some extent Mannheim must have felt this himself. In his later writings his claims to have wrought a revolution in epistemology were considerably muted. Rather than asserting that all thought is necessarily ideological and hence invalid, he now preferred a much less debatable argument, according to which perspectivistic thought is not necessarily incorrect but is one-sided by virtue of the social location of its upholders. Instead of the necessarily ideological character of all statements, we now get simply a warning that perspectivistic thought "might merely represent a partial view." This weakened version of the doctrine Mannheim called "relationism." Coupled as it is with the assertion that the social location of a thinker is "by no means irrelevant for the determination of the truth of a statement,"[21] the doctrine of relationism brought Mannheim fairly near to the position on value relevance (*Wertbeziehung*) that the neo-Kantians and Max Weber had elaborated long before him. The epistemological revolution had ended, or so it would seem, not with a bang but with a whimper.

When Mannheim used the sociology of knowledge as a concrete tool of

[21] *Ibid.,* p. 256.

research in substantive areas, he was much more successful than when he was diverted into dubious epistemological battles. His essays, for example, on "Conservative Thought," "The Problem of Generations," "Competition as a Cultural Phenomenon," "The Democratization of Culture," and "The Problem of the Intelligentsia"[22] are likely to be read widely at a time when Mannheim's sallies into epistemology will be of concern to only a few philosophers of science. Even in these papers Mannheim's propensity to vagueness of thought and expression, his tendency, for example, to bunch together under the blanket term "knowledge" elements as disparate as political beliefs, ethical judgments, categories of thought, and empirical observations, often detract from the value of his observation. Nevertheless, he helped open up a whole new field of sociological inquiry by showing in concrete detail how thinkers are deeply enmeshed in the historical and structural context to which they are existentially wedded. Mannheim taught us that men of knowledge are bound by many chains to the world of their fellows. He also taught us to appreciate again Rousseau's dictum that to know these chains for what they are is better than to deck them with flowers.

"Scepticism, driven to extremes," says Sir Isaiah Berlin, "defeats itself by becoming self-refuting."[23] But moderate scepticism, when it leads to inquiry on the possible sources of prejudice, bias, and distortion, can be a thoroughly liberating endeavor contributing to the perennial quest of man to know himself better.

THE SOCIOLOGY OF PLANNED RECONSTRUCTION

When Mannheim was forced to emigrate to England after the Nazi seizure of power, his whole intellectual orientation and plan of study suffered a sea change. He effectively abandoned sustained work in the sociology of knowledge and devoted himself for the remaining years of his life to a "Diagnosis of Our Time" and to the elaboration of a sociology of social planning and social reconstruction.

His English writings (as well as some of the work that dates from the period just before his emigration) differ dramatically from his early contributions. The fairly detached scholar with his somewhat muted left-wing sympathies now became a *sociologue engagé*. Mannheim now wrote like a man at bay. The rising tide of fascism threatened to engulf the whole of Europe, and Mannheim felt that no longer did it behoove the scholar to stay in his

[22] All these essays, as well as most of Mannheim's writings in the sociology of knowledge, outside *Ideology and Utopia,* are to be found in the following volumes: *Essays on Sociology and Social Psychology, Essays on the Sociology of Knowledge,* and *Essays on the Sociology of Culture* (New York, Oxford University Press, 1956).

[23] Isaiah Berlin, *Four Essays on Liberty* (New York, Oxford University Press, 1969), p. liii.

academic tower when all of civilization threatened to fall into the abyss of fascism.

Mannheim's diagnosis starts with the assertion that the contemporary crisis of civilization can be traced to a process of "fundamental democratization." While in previous ages elites had managed to keep the mass of mankind from having an effective say in political affairs, this political and cultural monopoly of the elites had now broken down. "Today a growing number of social groups strive for a share in social and political control and demand that their own interests be represented. The fact that these social groups come from the intellectually backward masses is a threat to those elites which formerly sought to keep the masses at a low intellectual level."[24] But the rise of the masses is not a threat to the elites alone. To the extent that these masses who are demanding a hearing in the political arena are driven by nonrational urges and emotions, they threaten the whole society. A society in which rational habits of thought are unevenly distributed is bound to be unstable.[25] It is likely to be engulfed in a revolt of disorganized and irrational mass movements if no new checks can be devised to channel and confine the wave of irrationality that emerges from the lower depth of mass society. The older elites have lost their hold, they are no longer able to lead, and at the same time society has become increasingly interdependent, rationalized, and organized, hence craving for leadership.

Within the organizations of mass society "functional rationality"—that is, the organization of series of action in such a way that they are highly calculable and efficient—has made great strides. But this process has at the same time led to a concomitant decline of "substantial rationality," that is, of "acts of thought which reveal intelligent insight into the interrelations of events."[26] "The more industrialized a society is and the more advanced its division of labor and organization, the greater will be the sphere of human activity which will be functionally rational and hence also calculable in advance."[27] But with this increasing regimentation, the chances have multiplied for substantially irrational behavior by men who wish to escape from the imprisoning rhythm of organized and rationalized life. The complicated world of modern functional rationality appears alien and incomprehensible to the ordinary man, especially in time of crisis when "the rationalized mechanism of social life collapses."[28] Men then experience a "state of terrified helplessness. . . . Just as nature was unintelligible to primitive man, and his deepest feelings of anxiety arose from the incalculability of the forces of nature, so for modern industrialized man the incalculability of the forces at work in the social system

[24] Karl Mannheim, *Man and Society in an Age of Reconstruction* (London, Routledge and Kegan Paul, 1940), p. 25. [25] *Ibid.*, p. 46. [26] *Ibid.*, p. 53. [27] *Ibid.*, p. 55. [28] *Ibid.*, p. 59.

under which he lives, with its economic crisis, inflation, and so on, has become a source of equally pervading fears."[29]

Palliatives devised by the old elites can no longer alleviate the fears and the panic of the masses of men. Hence, only a totally reconstructed social system, one that no longer relies on the uncoordinated activity of individuals held together by the forces of the market but on self-conscious planning, can hope to save western civilization. The present crisis requires the development of a new social style of thought that will again allow substantial rationality to dominate the affairs of men. Only at the level of "planned thinking" can the social world be brought under the ordering control of the democratic polity. Nothing less is required than a total restructuring of human thought and human will. Where the unseen hand of God has failed and brought us to our present predicament, democratic planning must be substituted. "All of us know by now that from this war there is no way back to a laissez faire order of society, that war as such is a maker of a silent revolution by preparing the road to a new planned order."[30]

Democratic planning, to Mannheim, is by no means only economic planning, though it is that also. Planning must lead to overall social reconstruction. It must, for example, lead to a reintegration of men into meaningful groups. "The great psychological and sociological problem in the future is . . . how to organize inarticulate masses and crowds into various forms of groups."[31] Not only the material well-being of the citizen of the future must be planned, but even his spiritual well-being can no longer be left to chance. This is why Mannheim, fundamentally an agnostic, was yet moved to advocate a revival of religion as a bulwark against disintegration. This is why he now assigned to the Christian churches the task of overcoming the weakening of moral values that had been the heritage of laissez faire society. The sociologist must realize "that for many reasons there is need of spiritual power to integrate people."[32] "In the old days religion was a stabilizer; today we turn to it again for assistance in the transition."[33]

Anything that helps reintegrate people and reestablish an order that has almost collapsed now appears to be in need of revitalization. "Education, adult education, social work, juvenile courts, child guidance clinics, parent education represent some of the institutions, old and new, which are instruments in our hands. . . . Denominational groups, local groups, interest groups, professional groups, age groups will develop a variety of approaches to valuations, but it is essential to supplement the divergence by a machinery of co-ordina-

[29] *Ibid.*

[30] Karl Mannheim, *Diagnosis of Our Time* (London, Routledge and Kegan Paul, 1943), p. 38.

[31] *Ibid.*, p. 93.

[32] Karl Mannheim, *Freedom, Power and Democratic Planning* (New York, Oxford University Press, 1950), p. 312. [33] *Ibid.*, p. 313.

tion and value mediation which culminates in a collectively agreed value policy, without which no society can survive."[34]

Mannheim believed that in the planned society of the future the selection of leaders cannot be left to chance.

> The current transformation of an unplanned society of group and personal competition into a planned society will result in increasingly systematic ways of selecting leaders. Instead of taking for granted that free competition will automatically bring the right man to the top . . . scientific selection promises a method of choice more strictly according to ability and merit. . . . Undoubtedly these still largely experimental methods promise to become efficient tools in selecting leaders.[35]

Mannheim was at pains to point out over and over again that the chosen scientific elite of social planners, new style sociologists, and moral leaders should always be responsive to other members of the society, and should not be tempted to impose their will on the community. But it is precisely on the often repeated point that social planning by an elite and democratic process are not incompatible that Mannheim's discourse is distressingly vague. He never really seems to have confronted the question of who guards the guardians and who plans the planners. Instead, he was wont to evade the issue by resorting to ambiguous formulations that often skirt the real issues. Mannheim distinguished between what he called arbitrary power and functional power. He claimed that in the good society of the future arbitrary power would disappear. "Our problem is how to gain control over the diverse centers of arbitrary power, how to coordinate and weld them into a more comprehensive pattern, how to discipline them gradually to function in the service of the community."[36] But what may be functional power to some may be arbitrary power to others. It all depends whose ox is being gored.

Mannheim was deeply beholden to democratic values. Yet one cannot suppress the suspicion that some of the means which he suggested the planners employ to revitalize democracy have the potentiality of killing the patient. He wished "to educate the individual out of his dependence on mass emotion,"[37] but he believed that for this aim to succeed, a

> conscious attempt at community reorganization and the readjustment of disintegrated personalities was needed. In the process of that primary conscious reintegration propaganda may play a valuable role. For propaganda, if rightly understood, does not necessarily mean the inculcation of false creeds, but the most successful way of dealing with impulses and desires which are not yet embodied in the groups in which we live. It is at once the simplest and most superficial form of reintegration.[38]

[34] *Diagnosis of Our Time*, p. 29. [35] *Freedom, Power and Democratic Planning*, pp. 95–96. [36] *Ibid.*, p. 69. [37] *Man and Society*, p. 359. [38] *Ibid.*

The writings of Mannheim's British period have not stood the test of time precisely because they were so very timely.[39] He grappled with many problems that still beset those of us who wish to bring about a planned society which yet safeguards democratic rights and the citizen's prerogatives. But his formulations tended to become flabby because of the urgencies of the hour in which he wrote. The promised synthesis of the idea of planning and of democracy, of manipulation and accountability, of scientific leadership and self-regulation turned out, upon inspection, to be largely a matter of verbal reconciliation. These problems are still with us. Even though the modern reader may derive great benefit from some of Mannheim's insights into the sources of our modern predicament and his sociological imagination might be stirred by the brilliant distinction between functional and substantial rationality, he will yet come away from these volumes with a sense of disappointment.

Granted, the disorders and distempers of the time called for drastic reconstruction. But the rage for order that animated Mannheim in his English period dragged him into a dangerous proximity to the ghost of Auguste Comte. The *sociologue engagé* did not resist nearly enough the demons first called into being by the spiritual son of Saint-Simon.

THE MAN

Karl Mannheim was born in Budapest on March 27, 1893, the only son of a Hungarian-Jewish father and a German-Jewish mother. His parents were solid, though by no means wealthy, members of the middle class. The young Mannheim attended the Budapest humanist *Gymnasium* and then took up philosophy at the local university. Soon thereafter he went to Germany, where in 1912–13 he studied for a year under Georg Simmel in Berlin. However, it was the situation in his native Budapest that was decisive for his further cultural and political intellectual development.[40]

Already as a very young man the precocious Karl Mannheim was an active participant in the small but increasingly self-conscious group of Budapest intellectuals. A high proportion of these men were, like himself, of Jewish origin. These intellectuals resembled in some ways the Russian intelligentsia of

[39] For a different interpretation which yet proved helpful to me in writing this section see Gunter W. Remmling, *Wissenssoziologie und Gesellschaftsplanung: Das Werk Karl Mannheims* (Dortmund, Ruhfus, 1968).

[40] My account of Mannheim's early Hungarian environment is largely based on David Kettler's detailed researches both in his *Marxismus und Kultur* (Neuwied und Berlin, Luchterhand, 1967) and in the first chapters of a full-length study of Mannheim which Professor Kettler is now writing. I am deeply indebted to both Kettler's book and his manuscript. I have also profited from a book on the prewar Hungarian intellectuals by the Hungarian historian Zoltan Horvath entitled *Die Jahrhundertwende in Ungarn,* German transl. (Neuwied und Berlin, Luchterhand, 1966). Cf. also Morris Watnick's fine study of Georg Lukacs in *Soviet Survey* (January–March 1958, April–June 1958, July–September 1958, January–March 1959).

the previous century. Like them, they were largely men without firm attachment to any of the major strata and classes of their society. They were conscious of their isolation and unhappily or proudly aware of their marginality.

THE INTELLECTUAL MILIEU OF BUDAPEST

The failure of the revolution of 1848 and the Austro-Hungarian Compromise of 1867 had created a Hungarian society and polity which was prosperous and seemingly stable but suffered from deep subterranean cleavages. The Hungarian state was run by an elite stratum of cosmopolitan aristocrats who cultivated a refined courtly style made possible through the revenues from their huge landholdings, and who tended to be oriented more toward Vienna than toward the still somewhat provincial Budapest. The machinery of government was mainly in the hands of members of a narrow-minded, chauvinistic, impoverished gentry who abhorred modern thought and progressive innovation and ruled over the peasantry in alliance with the Church. The peasantry, the bulk of the population, was economically oppressed, illiterate, politically disenfranchised, and docile. Even after the electoral reforms of 1913, less than one third of the male population had access to the ballot. About half the population was not of Hungarian origin and resisted more or less passively all efforts of the ruling strata to have them absorb and assimilate the culture of the Magyars and integrate in the Hungarian "national state." The industrial working class, though developing at the turn of the century, was still relatively small. In a population of 18 million, there were only 300,000 industrial workers around 1900, and of these only some 70,000 had joined unions by 1905.

The upper classes had but little contact with the peasantry, and the political and social life of the capital was almost completely severed from contact with the surrounding agrarian hinterland. Budapest was the only city in which a properous and relatively cultivated middle class had developed. This middle class, however, was largely Jewish in origin; no native Hungarian bourgeoisie had ever developed prior to World War I. The Budapest Jewish middle class had been freed from legal disabilities only in the 1860's. Isolated from other strata and feeling itself an island in a sea of nonbourgeois classes, it developed no strong political consciousness. It was intent on not offending the ruling aristocracy and gentry, and in fact was not averse to strengthening Magyar chauvinism through the newspapers and other media of communication it largely controlled. Content to manage and own most banking and commerce, it was ever ready to protest its loyalty to the powers that be.

Until the 1890's, the small intelligentsia of the capital largely accepted the prevailing state of things. Academic men in particular felt very much part of the establishment and defended its cultural prerogatives. But roughly around the turn of the century, the cultural scene changed drastically. All sorts of modern currents emerged simultaneously and a variety of intellectual doctrines of a nonconformist nature made their appearance. In the sciences, in music, in the fine arts, in literature, and in the social sciences modernistic and reforming thought flooded the cultural scene and overwhelmed the staid keepers of tradition. Some of the younger intellectuals who now came to the fore stemmed from the weak liberal wing of the impoverished gentry, others were drawn to it through the "Social Catholic" movement among reform oriented clergy and laymen, but most of them were sons and daughters of the Jewish middle class.

Insofar as politics and the social sciences were concerned, the innovating young intelligentsia found its main center in the *Society for Social Sciences* and its journal *The Twentieth Century* (*Huszadik Szazad*).

The Society sponsored translations of the works of, among others, Herbert Spencer, Lester Ward, Benjamin Kidd, Karl Kautsky, and Gustav Ratzenhofer. Deeply influenced by Comtean and Spencerian ideas, it resembled in many essentials the British Fabian society or the American Progressive movement. It propagandized for rational and scientific politics. Though programmatically committed to democracy, it had but little political contact with either the peasantry or the slowly emerging working class and its representatives in the Social Democratic Party. Moreover, a strong Hungarian national sentiment, which seems to have been at least as strong among recently assimilated Jewish intellectuals as among their Magyar counterparts, made all of them incapable of establishing contact with the national minorities. As a result, these intellectuals remained isolated, somewhat elitist in orientation, and condemned to political impotence. Zoltan Horvath, the historian of this group, writes: "In the progressive intellectual movements one always came across the same names; the movement was always limited to the same thin stratum, the few intellectuals who had gathered around radical sociology."[41]

Tied to the progressive intellectuals of the *Society for Social Sciences* by many ideological and personal connections was a special lodge of Freemasons, which arose a few years later. This lodge was named for the Hungarian revolutionary Ignaz Martinovics, and its members included many of the leading social reformers and some of the intellectual leaders of the Social Democratic Party. This lodge, in turn, was instrumental in founding a student society, the *Galileo Circle,* where the young reformist students first absorbed progressive literature and familiarized themselves with the "advanced" philosophy of William James and the positivism of Avenarius and Mach. It was in this intellectual milieu that the young Mannheim developed his intellectual outlook before leaving for Germany in 1912, and again after his return shortly before the beginning of the war.

During the first years of the war conditions did not change very much in Budapest. Most rich or educated young men were exempt from military ser-

[41] Horvath, *op. cit.,* p. 353.

vice. Academic activities as well as the lectures and discussions of the *Society for Social Sciences* continued as before. The political interests of the majority of the intellectuals remained severely restricted, emerging only again after the Russian Revolution.

Before the Hungarian revolution of 1918, there came into being yet another group of intellectuals, which, though even smaller than that around the *Society for Social Sciences,* had a decisive impact on subsequent Hungarian cultural history and on the development of Karl Mannheim. This was a discussion group led by Georg Lukacs, who had returned to Budapest from Heidelberg in 1915. Although he was then only thirty-one years old, he had made a name for himself as a literary critic and author of works in esthetics in both Hungarian and German. He had been close to Max Weber and had been singled out with high praise by Simmel. His philosophical orientation at the time was in the tradition of German idealism and historicism, though he had also read widely in German mysticism and vitalistic philosophy. Political concerns were then alien to him. Lukacs organized a weekly discussion group, which for three years met every Sunday in the house of a friend and admirer of Lukacs, the writer Bela Balazs. Karl Mannheim, as well as the art historian Arnold Hauser and other young intellectuals in their 20's and 30's, became regular members. Though they were all to be counted "on the left," they were hardly concerned with any kind of politics; if they opposed capitalist civilization it was in the name of *Geist* and idealism rather than in the name of socialism. In 1917, this group began to organize lectures and seminars under the name of *Free School for the Humanities,* stressing idealistic German philosophy in contradistinction to the positivism of the *Society for Social Sciences.*

The overall orientation of the Lukacs group appeared clearly in a lecture by Karl Mannheim entitled "Soul and Culture," which was given in the fall of 1917, and in a programmatic statement of the aims of the group, published in 1918 together with Mannheim's lecture. The introduction asserted that the time had come for a "reawakening of spirituality" and that "European culture now will turn away from the positivism of the nineteenth century and return to a metaphysical idealism." Mannheim's lecture affirmed that Marxist sociology and naturalism were *passé,* and he called for a return to Dostoievsky and Kierkegaard, as well as to Kant and Meister Eckart. Simmel's philosophy, and more particularly his analysis of the "Tragedy of Culture," were the dominant influence on Mannheim's exposition. He spoke as the exponent of a new generation, which, no longer content with the social science of its predecessors and its optimistic progressivism and positivism, searched for new spiritual nourishment. The new generation, Mannheim believed, needed to renovate human culture, reaffirm the dignity of the human spirit, and save the human soul from materialistic, positivistic, and scientistic shackles.

The opposition between the group of reformist sociologists that gathered in the *Society for Social Sciences* and the young defenders of *Geist* and idealism around Lukacs must not be overdrawn. To some extent this was a kind of family quarrel between intellectuals who were conscious of their minority position and their marginality and hence were drawn to each other regardless of doctrinal differences. Mannheim for one, despite his newly found allegiances, continued to attend the meetings of the *Society for Social Sciences* and retained his membership in the Martinovics Lodge. The lectures and seminars of the new Lukacs grouping were advertised in the meeting rooms of the *Society for Social Sciences,* and one of the leading members of the Lukacs group, the poet Anna Lezsnai, also happened to be the wife of the guiding spirit of the progressive social scientists, Oscar Jaszi.

The parting of the ways came only when Hungarian Revolution broke out. The members of the *Society for Social Sciences* became the intellectual mainstays of the Republican and mildly socialist Karolyi regime, which took power after the revolution of October 31, 1918. Members of the Lukacs circle played a very small part in this first phase of the revolution. But in December, 1918 Lukacs suddenly, and to the great surprise of his friends, entered the newly formed Communist Party. He was soon followed by a number of others in his group.

While the members of the *Society for Social Sciences* were in the main among the revolutionary moderates, the previous apolitical Lukacs group suddenly became the intellectual spokesmen for the Soviet regime when the Hungarian Soviet Republic was proclaimed on March 21, 1919. A good number of the lecturers of the *Free School for the Humanities* now turned from the soul to the revolution, and most of the fifty or so people who had at one time or another been among its audience turned to the Communist Party.

When the Soviet regime reorganized the University of Budapest in April 1919, almost all those who had been active in the *Free School* received positions or chairs at the University. Mannheim and Hauser never entered the Party like their spiritual mentor, but both taught, in philosophy and the theory of literature respectively, at the reorganized university. Nevertheless, Mannheim and Anna Lezsnai made an attempt to continue the group that Lukacs had founded and had now deserted.

The short-lived Communist regime collapsed at the beginning of July, 1919. It had never managed to gain support among the peasantry or to secure the countryside; nor did it succeed in reorganizing industrial and commercial activities in the provincial cities and in the capital. The Allies were determined to destroy it, and the old ruling strata preferred a humiliated and truncated Hungary to one dominated by Bela Kun and his revolutionary vanguard. Mannheim and all the other intellectuals who had taken a part in the Soviet regime, no matter how peripherally, were forced to flee from the White Terror.

During his subsequent academic career in Germany, Mannheim seems consciously to have avoided political involvements. It is nevertheless noteworthy that his first appearance before the German scholarly public was a review of a book by his friend and erstwhile mentor Georg Lukacs.[42] He continued to consider himself a man of the Left. He showed a certain amount of sympathy for the German labor movement and was linked in friendship with socialist intellectuals, including Paul Tillich and Emil Lederer.[43] But during the next decade or so Mannheim cultivated his academic connections and aspired to play an almost exclusively academic role. He continued his studies at Freiburg, where he attended Heidegger's lectures, and at Heidelberg. As Simmel had previously influenced his thought during his attendance at the University of Berlin, Alfred Weber may be counted the strongest influence on him at Heidelberg. Mannheim now lived as a *Privatgelehrte,* a private scholar, on an income provided by his family. He exposed himself in these years to a variety of currents of thought then contending for dominance in the hectic German intellectual world of the twenties. He was influenced by the Neo-Kantians, especially by Heinrich Rickert, but also by Husserl's phenomenology. At times he seems to have flirted with *Lebensphilosophie* and other antirationalist currents, but for the most part he fluctuated between adopting the cool critical position of a Heinrich Rickert and attempting to build a comprehensive new synthesis in the manner of a Hegel or Marx.

In his early years in postwar Germany Mannheim still considered himself a philosopher rather than a social scientist. His doctoral dissertation published in 1922, "Structural Analysis of Epistemology,"[44] is still, as the title indicates, conceived as a contribution to the philosophical analysis of knowledge. But soon sociological concerns began to dominate Mannheim's thought, partly because of the influence of Alfred Weber and of Max Scheler. His *Habilitationsschrift* "Conservative Thought,"[45] published five years later, is a sociological treatise.

In 1925 Mannheim was named *Privatdozent* (lecturer) at the University of Heidelberg. Two years later he was appointed Franz Oppenheimer's successor as professor of sociology and economics at the University of Frankfort. In 1925 he married the psychologist Juliska Lang, who was a fellow student at both Budapest and Heidelberg and who came from a Hungarian background very similar to his own. Mannheim's interest in psychology and psychoanalysis, especially in his later years, was mainly inspired by his wife, with whom he collaborated intimately.

Frankfort University, where Mannheim taught until he was forced to emigrate to England in 1933, was one of the centers of liberalism in Germany. Established originally through private funds and hence less dependent on governmental support, it was a harbor of liberal and even radical thought in the twenties and early thirties. (A few years after Mannheim arrived there, Max Horkheimer established his Institute for Social Research at the same

[42] Translated by Kurt H. Wolff in *Studies on the Left,* III, 3 (Summer, 1963).
[43] Paul Kecskemeti, personal communication, March 11, 1969.
[44] *Essays on Sociology and Social Psychology,* Chapter 1. [45] *Ibid.,* Chapter 2.

university). Little is known about Mannheim's years at Frankfort, except that he was an inspiring teacher who attracted and excited students. To judge from his intellectual output—both his masterpiece *Ideology and Utopia* and most of his other important contributions to the sociology of knowledge were written in Frankfort—these must have been comparatively serene years for Mannheim, even though toward the end the serenity was overshadowed by the rise of Nazism.

THE ENGLISH YEARS

His immigration to England in 1933, where he served as a lecturer at the London School of Economics and later as professor of education at London University, opened a totally new chapter in Mannheim's life. The emigration from Hungary to Germany had been relatively painless. No linguistic adjustment had been necessary, and Mannheim had already been a full participant in German cultural activities even before he came to live in Germany. The emigration to England was of a different kind. Mannheim now saw himself as a refugee in a culture and society which, to a large extent, was terra incognita to him. This involved fundamental adjustments: finding an entirely new audience and making an effort at self-transformation.

The change in Mannheim's style of thought was in effect so deep and decisive that there is a very sharp caesura between the "German" and the "British" Mannheim. The new intellectual context in which he operated led Mannheim decisively to shift his focus of interest and his general concerns. He almost totally abandoned the sociology of knowledge and devoted himself fully to the development of a sociology of democratic planning and social reconstruction. At the risk of some oversimplification, one might say that while Mannheim's German work stood under the shadow of Hegel and Marx and was focused on problems of social and intellectual change, his British work stood under the shadow of Durkheim. Jean Floud seems eminently correct when she writes that he now emerged "as a utopian of the right, seeking the security of an integrated society grounded in a common morality inculcated through education. Mannheim was a radical, but his radicalism was born of a deep conservatism. He yearned for stability. He wanted freedom . . . but freedom is impossible in a disordered society; change, social reconstruction is therefore unavoidable."[46] There is even reason to believe, as Jean Floud also notes, that just before his death in 1947 Mannheim reached beyond Durkheim to the latter's great French predecessor. "He was considering," writes Floud, "in a manner reminiscent of Comte, the possibility that sociology might provide the theology of a new social religion of democracy."[47]

[46] Jean Floud, "Karl Mannheim" in Timothy Raison, ed., *The Founding Fathers of Social Science* (Harmondsworth, England, Penguin Books, 1969), p. 204. [47] *Ibid.*, p. 213.

Mannheim's new interests were powerfully enhanced by a set of new acquaintances and friends he acquired soon after he moved to London. It would seem that he was never too well received by the established sociological fraternity at the London School. Instead, he came to be closely associated with a curious group of mainly religiously inspired and basically conservative men who went by the name of the Moot and who met quarterly to discuss problems of religious belief and the possible role of religion in the planned society of the future. Among the prominent members of the group were T. S. Eliot; J. Middleton Murry; Alex Vidler, a notable Anglican theologian and historian, then dean of Windsor Chapel; Joseph Oldham, an active Anglican social reformer; and other literary and academic men as well as senior civil servants and theologians.[48] It was before this group that Mannheim read a long paper, "Towards a New Social Philosophy: A Challenge to Christian Thinkers by a Sociologist."[49]

As Mannheim became increasingly interested in education as a means of bringing about reconstruction of society, he came to associate with a variety of educational reformers. Encouraged by Sir Fred Clarke, the director of the University of London Institute of Education, Mannheim lectured widely to a variety of groups interested in educational reform. These lectures, later gathered together in his *Diagnosis of Our Time,* were given originally before such disparate audiences as, to name but a few, an "International Gathering of Friends Service Council"; the "Week-End Summer Meeting of the Delegacy for Extra-Mural Studies at the University of Oxford"; a "Conference of Federal Union" at Oxford; the "New Education Fellowship" at Oxford; a "Youth Leaders' Conference" at Oxford arranged by the Board of Education. In the war years especially, Mannheim deliberately and self-consciously wished to transcend the purely academic audiences to which he had been almost completely limited in Germany. He desired to reach those educational leaders and public authorities who, so he believed, would have a hand at creating the planned society for which he was striving. Mannheim's effort to gain an audience wider than that of professional sociologists is perhaps best documented by the series of books he persuaded a leading British publishing house, Kegan Paul, Trench, Trubner and Co. (later Routledge and Kegan Paul) to publish under the characteristic title *International Library of Sociology and Social Reconstruction.* This library issued a great number of important studies in such traditional fields as "Sociology of Religion," "Sociology of Law," "Sociology of Art," "Sociology of Education," "Sociology of the Family," and "General Sociology." But it also had sections devoted to "Economic Planning," "Town and Country Planning," "Foreign Affairs—Their Social, Political and Economic Foundations," "Migration and Resettlement," "Anthropology and Colonial Policy," and "Sociology and Psychology of the Present Crisis." In addition to

[48] Edward Shils, "Karl Mannheim" in *International Encyclopedia of the Social Sciences* (New York, Macmillan, 1968). [49] *Diagnosis of Our Time,* pp. 100–65.

very fine studies in sociology, many of them of American origin or translated from Continental writings, the library also published books on important and timely questions, including *Plan for Reconstruction; Danger Spots in New Economic Controls; Patterns of Peacemaking* and *Creative Demobilization.* Mannheim's *International Library* was instrumental in introducing to a British public many works in sociology previously inaccessible, thereby helping to broaden the horizon of a rather insular British sociological fraternity. But the plan of the *Library* makes it amply clear that Mannheim intended to do more. He wished to impress on a wider public that the social sciences could vitally contribute to social reconstruction and the orderly planning of social affairs.

Mannheim died on January 9, 1947, shortly after the end of the war. It is idle to speculate whether, once the immediate pressures on the international scene were partly removed, he would have abandoned his activist stance and would again have concentrated his work on analysis and diagnosis rather than on prescriptions. As it was, he spent most of his abundant creative energies during his English years in passionate attempts to prepare for his adopted home country a way of life which the postwar welfare state has at least partly institutionalized since. While his sociological work of this period is not likely to rank with the output of his German period, he will be remembered as one of the architects of that post-capitalist society which has since spread from England over much of western civilization.

THE INTELLECTUAL CONTEXT

Mannheim's thought stands at the confluence of many intellectual currents and was shaped by all of them even as it slowly gained its own characteristic outlines. There are few doctrines and few intellectual, spiritual, and moral orientations from the end of the century to the turbulent years of the Weimar Republic and the Anglo-Saxon world of the thirties, that did not leave their mark on one or the other aspect of Mannheim's thinking. His was an amazingly adaptive mind which managed to turn to its own uses a variety of apparently contradictory approaches to philosophical, cultural, and sociological problems and queries.

Mannheim's native Budapest was almost completely dominated by German cultural influences, so that the ideas he absorbed in his youth were more or less similar to those that confronted a young intellectual anywhere within the reaches of German culture. Although the structure and form of life in Budapest was very different from that in Berlin or Vienna, the content of ideas surrounding a budding intellectual in Budapest differed only marginally from that experienced by his contemporaries in other centers of German culture.

In his *Gymnasium* days and probably in his first semesters at the University of Budapest, Mannheim was immersed to a large extent in the positivistic, optimistic, and reform-oriented stream of ideas that then dominated "advanced" thought in Budapest. Even though he reacted sharply against key aspects of these sets of ideas in his later career, it is readily apparent that he never abandoned them completely. One can discern in almost all of his writings, under layers of cultural criticism, of recondite *Geisteswissenschaft* and abstruse Hegelian formulations, sediments of the positivism and optimistic meliorism to which Mannheim was first exposed, together with the reformist intellectual elite of prewar Budapest.

When Mannheim went to Berlin on his first study trip abroad, he seems to have been much impressed with Georg Simmel. It is readily apparent from Mannheim's earliest published writings that Simmel's influence, both direct and soon thereafter mediated through his friend Georg Lukacs, dominated his thought for awhile. It was Simmel's philosophical ideas, not his formal sociology, which impressed Mannheim. By the time both he and Lukacs got to know the Berlin philosopher and sociologist, Simmel had left his sociological concerns behind and was mainly preoccupied with elaborating his critical and pessimistic analysis of the "tragedy of [modern] culture." Mannheim's first paper, based on a lecture entitled "Soul and Culture,"[50] which he delivered during the war in Budapest at the age of twenty-four, stands clearly under Simmel's shadow. In particular, the distinction between objective and subjective culture, or between culture as transmitted to each historical actor and the personal ideas and ideals this actor strives to realize, is purely Simmelian. In tune with Simmel, Mannheim here emphasized the tragic discrepancy between the individual soul and the objective culture in which it is immersed. He who wishes to create must necessarily submit to the direction of objective culture, yet such submission fosters inauthenticity, the crushing of the soul by the alien forces of an increasingly autonomous objective culture that has "no more relation to the soul than has a parasite to the host."[51]

While the Budapest lecture is imbued with the Simmelian sense of acute cultural crisis—a mood widely shared during the immediate prewar years—it does not indicate the subjacent resignation that Simmel expressed in that period. Mannheim, the young disciple, aware of the crisis, still reaches for a way out, a new departure. Granted, he wrote, that objective culture "surrounds us like an autonomous Leviathan,"[52] it cannot develop and continue without the devotion and collaboration of individuals. It is the mission of the young generation to strive in the future for a cultural renewal in which the claims of individual souls will not be crushed under the weight of the alien world of cultural objects.

[50] A German translation of this lecture is included in Kurt H. Wolff, ed., Karl Mannheim, *Wissenssoziologie* (Neuwied und Berlin, Luchterhand, 1964), pp. 66–84. [51] *Ibid.*, p. 74.

[52] *Ibid.*, p. 84.

What pervades Mannheim's Budapest lecture is a sense of the intellectual ferment and turmoil that the war had brought in its wake. Like most European intellectuals, the young Mannheim seems to have experienced the war as a catastrophe of such a magnitude that it became imperative to turn to new modes of thought. The old optimistic positivism had been shown to be inadequate; it had failed to account for, or to ward off, the collapse of western civilization that the war seemed to have brought in its wake.

MARXISM AND HISTORICISM

Soon after his return to Germany following the end of the Hungarian Soviet Revolution, Mannheim redirected his attention to Marxian thought. But this was no longer the staid, evolutionary, and largely positivistic Marxism in its Kautskyan form, which Mannheim first came to know in prewar Budapest. The new Marxism, as it was expounded by Lukacs, was activist, consciously revolutionary, and devoted to the furtherance of transforming *Praxis*. Influenced by the Russian Revolution and by Lenin's voluntaristic interpretation of Marxism, a new generation of young Marxist intellectuals, many of them members of the "front generation" who had lost their illusions in the trenches, now wished to take seriously Marx's old injunction that it was the philosopher's task not only to interpret the world but to transform it. Mannheim, who had been sceptical of the claims of Marxist doctrine in its reformist form, was much impressed by revolutionary Marxism. While never able to follow Lukacs into becoming a certified, even though slightly deviant, philosopher of the Communist Party, Mannheim nevertheless came largely to accept the view that the turmoils of the age presaged the end of the bourgeois era and the ascent of the revolutionary proletariat as a decisive history-making force. Although he was unwilling to accept Lukacs' contention that only proletarian thought "adequately" reflected reality and that all other class perspectives were necessarily subject to ideological distortions, Mannheim was predisposed to see in proletarian class consciousness a "perspective" which, because of its orientation toward the future, was likely to be more "relevant" than bourgeois thought wedded to the past and the *status quo*. And yet, despite these strong appeals of Marxism and the profound impact it had on all his subsequent thought, Mannheim never became an orthodox Marxist. The main reason for this was that while under Marxist influence he was simultaneously impressed by various relativistic doctrines within the tradition of German historicism, and these cast doubt on the absolutist claims emanating from the Marxist camp.[53]

German historicism stressed that no product of human culture, no meaningful event in human history, could be understood in a timeless and generalizing framework. In this view, human minds and human actions were restricted

[53] The following pages are indebted to Paul Kecskemeti's superb "Introduction" to Karl Mannheim, *Essays on the Sociology of Knowledge.*

to a temporal bound and could only be understood within it. Historicism enshrined historical relativism and stressed that each thought and each human action could only be understood and judged in terms of its cultural matrix. Historicism took its point of departure from Hegel's holistic cultural philosophy, according to which each cultural product of the past must be apprehended in relation to the stage in the progressive self-realization of the objective spirit which had been reached at a particular point in historical time. But, rejecting the Hegelian certitude of having discerned the course of the spirit's travail through human history, historicism as represented, for example, by Wilhelm Dilthey and Ernst Troeltsch, only asserted that each period in history, being inherently neither inferior nor superior to any other period, was to be judged by its own criteria and values rather than by the standards of the observer. Once the historian cultivated the ability to put himself imaginatively into the position of those historical actors and cultural creators he endeavored to understand (*verstehen*), he would be able to realize the significance and meaning of bygone periods, reveal their peculiar greatness and contribution, and thus preserve the monuments of past cultural achievements.

Mannheim accepted a large part of the historicist heritage. His sociology of knowledge can be seen as an outgrowth of historicist relativism, tempered and transformed by the Marxist emphasis on *Praxis* and supplemented by the programmatic assertion that systems of ideas need to be understood not only in terms of their autonomous and inherent development but also by reference to their embeddedness in social structures.

Mannheim was convinced that modern thinkers had to come to grips with historicism as an intellectual force, "just as in Athens Socrates was morally obliged to define his position vis a vis the Sophists."[54] He believed that

> historicism has developed into an intellectual force of extraordinary significance. . . . The historicist principle not only organizes, like an invisible hand, the work of the cultural sciences (*Geisteswissenschaften*), but also permeates everyday thinking. . . . Historicism is therefore neither a mere fad nor a fashion; it is not even an intellectual current, but the very basis on which we construct our observations of the socio-cultural reality.[55]

Despite these high tributes, Mannheim progressed beyond the position attained by historicist thought; he built upon the Marxist idea that ways of thinking were tied to ways of doing, and specified the multiple ties by which systems of ideas were bound to the *Praxis* of men located in concrete social structures. Mannheim moved from viewing ideas merely "from the inside" to perceiving them as responses to determinants emanating from the social structures in which thinkers were variously enmeshed.

[54] *Essays on the Sociology of Knowledge*, p. 84. [55] *Ibid.*, pp. 84–85.

GESTALT PSYCHOLOGY, NEO-KANTIANISM, AND PHENOMENOLOGY

While Mannheim reacted against the historicist tendency to interpret ideas in isolation from social conditions and utilized Marxism as an instrument to see ideas as functionally tied to the social world, he also appropriated other conceptualizations to buttress his holistic and structural emphasis. He profited from the development of *Gestalt* psychology, which rejected the atomistic associationism of previous psychological doctrine, and from the emphasis of this new psychology on configurational or structural aspects of psychological facts. The assertion of *Gestalt* psychologists that parts must be understood in relation to the wholes of which they are a part, that figures emerge only in relation to the ground against which they are perceived, served Mannheim well when he explored historical events or cultural products in relation to the historical and structural ground in which they are rooted.

The synthesizing and antiatomistic trend that Mannheim welcomed in *Gestalt* psychology also appealed to him in the new art history that was emerging. For example, Alois Riegl and Max Dvorák, rejecting the positivist method, attempted to apprehend a work of art through a synthetic interpretation in terms of the living context of a period and its culture. Instead of isolated "influences" or "motives," this new art history wished to penetrate to the meaning of a work of art by reference to its embeddedness in a complex of cultural symbols and objects. Mannheim's many references to this new trend in art history and his method of procedure in many concrete investigations testify to the influence of the new art criticism on his thought.

As has already been noted, Mannheim was influenced by his teacher Alfred Weber, especially by Weber's sociology of culture and his discussion of the role of intellectuals. In regard to the philosophical schools that contended for dominance in the Germany of the twenties, Mannheim can be shown to be indebted to many but beholden to none. He owes something to the neo-Kantians of the Marburg school, especially Rickert and Windelband, who had previously exerted their influence on the thought of Max Weber. Mannheim followed them in rejecting the methods of the natural sciences for the study of cultural phenomena, because he believed they had conclusively established that *Naturwissenschaft* and *Kulturwissenschaft* had to proceed with different methods since they had different *Erkenntniszwecke* (theoretical purposes). In particular, Rickert's notion of *Wertbeziehung* (value relevance), his stress on the fact that historians are apt to choose objects of investigation in terms of their relation to cultural values, made a considerable impression on Mannheim and pervades all his writings on perspectivistic thinking. The Marburg neo-Kantians, combined with Max Weber's interpretation of the notion of value relevance, may be deemed to have been among the major godparents of "perspectivistic thought."

Mannheim owes no less to Edmund Husserl's phenomenology, even though Husserl was intent upon breaking the hold that Kantian thought had for so long had on German academic philosophizing. What impressed Mannheim in Husserl's phenomenology was not the attempt to penetrate to knowledge of pure essences, to ideal mathematic objects, for example, but rather Husserl's emphasis on the "intentionality" of human thought. Husserl asserted that the sharp separation between knower and known and the essentially passive conception of the act of knowing in most modern philosophy had to be abandoned in favor of an activist conception of knowledge in which the subject was conceived as actively appropriating the objects of knowledge through "intentional" activity. Combined in various ways with the activist stance derived from Marxism, the phenomenological stress on the active transactions between the subject and the object of knowledge inform much of Mannheim's sociology.

Husserl's austere philosophy, centered as it was on the philosophy of mathematics, a subject largely alien to Mannheim, influenced him to a lesser degree than the work of one of Husserl's most gifted but also most erratic disciples, Max Scheler. Scheler attempted to broaden Husserl's concern with mathematical essences by asserting that the realm of values could also be approached phenomenologically, and that phenomenological analysis could disclose the existence of eternal and immutable value essences. Mannheim rejected this particular version of Platonism, but was stimulated by another seemingly unrelated aspect of Scheler's work. In 1924 Max Scheler published his paper *Problems of a Sociology of Knowledge,* later expanded in *Die Wissensformen und die Gesellschaft* (1926). In these works Scheler attempted to synthesize a Platonic doctrine of the immutability of a world of value essences with a comprehensive relativism. He described how different groups of men have striven, each in its socially and historically limited way, to grasp aspects of the eternal sphere of value essences. The infinite variety of subjective *a prioris,* the fact that different groups or periods or individual types elaborate their own forms of knowledge, meant to Scheler that men are striving to attain the value essences in different ways at different times rather than that the immutability of these essences is questionable. *Real factors* (such as biological, political, or economic constellations) favor or oppose the actualization of *ideal factors* (for example, moral or religious values), but they can never determine their content. They can only be facilitative "sluice gates of the spirit."

Although it can be shown that certain germinal ideas which culminated in the formulation of Mannheim's sociology of knowledge are already contained in his doctoral dissertation of 1922, *Structural Analysis of Epistemology*[56] and in several other papers antedating the publication of Scheler's work on the sociology of knowledge, there can be no doubt that Mannheim was influenced in crucial ways by Scheler. He set out almost immediately after Scheler's work

[56] *Essays on Sociology and Social Psychology,* Chapter 1.

had been published to discuss it in considerable detail in his *The Problem of a Sociology of Knowledge,* published in 1925. Rejecting Scheler's "doctrine of eternity" in the name of "present-day historical consciousness"[57] Mannheim yet pays high tribute to Scheler as the first to have elaborated a "comprehensive plan" for the sociology of knowledge and as possessing "the ability to observe thought both 'from within,' in terms of its logical structures, and 'from without,' in terms of its social functioning and conditioning."[58] Mannheim's sociology of knowledge differs from Scheler's in its rejection of neo-Platonic ideas, in its pronouncedly Hegelian and Marxian flavor, and in its activistic conception of the role of idea. Nevertheless, it seems incontrovertible that the publication of Scheler's work on the sociology of knowledge was among the "efficient causes" that led to the elaboration of Mannheim's mature thought.

In addition to some of the major sources of Mannheim's thinking—from Marxism to historicism, from *Gestalt* psychology and the new art history to neo-Kantianism and phenomenology—other influences left their impression on Mannheim. These include vitalism in biology as well as a variety of other strains of thought that stressed the dynamic and holistic character of cultural knowledge and were opposed alike to the alleged static quality of the methods of natural science and to positivistic views.

THE DEBT TO HEGEL

The great figure of Hegel, who stands at the origin of both Marxism and historicism, also stands behind the work of Mannheim. Even though he judged that "Hegel's venture in the philosophy of history . . . with its ready-made assumptions, had proved premature in content and method alike,"[59] Mannheim's own thought has a pronounced Hegelian cast. Hegel's resolute historicization of philosophical ideas, his stress on the historical conditioning of the human spirit and on the dialectical relationships between historical phenomena, and his "process thought,"—all these elements are part of Mannheim's intellectual equipment. It is as hard to conceive of Mannheim without reference to Hegel as it would be to conceive of Durkheim without reference to Comte.

During the final period of his life, Mannheim turned again to some of the reform-oriented ideas of his youth. His stay in Britain led him to "put into brackets" his previous activist Marxism and to attempt instead to transcend class-oriented thinking in favor of national planning. Earlier in Weimar Germany, Mannheim had reacted to a chaotic situation in which contending classes and strata opposed one another and fashioned justificatory ideologies in their contentions. What struck him later in the Anglo-Saxon world was the inherent consensual order that seemed to prevail in spite of the multiple conflicts in British and American society. A variety of interests opposed each other

[57] *Essays on the Sociology of Knowledge,* p. 167. [58] *Ibid.,* p. 180. [59] *Ibid.,* p. 34.

in England and in America just as they did on the Continent, but such conflicts of interests seemed much less able to call forth comprehensive ideologies and instead led to a variety of pragmatic adjustment, be it among policy makers or on the market place of ideas.[60]

THE TURN TOWARD PRAGMATISM

In trying to account for this sharp difference between the Anglo-Saxon countries and the European continent, Mannheim was moved to the study of pragmatism and its British empiricist antecedents. The historically oriented structural analysis of social reality that had informed his thinking in the German period was now largely displaced by a more concrete and pragmatic approach. With the spell of history once broken under the impact of the horrifying emergence of totalitarianism, Mannheim turned to Dewey and Mead and Cooley in his quest for aid in the elaboration of a concrete science of social reconstruction and human engineering. He now praised the positive significance of pragmatism for its contribution to social planning and interdependent thinking. Pragmatism, he wrote, "no longer sets an abstract barrier between thought and action . . . [it] was aware of that organic process by which every act of thought is essentially a part of conduct."[61] Much like Sidney Hook at roughly the same time, Mannheim found in pragmatic thought an analogue to the *Praxis* of Marxism, but one shorn of the Marxist chiliastic elements and infused by Anglo-Saxon practicality and an optimistic belief in the possibility of finding new ways of human adjustments. The frequent references to Dewey and Mead in Mannheim's later work are invariably favorable. Cooley's writings on primary groups and on the psychology of the self are also often cited with admiration and respect. While Mannheim tended to criticize traditional American sociology for its "isolating empiricism," for its failure to think in comprehensive structural terms, he was impressed by Dewey and his co-thinkers because of their ability to move from the particular to the general, from the close investigation of individual transactions to overall plans for a reconstruction of both philosophy and society.

Mannheim continued to think in structural terms after he moved to England, but he now conceived of the notion of structure in more comprehensive ways. He paid close attention to the psychological elements underlying social processes. In an effort to account for the emergence of the pathological and destructive forces that had emerged on the scene of history, Mannheim turned to psychoanalysis. Partly under the influence of his wife, who was trained in psychoanalysis, Mannheim immersed himself in the writings of Freud and his followers, both European and American. He groped his way toward a view in which fascism and war came to be seen, at least in part, as problems of

[60] The following pages owe much to Paul Kecskemeti's "Introduction" to *Essays on Sociology and Social Psychology.* [61] *Man and Society in an Age of Reconstruction,* p. 206.

psychopathology. Influenced by the work of Harold Lasswell and a number of American social psychologists, Mannheim came to believe that the "collective insecurity," the deep-seated anxieties that assaulted modern man, needed psychological analysis even though it had to be accompanied by simultaneous analysis of the institutional sources of such anxieties. Mannheim now called for a "sociological psychology" that would utilize the resources of psychoanalysis, as well as of other schools of psychology, to explain institutionally shaped individual behavior and to lead to a social engineering aimed at replacing "pathology" with "health" and "unreason" with "reason."

One last influence on Mannheim during his British period is hard to document in detail, although one has the distinct impression that it was fairly major. His close association with T. S. Eliot and other Anglican thinkers and theologians led Mannheim to revise his previous antireligious rationalism. His new emphasis on the importance of religion as a guide to conduct and on the group-binding forces of religious beliefs and practices was almost certainly stimulated by his association with the thinkers around Eliot and Middleton Murry. Mannheim hardly alluded to them in his published writings, and there are to my knowledge no detailed studies of Mannheim's relation to these thinkers. But there remains the strong impression that toward the end of his life Anglican Christian thought became a major ingredient in Mannheim's thinking, even though there is no indication that he himself ever became a Christian believer.

THE SOCIAL CONTEXT

THE HUNGARIAN BACKGROUND

Mannheim spent his formative years in a country in which the major societal forces had reached a kind of stalemate, effectively prohibiting creative innovation in political and social affairs. An essentially traditionalistic peasantry dominated by both Church and landholders seemed impermeable to novel ideas. Labor still had little weight in Hungary's premodern society, and its organizational endeavors in the unions and the Social-Democratic Party were more concerned with immediate bread-and-butter issues than with comprehensive reforms. The dominant aristocracy and the impoverished gentry, which did the dirty work for this aristocracy in the administration of the state, were committed to the maintenance of the existing state of affairs since social changes would undermine the basis of their domination. The oppressed minorities in the countryside, though suffering under the yoke of the Magyars, were isolated from one another and from the urban centers and were therefore unable to make themselves heard in the seats of power. The largely Jewish middle class was conformist to the core and dreaded any transformation that might upset its monopoly on financial and commercial affairs.

Given the stasis of the society, it is understandable that the small layer of alert and activistic intellectuals who gathered in Budapest around the turn of the century came to conceive of themselves as the sole voice and conscience of the nation. Even though they were doctrinally committed to the goal of democracy, conditions were such that they were almost ineluctably driven to an elitist stance. In their interstitial existence, they came to see themselves as reformers *par excellence*. Since there was little or no audience for their melioristic ideas, they alone, it seemed to them, could be the source of change, if it was to come at all. The ruling strata appeared to be wedded forever to ancient routines, corrupted by the exercise of unchecked power. Intellectuals concluded from this that enhancement of rationality in public affairs, the deliberate cultivation of new planning for fundamental change, would necessarily fall into their own hands, since they were the only stratum not tied to the use and wont of a static society. The intelligentsia could not tie itself to a party system that failed to represent the real interests of society. It could not accept party discipline. When intellectuals became party men, they were constrained to abandon the intellectual vocation. In Budapest at this time, as Mannheim used to say later, intellectuals saw themselves as the self-appointed guardians of the well-understood interests of the whole society.

The last sentence is one that often recurs in many of Mannheim's writings. He changed his political and sociological views a great deal over the course of his life career, but he never wavered in his belief in the redeeming qualities of "free-floating intellectuals." Though there have been other sources for the emergence of views that saw in men of ideas the preordained saviors of a fallen world, Mannheim's version was rooted in the Hungarian experiences of his formative years. When he later wrote that the intellectuals "might play the part of the watchmen in what otherwise would be a pitch-black night,"[62] he may have had his native Hungary in mind, but he was moved to extend his early views to all of western civilization. Wherever he looked, whether it was to the Germany of the twenties or the England of the thirties, he seemed to encounter the Hungarian experience writ large. In the turmoil, the breakdown, the sloth, and the stalemate of all western civilization, only intellectuals, removed from the contentions of the warring camps, might possibly constitute a self-chosen elite of custodians of reason and informed virtue. Among intellectuals, sociologists, because of their special skills in the analysis and guidance of social forces, would necessarily have to take pride of place. Sociologists as reformers, as the exponents of dispassionate scientific politics, might claim the special deference and respect due to men who did not succumb to the passionate

[62] *Ideology and Utopia*, p. 143.

appeals of the multitude and who managed to safeguard the well-being of the whole against the special pleadings of vested interests.

GERMAN SOCIETY IN THE TWENTIES

The Germany of the twenties, where Mannheim chose to live after his emigration from Hungary, was not a static society. It was the scene of continued clashes between antagonistic strata arrayed in warring ideological camps. Yet the incessant movement only concealed the fact that Germany was a stalemated society just as Hungary had been. The revolution of 1918 did not attack the major pillars of the Wilhelminian edifice. The state bureaucracy, the judiciary, the military, which were taken over from the Kaiser's regime, managed to maintain the authoritarian standards of the past and to checkmate the novel forces unleashed by the Republic. Racked by the crises of inflation and occupation, menaced by the extremist challenges of the Right and the Left alike, the Weimar Republic never gained a stable resting point. Intellectual culture flourished as it had rarely flourished before, but artists, literary men, and intellectuals generally performed a feverish dance on the edge of a volcano that might erupt any day.

In contrast to Hungary, Germany had a strong labor movement. Yet, powerful though it was, neither its dominant Social-Democratic wing nor its vigorous and radical Communist wing was able, most left-wing intellectuals agreed, to challenge in fundamental ways the existing state of affairs. The Social Democrats, having now gained a slice of that state power they had vainly craved during the Wilhelminian days, were contentedly reaping the benefits of office and position. Erstwhile revolutionary socialists relaxed in the belief that the Weimar Republic, in spite of all its blemishes, was after all the best of all possible worlds. It was not for them to pay attention to hair-brained and utopian schemes of fundamental reorganization. The Communists, however, were full of radical ardor. But after the final collapse of revolutionary hopes in 1923, they increasingly became an arm of the Comintern, manipulated and used as pawns in the games the Kremlin played. For this reason left-wing intellectuals tended to shun both the Communist and the Social-Democratic camps and to withdraw into political and cultural criticism. Their major organs, the *Weltbuehne* and the *Tagebuch*,[63] cursed both houses of labor and prided themselves on their independence. A Hungarian visitor to the coffee-houses frequented by Berlin or Munich intellectuals in the mid-twenties would have been easily reminded of the atmosphere of Budapest gatherings ten years earlier.

[63] Cf. Istvan Deak, *Weimar Germany's Left-Wing Intellectuals* (Berkeley, California, University of California, 1968).

The academy continued to be dominated by the "mandarins" who had called forth the wrath of Weber or Simmel, yet the changes from the prewar days were pronounced. Even though Peter Gay overstates the case when he says that in the Weimar days the "outsiders" suddenly became the "insiders,"[64] it is true that a number of previously marginal figures were now admitted into the halls of academe. In particular, some Jewish intellectuals were able to gain the academic recognition denied to them during the Kaiser's regime. As a result, a number of left-wing intellectuals now came to see the university as a haven, a relatively tranquil point of repair from which it was possible to study the passing scene *sine ira et studio.*

Mannheim's writings of the twenties show that he continued to be vitally concerned with the public scene and with the tumultuous happenings in the arena of politics, yet, perhaps as a reaction to his unhappy experience during the Hungarian Soviet Republic, it is also apparent that he had resolved to stand aside from direct political involvements. His major contributions during the German years appeared in academic publications addressed to an academic audience. He published, among others, in the organ of the neo-Kantians, *Logos,* in the *Yearbook for Art History,* in the *Yearbook for Sociology,* and in *The Cologne Quarterly for Sociology.* Several of his major papers appeared in the most prestigious social science journal, *Archiv fuer Sozialwissenschaft und Sozialpolitik,* which had been edited by Max Weber. *Ideology and Utopia* was published by a small publishing house, Friedrich Cohen, which catered in the main to an academic audience. Other of his writings were published by two equally academic houses, Ferdinand Enke and J. C. B. Mohr (Paul Siebeck), Max Weber's publishers. I know of only one contribution to a journal with a less specialized audience, a paper "On the Problematics of Sociology in Germany," which appeared in the *Neue Schweizer Rundschau* in Switzerland.

Not only the journals to which he contributed and the specialized houses that published his books, but his very style of exposition indicates that Mannheim wished to be considered an academic man in those years. Though he wrote with more clarity and lucidity than the run of German professors, his style makes hard demands on his readers, and he never popularized his thought. His writings bristle with footnotes and learned asides, and require of the reader a good deal of previous knowledge of the literature. He writes as an academic man addressing his peers.

Ideology and Utopia, published in 1929, was the first of Mannheim's publications that attracted some extra-academic attention. It was widely reviewed in the journals of the Left, but had a very mixed reception. It was "too strong stuff" for the official Social-Democratic spokesmen, recalls Paul Kecskemeti, and it was judged insufficiently revolutionary by the Communists and their intellectual hangers-on. Men like Herbert Marcuse and Theodor Adorno saw

[64] Peter Gay, *Weimar Culture* (New York, Harper & Row, 1969).

in Mannheim's yearning for scientific politics above the battle an abandonment of Marxist *Praxis*. The "regular" academic reviewers were even more lukewarm than the Social Democrats, and only a few maverick intellectuals on the Left, such as Emil Lederer, welcomed it with a measure of enthusiasm. The rising tide of Nazism and the inroads of the depression soon turned the attention of the public to more immediate concerns, and the debate over the book subsided. It is hard to say whether it would have had a broader impact on German readers under other circumstances. At it is, its author was forced to give up his academic chair and to move to England soon after Hitler came to power.

ENGLISH SOCIETY IN THE THIRTIES

English society appeared to Mannheim to be devoid of those deadly ideological struggles that had marked the German scene. While Germany seemed like a Tower of Babel where people talked past each other, Englishmen could still engage in a general dialogue because, despite their many differences, a common framework of ideas and shared symbols informed their discourse. In Germany Mannheim had felt that it was the task of intellectuals to evolve a way of reconciling divergent perspectives and of translating the assumptions of one group into the language of the other. He saw no such need in England. This was at least one reason he discontinued his work in the sociology of knowledge. Instead, he resolved to devote himself to the problems of social planning and social reconstruction which loomed so large in his mind ever since the catastrophe of Nazism.

As Mannheim's orientation to the passing scene changed drastically in England, it is all the more striking that he clung to his vision of the intellectuals as the saving remnant with extraordinary tenacity. He no longer used the term "free-floating intellectuals," to be sure. But the new elite of planners and educators he now called for and hoped to bring into existence was surely the same intellectual vanguard under another name. Its concrete tasks were now seen differently, but the societal functions of intellectuals as representatives of the interest of the whole remained essentially the same. A survivor of the prewar years in Budapest who had participated in the debates of the reformist social scientists in that city would have had no particular difficulty following Mannheim's discourse in London. The Budapest intelligentsia's dream of control of society by rational men devoted to the commonwealth had become the concern of intellectuals in the country of the Beveridge Plan. There was a neat fit between the Hungarian reformist ideas of prewar days and the new Anglo-Saxon concern with planning.

In tune with his new political activism, Mannheim now considered the academic tower a kind of half-way house from which he could make frequent forays into the surrounding world. This was facilitated by the fact that academic life in England was far less insulated than in Germany. English professors, and this holds even more for professors at London University where Mannheim taught than for those at Oxbridge, were accustomed to mix with journalists and newspaper commentators, to frequent the salons of the high and mighty, and to engage in a dialogue with political men in many a London club or at the high table of their college. Academic life in England was much less inbred than in Germany, and British mandarins and pundits were not averse to being heard on the B.B.C. or writing for the Sunday supplements and the weeklies.

Mannheim's ability to branch out from strictly academic work and to speak to non-academic men was enhanced by the fact that at the University of London he taught not only sociology but also education. Education as an applied subject had many more ties to all sorts of associations of teachers and educational administrators than had sociology, which was then still an almost exclusively academic subject and, moreover, had but little standing among English professionals and laymen alike. Mannheim addressed many and varied audiences, generally in the field of education and adult education. The same impression of variety and breadth of public is conveyed by the list of his publications. He rarely published in strictly academic journals, which had been his almost exclusive media in Germany. I could find only two papers by Mannheim in such journals, *Politica,* and *Sociological Review,* and both of these appeared at the very beginning of his stay in England. Almost all his other contributions appear in volumes entitled *Educating for Democracy, This Changing World, Peaceful Change,* and the like. Among the publications for which he wrote were *Tutors' Bulletin for Adult Education, Christian News Letter, The New English Weekly,* and, in tune with his new interest in psychoanalysis, the *International Journal of Psychoanalysis.* Even his publishing firm, Routledge and Kegan Paul, though a respected academic house, addressed a public much wider than the austere German academic publishers of an earlier day. The "International Library of Sociology and Social Reconstruction," which Mannheim directed for Routledge, was meant to reach a public of activist reformers at least as much as it hoped to attract academic attention.

Mannheim's style during the English years changed almost as much as his interests and audiences. Gone was the aloof abstractness that characterizes his German writings. The English works are much more readable and accessible than the German publications, which sometimes border on the hermetic. Yet, Mannheim paid a price for his successful efforts to reach a wider public. His style lost some of the logical rigor of the early days, it frequently became exhortatory, and, to the extent that he abandoned the analytical for the imperative mode, he tended to evade intellectual difficulties through recourse to often facile rhetorical devices. One is reminded, when reading the later Mannheim and visualizing him in his fervor of exhortation, of Durkheim's classical description of "a man speaking to a crowd."

> His language has a grandiloquence that would be ridiculous in ordinary circumstances; his gestures show a certain domination; his very thought is impatient of all rules and easily falls into all sorts of excesses. . . . Sometimes he even has the feeling that he is dominated by a moral force which is greater than he and of which he is only the interpreter. . . . The sentiments provoked by his words came back to him, but enlarged and amplified, and to this degree they strengthen his own sentiment. The passionate energies he arouses re-echo within him and quicken his vital tone.[65]

IN SUMMARY

Mannheim had a well-balanced mind and personality and hence can hardly be compared to the half-mad Priest of Humanity who used to address his Parisian audiences with religious fervor. And yet one senses some deep-seated parallelism between the late writings of Mannheim and those of Comte. They both lost some of their cool when they turned from diagnosis to prophecy in preaching to the Gentiles.

Not all of Mannheim's British writings were destined for wider audiences. *Man and Society in an Age of Reconstruction* (which was partly written in Germany) and the papers now published as parts III and IV of the *Essays in Sociology and Social Psychology* exhibit Mannheim's acute diagnostic ability as much as anything he wrote in his German years. But no matter how important Mannheim's output may have been for buttressing democratic institutions in a period of upheaval and heightened crisis, no matter how much they may have contributed to the emergence of the modern welfare state, their scientific status will be judged to be inferior to the bulk of his German writings.

Mannheim is one of the most appealing figures among sociology's great men. A profoundly human and humane person, he embodied in his analytical work and in his reformist passions the twin urges toward self-conscious understanding of man's vicissitudes on earth and toward active intervention in public affairs which, in varying degree, inform most sociologists. If he did not always keep those commitments in perfect balance, he is like many other sociologists, before and after him, who have not managed to do much better.

[65] Emile Durkheim, *The Elementary Forms of Religious Life* (New York, The Free Press, 1947), p. 210.

Pitirim A. Sorokin

1889-1968

THE WORK

Pitirim Sorokin's sociological theory is based on the well-known distinction between social statics (structural sociology in his terminology) and social dynamics. But because his discussion of statics did not have a profound impact on subsequent sociological analyses, it will be treated here in cursory fashion. By contrast, his thoughts on social and cultural dynamics, which have proved to be more fruitful and original, will be dealt with at some length.

THE OVERALL DOCTRINE

To Sorokin, the process of human interaction involves three essential elements: human actors as subjects of interaction; meanings, values, and norms that guide human conduct; and material phenomena that are vehicles and conductors for meanings and values to be objectified and incorporated into a sequence of actions. Not unlike Max Weber, Sorokin (except during his early years as an apprentice sociologist) rejected any attempt to study human affairs without reference to norms, meanings, and values. "Stripped of their meaningful aspects," he writes, "all the phenomena of human interaction become merely biophysical phenomena and, as such, properly form the subject of the biophysical sciences."[1]

Hence, in Sorokin's sociological thought the emphasis is on the importance of cultural factors, that is, of superorganic elements, as determinants of social conduct. To understand *personalities* as subjects of interaction, and *society* as the totality of interacting personalities, one must bear in mind that they rest on a foundation of culture—a culture that consists of the totality of meanings, norms, and values possessed by interacting persons and carried by material vehicles, such as ritual objects or works of art, which objectify and convey these meanings.[2]

In analyzing components of social interaction, Sorokin distinguishes between unorganized, organized, and disorganized forms. He discusses various types of legal and moral controls and speaks of solidary, antagonistic, and mixed systems of social interaction, as well as of familistic, compulsory, and

[1] Pitirim A. Sorokin, *Society, Culture and Personality* (New York, Harper, 1947), p. 47.
[2] *Ibid.*, p. 63.

mixed (contractual) types of social bonds. Having elaborated these different types of social interaction, Sorokin then proceeds to classify organized groups in terms of their functional and meaningful ties. Here he considers different degrees of intensity of group interaction and the related closeness or slackness of ties between group members. Furthermore, he states that groups may be unibonded, that is, they may be based on one main value, (as is the case, for example, with religious, occupational, or kinship groups), or they may be held together by multiple bonds (as in the case of a nation or a social class). In addition, he states that both unibonded and multibonded groups may be either open or closed.[3]

It is not necessary to elaborate on these classifactory schemes because, by and large, they have remained fairly sterile both for Sorokin's own substantive work and for that of others. In pointed contrast, his theory of social change, as well as his theory of social mobility and social stratification, deserve careful attention.

A PANORAMIC VIEW OF SOCIETY AND CULTURE

Sorokin's monumental *Social and Cultural Dynamics,*[4] in which he attempted to develop a full explanatory scheme for social and cultural change (with supporting evidence based on detailed statistical investigations), must be taken as the major exhibit for assessing his view of social change. The work as a whole, as Louis Schneider has suggested,[5] has a somewhat romantic cast: it presents a profusion of ideas and daring hypotheses, but lacks the poise, soberness, and careful marshalling of arguments that characterize the classical style. Such work is best approached by attention to its overall message and major contentions rather than by way of detailed criticism of particulars.

In this work, Sorokin attempts no less than a panoramic survey of the course of all human societies and cultures, supported by a series of general propositions to illuminate the historical variation in socio-cultural arrangements. He opposes any unilinear explanation of human evolution just as he opposes any approach that, as in the case of Spengler for example, conceives of the life cycle of cultures by way of quasi-biological analogies. Instead, he views socio-cultural phenomena as based on relatively coherent and integrated aggregates of cultural outlooks—which he calls *mentalities*—that impress their meanings on specific periods in the global history of humankind. What he is looking for, in his own words, is "the central principle [the reason] which permeates all the components" of a culture, "gives sense and significance to them, and in this

[3] *Ibid.,* Chapters I to V.

[4] Pitirim A. Sorokin, *Social and Cultural Dynamics,* four volumes (New York, American Book Co., 1937–1941).

[5] Louis Schneider, "Toward Assessment of Sorokin's View of Change" in George Zollschan and Walter Hirsch, ed., *Explorations in Social Change* (Boston, Houghton Mifflin, 1964), pp. 371–400.

way makes cosmos of a chaos of unintegrated fragments."[6] He does not claim that any culture is ever fully integrated, and he is aware that it will always contain fragments that are not fully reconcilable. Still, he stresses that sociocultural phenomena are not randomly distributed; rather, once analyzed from his specific angle of vision, they will reveal the operation of a few major *premises* that mark their overall character.

There are, according to Sorokin, only three fundamental premises for conceiving and apprehending the nature of reality. Either reality is felt to be directly accessible through the senses (*Sensate Culture*); or it is felt to be disclosed only through a view that transcends the world of the senses and achieves a transcendent vision of the eternal, as in Platonic idealism (*Ideational Culture*); or, finally, it takes an intermediate form (*Idealistic Culture*), which attempts to fuse and synthesize the other two in a dialectical balance between opposite principles.

Correspondingly, there are three irreducible forms of truth: sensory, spiritual, and rational. At various periods of history, one of the three basic premises achieves preeminence over the others and stamps its character on the main ways of thinking, feeling, or experiencing that distinguish an epoch. That is why the principal institutions of society (law, art, philosophy, science, and religion) exhibit at any particular time a consistent mental outlook that is the reflection of the predominance of one or the other of the three major cultural premises. During a *Sensate* period, for example, science will be rigidly empirical in its methods and procedures, art will strive for realism rather than for the imparting of transcendent visions, and religion will tend to be more concerned with the quest for concrete moral experience than for the truth of faith or reason.

Having been persuaded by his survey of world history that all the varieties of cultural constellations that have appeared on the human scene can be effectively encompassed as subvarieties of the three major *cultural* mentalities, Sorokin proceeds to explain why all major social change must be recurrent. The ceaseless flux of history, so he contends, has characteristic rhythms that are far from being random or subject to the whims of the Gods. Any culture, determined as it is by its major premises, follows a kind of inner necessity: it is subject to its own peculiar destiny. But the predominance of one fundamental *cultural mentality* carries within itself its own demise through the exhaustion of its own premises. This is what Sorokin, rejecting any explanation of social change through external factors, has called the principle of *immanent change*. As cultural systems reach the zenith of their full flowering, they "become less and less capable of serving as an instrument of adaptation, as an experience for real satisfaction of the needs of its bearers, and as foundation for their social and cultural life."[7] At this point, a cultural system, by driving to the limits the premises that gave it birth, exceeds the mark, distorts the portion of truth it once embodied through one-sided exaggeration, and prepares its own demise,

[6] *Dynamics,* I, p. 32. [7] *Dynamics,* IV, p. 743.

thereby giving birth to a new cultural system. This dialectic, which bears strong resemblances to the Hegelian, is at the heart of Sorokin's *principle of limits* and purports to explain the rhythmic periodicity of all socio-cultural phenomena. For Sorokin, just as for Hegel, change implies the rise of a new life at the same time as it imparts dissolution.[8]

The three major types of *cultural mentalities,* Sorokin contends, follow each other in reliable sequence. *Sensate* forms will be followed by *Ideational,* and they in turn by *Idealistic* forms of cultural integration. After this cycle has been completed, the recurrence of a new *Sensate* culture will initiate a new cycle. Since the days of the early Greeks and their *Sensate* culture, Western culture has completed two cycles of this sequence. We are now living at the end of a *Sensate* phase which has lasted for several hundred years. This stage is now overripe, it has reached its limits, and we live in the shadow of twilight among the debris of a disintegrating culture that is no longer able to give meaning and significance to our lives. Ideas once dominant and organizing no longer serve as guideposts, having fallen apart. We can already discern the first harbingers of a new *Ideational* integration sprouting like seeds beneath the snow. Ours is a world in which the center no longer holds and where even the best lack all conviction. But those who have the vision can have intimations of glad tidings of future redemption from the tyranny of the senses.

This is not the place to discuss the enormous statistical labors that went into establishing trends in the fluctuation of art forms, of philosophical, ethical, and legal norms and values, or of social relationships in ordinary times as well as during wars and revolutions—all of which are to be found in the first three volumes of Sorokin's *magnum opus.* They have been scrutinized by experts in these areas and have frequently been found to be wanting. One especially telling overall criticism was made long ago by Hans Speier, who has said that Sorokin's study of history "is imbued with the spirit of the doctrine that he desires to refute,"[9] since the methods he uses to establish the impermanence of *Sensate* and empirical culture are in themselves extremely empirical. Sorokin would probably have answered that it is given to no man to step out of his time, that even an attempt to refute the preeminence of Sensate empiricism must still avail itself of the tools that his age and time put at his disposal. Nevertheless, Sorokin's "romantic" contribution will have to be judged in the future not by any isolated concrete result of his investigation, but by the fruitfulness of the theoretical leads he has imparted to succeeding scholars. Viewed in this light, at least some of these leads may well survive, even if a number of his general contentions will have been swept aside. Furthermore, even though he may have been wrong on many counts, some of Sorokin's anticipations, written in the

[8] I borrow this characterization of the Hegelian logic from Carl E. Schorske's "Cultural Hothouse," *New York Review of Books,* Dec. 11, 1975.

[9] Hans Speier, "The Ideas of Pitirim A. Sorokin's Integralist Sociology" in Henry Elmer Barnes, ed., *An Introduction to the History of Sociology* (Chicago, The University of Chicago Press, 1948), p, 891.

1930's, indeed have a prophetic character. What he wrote then about the possible destruction of humankind by the pushing of buttons or about the coming celebration of hard-core pornography shows an almost uncanny sense of things to come in the world of the 1970's.

At a time when sociologists, under the impact of the debate about modernization and underdevelopment, have again begun to discuss the principles underlying the dynamics of socio-cultural change, Sorokin's stress on immanent change, as distinct from externally induced change, may have renewed significance. When scholars have increasingly wondered why the external impact of Western culture has had so widely differing results in many Third World nations, it might be well to assume Sorokin's angle of vision and to ask whether cultures in their *Idealistic* or *Ideational* phases might be more resistant to the importation of the *Sensate* cultures of the West than cultures, such as the Japanese or the Korean, that are already largely conditioned by *Sensate* sets of ideas. Why, for example, are modern methods of birth control readily acceptable in those countries while they have failed in India or Egypt? Could it be that they are "out of phase" in the latter, but not in the former, countries?

Turning to Sorokin's *principle of limits,* one again has the impression that if it were shorn of the somewhat dogmatic and grandiose manner in which it was first formulated, it could have interesting possibilities as a hypothesis. In fact, it has been one of the mainstays of Claude Lévi-Strauss's method of analysis. Whether or not Lévi-Strauss is familiar with Sorokin's work, the resemblances are striking. For example, Lévi-Strauss writes: ". . . In social undertakings mankind keeps manoeuvering within narrow limits. Social types are not isolated creations, wholly independent of each other, and each one an original entity, but rather the result of endless combinations, forever seeking to solve the same problems by manipulating the same fundamental elements."[10]

As should already be apparent, Sorokin's overall view is closely tied to his sociology of knowledge, a field to which, it is generally agreed, he made significant contributions.

SOCIOLOGY OF KNOWLEDGE

Sorokin's sociology of knowledge rejects any attempt to root ideas in the existential conditions of thinkers and their audiences. This contrasts sharply with most other sociological attempts to understand the rise and fall of ideas in relation to social structures, and is specifically in opposition to the theories of Marx, Weber and Mannheim, which have been examined earlier in this book. Although Sorokin has occasionally indicated that such an endeavor may be worthwhile, he himself did not take this route. Instead, his sociology of knowledge attempts to establish connections between concrete philosophical, religious,

[10] Claude Lévi-Strauss, "The Bear and the Barber," *Journal of the Royal Anthropological Institute,* vol. 93 (1963), pp. 1–11.

artistic, and scientific thought and the overall *cultural mentalities* in which this thought appears and flourishes. As has already been discussed, he attempts to document, for example, that in *Sensate* periods, scientific ideas tend to be based exclusively on sense experience and empirical proof and validation, whereas in periods of *Ideational* ascendancy, empirical science fails to develop, being replaced by varieties of *Naturphilosophien* that purport to attain intuitive insights into the nature of the universe.

Such attempts to link systems of ideas to supersystems and to derive every aspect of intellectual production from varying cultural mentalities, are open to the charge of tautological reasoning. As Merton has remarked, when Sorokin argues that "in a sensate society and culture the sensate system of truth based on the testimony of the organs of senses has to be dominant,"[11] he plainly argued in circles, "for sensate mentality has already been *defined* as one conceiving of 'reality as only that which is presented to the sense organs,'"[12] Sorokin's answer to such charges has not been very convincing. But even if his overall idealistic and emanationist explanation seems open to serious objections, this is not to say that his sociology of knowledge has been sterile. One need only dig beneath some of his grandiose characterizations of cultures to be rewarded by significant and worthwhile sets of concrete ideas.

Take, for example, Sorokin's discussion of the question: which cultural values penetrate and diffuse more easily when imported into an alien culture? In an effort to answer this question he does not simply refer to the overall compatibility of values between donor and recipient cultures, though he does this also; rather he points to the character of the human agents that first come into contact with the donor culture. "The kind of values," he says, "that penetrate first depends, primarily, upon the kinds of human agents that first come into contact with the other culture. If they are merchants . . . then various commercial commodities penetrate first; if they are missionaries . . . then the 'ideological values' penetrate first. If they are conquerors and soldiers, then partly material, partly non-material values penetrate simultaneously. If they are students of philosophy or social science . . . then they bring back and spread the theories and ideologies they studied."[13] This is a significant insight worth further elaboration, an insight, moreover, which points to the connection of ideas with the existential conditions of their carriers, and is hence not subject to the charge of tautology that must beset all emanationist theories in the sociology of knowledge.

Or consider Sorokin's first adumbration of a sociological theory of scientific discovery and technological invention, namely the idea that "any important new invention . . . or any important new discovery in the natural sciences

[11] Pitirim A. Sorokin, *Dynamics,* II, p. 5.

[12] Robert K. Merton, *Social Theory and Social Structure,* enlarged ed. (New York, The Free Press, 1968), p. 520. See also Merton and Barber's discussion of Sorokin's sociology of knowledge in Philip J. Allen, ed., *Pitirim A. Sorokin in Review* (Durham, N.C., Duke University Press, 1963).

[13] *Dynamics,* IV, p. 283.

. . . is the result of a long process, with a multitude of small discoveries made step by step, [so that] the really new element in any important invention or discovery is comparatively a very modest one."[14] In this case, Sorokin, to be sure, does not refer to the existential basis of scientific thought, yet he departs from his programmatic endeavors to link specific ideas to their matrix in overall cultural mentalities. He engaged, in fact, in an attempt to trace cumulative trends within scientific communities and to link specific innovators to the scientific tradition within which they operate.

Many of Sorokin's usable ideas in the sociology of knowledge do not come in his programmatic *magnum opus* but in a more modest companion volume, *Sociocultural Causality, Space, Time,*[15] published a few years later. Here, in a manner reminiscent of Durkheim and his school, Sorokin shows that the way a specific culture conceives of causality, space, and time is not identical with natural science conceptions and must be understood in relation to the specific socio-cultural context. Also following the Durkheimians, he argues moreover that even the space of the geometricians, for example, is "greatly conditioned and stamped by the sociocultural traits of the respective society and culture. The very units of the geometric distance—such as 'foot,' 'yard,' 'meter,' 'sajen,' 'finger,' 'rod,' and so on—bear the imprint of these [socio-cultural] conditions."[16] Sorokin shows further how, with the increase in communications between local societies and the wider world, parochial systems of thought recede before more universal representations of space. " 'To the right of Jones's house, about twenty rods' serves the purpose for a village where everyone knows where Jones's house is situated. But for the whole human population, such a point of spatial reference becomes indefinable and therefore unserviceable."[17] The difference between universalistic and particularistic codes of communication, which has been highlighted in our days by Basil Bernstein[18] and other scholars, can already be found *in nuce* in Sorokin's work.

It is worth noting Sorokin's observation that "the emergence of uniform . . . space of classical mechanics itself, with its system of reference, was conditioned by the sociocultural process of growth of cosmopolitan and international society and culture";[19] or his discussion of the fact that "when intercourse extends over many groups with different rhythms of sociocultural activities, and time indications, the concrete and local systems of sociocultural time cease to perform satisfactorily the functions of coordination and synchronization of their activities. Hence the urgent need to establish such a standardized system of time reckoning . . . as would serve equally all the groups as the

[14] *Dynamics,* IV, p. 182.

[15] Pitirim A. Sorokin, *Sociocultural Causality, Space, Time* (Durham, N.C., Duke University Press, 1943). Cf. also Pitirim A. Sorokin and Robert K. Merton, "Social Time: A Methodological and Functional Analysis," *American Journal of Sociology,* XXXXII 42 (1937), pp. 615–29.

[16] *Causality,* p. 146. [17] *Ibid.,* p. 146.

[18] Basil Bernstein, *Class, Codes and Control* (New York, Schocken, 1975), *passim.*

[19] *Causality,* p. 147.

uniform point of time reference for the coordination and synchronization of their activities."[20] Here Sorokin succeeds in showing in convincing detail that notions such as time and space do not simply emanate from overall mentalities but are rooted in the concrete exigencies of human communities; that they are, with apologies to Sorokin the emanist, existentially determined.

One further quotation will illustrate the great subtlety of Sorokin's sociological imagination. After having shown that in the modern world universal time-reckoning has largely replaced the community-rooted parochial ways of dealing with time, Sorokin turns around and makes the acute observation that the older qualitative time measures have by no means been fully replaced by quantitative time. In line with the art historian Wilhelm Pinder and reminiscent of what Mannheim called the "contemporaneity of the noncontemporaneous," Sorokin argues: "Within the same territorial aggregate composed of different religious, occupational, economic, national, and cultural groups, there are different rhythms and pulsations, and therefore different calendars and different conventions for the sociocultural time of these groups. . . . Compare . . . a Harvard calendar with one operating, say, among factory workers. . . . The calendar of the Roman Catholics in Boston—in part, at least—is different from that of the Protestant Bostonians. . . . Side by side with quantitative time (which itself is in a degree a social convention), there exists a full-blooded sociocultural time, with all its 'earmarks': it is qualitative, it is not infinitely divisible . . . , it does not flow on evenly . . . ; it is determined by social conditions, and reflects the rhythms and pulsations of the social life of a given group . . ."[21]

One ventures to think that this set of observations provides leads for several Ph.D. dissertations, even though the great French Durkheimian Maurice Halbwachs, probably unaware of Sorokin's work, has elaborated some of these ideas in his seminal work *The Social Framework of Memory* and elsewhere. Despite the fact that his ambitious overall scheme, like all closed total systems of sociological thought, may be found wanting, it should be apparent by now that Sorokin was a major force, a major thinker. Or, as a whimsical button worn by some graduate students at a recent convention of the American Sociological Association put it, "Sorokin lives."

SOCIAL STRATIFICATION AND SOCIAL MOBILITY

Sorokin holds a unique place in the study of social stratification and mobility. We owe to him the creation or definition of many of the terms that have become standard in this field. We also owe him a distinct vision of what the study of social mobility should be mainly concerned with, namely, the courses and consequences of demographic exchanges between groups, as distinct from the study of individuals who may move up or down or sideways in the social hierarchy.

[20] *Ibid.*, p. 188. [21] *Ibid.*, p. 196–97.

Sorokin defined social mobility in its broadest sense as the shifting of people in social space. He was not, however, interested in movements of individuals but in social metabolism, in the consequences of such movements for social groups differently located in the social structure.

"To find the position of a man or a social phenomenon in social space," Sorokin argued in the first place, "means to define his or its relations to other men or other social phenomena chosen as the 'point of reference.'"[22] Methods appropriate for the study of mobility are somewhat reminiscent of the system of coordinates used for the location of an object in geometrical space. But the analytical task is not completed when one has established a person's relations to specific groups. What needs further exploration is "the relation of these groups to each other within a population, and the relation of this population to other populations."[23] In other words, though the study of social mobility needs to concern itself with the movements of individuals, it also needs to pay close attention to the consequences of these movements for the social groups and the total structures that encompass these individual moves. Before considering social mobility we must know a good deal about the structure of stratification in which such movements occur.

Social stratification, to Sorokin, means "the differentiation of a given population into hierarchically superposed classes."[24] Such stratification, he held, is a permanent characteristic of any organized social group. Stratification may be based on *economic* criteria—for example, when one focuses attention upon the differentials between the wealthy and the poor. But societies or groups are also *politically stratified* when their social ranks are hierarchically structured with respect to authority and power. If, however, the members of a society are differentiated into various occupational groups and some of these occupations are deemed more honorable than others, or if occupations are internally divided between those who give orders and those who receive orders, then we deal with *occupational stratification*.[25] Though there may be other concrete forms of stratification, of central sociological importance are economic, political, and occupational stratification.

Sociological investigation must proceed to pay attention to the *height* and the *profile* of stratification pyramids. Of how many layers is it composed? Is its profile steep, or does it slope gradually?

Whether one studies economic, political, or occupational stratification, Sorokin contended, one must always be attentive to two distinct phenomena: the rise or decline of a group as a whole and the increase or decrease of stratification within a group. In the first case we deal with increases of wealth, power, or occupational standing of social groups, as when we talk of the decline of the aristocracy or the rise of the bourgeoisie; in the second, we are concerned with the increase or decrease of the height and steepness of the

[22] Pitirim A. Sorokin, *Social and Cultural Mobility* (New York, The Free Press, 1959), p. 4. (This volume was originally published as *Social Mobility* in 1927.)

[23] *Ibid.*, p. 5. [24] *Ibid.*, p. 11. [25] *Ibid.*, p. 11.

stratification pyramid in regard to wealth, power, or occupational prestige within groups—for example, when we say that the American Black population now has a higher stratification profile than it had at the turn of the century.

In contrast to evolutionary and "progressive" thought, and in tune with his overall view of the course of human history, Sorokin argued that no consistent trend toward either the heightening or the flattening of stratificational pyramids can be discerned. Instead, all that can be observed is ceaseless fluctuation. At times, differences between the poor and the rich may be reduced through the impact of equalitarian forces, but at other times inequalitarian tendencies will again assert themselves. Or at one point democratic participation will reduce differences in political power, while at another aristocratic and dictatorial politics will successfully increase the height of the political pyramid. In similar ways, some groups decline and others rise in ceaseless fluctuation.

Exterior features of the architecture of social structures having been sketched, Sorokin proceeds to summarize their inner construction, to wit: the character and disposition of the floors, the elevators, and the staircases that lead from one story to another; the ladders and accommodations for climbing up and going down from story to story.[26] This brings him to the concrete details of his study of social mobility.

Social mobility is understood as the transition of people from one social position to another. There are two types of social mobility, *horizontal* and *vertical.* The first concerns movements from one social position to another situated on the same level, as in a movement from Baptist to Methodist affiliation, or from work as a foreman with Ford to similar work with Chrysler. The second refers to transitions of people from one social stratum to one higher or lower in the social scale, as in ascendant movements from rags to riches or in the downward mobility of inept children of able parents.

Both ascending and descending movements occur in two principal forms: the penetration of individuals of a lower stratum into an existing higher one, and the descent of individuals from a higher social position to one lower on the scale; or the collective ascent or descent of whole groups relative to other groups in the social pyramid. But—and this is what distinguished Sorokin's orientation from that of many contemporary students of stratification and mobility—his main focus was upon collective, not on individual phenomena. As he puts it, "The case of individual infiltration into an existing higher stratum or of individuals dropping from a higher social layer into a lower one are relatively common and comprehensible. They need no explanation. The second form of social ascending and descending, the rise and fall of groups, must be considered more carefully."[27]

Groups and societies, according to Sorokin, may be distinguished according to their differences in the intensiveness and generality of social mobility. There may be stratified societies in which *vertical mobility* is virtually nil and others

[26] *Ibid.*, p. 128. [27] *Ibid.*, p. 134.

in which it is very frequent. We must therefore be careful to distinguish between the height and profile of stratification, and the prevalence or absence of social mobility. In some highly stratified societies where the membranes between strata are thin, social mobility is very high. In contrast, other societies with various profiles and heights of stratification have hardly any stairs and elevators to allow members to pass from one floor to another, so that the strata are largely closed, rigidly separated, immobile, and virtually impenetrable. Assuming that there are no societies in which strata are absolutely closed and none where social mobility is absolutely free from obstacles, one must recognize that Sorokin's distinctions, even though stated too metaphorically, are of considerable heuristic value.

In regard to degrees of openness and closure, Sorokin holds to his usual position: No perpetual trend toward either increase or decrease of vertical mobility can be discerned in the course of human history; all that can be noticed are variations through geographical space and fluctuations in historical time.

Attempting to identify the *channels of vertical mobility* and the mechanisms of social selection and distribution of individuals within different social strata, Sorokin identifies the army, the church, the school, as well as political, professional, and economic organizations, as principal conduits of vertical social circulation. They are the "sieves" that sift individuals who claim access to different social strata and positions. All these institutions are involved in social selection and distribution of the members of a society. They decide which people will climb and fall; they allocate individuals to various strata; they either open gates for the flow of individuals or create impediments to their movements.[28]

Without minutely detailing the many ways in which Sorokin illustrates the operation of these institutions or the way in which he shows why at a given time certain stratification profiles have called for specific mechanisms of selection, we should take note, however, of what he considers a "permanent and universal" basis for interoccupational stratification, namely: "The importance of an occupation for the survival and existence of a group as a whole." The occupations that are considered most consequential in a society, he states, are those that "are connected with the functions of organization and control of a group."[29]

In considering the impact of actual rates of social mobility, as well as the ideology of social mobility, on modern societies, we find Sorokin offers a fresh approach in the light of current experience. Far from indulging in unalloyed enthusiasm about high degrees of social mobility, Sorokin, like Durkheim, was at pains to highlight its dysfunctional and its functional aspects. He stressed, among other things, the heavy price in mental strain, mental disease, cynicism, social isolation, and loneliness of individuals cut adrift from their social moorings. He also stressed the increase in tolerance and the facilitation of intellec-

[28] *Ibid.*, p. 207. [29] *Ibid.*, p. 100.

tual life (as a result of discoveries and inventions) that were likely to occur with more frequency in highly mobile societies.

The analyst of social stratification, social mobility, and related matters can ignore Sorokin's work only at his or her expense. It still remains a veritable storehouse of ideas. Above all we need to take Sorokin's advice when he urges us to consider social mobility as a form of social exchange. Just as Lévi-Strauss brought about a revolution in the study of kinship (stressing that marriage is to be seen as an exchange between elementary families), so Sorokin presents the innovative idea that social mobility does not primarily concern the placement of individuals but is to be understood as exchange between social groups. By fostering the circulation of individuals in social space, such exchange increases or decreases the specific weight and power of the groups and strata between which they move. This central idea, if more fully elaborated, could be the impetus for a great deal of research in social stratification.

THE SOCIAL PHILOSOPHY

In a work on the history of sociological theories, Sorokin's "integralist" philosophy can be discussed only in a peripheral way, even though it undoubtedly loomed very large among Sorokin's preoccupations, especially in the last third of his life.

All of Sorokin's tracts for the times that deal with his philosophy are imbued with a pervasive distaste, one may even say hatred, for modern urban culture and all that it stands for. The *Sensate* world of the city jungle and the world of modernity as a whole are, to Sorokin, compounds of utter depravity, which he castigates in the accents of Old Testament prophets or Russian itinerant preachers. Consider the following lines from the final chapter of his autobiography: ". . . In the human world around me the deadliest storm is raging. The very destiny of mankind is being weighed in the balance of life and death. The forces of the dying Sensate order are furiously destroying everything that stands in their way. In the name of 'God,' 'progress,' 'civilization,' 'communism,' 'democracy,' 'freedom,' 'capitalism,' 'the dignity of man,' and other shibboleths they are uprooting these very values, murdering millions of human beings, threatening man's very survival and tending to turn this beautiful planet into an 'abomination of desolation.' "[30]

Sorokin's was an apocalyptic vision; he expected the fire next time. Yet, instilled as he was by a philosophy of history that rested on the notion of cyclical fluctuations in human affairs, he seems never to have doubted that the collapse of Western *Sensate* culture would be followed in its turn by a rebirth under different stars. It is this new *Ideational* culture that Sorokin sought to anticipate in his Integralist philosophy. In times to come, the present desert of

[30] Pitirim A. Sorokin, *A Long Journey* (New Haven, Conn., College and University Press, 1963), p. 324.

love would be superseded by a harmonious civilization in which altruistic love—which he studied intensely in the last period of his life—would overcome the competitive strivings of *Sensate* mentalities; here people would again find a secure footing in revitalized communities of their fellows. Then "the supreme Trinity of Truth, Goodness, and Beauty, wrongly divorced from one another by Sensate mentality"[31] will be reinstalled in "one harmonious whole." Men and women, now mired in the slough of despond, will again grow to truly human stature. Sorokin fervently believed, that after the *Goetterdaemmerung* of the dying *Sensate* order, humankind would again enter into its true kingdom. Having "deliberately become a 'stranger' to the glittering vacuities, and short-lived 'successes'" of *Sensate* decay, having "alienated [himself] from its hollow values, sham-truths, and grandiose pretenses,"[32] Sorokin saw himself as another Moses who, even though he could not enter the promised land, was still able, owing to his cultural estrangement, to forecast its main features in his Integralist philosophy. Let him who has never dreamt of a redemptive Utopia of the future cast the first stone.

THE MAN

On February 27, 1917, the first day of the mass demonstrations that were to presage the Russian Revolution, an ardent young intellectual and rebel, who had twice been imprisoned by the Czarist authorities for his revolutionary activities, noted in his diary: "It has come at last. At two o'clock in the morning . . . I hasten to set down the stirring events of this day. Because I did not feel too well and since lectures at the University had virtually ceased, I decided to stay at home and read the new work of Vilfredo Pareto, *Trattato di Sociologia Generale*."[33] If the writer of this entry had written nothing else in his life, these sentences would stand as a classic example of the tortuous love affair between intellectuals and revolution, of the complicated tension between theory and *Praxis*. The writer was Pitirim A. Sorokin.

FROM IKON PAINTER TO PROFESSIONAL REVOLUTIONARY

Sorokin was born on January 21, 1889, in a remote village in northern Russia's Vologda Province, inhabited by a non-Russian people of Ugro-Finnish origin, the Komi. The area consisted mainly of primeval forest stretching for

[31] *Ibid.*, p. 325. [32] *Ibid.*, p. 325.

[33] *A Long Journey*, p. 106. My main source for this section are Sorokin's three autobiographical statements. In addition to the full account in *A Long Journey*, see *Leaves from a Russian Diary* (New York, E. P. Dutton, 1924), and "Sociology of My Mental Life" in Philip J. Allen, *op. cit.* For a somewhat different account of Sorokin's relation to Lenin and some additional information cf. Jean Floud's review of Sorokin's *Fads and Foibles* in *British Journal of Educational Studies*, VI, 1 (November 1957), pp. 84–86.

many hundreds of miles in all directions. The small villages of the Komi were like tiny islands in a huge and engulfing forest vastness. The Komi spoke their own language but almost all were fluent in Russian as well. Industrialization and urbanization had not yet come to their land, and they subsisted mainly by farming, supplemented by fishing, hunting, lumbering, and trapping. The Komi never knew the serfdom that had marked most of the rest of Russia for many generations. They managed their local affairs autonomously through village self-governments similar to the Russian *mir* or communal peasant community. Land was held in common by the village; from time to time it was distributed and redistributed among individual families according to their needs and size. The houses of the village leaders and elders, of the priests, teachers, doctors, storekeepers, and village policemen were more spacious and comfortable than those of ordinary villagers, but otherwise the conditions of the inhabitants were nearly equal. Sorokin, the future analyst of social stratification, had little to draw upon from childhood memories, except by way of contrast, when he set upon this task many years later in a totally different environment, the state of Minnesota.

Sorokin was only three years old when his mother died—her funeral was the first conscious recollection etched in his mind. His father was of Russian origin, born in Veliki Ustyug, an ancient northern city that was a center of arts and crafts. He had served his apprenticeship in one of the artisan guilds and had gained his diploma as "a master of golden, silver and ikon ornamental works." He subsequently moved to a Komi village and there married a young woman who bore him three sons—Vassily, Pitirim, and Prokopiy.

After the death of their mother, the two older boys, Vassily and Pitirim, lived with their father; the youngest lived with an aunt. At times their father presented the loving image of a conscientious, affectionate, and protective guardian who took great pride in his craftsmanship and his standing in the many villages through which he wandered in search of work. At other times, however, he was given to long sprees of drunkenness that often resulted in *delirium tremens*. During one of his drunken outbursts, depressed, violently irritated, and enraged at his sons, the father snatched a hammer and struck both brothers. As a result, Pitirim's upper lip was somewhat misshapen for many years. Deeply affected, the ten-year-old Pitirim and the fourteen-year-old Vassily left their father's house, never to return. They immediately decided to make use of their exposure to the father's craft and to start independent careers as itinerant craftsmen, moving from village to village in search of customers. They never met their father again and heard of his death about a year later.

Young though they were, the boys managed to get commissions for painting and decorating churches, even a cathedral, gilding and silvering ikons and candelabras and making copper or gold ikon covers. Only sporadically did they attend various elementary schools. Nevertheless, after a few years of this nomadic life, Pitirim, at the age of fourteen, secured a modest scholarship at the

Khrenovo Teachers' Seminary. Travelling to the seminary by steamer and railroad, the young country lad had for the first time an intimation of the characteristics of big cities and industrial regions. The world of peasant culture, of rural folkways, of religious custom and of semipagan folklore now lay behind him, never to be reentered except for short periods, but always to be retained in his imagination and memory. Though he was to go on to live in the rapidly evolving urban and industrial *Gesellschaft* of Russian, and later, American cities, his life work was shaped to a large extent by his formative years in the village *Gemeinschaften* of the Komi people of the northern forest.

The city people and their sons in the Khrenovo Seminary at first treated Sorokin as a yokel because he lacked urban polish and sophistication. While he suffered from their contempt, the youngster himself, still in his homespun clothes, was inclined to agree with their judgement of him. But it did not take him long to acquire urban ways and manners and to buy his first ready-made suit. He soon was the leader of his class, despite his previous nomadic life and his previous sporadic schooling. The seminary, which was run by the Russian Orthodox Church, was concerned primarily with training teachers for the Church's elementary schools. But because it was located near sizable urban and industrial centers—and hence open to the winds of new doctrines—the school actually provided a quality of education more advanced than most other seminaries. Students and teachers freely interacted with townspeople, with the local intelligentsia, and with leaders of political opinions of all shades, from monarchists to Social Revolutionaries and Social Democrats. Immersing himself in the study of a variety of new books, journals, and newspapers that his newly won friends and acquaintances had thrust upon him, Sorokin soon shed his previous Orthodox religious and philosophical beliefs. The new ideas he was exposed to and his growing awareness of the miserable social and political conditions of Imperial Russia soon turned the peasant youth into an urban agnostic, a believer in scientific theories of evolution, and an active revolutionary. (The ferment created by the Russo-Japanese War of 1904 and the harbingers of the revolution of 1905 also contributed to this transformation.) Nevertheless, because he still clung to his earlier belief in self-help and individualism, he was repelled by the Marxist determinism of Social Democracy; young Sorokin became instead an ardent member of the populist Social Revolutionary party. Though now an urbanite, he was still powerfully attracted by the *Gemeinschaft* populism of the Narodniki, whose gospel he was helping to spread among students and factory workers, as well as the peasants of the surrounding countryside.

On the eve of the school's Christmas vacation in 1906, Sorokin was scheduled to address a group of workers and peasants. As he entered the meeting hall the police arrested him, escorted him to a horse-and-sleigh, and delivered him to a local prison. Prison treatment during the last years of the Czar's regime was no longer as harsh and inhuman as it had been in previous days. Prisons by now in fact became "graduate educational institutions" for revolutionaries, who gathered in interminable discussions of revolutionary theory and used their enforced leisure to read the works of Marx and Engels, of Kropotkin and Lavrov, of Tolstoi, Plekhanov and Lenin, as well as Darwin, Spencer, and other evolutionist and "progressive" thinkers. Sorokin probably learned more in prison than he could have absorbed in an entire semester's work at his Seminary.

Prison also afforded Sorokin his first acquaintance with common criminals, and this led to his choice of criminology and penology as his area of specialization during his later stay at St. Petersburg University. In addition, Sorokin transmuted his lived experience into academic knowledge: his first book, *Crime and Punishment, Service and Reward,* was published seven years after his first imprisonment.

Sorokin remained in prison four months before he was released. Though discharged from his school, he was received by most teachers and students as a hero of the revolution; yet stigmatized as a revolutionary, he could not be admitted to another school nor could he find any type of employment in the region. He therefore resolved to become an itinerant preacher spreading the revolutionary message, not unlike his earlier experience with painted ikons. Pitirim Sorokin, sought by the police for escaping from their supervision in his place of residence, disappeared, and an anonymous "Comrade Ivan" emerged as an organizer, speaker, and instructor among factory workers, students, and peasants throughout the Volga region. Most of the meetings he addressed and the demonstrations he led were peaceful affairs, but on one occasion, with a large group gathered together, Comrade Ivan, standing on a tree stump high above the crowd, fiercely denounced the regime. The meeting was broken up by the police with whips and sabers, which resulted in the deaths of two workers and a police officer and the wounding of several Cossacks, workers, and policemen. Thereafter, upon the urgings of his friends, Comrade Ivan retired to his aunt's house in the Komi village of Rymia, where he stayed for two months, helping with the farm work and visiting with boyhood friends. With no hope of continuing his education or of finding employment, Sorokin resolved in the fall of 1907 to make his way to St. Petersburg.

STUDENT AND SCHOLAR AT ST. PETERSBURG

It was easier for Sorokin to decide to go to St. Petersburg than it was for him to get there. The cheapest fare by steamer to Vologda and from there by train to St. Petersburg was approximately sixteen rubles; Sorokin had but one. He increased his funds to some ten rubles by painting two peasant homes, which paid for third-class accommodations on the steamer. But in Vologda he learned that the train fare to St. Petersburg was eight rubles, five more than he possessed. He therefore decided to buy a ticket to a point not far from Vologda and to travel the rest of the way as a stowaway—the "rabbit" class, as it was then called in Russia. He was soon discovered, however, but fortunately by a kind and understanding conductor. Sorokin explained that he was travelling to the capital to pursue his education; the conductor, an older man endowed with the Russian respect for things of the spirit, allowed the young man to continue on the trip on condition that he would earn his fare by cleaning cars and lavatories and also assisting the engine-stoker. With the help of this *Praxis,* Sorokin was sped on in his search for theory; when he reached St. Petersburg he had an unexpended balance of fifty kopecks in his pocket.

Having managed to be hired by an upward-mobile employee of the central electric station as a tutor for his two boys (in exchange for room and meager board), Sorokin set out to gain admission to the University. This was by no means easy. Since he had been expelled from his seminary and had never even attended *gymnasium,* there was only one way to gain admittance. He would have to pass a stiff "examination of maturity" for all eight grades of *gymnasium* and some additional materials required of "externs"—those who had not graduated from *gymnasium.* Largely ignorant of Latin and Greek, French and German, as well as mathematics, Sorokin could pass the examination only by attending one of the night schools that offered such training. When he learned that one of the teachers at a well-known night school was the first man from Komi to become a professor at the university, Sorokin presented himself at the professor's apartment and told the latter's astonished wife that he had just arrived from the Komi people and would like to see the Komi professor. K. F. Jakov, the man in question, not only arranged for Sorokin's free admission to night school, but opened up his own house to him, introduced him to some of the leading intellectuals, and thus paved his entrée to several philosophical, literary, and artistic circles in the university. The Komi professor also played a major role in the personal life of his student, for it was at one of Jakov's receptions that Sorokin met his future wife.

Through Jakov's recommendations, Sorokin soon obtained additional tutorial work that enabled him to earn a small wage while attending three semesters of night school. This school, as was the case with so many throughout Russia, was a hotbed of revolutionary ideas; Sorokin learned much in the give-and-take discussions among his like-minded peers—probably more than he did in the formal course of instruction.

After two years of study and extensive exposure to St. Petersburg's cultural offerings and intellectual stimulations, Sorokin returned to Veliki Ustyug, his father's hometown, to prepare for the final examination. The reason for this move was not so much to return to his roots (as current conceit has it); rather, he could live more cheaply with his uncle and aunt than was possible in the capital. In May 1909 he passed the examination with the grade of "excellent" in all subjects.

Back in St. Petersburg, Sorokin first enrolled in the newly opened Psycho-

Neurological Institute. A number of factors influenced his choice. First, the institute program was less rigid than that of the university; second, the university offered no instruction in sociology whereas two renowned sociologists, M. M. Kovalevsky and E. de Roberty, taught at the institute; finally, the institute's student body was largely of peasant and lower-class origin, who were more open to revolutionary ideas than students at the university. During his first year at the institute Sorokin attracted the attention of several of his instructors and was considered one of the top students. However, since university, but not institute students were exempt from serving in the military, he had to leave the institute and enroll at the university in order to escape the draft. But throughout the next few years his ties to the institute remained so strong that he became secretary and assistant to his teacher M. M. Kovalevsky, and, in his first year of graduate work, he was appointed a lecturer in sociology at the institute.

Despite the fact that the university did not officially recognize sociology as a field for matriculation, the subject was taught in courses listed under law or economics, criminology or history. As most of these courses were given in the faculty of law and economics, Sorokin chose that department as his field of specialization and was exposed to the guidance of such internationally known scholars as M. I. Tugan-Baranovsky in economics and M. I. Rostovtzeff in the classics. Sorokin proved himself to be a brilliant student and managed, even as an undergraduate, to publish a number of studies in sociological, anthropological, and philosophical journals. His first substantial volume, the previously mentioned *Crime and Punishment, Service and Reward,* was published in his junior year.

Though it seemed evident even in his early years at the university that he was destined for a brilliant academic career and soon would be accepted in the various circles of St. Petersburg's intelligentsia, Sorokin did not let his intellectual life interfere with his revolutionary activities. Indeed, his academic career was temporarily interrupted when the police raided his home to arrest him, but he happened to be away at the time. To escape the further attention of the police, Sorokin procured a false passport and the uniform of a student officer of the Military Medical Academy; he then went to the Riviera as a male nurse and companion to a fellow revolutionary who suffered from tuberculosis. These unusual circumstances allowed the young provincial from the northern forests to get his first glimpse of European upper-class culture. He even gambled at the Monte Carlo casino and won a few hundred francs. It may have been with those francs that he bought a copy of the recently published *Soziologie* by one Georg Simmel. After a few weeks, the student "disorders" at the university had abated, and the police relaxed its vigilance so that Sorokin could return to the capital and resume his studies.

Having escaped police arrest in 1911, Sorokin was not so lucky in 1913. He had written a pamphlet about the crimes and the misrule of the Romanov dynasty as a counterpoint to the tercentenary celebrations of that dynasty's reign. Thereupon he was betrayed by an *agent provocateur* and was arrested. The young revolutionary was placed in a relatively comfortable cell, had access to a good prison library, and simply continued his work. He also read a number of lighter volumes, among them Mark Twain's *Life on the Mississippi*. "It did not occur to me then," he later wrote in his autobiography, "that sometime in the future I would be living on the banks of this river [in Minneapolis]." But that time was not yet. Having no proof that Sorokin had in fact written the incriminating pamphlet and being hard pressed by many of Sorokin's professors, the police soon released him so that he could again devote himself to his formal education.

In 1914 Sorokin graduated with a first-class diploma from the university and was immediately offered the position of a "person left at the university to prepare for a professorship." He gladly accepted the offer, especially since a fairly good stipend went with it. For the first time he was able to live in a style to which most of his peers had long been accustomed. The stipend was granted for a four-year period to allow him to prepare for the *magister* (master) degree and a position as a *Privatdozent* (lecturer). Since sociology was still not an approved discipline, Sorokin chose criminology and penology as his major subject and constitutional law as his minor.

The master's degree was much more highly regarded in Russia than in the United States. In fact, most academicians held only such a degree; but a very few outstanding professors wrote distinguished dissertations that earned them a Ph.D. The oral examination for the magister degree took three full days, a fourth day being devoted to a substantial essay on a topic assigned by the body of examiners. It usually took at least four years to prepare for this examination but after only two, Sorokin passed in late 1916. He was now entitled to become a *Privatdozent* at the university; in order to receive the degree of "magister of criminal law," however, he still had to submit a dissertation and to defend it in a rigorous dispute with all the official opponents appointed by the university, as well as with unofficial faculty opponents and public challengers. Sorokin had planned to submit his volume on *Crime and Punishment, Service and Reward* as his dissertation, and his professors had agreed tentatively to schedule the defense for some day in March of 1917. But the Revolution prevented this. After March 1917 all university life practically ceased for several years. Sorokin had to wait until April 1922 to defend two volumes of his *System of Sociology* as a dissertation for the degree of doctor of sociology.

THE REVOLUTION AND AFTER

During the war years Sorokin by no means ceased his opposition to the Czarist regime. Nevertheless, he agreed with the majority of his Social Revolutionary comrades, as well as such Social Democratic luminaries as G. Plekhanov, to support the war effort (if rather critically) and to oppose those on the Left who called for a speedy end to the war and a separate peace with Germany. Those on the internationalist Left now called him and his co-thinkers Social Patriots.

When the revolution broke out, most of the political leaders of whatever camp were caught by surprise. The Social Patriots greeted it with a high degree of ambivalence. They had hoped for it during many years of underground struggle, but were fearful that the revolutionary events would undermine Russia's ability to continue the war at the side of its Western allies. Moreover, many intellectuals who had long been enthusiastic for revolution in the abstract found themselves repelled by many features of the revolution in the concrete. Sorokin's diary of those days clearly exhibits his ambivalence. No question, he rejoiced at the fall of the old regime. Yet caught in the whirlpool of revolutionary disorder, observing "unruly crowds" and "wildly firing men," witnessing manhunts for policemen, counterrevolutionaries, and informers, and learning of the massacres of officers, Sorokin could not suppress a deep repulsion about what he felt to be the rule of the mob in the streets of his beloved St. Petersburg.

After the abdication of the Czar and the installation of a Provisional Government, Sorokin engaged in a frantic round of activities. He agreed to become an editor of a new Social Revolutionary newspaper, only to discover that the editors were split between Social Patriots and Internationalists. Thus the paper would print an article on page one that was mercilessly savaged on page two. He went from meeting to meeting, from conference to conference, trying desperately to hold the right wing of his party together. He helped organize an All-Russian Peasant Soviet to counterbalance the radical Workers' Soviet. It all seemed futile. He finally left for his northern homeland to try to convince the peasants there that support of the Provisional Government against its enemies on the Left was the only road to salvation. He then wrote in his diary: "What a relief to leave the capital with its constantly moving crowds, its disorder, dirt, and hysteria, and to be again in the tranquil places I love." Having come face to face with the revolution he had so ardently desired in the past, Sorokin had fast become thoroughly disillusioned. How beautiful it had looked during the Czar's reign and how ugly it had turned out to be. "I sometimes feel like a homeless dog," he jotted down in his diary.

The frantic round of activities continued after Sorokin returned to Petrograd. He exhausted his energies in meeting after meeting, being alternately tired and weary, excited and alert. In the midst of it all, at the end of May, he married Elena Petrovna Baratinsky, a fellow student and botanist. After the church ceremony, to which he had come from an important meeting, his new wife and some friends went to lunch, which could last no longer than half an hour, for the groom had to hurry off to another "cursed conference."

In July 1917, in the midst of new riots and with the Provisional Government now headed by Kerensky fighting for its life, Sorokin agreed to accept the post of Secretary to the Prime Minister. There was little he could do. The Bolsheviks were waiting in the wings and could not be stopped. In a few months they succeeded in overthrowing the Kerensky government and proclaimed the Russian Soviet Republic. Sorokin and his friends continued a rearguard fight in the shortlived constitutional assembly and elsewhere but they knew that their cause was lost. They now were counted among the "former people," not unlike the Czarist officials against whom they had battled for so many years.

During the Civil War and the period of starvation and exhaustion that followed, Sorokin, who had for a short period sat next to the seats of power, became one victim among many. Early in January 1918 he was arrested at the offices of the anti-Bolshevik newspaper which he was editing. Released after two months, Sorokin and his wife went to Moscow in hopes of revitalizing the coalition of anti-Bolshevist groups in that city. He helped to start another newspaper, only to see its presses smashed soon after the first copy had appeared. Soon after, he returned to the northern country, worked underground under an assumed name, and hoped that the Bolshevist regime could be defeated with the help of a British expeditionary force that had landed in Arkhangelsk. But the British provided only limited aid, and the antirevolutionary forces, after some initial successes, were thoroughly routed. Sorokin was now forced to wander from village to village, his life in jeopardy, his name on the Bolsheviks' "wanted" list as a counterrevolutionary. For several months he hid in the forest. Finally, he made his way back to his home town, where he found shelter with his family, but decided that a prolonged stay would endanger his kin. Sorokin went to the local office of the secret police, the Chekha, and gave himself up. He was committed to the prison at Veliki Ustyug and fully expected to be executed any day. Instead he was released on December 12, 1918, on direct orders from Lenin himself.

A few days earlier, writing in *Pravda,* Lenin had announced a major change in the government's policy concerning the intelligentsia, arguing that it was important to gain the allegiance of the educated, especially those from the peasant strata who had now turned against the new regime after valiantly having fought against the Czar. The Communists should cease to persecute them, Lenin argued, and attempt to convert them into allies. It was in pursuance of that new directive that Sorokin was released and sent to Moscow. It turned out that one of his former students, now a Commissar, had pleaded with members of Lenin's cabinet who knew him well. They had agreed to talk to Lenin. Lenin was persuaded, wrote the *Pravda* article, revoked Sorokin's death sentence, and ordered his release. At the end of 1918 Sorokin returned to Petrograd University and resumed his academic duties. The days of his activist involvement were over.

Half-starved, and living under the most trying personal circumstances, Sorokin not only managed to give regular courses of lectures at the reopened university, but to launch a series of major writing projects. Besides two elementary textbooks in law and in sociology, he finished the two substantial volumes of his *System of Sociology*. To get these volumes published required almost as much energy as writing them. The work could clearly not pass the strict Communist censorship. Some of Sorokin's friends in a publishing house and at two nationalized printing presses managed to print the more than 800 pages secretly. The censorship permission on the title page was forged, ten thousand copies of each volume were published—all of which were sold within two or three weeks. When the government learned of the publication, it ordered all copies confiscated, but there was nothing left to confiscate. Shortly thereafter, Sorokin, who by then had been elected chairman of the newly founded department of sociology, submitted these illegally published volumes to the Juridical Faculty as his doctoral dissertation. After a typically extensive dispute, the faculty voted unanimously to accept the work as meeting all university requirements, and on April 22, 1922, Sorokin finally acquired his Ph.D. degree. It had been a long and tortuous journey; even so, Sorokin received his degree when he was only thirty-three years old, an age at which many American students of sociology will not yet have received theirs.

Having published two volumes of the planned three volumes of his *System,* Sorokin decided to postpone the writing of the last volume in order to do a first-hand study of mass starvation in the famine districts of Samara and Saratov. The book setting down the results of this inquiry, *The Influence of Hunger on Human Behavior, on Social Life and Social Organisation,* was published in May 1922, but only after the censors had severely mutilated it, cutting away many paragraphs and some entire chapters. The book has recently been republished in an English edition edited by Sorokin's widow shortly before her death.[34]

During 1922 a new wave of arrests of the non-Communist members of the intelligentsia hit Petrograd. Sorokin escaped by moving to Moscow, where he was less well known. When he learned that all those arrested were to be banished abroad, he voluntarily presented himself to the Chekha, and, after the usual delays, was given a passport. On September 23, 1922, he left Russia, never to return.

THE FIRST YEARS IN AMERICA

After a year's sojourn in Czechoslovakia, where he had been invited to stay at the request of President Masaryk, whom he knew well, Sorokin accepted the offer of two prominent American sociologists, Edward C. Hayes and Edward A. Ross, to come to America to deliver a series of lectures on the Russian Revo-

[34] Pitirim A. Sorokin, *Hunger as a Factor in Human Affairs,* edited and with an introduction by Elena Sorokin (Gainsville, Fla., The University Presses of Florida, 1975).

lution. Arriving in New York in October 1923, Sorokin first resolved to learn some English by attending lectures and meetings as well as various church services. Having gained a sufficient, though by no means full, command of the language, he gave his first lecture at Vassar College. In his early months in America, he also worked on his book, *The Sociology of Revolution*[35] and drafted major parts of his *Leaves from a Russian Diary*. Proceeding to the Universities of Illinois and Wisconsin, he delivered a series of lectures on the Russian Revolution and related matters. Predictably, he encountered a great deal of opposition from younger academics who regarded him as a disgruntled political emigré who had forgotten nothing and learned nothing. Yet this opposition abated when a number of prominent sociologists, Cooley, Ross, and Giddings among them, came to his defense. Sorokin continued to lecture at various universities, and in 1924 he was invited by the head of the sociology department at Minnesota, F. S. Chapin, to teach a course during the summer session. This led to an offer of a visiting professorship for the next year at half the normal salary for full professors of the University. Soon after, he was given a full professorship, though still at a salary substantially below that given to his American colleagues. During his years at Minnesota, Sorokin trained a number of distinguished students, C. A. Anderson, Conrad Taeuber, T. Lynn Smith and O. D. Duncan (the elder) among others, who later made major contributions, especially in rural sociology.

In the meantime, Sorokin's wife decided to continue her graduate work in botany and received her Ph.D. in 1925. The University's strict nepotism rules prevented her from receiving a teaching position at the University, and so she accepted a professorship of botany at neighboring Hamlin University.

Sorokin's scientific output during his six years in Minnesota was truly amazing. *The Sociology of Revolution* was published in 1925. *Social Mobility,*[36] the pioneering work on which all subsequent research in the area has depended heavily, followed in 1927. Only a year later his monumental critical survey, *Contemporary Sociological Theories,*[37] appeared. Collaboration with C. C. Zimmerman, who was to become his life-long friend, produced *Principles of Rural-Urban Sociology*[38] in 1929, and three volumes of *A Systematic Source-Book in Rural Sociology,*[39] with Zimmerman and C. J. Galpin as co-authors, were published in 1930–32. When one considers that Sorokin was still not fully conversant with the English language, that he faced all the usual difficulties of adjustment in an unfamiliar academic environment, his is an astonishing achievement.

[35] Pitirim A. Sorokin, *The Sociology of Revolution* (Philadelphia, Lippincott, 1925).

[36] Pitirim A. Sorokin, *Social Mobility,* (New York, Harper, 1927).

[37] Pitirim A. Sorokin, *Contemporary Sociological Theories* (New York, Harper, 1928).

[38] Pitirim A. Sorokin with C. C. Zimmerman, *Principles of Rural-Urban Sociology* (New York, Holt, 1929).

[39] Pitirim A. Sorokin with C. C. Zimmerman and C. J. Galpin, *A Systematic Source-Book in Rural Sociology,* 3 vols. (Minneapolis, University of Minnesota Press, 1930–32).

These books established Sorokin's place in the forefront of American sociology, even though they received mixed reviews. Some reviewers harshly criticized them; others, including such leaders of the field as Cooley, Ross, Giddings, Chapin, and Sutherland, warmly praised them. As a result, Sorokin was offered professorial appointments by two major universities, which he declined. But when President Lowell invited him to accept the first chair of sociology at Harvard, he went to Cambridge where he taught from 1930 to 1955. He continued to direct his Research Center in Creative Altruism at the University until his full retirement at the end of 1959 at the age of seventy.

THE HARVARD YEARS

It was during his Harvard years that Sorokin made some of his most significant and creative contributions to American sociology. When he first arrived at Harvard, a Department of Sociology did not yet exist, and Sorokin's chair was organizationally placed in the Department of Economics. But at the end of the first semester of the 1930–31 academic year, the administration finally approved a separate Department of Sociology and Sorokin became its chairman the next year. The man who had established the first Department of Sociology at Petrograd University in 1919–20 was given the opportunity to organize and guide Harvard's first such department a dozen years later.

Although relatively small, the department soon acquired considerable renown. Sorokin induced his Minnesota friend Carle Zimmerman to come as an associate professor and Talcott Parsons, who was teaching in the Department of Economics, became a sociology instructor. Special lectures or courses were offered by such eminent Harvard men as A. D. Nock in the sociology of religion, Dean Roscoe Pound in the sociology of law, Sheldon Glueck in criminology, and Gordon Allport in social psychology. Sorokin also brought a distinguished array of outside lecturers, including W. I. Thomas, Howard P. Becker of Wisconsin and Leopold von Wiese of Cologne.

Talcott Parsons, who was then working on his *Theory of Social Action,* had, next to Sorokin himself, the most powerful influence on the brilliant cohort of graduate students who flocked to the department soon after its inception. Many of the men who were to assume a leading position in sociology after their graduation from Harvard—for example, Robert K. Merton and Wilbert Moore, Kingsley Davis and Robin Williams—were influenced by both Sorokin and Parsons, though the Parsonian influence proved to be more enduring. Others, such as N. DeNood, E. A. Tiryakian, and R. DuWors, followed more closely in Sorokin's footsteps.

Sorokin was an unconventional teacher with a distinctive mode of presentation and style of delivery. He never lost his pronounced Russian accent, and when he ascended the platform and began speaking some of his auditors felt that they were listening to a rousing church homily rather than a classroom lecture. His best-known course for undergraduates, Principles of Sociology (officially listed as *Sociology A*), was commonly called *Sorokin A* by the Harvard Crimson Confidential Guide.[40]

One of Sorokin's students, Robert Bierstedt, has vividly described his way of teaching. He writes, "As a lecturer, Sorokin had no histrionic peer. A man of astonishing physical vigor, he would mount huge attacks against the blackboard, often breaking his chalk in the process. One of his classrooms had blackboards on three sides. At the end of the hour all three were normally covered with hieroglyphics, and clouds of chalk dust hovered in the air. If he was dramatic, he was also often melodramatic. For no American sociologist did he have a word of praise—always, in fact, the contrary. . . . His response to George Lundberg was typical. He arrived in class one morning, waved one of Lundberg's recently published papers before us, and declaimed . . . 'Here is a paper by my friend Lundberg on a subject about which, unfortunately, he knows nothing! It is a disease with him! He was not born for this kind of work.' On another occasion [he said to me] 'John Dewey, John Dewey, John Dewey! I read a book by John Dewey. I read another book by John Dewey. I read a third book by John Dewey. Nothing in them.' "[41]

Soon after coming to Harvard, Sorokin set to work on the four-volume treatise entitled *Social and Cultural Dynamics,* eventually published between 1937 and 1941. To accomplish this immense task, Sorokin enlisted a number of Russian emigré scholars, as well as some of his students, such as Robert K. Merton and John H. Boldyreff, as collaborators. They did much of the spade work in gathering data, computing statistics, and consulting reference works. Harvard assisted the work by a four-year grant amounting to roughly $10,000.

Sorokin was now at the pinnacle of his career, but even his Harvard years were accompanied by considerable stress. Departmental chairmen at Harvard as elsewhere in America were by no means as powerful as were their counterparts in Europe, and Sorokin probably still hankered after the European model. Though firmly ensconced in his position, he did not succeed in dominating the Department. Highly respected, even admired, by many of his students, he was not singular in the influence he had over them. That role he was forced to share with Talcott Parsons, despite the fact that Parsons was initially a young instructor when Sorokin held the only full professorial chair. Parsons and Sorokin shared a number of ideas, more particularly in regard to the central role of cultural symbols in the determination of social action, yet they never managed to reconcile their views. Their relations throughout the period could best be characterized as frigid competitive coexistence. It is fair to say that Sorokin indeed put Harvard's Department of Sociology on its feet, but he did not succeed in giving it his own distinctive imprint.

Sorokin's cast of mind in those years was conservative, and it is conceivable

40 Arthur K. Davis, "Lessons from Sorokin" in Edward A. Tiryakian, ed. *Sociological Theory, Values, and Sociocultural Change, Essays in Honor of Pitirim A. Sorokin* (New York, The Free Press, 1963), pp. 1–7.

41 Robert Bierstedt, *Power and Progress* (New York, McGraw-Hill, 1974), p. 2.

that this factor was instrumental in his being appointed to the Harvard faculty during a period of deep social crisis and the consequent ascendancy of a variety of Marxian or non-Marxian radical ideas. Yet the man from the Komi people was a conservative of a peculiar kind. As a conservative libertarian, a Christian anarchist, he never lost his peasant distrust of the centralizing state, a distrust that was reinforced by his experiences during the Russian Revolution. Thus, Sorokin had little in common with his American counterparts. Arthur Davis, one of his students, tells a revealing anecdote. Davis had been arrested by the Boston police for handing out leaflets for a CIO union during an organizing drive. The magistrate let him off, but one of his professors warned him that the arrest might have jeopardized his scholarship. When the matter came to Sorokin's attention in his capacity as departmental chairman, he brushed it aside with the comment that he himself had been arrested six times, three times by the Czar and three times by the Bolsheviks. . . .[42]

Sorokin never relished his administrative duties. He has reported that his requests to be relieved of them were twice turned down by the administration. Finally in 1942, having served for ten years, Sorokin's resignation as chairman was accepted. Soon after, the department was reorganized under Parsons's leadership and became the Department of Social Relations. From that point on, Sorokin played only a marginal role in the development of Harvard sociology. I remember coming to the Department's building in Emerson Hall in the early fifties, and, not finding Sorokin's office where I expected it (namely on the floor where most of the activities went on), was told that Sorokin (and Zimmerman) had their offices on an upper (desolate looking, as I recall) floor. Nor is it pleasant to note, on the other hand, that after the publication of Parsons's *The Social System,* Sorokin put under the door of the Department's offices a mimeographed statement in which he attempted to prove that the major ideas of this book had been anticipated in his own work.

Sorokin's alienation from the Department was at least partly compensated for by his establishment in the late forties of the *Harvard Research Center in Creative Altruism*. Sorokin had originally planned to carry on research in this field without financial assistance or a research staff. Quite unexpectedly, he received a letter from Ely Lilly, head of a large drug company and a well-known philanthropist, expressing an interest in aiding Sorokin in this venture. There followed a grant of $20,000. After Sorokin had begun to publish some of the results of his investigations, Mr. Lilly said he would like to meet him. When Sorokin informed him that he had so far spent exactly $248 out of the $20,000 grant, Mr. Lilly, with typical American impatience, queried, "Can't you put more steam into the business?" Sorokin agreed, and he received an additional grant of $100,000 for five years, which underwrote the Center's expenses. I hesitate to say much about the value of the inquiries of the Center. Even though

[42] Arthur K. Davis, *op. cit.*

not all its results were as startling as the find that "altruistic persons live longer than egoistic individuals," I do feel that little of enduring merit resulted from its labors.

Sorokin's influence at Harvard had originally been strong. But what the British literary critic John Gross once said about his fellow critic F. R. Leavis seems also to have applied to Sorokin: "Good students welcomed him as an emancipator, and then found that they had to spend years to escape from his liberating influence."[43] This was especially true, perhaps, after the publication of *Social and Cultural Dynamics,* when Sorokin's thought became increasingly rigid and dogmatic and when he largely veered in the direction of social prophecy and away from detached scholarly inquiry. Two of his works in the forties, *Sociocultural Causality, Space, Time* (1943)[44] and *Society, Culture and Personality* (1947)[45] still continued in the tradition of his earlier contributions, but the titles of other books published during and after the forties indicate his now prepotent inclination to serve as a prophet of doom and disaster: *Crisis of Our Age* (1941), *Man and Society in Calamity* (1942), *Reconstruction of Humanity* (1948), *Altruistic Love* (1950), *Social Philosophies of an Age of Crisis* (1950), *Explorations in Altruistic Love and Behavior* (1950), *S.O.S. The Meaning of Our Crisis* (1951), *The Ways and Power of Love* (1954), *The American Sex Revolution* (1957), and *Power and Morality* (1959). Whatever their value as tracts for the times or as prophetic indictments of the sins and errors of his contemporaries, they do not warrant analysis in a work devoted to sociological theory.

Only twice in those late years did Sorokin return to more strictly sociological concerns. His *Fads and Foibles in Modern Sociology and Related Sciences* (1956)[46] was a fierce indictment of practically all of contemporary sociology in general and of most empirical and statistical inquiries in particular. Though it made many telling critical observations on misuses and abuses of empirical research methods, it was couched in so all-encompassing and global terms that it missed its mark. The book also laid itself open to the fairly obvious observation that it hardly behooved an author who had used statistical techniques throughout his work (and who had often used them in ways which seemed questionable to most statisticians) now to indict practically all contemporary sociology as having succumbed to "quantophrenia," the madness of numbers. As a whole, the book proved an embarrassment even to Sorokin's most devoted former students.

A sequel to his renowned *Contemporary Sociological Theories,* entitled

[43] John Gross, *The Rise and Fall of the Man of Letters* (London, Weidenfeld and Nicholson, 1969), p. 284.

[44] Pitirim A. Sorokin, *Sociocultural Causality, Space, Time* (Durham, N.C., Duke University Press, 1943).

[45] Pitirim A. Sorokin, *Society, Culture and Personality,* (New York, Harper, 1947).

[46] Pitirim A. Sorokin, *Fads and Foibles in Modern Sociology and Related Sciences* (Chicago, Regnery, 1956).

Sociological Theories of Today[47] received a more favorable reception. Though replete with many poisoned barbs directed at most of his contemporaries and predecessors, it nevertheless showed Sorokin's capacity, even in his old age, to deal in a serious manner with sociological ideas and theories that he personally rejected wholeheartedly.

Sorokin was never a man to underestimate his own merit. In fact, he occasionally was heard comparing his contributions to those of Aristotle. It is understandable, therefore, that he clearly suffered in his later years from the comparative neglect of his contemporaries. But he never lost confidence. The peasant lad from the Komi people had initially been rejected by the urban sophisticates of St. Petersburg and yet had come to surpass almost all of them; why should he now worry about being shunned by representatives of a decaying *"Sensate"* culture? Sorokin plodded on, literally cultivating his own garden. He was probably as proud of the awards he received from horticultural societies for his magnificent flower garden in suburban Winchester as he was of all the honors, including the presidency of the American Sociological Association, which his colleagues bestowed on him. His two sons, both scientists like their mother, and his extended range of friends and admirers throughout the world, saw to it that Sorokin in his declining years was surrounded by the love which, so he had reiterated again and again, makes the world go around. When the old fighter died on February 11, 1968, even those he had attacked with his sharp strikes and his pointed arrows agreed that he was one of a kind—a kind that doesn't seem to appear any more.

I shall never forget the gaunt old man standing erect on a platform in an ultra modern lecture hall at Brandeis University, exhorting his audience to turn away from the lures and snares of a *"Sensate"* culture, to recognize the errors of their way, and to return to the path of *ideational* righteousness. It was as close as I would ever come to understand what it might have been like to be addressed by an itinerant preacher who had come out from the wild forest to instruct the erring flock of peasant sinners in the true ways of the Lord.

THE INTELLECTUAL CONTEXT

Even a superficial glance at Sorokin's major works reveals that his was an encyclopaedic mind. The scope and range of his *Contemporary Sociological Theories,* for example, give evidence that he read almost everything of any pertinence in the social sciences, in legal studies, and in most fields of philosophy. It therefore is impossible even to list the multitude of authors Sorokin was familiar with and who influenced him. Most of the masters discussed in this volume, from Comte to Weber, from Marx to Simmel and Pareto, for example,

[47] Pitirim A. Sorokin, *Sociological Theories of Today* (New York, Harper & Row, 1966).

had a decided impact on Sorokin's receptive mind, though he dissected their contributions with his renowned critical scalpel. It is appropriate, therefore, to limit the account of Sorokin's intellectual inheritance to major Russian thinkers of the nineteenth and twentieth centuries, most of whom are known only imperfectly to most Western scholars.

Sorokin stood at the confluence of two divergent streams of thought in Russian intellectual history—Populist idealism, and positivistic and deterministic behaviorism. These two major intellectual traditions, with, in addition, various philosophies of history, notably those of Danilevsky and Kovalesky which emphasized stage theories of human development, account for much of Sorokin's intellectual background but they cannot explain all of it.

POPULIST THOUGHT: HERZEN, LAVROV AND MIKHAILOVSKY[48]

The Populists, those nineteenth-century revolutionary enemies of Czardom, preached "going to the people" as the only road to salvation. Yet to call them "idealists" would not have met with their wholehearted approval. Most, if not all, were in one way or another believers in scientific determinism and some form of positivist doctrine. Yet they were also voluntarist individualists who stressed the importance of subjective definition of situations in the historical process as much as they may have worshipped the objective laws of historical development. Veering back and forth between Comte and Kant, between deterministic positivism and transcendental or romantic idealism, they seem never to have reached a stable resting ground. Immersed as they were in an ever changing flux of ideas, open to the winds of doctrines that reached them from Germany, France, and England, they seem to have been united only in respect to one overriding idea: salvation would come only from the *narod,* the people. Most of them came from noble origins, but they had turned in horror from the upper-class culture in which they had been born and bred. They realized that the refinement of that culture was bought at the price of the exploitation and dehumanization of the peasantry and that the core of that culture was utterly rotten. Hence, as one of them put it, "Let us go to the village . . . Let us gather together all who believe in the people . . . Only there amidst the great people in the village, in the *obshchina,* can salvation and reason be found."[49]

"Alexander Herzen (1812–1870), like Diderot," Sir Isaiah Berlin has written, "was an amateur of genius whose opinions and activities changed the di-

[48] My general account of Populist thought is largely based on two works, Thomas G. Masaryk, *The Spirit of Russia,* vols. 1 and 2 (New York, Macmillan, 1955), and Franco Venturi, *The Roots of Revolution* (New York, Knopf, 1960).

[49] V. S. Prugavin, quoted in James H. Billington, *Mikhailovsky and Russian Populism,* (Oxford, Oxford University Press, 1958), p. 94. This book has been most helpful not only on Mikhailovsky but on other Populist thinkers.

rection of social thought in his country."[50] He became the pioneer of Russian radical Populism following his disappointment in the failure of the revolution of 1848 in France. He turned from his previous belief in European liberal and French socialist ideas, from his faith in the ineluctable course of progress and enlightenment, to the conviction that only the power of the unspoiled Russian peasant people, gathered in its communal institutions, would be able to realize the unfulfilled hopes of the European radical tradition. After the failures of 1848, Herzen became convinced that the socialist folk society he wished to establish would only come about if it were firmly rooted in the existence of the great majority of the Russian peasantry. The foundation of the new Russia, which was to succeed the corrupt and decaying imperial regime, was to be the *mir*—the peasant community.

Herzen saw three elements of exceptional value in the *mir:* the right of every individual to the land, community ownership of the land, and self-government of the village community. His thought went through distinct phases during his lifetime, but, after 1848, he tenaciously clung to this core idea. Faced with the objection by Marxists and other historical determinists that Russia would first have to go through a phase of capitalist economic development before it could reach the higher stage of socialism, Herzen replied that it was fallacious to believe in one uniform historical law of development because many historical possibilities are always open. Upon the foundation of the *mir,* but without the bourgeoisie or the dead hand of Roman Catholicism, Russia could advance straightforward to a higher level of development. Its socialism could avoid the corruptions and the exploitation of Western capitalist societies as well as the centralizing and deadening effects of Western state-oriented socialist doctrine. Rather, Russian socialism, firmly rooted in peasant tradition, would inaugurate a decentralized communitarian and federalist socialism free from the disfiguring stigmata of European proletarian socialism and communism.

Unfortunately, Herzen's writings were neither consistent nor systematic. Succeeding generations of Populists attempted to remedy these deficiencies without fully succeeding.

Peter Lavrov (1823–1900), the first Populist pioneer of sociology, was as fully committed to the ideal of the *mir* as was Herzen, but he attempted to ground his creed in a systematic philosophy of history. Greatly influenced by Auguste Comte, Darwinian evolutionism, and the writings of Herbert Spencer, Lavrov nevertheless insisted that scientific laws had little relevance to history, which is moved by "those mental and moral aims which in every epoch are recognized by the most developed personalities as the highest aim, as truth and the moral ideal."[51] Lavrov's faith in progress was unbounded, yet counterbalanced by a Kantian concern with human individuality and the autonomous capacity of human beings to strive for the realization of their ideals. Human history was

[50] Isaiah Berlin, "Introduction" to Alexander Herzen, *My Past and Thought* (London, Chatto and Windus, 1968), p. XIII.

[51] Billington, *op. cit.,* p. 37.

a developmental process, yet, although humankind was subordinated to historical constraints, it was at the same time empowered through growing awareness of its predicaments to shape its own destiny.

Consciously aware human beings, according to Lavrov, choose aims for themselves in the light of ethical ideas. Thus he reached what he considered a reconciliation of objectivism and subjectivism, of Comte and Kant. He believed in inevitable historical progress, but progress came to be defined in terms of the growing powers of human subjectivity as "The development of individuality alike, physically, mentally, and morally; the incorporation of truth and justice in social forms."[52]

Lavrov held fast to human consciousness and championed individuals and their liberty against the claims of historical and societal constraints. To Lavrov, the state was devoid of ethical or metaphysical dignity; it was an external order operating through coercion. The aim of progress was to reduce the powers of the state to a minimum. In the future, a federation of communes would be the institutional foundation through which the Russian folk would be enabled to express its distinctive communitarian culture.

Lavrov was a somewhat aloof figure who did not immerse himself in the revolutionary movement even though he influenced its development. In contrast, his contemporary, Nicolai K. Mikhailovsky (1842–1904), had a more direct and potent influence on the Populist movement, in which he was an active participant. But just like Lavrov, who has often been called the first Russian sociologist, Mikhailovsky became a leading non-Marxist sociological scholar identified with the Populist movement. Like Lavrov too, Mikhailovsky borrowed heavily from Comte. He developed a theory of three major stages in human evolution which in many respects resembled the Comtean prototype, with one important exception. His third stage had little in common with Comte's technocratic ideal; it was to be marked by the apotheosis of individuality. To Mikhailovsky there was no higher aim in history than the struggle of individuals to be themselves. In the third stage of human development, humanity regains the idea that human beings are the measure of all things, but adds to it a mastery over nature that was denied earlier generations. In the third stage, human brotherhood will be the cornerstone of human individuality. The *mir*-based society will allow an unprecedented development of the human personality, freed from the constraints of marketplace and coercive state power.

In Mikhailovsky's sociological ideas, just as in Lavrov's, there is a stress on the need for both "objective" and "subjective" methods in sociology. They both taught that social and historical facts demand a material and a social-psychological explanation. Since human beings are goal-directed animals, the neglect of human ends, wishes, and desires must lead to an impoverished social science. Mikhailovsky hence was in the forefront of the critics of social Darwinism in Russia. In human society, he argued, concepts like chance variation and natural

[52] *Ibid.*, p. 12.

selection were inapplicable, for they implied purposeless struggle; rather, what characterized human strife and contention was purposes and goals. The thinking, feeling, desiring personality—not the biological organism—must be the center of sociological understanding; only in those terms can progress be measured. Throughout his life, and despite many variations in his views, Mikhailovsky remained a radical humanist.

Even this rapid survey of a few representative figures in the Populist movement shows the extent to which Sorokin's work has been shaped by the Populist tradition in which he immersed himself from an early age. His reformer's zeal, his rejection of value neutrality in the social sciences, his passionate individualism coupled with his admiration for peasant culture and his distrust of the sensate excesses of urban culture—these and many other elements in his world of ideas were rooted in his self-conscious adherence to the Populist tradition. Much of his philosophy of history, however, had other roots, among which the work of Nikolai Danilevsky (1822–1885) looms large.

DANILEVSKY AND THE REVOLT AGAINST THE IDEA OF LINEAR PROGRESS

Nikolai Danilevsky was a polymath who wrote profusely on a variety of subjects from biology to economics, from political science and linguistics to history. He is now remembered only as the author of the influential *Russia and Europe,* a slavophile tract for the times but also an important contribution to the philosophy of history. Danilevsky belonged to a very different social and cultural milieu than the Populists. A government official in the Ministry of Agriculture, later the head of the Russian Commission on Fisheries, he was a loyal subject of the Czar, even though in his youth he had been involved with Dostoievsky in the anti-Czarist Petrashevsky conspiracy. While the Populists aimed at undermining the Czarist regime, Danilevsky wanted to provide the ideological justification to extend its sway.

Though Sorokin never shared Danilevsky's political and ideological predispositions, he was influenced by Danilevsky's philosophy of history. He has written that *Russia and Europe,* "Begun as a political pamphlet of the highest grade, . . . demonstrated its political contentions to such a degree that it became a brilliant treatise on the philosophy of history and cultural sociology, and ended up by being an unusually shrewd and essentially correct piece of political prognostication and prophecy."[53]

The major burden of the work is contained in its attack on the idea of linear progress and evolution. Human history, Danilevsky argued, proceeds by multi-linear and multi-directional movements. There can be no general evolution of all humanity, since various civilizations are subject to their own dis-

[53] Pitirim A. Sorokin, *Social Philosophies in an Age of Crisis* (Boston, Beacon Press, 1950), p. 71. My account of Danilevsky's work is largely based on Sorokin, with assists from Masaryk, *op. cit.*

tinctive historical trajectories. Danilevsky believed that in studying human development—just as in studying botany and zoology, the subjects in which he was trained—scholars will make progress only when they have abandoned artificial unilineal evolutionary ideas and replaced them by classifications into different types of organisms and their different genera and species. Each civilization or historico-cultural type produces distinctive and unique achievements. Only within the life-history of each of these types, but emphatically not of humankind as a whole, can one talk of ancient, middle, and modern phases of development.

Danilevsky distinguished ten major types of civilization: Egyptian, Chinese, Assyrio-Babylonic, Indian, Iranian, Hebrew, Greek, Roman-Arabian, Slavic, and Teutono-Romanic or European. In due course, the Slavic type is destined to separate from its European roots and will develop a synthesis of those elements that have only been partly developed by the other types. Thus, while the Jews achieved high success in the cultivation of religion, the Greeks in aesthetic culture, the Romans in the art of government, and the Europeans in the political and cultural fields, the Russians will be the first to achieve an organic union of these four chief elements of civilization. They will reject the one-sided scientific and industrial character of European civilization; they will cast aside the materialism of its philosophical outlook and the religious anarchy that beset Europe ever since the Reformation; they will overcome the excesses of political democracy and economic feudalism. Once Russia will have organized a Slav federation it will become the beacon for all other civilizations, a Third Rome.

It was not Danilevsky's political perspectives, however, that attracted Sorokin. Rather, or so one can surmise from his discussion of Danilevsky's work, Sorokin was impressed by Danilevsky's pluralism, his rejection of the prevalent view that Germano-Romanic civilization was identical with universal human civilization, as well as by his pointed criticism of the excesses of European "materialist" culture.

It must be emphasized, however, that despite Danilevsky's quasi-biological analogies, he did not fall into the trap which disfigured much of Spengler's thought—namely, of believing that each civilization followed exclusively the laws of its own development. Stress on distinctive civilizational styles, he argued, does not mean that each cultural unit follows its own path irrespective of its neighbors. To the contrary, colonization, grafting, and crossfertilization are main avenues of cultural diffusion. But despite borrowings and diffusion, as long as a civilization is alive and creative it will continue to incarnate its specific and unique cultural style.

Perhaps the one aspect of Danilevsky's work that had the most influence on Sorokin was the former's views about the different phases any particular civilization is bound to traverse in its development. In the first phase, a patterned form of civilization emerges from an initial congeries of diverse elements. In the second, cultural and political independence is achieved. In the third, all creative potentialities are realized. This last phase of blossoming, Danilevsky contends, lasts only a few centuries, whereas the preparatory stages may have lasted for millennia. This period ends when the creative powers of the people have become exhausted. All that remains after that is a period of petrification or decay, of apathy or despair. The stage of decline and disintegration sets in earlier than can readily be observed—in fact, when contemporaries may still believe that their culture is at its height. Senility may have already begun even when a civilization still appears at its zenith.

While Sorokin seems not to have been impressed by the quasi-biological aspects of Danilevsky's doctrine or his panslavism, Danilevsky's sociology of knowledge and science left their mark on his own thought. According to Danilevsky all cultural products partake their key characteristics from specific mentalities prevalent in specific cultural environments and from the respective stages of development through which all civilizations must pass. It is also most probable that Sorokin's views on immanent, as distinct from externally induced, change and on the principle of limited possibilities owe a good deal to Danilevsky.

The works of the scholars treated so far were, of course, known to Sorokin only through the reading of their books. The more direct influence came from his teachers and colleagues.

ST. PETERSBURG TEACHERS AND PEERS

Sorokin had the unusual advantage of coming to St. Petersburg University and the Psycho-Neurological Institute at just the period when a number of brilliant scholars had begun the elaboration of novel psychological and sociological ideas within an academic setting. He was exposed to the teachings of pioneers who self-consciously felt that they were upon the point of conquering hitherto unknown territories of the human mind and of human social organization. Among these scholars Maksim M. Kovalesky assumes pride of place, both objectively and because of his influence on Sorokin.

Kovalesky (1851–1916) was a social historian and sociologist of international stature.[54] He meant to follow in the footsteps of Sir Henry Maine in the comparative study of social institutions within an evolutionary framework, as he revealed in the title of some of his works written in the eighteen-eighties: *Modern Custom and Ancient Law; Primitive Law; Law and Custom in the Caucasus; Comparative Historical Method in Jurisprudence; Agrarian Communities.* Later works such as *The Economic Growth of Europe up to the Rise of Capitalism* continued in the same tradition. In the years before World War I, Kovalesky turned his attention from comparative institutional history

[54] Cf. N. S. Timasheff, "The Sociological Theories of Maksim M. Kovalesky" in Henry Elmer Barnes, ed., *An Introduction to the History of Sociology* (Chicago, The University of Chicago Press, 1948), pp. 441–57.

to sociology, publishing, among other works, a review of the sociological theories of his time, *Contemporary Sociologists,* as well as a discussion of the scope and methods of sociology.

The son of a rich landowner, Kovalesky possessed independent means so that he did not have to rely on his earnings as a professor of constitutional law at Moscow University. This put him in good stead when the government, appalled by his widely proclaimed conviction that constitutional reform was unavoidable, dismissed him from the university in 1889. As a consequence, Kovalesky, who was a liberal but neither a Populist nor a revolutionary, went into self-imposed exile and spent his next fifteen years as an independent scholar in France and lectured occasionally at many European universities. Returning to Russia after the upheavals of 1904–1906, he became a professor at St. Petersburg University and the holder of the first chair in sociology at the Psycho-Neurological Institute.

The notion of unilinear evolution was very much in the center of Kovalesky's theoretical preoccupations. Though critical of some evolutionists and opposed to their organic theories of society, he was never able to free himself from the presuppositions of evolutionary theory. Despite doubts and reservations, he essentially held to the comforting nineteenth-century idea that the basic law of sociology was that of uniform evolutionary progress. "The similarity of economic conditions," he wrote, "the similarity of legal relations . . . , the similarity in the level of knowledge, formed the cause of the fact that people of different races and belonging to different epochs began their development from identical stages."[55] In later developments also, he argued, the emergence of similar structures and institutions among cultures that had nothing in common with one another testified to the operation of uniform laws of developmental stages.

Sociology, Kovalesky argued, had as its major task the study of the collective mentalities of social groups in so far as these are related to the evolution of their social organizations. Following in the footsteps of Auguste Comte, Kovalesky contended that sociology must study social order and social progress. Far from being only a descriptive science, it must also contribute to social policy by discovering all the causes on which both order and progress depend. Progress consists of gradual changes in social and economic structures and will hence yield objective criteria that can be used by the lawmaker in maintaining social order by adjusting institutions to the requirements of change.

Kovalesky's overall evolutionary scheme, which he used in a number of his historical investigations and in his ethnographic field works in the Caucasus, need hardly detain us. It bears a strong ressemblence to similar schemes by Spencer and Morgan and the British nineteenth-century anthropologists. What needs to be noted, however, is Kovalesky's oft-repeated insistence that any monistic theory should be rejected, be it based on economic factors or on demo-

[55] Quoted in *Ibid.*

graphic determinism. Only consideration of a variety of causative factors, he taught, could do justice to the complexity of evolutionary phenomena. He achieves his most telling effects when he describes the interrelation between many different factors—demographic, political, legal, economic—in bringing forth a new stage in evolutionary development. Even though he studied demographic determinants in more detail than others, he nevertheless remained a strong believer in the plural character of social causation. He always stressed that even when demographic factors seem to be the decisive element in explaining, say, economic developments, as with the Black Death of the late Middle Ages, they never worked alone.

Although Sorokin abandoned his teacher's confident belief in progress and beneficent evolution after the searing experiences of the Russian Revolution, it would seem that Kovalesky's penchant for large-scale historical generalizations, combined as it was with minute attention to specific ethnographic and descriptive detail, left its mark on his pupil. No doubt, Kovalesky's stress on the influence of the social organization on the people's collective mentalities helped stimulate Sorokin's later interest in the sociology of knowledge. Sorokin's life-long insistence that sociology must be concerned with the data of history and that historians and sociologists should be allies, rather than competitors, in the endeavor to unravel the secrets of the human predicament surely owes a good deal to Kovalesky.

The impact of Sorokin's other teachers was probably less pronounced, and there is less information available on them. Next to Kovalesky, Sorokin seems to have worked most closely with Leon Petrajitzki (1867–1931),[56] the pioneer of the Russian branch of the sociology of law, who was also the teacher of the renowned sociologist George Gurvitch, later of the Sorbonne, and of T. S. Timasheff, later a distinguished sociologist of law in the United States. Sorokin stressed his influence on him in his writings and lectures. Petrajitzki taught that students of law should not restrict themselves only to the formal study of statute law, but should consider the socio-psychological foundations on which enacted law necessarily rested. Law, he asserted, was first and foremost based on subjective experience. Moral and juridical emotions are the cornerstone of the law, and these emotions, rather than the law itself, are the guides to conduct. Furthermore, he argued, the state is by no means the only source of law. Much of law is, in fact, "unofficial law," so that in any society one is not faced with a monolithic legal structure but with juridical pluralism. Concerned as he was with "humanizing" the law, Petrajitzki aimed at developing a "politics of law," which was to achieve an enduring reconciliation of law with the ideal of love and brotherhood. Rejecting hedonistic and utilitarian approaches to law, Petrajitzki wanted to develop a subjectivistic and phenomenological approach resembling in some ways Max Scheler's contributions, to which Gurvitch was drawn after his emigration from Russia.

[56] Cf. George Gurvitch, "Leon Petrajitzki" in *Encyclopaedia of the Social Sciences* (New York, Macmillan, 1938), vol. XII, pp. 103–4.

Petrajitzki's "psychological sociology" of legal and moral phenomena exerted a strong influence on Sorokin. He has said that Petrajitzki's theory "is quite original, extraordinarily logical, and at the same time quite factual and inductive. And what is more important, it works in an analysis of the most complex and concrete social phenomena."[57] Sorokin's later insistence on the importance of studying meaning structures and collective mentalities as clues to stages of civilization seems to have its source in Petrajitzki's teaching. His late writings on the theoretical and practical importance of love and altruism probably owe as much to the influence of Petrajitzki as they do to Populist thought.

Though Kovalesky and Petrajitzki taught at the Psycho-Neurological Institute, they seem to have exerted only a marginal influence. The predominant atmosphere in that Institute was created by the strict positivistic behaviorist Vladimir Bekhterev (1857–1917).[58] Next to Ivan Pavlov, who taught Sorokin at St. Petersburg University, Bekhterev is the co-founder of modern behaviorism. A neurologist and physiologist of genius, Bekhterev's experiments in reflexology deeply influenced John B. Watson and, together with Pavlov's work, provide the foundation for all subsequent research in behavioral psychology in Europe and America.

Sorokin's earliest work is imbued with a strictly behaviorist view of human conduct. He then could write: "Human conduct is an extraordinary complex phenomenon, determined in an immense variety of cases by inborn reflexes and their stimuli . . . The balance of conduct is achieved by way of self-restriction and a complex of struggle of various stimuli and reactions."[59]

After his disillusion with the Russian Revolution, Sorokin came to reject behaviorism and positivism entirely. They seemed to him to have failed because of their reductionist approach to human conduct. Yet one could say that Sorokin's later concern with backing his "integralist" philosophy with elaborate statistical investigations can be accounted for, at least in part, by his exposure to the strongly positivistic, scientistic, and behaviorist training he received at St. Petersburg. Furthermore, it would be wrong to put too sharp a dividing line between the idealist and the positivistic traditions in Sorokin's Russia. They often overlapped in very characteristic, if not characteristically Russian, ways. Consider the following pronouncement by Ivan Pavlov, "[I have the] deep, irrevocable and ineradicable conviction that [the study of conditioned reflexes] is the path of the final triumph of the human mind over its last and uppermost problem—full knowledge of the laws and mechanisms of human nature and thus full, true, and permanent happiness."[60] The pathos of these lines is deeply

[57] Pitirim A. Sorokin, "Russian Sociology in the Twentieth Century." *Publications of the American Sociological Society,* XXI (1926), pp. 57–69.

[58] Cf. Gregory Razran, "Vladimir Bekhterev" in *International Encyclopaedia of the Social Sciences* (New York, Macmillan, 1968), vol. II, p. 45.

[59] Pitirim A. Sorokin, *The Sociology of Revolution* (Philadelphia, Lippincott, 1925), p. 31.

[60] Quoted in Gregory Razran, "Ivan Pavlov" in *International Encyclopaedia of the Social Sciences* (New York, Macmillan, 1968), vol. XI, p. 486.

rooted in Russian tradition, and it is that tradition, over and above all diversities, that comes to life in the work of Pitirim Sorokin.[61]

THE SOCIAL CONTEXT

AN ABORTIVE REVOLUTION

Pitirim Sorokin grew into young manhood in the years immediately following Russia's defeat in the war with Japan and the abortive revolution of 1905.

Popular discontent had mounted throughout Russia in 1905. At the end of October of that year a general strike paralyzed the empire. Delegates of strike committees formed a *soviet* (council) of workers' delegates in St. Petersburg, which for a while seemed to develop into a power seriously challenging the established authorities. Czar Nicholas II was forced reluctantly to issue a manifesto promising an elected legislature (*duma*) and the establishment of full civil and political liberties. Through these concessions he managed to quiet much of the popular discontent and to divert revolutionary energies. Order was re-established, peasant revolts subsided, and the power of the *soviets* came to an end. It soon became apparent to most of Russia's liberal and radical intelligentsia that, though some concessions had been won, the revolution had failed.

Marxists and peasant-oriented Populists boycotted the elections to the first *duma,* arguing that it had no real power to affect political events. As a result, moderate reformers and members of a Labor group, made up of Populists who had stood for election despite their party's boycott, dominated the *duma.* When the majority developed a far-reaching reform program involving, among other things, the division of large landed estates among the peasantry and a full amnesty for all political prisoners, the Czar dissolved the *duma.* The second *duma,* in which the Left now took part, was even more radical in its demands than the first. It met for only three months in 1907 and then was dissolved. A new electoral law was now passed that sharply reduced the franchise. The law was designed to strengthen representation of the well-to-do at the expense of workers and peasants and to reduce the representation of the non-Russian nationalities. In consequence, rightists dominated in the succeeding *dumas,* and the hopes and promises of 1905 had come to naught. The Czar was again fully in the saddle. A deep feeling of discouragement and depression now prevailed among Russia's radicals and among most liberals.

Though democracy had been defeated, the new political system differed significantly from the old. Under an energetic Prime Minister, P. A. Stolypin,

[61] For a general sociological description of the prerevolutionary Russian intelligentsia see Lewis A. Coser, *Men of Ideas* (New York, The Free Press, 1965).

the government attempted in Bismarckian manner to accomplish by administrative reform from above what it had refused to concede to pressures from below. Political parties and trade unions could now be legally established, though the unions were still not permitted to strike. Censorship of the press was relaxed, and book censorship practically ended.

From 1908 on, the economy, aided by the state, made considerable strides forward. Most importantly, Stolypin initiated a series of agricultural reforms that had a profound impact on the countryside. He aimed to break up the traditional peasant commune and to encourage individual ownership. His measures created a deep cleavage between the well-to-do peasantry, whose major discontents were allayed by the prospect of becoming independent peasant proprietors, and the landless peasantry. The latter, it was reckoned, being condemned to perpetual poverty, would be forced to leave the countryside and provide manpower for the growing industry. In the meantime, the large landed estates remained in the hands of their previous owners and were protected from the wrath of their landless tenants. In summary, the Stolypin reforms aimed at the destruction of the old communal village system with its egalitarian features and at the creation of a capitalist, market-oriented system of agriculture, based on the self-interest, the enterprise, and the greed of the rich and middling peasantry.

While Stolypin's agrarian measures aimed to destroy the peasant basis of the Populists and Social Revolutionaries, his policies in the field of ethnic relations undercut the power of the non-Russian nationalities through a concerted drive of Russification. The cultural organizations of the non-Russians that had sprung up in the wake of the revolution were dissolved, the representation they had enjoyed in the first two *dumas* was sharply reduced, and Russian culture was given unquestioned preeminence over all others. Hence, despite his reforms, despite economic advance, social tension increased during the prewar years, and finally erupted in revolution during the war.

It was predictable that Sorokin, along with most intellectuals from non-Russian nationalities and the majority of the intelligentsia of the empire, would align himself with the enemies of the regime. He was deeply attached to the peasant communal life styles of his northern region and therefore opposed to the procapitalist agrarian policies of the government. Having come from a region dominated by non-Russian stock and himself part Komi, and, in addition, being a member of the intelligentsia thirsting for freedom and democracy, it was almost preordained that he would join the anti-Czarist camp and consider himself a revolutionary,[62] but a revolutionary of a very special kind.

[62] The above sketch of Russian history in the decade before the outbreak of World War I is based on B. H. Sumner, *Survey of Russian History* 2nd ed. (London, Duckworth, 1948); and G. Vernadsky and M. Karpovich, *A History of Russia,* 4 vols. (New Haven, Yale University Press, 1943–59).

THE PERPETUAL LONER FROM THE KOMI PEOPLE

There is no better clue to an understanding both of Sorokin's political view in prerevolutionary days and of his subsequent writings than the fact that, throughout his career in Russia and in America, he was a loner suffering from socially induced strain and ambivalence. His culture was Russian, yet he had acquired it in peasant communities that were largely non-Russian. He came from the village *Gemeinschaft* of the Komi people, yet had no secure roots in it. He was only part Komi and throughout his youth he had lived as a perpetual wanderer, estranged from the roots for which he yearned. He loved the folk culture, the semipagan folk religion, the simplicities and naive pieties of the Komi villager; yet, once he had gone to the seminary, he came to regard them as remnants of a past that was largely obsolete.

Like Veblen before him, Sorokin never lost his distrust of urban life-styles, of the indulgences and stimulations of city life. Like Veblen, he was ever suspicious of cosmopolites, regarding city civilization as the whore of Babylon—yet he was himself a sophisticated urbanite. His enduring yearning for *Gemeinschaft* in the wilderness of the cities was grounded in nostalgia for the simple village communities in which he grew up. Yet, here again, much like Veblen, he had been as marginal in that *Gemeinschaft* as he was later to be in the big city.

Like many others who lost their mothers at an early age, Sorokin seems throughout his life to have yearned for the embrace of true "mothering" communion, an experience which always eluded him. His father had been alternately protective and despotic, so it is not surprising that the young boy had strongly ambivalent feelings about him. It is interesting to speculate that the young Sorokin probably projected the disappointments of his personal life onto the larger societal scene. If even parental authority could not be trusted, then other authorities could be relied on even less. Far better to be entirely on one's own, trusting no one invested with authority. This background accounts in part for the strange combination in Sorokin's make-up: pronounced communitarian and anti-individualist tendencies with an equally pronounced stress on an almost anarchistic libertarianism.

When he left the Komi people to cast his lot with Russian culture and urbanized life-styles, Sorokin did not yet abandon all his previous allegiances. To be sure, he now acquired the mental cast of the student intelligentsia, believing in evolution, progress, and enlightenment. But it is significant that he chose to align himself with the decentralist, peasant-oriented Populists rather than with the Marxists. The man from Komi would never lose his distrust of the centralizing state and its levelling tendencies. He became for a time a revolutionist and a socialist, but never a Marxist.

I have no evidence that indicates Sorokin was particularly lonely or isolated during his student days. Many years later he still spoke with warmth and affection of his many friends and associates at St. Petersburg. Yet between the lines of his autobiographical writings one can detect that he remained conscious of being an outsider. It is at least plausible that his almost monomaniacal drive for learning was largely motivated by his desire to show the insiders that he, the outsider, could surpass them in command of vast bodies of literature. The man from Komi, who had never attended *gymnasium,* would demonstrate that he could master the ways of their culture more deeply and extensively than could they. His ambivalent desire for both acceptance and autonomy is reflected in the habit that was never to leave him: he would pile footnote upon footnote to indicate that he was at home in the whole storehouse of Western culture, while at the same time critically and often violently attacking almost all contemporary thinkers. He would show his colleagues that, though conversant with all the contributions of past and present thinkers, he remained his own man.

The revolution of 1917 shattered much of the positivistic, evolutionary, and scientistic outlook that Sorokin had shared with his companions. Witnessing the atrocities, the disorders, the inhumanities of that revolution, and unable to excuse them in terms of some higher purpose, Sorokin broke with his previous intellectual commitments and worked his way to the anti-sensate philosophical positions that underlay his subsequent work. In a sense, the revolutionary experience created a sea change in his world view. One can nevertheless discern continuities between the mental outlook of his younger days and his mature doctrine. Over and above all change in intellectual development, Sorokin was marked, before as well as after his disillusionment with the revolution, by his background first as a semioutsider among the Komi, then as a stranger from Komi among the Russian intelligentsia, and finally as a Russian among Americans.

A LONER IN AMERICA

The lot of the emigré is never easy. To make one's way in a strange society and an alien culture always taxes energies and induces strain. Even the emigré who is received with open arms by his hosts finds it hard to shed a sense of his distinctiveness, a distinctiveness which he may prize, even over-value, but which he nevertheless perceives as an indelible stigma. The ways of the host people are not his ways, and their language remains alien even if he manages to master its intricacies. Severed from previous commitments to kin and friends, from institutional loyalties and communal bonds, the emigré is likely to feel "lonely and afraid in a world he never made." Even those emigrés who acquire new friends and colleagues and forge new bonds of affection are likely to remain somewhat alienated if one considers, for example, that most adult friendships are based on common experience in school or neighborhood. The emigré is forever excluded from these bases of communality.

However, many, if not most, emigrés manage after some period of time to shed at least part of their initial fear of rejection and to experience the sense of elation that comes from being accepted in the host community. Such, it would seem, was never fully the case with Sorokin. Instead, his sense of marginality remained even more pronounced in America than it had been in Russia.

Americans, to be sure, were not likely to know about his Komi background and considered him one among many Russian refugees. But not matter, it would seem that Sorokin in Minnesota, and more especially at Harvard, never felt fully accepted; nor was he himself fully accepting. He received sustained support and encouragement from a number of eminent sociologists, yet his pronounced anti-Soviet views, which he displayed with characteristic vigor and openness, made him the *bête noire* of many liberals and radicals in the discipline and outside, who regarded him as a dyed-in-the-wool reactionary. His books were widely reviewed and sold well, but he was more often savaged than praised by reviewers. What is even more revealing is the fact that the favorable reviews he received came more often in the popular journals, while the learned journals tended to be lukewarm or negative. A. E. Tibbs, who has tabulated all reviews of *Social and Cultural Dynamics,* finds that of seven reviews in popular journals, only two (by Sidney Hook and Lewis Mumford) were unfavorable. In contrast, of six reviews by specialists other than sociologists, four were negative, one neutral, and only one favorable. Finally, of eleven reviews in sociological journals, six were ambivalent, four were negative, and only one was favorable. Moreover, the reviews by Robert MacIver and Hans Speier in the *American Sociological Review,* the official journal of the American Sociological Society, were harshly critical, and Robert Bierstedt, writing in the same journal, was even more rejecting.[63] Soon after completing his work on *Dynamics,* Sorokin largely turned away from attempts to convince his sociological peers who had rebuked him and wrote increasingly for the popular audience which he deemed more receptive.

Sorokin made some friends among his American associates, but his closest ties were with Russian emigrés whom he knew from Petrograd days. These included the conductor Serge Koussevitzky and the historian Michael Rostovtzeff, two friends to whom he dedicated his *Dynamics.* In his autobiography Sorokin speaks affectionately of a great number of American men and women, yet none were as close to him as his Russian friends. In Minnesota, especially on long camping trips with the Chapins or the Zimmermans, he found more congenial companionship than he later experienced at Harvard. The open friendliness that can be found in the midwest is not particularly characteristic of the Harvard atmosphere. One has the impression that the Russian emigré, with his distinctive speech pattern, his unfashionable opinions, and

[63] I take these data from A. E. Tibbs, "Book Reviews of Social and Cultural Dynamics, A Study in Wissenssoziologie," *Social Forces,* XXI (May 1943), pp. 473 ff.

strange peculiarities remained forever an alien on the Harvard yard. What was true of Harvard in general was also true in regard to Sorokin's colleagues in the Department. Apart from his friend C. C. Zimmerman, whom he had induced to follow him from Minnesota to Harvard, Sorokin did not enjoy a strong collegial relationship with his departmental associates, either during his chairmanship or after. When he mentions Harvard colleagues, they turn out to be economists, historians, scientists, or musicians—hardly ever sociologists. There were his students, of course, but despite their initial enthusiasm most of them did not become his disciples.

Sorokin was never at home at Harvard and always felt on the defensive. He had already been predisposed to be highly critical of the contributions of others, and this tendency became accentuated at Harvard and sometimes assumed grotesque features. Especially after having relinquished the Department's direction, he engaged in an almost incessant combat against all comers. In the process he alienated a fair number of colleagues in the sociological community who might have been well disposed to him initially and potentially receptive to at least some of his ideas. As a result of his rebuffs, Sorokin was moved to look for a different audience, for people who were inclined to listen to his message of doom and disaster.

Yet another reason for this turn of attention is to be found in the incentives provided by America's depression and crisis. During the first few years of Sorokin's stay in America, this country enjoyed an unprecedented prosperity, and social questions remained relatively muted. This may in part account for the fact that Sorokin did not seem overly concerned with American social affairs. He was still trying to come to terms with his disastrous Russian experiences and felt the need to instruct his American audiences about what he felt were the horrors of the Russian Revolution. But otherwise in his Minnesota writings he addressed himself to such scholarly inquiries as social mobility, the history of sociological theory, and rural sociology. But by the time he reached Harvard the depression was in full swing and urgent social questions were on the agenda. Left-wing social thought of a Marxist or near-Marxist variety began to make major inroads on the groves of academe. Sorokin then resolved, in reaction, to popularize his antirevolutionary philosophy and to develop his own distinctive socio-political message in a series of tracts for the time. In the beginning, his direction of the Department's affairs took much of his time, and the monumental task of writing the four volumes of *Social and Cultural Dynamics* preempted the rest. But after this work was finished and he gave up the chairmanship, Sorokin began to publish his works of moral and political exhortation, beginning with *The Crisis of Our Age*. Moreover, as was discussed earlier in this chapter, the *Dynamics* itself was by no means free from sociocultural pleading. It would then seem that Sorokin's turn toward the explicit formulation of remedies for the ailments of the age can be traced, at least in part, to the stimulation provided by time and place.

IN SUMMARY

The isolation of Sorokin, though pronounced, was never total. He was encouraged by a number of eminent European philosophers and historians, as well as by some non-American sociologists of an older generation. Arnold Toynbee held him in high esteem; Corrado Gini, the Italian statistician, Lucio Mendieta y Nuñez, the leading South American sociologist, and Leopold von Wiese of Germany followed his work with sustained attention. But the fact is that there were few, very few, friends and colleagues who favored Sorokin with sustained critical attention. He had at times many students and always some devoted disciples, but there were apparently few persons within his intellectual circle who were his equal in intellectual attainments or eminence. Had he had such peers, one ventures to think, many of the flaws of his sociological works might have been remedied, and surely some of the obvious and glaring incongruities in his later "prophetic" writings might have been omitted. Lacking such sustained critical colleagueship, Sorokin came increasingly to divide the world in a somewhat manichean manner into friends and enemies, with most American sociologists being counted among the latter. Some of his former students—Robert K. Merton, Wilbert Moore, Bernard Barber, and Edward Tiryakian, among others—remained attached to him, but one does not have the impression that they maintained a sustained intellectual dialogue with him after they left Harvard. And thus, like Auguste Comte in his latter days, being excluded or having excluded himself from sustaining social networks and social circles, Sorokin's voice became more and more shrill and his view increasingly eccentric. Many of his later works, it must be said, make rather painful reading. He paid a heavy price for his social and intellectual isolation.

Being a perpetual loner, an outsider who wished to show the insiders the error of their ways, provided the motivation and emotional energies that enabled him to do the prodigious amount of scholarly work that he accomplished. Yet this loner's stance also alienated him in the end from much of his potential audience. Despite the fact that two *Festschriften* were published in his honor,[64] and in 1963 he was elected to the presidency of the American Sociological Association, he was almost a forgotten man in the last decade or so of his life.

It is my hope that these pages will help to restore Pitirim A. Sorokin to the place he so surely deserves. Yet they must also take notice of the heavy price he paid in eccentricity, intellectual arrogance, and self-righteousness—the fruits of his socially induced and self-willed isolation.

[64] Philip J. Allen, ed., *Pitirim A. Sorokin in Review* (Durham, N.C., Duke University Press, 1963), and Edward A. Tiryakian, ed., *Sociological Theory, Values, and Sociocultural Change, Essays in Honor of Pitirim A. Sorokin,* (New York, The Free Press, 1963).

William I. Thomas

1863-1947

Florian Znaniecki

1882-1958

THE WORK

The names William I. Thomas and Florian Znaniecki have come to be linked in the minds of generations of scholars because *The Polish Peasant in Europe and America*[1] is their common masterpiece. It is for this reason, although their cast of mind and even their personalities differed in many ways, they will be treated together in this chapter. Their work is intertwined in the history of sociology, and their lives may be best approached in terms of their contrapuntal relationships.

Given this focus on their common work, *The Polish Peasant* will be discussed first, even though both authors, and Thomas particularly, had already made other noteworthy contributions prior to their joint enterprise. The purpose of *The Polish Peasant* was to provide a documented sociological treatment of the life-experiences of Polish countrymen as they came to be involved in the major social changes that attended their moves from the relative security and rootedness of their native villages to the uprooting wilderness of American urban life.[2] My emphasis, however, here, as elsewhere, is not on the detailed findings of this work, but on the major theoretical underpinnings that give it a significance well beyond its stated purpose.

THE POLISH PEASANT—A LANDMARK

The Polish Peasant is a monumental achievement, the earliest major landmark of American sociological research. Being centrally concerned with issues of ethnic identity and ethnic subcultures, it should be of special interest at present when these issues have again assumed a salience they seemed to have lost for a time since Thomas's and Znaniecki's days.

1 William I. Thomas and Florian Znaniecki, *The Polish Peasant in Europe and America,* 2 vols. (Dover, 1958). First edition in 5 vols., (Boston, Richard Badger, 1918–1920); the first two vols. were originally published by The University of Chicago Press in 1918.

2 This section owes a great deal to the following: Morris Janowitz, "Introduction" to Morris Janowitz, ed., *William I. Thomas on Social Organization and Social Personality* (Chicago, The University of Chicago Press, 1966); Robert Bierstedt, "Introduction" to Robert Bierstedt, ed., *Florian Znaniecki on Humanistic Sociology* (Chicago, The University of Chicago Press, 1969); Hyman H. Frankel, *The Sociological Theory of Florian Znaniecki,* unpublished Ph.D. dissertation, (University of Illinois, 1958); and John Madge, *The Origins of Scientific Sociology* (New York, The Free Press, 1962), Chapter III.

The raw materials of the book (which are reported in exhaustive detail) are derived from life-histories of Polish immigrants to Chicago. These materials—personal letters, autobiographies, diaries, and other personal documents—are extremely rich in their peculiar specificity. The purpose here is not to delve into the documentary evidence at length, worthwhile task though that would be; rather, my aim is to delineate the ways, sometimes successful, sometimes not, in which the authors captured the peculiarities of their detailed accounts within a net of generalizing abstractions.

Thomas and Znaniecki self-consciously rejected the fallacy that any science ever consists in the accumulation of facts. "A fact by itself," they wrote, "is already an abstraction. . . . The question is only whether we perform this abstraction methodologically or not, whether we know what and why we accept and reject, or simply take uncritically the old abstraction of 'common sense.' "[3] Methodical abstraction would allow them to do justice to their material and yet transcend it, thus providing a theoretical frame that could be used on other materials that had no concrete resemblance to the Polish data they report in their work.

THE POLISH PEASANT—ITS THEORETICAL UNDERPINNINGS

The theoretical scheme underlying *The Polish Peasant* may be best understood as an attempt to go beyond both a purely individualistic or subjectivistic approach to sociological data and a generalized "objectivistic" interpretation of social life and social change in which acting, feeling, thinking individuals would be granted no analytical attention. They wished to avoid the trap of psychologistic interpretation found, for example, in the work of their contemporary Franklin Giddings, where most of humankind's travail is considered as the result of "consciousness of kind" and similar psychological constructs. Yet they also wished to avoid a type of theorizing of a certain positivistic variety, which emphasized the determinant influence of geography, climate, or race on human behavior, or of a vulgar Marxism. In short, they objected to seeing people as playthings of forces over which they had no control.

In their attempt to do justice to both objective and subjective factors, they developed a scheme in which only the conjoint interplay of individual attitudes and objective cultural values was seen as adequate to account for human conduct. By attitude they understood, "a process of individual consciousness which determines real or possible activity of the individual in the social world."[4] An attitude is a predisposition to act in relation to some social object; it is not a purely psychic inner state. A social value, on the other hand, is understood as "any datum having an empirical content accessible to the members of some social group and a meaning with regard to which it is or may be an object of activity."[5] The authors specified further that only certain classes of values, namely

[3] *The Polish Peasant,* I, p. 37. [4] *Ibid.,* p. 22. [5] *Ibid.,* p. 21.

those that are embodied in norms and rules of conduct, come within the purview of sociological investigation. These values consist of the ". . . more or less explicit and formal rules of behavior by which the group tends to maintain, to regulate, and to make more general and more frequent the corresponding types of actions among its members. These rules [are] . . . customs and rituals, legal and educational norms, obligatory beliefs and aims, etc."[6]

The main focus of their investigation is social change. They proceed to show that it is always the result of an interplay between attitudes and values. As they put it, "The cause of a social or individual phenomenon is never another social or individual phenomenon alone, but always a combination of a social and an individual phenomenon. Or, in more exact terms: The cause of a value or of an attitude is never an attitude or a value alone, but always a combination of an attitude and a value."[7]

Thomas and Znaniecki formulated this basic approach in a variety of ways, as when they speak, for example, of the "reciprocal dependence between social organization and individual life organization."[8] But their underlying stress on conjoint investigation of the objective and the subjective dimensions of social behavior remains constant throughout their work. It will be remembered from earlier chapters of this book that this general orientation is closely related to the social psychology and sociology of Cooley and Park and that it has its roots in the pragmatic philosophy of William James, Mead, and Dewey. What is perhaps less obvious is that it is closely related to Marx's stress that people make their own history but they don't make it as they please; they are constrained by the play of social forces they encounter on their scene of action. It is also closely related to Robert K. Merton's later insistence that social actions need always to be explained in terms of individual choices between socially structured alternatives.[9]

To Thomas and Znaniecki the influence of external or objective factors upon human conduct assumes importance only to the extent that they are subjectively experienced. Hence, it is the task of the analyst to try to show how subjective predispositions, or attitudes, molded by experience, determine the response of individuals to the objective factors that impinge upon them. Thus, it is not the social disorganization of city slums that determines deviant behavior of recent immigrants, but it is experienced loosening of normative constraints in the slum that results in deviant reactions in individual slum dwellers.

In an effort to conceptualize a set of basic dispositions that could then be related to the interplay of attitudes and values, the authors developed their well-known classification of the four basic human wishes: (1) the desire for new experience; (2) the desire for recognition; (3) the desire for mastery; and

[6] *Ibid.*, p. 31. [7] *Ibid.*, p. 44. [8] *Ibid.*, II, p. 1128.

[9] Cf. Arthur L. Stinchcombe, "Merton's Theory of Social Structure" in Lewis A. Coser, ed., *The Idea of Social Structure: Papers in Honor of Robert K. Merton* (New York, Harcourt Brace Jovanovich, 1975), pp. 14 ff.

(4) the desire for security.[10] Though this classification is more often cited than any other discussion in *The Polish Peasant,* it seems to be among the least valuable aspect of the work. To establish such lists of basic wishes or drives is a sterile enterprise. Other authors have established similar lists consisting of ten or many more such basic predispositions which are equally plausible and equally powerless to account for the complicated motivational repertory of the human animal. (Indeed, both Thomas and Znaniecki became quite sceptical about this aspect of methodology in *The Polish Peasant* at a later stage in their careers.)[11]

Thomas and Znaniecki's incursion into general psychology by way of the so-called theory of basic wishes resulted in failure. Their development of the rudiments of a social psychology, on the other hand, has borne abundant fruit. They sharply distinguished psychical states from attitudes, assigning the study of the first to general psychology and of the second to social psychology. "By its reference to activity," they stated, "and thereby to the social world the attitude is distinguished from the psychical state. . . . A psychological process is . . . treated as an object in itself, isolated by a reflective act of attention, and taken first of all in connection with other states of the same individual. An attitude is a psychological process treated as primarily manifested in its reference to the social world and taken first of all in connection with some social value. . . . The psychological process remains always fundamentally a *state of somebody;* the attitude remains always fundamentally an attitude *toward something.*"[12]

Even if one conceives of social psychology as the science of social attitudes, it would still be possible to restrict one's focus largely to attitudes of individuals. This was, however, not what Thomas and Znaniecki had in mind. As they put it: "The more generally an attitude is shared by the members of the given social group and the greater the part it plays in the life of every member, the stronger the interest which it provokes in the social psychologist. . . . Thus, the field of social psychology practically comprises first of all the attitudes which are more or less generally found among the members of a social group, have a real importance in the life-organization of the individuals who have developed them, and manifest themselves in social activities of these individuals."[13] What the authors are concerned with, in other words, are not the idiosyncratic responses of particular individuals, but rather attitudes that these individuals share to a greater or lesser extent with other members of the groups in which they are variously placed. Social psychology, in this view, is the "science of the subjective side of social culture."[14]

[10] *The Polish Peasant,* I, p. 73.

[11] Everett Hughes writes in a personal communication (September 24, 1969): "When I was a graduate student, Wirth organized a dinner to meet Thomas once when Thomas was passing through Chicago. . . . The older students asked him questions about the four wishes. Thomas asked: 'Now which wishes did we finally use in the introduction to *The Polish Peasant?*' He seemed entirely unconcerned about any defense of them, but did indicate that Znaniecki always insisted on being systematic."

[12] *The Polish Peasant,* I, p. 22. [13] *Ibid.,* p. 29. [14] *Ibid.,* p. 31.

On the other hand, the objective side of culture, the investigation of social values, is the proper domain of sociology. Social values are objective cultural data that confront the individual, as it were, from the outside. "These values cannot be the object matter of social psychology; they constitute a special group of objective cultural data . . . the rules of behavior, and the actions viewed as conforming or not conforming with these rules, constitute with regard to their objective significance a certain number of more or less connected and harmonious systems which can be generally called *social institutions,* and the totality of institutions found in a concrete social group constitutes the *social organization* of this group. And when studying the social organization as such we must subordinate attitudes to values. . . ."[15]

It was the peculiar genius of Thomas and Znaniecki to balance their emphasis on attitudes, subjectively defined meanings, and shared experience, by an equally strong emphasis on the objective characteristics of cultural values and their embodiment in specific institutions. This is why their analyses in *The Polish Peasant* move from consideration of microsociological units, such as primary groups and family structures, to the larger institutional settings in which these smaller units are embedded. Linking the study of primary groups to the larger institutional context, Thomas and Znaniecki studied the community in which primary groups in general, and the family and kingroups in particular, flourished; they then proceeded to investigate the still wider frame of social organization, which included the educational system, the press, voluntary organizations, and the like. Though each of these, they argued, could not be analyzed in isolation, each provided distinct arrangements of social values that assumed salience, in different and varying degrees, as objects to which attitudes were directed even as they themselves shaped these attitudes.

The main chord that Thomas and Znaniecki strike over and over again is the reciprocal relation between attitudes and values, between individual organization and social organization, between individual behavior and the social rules that attempt to control it. This meant to them a continued interplay involving not only individual adaptation but also disruption of social order. Like their contemporary Robert Park, they believed that equilibrium between individual desires and social requirements was at best a marginal and exceptional condition. In general, social controls and social norms never succeeded in completely suppressing individual efforts to break the bonds imposed by social organization. The dialectic of social change involved efforts on the part of the group to bend members to its requirements and, at the same time, attempts on the part of these individuals to break group-imposed constraints in order to realize aspirations not condoned by the norms of the group.

Thomas and Znaniecki were intent upon countering the prevalent moralistic pronouncements about such serious social problems as crime and delinquency by stressing that the roots of the problems were in social conditions

[15] *Ibid.,* pp. 32–33.

rather than individual failings. Hence, when they introduced the notion of social disorganization they defined it as "a decrease of the influence of existing social rules of behavior upon individual members of the group."[16] But they took pains to emphasize that this notion "refers primarily to institutions and only secondarily to men."[17] That is, like Durkheim's notion of *anomie,* the concept of social disorganization refers primarily to a disordered state of society rather than to a condition of individuals. Moreover, they also pointed out that there was never a one-to-one association between social and individual disorganization, so that even in disorganized areas of a city, for example, one could expect to find a number of individuals who manage to organize their lives in a satisfactory manner. "The nature of [the] reciprocal influence [of life-organization of individuals and social organization] in each particular case is a problem to be studied, not a dogma to be accepted in advance."[18] To Thomas and Znaniecki social disorganization never meant a static condition but rather a social process subject to a great deal of variation in impact and extensiveness.

A TYPOLOGY OF HUMAN ACTORS

In an effort to explore further the interplay between social organization and individual attitude, between social constraint and individual response, Thomas and Znaniecki developed a suggestive typology of human actors, distinguishing three typical cases in terms of the variant responses of people to cultural demands. This typology, it should be noted, as distinct from their abortive attempt to delimit basic wishes, has had a considerable influence on the subsequent typologies of David Riesman[19] and other current scholars.

Thomas and Znaniecki first describe the *Philistine* who is "always a conformist, usually accepting social tradition in its most stable elements. . . . Every important and unexpected change in the condition of life results for such an individual in a disorganization of activity."[20] His type of adjustment has become so rigid as to preclude the development of any new attitudes except through the slow changes brought about by age in the individual and by time in his social milieu. The polar opposite of this type is the *Bohemian,* "whose possibilities of evolution are not closed, simply because his character remains unformed."[21] In this type, "we find an undetermined variation of schemes."[22] He may be highly inconsistent, "but on the other hand he shows a degree of adaptability to new conditions quite in contrast to the *Philistine*."[23] While the first type is a conformist and the second a rebel, the *creative man* is an innovator adaptable to new conditions, displaying variegated interests. These are "compatible with a consistency of activity superior to that which tradition can give if the individual builds his life-organization not upon the presumption of the

[16] *The Polish Peasant,* II, p. 1128. [17] *Ibid.,* p. 1127. [18] *Ibid.,* p. 1128.
[19] David Riesman et al., *The Lonely Crowd* (New Haven, Yale University Press, 1950).
[20] *The Polish Peasant,* II, p. 1853. [21] *Ibid.,* p. 1853. [22] *Ibid.,* p. 1855. [23] *Ibid.,* p. 1855.

immutability of his sphere of social values, but upon the tendency to modify and to enlarge it according to some definite aim."[24] The *creative man* does not simply act within the grooves of tradition, nor is he indiscriminately rebellious when it comes to societal requirements; rather, with a judicious blend of innovation and tradition he clears a new path through the forest of the customary and can hence be a creative guide in efforts to bring about social change.

Thomas and Znaniecki made it clear that what they were delineating here were ideal types, never fully realized in any particular personality. As they put it, "None of these forms is ever completely and absolutely realized by a human individual in all lines of activity; there is no *Philistine* who lacks completely *Bohemian* tendencies, no *Bohemian* who is not a *Philistine* in certain respects, no *creative man* who is fully and exclusively creative. . . ."[25] They were aware that these general types "include . . . an indefinite number of variations."[26] But, like the more elaborate and sophisticated ideal types depicted by Max Weber, these general types may well serve as rough guides in efforts to classify the immense variety of human personalities along a continuum based on their variant orientations to the requirements of social living. It is important to note that at a time when John B. Watson and others conceived human beings as infinitely manipulable by their social environment, Thomas and Znaniecki insisted that though *Philistines* were all around and *Bohemians* might exhaust themselves in futile rebellion, there also existed innovative and creative people who attempted, while acknowledging limits, to transcend them in the image of their desire.

The range of subjects touched upon in *The Polish Peasant* is wide indeed. Its authors displayed a sympathetic interest in the huge diversity of personalities, cultural patterns, and institutional arrangements they encountered in their research on both the old continent and the new. In America they dealt with city politics and prostitution, the press and the dance hall, family quarrels and nostalgic longings for a lost home—all discussed against the backdrop of conditions in Poland. And while engaged in sociological investigation of typical behaviors, they always displayed a loving concern for the varied ways unique persons came to terms with their predicaments. And yet, despite this diversity of topics, there was a strong unity in their work. They were concerned throughout to document and analyze the impact of urbanization, industrialization, and modernization in the modern world. They showed how the traditional forms of social control were replaced by the looser and more tenuous controls that attempt to guide the conduct of modern men and women. They documented the sea change from a kin-dominated culture to one based on urban associations or loose neighborhood ties. Although they appear at times to be lost in a welter of details, their work is marked throughout by concerns very similar to those that moved most of the other masters of modern sociology, from Marx to Mannheim.

[24] *Ibid.*, pp. 1855–56. [25] *Ibid.*, p. 1856. [26] *Ibid.*, p. 1857.

What is more, like many of their intellectual forbears and contemporaries, they saw in sociology not only an analytical discipline but one capable of providing guidance to social policy. They were convinced that common-sense knowledge, on which humankind had relied through the millennia, is no longer an adequate basis for social control. They believed that the systematic knowledge they aimed to provide would furnish the rudiments of a science of purposeful social intervention and rational control. They even went so far as to state, ". . . It is always the question of an ultimate practical applicability which . . . will constitute the criterion—the only secure and intrinsic criterion—of a science."[27]

At first blush, Thomas and Znaniecki's stress on rational control and social techniques might suggest that they were seduced by some technocratic ideal of overall planning. But such was emphatically not the case. To the contrary, they emphasized that their analyses and findings were in the first place meant to increase the awareness and knowledge possessed by the individual subjects they studied. In a passage that could as well have been written by a contemporary sociologist such as Jürgen Habermas, they stated that, "it is desirable to develop in the individuals the ability to control spontaneously their own activities by conscious reflection."[28] It was to such an increase in the conscious awareness of their subjects that they dedicated their work. "While in earlier stages," they argued, "the society itself provided a rigoristic and particularistic set of definitions in the form of 'customs' or 'mores', the tendency to advance is associated with the liberty of the individual to make his own definition."[29] The sociological analyses they provided were intended to further that development.

The subtleties of the theorizing in *The Polish Peasant* should not blind us to some of its deficiencies. Too often, conceptual distinctions that appear clear-cut in the methodological discussion become blurred in concrete exposition. Even such key concepts as attitude and values, as the authors were later to acknowledge, often come to be used almost interchangeably. At times it is difficult to disentangle subjective factors and their objective correlates, precisely because the objective world is always dealt with only to the extent that it enters subjective experience. Such methodological criticisms were elaborated in detail in Herbert Blumer's exhaustive critique of the work.[30] Nevertheless, despite the fact also emphasized by Blumer, that there are considerable discrepancies between the theoretical guidelines and the substantive contributions, *The Polish Peasant* has aged very well indeed. It remains one of the great landmarks of American sociological investigation, and, despite its flaws, its theoretical framework may still inspire emulation by those who possess more developed theoretical tools.

[27] *The Polish Peasant,* I, p. 20. [28] *Ibid.,* p. 72. [29] *Ibid.,* p. 72.

[30] Hubert Blumer, *An Appraisal of Thomas and Znaniecki: The Polish Peasant in Europe and America* (New York, Social Science Research Council, 1946).

WILLIAM ISAAC THOMAS—FROM ETHNOGRAPHER TO SOCIAL PSYCHOLOGIST

An admiring student, Kimball Young, said in his obituary of W. I. Thomas that he "never regarded himself essentially as a theorist."[31] This was probably so, but he surely was a theorist despite himself. What is more, he attempted throughout his life to gain greater intellectual clarity and analytical depth, rather than pursuing a fixed initial line of thought. To follow him on his intellectual voyage is a moving experience.

Thomas's early writings—for example, his *Sex and Society*[32] published in 1907—still show heavy traces of the biologistic biases of the times, even though they also indicate the author's efforts to free himself from these influences. Only those devoid of a sense of historical context will bridle today at such pronouncements as, "Morphologically the development of man is more accentuated than that of woman. Anthropologists . . . regard women as intermediate between the child and the man."[33] Statements such as these, moreover, ought to be read in conjunction with Thomas's fervent pleas in this work for an end to the subjection of women. At this stage in his thinking he may still have been partly in the throes of sexist reasoning, but he could also write in the same book, ". . . When we taken into consideration the superior cunning as well as the superior endurance of women, we may even raise the question whether their capacity for intellectual work is not under equal conditions greater than in man."[34] The book ends with a magnificent sentence which should help wash away many of Thomas's early sins: "Certain it is that no civilization can remain the highest if another civilization adds to the intelligence of its men the intelligence of its women."[35] What applies to his treatment of women also applies, *grosso modo,* to his writings on race relations and American Blacks.

Just as the biologistic bias in Thomas's early writings cannot be ignored, neither can his psychologistic bias. It would be a mistake, however, not to recognize that he overcame that bias in his later work. Still, it is surely a bit unsettling to learn from the early Thomas that the rules of exogamy "doubtless originate in the restlessness of the male" and his tendency "to seek more unfamiliar women."[36] Many other such naive psychologistic interpretations of institutional arrangements can be found in this book. But such *gaucheries* stand side by side with little gems of sociological reasoning, such as: "The degree to which abstraction is employed in the activities of a group depends on the complexity of the activities and on the complexity of consciousness in the group."[37]

During the first stages of his career Thomas slowly developed from a traditional ethnographer, reared in the German tradition of *Voelkerpsychologie,*

[31] Kimball Young, "William I. Thomas," *American Sociological Review,* XIII, I (1948), p. 104.
[32] William I. Thomas, *Sex and Society* (Chicago, The University of Chicago Press, 1907).
[33] *Ibid.,* p. 18. [34] *Ibid.,* pp. 312–13. [35] *Ibid.,* p. 314. [36] *Ibid.,* p. 57.
[37] *Ibid.,* p. 267.

to a sophisticated social psychologist with a sociologist bent, as evidenced by *The Polish Peasant* and the works immediately following. His early works must be read as stepping stones on the way. Only a year after the publication of *Sex and Society,* Thomas's *Source Book for Social Origins*[38] appeared. A careful reader could already perceive that the author, while providing a wealth of ethnological data as source materials and still operating with such psychological notions as "attention," "habit," and the like, was on his way to developing sociological interpretations that owed relatively little to the biologistic and evolutionary propensities of most of his contemporaries.

Thomas's genius came to full flowering in *The Polish Peasant,* a book free from biologistic and psychologizing biases, as well as the occasional racist overtones of his early works. In his later works Thomas continued to develop theoretical leads to social psychology first adumbrated in *The Polish Peasant.* It would seem that by some subconscious division of labor, Znaniecki in his later writings elaborated the notion of social values, which he called "cultural reality," while Thomas's concerns were in the main directed to the social psychological approach characterized by the notion of attitudes.

THOMAS'S SITUATIONAL ANALYSIS

Perhaps the highpoint in the development of Thomas's social psychology came with his elaboration of the famous notion of *the definition of the situation.*[39] The notion is so central that an extended quotation is in order:

> ". . . the higher animals, and above all man, have the power of refusing to obey a stimulation which they followed at an earlier time. . . . We call this ability the power of inhibition. . . . Preliminary to any self-determined act of behavior there is always a stage of examination and deliberation which we may call *the definition of the situation.* . . . Not only concrete acts are dependent on the definition of the situation, but gradually a whole life policy and the personality of the individual himself follow from a series of such definitions. But the child is always born into a group of people among whom all the general types of situation which may arise have already been defined and corresponding rules of conduct developed, and where he has not the slightest chance of making his definitions and following his wishes without interference. . . . There is therefore always a rivalry between the spontaneous definition of the situation made by members of an organized society and the definition which his society has provided for him. The individual tends to a hedonistic selection of activity, pleasure first; and society to a utilitarian selection, safety first. . . . It is in this connection that a moral code arises, which is a set of rules of behavior norms, regulating the expression of the wishes, and which is built up by successive defi-

[38] William I. Thomas, *Source Book for Social Origins* (Chicago, The University of Chicago Press, 1909).

[39] The notion was first introduced, in a rather casual manner, in *The Polish Peasant,* I, p. 68; its full elaboration came later.

nitions of the situation. In practice the abuse arises first, and the rule is meant to prevent its recurrence."[40]

The notion of the definition of the situation provided Thomas with a secure vantage point from which he could criticize all instinctivistic or biologistic interpretations, as well as the crude behaviorism of John B. Watson and his followers. Only close analytical attention to the subjective ways in which human beings filtered the crude data of their senses, only sustained concern with the mediating functions of the human mind could help explain the root fact that though two individuals might be presented with an identical stimulus, they might react to it in utterly different ways. This could be seen in operation both between categories of individuals and between culturally differentiated groups. A well-dressed woman, for example, may be perceived by males in terms of her sexual attractiveness, while women might focus attention on the design of her clothing. A teddy bear might be a protective talisman to a child, but is only a plaything to an adult. A record player may be a means for filling empty leisure time to a jaded city dweller, while it may be the voice of a god to a primitive. Unless analysts attend to these subjective meanings, these definitions of the situation, they will be as unable to understand fellow human beings as they will be incapable of understanding other cultures.

But there is still more. Human actions can make sense to us only if we become aware that all meanings come to be constructed by definitions through which the prism of the mind orders perceptual experience. Ponder carefully the following sentence, the most pregnant sentence that Thomas ever wrote: "If men define situations as real, they are real in their consequences."[41]

What Thomas was saying was that people respond not only to the objective features of a situation, but also, and often mainly, to the meaning that situation has for them. And once such meanings have been assigned, their consequent behavior is shaped by the ascribed meaning.[42] If people believe in witches, such beliefs have tangible consequences—they may, for example, kill those persons assumed to be witches. This then is the power the human mind has in transmuting raw sense data into a categorical apparatus that could make murderers of us all. Once a Vietnamese becomes a "gook," or a Black a "nigger," or a Jew a "kike," that human being has been transmuted through the peculiar alchemy of social definition into a wholly "other" who is now a target of prejudice and discrimination, of violence and aggression, and even murder. It stands to reason, of course, that there are benevolent as well as malevolent consequences of such definitions of the situation; peasant girls can become saints and politicians high-minded statesmen. In any case, and regardless of the con-

[40] William I. Thomas, *The Unadjusted Girl* (Boston, Little, Brown, 1923), pp. 41–43.

[41] William I. Thomas (with Dorothy Swaine Thomas), *The Child in America* (New York, Alfred A. Knopf, 1928).

[42] This formulation is largely borrowed from Merton's discussion of the "Thomas Theorem" in his *Social Theory and Social Structure, op. cit.*, pp. 475–76.

sequences, definitions always organize experience; they are "equivalents to the determination of the vague."[43] It would be superfluous to adduce the numerous progeny that Thomas's notion has engendered. Anyone, for example, writing on prejudice and discrimination can ill afford to neglect it.

During the nineteen twenties and in the last stages of his career, Thomas's thought moved increasingly away from his previous concerns with basic motivational structures and wishes. In tune with his fully developed notion of the "definition of the situation," he now concerned himself with what he described as "situational analysis." By this he meant, to quote from his Presidential Address to the American Sociological Society, that "the particular behavior patterns and the total personality are overwhelmingly conditioned by the types of situation and trains of experience encountered by the individual in the course of his life."[44]

In *Old World Traits Transplanted* (originally published as a work by Robert Park *et al.*, but in fact mainly written by Thomas),[45] in *The Unadjusted Girl, The Child in America* (with Dorothy S. Thomas) and in *Primitive Behavior*[46] situational analysis, in which the definition of the situation assumed pride of place, was applied to a diversity of concrete topics. In all of them, Thomas clung to his view that society and individuals should always be conceived of as being involved in reciprocal interaction. As he put it in *The Unadjusted Girl,* "Society is indispensable to the individual because it possesses at a given moment an accumulation of values, of plans and materials which the child could never accumulate alone. . . . But the individual is also indispensable to society because by his activity and ingenuity he creates all the material values, the whole fund of civilization."[47] Thomas was prepared to subscribe to Cooley's dictum that the individual and society are twin born, but only if he were allowed to specify that they were not identical twins. He was much more aware than Cooley of the crises and dislocations that are bound at times to disrupt the harmonious interplay between them.

Later works also extended Thomas's concern with typologies as in the suggestive chapter of *Old World Traits Transplanted,*[48] in which he distinguishes among the following immigrant types: The Settler, The Colonist, The Political Idealist, The Allrightnik, The Cafone, and The Intellectual. Each of these types, he suggested, reacted to the immigrant experience in a distinctive and characteristic manner. Typological distinctions, he felt, were most useful in

[43] *The Unadjusted Girl,* p. 81.

[44] William I. Thomas, "Situational Analysis: The Behavior Pattern and the Situation" in Janowitz, *op. cit.,* pp. 154–67.

[45] Robert E. Park and Herbert A. Miller, *Old World Traits Transplanted* (New York, Harper, 1921). This work was mainly authored by W. I. Thomas.

[46] William I. Thomas, *Primitive Behavior: An Introduction to the Social Sciences* (New York, McGraw-Hill, 1937).

[47] *The Unadjusted Girl,* pp. 233–34.

[48] *Old World Traits Transplanted,* Chapter V.

breaking down global categories such as "immigrants" into subcategories, displaying distinctive behaviors in their interaction with the host community. Such typologies were further developed in the work of Florian Znaniecki.

FLORIAN ZNANIECKI—PHILOSOPHER TURNED SOCIOLOGIST[49]

As we saw in *The Polish Peasant,* Znaniecki's collaborative work with Thomas, the twin notions of attitudes and values provided the major theoretical scaffolding. Yet neither of its authors was content with these notions in his subsequent writings. While Thomas progressively discarded the theory of basic wishes, which had been closely limited to his notion of attitudes, and worked his way toward a situational analysis independent of assumptions about basic motivational drives, Znaniecki, on his part, abandoned the notion of attitude altogether.

Although *The Polish Peasant* in general, and the Methodological Note that introduces it in particular, were the joint product of both authors, it is evident that the emphasis on attitudes was mainly Thomas's, whereas, the focus on values came mainly from Znaniecki. He had devoted his earliest philosophical work, published in 1910, to "The Problem of Values in Philosophy."[50] Even though he had moved from philosophical to sociological investigations, primarily under the impact of his collaboration with Thomas, he remained preoccupied with the function of values, with the construction of *Cultural Reality,* the title and subject matter of the first book he published in English.[51] Social psychology was never to be his *forte.*

For some years after their collaboration on *The Polish Peasant* had ended, Znaniecki struggled with various attempts to come to a successful resolution of the difficulties in the attitude-values distinction of the joint work that many critics, Herbert Blumer in particular, have pointed out. He explains in the preface to *Social Actions* that his attempts to build a theory of psychological tendencies cost him ten years of frustration. He now concluded that he had decided "to get rid of the assumption that the whole variety of social actions of men has to be deduced from a few permanent and fundamental psychological forces, essential attitudes, wishes, desires, or what not."[52] He adopted instead a theoretical strategy that focused on these actions "in their empirical concrete-

49 I am greatly in debt to Helena Znaniecki Lopata, Florian Znaniecki's daughter, for a variety of materials she put at my disposal. This section borrows liberally from her paper *Florian Znaniecki: Creative Evolution of a Sociologist* (mimeoed), originally presented at the conference on "Florian Znaniecki and his Role in Sociology," organized by the Sociological Institute of Adam Michiewicz University and the Poznan branch of the Polish Sociological Society, December 15–16, 1972, in Poznan, Poland. The paper was later revised and enlarged.

50 Florian Znaniecki, *Zagadnienie wartosciw filozofji* (*The Problem of Values in Philosophy*), Warsaw, 1910; published by *The Philosophical Review.*

51 Florian Znaniecki, *Cultural Reality* (Chicago, The University of Chicago Press, 1919).

52 Florian Znaniecki, *Social Actions* (New York, Farrar and Rinehart, 1936), p. VIII.

ness and variety, and [tried] to order them such as they are, without any prior assumptions concerning the psychological sources from which they spring."[53]

As shall soon be seen, Znaniecki never abandoned his stress on the importance of subjective meanings in the determination of social action. However, as Frankel puts it, "he [now] conceives of [the subjective factor] not as psychological in its constitutive relatedness to social action. Rather, the subjective factor is logically converted into *social data.* That is, as a component of the 'social system' which Znaniecki constructs and investigates inductively, the 'attitudes' and 'tendencies' of human agents have the same quality of empirical content as other social data, such as values, norms, and rules of social behavior. In this way, Znaniecki seeks to avoid what he considers the logical pitfalls of including psychological analysis of social systems."[54] Thus the *noblesse oblige* of the aristocrat or the inquisitiveness of the scientist need not be explained psychologically but can be seen as constituent elements of their behavior in the social circles in which they are moving by virtue of their differentiated roles.

The shift is already evident in his *The Method of Sociology,* published in 1934, and it became more pronounced in his later work. Znaniecki moved from social-psychological preoccupations to a purely sociological vision in which actors as *social persons* are understood largely in terms of the *social role* they enact within *social circles.* Abandoning the attempt to capture the totality of human personality in his theoretical net, Znaniecki decided to restrict himself to a sociological approach in which the human individual was studied as a participant "in social life and culture,"[55] in the world of human interaction and cultural values.

Following Park and Burgess, he now defined the term *person* (in the Latin meaning of the word *persona*) as "an individual's conception of his role" and showed that an individual tends to behave in accordance with this conception.[56] Just as an actor performs a number of distinct roles, individuals play several different social roles depending on the social circles in which they variously move. "No individual can play the role of Hamlet alone. He must have a circle of other actors and actresses playing the roles of the Queen, the King, Horatio, Ophelia, Polonius etc., all of whom accept him as the impersonation of Hamlet."[57] In the same way, "we shall find in every social role a social circle within which the individual performs it, that is a set of agents who accept him and cooperate with him."[58] "Every social role presupposes that between the individual performing that role, who may thus be called a 'social person' and a smaller or larger set of people who participate in his performance and may be termed his 'social circle' there is a common bond constituted by a complex of values which all of them appreciate positively."[59] Different social circles, in other

[53] *Ibid.* [54] Frankel, *op. cit.,* pp. 79–80.

[55] Florian Znaniecki, *Social Relations and Social Roles* (San Francisco, Chandler, 1965), p. 202.

[56] *Ibid.,* p. 202. [57] *Ibid.,* p. 203. [58] *Ibid.,* p. 203.

[59] Florian Znaniecki, *The Social Role of the Man of Knowledge,* with a new introduction by Lewis A. Coser (New York, Harper Torchbooks, 1968), pp. 14–15.

words, are distinguished by the set of values that they uphold and enforce and in terms of which they react, be it positively or negatively, to the persons who enact their roles in the view of these circles—the persons who constitute the audience of the performer.

The notion of social role, as developed by Znaniecki, differs in important particulars from that developed by Ralph Linton and the long line of theorists who have taken their lead from him. In Znaniecki's view, roles are not anchored in status positions and sets of generalized expectations about behavior. Instead, his notion specifically directs attention to the dynamic relations that link role players to the circles in which they are variously enmeshed. As Helena Znaniecki Lopata puts it, "the social circle, whether preceding the social person or being drawn together by him or her, includes everyone toward whom there are role duties and everyone who grants rights facilitating the performance of the function. . . . They must grant rights to perform actions and they must undertake specific actions on their own without which the social person cannot carry out his or her part in the manner designated by their common values and norms."[60]

Znaniecki stressed that "all generalizations about social role require . . . an inductive, comparative study of particular roles, as actually performed by individuals in cooperation with their circles."[61] He wished to draw particular attention to individual variations in the performance of roles, stressing that actors do not mechanically respond to role expectations: sometimes they may underperform; other times they may overperform. Creative individuals, he noted, may well initiate major departures from expectations, thereby leading to the emergence of new kinds of role. This is why, in his later work, he abandoned the notion of status which he had used "to denote the totality of rights which an individual is granted by the social circle within which he performs a certain role."[62] The notion of status, he came to argue, "neglects or fails to solve . . . changes in the valuation of the person, as his role evolves; the process of widening and narrowing the circle within which a role is performed; dynamic relations between simultaneous and successive roles of the same individual and of several individuals; and, finally, the gradual creative emergence in the course of history of new roles, with new standards and norms."[63]

When Znaniecki talks about social persons and social roles, about social relations and social groups, he means that all such notions make sense only if they ultimately rest on a cultural basis, on shared knowledge, norms, and values. "The cultural pattern of a social system," he argues, "includes certain axiological [value] standards which participants in the system are supposed to apply in evaluating each other and the system as a whole, as well as certain norms by which they are expected to be guided in their actions. In so far as they

[60] Helena Znaniecki Lopata, *op. cit.*, p. 15. [61] *Social Relations and Social Roles, op. cit.*, p. 207.
[62] *Ibid.*, p. 207. [63] *Ibid.*, p. 208.

accept and conform with these standards and norms, the social system manifests a dynamic inner order which can be termed axionormative."[64]

If it is true that human activities cannot be understood without reference to the values which human actors uphold in their intercourse with others, then it stands to reason that any sociological analysis is seriously amiss if it fails to pay attention to human meanings. This is what Znaniecki called the "humanistic coefficient." As he explained it, "the data of the cultural student are always 'somebody's,' never 'nobody's' data. This essential character of cultural data we call the *humanistic coefficient,* because such data, as objects of the student's theoretical reflection, already belong to somebody else's active experience and are such as this active experience makes them. If the humanistic coefficient were withdrawn and the scientist attempted to study the cultural system as he studies the natural system, i.e., as if it existed independently of human experience and activity, the system would disappear and in its stead he would find a disjointed mass of natural things and processes, without any similarity to the reality he started to investigate."[65]

One can appreciate Znaniecki's thought without succumbing to the occupational disease of historians of ideas, which consists, in part, in discovering "anticipations" of every new idea by previous thinkers.[66] Yet it is interesting to note that Znaniecki's formulation of the humanistic coefficient already contains major elements of what is today modishly called the "reflexive" or phenomenological approach to sociological data. More than a generation ago, Znaniecki hammered away at the basic proposition that emphasis on the humanistic coefficient distinguished the study of human actors from other branches of sciences based on a naturalistic, hence unreflexive, approach.

Not all of Znaniecki's work has stood the test of time. I have no access to the works he published in Polish. Of his books in English, it is evident that *Cultural Reality* is still largely a work of philosophical analysis rather than a sociological treatise and that the book on *The Laws of Social Psychology*[67] embodies ideas that Znaniecki was largely to abandon in his subsequent work. *The Method of Sociology* is a lucidly written treatise in which he elaborates the major differences between the natural and social sciences and in which he outlines the methodological approach that is appropriate for the study of cultural—as distinct from natural—systems. Here one can also find Znaniecki's cogent defense of sociology as a value-free discipline, studying what is rather than what ought to be. Its methodological reflections very much deserve rereading by contemporary sociologists. *Social Actions,* which followed *The Method,* is, on the other hand, largely an attempt at classifying various types of

[64] Florian Znaniecki, "Sociometry and Sociology," *Sociometry* V, 3 (1943), pp. 225–53 as quoted in Helena Znaniecki Lopata, *op. cit.,* pp. 5–6.

[65] Florian Znaniecki, *The Method of Sociology* (New York, Rinehart, 1934), p. 37.

[66] Cf. Robert K. Merton, *op. cit.,* pp. 8 ff.

[67] Florian Znaniecki, *The Laws of Social Psychology* (Chicago, The University of Chicago Press, 1925).

social actions. There seems little there, beyond the general orientation already developed elsewhere, that warrants attention now. His last books, *Cultural Sciences*[68] and *Modern Nationalities,*[69] though erudite and insightful, hardly add to his major work. The posthumously published *Social Relations and Social Roles* contains the most systematic development of his role theory but is otherwise an unfinished sketch of a work on *Systematic Sociology,* which he was not able to complete.

The Social Role of the Man of Knowledge remains his masterpiece. It is not only a major contribution to the sociology of knowledge, but the most incisive presentation of his distinctive style of sociological analysis and of his peculiar vision of the contribution the sociologist can make to the study of human culture and social organization.

ZNANIECKI'S SOCIOLOGY OF KNOWLEDGE

In *The Social Role of the Man of Knowledge,*[70] Znaniecki resolved to impose upon himself a strict self-denying ordinance: he was to resist every temptation to deal with epistemological questions. His was to be strictly a scientific and substantive inquiry. In tune with his earlier methodology he was only to assume that every thinker claims that his system of knowledge is true and objectively valid. It was not the business of the sociologist, he believed, to investigate or invalidate these claims to truth. "The sociologist is bound to abide by whatever standard of validity those individuals or groups apply to the knowledge in which they take an active share."[71] It is not the investigator's "definition of the situation" but the subject's that must inform the study. Whether systems of knowledge may be judged true or false, valid or invalid does not concern the sociologist, who must remain content to trace their origins and consequences. Znaniecki summed this up eloquently: "When he is studying their social lives, he must agree that, as to the knowledge which they recognize as valid, they are the only authority he need consider. He has no right as a sociologist to oppose his authority to theirs: he is bound by the methodical rule of unconditional modesty. He must resign his own criteria of theoretical validity when dealing with systems of knowledge which they accept and apply."[72]

Not only did Znaniecki reject all epistemological and metaphysical speculations, but he restricted his attention to what Werner Stark has called the "microsociology of knowledge."[73] That is, he did not concern himself with "the total intellectual atmosphere of society" or "the total historical movement of the social system."[74] He more modestly limited himself to the study of the social

[68] Florian Znaniecki, *Cultural Sciences* (Urbana, Ill., University of Illinois Press, 1952).
[69] Florian Znaniecki, *Modern Nationalities* (Urbana, Ill., University of Illinois Press, 1952).
[70] The following pages are adapted from my Introduction to *The Social Role of the Man of Knowledge, op. cit.*
[71] *The Social Role of the Man of Knowledge, op. cit.*, p. 5.
[72] *Ibid.*, p. 6.
[73] Werner Stark, *The Sociology of Knowledge* (London, Routledge and Kegan Paul, 1958).
[74] *Ibid.*, p. 30.

roles of creators and carriers of knowledge and of the social and organizational structures within which they function.

Znaniecki set himself a twin task: to develop a typology of the variety of specific social roles that men of knowledge have played, and to investigate the normative patterns that govern their behavior. A central tool for the investigation of both these problems is the notion of "social circle," that is, the audience or the public to which thinkers address themselves. Znaniecki shows that thinkers, at least in heterogeneous societies, are not likely to speak to the total society but rather to selected segments or publics. Specific social circles bestow recognition, provide material or psychic income, and help shape the self-image of the thinker internalizing the normative expectations of the audience. Thinkers are expected to live up to certain demands of their circles, and these in turn grant certain rights and immunities. Men of knowledge anticipate the demands of their public, and they tend to define data and problems in terms of these actual or anticipated audiences. Thus, thinkers may be classified in terms of their audiences and the performances that are expected of them within the social context in which they are variously enmeshed.

A major part of the book is devoted to Znaniecki's classification of various social roles that men of knowledge can play. He distinguishes, *inter alia, Technological Advisors; Sages*—that is, those who are expected to provide ideological justifications for the collective aims of their groups; and *Sacred* and *Secular Scholars* (who in turn fall into various subtypes from "discoverers of truth" to "disseminators of knowledge," from "systematizers" and "contributors" to "fighters for truth"). He also deals with *Creators of Knowledge,* who in turn may be *Fact-Finders* or *Discoverers of Problems.*

This is by no means an arid exercise in classification. Znaniecki shows that the demands of the social circle on the man of knowledge vary with the specific role he is expected to play. Thus, technological leaders are not expected to search for new facts that might undermine belief in the correctness of previously programed activities. They are institutionally expected to regard new facts with suspicion. In contrast, *Creators of Knowledge* are rewarded for the discovery of new facts. Each particular social role that the man of knowledge assumes carries with it certain types of expectations; each social circle rewards and punishes particular types of intellectual performance.

Znaniecki's classification provides important clues for the study of the reception or rejection of novel ideas, as Robert K. Merton recognized in a review written shortly after the book appeared. It allows us to specify "the ways in which various social structures exert pressure for the adoption of certain attitudes toward new empirical data."[75] For example, the *Sage,* whether a reformer or

[75] *American Sociological Review* VI, 1 (1941), pp. 111–15. Reprinted in Lewis A. Coser and Bernard Rosenberg, *Sociological Theory* (New York, Macmillan, 1957), pp. 351–55. The quotation is on p. 353 of the reprint.

an apologist for the existing order, knows the answers and hence cannot search for new facts that might prove to be unsettling. *Scholars,* on the other hand, "have positive or negative attitudes toward genuinely new facts, depending on the extent to which the school's system is established: in the initial stage new facts are at least acceptable, but once the system is fully formulated the intellectual commitment of the school precludes a favorable attitude toward novel findings."[76] By focusing attention on the structural sources of *neophobia,* Znaniecki therefore allows us to move a considerable distance from the global assertion that all organizations and social structures are necessarily conservative and disinclined to recognize innovation. Had Znaniecki written today, he might have found it profitable also to investigate the complementary structural conditions for *neophilia,* that is, the one-sided value emphasis on what is new. This emphasis is most pronounced nowadays among certain unattached intellectuals whose audience demands of them a restless search for new stimulants to tickle jaded intellectual or aesthetic palates.

Znaniecki is not merely content to delineate a variety of social roles for men of knowledge; he also provides important clues to understanding the process through which such roles may be transformed and superseded. He shows, for example, that certain schools of religious thought can perform their tasks to an optimum extent only when they succeed in insulating their practitioners from contact with rival schools. As a sacred school loses its monopoly and is forced to contend with others, it can no longer rely on unexamined faith but must develop rational modes of persuasion. The challenge of conflicting belief systems contributes to a process of gradual secularization of major portions of sacred knowledge, and fields previously preempted by *Sacred Scholars* gradually are taken over by their *Secular* counterparts. Conflicts of ideas, Alfred North Whitehead once argued, are not a disaster but an opportunity. Znaniecki would have readily agreed. They are an opportunity, above all, for replacing the closed mental world of the *Sage* with the open universe of the *Explorers of Knowledge.*

These few examples of Znaniecki's creative approach to the sociology of intellectual life will, I trust, move readers of this book to think of particular problem areas that deserve to be investigated from the perspective of Znaniecki's conceptual framework. This is indeed his chief merit. He provides a storehouse of suggestive leads and concepts for a well-rounded future sociology of men of knowledge.[77] Znaniecki, in his modest way, did not set out, as did so many of his forebears, to provide all the answers. His is an open-ended work of scholarship, and his role was that of the *Explorer of Knowledge,* rather than the *Sage.* He desired his future readers to become explorers with him rather than his disciples.

[76] *Ibid.,* pp. 353–54.

[77] For an attempt to use some of Znaniecki's categories see Lewis A. Coser, *Men of Ideas, A Sociologist's View* (New York, The Free Press, 1965).

THE MEN

William I. Thomas and Florian Znaniecki, despite their close collaboration for a number of years and the high esteem in which they held each other after that collaboration had ceased, were men of sharply different personal characteristics and came from widely different social backgrounds. It might be supposed that they would have had difficulty establishing intellectual rapport: one the earthy, expansive, vital, extrovert son of southern dirt farmers; the other the gentle, genteel, introvert, somewhat stiff professorial descendant of a long line of aristocratic Polish landowners. Yet they overcame their differing personal backgrounds and intellectual stances. The earthy "pragmatist" from the southern hills and the inveterate theorist and systematizer from Poland's nobility managed, when the course of events threw them together, to create a joint work which, though not a seamless web, was nevertheless a common product.

WILLIAM I. THOMAS[78]

Thomas was born in Russell County, an isolated region of old Virginia, on August 13, 1863. His father, Thadeus Peter Thomas, combined preaching in a Methodist church with farming. His son said that the social environment in which he grew up, twenty miles from the nearest railroad, resembled that of the eighteenth century. He felt that in his subsequent moves to a southern university town and later to the metropolitan cities of the Middle West and the North he had lived "in three centuries, migrating gradually to the higher cultural areas."

That this became possible, Thomas stated, was "due to some obscure decision on the part of my father to attend an institution of learning—Emory and Henry College, Virginia." His father's father, Thomas's grandfather, was a stubborn Pennsylvania Dutchman, rich in land but with narrow peasant prejudices against cultural pursuits. He opposed his son's search for booklearning and punished him by sharply reducing his inheritance and forcing him to take up farming in an undesirable geographical location and on poor and marginal soil.

Thomas's father, however, remained deeply attached to the idea of learning. When he realized that his seven children had no adequate educational opportunities in the provincial backwater where he was making a poor living, he moved with his family to Knoxville, Tennessee, the seat of the state university.

Young Thomas spent his childhood and early adolescence with the moun-

78 This section is based on Morris Janowitz's "Introduction," *op. cit.*, and on William I. Thomas's "Life History" published by Paul J. Baker in *The American Journal of Sociology*, vol. 79, 2 (Sept. 1973), pp. 243–50. This autobiography was not available to Janowitz at the time he wrote the "Introduction." I followed Thomas in the few instances where there are discrepancies between his account and that of Janowitz.

tain people, sharing their passionate interest in shooting and hunting. "My zeal for this," he writes, "was fanatical. I reckon that I passed no less than seven years of my youth in the woods alone with a rifle, without a dog, shooting at a mark, regretting the disappearance of large game and the passing of the Indian and of pioneer life." There exists no record of the impact that the new urban environment of Knoxville must have made on the young mountain boy, but it would seem that he managed the cultural transition without experiencing a major shock. Having enrolled at the University of Tennessee in 1880 and majoring in literature and the classics, Thomas soon became a leader among the undergraduates, excelling not only scholastically but socially as the "big man on campus." He won honors in oratory, became president of the most prestigious literary society, and at the same time captained the university's officer training unit.

During his first two years at the University, Thomas's zest for learning was less than conspicuous. But after that, under the influence of two teachers, Professors Alexander and Nicholson (the first a Greek scholar, the latter a devoted Darwinian who taught zoology, geology, and other natural sciences), Thomas decided to become a scholar. "I recall," he has written, "that on a hot August day in the summer vacation, between the sophomore and the junior year, I had a conversion. After some . . . profound reflection I determined that I was to go in for scholarship." This decision taken, he immediately paid a visit to Professor Alexander and announced his life plan. He also recalls that soon afterward, impressed by German scholarship, he resolved to seek further enlightenment in German universities. (At the time, it was generally assumed that German universities provided graduate instruction vastly superior to what was available in America. Hence, young academics were motivated by values and attitudes to study in Germany.) When friends inquired about his future career, he replied: "I am going to Germany." But that time was not yet. After graduation he stayed on at the University as an instructor, teaching Greek, Latin, German, French—most of them, as he later admitted, rather inadequately. Now carrying the honorific title of Adjunct Professor, he was also entrusted with instruction in natural history. The newfangled idea of specialization, it would seem, had not yet reached the University of Tennessee.

Throughout this period, the eager and ambitious young instructor never abandoned the idea of going to Germany. He finally obtained a leave of absence for a year's study and spent the academic year 1888–89 at Berlin and Goettingen. This year was decisive in determining his future intellectual orientation. It was in Germany that his interests changed from natural history and philology to ethnography, although this interest was not entirely new. Already at Tennessee reports of the Bureau of Ethnology had come to his attention. Moreover, as an adolescent he had roved over the Cumberlands and the Smoky Mountains in search of game, and, as he noted in his autobiographical sketch, he had later collected "a list of about 300 'Chaucerian' and 'Shakespearian' words surviving in the speech of the mountaineers." These early interests led him in Germany to immerse himself in the writings of the German folk psychologists Lazarus and Steinthal and to pay close attention to Wilhelm Wundt's *Voelkerpsychologie*. At the same time he attended courses in old English, old French, and old German, given by some of the leading German experts in these fields; he also continued his study of Greek culture under the great German classicist Wilamowitz.

Returning from Germany, his cultural horizons having been decisively broadened, he resolved not to go back to the University of Tennessee, and instead accepted a professorship in English at Oberlin. This was a traditional subject, to be sure, but Thomas taught it mainly within a comparative framework. His concern with ethnography also led him to a careful perusal of Herbert Spencer's *Principles of Sociology* and to further comparative studies suggested by Spencer. His three years at Oberlin were among the most satisfactory of his life. "I was not at that time sufficiently irreligious," he noted later, "to be completely out of place, and yet a sufficient innovation to be a novelty."

Nevertheless, when the news reached him of the opening of the first American Department of Sociology at the University of Chicago, he gave up what looked like an established career at Oberlin to become a graduate student at Chicago. Though attracted by the department's offerings in sociology and anthropology, Thomas took relatively few formal courses in the department, doing most of his work in courses marginal to sociology, including biology, physiology, and brain anatomy. Although he paid but scarce attention to his directors of study, Albion Small and Charles Henderson, and seemed more inclined to explore the city of Chicago than the departmental library, Thomas must clearly have impressed his mentors. After only one year in residence he was invited to offer his first course in sociology in the summer of 1894. In 1895 he served as an instructor, and in the following year, having completed his doctoral work (his thesis was entitled "On a Difference in the Metabolism of the Sexes"), he became an assistant professor. In 1900 he was promoted to associate professor, and in 1910, having by this time assumed a prominent position in the department, he became a full professor.

While Albion Small's teaching focused on theoretical issues and historical data, and Charles Henderson's on social problems and their remedies, Thomas's interest was mainly in ethnographic and comparative studies. At that time the Chicago Department was a joint department of sociology and anthropology, and Thomas offered courses in what today would be called cultural and physical anthropology. In line with this orientation he returned to Europe immediately after receiving his doctoral degree to visit a variety of cultural settings. He travelled as far as the Volga, preparing to write a comparative study of European nationalities. This project was shelved, but he returned to it around 1909 when he revisited Europe "for the purpose of studying peasant backgrounds with reference to the problem of immigration."

the founder of Hull House, offered
ımigration. For the next ten years he
ce Psychology, which enabled him to
the publication of *The Polish Peasant.*
ılikely that the work would ever have
ıake a number of trips to Poland in
ered other research expenses.
tudy a variety of Eastern European
being too ambitious an undertaking.
gest and most visible ethnic group in
mber of social problems, from family
hat this son of a southern rural min-
prooted sons and daughters of Polish
ı the urban jungles of metropolitan

y on the Polish community, Thomas,
d following established procedures
sh language. He then set out to de-
ommunity in Chicago, as well as to
Thomas still used methods that had
ples and did not yet think of gather-

wn the back alley behind his house,
garbage which someone was throw-
at his feet, a long letter fell out. He
d that it was written in Polish by a
It was addressed to her father and
ls. It then occurred to Thomas that
ters. This was the unlikely accident
…fe-history method for which he has since become famous. Let no one be tempted to interpret the incident as confirmation of the "accidental theory of history." It took a very peculiar kind of man with very special gifts and training to pay attention to a bag of garbage thrown at his feet.

For more than a decade after this incident, Thomas moved back and forth between the Chicago Polish community and communities in the old country to gather written materials to supplement oral information. The 2,244 pages of the final work are largely given to the reproduction of these materials. Thomas used 754 letters acquired through an advertisement in a Chicago Polish-language journal, apparently offering 10 to 20 cents for any letter received from Poland. He used some 8,000 documents bought from the archives of a Polish newspaper that he approached during a visit to that country in 1909–10. He also used data and documents from Polish parish histories in Chicago, from immigrant organizations, from the files of charitable and legal aid associations, and from diaries of Polish immigrants (for which he paid the authors).

During his trip to Poland in 1913, Thomas met the Director of the Polish Emigrants Protective Association, Florian Znaniecki, a young philosopher who was not allowed to teach in Russian-dominated Poland because of his commitment to the idea of Polish nationalism. Znaniecki proved to have a wide knowledge of Polish peasant life—a rarity among members of Poland's gentry intelligentsia. The materials he collected for Thomas from the archives of the Polish Emigrants Protective Association proved invaluable. A year later, when World War I broke out and Germany invaded Poland, Znaniecki left his home country and went to see Thomas at Chicago. It is not entirely clear whether Thomas had formally invited him or not, but the important fact is that Thomas asked him immediately to join his project as a research worker. Soon thereafter Znaniecki became his co-author, working closely together with him until the completion of the monumental work.

During the many years of preparation for the book, Thomas and his wife Harriet Park, whom he had married in 1888, actively participated in the social and intellectual life of Chicago. They had close connections with various social-work agencies and were identified with many of the social-reform activities described in earlier chapters of this book. At times, Thomas's "advanced views" on such social problems as crime and delinquency did not suit the established powers. The Chicago Vice Commission, for example, which was set up by well-meaning but timid establishmentarian souls, seemed to recoil in horror at some of the "progressive" suggestions of Thomas, who had done considerable research work for the Commission's use. Not only Thomas's views, but also his life-style offended some of the *bien pensants.* He certainly did not conform to the image, prevalent at the time, of a staid and withdrawn academic. He dressed well, enjoyed the company of attractive women, mixed in bohemian quarters, and dined in posh restaurants as well as local dives. He was, as they say, a controversial figure. His unfashionable ideas and flamboyant life-style made him attractive to students but also aroused a good deal of animosity, even enmity, among the more settled denizens of the faculty club and administration building.

In 1918, those who had been secretly gunning for him finally had an occasion to move in for the kill. The *Chicago Tribune,* which had long been perturbed by the "unsound ideas" of professors at the University, announced one day in big headlines that Thomas had been arrested by the Federal Bureau of Investigation. The charges? Alleged violation of the Mann Act (which forbade the transport of young women across state lines for "immoral purposes") and false hotel registration. These charges were later thrown out of court, but in the meantime the publicity had been extensive, especially since the lady with whom he was involved, one Mrs. Granger, reported that she was the wife of an army officer then serving with the American forces in France.

Why the F.B.I. got involved in this case is unclear, but it has been suggested that Thomas's wife was under surveillance for her pacifist activities and that the F.B.I. might have thought it expedient to discredit the husband so as to humiliate the wife. While such an interpretation might have seemed farfetched a few years ago, it does not seem so now.

What followed constitutes one of the shameful chapters in the history of American universities. The president of the University of Chicago, Henry Pratt Judson, supported by the trustees, moved immediately to dismiss Thomas. Albion Small, the chairman of his department, offered no public defense, although he made some private moves to protect Thomas and wept in his office over the loss of his prize student and colleague. There was no faculty protest and hardly a voice was raised from the ranks of Thomas's immediate colleagues. Everett Hughes writes me that this could not have happened at Harvard. No Boston paper would have mentioned an incident involving a Harvard professor. "Chicago was too parvenu to control the papers." (Personal communication, April 12, 1976.)

Thomas's career was shattered at the age of 55, and he never again was given a permanent position at any university. The University of Chicago Press, which had issued the first two volumes of *The Polish Peasant,* broke its contract with the authors and refused to publish the succeeding volumes (which were later issued by an obscure house, Richard G. Badger of Boston). Despite his twenty years' services, the University of Chicago and its minions did everything possible to drop his name into an Orwellian memory hole. Even the University of Chicago archives contain nothing to remind one of Thomas, except for a few administrative letters.

The Carnegie Foundation behaved just as badly. It had earlier commissioned Thomas to write a volume in their Americanization Studies series. When, after the unfortunate incident, the manuscript, *Old World Traits Transplanted,* was delivered, the Foundation insisted that Thomas's name not appear as the author; the book was published under the names of Robert E. Park and H. A. Miller, who had done some minor work on the volume. Only in that way could the reputation of the Foundation and of the social sciences be protected. A recommendation for Thomas's appointment to the staff was vetoed by the directors. It was a famous victory for the philistines.

After the Chicago disaster Thomas moved to New York. He lectured for a number of years at the New School for Social Research, then a haven for such unconventional scholars as Thorstein Veblen, Charles Beard, and Harold Laski, but at that time it was nonetheless a marginal academic institution. In 1936–37 Pitirim Sorokin, one maverick recognizing another, appointed him to a visiting lectureship on the Harvard faculty, where he was lionized by the graduate students and instructors. This was his last academic position.

During the New York years, Thomas, despite his public hounding, nevertheless was able to do a good deal of research, much of it sponsored by

Mrs. W. F. Dummer of Chicago, a wealthy woman philanthropist who never faltered in her support of him. In later years he also received grants from the Laura Spelman Rockefeller Memorial and the Bureau of Social Hygiene. In the late thirties he served for a while as a staff member of the Social Science Research Council and was closely associated with the Social Science Institute of the University of Stockholm.

Thus, even without a regular university appointment Thomas was given the opportunity to continue his research. Yet the philistines did not relent easily. When some of the Young Turks of sociology, backed by Robert Park, argued in 1926 that it was high time that Thomas be offered the presidency of the American Sociological Society, leading sociologists, among them the ministerial Charles A. Ellwood, argued that this would be inappropriate and would sully the honor of American sociology. When his name was entered for nomination, the "old guard" sought to find an appropriate candidate to defeat him. Thomas considered withdrawing his name under these circumstances and was only persuaded to stay in the race by Ernest Burgess who assured him that the Young Turks, Louis Wirth, George Lundberg, Stuart Chapin, Stuart Rice, Kimball Young and others, would mobilize their younger colleagues on his behalf. They did, and he won by a wide margin.

Despite his trials and tribulations, Thomas, the dirt farmers' tough son from the Virginia hills, seems never to have been discouraged. His zest for life stood him in good stead. He managed to cope with whatever problem he tackled, in work or in private life. Earlier in his career, when he was dissatisfied with the finish on his dining table, he invented a better furniture polish. Later, disliking his inferior golf balls, he invented a better one—and enjoyed the proceeds of his patent. In 1935, after his first marriage had broken up, the seventy-two-year-old man married his thirty-six-year-old research associate Dorothy Swaine, who later became a leading student of demography and the first woman president of the American Sociological Society. Nothing in his life, and a rocky life it was, could defeat William I. Thomas. Even in his last years of semiretirement he continued his research in New Haven and Berkeley. He died at the age of 84 in December 1947.

FLORIAN ZNANIECKI[79]

Moving from the life of William I. Thomas to that of Florian Znaniecki, we encounter quite another social landscape, quite a different personal trajectory.

Florian Znaniecki was born into a noble Polish family of landowners who

[79] This selection could not have been written without the invaluable help of Helena Znaniecki Lopata. In addition to her paper (cited earlier), I have profited a great deal from her autobiographical account "A Life Record of an Immigrant," *Society,* November–December 1975, vol. 13, 1, pp. 64–74, and from an autobiographical letter by Znaniecki addressed to one Father Mulvaney dated 27th February, 1945, which she kindly has made available to me.

traced their history to the fifteenth century. It was a family with a rather complicated and cosmopolitan line of descent. Znaniecki's mother came from a Saxon professional family, and among her ancestors was a physician to King August II of Saxony and Poland. Both of Znaniecki's grandmothers were French; two of his uncles had been officers of the Prussian Royal Guards, married to German women. His maternal granduncle became a Turkish Pasha. The tradition of Polish patriotism ran deep in the family, yet Znaniecki's grandfather and three of the latter's sons fought as officers with the Prussian Hussars during the Franco-Prussian wars.

The Znanieckis were not only remarkable for the cosmopolitan complexity of their family tree. Znaniecki's daughter, Helena Znaniecki Lopata, reports that one of her uncles traced the family history—before the Nazis killed him. This uncle unearthed three documents dating back to an ancestor in the fifteenth century. One reveals that a man accused an ancestor of Znaniecki of unlawfully adding a coat of arms and the "cki" ending to his name. The man had to offer a humiliating apology: he had to crawl under the dining table at the King's court and withdraw the accusation publicly. A second document reported this ancestor as having killed the same man and his whole family at the altar of a church to which they had fled for safety. The third document finds the same Znaniecki to be a judge in the very district in which he had allegedly committed the murders only a few years earlier.

Znaniecki was born in 1882 near Swiatniki in German-ruled Poland. His father had lost his estate when the son was only a few years old. Since he had no other marketable skills than the management of estates, he was fortunate that one of his friends offered him such a position in Russian-ruled Poland. The children (two daughters and the son Florian) spent their earlier years, as was the custom of the nobility, with private tutors. Znaniecki learned Polish literature from his mother, German literature from a German governess, and French literature from a French tutor. He taught himself English and Russian and gained a knowledge of Greek and Latin in gymnasiums in Czestochowa and Warsaw.

Znaniecki was a rebellious youngster, ever ready to oppose Poland's Russian overlords. The Russian authorities severely restricted the subjects in which Polish students could be instructed, and so the students organized underground study-groups to learn forbidden subjects. Znaniecki became the philosophy expert of the "school" and, by age eighteen had digested the work of many Western philosophers and was especially enamored with Kant. The Russian-oriented school authorities found it hard to cope with the young student leader. He was once expelled for using a private calling card to gain entry to the principal's office as a representative of protesting students. Yet he had some well-wishers among the teaching staff. After he had flunked mathematics and was in danger of not graduating, a teacher quietly interceded, because he had been impressed by a book of poems about Cheops, builder of the great pyramid at

Giza, that the precocious young man had written and managed to have published.

Znaniecki's university career proved as eventful and lively as his high school (gymnasium) days. After earning his first degree at the University of Warsaw, Znaniecki studied at Western European universities. He went to the University of Geneva to study philosophy and after gaining the equivalent of a master's degree, he transferred to Zurich and later to the Sorbonne where he planned to work on a doctoral thesis. His sponsor, however, suddenly died, and Znaniecki returned to Poland to earn a Ph.D. in philosophy at Cracow University in 1909.

Thus far this sounds like a fairly normal academic career, but it was not. While in Geneva, Znaniecki fell desperately in love with his best friend's wife, dramatically left his clothes on the shores of Lake Geneva, and vanished for two years. The desperate young man had joined the French Foreign Legion, and not even his mother knew whether he was alive or dead. After discovering that the Legion failed to live up to his romantic expectations, he managed to get an honorable discharge, having wounded himself in the chest and thumb, allegedly while falling asleep on his gun during guard duty. It is also worth mentioning that after the young and by now somewhat sobered philosopher returned to his studies, he still found time to edit a French literary magazine. His was not the typical academic career.

Within four years after his doctoral graduation, Znaniecki published two books, *The Problem of Values in Philosophy,* and *Humanism and Knowledge,* and translated Bergson's *Creative Evolution* into Polish. Yet there was little chance for him, a patriotic Pole, to join the faculty of any university under Russian administration. Instead, Znaniecki accepted a position as the Director of the Polish Emigrants Protective Association. It was there that W. I. Thomas met him in 1913 on one of his field trips in search of materials for what was to become *The Polish Peasant.* Thomas was impressed by Znaniecki's intimate knowledge of Polish peasant life and by the mounds of materials that Znaniecki was able to provide from the archives of his organization. He seems to have suggested to Znaniecki—this matter is not entirely clear—that he come to Chicago to aid him in his further investigations. When World War I broke out a year later and the Germans once again invaded Russian-ruled Poland, Znaniecki decided to leave for America and found his way to Thomas's office. He had hardly more than a nickel in his pocket—in fact, he had to leave his wife at the Chicago train station because he did not have enough money for both of them to reach the campus.

At this time Znaniecki was basically unfamiliar with sociological research, although he was interested in it and had done some research in the sociology of emigration. Thomas nevertheless immediately added him to his research staff and soon thereafter offered him the co-authorship of *The Polish Peasant.* It must be stressed that Znaniecki was already familiar with the works of most

European sociologists. He learned the tools of the research trade from Thomas and his collaborators, but his theoretical knowledge, even at this early point, was at least as extensive as that of his mentor. Nevertheless, Znaniecki accepted Thomas's suggestion that he take a doctoral degree in sociology. This meant that he had to give up his hopes and efforts of developing a new philosophical system. As a doctoral candidate he attended seminars and took active part in the discussions. Yet, as he himself reports, "After a month Thomas conveyed to me the request of the professors that I cease to come." Why this happened remains a mystery to this day. But Znaniecki was undaunted and now concentrated entirely on his joint work with Thomas. At the risk of seeming a touch disloyal to the sociological discipline, one may speculate that a Chicago Ph.D. in sociology would probably not have added appreciably to his contributions.

Soon after their arrival in America, Znaniecki's first wife died suddenly. His second wife, Eileen Markley, whom he met in Chicago, was a Connecticut-born lawyer of Irish descent, whose father was a lawyer and who had made the then unusual career decision to become a lawyer herself. She received her B.A. degree from Smith College, her M.A. in history from Columbia, and, in 1915, her LL.D. from the University of Chicago. After her marriage she dropped her work with the Legal Aid Society and helped Znaniecki with his work on *The Polish Peasant.* Znaniecki would return home after having conferred with Thomas and proceed to write up his ideas in longhand. His wife would then correct his English and type the manuscript. She continued to do this throughout Znaniecki's life, typically and perhaps unfortunately giving up her own hard-won career for his. And his was the better for it.

Znaniecki could very well have stayed in America at that time. His wife's family certainly urged him to do so. Although he did not have a regular position at the University of Chicago, he taught Polish History and Institutions there; and the prospect of a regular position at Chicago or elsewhere would presumably have been quite good after *The Polish Peasant* was published. Two events made him decide not to stay. Thomas was suddenly dismissed from the University under the apalling circumstances reported earlier; and just at that time Znaniecki received an invitation from the new Polish University of Poznan to join its staff as an Associate Professor of Philosophy. Znaniecki's decision to accept that post must have been hard for his wife, for she did not speak Polish and having already given up her career, she now had to give up her citizenship and her country.

Immediately after the family's arrival in Poznan in 1920, Znaniecki had his chair in philosophy changed into a chair of sociology. With great zest he threw himself into the work of intellectual reconstruction of newly independent Poland. Sociology had not been taught in Poland up to that time, but Znaniecki soon gathered a number of enthusiastic students around him. With their help he founded the Polish Sociological Institute and started the *Polish Sociological Review.* During his stay in Poznan, nine students took doctoral degrees in sociology and the number of students on the graduate level increased from six to fifty.

In 1932–34 Znaniecki returned to the United States on a leave of absence, serving as a visiting professor in the sociology department of Columbia University, then chaired by his friend Robert MacIver. During these two intensively stimulating years at Columbia Znaniecki supervised a number of dissertations, published *The Method of Sociology* and wrote major parts of his *Social Actions,* published soon after his return to his homeland. These volumes, written in English, had been preceded by two massive volumes written in Polish, *Introduction to Sociology* (1922) and *Sociology of Education* (1928–1930).

Although the erroneous belief still persists that Znaniecki was primarily a theorist and only peripherally interested in research, his main work in Poland was devoted to training researchers. The major emphasis in the Institute and in Znaniecki's courses of instruction was on empirical investigations and especially, following the pattern of *The Polish Peasant,* on life-histories as sources of research data. Over the years numerous manuscripts prepared by workers and peasants were collected, as well as writings of more highly educated Poles. A single competition for workers' autobiographies drew three-hundred manuscripts; the Institute published at least parts of over one hundred of them. These primary documents were later burned by the Nazis. But in gathering and evaluating them a number of young sociologists had learned their trade, and these were the men and women who helped rebuild Polish sociology after World War II.

The Znanieckis' daily life in Poland was surely different from that in America. They first lived on an estate outside of Poznan, and his daughter, who was born there in 1925, remembers his climbing on his horse every day on the way to the University. The horse was tied up near the railroad station and Znaniecki then took the train to the city. Znaniecki and his wife often rode their horses when visiting friends in the surrounding countryside. Finally, Mrs. Znaniecki revolted against this way of life and the family moved to the city, where she felt less isolated. Znaniecki's life-style was distinctive in several ways. Throughout his life he wrote in bed, after being served breakfast, from eight o'clock until noon. During that time his wife typed what he had written earlier. Both taught at the University in the afternoon. Mrs. Znaniecki had no regular faculty appointment but taught various courses in American literature and history.

In the late thirties the Znanieckis bought land in the countryside and were supervising the building of a home when Znaniecki was invited to give a series of lectures at Columbia during the summer of 1939. His wife and daughter decided to stay behind to see to the finishing touches on the house. Just then World War II broke out and the Germans occupied Poland. Mrs. Znaniecki and her daughter were interned in a Nazi concentration camp. Mrs. Znaniecki, who must have been a formidable woman, persuaded the commander of the camp that she was an important person in America, and the scared commander released mother and daughter (America had not yet entered the war). They managed to flee to Italy and then to return to the United States.

His summer's work at Columbia having come to an end, and without news from his family, Znaniecki insisted—against the advice of his friends—to return to Poland. Always a stubborn man, he embarked on a liner to Europe not only to look for his family, but to prepare to write a sociological history of the Polish resistance. Luckily the liner on which Znaniecki travelled was intercepted by a British submarine and brought into a British port. It now became clear that he could not return to Poland. That country was now occupied by Germany and Russia, and Znaniecki had the honor of figuring prominently on the blacklist of both governments. He therefore returned to America and was soon joined by his family.

It seems obvious that Znaniecki would have liked to have stayed at Columbia where he had many friends and where he had just given a successful course of lectures that would soon be published as *The Social Role of the Man of Knowledge*. But since there was no position open at Columbia, he accepted the offer of a professorship in the Department of Sociology at the University of Illinois. He spent the last years of his active career and his retirement years at Urbana. His colleagues honored him by electing him president of the American Sociological Society for 1953–54. He published two major studies and several minor ones while at Urbana, and up to his death on March 23, 1958, he was hard at work on what he liked to call half-humorously his *magnum opus*—*Systematic Sociology,* portions of which have been published posthumously by his daughter.

I remember the tall, sparse, somewhat stiff and shy, even awkward, and very professorial figure of Znaniecki at the Urbana campus when the American Sociological Society met there during his presidency. He seemed to me then the perfect exemplar of the European academic man. Somewhat aloof, perhaps slightly bewildered by the hustle and bustle of the convention, he seemed like a gentle and genteel stranger who had fallen among wheelers and dealers on the academic marketplace. That there was some truth to this impression will soon be shown.

THE INTELLECTUAL CONTEXT

WILLIAM I. THOMAS

Thomas was a widely read man, not only in sociology and social psychology but in anthropology, psychology, biology, literature, history, Egyptology, Assyriology, and related fields. Nonetheless, he was never attracted by encompassing theoretical systems. In particular, he "never became influenced by philosophy as offering an explanation" of social life.[80] Much like Spencer in his time, Thomas drank from many sources and gleaned from many fields, without, however, ever wanting like Spencer to develop a "system" of his own and without being attracted by thinkers who endeavored to construct self-contained philosophical or sociological systems. In this, as shall be seen, he differed markedly from Znaniecki. Both were attracted in one way or another by pragmatic philosophy, but Thomas was also "pragmatic" in the nonphilosophical sense: he wanted to extract from the literature facts and ideas that "worked" for his own purposes. As he said, "I think it is true that no book deserves a complete reading." Nevertheless, a few names stand out among those contemporary and near-contemporary figures who seem to have had a measure of influence on Thomas's intellectual trajectory.

Next to his teachers at the University of Tennessee, the men whose lectures he attended at Berlin and Goettingen must be counted as important early influences on Thomas's thought. He was set by them on the path of comparative anthropological studies that marked much of his early work, and to which he returned in his last book, *Primitive Behavior.* Wilhelm Wundt's *Voelkerpsychologie,* which has been discussed in the Durkheim chapter of this book, and the related comparative ethnography of Moritz Lazarus and Heymann Steinthal were the key influences.[81] He was impressed by their meticulous and scientifically detached ways of gathering comparative data on nonliterate societies and on the peasant cultures of preindustrial Europe. His propensities for comparative studies were reinforced after his return from Europe by his immersion in the work of Herbert Spencer. Thomas, as he said himself, "was influenced by [Spencer's] evolutionary and anthropological view of the development of institutions, but . . . never [became] a 'Spencerian'." This was mainly because he was repelled by Spencer's tendency to put all his data into a preconceived theoretical framework. "His suppression of inconvenient data and selection of convenient data was little less than dishonest." Comparing Spencer's generalization in his *Principles of Sociology* with the data collected by Spencer's collaborators in his *Descriptive Sociology,* Thomas discovered that "he had ignored all the data which did not confirm his theories." This must have reinforced Thomas's distrust of all system builders.

Thomas was lured to the University of Chicago as a graduate student by the attractive courses in sociology and anthropology. But, as it turned out, the theoretical and historical teachings of Albion Small, the chairman of the department, left him cold. He was even less attracted by the Christian social meliorism of Charles Henderson. Instead, as has been mentioned earlier, Thomas took courses in areas that were marginal to sociology. He studied physiology and

[80] All quotations are from his "Life History" ed. by Paul J. Baker, *op. cit.*

[81] On Steinthal's and Lazarus's influence on American social psychology cf. F. B. Karpf, *American Social Psychology: Its Origin, Development and European Background* (New York, McGraw-Hill, 1932), pp. 41–51.

experimental biology with Jacques Loeb, the pioneer of artificial parthenogenesis (the artificial activation of unfertilized eggs as an alternative to sexual reproduction). He also took work with Adolf Meyer, the prominent psychiatrist who, at that time, lectured mainly on brain anatomy. Such courses turned him away from what was still left of his early Christian upbringing and made him espouse, to use the title of one of Jacques Loeb's books, a "mechanistic [i.e., materialistic] conception of life."

Both in Chicago and earlier, Thomas took great care not to fall under the sway of a "master." He was one of those masterless men whom Veblen, and later C. Wright Mills, lovingly depicted in their writings and tried to emulate. "It is certainly a misapprehension of the truth," Thomas wrote, "to trace influence predominantly to personalities or 'masters'. This represented the truth more completely at the time when primary group norms prevailed in society, when outstanding personalities assembled disciples and followers and created cults and schools. But at present the influences are as diverse as the 'great society' is diverse in its models and attitudes. We tend to be more influenced by trends of thought and method than by particular persons, and we tend to be influenced by dissent from, as much as acquiescence in, the system of other persons." Whatever the correctness of this generalization, it was certainly true for his own intellectual development.

It has often been said, quite correctly, that Thomas was beholden for much of his general outlook to the pragmatic philosophy of Dewey and Mead, both of whom, it will be remembered, taught at the University of Chicago during Thomas's stay there. Yet in a letter written in 1928 to Luther L. Bernard who had solicited information on who had influenced him, Thomas wrote: "I have added the names of Mead and Cooley to those who influenced me. I have preferred to say nothing about Dewey. When he came to the university I was already offering a course on Social Origins. I gave him materials used in his address as President of the Philosophical Society about that time and it would be more correct to say that he came under my influence than that I came under his. It was true that I was interested in his thought and certainly attempted to use some of it in my classes, but Dewey has always seemed to me to be essentially a mystic and a metaphysician and I found—or thought I found—that I was repudiating almost everything he said, or ignoring it. It may be nevertheless, that he had more influence on me than I remember. The same of Mead."[82]

There is something of ambivalence in these lines, and one feels that in his last sentences Thomas admitted guardedly that his assessment of Dewey's and Mead's influence may have been somewhat of an understatement. Yet it is true that, even though his thought is rightly classed as moving within the orbit of the pragmatist tradition, Thomas was never willing to commit himself explicitly to this or any other philosophical system.

Among his contemporaries within the social sciences, Charles H. Cooley, as

[82] The letter is reproduced in Paul J. Baker, *op. cit.*

he mentioned in his letter, had a decided influence on Thomas. The notion of the "primary group," though used in a somewhat different sense from Cooley's, played a considerable role in Thomas's work ever since *The Polish Peasant*. It takes no great ingenuity to ferret out the influence of Cooley, as of Mead, when it comes to Thomas's notion of the *definition of the situation*. It would also seem that the social behaviorism of Mead and Cooley may have been one of the reasons Thomas, though admittedly influenced by John B. Watson, "never accepted behaviorism as he formulated it"; that is, he never succumbed to the crude physiologistic and antimentalistic stance of Watson.

Among those with whom Thomas worked closely, Robert E. Park and Florian Znaniecki surely influenced him most. After Thomas's crucial meeting with Park, and his successful attempt to bring Park to Chicago (see the chapter on Park in this book), Thomas "enjoyed a very long and profitable association with him." He has said that, "Park was not only ruminating all of the time but imposing his ruminations on me, with eventual great profit to myself." A comparison of the present chapter with that on Robert Park will show that there must have been a close elective affinity between these two men who, despite Park's superior philosophical training, were much alike in their empirical bent and their passionate desire to create a scientific sociology, anatomizing societal trends and phenomena so as to contribute to a reformed America within the progressive tradition. I shall comment on Znaniecki's influence in the section devoted to him.

Without being specific, Thomas has said that he was influenced by the work of the anthropologist Franz Boas. One can only surmise that Boas's determined attacks on racialist thinking helped remove whatever slight traces of racial bias were contained in Thomas's early work. Moreover, Boas's demolition of the unilineal evolutionism of Spencer stood Thomas in good stead when he broke the ties to this point of view, all found in his early work.[83]

Finally two intellectual orientations must be mentioned to which Thomas does not refer in his writings but to which, I deduce from internal evidence, he was in considerable debt. As has been seen, Thomas took courses with the psychiatrist Adolf Meyer (1866–1950) when at the University of Chicago. At this time, however, Meyer had not yet embarked on the major work that was to make him into a great pioneer of modern American psychiatry. His later approach, however, has so many points of similarities with Thomas's that I find it hard to believe that, in an effort to keep up with the work of a former teacher, Thomas would not have been familiar with it. Meyer termed his approach to psychiatry "psycho-biology," by which he meant that human beings as biological units could be understood only as being integrated through psychological mechanisms. Combating the biologistic and physiological view of mental illness that had been prevalent up to this time, Meyer stressed that in diagnosis

[83] On Thomas's debt to Boas, cf. George W. Stocking, *Race, Culture, and Evolution* (New York, Free Press, 1968), pp. 260–64.

and treatment psychological factors must be considered medically pertinent. Meyer's view of the human personality centered attention on social and cultural factors as being of crucial importance in the etiology of both health and illness and saw mental disturbances as "progressive habit formations." What is more, he emphasized the need to study the *life-history* of individuals in order to discover and trace various stages of personality development. Individuals, he was wont to stress, are both the products and the victims of their life experience. Meyer's influence on American psychiatry was very deep indeed. By cutting it loose from its previous anchorage in physiology and its preoccupations with brain damage and related notions, he pioneered the emphasis on life experience and socio-cultural factors that later psychodynamic and psychoanalytical methods have tended to elaborate. That Thomas profited from Meyer's stress on life-history, habit formation, and life experience seems evident.

In his New York years, Thomas came into personal contact with representatives of American psychoanalytical thought. At Harvard, his seminar focused on depth psychology. I find no evidence that he was particularly influenced by orthodox psychoanalysis and its theoretical grounding in the theory of libido and the dynamics of the relationships between ego, id, and superego. In fact, he made disparaging comments on the Oedipus complex. But Thomas seems to have had much sympathy with the attempts of Harry Stack Sullivan, himself a follower of Meyer, to recast psychoanalytical thought in interactionist, and largely Meadian, terminology.

It would seem to me, though I have no way of proving this, that the thought of Alfred Adler, the founder of *Individual-Psychologie,* must have been familiar to Thomas. Adler had broken with Freud before World War I, rejecting much of his psychodynamic emphasis. Instead, Adler developed a doctrine in which ego psychology in general and the *Lebensplan* (life plan) of the individual, as shaped through attempts to come to terms with life experience and environmental stresses, assumed primary importance. Here again the parallelism between these conceptions and Thomas's work, especially in its later phases, seems very pronounced and not likely to be a case of wholly independent development.

A fuller account would have to dwell on the studies in animal psychology and animal behavior which influenced Thomas, from the investigations of animal "tropism" initiated by his former teacher Jacques Loeb and later pursued by Jennings, Vervorn and others, to the animal studies, more particularly of ape and monkey behavior, by Yerkes and Wolfgang Koehler. It is also worth noting that Thomas's late preoccupations with childhood behavior, as well as Dorothy Thomas's correlative work, profited from the research of Charlotte Buehler (who was also Paul Lazarsfeld's teacher) in early childhood development. But enough has been said to indicate that Thomas remained true to his early resolve to be open to a wide variety of influences without succumbing fully to any of them.

In the last period of his life, Thomas stated that he had now arrived at a point where his most stimulating contacts were with younger sociologists, many of whom had been his pupils. The illustrious group of former Chicago students who dominated American sociology from roughly 1920 to 1935 were all influenced and largely shaped by Thomas. Ernest Burgess studied under him. Ellsworth Faris, Louis Wirth, and Everett and Helen Hughes all knew Thomas personally, though they were mainly trained by Park after Thomas had been forced to leave. Samuel Stouffer's interest in attitude research was stimulated by Thomas and built on the work of Thurstone, who had also been under Thomas's influence. Donald Young, Kimball Young, Leonard Cottrell, Edward Reuter, Clifford Shaw, and Stuart Queen were either influenced by Thomas in their student days in Chicago or subject to his influence from a distance. Thomas's emphasis on intensive social observation was continued by Robert Park and, after 1938, by Everett Hughes, who taught at Chicago until after World War II and helped fashion yet another generation of distinguished sociologists. Herbert Blumer at Chicago and later at Berkeley developed a symbolic interactionist perspective which, though mainly beholden to Mead, also contained many elements derived from Thomas's work.

Nor was Thomas's influence restricted to scholars associated with the University of Chicago. Robert K. Merton, in particular, though having wholly different academic roots, was deeply indebted in his work to Thomas, as he has stated repeatedly. Merton's influential paper on "the self-fulfilling prophecy" constitutes in effect a creative extension of the line of thought developed by Thomas's definition of the situation, and Thomas's work provided critical building blocks in what became Merton's theory of reference group behavior.[84]

The philistines succeeded in dimissing Thomas from Chicago; what they could not do was to prevent the spread of his intellectual influence. That influence proved decisive in shaping the work of whole generations of American sociologists. Once again the pen had been mightier than the sword wielded by the policemen of the mind.

FLORIAN ZNANIECKI

Znaniecki was trained in philosophy and accordingly carried much heavier philosophical baggage as a sociologist than W. I. Thomas. Moreover, while

[84] This account of Thomas's intellectual progeny omits the influence of *The Polish Peasant* on subsequent researchers using the life-history method in the manner pioneered by this work. They are too numerous to mention here. But it might be of some value to list three volumes which attempted to codify and assess this method: John Dollard, *Criteria for the Life History* (New York, Peter Smith, 1949); Gordon Allport, *The Use of Personal Documents in Psychological Sciences* (New York, Social Science Research Council, Bulletin 49, 1942); Louis Gottschalk et al., *The Use of Personal Documents in History, Anthropology and Sociology* (New York, Social Science Research Council, Bulletin 53, 1945), see esp. the chapter by Robert Angell on sociology.

Thomas had no desire to build a system of his own, Znaniecki's thought was nothing if not system oriented.

After his first visit to America, Znaniecki wrote in the introduction to his first book published in English, "The primary source of the views on which I am trying to build a philosophy of culture lies . . . in Polish historical idealism. Of all my later debts none is greater than the one I owe to pragmatism of which, in fact, I am inclined to consider myself a disciple."[85] What he said here of his philosophical writings also applies, *grosso modo,* to his later sociological contributions. Not being familiar with Polish philosophical idealism, I shall emphasize in what follows the German idealistic tradition from which, I conclude, it largely derived.

Znaniecki's debts to the idealistic tradition are many, but none is greater than that which led him throughout his work to reject any mechanistic or deterministic explanation of human behavior and to continue to insist on the "conscious purposiveness" of social action. Kant's sharp distinction between the world of nature and the world of man, his fundamental premise that humans are free and self-determining agents in the realm of culture, (though like all other physical bodies they are determined by the laws of nature), informs Znaniecki's thought just as it informed the thought of most German nineteenth-century thinkers in the tradition of classical idealism and *Geisteswissenschaft.* This tradition has been discussed in the chapter on Max Weber. Znaniecki's notion of the "humanistic coefficient," his emphatic conviction that any human factor must be considered in terms of the experiences of human agents, "not because of what it 'is' as a natural datum, but because of what it 'means' as a humanistic cultural datum"[86] places him directly in the German idealistic tradition and its offshoots in Dilthey's and Neo-Kantian thought.

The impact of this tradition on Znaniecki's views of culture as a realm separate from nature, but also from individual psychology, is readily apparent. Already in his early books in Polish, Znaniecki endeavored to defend the thesis that the world of culture rested on the existence of values which were not reducible either to natural objects or to purely subjective processes. Znaniecki has said that he took the notion of "value" to denote cultural phenomena from the works of Friedrich Nietzsche.[87] But his elaboration of the notion of culture as a third realm, distinct both from the world of natural objects and from individual subjective experience, owes a great deal to the various exponents of German *Geisteswissenschaften.* (It might be of interest to point out that this distinction has recently been revived in the writing of Sir Karl Popper.)[88]

While Znaniecki can be considered an heir of the idealist tradition and its later offshoots, it is also important to note that he turned away from it in other

[85] *Cultural Reality,* pp. XIII–XIV. [86] *Social Actions,* p. 13.

[87] *The Method of Sociology,* p. 84.

[88] Cf. Paul Schlipp, ed., *The Philosophy of Karl Popper* (La Salle, Ind., Library of Living Philosophy, 1974).

respects. As he explained in *Cultural Reality,*[89] this tradition, though unassailable on purely logical grounds, had proved over time to have been substantively sterile, while the opposing realistic or naturalistic school of thought had developed a large and continually growing body of positive empirical knowledge in the study of mankind and its works. This did not induce Znaniecki to accept Watsonian behaviorism or any variety of positivistic thought. He felt that idealism and positivistic naturalism had to be transcended in a new synthesis. Such a synthesis would stress the preeminence of culture in the explanation of human behavior while yet not succumbing to the extreme idealistic view that the realm of ideas is located somehow outside the world of human experience. "If therefore modern thought intends to avoid the emptiness of idealism and the self-contradiction of naturalism, it must accept the culturist thesis. It must maintain against idealism the universal historical relativity of all forms of reason and standards of valuation as being within, not above, the evolving empirical world. It must maintain against naturalism that man is not a product of the evolution of nature, but that on the contrary, nature, in a large measure at least, is the product of human culture. . . ."[90]

It was in his effort to transcend both crude positivistic naturalism and extreme idealism that Znaniecki encountered pragmatist thought and largely accepted its general orientation. Znaniecki could not bring himself to accept the details of the pragmatist position "such as the biological conception of activity, the instrumental definition of truth, and several others."[91] What he found congenial in it was the emphasis on the close connection between human ideas and values and human activities, its relativistic views of cultural realities, its emphasis that, to quote a phrase of Dewey's, "Every living thought represents a gesture made toward the world, an attitude taken to some practical situation in which we are implicated."[92]

There is no need to discuss here the details of the pragmatist conception and its insistence on the close interconnectedness between thought and action and between ideas and their settings in concrete human communities, issues that are dealt with in the chapter on Mead. It is noteworthy here that Znaniecki's attempts to develop a distinctive sociology of knowledge, most successfully in *The Social Role of the Man of Knowledge,* are made from a pragmatist perspective. Pragmatism allowed him to explore cultural data without reducing them to individual subjective experiences, sense impressions, prepotent reflexes, or responses to Pavlovian stimuli.

While Znaniecki's indebtedness to the offshoots of German idealism in *Geisteswissenschaft* and to the American pragmatic tradition cannot be disputed, other influences are considerably more complex. Most of his works are

[89] *Cultural Reality,* p. 1 ff. [90] *Ibid.,* p. 21. [91] *Ibid.,* p. XIV.

[92] John Dewey, *German Philosophy and Politics* (New York, Holt, 1915), p. 7; as quoted in Frankel, *op. cit.*

studded with references to a variety of writers, both philosophical and sociological, and to both classical as well as contemporary statements. The annotated references to *The Method of Sociology,* for example, occupy not less than 57 of the total 336 pages. All major German, French, and American sociologists can be found in Znaniecki's references, nor could I find many philosophers to which Znaniecki did not refer at one time or another. It would serve little purpose to single out some of them here, especially since there seems no way of deciding who among these many scholars deserves to be ranked higher than another in Znaniecki's personal pantheon.

The influence of one British philosopher, however, F. C. S. Schiller, needs to be mentioned, since his work had a very important impact on Znaniecki. In one of his earliest books, *Humanism and Knowledge* (in Polish), Znaniecki followed closely in the footsteps of Schiller's argumentation which had been developed in the latter's "Studies in Humanism" published a few years earlier (London, 1907). Schiller was a pragmatist and voluntarist who opposed idealism by arguing that man is the creator of values and the maker and remaker of the "reality" in which he is immersed. Schiller opposed naturalism and behaviorism because, so he contended, they ignored the unique capacity of human beings to give meaning to their experience and to act accordingly. It seems evident that Znaniecki's later development of the notion of "cultural reality" and of the "humanistic coefficient" owes a good deal to the impetus he had received from Schiller's work. (Personal communication from Theodore Abel, May 12, 1976.)

In regard to his intellectual debts, Znaniecki noted in a short autobiographical statement: ". . . I am a self-made sociologist. I never took a course in sociology in my life [though he evidently tried at least once in Chicago, L. A. C.]. Even in philosophy, I was always a rebel. I got some stimulation from personal contacts with such sociologists as Durkheim, Lévy-Bruhl, Célestin Bouglé, W. I. Thomas, Albion Small; but whatever I know, I learned from books and sociological research."[93]

Znaniecki seems to have been a bit unfair here. He probably knew the first three only fleetingly during his student days at the Sorbonne, whereas, as he himself has written elsewhere, he was profoundly influenced by Thomas during the years of their association. And completely omitted from the roster is the name of Robert MacIver, who clearly had a major impact on his thought in America. His preface to *The Method of Sociology* seems to strike a more balanced note. Here he wrote: "My obligations as a sociologist are too numerous to be recorded. But there are two men to whom above all others I wish to express my gratitude. . . . One is William I. Thomas, a long and intimate association with whom was the best possible introduction a philosopher could have into sociological reality. The other is Robert M. MacIver. . . ."[94]

[93] Letter to Father Mulvaney, *op. cit.*

[94] Florian Znaniecki, *The Method of Sociology, op. cit.,* p. IX.

The association of Thomas and Znaniecki in the writing of *The Polish Peasant* was unusually close. The overall inception of the work was, of course, Thomas's, who had worked on it long before he met Znaniecki. The Methodological Note, on the other hand, was largely written by Znaniecki in an effort to combine and to reconcile Thomas's concern with attitudes and wishes and his own involvement in the investigation of cultural values. As has already been mentioned, Znaniecki later gave up Thomas's concerns with attitudes and wishes, evolving his own interpretation of the data of human experience. But it remains, however, that his methodological discussion of the inferior value of simple enumerative induction (as used for example in the work of Sumner or Spencer) in contrast to analytical induction (the study of typical cases) rests almost entirely on W. I. Thomas's use of the case study method.[95]

Robert MacIver was a close personal friend of Znaniecki. Although personal friends do not necessarily influence each other's thought, the family resemblance between Znaniecki's "humanistic coefficient" and what MacIver called the "dynamic assessment" is so close that it must be assumed that these two friends largely shared a common scholarly orientation. MacIver wrote in *Social Causation,* "In all conscious behavior there is . . . a twofold process of selective organization. . . . The inner, or subjective, system is focused by a dynamic valuation; and the outer, or external, system is 'spotlighted' in that focus, the part within the spotlight being transformed from mere externality into something also belonging to a world of values, as vehicle, accessory, hindrance, and cost of the value attainment."[96] It is readily apparent that, apart from differences in terminology, Znaniecki might have written this as well. They surely worked within the same universe of ideas, and it is quite impossible to decide who owed more to whom in their intellectual transactions.

Znaniecki, who left a whole school of disciples in Poland, had hardly any disciples in America (except of course for those men and women who drew major inspiration from *The Polish Peasant*). Why this was so can largely be accounted for by sociological, rather than purely intellectual, reasons.

THE SOCIAL CONTEXT

WILLIAM I. THOMAS

The social context in which Thomas developed his personality and created his work has been described in the chapters on Park and Mead. Thomas lived and worked in the progressive era; he was marked by the reformist and meliorist winds of doctrine that swept through America in the first quarter of the twentieth century, and he was at least as deeply immersed in the social reform movements of Chicago as Park and Mead had been. He was more particularly

[95] *Ibid.* chapter VI. [96] Robert MacIver, *Social Causation,* (New York, Ginn, 1942), p. 292.

and more persistently concerned than were Park or Mead with urban disorganization, with the breakdown of moral norms, with deviance, criminality and the like, but these were matters of greater personal emphasis not divergent orientations. By and large, Thomas, Park, and Mead shared a common universe of ideas and values as they shared a common vantage point as academic men sensitive to the ills of transition in urbanizing America.

One matter, however, deserves some comment: Thomas's persistent refusal to address any but academic audiences. Park spent a major part of his life as a muckraking journalist attempting to alert a popular public to the social problems of the age. Even after becoming an academic man at the age of fifty, a wider audience was never far from his mind, even though he now directed most of his writings to his colleagues and students in the social sciences. The same can be said of Mead. Although he was hampered by a ponderous style and an inability to write with ease, he seems to have made some efforts at least to broadcast his reforming ideas to an audience wider than that of the university. In contrast, though Thomas served as a consultant to reform organizations and occasionally a speaker before reform audiences, he hardly made any attempt in his writings to reach out beyond the academy. Given his plastic style and easy manner of exposition, his reformer's zeal and activistic propensities, he might have been expected to write frequently for those organs of opinion that addressed an audience wider than his academic colleagues and students. Yet, except during the years 1908–09, when he wrote a series of articles for the *American Magazine* on such topics as "The Mind of Woman" and "Eugenics: the Science of Breeding Men," Thomas published only in scholarly publications and in books destined mainly to be read by social scientists.

This seems even more remarkable when one considers that other American sociologists, including Veblen and Sorokin, turned to a wider audience when they found themselves rebuffed by university authorities and academic peers. Thomas, who probably suffered more seriously in this respect than these men, refused to avail himself of the more popular media even after his expulsion from the University of Chicago. Given the lack of biographical and autobiographical information, one can only speculate about the reasons for this.

Thomas did not acquire his learning lightly or with ease. The mountain boy from rural Virginia had faced a rocky road on his way to learning; once he had made the decision to become a man of knowledge, he probably valued the academic life with an intensity superior to that of persons who had grown into it, so to speak, organically. What he had won by such fierce determination, that in which he had invested much, was treasured with great intensity. As Simmel and others have remarked and much later psychological research has confirmed, we fight intensely not only when goals are valued highly, but the very intensity of struggling for a goal makes us value it more highly than if it had been reached with ease. Thomas had fought hard to gain the ear of the academy and he was not to be detracted from his commitment to it, even when he was rebuffed.

Veblen and Sorokin and other sociologists had also struggled on their way to knowledge and still searched for a larger audience. Yet another more important factor seems to have been at play for Thomas but not for them. Veblen and Sorokin, though attracting some followers, did not manage to gather around them large numbers of admiring students, let alone disciples. Thomas, in contrast, never lost his following of students and former students, even after his trying Chicago experiences. They stood with him and managed, *inter alia,* to have him elected to the presidency of the American Sociological Society despite the resistance of many of their elders. This fact is probably the main reason for Thomas's persistent clinging to an academic audience. Finding much needed support among students and former students, being sustained by their admiration of his work and their devotion, he did not feel that need to turn to an altogether different audience even after his rebuff. Moreover, as some of these men and women assumed major positions in various foundation offices and research establishments, they saw to it that Thomas was supported and encouraged by these institutions, thus making it psychologically possible for him to remain within the circle of academic or near-academic scholars.

Thomas's fidelity to his academic audience is all the more remarkable when one discovers that the sales of his books were, to say the least, unimpressive. The number of sociologists in the United States during the twenties was small, and even when one adds to their number social workers and other professionals, this was not yet a public large enough to sustain major book sales. Hence, the first edition of 1500 copies of *The Polish Peasant* was not exhausted until almost eight years after publication. This may have been partly due to the fact that it was brought out by a small house after the University of Chicago Press had reneged on its contract. But even the second edition, now under the prestigeful imprint of Alfred A. Knopf, sold only 1500 copies in ten years. It is only in our days, with a much wider audience for sociological books, that *The Polish Peasant* has done better. A reprint edition by Dover in 1958 sold more than 3000 copies in three years. I do not have the sales figures for Thomas's other books, but they cannot have been large, and after he was forced to leave Chicago, the University of Chicago Press let them go out of print and refused to republish them.[97] *Old World Traits Transplanted* has only recently been reissued, finally under the name of its rightful author.

Thomas's dogged persistance in addressing an academic audience—and his refusal to look for popular acclaim—was altogether remarkable.

[97] I take these publishing data from Janowitz, *op. cit.*

FLORIAN ZNANIECKI

Znaniecki's background and social context involves exploration of territory much less familiar to American readers than the background and social context of Thomas. He was very much a Pole in his make-up, despite the many years he spent in this country, and so his roots in the tradition of the Polish gentry and the Polish intelligentsia must be sketched before his later career in America is considered.

From the time of the Middle Ages, Polish society, like Mannheim's Hungary, was distinguished from Western Europe by the absence of a middle class. Until just recently Polish culture rested almost exclusively on a basis in aristocratic and gentry strata.[98] The vast majority of peasants were not allowed the means of cultural expression, and the nobility dominated the field. Forbidden by law and custom to work in commerce and industry, members of the nobility could only be landlords and warriors. Fiercely individualistic, contentious, unwilling to accept the yoke of subordination even to their own kings, the higher aristocracy and gentry cultivated elaborate and refined feelings of honor and personal dignity, of patriotism and national pride, but they were unable to engage in organized and collectively shared political efforts. The curious organization of the gentry diet with its *liberum veto* (that is, the procedural rule that a single veto by one of its members could prevent any action) symbolizes some of the Polish gentry's scale of values. When Poland lost its independence and was partitioned among Russia, Germany, and Austria in the late eighteenth century, at least one major reason surely was the political ineptitude of its dominant stratum.

In the nineteenth century, now under foreign domination, the peasantry kept its language, tradition, and national folk culture, but the main effort to throw off the foreign yoke rested with the gentry. The successive Polish insurrections of the last century were inspired, led, and largely manned by young people stemming from the nobility. Yet the nineteenth century also witnessed the gradual erosion of the gentry's social basis in landholding. The repressions following each successive uprising, together with the enfranchisement of the peasantry in 1864, led to a gradual decline of noble estates and to the decay of their accustomed forms of social and cultural life.

As more and more members of the gentry lost their estates, they flocked to the cities and took over most of the emerging professional and higher white-collar occupations. It is from their ranks that the Polish intelligentsia gradually developed, a stratum that has no counterpart in the West, though it is also a distinctive feature of the Russian nineteenth-century scene. The word "intelligentsia" emerged only in the second half of the nineteenth century to describe the new stratum that then made its appearance. It might be defined, following

[98] On the Polish gentry and the Polish intelligentsia see, Alexander Hertz, "The Case of an Eastern European Intelligentsia," *Journal of Central European Affairs* XI, 1 (January–April, 1951), pp. 10–26; and Jan Szczepanski, *Polish Society* (New York, Random House, 1970).

the Russian historian Alexander Kornilov, as "The intellectual body composed of men of various orders and classes, standing apart by virtue of their education and consciousness of ideals as well as by their aim not only to build up consciously their own life, but to exercise their influence on the life structure of the whole nation according to their ideas and views."[99]

In countries in which large masses of the population were either illiterate or possessed only the rudiments of booklearning, education was seen as a personal asset setting individuals apart and giving them entry to a higher social and cultural scene. It not only opened the gates to professional status but imposed general cultural responsibilities. Particularly in Poland, it implied the duty to strive for the preservation of the national culture. A university diploma was therefore comparable to a title of nobility in that it symbolized *noblesse oblige,* an exalted dignity but also a commitment to peculiar cultural obligations.

This is why in the last half of the nineteenth century the Polish intelligentsia took over most of the cultural leadership and moral authority that had previously rested in the hands of the gentry. This intelligentsia, however, continued to be mainly recruited from the ranks of the impoverished gentry.

In Russian-dominated Poland—things were somewhat better in the territories dominated by Austria and Germany—university-educated persons who came from the new academic centers of Vilna and Warsaw found few careers open to them in the Russian civil service; even the military, though somewhat more accessible, was not widely receptive to Poles. As a result, the sons of impoverished noblemen flocked into the professions, for such careers allowed them to live in the cities while still maintaining a high social standing in the eyes of their former rural peers. From these circles emerged the first nucleus of nineteenth-century patriotic and liberal reformers. After the collapse of national autonomy and sovereignty, they became the mainstays of efforts to defend national culture. The first scientific societies, the first scientific journals, the first dictionary of the Polish language, the first museums and collections of national treasures—these were all organized and directed by the gentry intelligentsia. Toward the end of the nineteenth century its ranks were swelled by new recruits from the emerging middle class, from Jews and from the peasantry; even then the intelligentsia remained dominated by values and lifestyles that had characterized it from its inception.

What marked that style of life above all was a very high esteem for intellectual and artistic creativity. Creativity in any field was regarded not only as valuable in itself, but as a "service to the Polish nation." Seen as the basis of national existence it was valued more highly than achievements in business, industry, or politics. Together with faith, honor, and freedom, intellectual or artistic accomplishments were more highly prized than such middle-class traits as thrift, frugality, success in business, or hard work.

[99] Quoted in Hertz, *op. cit.*

By the turn of the century, during the period in which Znaniecki grew up, the intelligentsia had taken over from the gentry, from which it was still largely descended, the claim to lead the nation. By that time, in addition, young members of the intelligentsia had also assumed the leadership of the slowly emerging labor and peasant movements.

Florian Znaniecki, the son of impoverished landowners of gentry origin, was a self-conscious member of the intelligentsia. His lifelong emphasis on the central importance of cultural values, his deep-felt commitment to scholarly excellence, his impassioned defense of the life of the mind against any encroachments from the powers to be, his personal life-style and pronounced individualism, his enduring concern with education and citizenship—all these characteristic traits can best be understood as rooted in the social background of the Polish intelligentsia. In other countries it would have been somewhat surprising to find a young Ph.D. in philosophy turning up as the head of an Emigrant Protective Association. Not so in Poland; the intelligentsia took it as an obligation to serve the Polish people in whatever manner was feasible at the time. If one couldn't teach at a university because of Russian proscriptions, one served one's people in other, perhaps humbler, lines of activity.

When Znaniecki came to America, he must have realized after a while that intellectuals did not rank as highly in the American status structure as in the Polish. Academic men and women in the United States were not expected to stray from their specific university duties by attempting to become teachers and guides to the nation as a whole. Twice during his stay in America Znaniecki tried to propose major reforms of the educational system in order to influence the training of national leaders. In both cases he found little response.

While at Teachers College of Columbia University in 1931–1933, he wrote a long memorandum on national leadership with a detailed plan for the organization of a "school or institute for the training of social leaders." Dean William Russell of Teachers College, to whom the memorandum was addressed, replied that he was "convinced by the logic of the memorandum," and would like to see such an experiment put into practice. He even stated that "the country which first has the courage to try your experiment . . . will be likely to assume a position of world leadership in education."[100] Professor David Snedden of Teachers College wrote Znaniecki in a similar vein. But they apparently did nothing to put his proposals into effect, and Znaniecki surely did not possess the manipulative skills to push it through the jungle of committee deliberations required for any kind of action.

Many years later, at the University of Illinois, Znaniecki wrote a lengthy manuscript entitled *The Social Role of the University Student* that contained elaborate recommendations to the University of Illinois for the revamping of its educational offerings. The then president of the University did not take kindly

100 Copy of letters from Russell to Znaniecki dated June 22, 1933, and from Snedden to Znaniecki dated August 1, 1933, provided by Helena Znaniecki Lopata.

to Znaniecki's emphasis on the inadequacies of the university's educational system and to his critical stance regarding the American system of higher education as a whole. He made no effort to put any of Znaniecki's recommendations into effect.[101]

Znaniecki's attempts to live up to the calling of the Polish intelligentsia to provide leadership for the nation fell on fallow ground in the United States. Few people in positions of power and authority were ready to listen to a professor, and a foreign professor at that, who presumed to provide guidelines for national leadership.

Znaniecki also faced some difficulties in the more usual professorial and scholarly activities. While at the University of Chicago, Thomas smoothed Znaniecki's path, and the latter soon gained recognition from some members of the Chicago faculty. Yet there was also strong, still undiagnosed resistance to him when he made an effort to gain a Ph.D. in sociology. Moreover, his standing was diminished when Thomas, his sponsor and collaborator, was ostracized.

The ensuing years in Poland seem to have been very satisfying to Znaniecki. In his homeland he was able to gather around himself a large number of enthusiastic students and junior colleagues who accepted his guidance and teaching and with whose help he built and shaped the Polish school of sociology. He found few such idealistic students at the University of Illinois after his return to America. As his daughter wrote me, "The University of Illinois students were more mundane and he was not able to influence them as deeply. I remember life in Poland with students constantly around, discussing, arguing, assuming that they could change the world, particularly through changing the educational system."[102] Such students did not flourish at the University of Illinois, and this must have been quite galling to a man who, as evidenced by his writings, was acutely conscious of and sensitive to the relations between a teacher and his circle.

His years at Illinois, one gathers, were by no means unhappy—he dedicated *Cultural Sciences* "to the University of Illinois in gratitude for ten free, happy, and productive years as a member of its faculty"—but as his daughter has written, he experienced a loss of status upon coming to Illinois. He had a great deal of influence in Poland and was known throughout the intelligentsia and governmental circles.[103] He enjoyed neither of these advantages in the United States, especially at the University of Illinois.

Among his works in English after his University of Chicago period, *The Method of Sociology* and *The Social Role of the Man of Knowledge,* outrank the rest. It is worthy of note that both these books were written at Columbia University, where Znaniecki had the close intellectual companionship of Robert MacIver, John Dewey, George Counts, and other such peers. Participating in seminars and discussion groups, lecturing before congenial academic audiences,

[101] Helena Znaniecki Lopata, *Florian Znaniecki, op. cit.*

[102] Helena Znaniecki Lopata, personal communication, January 20, 1976. [103] *Ibid.*

Znaniecki profited a great deal from interchanges within a dense social network of colleagues at Columbia University. Here he felt appreciated and stimulated through continued social and critical intercourse with people he deemed his equals. The impact of these associations is reflected in the clear and logical structure of the books written at Columbia, their clarity of style and convincing argumentation. His other books, written under less congenial surroundings, suffer by comparison.

I cannot help but feel that he was less closely tied to his colleagues during the University of Illinois period and that these colleagues themselves were not of the calibre of his associates and peers at Columbia. Robert Bierstedt has written me that I was mistaken in my impression that Znaniecki was somewhat lonely there. He points out that Znaniecki "had many warm friends there; he and Eileen carried on a lively social life; and he was held in high respect not only by his colleagues in the department—Donald Taft, E. T. Hiller, and William Albig among them— but outside the department as well."[104] This may all have been the case, yet his daughter seems closer to the mark when she writes: "I don't think that father suffered from isolation from colleagues at Illinois any more than any place before [in America, I presume], *with the exception of New York*."[105]

He was by no means totally isolated at Illinois. The young Robert Bierstedt, in particular, carried on a sustained intellectual dialogue with him, and Znaniecki valued that exchange so highly that he even consented to give up his lifelong habit of staying in bed during the morning in order to have a chance to carry on discussions with Bierstedt. But apart from the brilliance of the young Bierstedt, it may be that Znaniecki valued their conversations so highly just because he had few other such stimulating partners. After the war other members of the Polish intelligentsia settled in Urbana and encompassed the Znanieckis in their circle of intimate friendship, but such friendship seems to have rested in large part on nostalgia. It is revealing that, as his daughter writes, "Father made a point of becoming an American citizen and was very proud of that. Yet had it not been for men like Gidynski who convinced him that his return to Poland would be a blow to its eventual freeing from Soviet communism, I think he would have liked to return to Poland."[106]

Throughout the Illinois years, even as before, the Znanieckis remained close to the MacIvers, spending summers with them at their Martha's Vineyard retreat or playing bridge at their house in the Palisades. The Bierstedts—Betty Bierstedt is MacIver's daughter—too remained close friends. Over the years Znaniecki was also sustained by his close friendship with his former student Theodore Abel who, after having received a scholarship at Columbia University upon Znaniecki's recommendation, had later joined the staff of Columbia's sociology department. Znaniecki had been instrumental in persuading the

[104] Robert Bierstedt, personal communication, November 15, 1975.

[105] Helena Znaniecki Lopata, personal communication, *op. cit.* [106] *Ibid.*

young Abel to switch his interests from philosophy to sociology, and he was the first of his students to get his doctoral degree at the University of Poznan under Znaniecki's guidance. The two men remained close friends in America. It was Abel's recommendation, strengthened by his translation of the main parts of Znaniecki's "Sociology of Education," that convinced the Columbia faculty that he should be made the recipient of a two-year grant to study the issue of education and social change. It was also Abel who arranged Znaniecki's visit to Columbia in 1939 to teach in the Summer Session of which he was in charge. This appointment probably saved Znaniecki's life by keeping him in America when the Nazi's invaded Poland.

And yet, despite close friendships he developed and despite many indications of recognition and esteem accorded him by American sociologists—from Albion Small and Howard P. Becker to Robert K. Merton—Znaniecki remained somewhat of an outsider in the American academy. He was elected to the presidency of the American Sociological Society, to be sure, but it should be noted that this election was rather belated, coming as it did only in 1953, just five years before his death at the age of seventy-six.

One other matter needs some comment. Even a fairly superficial reader of Znaniecki's work must be struck by the similarities between many of his ideas and those of Talcott Parsons. Both were committed to a voluntaristic theory of action, sharing a commitment to an antipositivistic and antipsychologistic conception of human behavior. Both attempted to devise sociological systems in which the notion of social role plays a salient part. Both shared the conviction that only through the absorption of the sociological and philosophical heritage of Europe would American sociology be protected from the temptations of atheoretical fact-finding and empiricism. Yet, Parsons achieved a towering influence on American sociology while Znaniecki had relatively little impact. One reason for this is surely that Znaniecki never succeeded in constructing the full sociological system to which he aspired, but another is to be found in the respective location of the two men within the academic world in general and the world of sociology in particular. Parsons was securely placed at Harvard, one of the centers of the sociological enterprise, whereas Znaniecki's location was on the periphery. While Parsons in the late 1930's had already begun to train a brilliant group of students (as will be shown in the next chapter), Znaniecki, though he trained first-rate graduate students in Poland, had virtually none in the United States. Parsons became the fountainhead of a school of sociology, whereas Znaniecki's voice remained the voice of one man alone. Not unlike the case of Gabriel Tarde and Emile Durkheim, the work of the man in the center overshadowed that of the man on the periphery.

Had he been born under different stars, had he not been forced to shuttle back and forth between two cultures, had his academic location been more central, Znaniecki might have produced even more significant work than in fact he did. But in light of the factors that hampered his creativity, it is wondrous indeed that he managed to gather the abundant fruits that make him one of our masters.

IN SUMMARY

Thomas and Znaniecki came from very different backgrounds and were in many ways dissimilar in their personal make-up, yet they managed to collaborate harmoniously on the monumental *The Polish Peasant in Europe and America* which, without any doubt, is the first major landmark in the development of American social research. It will long be remembered not only for its concrete findings and methodological approaches, but also, and perhaps mainly, for the theoretical framework jointly provided by its authors.

Far from resting on their laurels after the publication of their joint work, both authors went on to make individual contributions which matched their previous work. Elaborating on his earlier concern with social attitudes, Thomas developed a sophisticated social psychology, based on the central notion of "the definition of the situation," which still informs a good deal of sociological thought at the present time. Znaniecki in his turn, elaborating on his earlier structural notions, moved on to develop a highly stimulating version of role theory, and, in *The Social Role of the Man of Knowledge,* made one of the few really important contributions to the sociology of knowledge to be written in America.

One is hard put to imagine what the course of American sociology would have been without the work of these two men. One thing is certain; without the impact of these masters, American sociology would have been much the poorer.

Recent Trends in American Sociological Theory

This chapter will concentrate on those recent trends in American sociological theory that are of general significance for the discipline and have had a marked impact on it.* Space does not permit covering any specialized fields of inquiry—for example, the impressive developments in demographic theory in the last few decades or the efflorescence of theoretical thought in urban sociology. One reader or another may be disappointed that a particular and no doubt important theoretical development has not been included. It can only be said that I have attempted to keep personal predilections in check in order to depict what I take to be the overall consensus about the relative importance of sociological theories that came to the fore between the nineteen forties and the mid-nineteen sixties.

Since the varieties of functional analysis took pride of place during most of the period covered here, the first part of this chapter is devoted to considering them. Symbolic interactionism and its offshots in Goffman's dramaturgical approach, labeling theory, exchange theory, "conflict theory," and related developments will be discussed in some detail in the second part of this chapter.

THE RISE AND HEGEMONY OF FUNCTIONAL ANALYSIS

Earlier chapters of this book have documented the lengthy dominance of the Chicago Department of Sociology over the rest of American sociology. The end of the Chicago dominance may conveniently be dated in 1935 when the American Sociological Society, until then largely, though not wholly, dominated by the Chicago department or Chicago-trained scholars, decided in a minor *coup d'état* to establish its own journal, *The American Sociological Review,* thus severing the long-time formal and informal links of the discipline to the Chicago department. While to this day Chicago has continued to be among the most prestigious and influential centers of sociological research and training, it has not regained the dominant position it once enjoyed in American sociology.

* This chapter is a considerably revised and enlarged version of a paper entitled "Sociological Theory from the Chicago Dominance to 1965," which appeared in volume 2 of the *Annual Review of Sociology* in the Fall of 1976.

A NEW COURSE IN SOCIOLOGY

Although the importance of Parsons's *The Structure of Social Action* (1937)* was not immediately recognized, it may be said in retrospect to constitute the other watershed in the development of American sociology in general and sociological theory in particular. This work was a landmark in that it set a new course—the course of functional analysis—that was to dominate theoretical developments from the early 1940's until the middle of the 1960's.

Functional analysis is here defined as a theoretical orientation concerned, as other are orientations, with the interrelations between social phenomena in general and, more specifically, with the consequences of given items for the larger structure or structures in which they are variously embedded. (This definition largely follows statements set forth by Merton [1968] and Stinchcombe [1968].) Functions are those observed consequences that make for adaptation or adjustment of given structures; dysfunctions are those observed consequences that lessen adaptation or adjustment. Functional analysis, moreover, focuses attention on the causal loop through which the consequences of given courses of action act back on the item under observation, bringing about, as the case may be, its persistence or modification.

It would be too facile to say, as has often been asserted, that American sociology was liberated from an atheoretical empiricism during the Chicago period by Parsons's daring synthesis of several major European sociological traditions. Many of the major Chicago figures, as has been shown, had studied in Europe and were well acquainted with European sociological and philosophical thought. Several of them, Small and Park in particular, were familiar with the work of Georg Simmel, for example, which they helped to introduce to the American scholarly public (cf. Levine 1976). A simple glance at Park and Burgess's influential textbook readily shows that far from being parochial, they attempted to introduce their students to a great deal of European sociological thought.

Nonetheless, the Chicago reception of European sociological contributions proceeded by bits and pieces. Chicago scholars made use of one or another aspect of European work, but they did not succeed in assimilating it in a systematic manner. This was precisely what the Harvard group, under the guidance of Parsons, managed to accomplish in the wake of the publication of *The Structure of Social Action*. This book widened the vistas of American sociologists, making them receptive to the rich heritage of the European sociological tradition. In this work Parsons attempted to develop a "voluntaristic theory of social action" by way of a creative synthesis of Durkheim, Weber, and Pareto. (The work of the British economist Marshall was also considered in detail but later was somehow largely dropped from consideration.)

* Throughout this chapter I have followed a standard form of reference, citing authors and year of publication, which are readily identified in the bibliography on page 582.

Surveying the major assumptions and theoretical premises of utilitarianism, idealism, and positivism, Parsons set out to analyze them critically and to indicate in what respects they might be useful in elaborating the new synthesis for which he was striving. Agreeing with the utilitarian view of individuals as purposive and goal-oriented actors, he rejected what he conceived to be its atomistic and overly rational orientation and its attendant incapacity to account for the emergence of a social order regulating the goal-oriented activities of individual actors. Positivism was attacked for its reductionism—its propensity to explain individual behavior in terms of physiological, psychochemical, genetic, or geographical influences—and its consequent inability to account for the voluntaristic, choice-making, and goal-striving tendencies of social actors. Finally, the German idealistic tradition was praised for its emphasis on the influence of cultural determinants such as ideas or symbolic processes, while it was criticized for not giving satisfactory explanations for the complex interrelations between social structures and the world of ideas. This tradition, so Parsons argued, was bound to an "emanationist" conception of cultural determination, which held that differences in the behavior of social actors at different times and in different places could be accounted for solely in terms of ideational or cultural determinants. In such a conception, social structures always emanate from the world of ideas. Parsons argued that idealist theorizing could never explain the tensions and discrepancies between the world of ideas and the world of social activities. If, as he contended, ideas and social structures were bound to each other through dynamic interplays and interchanges, a theory that saw social structure simply as an emanation of ideas was surely inadequate. Furthermore, if the character of each particular society was said to be determined by its values and ethos, it would be impossible to develop a generalizing theory of society to account for human actions across the resulting cultural diversities. This was precisely what Parsons attempted to do.

Parsons developed a series of abstract analytical concepts that were to be ordered in such a manner as to account for central features of all human societies without having to deal with the myriad of empirical phenomena that threatened to drown the researcher in a sea of particularities. He wanted to highlight the salient and systematic features of human action.

In *The Structure of Social Action* these central features were constructed from the following basic building stones: (a) actors, capable of voluntary striving, emphatically not behaving and reacting bodies; (b) goals that these actors were striving for; (c) choices between alternative means these actors were using in their pursuits; (d) situational constraints coming from both biological and environmental conditions, which set bounds to the selection of means and the accomplishment of ends; and (e) sets of norms and values that channeled the actors' choices of both means and ends.

In sum, human actors were seen as capable of making choices of courses of action, but these choices were constrained by biological and environmental conditions and, more importantly for Parsons, by the values and norms governing the social structures in which they were variously enmeshed.

This conceptual scheme, as *The Structure of Social Action* shows in instructive detail, was derived from the synthesis, among other things, of the Durkheimian emphasis on structural determinants and collective consciousness, the Weberian stress on the determining functioning of sets of ideas and values, and the Paretian notion of moving societal equilibria resulting from the interplay of actors possessed in varying degrees of a set of fundamental "residues" or prepotent drives. (At a later date Freud largely replaced Pareto in Parsons's theoretical edifice, and the functionalist theories of Malinowski and Radcliffe-Brown became major building blocks of the Parsonian synthesis.)

In the later development of Parsons's theoretical scheme, interaction came to displace the emphasis on social action of individuals. In his second major work, *The Social System* (1951), the systematic interrelations between human actors and the relatively stable patterns built out of institutionalized expectations that constrain their actions are the focus of attention rather than consideration of individual actions. While it may be true that this shift in perspective has involved a toning down of Parsons's earlier stress on the voluntary character of social action, he nevertheless continued to hold that a social system can operate only if its component actors are sufficiently motivated to act in terms of the requirements of that system.

In *The Social System,* Parsons emphasizes the central importance of institutionalized values and norms and differentiated social roles corresponding to differentiated status positions. The foundations of a social system, or of one of its subsystems, are motivated actors who play roles governed by the expectations of other actors involved with them in a web of social interaction. In a relatively stable system, the role partners of particular status incumbents serve to hold them in line through their expectations and their power to exercise negative or positive sanctions. The central values and norms of the system are upheld when properly socialized actors are motivated to live up to role requirements and when they are impelled to uphold and defend these institutionalized requirements in their interaction with other actors. The primacy of values and norms in Parsons's system makes it appropriate to call this system "normative functionalism."

This main line of Parsons's system has had a strong impact on American sociology. Toward the end of this chapter I shall return to the later development of Parsons's thought.

Parsons's work is intimately associated with Harvard University, yet the Harvard Department of Sociology, as has been shown in an earlier chapter, was not originally dominated by Parsons. He became an instructor in sociology at Harvard in 1931, a year after the founding of the department, and served in that rank for fully five years. The founder and first chairman of the department, Pitirim Sorokin, was highly critical of Parsons's work from the beginning, and so it was that the two men never achieved a close intellectual relationship although they shared a number of central ideas, most particularly concerning the importance of values in the determination of human conduct. Nevertheless, the small elite group of uncommonly gifted students who gathered at Harvard in the 1930's all seem to have been influenced, though to different degrees, by both Sorokin and Parsons. The most prominent sociology students at pre-World War II Harvard were George Homans (who was a junior Fellow in the Harvard Society of Fellows), Robert K. Merton, Kingsley Davis, Wilbert Moore, and Robin Williams. All of them have left an enduring mark on the subsequent development of sociological theory.

One other seminal influence on them, that of the physiologist and Pareto specialist, J. L. Henderson, needs to be mentioned briefly. His famous seminar on Pareto attracted such outstanding graduate students as Robert K. Merton, George Homans, and Kingsley Davis, as well as members of the Harvard faculty in the early 1930's (cf. Barber 1970, and the Pareto chapter in this volume).

George Homans

Homans was greatly influenced by Henderson, and his first major work (written with Curtis in 1934) was an introduction to the work of Pareto. He subsequently turned to work in English social history, which culminated in his *English Villagers of the Thirteenth Century* (1941). Though this book was highly praised by historians, it did not have much impact on American sociology. Such was not the case with his subsequent work. *The Human Group* (1950) presents a theoretical reanalysis of a series of previous studies of such diverse subjects as work groups in factories, street gangs, the kinship system in primitive societies, and the structure of a declining New England community. In this work, Homans attempted to develop a theoretical scheme of interrelated propositions derived from observed regularities in the initial accounts of these studies. He then used an inductive strategy much at variance with that of Parsons. However, the book was at least partly rooted, like Parsons's own work, in the functionalist approaches of Durkheim and of the British anthropologists Malinowski and Radcliffe-Brown. Homans's strategy set out to extract from the studies under investigation a number of propositions and to establish the conditions under which such propositions would in fact hold. He showed, for example, that increased interaction between persons would increase their liking for one another, but qualified this statement by noting that this would only be the case if they had roughly equal status positions, one not holding significant authority over the other. While *The Human Group* may still be said to be largely congruent with the emergent functionalist perspective, Homans's subsequent work, notably his *Social Behavior, Its Elementary Forms* (1961), abandons this perspective in favor of an exchange theory largely constructed from building blocks provided by the Skinnerian version of psychological behaviorism and classical utilitarian economic theory. This work will be discussed later.

Robert K. Merton

Robert K. Merton, who was to become the only serious rival of Parsons as a central figure in the theoretical development of American sociology during this period, studied under both Parsons and Sorokin. He was clearly influenced by both, though Parsons's impact was more pronounced. His thought was affected by a variety of European thinkers to whom he was largely introduced by Sorokin and Parsons, especially through Parsons's lectures that led to *The Structure of Social Action*. Merton's theoretical stance owes much to that book and, to a lesser extent, to Parsons's subsequent work. Merton's writings in the sociology of science were in part also stimulated by Sorokin, with whom he collaborated in parts of the latter's monumental *Social and Cultural Dynamics.*

Still, long before Merton published his highly influential *Social Theory and Social Structure* (1949, 1957, 1968), consisting mainly of previously published papers, it had become apparent that Sorokin's influence on Merton had become attenuated. Moreover, while Merton held a broadly functional perspective, his path began to diverge from that of Parsons as he refined the method of functional analysis. Largely rooting his thought in the same set of thinkers that Parsons had highlighted (though adding Karl Marx and Georg Simmel to Parsons's set of seminal Europeans), Merton rejected Parsons's attempt to develop a general all-encompassing theory in favor of an apparently more modest aim: the development of theoretical propositions of middle range, purporting to analyze a limited set of empirical phenomena (cf. Parsons 1949, Merton 1968). Merton argued that in view of the general status of sociological knowledge and theory Parsons's enterprise was overambitious. Sociology did not yet have its Kepler, let alone its Newton, and attempts to build a general theoretical system at this stage were, according to Merton, condemned to failure. Pluralistic theories of the middle range, on the other hand, could elucidate limited sets of empirical phenomena, could be susceptible to empirical testing, and could be consolidated into more wide-ranging theories.

Yet Merton did not merely forward a series of brilliant detailed studies in delimited areas; he had an overall theoretical vision. This perspective, as Stinchcombe (1975) has shown, focuses on motivated actors whose consequential choices are largely, though never wholly, constrained by their differential location in the social structure. People, Merton argues in all of his work, are not free to act as they please, but have alternative modes of action. These, however, are structurally patterned and institutionalized. Most of Merton's work aims to elucidate structural sources of variations in patterns of choice. His apparently disparate contributions—whether in the study of anomie or the sociology of science, whether in the analysis of the functions of political machines or of reference groups—are rooted in this overall perspective. While rejecting the Parsonian attempt to build an all-encompassing general theory at this stage of sociology's development, Merton nevertheless taught his students the art of approaching a variety of substantively different theoretical problems under a unified theoretical angle of vision.

In addition, Merton endeavored to counteract the rigidity of previous functional theory by suggesting a number of paradigms and a protocol for functional analysis, which, among other things, stressed the need to consider dysfunctions as well as functions, questioned Malinowski's assumption that every social phenomenon necessarily had a social function, and attacked the conservative implication that any item was indispensable to the operation of a given social structure. By highlighting the twin notions of functional alternatives and dysfunctions, Merton did yeoman's work in banishing the Panglossian optimism that all was always to the best in all possible (functional) worlds. His analyses stressed instead the need to be aware of basically structural sources of disorder, of socio-cultural contradictions, and of divergent values within given structures. To Merton, social actors are always faced by sociological ambivalence, ambiguities, conflicting expectations, and dilemmas of choice; and societies, far from being rigidly unified wholes, contain in their structures discrepancies and incongruities that preclude the possibility of treating them as unambiguously unified wholes (Merton, 1976).

His closely argued distinctions between manifest and latent functions (those consequential activities that are present in the actor's mind and those that are not) and his distinguishing of individual purposes from functional effects helped to remove some of the teleological implications that many critics had discerned in the writings of some of his predecessors and contemporaries.

There is no need to indulge in invidious comparisons on the respective, overall influence of Parsons's and Merton's work on subsequent theorizing. There is, however, little doubt that Merton's theoretical stress on problems of the middle range has been more pronounced in its impact on empirical research than has the Parsonian grand theory.

Kingsley Davis

Kingsley Davis received his Ph.D. from Harvard in 1936, the same year Merton did. Although he later described functional analysis as a dominating and therefore not distinctive orientation (1959), and although his work in recent years has been almost completely devoted to specialized demographic studies, he must be reckoned among the handful of figures who helped to establish a functional style of analysis as the predominant theoretical mode in the 1940's and 1950's. His textbook *Human Society* (1949) endured for many years as the most thorough and systematic attempt to present a general view of social structures and social functions from a largely Parsonian-Mertonian perspective. It was superseded only in 1960 by H. M. Johnson's *Sociology,* a much less imaginative and considerably more rigid presentation of the major lines of Parsons's and Merton's thought. Davis also developed a series of analytical papers on the sociology of the family, the sociology of prostitution, and related areas in which functional analysis was exemplified in his characteristically lucid fashion. Although evidently beholden to the teachings of Parsons, these papers do not follow him in his grand design but exemplify a Mertonian type of middle-range strategy. They still serve as examples of functional theorizing at its best.

Wilbert Moore and Robin Williams

Wilbert Moore, who received his Ph.D. from Harvard in 1940, and Robin Williams, who received his in 1943, are other major figures who helped establish functional analysis as the dominant perspective in the fifties and early sixties. Moore did this through a series of works in the sociology of industrial relations (1951) and the sociology of modernization and social change (1963).

Williams's contributions to functional analysis were chiefly made through his work in inter-group relations (1947), his collaboration (with Stouffer et al) in *The American Soldier* (1949), a landmark in sociological research, and his influential textbook *American Society* (1951), the first major attempt to understand the whole of American society in terms of functional analysis.

Marion Levy

Marion Levy, who received his Ph.D. from Harvard in 1951, wrote a major book, *The Structure of Society* (1953), which attempted, very much along Parsonian lines, to present a grand synthesis of functional analysis. His work on the Chinese family (1949) and on the theory of modernization (1966), though marginally differentiated from Parsons, follows closely in the footsteps of his erstwhile teacher.

HARVARD IN THE FIFTIES

In the 1950's other Harvard-trained sociologists, too numerous to mention here, continued the tradition of their predecessors. By that time Parsons and his colleagues had succeeded in transforming the Harvard Department of Sociology into the Department of Social Relations through the amalgamation of social and clinical psychology, social anthropology, and sociology. Parsons chaired that department for ten years. Though not all of his colleagues shared all aspects of Parsons's vision, he nevertheless dominated the department as a whole, both organizationally and intellectually, and it served as a major vehicle in spreading the message of his own style of theorizing.

By this time, Parsons's earlier students had now assumed leading positions in other universities—Merton at Columbia (where Davis also taught before going to Berkeley), Williams at Cornell, and Moore and Levy at Princeton. A number of other Harvard-trained sociologists continued to work in the general Harvard tradition, though most tended to diverge to a greater or lesser degree from Parsons's grand scheme of analysis as time went by. Merton's students at Columbia—Selznick (1949), Blau (1975), and Gouldner (1955), for example—continued to work in a broadly Mertonian tradition. Other prominent sociologists like Goode (1963, 1973) and Gross (1958) also patterned their work in the mode of Parsons or Merton although they did not receive their doctorates from departments in which functional analysis predominated. (Goode worked under Kingsley Davis, the major theorist at Pennsylvania State University, but the department as a whole did not share Davis's perspective.) By around 1950 this mode had clearly become predominant in American sociological theory.

PARSONS'S NEW DIRECTIONS

In the meantime, Parsons's own work developed in several new directions. In 1951, he collaborated with Shils in publishing *Toward a General Theory of Action*. The authors developed a set of concepts characterizing, so they claimed, all action systems. These they termed *pattern variables,* which were supposed to account not only for the variant normative priorities of social systems, but for the dominant modes of orientation in personality systems and the patterns of values found in cultural systems. Essentially a massive elaboration and refinement of the *Gemeinschaft-Gesellschaft* dichotomy of Toennies, these pattern variables were presented as dichotomous alternatives between affectivity and affective neutrality, between universalism and particularism, between diffuseness and specificity, or between achievement and ascription.

Affectivity-affective neutrality refers to the amount of emotional involvement allowed to enter into an interactive situation. Modern physicians, for example, could not perform their tasks were they to be affectively involved with their patients, whereas high affective involvement might be a condition of success for the primitive medicine man.

The dichotomous alternative of universalism-particularism pertains to the standards of evaluation of others in an interactive situation made up of individual specimens of general categories of persons (as in the procedures of modern bureaucracies) or of particular human beings (as in courtship). Such distinctions might have appeared rather "academic" at the time they were first advanced, but with recent arguments over affirmative action, hiring policies, and related matters it has now become evident that they are of considerable importance when it comes to public policy.

Diffuseness and specificity refer to the nature of obligations in interactive situations, whether they should be narrowly defined (as in a modern labor contract) or be of a more diffuse nature (as in a marital relationship).

Finally, the distinction between achievement and ascription rests on whether status incumbents are judged on what they do rather than who they are: for example, a modern civil servant being evaluated in terms of his or her performance, as opposed to a medievel noble who is judged in terms of who he is.

These pairs of variables were thus seen as focal points of individual decisions, normative demands, and value orientations. They were said to channel the actions of actors through the twin mechanisms of socialization and social control. Proponents of this theory claimed that these pairs of variables, being built into the personality system, ensured a fit between individual actions and societal requirements. Social actors, it was contended, would learn, be it in childhood or in later adult socialization, which particular set of orientations would be appropriate in specific interactive situations. In addition, other types of social control would be activated in order to ensure that actors within given structures deviated as little as possible from normative demands to adhere to specific orientations in particular situational contingencies.

Only two years after the publication of *Toward a General Theory of Action* (1951), Parsons, again joined by Shils and for the first time by his Harvard colleague Bales, published another book, *Working Papers in the Theory of Action* (1953), in which he presented yet another theoretical extension of his previous scheme of analysis. Building on ideas in *The Social System* as well as on the results of small-group research previously conducted by Bales, Parsons and his collaborators now suggested that all action systems were faced with four major problems if they were to survive and develop. They must secure sufficient resources from their environment and distribute these within the system. This is termed *adaptation*. They must mobilize resources for the attainment of system goals and establish priorities among these goals. This is called *goal attainment*. They must coordinate and adjust relations within the system and hence have mechanisms for *integration*. Finally, there must be ways of ensuring that component actors are sufficiently motivated to play their parts (*pattern maintenance*), as well as mechanisms devoted to internal *tension management*. These last two functions are grouped under the term latency. (This entire set of functional requirements was called the A.G.I.L. scheme.) Any item under sociological analysis, it was now suggested, would have to be assessed in terms of its functional contribution to the general requirements of the system.

Space does not allow extended consideration of other aspects of Parsons's amazingly fertile sociological imagination as exhibited in works published in the 1960's. In a series of interrelated papers he now focused attention on what he termed generalized media of exchange, such as money and power. He argued that in any type of exchange transactions are facilitated by symbolic media. When it comes to the buying and selling of goods in an economy that is no longer based on barter, money is used so as to facilitate transactions. What is more, money deposited in a bank by many individual depositors allows the bank to inject much larger sums of money into the economy, thus allowing an otherwise unattainable expansion of economic transactions. In similar ways, if many individuals empower political representatives and governmental personnel through the electoral process to act in their behalf, governmental action acquires the necessary power to expand the social and political system's effectiveness (1963).

In a related series of papers, Parsons further developed the fairly idealistic underpinnings of his thought through the notion of an information (or cybernetic) hierarchy of social control (1970). He now asserted that in the last analysis symbolic processes have primacy over social structural factors, since institutions are at bottom communication systems. Transactions and exchanges within social systems and between the various component parts of such systems are carried out by way of symbolic media such as money, power, influence, and commitment. These media can be seen as informational controls that channel, delimit, and expand activities within social structures. Parsons now argued that since symbolic media are a major part of all cultural systems, cultural systems have directing control over social systems, just as social systems in turn control the personality systems of component actors.

In the 1960's and early 1970's Parsons, who had once rejected Spencer's thought as entirely obsolete, returned to a Spencerian evolutionary scheme in an attempt to counter critics who accused him of being unable to offer an explanation of social change. In his *Societies: Evolutionary and Comparative Perspectives* (1966) Parsons argued that a process of increasing differentiation marked the evolution of all human societies and of particular social systems. In earlier stages of human evolution, kinship roles and political and occupational roles were fused in the same persons; for example, heads of families also exercised political power as village elders and acted as managers of agricultural enterprises. But in modern times such roles are no longer fused and in the possession of the same persons, but rather are allocated to different, functionally specific, role incumbents. The priest-magician-mathematician-medicine man of old has now been succeeded by a number of persons in a number of differentiated positions, exercising their roles and tasks unencumbered by distracting overlaps. In such ways, Parsons argues, modern societies have evolved into highly differentiated structures capable of efficient controls over the environment; they have attained not only economic but cultural productivity that people in earlier evolutionary stages could never have imagined.

Parsons's work became the target of a number of attacks in the 1950's and

1960's (Lockwood 1956, Coser 1956, Mills 1959, Dahrendorf 1958, Gouldner 1970). His critics complained of a built-in bias toward conformity, an absence of concern with social conflict, an inability to perceive the central place of material interests in human affairs, a persistent Panglossian optimism, and a disproportionate concern with integration and consensus at the expense of concern with radical change and instability. Although these persistent critical onslaughts were important, they were not wholly responsible for the eclipse of Parsonian thought in the last ten years or so. Rather, that eclipse was due more to a general shift in concern away from the macrosociological and structural features of Parsonian theory in particular and of structural-functional analysis in general.

THE RESURGENCE OF MICROSOCIOLOGICAL AND CONFLICT THEORIES

EXCHANGE THEORIES

A first intimation of new concerns can be seen in Homans's shift of analytical attention from the system approach in *The Human Group* (1959) to a psychological exchange perspective fully developed in his *Social Behavior: Its Elementary Forms* (1961). In the latter work, Homans mounted a full-scale attack on sociological system theories and asserted that a comprehensive explanation of human behavior would never become possible on the sociological level, but had to proceed on the psychological plane. Borrowing largely from the particular form of behaviorism developed by his Harvard colleague B. F. Skinner, as well as from utilitarianism and classical economics, Homans argued that self-interest was the universal motive that made the world go around and that men and women, just like Skinnerian pigeons, modified their behavior in terms of positive or negative reinforcement provided by their environment. Homans's social world now consisted of interacting individuals exchanging rewards and punishments. As distinct from the nineteenth-century image of economic man, Homans's incentives to action consisted not only of money or commodities, but of approval, esteem, love, affection, and other nonmaterialistic or symbolic tokens. Homans's person was seen as a rational calculator of pleasures and pains, forever intent on maximizing returns and minimizing losses. Homans now tended to couch his arguments in terms of chains of deductive reasoning, starting with such axioms as "Men are more likely to perform an activity, the more valuable they perceive the reward of that activity to be." He proceeded from there through a series of derivations to explain why in concrete settings particular persons were motivated to adapt their behavior because of the incentives and disincentives present in a given social environment.

Homans was attacked as a reductionst by several of his critics, who attempted to show that his deductive schemes tended to be either tautological or *ad hoc*. They charged, in particular, that he was unable to explain such basic sociological variables as level of industrialization or degree of literacy with his reductionist scheme. His critics also contended that by neglecting the symbol-using nature of the human animal, Homans was incapable of explaining the world of values and norms that largely determined the course of human actions. They further argued that he neglected those attributes of social structure that could not be reduced to individual propensities.

Peter Blau, though clearly much influenced by Homans's work, proceeded in his *Exchange and Power in Social Life* (1964) to remedy some of the deficiencies of Homans's conceptualizations and to reconcile them with the structural perspective that had previously dominated his own work and to which he was later to return (Blau, 1975).

In the first part of his book, Blau follows Homans's lead and develops an elementary model purporting to account for "an exchange of activity, tangible or intangible, and more or less rewarding and costly, between two persons," even though he is more sharply aware than Homans that purely rationalistic economic models of human transactions are inadequate whenever there is no accepted medium of exchange such as money. He acknowledged that wherever there is no standard measure of value, the notion of exchange must lose much of its precise meaning and may be largely a matter of analogy.

Blau followed Homans in arguing that in addition to money, people find social approval, respect, and compliance with their wishes inherently desirable. Actors compete with one another in order to maximize these rewards, and their competitive exchanges always proceed under the assumption that people who can bestow rewards will receive rewards in turn. Blau parted company with Homans, however, when he stated that while ideally norms of reciprocity prevail among exchange partners, in fact these norms are systematically infringed, creating imbalances and deprivations that always threaten the smooth operation of social systems. People being differentiated in terms of the resources they possess create power bases through which they may be able to exploit those deprived of such bases. In this part of the book, though following some of Homans's main leads, Blau tones down the latter's emphasis on balance and equilibrium and highlights sources of conflict and contention.

In the second part of his book, Blau proceeds to modify considerably the rather bleak Hobbesian model of society that he presented in the first. Abandoning Homans and returning to a macrosociological perspective, Blau shows that processes of institutionalization, value commitment, and normative regulation make it impossible to explain the workings of society in reductionist terms. While the first part of the book limits itself to elementary exchanges based on the maximization of advantages or the processes of interpersonal attraction and repulsion, in the second part the shared values of the functionalist reenter the scene, and macrosociological issues replace concern with the minutiae of microsociological exchange processes. Almost like the return of the previously repressed, the symbolic nature of the human animal and its immersion in a universe of norms and values now came to the fore of analytical attention. It now turns out that human actors may well be moved by adherence to legitimating values, even though this may involve costs in self-interest and the maximization of advantages. Shared values, it turns out, control exchange relations, just as in Durkheim's structural explanation where contracting individuals can proceed in their dealings only within a matrix of previously established norms.

SYMBOLIC INTERACTIONISM

There exists a tension in Blau's work between a theoretical commitment to the primacy of a micro-level exchange model and a concern with a structural explanation of human conduct on the macro-level. In symbolic interactionism the structural level of analysis is all but abandoned, and the scene is almost completely occupied by interacting individuals who modify their respective conducts regardless of position in the social structure, socio-cultural climates of values and norms, or institutional settings. As Jonathan Turner (1974, p. 178) puts it, "Symbolic interactionists tend to conceptualize human interaction and society in terms of the strategic adjustments and readjustments of players in a game. While games have rules, symbolic interactionists are likely to focus attention on how players interact in ways that, depending upon the course of their interaction, create, maintain, and change the rules of the game."

The theoretical scheme of symbolic interactionism is largely based on a systematization and elaboration of the intellectual heritage of Mead (and to a less extent, Dewey and James). Since an earlier chapter of this book is devoted to Mead, my account of symbolic interactionism can be relatively brief.

Symbolic interactionism's basic tenets, as formulated by its *spiritus rector,* Herbert Blumer (1969), and his disciples and co-thinkers, can be briefly summarized: Human beings act toward social objects mainly in terms of the meaning they attribute to those objects rather than to their intrinsic character. (It should be readily apparent to readers of the chapter on W. I. Thomas that this conceptualization owes as much to Thomas as it owes to Mead.) Such meanings are constructed and reconstructed in the process of social interaction. Shaped as they are by the actual or anticipated response of others, human actions cannot be accounted for by background characteristics, prepotent impulses, structural requirements, or external stimuli. Social reality, far from being stable, is the result of ongoing negotiations between mutually involved sets of actors. These actors are always engaged in fluid interpretative, evaluational, and definitional processes so that only strictly inductive procedures can help elucidate their behavior. Take, for example, the conduct of two young persons who are having a first date. In general American culture or in particular status groups there are, to be sure, certain broad and general norms that govern such encounters, but the actual behavior of these two young persons can never be predicted on the basis of these norms. In fact, they will have to negotiate and renegotiate their mutual conduct in terms of a series of complicated moves and countermoves that gradually will allow them to develop courses of action that are acceptable and pleasurable to both. Only in and through such interactive exchanges do they attain proximate definitions of who their partner *really* is, and how to behave appropriately toward the other.

Symbolic interactionism claims that any sociological theory that proceeds deductively or attempts to build law-like propositions is bound to founder on the rock of the inevitable particularities and the ever-changing character of human conduct. Hence, symbolic interactionism is at bottom an antitheoretical sociological theory that refuses in principle to transcend the peculiar characteristics of social processes in the here and now. In effect it goes far toward rejecting conceptual generalization and abstraction and allowing concepts to perform at best a sensitizing function. Since the social world is constructed from interpretative processes arising in transactions between individuals, it is only amenable to careful description aided by sensitizing, as opposed to theoretically grounded, concepts. Only by taking the role of others and inserting himself or herself imaginatively in the flux of social interchanges between actors can the sociological researcher make sense out of data. Blumer and his co-thinkers in fact want to teach a lesson of humility to the sociological theorist, who is seen as incapable of constructing enduring, objective, theoretical structures, but who must, in their view, be attentive to the subjective interpretations, the definitions of the situations, and the emergent meanings that arise in human interaction, and be content with that.

Although functional analysts as well as other sociological theorists have availed themselves of many particular insights provided by Mead and his successors in the elucidation of social-psychological processes, they have tended to reject what many of them came to see as the idiographic bias of symbolic interactionism. Yet symbolic interactionism continues to be a lively tradition in American social psychology. In addition, it has in the last two decades given rise to highly significant outgrowths in the dramaturgical analyses of Erving Goffman and the so-called labeling approach developed by Edwin Lemert, Howard Becker, and their numerous disciples and followers.

DRAMATURGICAL ANALYSIS

Canadian-born, Goffman received his Ph.D. from the University of Chicago. Although he has developed a quite distinctive approach, the influence of Thomas and Mead and of the symbolic interactionists on his work is unmistakable. Goffman has enriched social psychology and microsociology in a variety of ways, but his development of role theory through conscious elaboration of a dramaturgical model is his most distinctive and important contribution. Many role theorists before Goffman have quoted a well-known passage from Shakespeare's *As You Like It,*

> All the world's a stage
> And all the men and women merely players:
> They have their exits and their entrances;
> And one man in his time plays many parts.

But it was Goffman who transformed a rather vague analogy into a powerful dramaturgical vision. Beginning with his still best-known work, *The Presentation of Self in Everyday Life* (1959), Goffman attempted to illustrate and analyze the complicated ways in which men and women construct images of their selves in encounters with significant others. Like actors on the stage, he argues, we are perpetually concerned with presenting images of ourselves to the various audiences we engage. Our conduct and demeanor is shaped by our desire to leave an acceptable impression in the minds of those we deem important to us. In order to do so, we must hide unacceptable aspects backstage so as to present an unblemished image frontstage. Social actors are perpetually engaged in managing their encounters with others so that the impressions they leave maximize their impact on their audience and provide favorable responses which, in turn, feed the narcissistic resources of the self. It has been observed that experienced stage actors find it difficult, if not impossible, not to act, be it on the stage or off. So, it would seem, Goffman's model of human actors assumes that it is senseless to ask what a man or a woman *really* is since we are always acting. We are forever on stage, even when we may believe that we are most spontaneous and sincere in our responses to others. Ego's conduct is always molded through dramaturgical encounters with various alters. We may play the role of deferential students in encounters with professors, ardent suitors with our beloved, dutiful sons and daughters with our parents, or ambitious young executives impressing our superiors in bureaucratic structures. What we can never be, so Goffman argues, is men and women *tout court.* We are what we pretend to be.

Forever bound to the Ixion's Wheel of impression management, forever imprisoned in the frames of situational contingencies and determinants, we must continue to act out the tragedy or comedy of our lives; and the show must go on as long as we live. To be sure, we may at times depart somewhat from our scripts, we may "ad lib" a bit and attempt to establish some "role distance" by withholding some aspects of the self from immersion in particular performances. But these, Goffman suggests, are in the last analysis only marginal freedoms, allowing us at times a bit of a safety valve when the pressures of others threaten to become unbearable. According to Goffman, we can never manage, even in madness, to escape the presence of others and the prepotent tendency to shape ourselves according to their expectations. Jean-Paul Sartre once proclaimed that others are our hell. Goffman would not use such heated language; he simply proclaims coolly that others are our perpetual companions on our journey through life and that none of us can ever manage to construct a self that is not intimately involved with other selves that play their roles on the same stage. Just as we cannot possibly conceive of Hamlet except in relation to the King and the Queen, to Ophelia, to Polonius and to all the other players, so we each define ourselves—and in turn can be defined by others—in the intermeshing of our conduct with that of all the persons who accompany each of us through our life's journey.

Critics have often objected that much of what Goffman describes may apply to "other-directed" members of America's middle and professional classes, but is less applicable to other classes in America or to other cultures or historical epochs. This may indeed be the case. But it remains that Goffman's amazingly acute observations of interactions and interchanges, his marvellously trained sociological eye for all the nuances of human conduct under the gaze of others, his Simmelian ability to unravel the intricacies of human transactions, have largely enriched our knowledge of microsociological processes. Only the future will tell whether his type of sociology can be so codified that it can be transmitted to other, perhaps less gifted, analysts.

LABELING THEORY

Labeling theory is as much rooted in the Chicago tradition of Mead, Thomas, and Blumer as is the work of Goffman. I shall only briefly sketch its major tenets since most of its contributions are concerned only with one subfield of sociology, the study of deviance.

While most theories of deviance prior to the emergence of labeling theory were mainly concerned with the study of the causes and consequences of various forms of deviance, labeling theory attempted to shift the major focus of attention from those engaging in deviant behavior to those who make the rules that design certain men and women as deviants in the first place. Labeling theory, very much within the Chicago tradition, stressed that one could not understand deviant acts in terms of the behavior of deviants alone but that such acts lend themselves to full sociological analysis only if and when it is realized that, just like all other social acts, they involve interactive relationships.

In the first formulation of what later came to be called labeling theory, Edwin Lemert (1951) made a crucial distinction between what he termed primary and secondary deviance. Primary deviance, he contended, encompassed particular acts—a homicide, a theft, an episode of mental breakdown. Secondary deviance, on the other hand, occurred when those having been involved in primary deviance were categorized and perceived by others as murderers, thieves, or mental patients. Secondary deviance hence involved the action of others who, in effect, categorized particular actors and assigned them to special stigmatized categories of people. Moreover, the persons so categorized acquired a new sense of identity by internalizing these judgments of others and conceiving themselves as murderers, thieves, or mental patients.

Lemert did not yet use the term labeling. This was coined by Howard S. Becker (1963) who argued that the analytical focus of theories of deviance ought to be shifted from deviant acts to those "moral entrepreneurs" who labeled others as deviants. This might at first appear a rather trivial observation since nobody can doubt that jay walkers or auto thieves become such only after officers of the law define these activities as punishable offenses. Yet the matter becomes nontrivial if it is realized, for example, that while the population at large has many individuals who display symptoms of mental instability, only a certain proportion of all those afflicted will ever come to the attention of psychiatrists or will ever be confined to mental hospitals. Men and women in the latter category may then be persons displaying the same tendencies as those found at large, but they have been labeled by others, whether their intimates or public officials, as mentally ill.

Deviance, so the labeling theorists assert, is always a result of interaction between those who are labeled deviants and those who so label them. The act of stealing does not make one into a thief; a person becomes a thief in the minds of others and also of himself or herself only if and when apprehended and labeled in a criminal procedure. An identical act by a juvenile may be deemed a "behavior disorder" in a middle-class suburb and juvenile delinquency in Harlem. A man engaged in homosexual activities will become a homosexual only if and when others so define him and assign a homosexual identity to him. Deviant roles, in this view, always involve more than particular types of acts; they always require public labeling of these acts as deviants. Labeling theorists are centrally concerned not with acts in themselves but with societal reactions to these acts.

Critics have pointed out that labeling theorists have often neglected the objective circumstances of primary deviance and have focused almost exclusively on those others who label and stigmatize these acts. This would lead to the rather absurd conclusion that behavior contrary to a norm is not deviant unless it is discovered. (Gibbs 1966) In hands less skillful than those of Lemert or Becker, labeling theory has often become a rather blunt tool, which lends itself more easily to efforts at debunking the social order than to probing analysis of its functioning. It remains true, however, that like Goffman's dramaturgical analysis, labeling theory has sensitized contemporary sociologists to the old Simmelian notion that all social behavior involves human interaction and cannot be understood except as a transaction between actors and those who categorize their activities. Not their acts in themselves, but reactions to these acts assign deviants to special stigmatized or devaluated status positions.

"CONFLICT THEORIES"

Critics of symbolic interactionism as well as of its various offshots have criticized these theories for their neglect of macrosociological variables such as power constellations or class conflicts. It is precisely the analysis of those matters that stands in the forefront of the attention of scholars who are said to belong to the "conflict school." I have advisedly used this cautious formulation since some sociologists, including myself, who are often said to belong to that school have rejected such labeling. More generally, it may be said that this "school" has a somewhat protean shape. The term is sometimes simply used as a code word for Marxism. But it also refers to sociologists who have made contributions to the sociological study of conflict and who have highlighted the importance of conflict-ridden interaction in society without, however, claiming that "conflict theory" presents an encompassing theoretical scheme such as, say, Ptolemaic astronomy in relation to Copernican. Gluckman (1956) and Coser (1956, 1967) have maintained instead that there can be only one general sociological theory even though it may consist of various conceptual schemes and sets of partial theories of the middle range considered important for understanding particular social dimensions.

Although he wrote before the term had gained currency, the work of C. Wright Mills (1956, 1959) is best considered as one version of "conflict theory." Mills had done his undergraduate work at the University of Texas where he had been influenced by the pragmatic philosophy of Dewey and Mead; he then moved on to the University of Wisconsin where he came under the influence of Hans H. Gerth, a German refugee scholar steeped in the tradition of Max Weber and Karl Mannheim. At Wisconsin and during his later years at the University of Maryland and at Columbia University (where he taught up to his untimely death in the early 1960's), Mills evolved a sociological stance distinctively his own, although he was beholden to a variety of partly divergent traditions of theorizing.

Mills's early work in the sociology of knowledge followed in the broad tradition of Karl Mannheim, but it was probably more deeply in debt to American pragmatism in general and to the thought of the literary critic Kenneth Burke in particular. As time went on, Mills moved from concern with problems of sociology of knowledge to broader macrosociological investigations. In these later works, Mills elaborated a radical perspective which, while borrowing much from Marx, relied at least as heavily on Thorstein Veblen and Max Weber, as well as on the Italian theorists Pareto and Mosca.

Mills can best be understood as a belated offspring of midwestern populism.

He battled against corporate and military elites, and "the interests." He criticized the fallen world of corporate America in terms of an idea of participatory democracy that, so he thought, had once existed on the American frontier. His radicalism was more closely comparable to that of Veblen, whom he greatly admired, than to the Marxist tradition. His most influential and enduring work, *The Power Elite* (1956), presented a powerful challenge to much previous research in stratification and class analysis. The book gained its strength more from this challenge than from the data he adduced to show that a relatively cohesive elite of corporate and military leaders had usurped the major decision-making power in America and had taken it away from the population at large. He was unconcerned with analysis of the minutiae of status differentials and channels of social mobility. He focused instead, with a characteristic sense for the jugular, on the major conflicts and contentions between key holders of societal power and the historical drift of such power from local and popular centers to the commanding heights of military and corporate bureaucracies. To Mills, any macrosociological analysis worth its salt had to be grounded in concern with the struggle for power between conflicting classes, between rulers and ruled, between the high and mighty and the common man. His formulations often tended to lack precision, and many of his generalizations have hardly stood up under the test of subsequent research. But his distinctive version of "conflict theory," with its central emphasis on macrosociological forces and the contentions of power between classes of corporate actors, helped revive an almost buried radical perspective within the sociological tradition.

Readers of the early work (1958, 1959) of the bilingual German sociologist Ralf Dahrendorf often erroneously assumed that his critique of functional analysis in general and of Parsonian theory in particular stemmed from a radical Marxist position. It soon became apparent, however, that although Dahrendorf had indeed been much influenced by Marx, he argued for a conflict perspective in sociological theory that had more in common with nineteenth-century classical liberalism than with the socialist tradition. His was an ambitious attempt to lay the groundwork for a general theoretical system sharply at variance with functional analysis and premissed on the idea that all human societies can best be understood as arenas for perpetual struggles for power and authority that cease only in death.

Dahrendorf's point of departure is the assertion that all social organizations are in fact based on hierarchies of power in which the powerful are able through various means, among which coercion is central, to extract conformity to their expectations from the less powerful. Power and authority are conceived as scarce resources, and the component actors of every society are said to be perpetually engaged in struggles over the distribution of these resources. At times their contentions may be latent or muted, but they are never absent from any social structure. Societies are always in a state of conflict and the interests of some human actors are always opposed to those of others. These interests are not primarily seen in economic terms, as in the Marxian scheme, but rather in terms of contentions over the distribution of power. Conflicts can never be eradicated since every particular solution to a conflict of power creates a new constellation of interests that must give rise to new conflicts.

In Dahrendorf's scheme the inexorability of conflicts of interests has as its corollary the assertion that societies are always in flux and that social change is hence a ubiquitous feature of society. Any attempt, as in Parsonian theory, to postulate equilibria in social functioning is rejected. The details of Dahrendorf's work are concerned, by way of discussing a variety of intervening structural factors, with specifying conditions that help exacerbate or mute conflicting interactions. Throughout his work he holds firmly to his major assertion that though conflicts may be channeled, institutionalized, and shorn of their more violent manifestations, they can never be eradicated from the human scene. Since power and authority are, to use a terminology that he would reject, "functional prerequisites" of any social system, and, since they must necessarily invite contention, social conflict, and social change, they are the nodal points of any explanations of human affairs.

In briefly evaluating Dahrendorf's contributions, one may note that his panconflict imperialism suffers from the same one-sidedness as Parsons's panconsensus views. One may also assert, however, that his work, together with that of Marxian sociologists and the other so-called conflict theorists, has contributed to growing dissatisfaction with those versions of functional theory that clung to equilibrium models and assumed that societies are mainly held together by normative consensus. These conflict theorists have highlighted those societal processes where consensus, far from being spontaneously forthcoming, has been achieved through coercion, manipulation, or all those other means that are available to the powerful in their attempt to maintain their domination over the powerless.

My own work on the functions of social conflict (1956, 1967), while highlighting the central importance of conflict in human societies, eschewed the temptation to see in conflict the preeminent form of social interaction. I argued instead for a view that stressed the need to investigate the roots of consensus as well as the roots of conflicts between individuals and classes of individuals. A critical discussion of my contributions to "conflict theory" can be found in Turner (1974).

IN SUMMARY

A balanced assessment of the theoretical trends discussed in this chapter will become possible only after considerably more time has elapsed. We are still too closely involved with them. Like young trees that have only begun to bear fruit, these theories will have to be judged by a generation that is able to evaluate the quality of their products, their ultimate worth. Some of them, no doubt, will turn out to have been barren, while others will have produced an abundant harvest.

Nevertheless, one conclusion can already be made with some confidence: American sociology has come of age during the period under consideration. It is no longer mired in the swamp of *ad hoc* explanations or raw empiricism. It is no longer content with genuflections before closed theoretical systems, whether homegrown or imported from Europe. American sociology, largely under the impact of the theoretical thought discussed in these pages, is now equipped with a remarkable array of theoretical notions, including those developed so recently that they are not discussed in this historical account. Such an array should allow the discipline to contribute mightily in the future to that major task its founder envisaged for it from the beginning: to provide a reasoned explanation of the social roots of the human predicament.

LITERATURE CITED

Barber, B. (ed.) (1970) *L. J. Henderson on the Social System.* Chicago: The University of Chicago Press.

Becker, H. S. (1963) *Outsiders: Studies in the Sociology of Deviance.* New York: Free Press.

Blau, P. (1964) *Exchange and Power in Social Life.* New York: Wiley.

Blau, P. (ed.) (1975) *Approaches to the Study of Social Structure.* New York: Free Press.

Blumer, H. (1969) *Symbolic Interactionism: Perspective and Method.* Englewood Cliffs, N.J.: Prentice-Hall.

Coser, L. A. (1956) *The Functions of Social Conflict.* New York: Free Press.

Coser, L. A. (1967) *Continuities in the Study of Social Conflict.* New York: Free Press.

Coser, L. A. (ed.) (1975) *The Idea of Social Structure: Papers in Honor of Robert K. Merton.* New York: Harcourt Brace Jovanovich.

Dahrendorf, R. (1958) Out of utopia: Toward a reorientation of sociological analysis. *American Journal of Sociology.* 64:115–27.

Dahrendorf, R. (1959) *Class and Class Conflict in Industrial Society.* Stanford, Calif.: Stanford University Press.

Davis, K. (1949) *Human Society.* New York: Macmillan.

Davis, K. (1959) The myth of functional analysis. *American Sociological Review.* 24:757–72.

Gibbs, J. (1966) Conceptions of deviant behavior: The old and the new. *Pacific Sociological Review.* 9:13.

Gluckman, M. (1956) *Custom and Conflict in Africa.* New York: Free Press.

Goffman, E. (1959) *The Presentation of Self in Everyday Life.* New York: Doubleday & Co.

Goode, W. (1963) *World Revolution and Family Patterns.* New York: Free Press.

Goode, W. (1973) *Explorations in Social Theory.* New York: Oxford University Press.

Gouldner, A. (1955) *Patterns of Industrial Bureaucracy.* New York: Free Press.

Gouldner, A. (1970) *The Coming Crisis of Western Sociology.* New York: Basic Books.

Gouldner, A. (1973) *For Sociology.* New York: Basic Books.

Gross, N. (1958) *Exploration in Role Analysis.* New York: Wiley.

Homans, G. (1941) *English Villagers of the Thirteenth Century.* Cambridge, Mass.: Harvard University Press.

Homans, G. (1950) *The Human Group.* New York: Harcourt Brace Jovanovich.

Homans, G. (1961) *Social Behavior: Its Elementary Forms.* New York: Harcourt Brace Jovanovich.

Homans, G., and Curtis, C. P. (1934) *An Introduction to Pareto.* New York: Knopf.

Johnson, H. M. (1960) *Sociology, a Systematic Introduction.* New York: Harcourt Brace Jovanovich.

Lemert, E. (1951) *Social Pathology.* New York: McGraw-Hill.

Levine, D. (1976) Simmel's influence on American sociology. *American Journal of Sociology,* 81, 4:813–42 and 81, 5:1112–32.

Levy, M. (1949) *The Family Revolution in China.* Cambridge, Mass.: Harvard University Press.

Levy, M. (1953) *The Structure of Society.* Princeton, N.J.: Princeton University Press.

Levy, M. (1966) *Modernization and the Structure of Societies.* Princeton, N.J.: Princeton University Press.

Lockwood, D. (1956) Some remarks on "the social system." *British Journal of Sociology.* 7:134–46.

Merton, R. K. (1968) *Social Theory and Social Structure.* New York: Free Press. Revised ed. Originally published in 1949 and revised in 1957.

Merton, R. K. (1976) *Sociological Ambivalence and Other Essays.* New York: Free Press.

Mills, C. W. (1956) *The Power Elite*. New York: Oxford University Press.

Mills, C. W. (1959) *The Sociological Imagination*. New York: Oxford University Press.

Moore, W. (1951) *Industrial Relations and the Social Order*. New York: Macmillan.

Moore, W. (1963) *Social Change*. Englewood Cliffs, N.J.: Prentice-Hall.

Mullins, N. C. (1973) *Theories and Theory Groups in Contemporary American Sociology*. New York: Harper & Row.

Parsons, T. (1937) *The Structure of Social Action*. New York: McGraw-Hill.

Parsons, T. (1949) *Essays in Sociological Theory*. New York: Free Press.

Parsons, T. (1951) *The Social System*. New York: Free Press.

Parsons, T. (1963) On the concept of political power. *Proceedings of the American Philosophical Society*. 107:232–62.

Parsons, T. (1966) *Societies: Evolutionary and Comparative Perspectives*. Englewood Cliffs, N.J.: Prentice-Hall.

Parsons, T. (1970) Some problems of general theory. In *Theoretical Sociology*, ed. J. C. McKinney, E. A. Tiryakian. New York: Appleton-Century.

Parsons, T., Shils, E. (eds.) (1951) *Toward a General Theory of Action*. Cambridge, Mass.: Harvard University Press.

Parsons, T., Bales, R., Shils, E. (1953) *Working Papers in the Theory of Action*. New York: Free Press.

Selznick, P. (1949) *TVA and the Grass Roots*. Berkeley: University of California Press.

Stinchcombe, A. (1968) *Constructing Social Theories*. New York: Harcourt Brace Jovanovich.

Stinchcombe, A. (1975) Merton's theory of social structure. In *The Idea of Social Structure: Papers in Honor of Robert K. Merton*. (ed.) L. A. Coser. New York: Harcourt Brace Jovanovich.

Stouffer, S. A. et al. (1949) *The American Soldier*. Princeton, N.J.: Princeton University Press.

Turner, J. H. (1974) *The Structure of Sociological Theory*. Homewood, Ill.: Dorsey.

Williams, R. M. (1947) *The Reduction of Intergroup Tensions*. New York: Social Science Research Council.

Williams, R. M. (1951) *American Society*. New York: Knopf.

A Selected Reading List of Recent Works

Stanislav Andreski, ed., *Herbert Spencer: Structure, Function and Evolution* (London: Joseph, 1971).

An excellent selection of Spencer's most pertinent sociological writings with a concise introduction by the editor.

Shlomo Arineri, *The Social and Political Thought of Karl Marx* (Cambridge: Cambridge University Press, 1968).

A noteworthy study of the subject.

Reinhard Bendix and Guenther Roth: *Scholarship and Partisanship: Essays on Max Weber* (Berkeley: University of California Press, 1971).

A series of interrelated essays centering on Weber's social and political thought and its subsequent impact. A valuable reassessment and commentary by two leading American Weber scholars.

Dominick La Capra, *Emile Durkheim: Sociologist and Philosopher* (Ithaca, N.Y.: Cornell University Press, 1972).

A somewhat unorthodox new assessment by a young historian of ideas.

Terry Nicholas Clark, *Prophets and Patrons: The French University and the Emergence of the Social Sciences* (Cambridge, Mass.: Harvard University Press, 1973).

A fine study of the social, political, and intellectual context in which the Durkheimian school developed.

Anthony Giddens, ed., *Emile Durkheim/Selected Writings* (Cambridge: Cambridge University Press, 1972).

New translations of selected Durkheim texts with an informative introduction by the editor.

Anthony Giddens, *The Class Structure of the Advanced Societies* (New York: Barnes and Noble, 1973).

Contains exceptionally stimulating critical assessments of Marx's and Weber's theories of social class.

Donald N. Levine, ed., *Georg Simmel on Individuality and Social Forms: Selected Writings* (Chicago: The University of Chicago Press, 1971).

An indispensable selection of Simmel's writings with a sophisticated introduction by the editor, a leading Simmel scholar.

Stephen Lukes, *Emile Durkheim: His Life and Work* (New York: Harper & Row, 1972).

The definitive intellectual biography of Durkheim, a superb work.

David McLellan, *Karl Marx: His Life and Thought* (New York: Harper & Row, 1974).

A full and comprehensive intellectual biography that supersedes most previous work.

Robert A. Nisbet, *The Sociology of Emile Durkheim* (New York: Oxford University Press, 1974).

A superb Durkheim primer.

Bertell Ollman, *Alienation: Marx's Conception of Man in Capitalist Society* (Cambridge: Cambridge University Press, 1971).

A probing, though turgidly written, reexamination of Marx's philosophical premises.

J. D. Y. Peel, ed., *Herbert Spencer on Social Evolution: Selected Writings* (Chicago: The University of Chicago Press, 1972).

Many fine selections with a helpful and wide-ranging introduction by the editor.

J. D. Y. Peel, *Herbert Spencer: The Evolution of a Sociologist* (New York: Basic Books, 1971).

An excellent and critical intellectual biography.

W. G. Runciman: *A Critique of Max Weber's Philosophy of Social Sciences* (Cambridge: Cambridge University Press, 1972).

A highly sophisticated critique of Weber's methodology from a British sociologist steeped in Wittgensteinian philosophy.

Otto Stammer, ed., *Max Weber and Sociology Today* (New York: Harper Torchbooks, 1972).

A translation of some of the proceedings of the 15th German Sociology Congress held in Heidelberg to commemorate the centenary of Max Weber's birth, with contributions from most leading Weber scholars.

Marrianne Weber, *Max Weber, A Biography,* translated by Harry Zohn (New York: Wiley, 1975).

The long awaited translation of the classical biography by Weber's widow on which all subsequent work is largely based.

Kurt H. Wolff, ed., *From Karl Mannheim* (New York: Oxford University Press, 1971).

A wide-ranging collection of Mannheim's essays with a searching introduction by the editor, a leading Mannheim scholar.

Index

Index

7
B 8
C 9
D 0
E 1
F 2
G 3
H 4
I 5
J 6